CATHOLIC RECORD SOCIETY
PUBLICATIONS

RECORDS SERIES
VOLUME 85

Alexander Goss, Bishop of Liverpool (from a
photograph probably taken in the late 1850s)

*Reproduced by courtesy of the Archives of the
Archbishop of Liverpool*

The Correspondence of Alexander Goss, Bishop of Liverpool 1856–1872

Edited by
PETER DOYLE

PUBLISHED FOR
THE CATHOLIC RECORD SOCIETY
BY
THE BOYDELL PRESS

2014

First published 2014

ISBN 978–0–902832–28–2

A Catholic Record Society publication
published by The Boydell Press
an imprint of Boydell & Brewer Ltd
PO Box 9, Woodbridge, Suffolk IP12 3DF, UK
and of Boydell & Brewer Inc.
668 Mt Hope Avenue, Rochester, NY 14620–2731, USA
website: www.boydellandbrewer.com

A CIP catalogue record for this book is available
from the British Library

The publisher has no responsibility for the continued existence or
accuracy of URLs for external or third-party internet websites referred to
in this book, and does not guarantee that any content
on such websites is, or will remain, accurate or appropriate

This publication is printed on acid-free paper

Printed and bound in Great Britain by
TJ International Ltd, Padstow, Cornwall

CONTENTS

ACKNOWLEDGEMENTS

I wish to thank a number of individuals and the staff of various institutions for their assistance in collecting the materials for this book and their generous support and advice during its preparation. First of all, Dr Meg Whittle, archivist of the Archdiocese of Liverpool, for her advice, expertise and encouragement throughout the project and specifically for arranging the temporary transfer of Goss's letterbooks to the Archives of the Archbishop of Liverpool for easier reference. Among other individuals, special mention must go to two long-standing members of the North West Catholic History Society, Tony Hilton and Brian Plumb. Both have been invaluable sources of information; while the former's scholarly work as editor of *North West Catholic History* has made available to historians a great deal of carefully researched material on the history of Catholicism in the north-west of England, without Brian Plumb's invaluable biographical dictionary, *'Found Worthy'*, I could not have embarked on editing these letters.

I must also thank Fr Peter Phillips for alerting me to the early Goss letters in the Lancashire Record Office; Canon J. A. Harding for allowing me to use material from his biography of Bishop Clifford of Clifton; Dr Serenhedd James for information on the Errington family, and finally Fr John Broadley, my successor as volumes editor for the Society, for his careful editing of the text.

I am also grateful to a number of archivists and their staff: those at the Lancashire Record Office, as the major repository of Goss's correspondence; Fr Nicholas Schofield and his staff at the Archives of the Archbishop of Westminster; Dr Jonathan Bush at Ushaw; the Rev. Michael Dolan of the Talbot Library in Preston; Greg Harkin of All Hallows College, Dublin; the staff of the Propaganda Archives in Rome, and Andrew Alexander, deputy head of the map department of Cambridge University Library.

I also wish to thank the often unsung authors of parish histories who have made my task that much easier.

My apologies to others whom I have forgotten to mention and to any copyright holders whose permission to publish has inadvertently not been obtained.

I (and my wife) have lived with Bishop Goss for too long; perhaps he may now be allowed to rest in peace, with a final word of gratitude for all he did to help the growth of the Church in the north-west of England.

Peter Doyle

ABBREVIATIONS

AAA	Archives of Ampleforth Abbey
AAL	Archives of the Archbishop of Liverpool
AAW	Archives of the Archbishop of Westminster
ABO	Archive of the Birmingham Oratory
APF	Archives of the Sacred Congregation of the Propagation of the Faith, Rome. Two collections are used in this work (see Note on Sources for full details):
	APF, *Anglia*, vol. no./item no.
	APF, *Lettere*, vol. no./item no.
CDA	Archives of the Diocese of Clifton
CI	The Catholic Institute school, Liverpool
CPSC	The Catholic Poor School Committee
CRS	The Catholic Record Society
DDC	*Dictionnaire de droit canonique* (Paris, 1965)
Dessain	Dessain, C. S. *et al.* (eds), *The Letters and Diaries of John Henry Newman*, 32 vols (London and Oxford, 1961–2008)
DIB	*Dictionary of Irish Biography* (Cambridge, 2009)
DIP	*Dizionario degli Istituti di Perfezione* (Rome, 1974–)
Directory	*The Catholic Directory*: an annual publication that changed its name but remained basically the same in purpose; see Note on Sources, p. xv
DTC	*Dictionnaire de théologie catholique*, 17 vols (Paris, 1899–1950)
Extracts	Octavo volume of random extracts from *Liverpool Diocesan Directory & Ordo* in the 1880s and 1890s; numbering of the pages has been added later, by hand, in red ink; deposited in AAL.
fol./fols	folio/folios
Fitz-L	Charles Fitzgerald-Lombard OSB (ed.), *English and Welsh Priests 1801–1914: A Working List* (Bath, 1993)
LRO	Lancashire Record Office
LRO, RCLv	Roman Catholic material relating to the original Liverpool Diocese in the Lancashire Record Office
MR	Missionary Rector
NWCH	*North West Catholic History*, the journal of the North West Catholic History Society (Wigan, 1969–)
ODCC	*The Oxford Dictionary of the Christian Church* (2nd rev. edn, Oxford, 1983)
ODNB	*The Oxford Dictionary of National Biography* (Oxford, 2004)

OED	*The Oxford English Dictionary*
PL	Pastoral Letter
RH	*Recusant History*, the journal of the Catholic Record Society
SCH	*Studies in Church History*, the annual volume published by the Ecclesiastical History Society
SEC	St Edward's College, Everton, Liverpool, Goss's official residence
Synodi	*Synodi Liverpolitanae I–VIII* (Liverpool, n.d.) in AAL, Liverpool Synods 1853–1955
UC	Ushaw College archive
VA	Vicar Apostolic
VCH	*The Victoria History of the Counties of England*: *Lancashire*, 8 vols (London, 1906–14; repr. 1966)
VEC	The archive of the English College, Rome
VF	Vicar Forane or Dean
VG	Vicar General

Religious orders and congregations

CAP	Order of Friars Minor Capuchin: Capuchins
CM	Congregation of the Mission: Vincentians
CP	Congregation of the Passion: Passionists
CSO	Cistercians of the Strict Observance: Cistercians
CSSR	Congregation of the Most Holy Redeemer: Redemptorists
FCJ	Faithful Companions of Jesus
IC	Institute of Charity: Rosminians
OFM	Order of Friars Minor: Franciscans
OMI	Oblates of Mary Immaculate
OP	Order of Friars Preachers: Dominicans
OSB	Order of St Benedict: Benedictines
SJ	Society of Jesus: Jesuits
SND	Sisters of Notre Dame of Namur

Biographical abbreviations

b.	born
bp.	bishop
c.	curate
d.	death (in the case of a priest, the absence of a date of death usually denotes the person left the priesthood)
edu.	educated
md.	married
o.	ordained
r.	rector

Abbreviations commonly used by Goss in his letters

B.S.	Blessed Sacrament
Dr. E.	Archbishop Errington
H.E./H.Em	His Eminence
H.F.	Holy Father
HS/H.S.	Holy See
J.C.	Jesus Christ
Prop./Prop:	Propaganda
P.S.	Poor School (Committee)
Xt.	Christ

Latin phrases commonly used by Goss in his letters

cura animarum	the pastoral care of souls
in fraudem legis	in comptempt of the law
pro popolo	for the people = a Mass without stipend offered for the people of a particular mission
relatio status animarum	an account of the religious state of a diocese/ mission
status animarum	the state of souls, usually referring to a priest's religious census of his mission or district

NOTE ON SOURCES

Manuscript sources

For his day-to-day correspondence Goss used a copying machine that produced copies on flimsy paper, each page approximately A4 in size and numbered. The bound copies were known as 'press books'.[1] Unfortunately, he did not generally keep copies of correspondence he received unless it was from Rome; there are a few letters to him in LRO RCLv (unsorted) and in the Ushaw College archives.

The main collections of Bishop Goss's letters are as follows:

1 The principal collection comprises five volumes of letter-books (or 'press books') in the Lancashire Record Office, Preston (LRO); each volume contains 400–500 pages of copied letters bound in half-leather. The full reference for this collection is LRO, RCLv Box 14, Letter-books of Bishop Goss; the individual books are numbered 5/1–5. In this edition a shortened archival reference at the head of each letter gives the letter-book number and the item number (so, for example, the archival reference for letter 74 is 5/1/272). The last letters in these volumes are dated December 1868. Also in the Lancashire Record Office are two volumes of his secretaries' letters, LRO, RCLv Box 15, 5/6/1, and 5/6/2; a few items from these letter-books are included here.

2 Additionally, the Lancashire Record Office has a box of unsorted documents containing a few of the Bishop's letters dating from when he was on the staff of St Edward's College, Liverpool. The two transcripts from this source are given the box reference, LRO, RCLv 76, the addressee and the date.

3 The extensive archives of the Archbishop of Liverpool (AAL) are arranged principally into a number of collections; the relevant one here is the Early Bishops' Collection (or EBC). Each collection is sub-divided into series, indicated by S1, S2, etc, containing papers arranged thematically (e.g. Rome; other bishops; education). The series are further sub-divided into numbered boxes, with individual documents then listed A/1, etc. In this volume, references to this collection are generally referenced AAL (without EBC), followed by the appropriate series, box and item number. The EBC Collection contains some loosely gathered, paginated copies of important

---

[1] See www.officemuseum.com/copy_machines. Which type of machine the bishop used is not known.

Goss letters, not in the normal letter-books though copied onto letter-book paper; transcripts from this collection are referenced as Add. Lttrs, with the page number. Also in AAL are a small number of loose letters, referenced as EBC, S1/3/C/item no; some of these letters are in draft form and it is not always clear whether a letter was sent or not. Additionally, there are Chapter Minute Books, the first volume covering December 1853–November 1877 (at S4/1/A/1). The EBC also contains Goss's Pastoral Letters 1855–72 (at S1/2/C/1–20) and an incomplete set of his Ad Clerum letters, 1855–72 (at S1/3/C/1).

4   The letters contain several references to funds and trusts, most of them established in aid of ecclesiastical education. In AAL the relevant documents are filed alphabetically and catalogued as FDC/S4/2/B/1–; information on most of the older funds is patchy.

5   AAL also has a bound collection of extracts from the *Diocesan Directories* of the 1880s and 1890s, entitled *Biographies Etc*; most are obituaries but there are also statistical tables and a few local histories, including one of Catholicism in the Isle of Man. The pages carry their original pagination, but a continuous numbering has been added by a modern hand; the volume contains 450 pages, and is referred to as *Extracts* in the notes here.

6   There are a number of letters in the Ushaw College Archive, referenced here as UC followed by the archive reference; for example, UC/PA refers to the President's Archive, followed by the item number. There is a large collection of documents on permanent loan to Ushaw College from the Archdiocese of Liverpool, used by Dr David Milburn for his history of the college (Ref: GB-0298-UC/P42; generally the reference is UC/P42/item number). These have only recently (autumn 2013) been catalogued. As well as containing a small number of letters to Goss, the collection is useful in showing the involvement of all the northern bishops in the various disputes with Ushaw, as well as the extent of Propaganda's involvement.

7   The archives of the English College, Rome: the Talbot Collection contains two letters from Goss to Mgr Talbot, which are included here (reference is VEC: Tal/item number). Other letters in the collection mention Goss, mainly in connection with the quarrel about Ushaw and written by Mgr Newsham or Cardinal Wiseman, but these are not reproduced here.

8   Occasional letters from other archives are identified by the official abbreviation for the archive in question, followed by any particular reference used in that archive. A list of these abbreviations may be found on page x–xi.

9   The archives of the Sacred Congregation for the Propagation of the Faith (Propaganda) in the Vatican contain two collections of particular relevance here. The first contains the letters and documents sent

to the Congregation from England, including from the bishops; most have been translated into Latin or Italian, occasionally into French. These make up the multi-volume collection known as *Scritture Riferite nei Congressi Sacrae Congregationis, Anglia*; each volume covers a number of years and the relevant ones for this work are vols 13: 1852–54; 14: 1855–57; 15: 1858–60; 16: 1861–63; 17: 1864–66; 18: 1867–70; 19: 1871–74. This collection is referenced here as APF, *Anglia*, vol. no., followed by item number. Some documents in this very important collection may also be found in the English sources already listed, but there are many for which the English original is missing. Of special value is the fact that the correspondence of the several parties to a dispute has been preserved, so that one gets a more balanced picture; in the dispute between Bishop Goss and the Rev. Henry Gibson, for example, while the English sources give nearly all Goss's letters they contain none of Gibson's, but these are in APF; this particular dispute takes up over 150 pages!

The second APF source is less important in this context: it is *Lettere della S.C. de Propaganda Fide*, referred to here as APF, *Lettere*. These are the replies sent from Propaganda; the collection comprises hundreds of volumes; relevant material (unfortunately not sorted by country) may be found in volumes 346–63, covering the years 1855–72.

Printed sources

Burke, Thomas, *Catholic Liverpool* (1910): a useful source, particularly for local political issues; it is uncritical of anything clerical and written as though the diocese was limited to the town.

Decreta Quatuor Conciliorum Provincialium Westmonasterium, 1852–73 (2nd edn, London, n.d.): the source for the official decrees of the four Provincial Councils or Synods, and of letters and decrees of Propaganda and other Roman documents. There was also an English edition: Robert E. Guy (ed.) *The Synods in English, being the Text of the Four Synods of Westminster* (Stratford-upon-Avon, 1886).

Directory: a publication with the same purpose but different titles throughout the nineteenth century; published annually in London; *Directory* and year of publication is the default reference used here.
The Laity's Directory (before 1840).
The Catholic Directory, Almanack and Ecclesiastical Register (1848).
Ordo Recitandi Officii Divini et Missae Celebrandae and Directory (1849).
The Catholic Directory and Ecclesiastical Register (1850).
The Catholic Directory, Ecclesiastical Register and Almanac (1858).

Kelly, Bernard W., *English Catholic Missions* (London, 1907, repr. 1995): very useful, but occasionally inaccurate.

Liverpool Catholic Directory and Family Almanack (Liverpool, 1885–).
Questions Addressed to the Clergy of the Diocese of Liverpool at the Visitation of 1855 (Liverpool, 1855).
Questiones Morales de Quibus Deliberabitur in Conventibus sub Praesidentia V.F. Dioeceseos Liverpolitanae (Liverpool, 1855–62).
Synodi Liverpolitanae I–VIII (Acta et Statuta) (Liverpool, n.d.).
The Tablet, 1840–.

Biographical sources

Biographical information has been drawn from a number of printed sources. For clergy in the diocese of Liverpool, Brian Plumb's excellent *'Found Worthy'* is essential and has been used throughout. The lists edited by Charles Fitzgerald-Lombard OSB have also been indispensable, especially for priests from other dioceses and for members of religious orders (referenced as Fitz-L). Where not otherwise noted, biographical details are from these two works. Goss's use of 'Mr' to refer to clergy sometimes causes uncertainty as to whether a priest or a lay person is being referred to.

Plumb, Brian, *Arundel to Zabi: A Biographical Dictionary of the Catholic Bishops of England and Wales (deceased) 1623–1987* (Warrington, 1987).
Plumb, Brian, *'Found Worthy'. A Biographical Dictionary of the Secular Clergy of the Archdiocese of Liverpool (Deceased), 1850–2000* (2nd edn, Wigan, 2005).
Fitzgerald-Lombard OSB, Charles (ed.), *English and Welsh Priests 1801–1914: A Working List* (Bath, 1993).

Other useful biographical sources have been:
Anstruther, G., *The Seminary Priests*, 4 vols (Ware and Ushaw, Great Wakering, 1968–77).
Bellenger OSB, Dominic Aidan (ed.), *English and Welsh Priests 1558–1800. A Working List* (Bath, 1984).
Gillow, J., *A Bibliographical Dictionary of the English Catholics*, 5 vols (London, 1885–1902).

Note on the maps

The diocese of Liverpool comprised the Lancashire hundreds of Lonsdale, Amounderness, Leyland and West Derby (the areas coloured yellow and pink on the map) and the Isle of Man. The other two hundreds, Salford and Blackburn (coloured green and orange on the map), were part of the diocese of Salford.

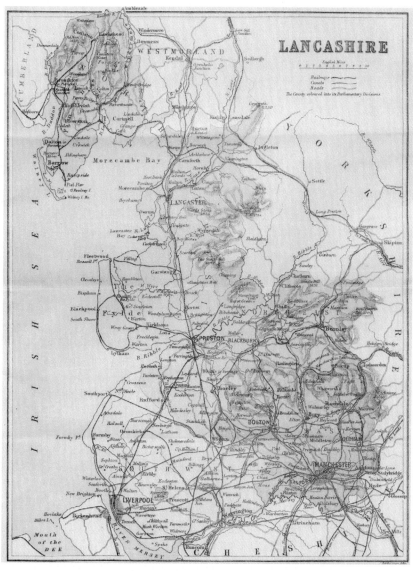

Lancashire c.1870: map by Bartholomew, from G. R. Emerson, *Geography of Lancashire: adapted to the new code* (London, 1872)

See Note on the maps opposite

The Isle of Man c.1870: map from Sidney Hall, *A travelling atlas of the English Counties* (London, *c*.1874)

INTRODUCTION

This volume presents a small selection of the more than 2,500 letters left by Bishop Goss of Liverpool, in the hope that they will help towards an understanding of the issues and complexities facing the restored hierarchy after 1850. Goss's over-riding aim was the advancement of religion in his diocese, and to this end he acted and wrote, as he put it, 'without restraint or reticence'. The letters range in content from the often humdrum daily business of a missionary bishop to his attempts to impose and defend episcopal authority locally and nationally, along with his involvement in a number of national issues. He was instrumental in laying out the foundations and setting the tone of one of the major dioceses in England and Wales and had an impact on how the hierarchy saw itself for the next half century. The letters reveal the complex personality of a man moulded by both English recusant traditions and the Victorian values of the day.

The restored hierarchy

The restoration of the hierarchy in England and Wales in 1850 established a single metropolitan see (Westminster), with twelve suffragan sees, of which Liverpool was one. What was established was not a fully independent hierarchy, for the bishops continued to be under the Roman Congregation for the Propagation of the Faith, or Propaganda, whose brief was to watch over and control the Church in missionary territories. By the decree of restoration, England and Wales had, in one sense, rejoined the visible family of the institutional church, but it was still a junior member, not fully trusted to act as an adult. Moreover, the decree said nothing about how the respective bishops should work together as a hierarchy, the rights of the individual bishops or their relationship with their Roman master, the Congregation of Propaganda. These issues were worked out, at least in part, over the next half century or so, largely by trial and error, but relationships and working arrangements remained uneasy and liable to disruption. For its part, Propaganda gave no overall guidance: individual questions were asked and (eventually) answered. If they had been asked for a model, the Roman authorities would no doubt have pointed to the Council of Trent and the saintly Charles Borromeo as providing sufficient guidance to any of the diocesan bishops setting out to re-establish episcopal authority in England and Wales after 1850.

Some of the resulting issues were to be expected as the bishops worked out how they should act as a hierarchy. Who was to convene and set the agendas for their regular meetings, as well as for their more important provincial synods? At these meetings, did the bishops have a decisive or only a consultative voice? Should they issue joint statements or pastoral letters on disputed matters or decrees from Rome; how far should they seek a common approach to pastoral practice or coordinate their reactions to government legislation, regarding, for example, the registration of Catholic charities or the provision of schools? Other questions had, perhaps, a more practical immediacy. How were the funds of the former districts to be distributed when the boundaries of the new dioceses were different (what had been the Lancashire District in the 1840s was now divided between the three dioceses of Liverpool, Salford and Shrewsbury)?[1] Who controlled the three major colleges (established when there were only four Vicars Apostolic for the whole of England and Wales) – the seminary rectors, the individual bishops of the dioceses in which they were located, or groups of the bishops most directly affected? There were important practical questions involved here: the right to claim clergy from the co-interested dioceses for the staff, and the distribution and control of funds (some of long standing) for the training of the clergy.

Although by 1850 it had been established that control in the Church in England and Wales would be firmly clerical, it still had to be worked out how far that control would be episcopal. For their part, several of the Secular clergy (perhaps especially in the north of England) had hoped that the restoration of a hierarchy would bring them greater freedom from the control of the Vicars Apostolic and a greater voice in establishing local ecclesiastical policy. Such hopes were to be disappointed: even a cursory reading of the letters of Bishop Goss shows he had no doubt that the acceptance of a firmer authority and stricter regulation by the clergy was essential for the advancement of religion. And the people served by these clergy? Did the changes of 1850 mean anything other than a change of name to most of them? Almost certainly not, though they might see the bishop more regularly on visitation, listen to more pastoral letters and be approached more systematically for money. For the better off, who had perhaps enjoyed privileges under the Vicars Apostolic (such as having their own private chapel and appointing priests to serve them, even when they also acted as the local missioner[2]), the imposition of

---

[1]   For other cases see Richard J. Schiefen, *Nicholas Wiseman and the Transformation of English Catholicism* (Shepherdstown, WV, 1984), 230–4, 241–2.

[2]   The 1850 restoration did not re-establish canonical parishes, as the clergy had hoped; territorial divisions of the dioceses remained missions, the term usually used in missionary territories. Priests serving such missions were technically missioners, although most of them regarded themselves as the equivalent of parish priests. Apparently the Vicars Apostolic had been against the setting up of parishes as being too permanent in a rapidly expanding Catholic population; see M. V. Sweeney, 'Diocesan Organisation and Administration', in G. A. Beck (ed.), *The English Catholics 1850–1950* (London, 1950), 119–21, 148–9.

a more canonical regime could come as a cold surprise, especially if it led to a questioning of their right to have such a privilege, which it did in the great majority of cases. In such a new situation much would clearly depend on the personalities of the bishops involved and what they saw as their rights and responsibilities. Several of them had been Vicars Apostolic, with ill-defined though relatively extensive powers, working largely independently of each other.

An important issue they needed to address as a body arose from the large number of Regular clergy, especially Jesuits and Benedictines, serving missions and living outside their religious houses, often on an individual basis; in Lancashire they were almost equal in numbers to the Secular clergy. They had played an indispensable role in keeping Catholicism going during the penal years, although not without frequent friction and worse between themselves and the Seculars. A delicate relationship had not been improved when Faber preached at Goss's consecration in 1853 on the superiority of the Secular clergy, 'the life of the Church', over the Regulars, 'only its ornament'.[3] They had enjoyed at least a practical semi-independence from the Vicars Apostolic and some of them regarded the newly established bishops with suspicion, insisting on carrying on as before, even though the decree of restoration had expressly abolished their privileges; it was to be many years before their relationship with the bishops was regulated and standardised.

The restoration, although essentially a matter of internal reorganisation, caused a public outcry, sometimes accompanied by violence, at the supposed pretensions of papal authority. Anti-Catholicism was endemic in the wider society, although by mid-century it was generally non-violent.[4] It may be difficult in many cases to distinguish between anti-Catholicism and anti-Irish feeling, but it made little difference to those on the receiving end of prejudice whether they were the victims of the one rather than the other. Lancashire had the largest proportion of Irish migrants in the country, with about 25 per cent of the total in the 1840s and 1850s, and Liverpool Catholics were not alone in experiencing hostility[5] as numbers flooded in after the famine. Catholics might no longer be under siege but they could still exhibit a siege mentality faced

---

[3] Reported in *The Tablet*, 1 October 1853.

[4] Much has been written on this topic; see J. Belchem, *Irish, Catholic and Scouse. The History of the Liverpool Irish 1800–1939* (Liverpool, 2007); Jonathan Bush, *'Papists' and Prejudice: Popular Anti-Catholicism and Anglo-Irish Conflict in the North-East of England, 1845–70* (Newcastle upon Tyne, 2013); Frank Neal, *Sectarian Violence: The Liverpool Experience, 1819–1914* (Manchester, 1988); Edward R. Norman, *Anti-Catholicism in Victorian Britain* (London, 1968); D. G. Paz, *Popular Anti-Catholicism in Mid-Victorian England* (Stanford, CA, 1992).

[5] See, for example, D. M. MacRaild, *Faith, Fraternity and Fighting: The Orange Order and Irish Migrants in Northern England, c. 1850–1920* (Liverpool, 2005).

by a hostile press and obstruction by local officials refusing to allow them their rights.

The Diocese of Liverpool

Geographically, the diocese extended from the Mersey to the mountains seventy-odd miles to the north. It took in the Lancashire hundreds of Amounderness, West Derby, Leyland and Lonsdale, as well as the Isle of Man. The other hundreds, Salford and Blackburn, were in the new Diocese of Salford.[6] As a result, the diocese comprised both heavily urban centres (Liverpool, Preston, Wigan, for example) and rural areas (the Fylde being the most obvious). The new diocese covered an area with a rich and unbroken tradition of Catholicism; it had the largest number of Catholics, priests and churches of any diocese in the country. While it was immediately and irrevocably affected by mass Irish immigration, this did not destroy its native traditions. It is not possible to give an accurate figure for the number of Catholics living in it, but an estimate of between 190,000 and 200,000 seems to be reasonable.[7] In 1840 it had probably been between 115,000 and 120,000. The number of churches where public Mass was available was eighty-four (increased from sixty-eight in 1840), and the number of priests serving on the mission was 122 (increased from eighty-seven). The increase in the number of Catholics was due principally, though by no means entirely, to Irish immigration, something that had been a well-established factor since the early years of the century. The 1841 census gives a figure of 49,639 Irish-born for Liverpool and 105,916 for the whole county. About 85 per cent of these immigrants were almost certainly Catholic. Ten years later, the Irish-born population of the county had risen to 191,500, an increase of almost 81 per cent. Most of this increase was due to the very large number of people leaving Ireland in the post-famine years after 1846: in 1846 itself, over 280,000 landed in Liverpool, in 1847, over 300,000; in 1848–50, about 200,000 landed there each year, and in 1851, about 250,000. But most of these immigrants moved on from Liverpool, so that by 1861 the number of Irish-born in Lancashire had only risen to 217,320, and

---

[6]   Originally Leyland Hundred had been placed in the diocese of Salford, but before a bishop had been appointed there Bishop Brown had objected because it meant his diocese was split into two parts; in 1851 he persuaded Propaganda to transfer the hundred to Liverpool, where it remained despite objections from Salford.

[7]   Various attempts have been made to arrive at an approximate figure. The most detailed is by Philip Hughes: 'English Catholics in 1850', in Beck, *The English Catholics*, 42–85; see also John Bossy, *The English Catholic Community, 1570–1850* (London, 1975), ch. 13; J. A. Lesourd, *Les catholiques dans la société anglaise, 1765–1865*, 2 vols (Lille/Paris, 1978). Goss's treasurer, T. E. Gibson, used the Lenten Returns to arrive at an estimate of 199,000 for 1850: RCLv, 'Diocese of Liverpool 1850–71'.

by 1871 it had dropped to 200,061. The diocese, of course, was not co-terminus with Liverpool: Wigan had 5.8 per cent Irish-born in 1851, rising to nearly 7 per cent ten years later; the figures for Preston were 6 per cent and 7.4 per cent, and for Warrington 10 per cent and 8.8 per cent. Even the rural Fylde had 3.3 per cent in 1851, rising to 5.7 per cent in 1861, but Lancaster only moved from 1.5 per cent to 1.9 per cent. Whatever the figures for individual towns and areas, it is true to say that there was hardly anywhere in the diocese that did not experience an increase of Catholics due to Irish immigration.

The process of Irish immigration to England was long established, though its scale in the late 1840s and early 1850s was immense. This meant that there were settled communities of Irish for the newly arrived to relate to and integrate into, and the Church in Lancashire had been dealing with its effects for some time. Between 1840 and 1850 Bishop Brown had opened fourteen new churches, eight of them in Liverpool and Bootle, had encouraged the building of schools and introduced new religious orders to help run them. The social ills attendant on this immigration have been fully documented. They were greatest in Liverpool, but not evenly distributed: certain parts of the borough were unaffected and experienced an Irish presence only in their well-established and frequently respectable second- and third-generation descendants.[8] Such middle-ranking and sometimes professional Irish Catholics were represented in every social group in the town – merchants, bankers, medical men, businessmen. As the new arrivals settled, few of them made it from 'rags to riches', but many moved from 'rags to respectability'. The majority of Catholics throughout the diocese, however, remained in the working classes and this meant that they were for the most part engaged in unskilled or lower-skilled jobs. They shared in the poverty, and must on occasion have fallen into the pauperism that was the lot of such workers in Victorian England.

It is important to stress, however, that what was achieved by way of expansion in the 1840s to 1860s could not have been achieved without the considerable support of wealthy and comfortably-off Catholics, English and Irish. There were 'county' families with considerable landed and commercial wealth, like the Gerrards of Garswood, the de Traffords of Croston, the Blundells of Little Crosby, the Weld Blundells of Ince Blundell, the Daltons of Thurnham, the Orrells of Blackbrook, the Brockholes of Preston, Lady Scarisbrick of Scarisbrick Hall, the Gillows of Clifton and the Whitesides of Lancaster, all of whom at times headed

---

[8]   See Bossy, *The English Catholic Community*, 306–43; W. J. Lowe, *The Irish in Mid-Victorian Lancashire: The Shaping of a Working-Class Community* (New York, 1989), and n. 5, above.

subscription lists for annual charities or one-off appeals. The Liverpool had its annual Catholic Charities Ball, held in the Town Hall, which was one of the major events of the social calendar, attended by several hundred people (though not all of them were Catholics) who each paid a substantial entrance fee. The Catholic Club (founded 1844) attracted a middle-class membership, concerning itself with liberal politics and Catholic charities, while the Catholic Benevolent Society (founded 1810) charged variously ten shillings or a pound annually and as its main aim supported Catholic orphanages and asylums.[9] Similar, predominantly lay, bodies existed outside Liverpool: Preston's Catholic Brethren dated from the early eighteenth century (1731), and the Broughton Catholic Charitable Society (1787) helped 'needy persons, families and charitable organisations'. In 1869 it was worth advertising in the Catholic press a week's residential retreat for 'lay gentlemen'; who but the comparatively well-to-do could afford to go? The idea that the new churches and schools were built from 'the pennies of the poor' has a long history but is little more than a romantic legend. Where there was no or only a little support from the well-to-do, missions might carry heavy building debts for years: the country mission of Burscough, for example, where the church had been opened in 1819, at a cost of a little over £1,500, still owed £800 in 1850.[10]

The Bishop

Alexander Goss was born in Ormskirk, Lancashire, in July 1814. On his mother's side he was descended from old Lancashire recusant stock; his uncle was Rev. Henry Rutter and his great-uncle Rev. Robert Banister.[11] His father, John Goss, was a Protestant. Goss was educated at Ushaw and then, taking advantage of money left to him by Rutter, he went to the English College, Rome, where he was ordained in 1841. He spent a short time as a curate at SS Peter and Paul's Church, Mawdesley, before being appointed in October 1842 as Vice-President of the newly established St Edward's College, Liverpool, a boarding school and, later, the junior

---

9   See Thomas Burke, *Catholic History of Liverpool* (Liverpool, 1910), for the various Catholic social agencies in Liverpool.

10   Gillian Goddard, *St John the Evangelist Catholic Church, Burscough. A Celebration of the Tercentenary of the Foundation of Burscough Hall Mission (1700–2000)* (Burscough, 2000) 26. See letters 227 and 191 below for other examples: St Oswald's, Old Swan and St Joseph's, Liverpool.

11   For biographical details, see Brian Plumb, *Arundel to Zabi: A Biographical Dictionary of the Catholic Bishops of England and Wales (Deceased) 1623–1987* (Warrington, 1987); also P. Doyle in *ODNB*. There is an interesting short account in F. J. Cwiekowski, *The English Bishops and the First Vatican Council* (Louvain, 1971), 43–4.

seminary for the Liverpool diocese; it was to be Goss's home until his death in 1872.[12]

It is to the President of St Edward's (and Goss's last VG), Canon John Henry Fisher,[13] that we owe a personal sketch of the bishop. He was writing to Mgr Talbot in Rome, who had accused Goss of being 'cold and indifferent' for not answering a letter, and stressed that Goss was a 'shy, retiring and reserved' person, who 'lives apart from the world. He has no thought nor care for anything but his Diocese. He may be *obditus negotiis et totus in illis*,[14] but they are the concerns of his Diocese ... He can only think and work for his flock.' Such a description would probably have surprised those who had to deal with Goss in public disputes and to whom Manning's description of him as 'strong and resolute almost to vehemence', and going into battle with 'his usual rough violence – the crozier, hook and point', would have seemed more appropriate.[15] Perhaps he over-reacted as shy people sometimes do when they have to speak out in public; he certainly exaggerated at times to make a point. He described himself as a 'rough and ready speaker', able to speak his mind to 'plain, homely Lancashire folks' but no more. He decried what he saw as the plotting, double-dealing and rumour-mongering of his opponents, especially in Rome, and lamented the absence of 'truth, simple English truth' from their statements, though it is clear from his letters that he was not above a certain amount of plotting and manoeuvring himself.[16] Though implacable against any invasion of his rights as a diocesan bishop or any weakening of his authority, he bore no grudges, as Manning himself conceded, and was open to persuasion 'with a delicacy of the highest kind in balancing justice'.[17]

All the evidence points to a life of unceasing work: on visitation he might preach (rarely for less than an hour) three or four times a week, and twice on Sundays, for two months together; he officiated and preached at some church every Sunday, even supplying for absent clergy; he could spend twelve hours a day at his desk and still be up very early the next

---

[12] On St Edward's, see P. Doyle and L. McLoughlin, *The Edwardian Story* (Wirral, 2003); Burke, *Catholic History*, 72. It is said that, while at Mawdesley, Goss 'astonished the natives by his energy and eloquence, earning a great reputation amongst them' (A. Hewitson ('Atticus'), *Our Country Churches and Chapels. Antiquarian, Historical, Ecclesiastical and Critical Sketches* (Preston and London, 1872), 239).

[13] John Henry Fisher, 1812–89, at St Edward's 1842–84. Appointed a canon in 1851, he became VG in 1868 and virtually ran the diocese during Goss's later illnesses. Two brothers were priests in the diocese: James, 1814–83, also a canon and Goss's treasurer, and George, 1810–97, dean.

[14] Trans: 'burdened with business and totally taken up with it'. On Talbot, see n. 379.

[15] Manning in his eulogy, published as *The Good Soldier's Death* (Liverpool, 1872).

[16] See letters 175, 279, 440.

[17] Manning, op. cit.

morning to attend to a sick call from a priest. His way of life was frugal: in 1856 he claimed to be still using his student cassock. He hardly ever rang for servants and never ordered a dish when he did not like what was on the table, even though he knew another was available; indeed, he claimed never to order 'as much as a cup of tea'. He had no house of his own and insisted on paying for his keep at St Edward's 'because he was of no service' to it. He did not keep a carriage, travelling on visitations by train and begging lifts from better-off members of his flock. It was the life of an active, missionary bishop.

The first bishop of Liverpool was George Hilary Brown, 1786–1856, the former Vicar Apostolic of the Lancashire District (set up in 1840).[18] He appointed Goss to his Chapter in 1851 and made him Canon Theologian. Brown's deteriorating health soon made it necessary for him to have a coadjutor and Goss was appointed to the post in June 1853, very much against Brown's wishes.[19] Cardinal Wiseman consecrated Goss Bishop of Gerra in September in the pro-cathedral of St. Nicholas in Liverpool. Brown and Goss never got on and as Brown's health deteriorated his distrust of his coadjutor grew; he believed Goss was in league with members of the Chapter against him and refused to give him any definite work or financial allowance.[20] A particular issue was the visitation of the diocese: Goss wished to start this and drew up a list of questions which the clergy were to answer beforehand; Brown derided these and Goss found it difficult to find out from Brown whether he had the faculties to carry out the visitation or not. This issue of faculties was key: Goss believed that Brown regarded a coadjutor as a type of

[18] Brown had taught at Ushaw for ten years before becoming rector of St Peter's, Lancaster, for twenty-one years; he was consecrated Bishop of Bugia (later transferred to Tloa) in August 1840 and appointed Vicar Apostolic of the new Lancashire District. He was a poor administrator, frequently quarrelling with those whom he had appointed; increasing bad health made matters worse. For all his failings, however, his years in charge had not been barren: seventeen new missions had been opened, several new religious orders had been introduced, a unique Catholic Blind Asylum and other social agencies had been established, St Edward's College and the Catholic Institute school had opened to offer secondary education, while a Teacher Training College for girls provided teachers for the growing number of Catholic elementary schools. He ended the last vestiges of lay control and patronage of missions and established a number of important diocesan funds, including the Diocesan Mission Fund and that for Ecclesiastical Education, with annual collections throughout the diocese. See N. Schofield and G. Skinner, *The English Vicars Apostolic 1688–1850* (Oxford, 2009), 187–90; Hilton, *ODNB*; P. Doyle, '"A Tangled Skein of Confusion": The Administration of George Hilary Brown, Bishop of Liverpool 1850–56', *RH* 25:2 (October 2000), 294–303.

[19] Brown had had problems with his previous coadjutor, Bishop James Sharples, 1799–1850, an energetic and fiery personality. Wiseman had been instrumental in Goss's appointment. See Doyle, 'Tangled Skein', at 297–8.

[20] APF, *Anglia*, 14, fols 207–8; 1111–13. Goss stated his case at considerable length in letters to Wiseman, below, letters 5 and 6, and Appendix 2.

personal assistant or chaplain, and not as someone with episcopal power who could help in running the diocese. Goss asked for specific faculties in writing and thought Brown was offering him (and that verbally) only those of a vicar general. On his side, Brown complained of Goss's 'youth and presumptiousness' and lack of pastoral experience; it cannot have helped when Goss continued to sign his letters 'Your affectionate brother in Christ', implying an equality of status that Brown simply did not understand. Goss later admitted he had not been without fault, taking his stand too unbendingly on points of principle, a point Wiseman also made. In the end their quarrels were to some extent patched up by Propaganda and Wiseman, but Brown's administration came under increasing criticism and is perhaps best summed up by Goss's phrase 'a tangled skein of confusion'.[21] Goss succeeded Brown as bishop in January 1856.

Relations between the bishops

While most of Goss's energy went on diocesan matters such as opening new missions and providing sufficient clergy to staff them, he was heavily involved in a number of national issues that affected the English and Welsh Catholic body in different ways and which were to have lasting effects on its constitution and outlook. At stake was the question of authority and the role of the bishops. The leader of the new hierarchy was Cardinal Wiseman, a hugely talented, colourful (even flamboyant) figure, devoted to Rome and its ways.[22] He was, however, a weak and dilatory administrator and a poor judge of people, delaying dealing with routine business to an embarrassing extent. Gradually Goss lost patience with him and their former respectful relationship disintegrated into bitterness as the bishop felt Wiseman's lack of action was causing him and the other bishops more and more trouble. In a letter of August 1858, for example, he complained that nothing had been done to solve the Youens/Sherburne dispute (see below) even though arbitration had been agreed years before. As a result, money was not being provided for apprenticeships for poor boys and a wealthy and good landed gentleman was thinking of instructing his solicitors on the matter.[23]

---

[21] David Milburn, *A History of Ushaw College: A Study of the Origin, Foundation and Development of an English Catholic Seminary* (Durham, 1964), 213. Appendix 2 contains a diary of the lengthy correspondence that resulted from their quarrels as well as extracts from two of the letters. Goss certainly felt his inexperience did not help him when dealing with senior members of the clergy even apart from the bishop.
[22] On Wiseman, see Schiefen, *Nicholas Wiseman*; Wilfrid Ward, *The Life and Times of Cardinal Wiseman*, 2 vols (London 1897); J. Derek Holmes, *More Roman than Rome* (London, 1978); Brian Fothergill, *Nicholas Wiseman* (London, 1963).
[23] Letter 5/2/274–7; the letter is incomplete, with at least three pages missing; it is not in AAW.

Moreover, Goss felt that the cardinal's autocratic manner added to the problems: Wiseman, Goss thought, could only be propitiated 'by having the hierarchy prostrate before him'. On the question of the right to convene the bishops, he added, the cardinal thought he alone could do so, while the other bishops thought they could do so as a group; it was, he felt, time to sort this out 'for we are in the 11th year of our hierarchical existence'.[24] Goss advised another bishop who was writing about their problems to Propaganda to stress that 'in an age of republican equality' there was great danger in 'humbling the Episcopal authority of the ordinaries in England in order to smooth the morbid sensibility of an invalid'.[25] Here again, Goss over-reacted to the situation, as he had done in his quarrels with Brown, but underneath the sometimes petty-seeming disputes lay important points concerning episcopal authority. When Wiseman asked Propaganda to quash the decrees of the Third Provincial Synod (1859) because he believed the bishops did not have the right to legislate as a body about the seminaries, Goss led the opposition and in 1860 went to Rome to plead the bishops' case; two years later he organised his colleagues in a final appeal to Propaganda, even writing draft letters for the other bishops to send to Rome. In the meanwhile he decided that it would be dishonourable to attend the annual meetings of the hierarchy convened by the cardinal and so organised a partial boycott of them in 1862 and 1863.

While Goss believed that the cardinal's way of acting in general lessened the authority of the other English and Welsh bishops (an authority already under pressure, he believed, from the centralising tendencies of the Roman authorities), it is clear from these letters that a principal cause for concern was the position of Ushaw. It had been opened as the northern successor to Douai at a time when the whole of northern England comprised the old Northern District with a single Vicar Apostolic. When this was split by the establishment of additional districts in 1840, and still more when the new dioceses were established ten years later, questions arose about the control of the college and its funds: it lay in the diocese of Hexham and Newcastle and both the college authorities and the local bishop, Hogarth, claimed it was now essentially a diocesan college that other bishops might send their students to if they wished, but only on the terms laid down by the college. They also claimed total control over the funds that had been set up over the years for the education and training of northern priests. The other northern bishops (of Beverley, Liverpool, Salford and Shrewsbury) argued that this was unjust and that they jointly with Hexham and Newcastle, had equal rights over the college

---

[24]   To Ullathorne, 5/4/103, May 1861, and see letter 336 below.
[25]   To Menevia, 17 January 1862, (5/4/276), and see n. 601.

and owned a pro rata share of its funds. Again, Goss appointed himself leader of the disaffected bishops. A peaceful resolution of the issues involved was made all the more difficult to attain because Wiseman had been appointed Apostolic Visitor of Ushaw in 1850; he sided with the college authorities and used his standing in Rome to support their case (partially, at least, because of his desire to have sole control over St Edmund's, Ware, in his own diocese). The question of the constitution of the three colleges was discussed at the third Provincial Synod in 1859 and settled in favour of joint episcopal control.[26] It was these decrees that Wiseman asked Propaganda to turn down; he seemed to have won the day when Propaganda asked the bishops to put forward their views individually for further consideration, but in the end it found in favour of the bishops against Wiseman and the college authorities. The cardinal had over-estimated his influence in Rome, as also had Goss and the other bishops.[27]

Propaganda also found in favour of the bishops and against the college in two other major disputes, both concerning funds. The first was about the Sherburne Trust. Thomas Sherburne[28] had been a generous bene-factor of Ushaw for some years, funding much of the extensive building works between 1849 and 1854. He also set up a trust with the extensive property left him by the local squire, William Heatley, for general chari-table purposes and especially the education of northern ecclesiastical students; he did not specify that they had to be trained at Ushaw, although this was undoubtedly his intention. When there was talk of setting up a junior seminary in Lancashire (St Edward's College, Liverpool, which Bishop Brown did make into a junior seminary in 1850) Sherburne and the college authorities feared that some of the money would go there instead, and so tried to alter the terms of the trust, but failed in their attempts to do so. Goss and the other northern bishops claimed that they, and not the college authorities, should control the funds and use them as they thought best for their dioceses.

The second case also involved Sherburne. Thomas Youens[29] had provided over £12,000 to Sherburne in 1841 (the money had come origi-nally from Heatley). Sherburne had used this money to defend himself

---

[26] *Decreta*, 170–2; Schiefen, *Nicholas Wiseman*, ch. 13: 'The Colleges'.
[27] See Milburn, *History of Ushaw College*, 250–2; Judith Champ, *William Bernard Ullathorne 1806–1889: A Different Kind of Monk* (Leominster, 2006), 266; Schiefen, *Nicholas Wiseman*, 310–11.
[28] Thomas Sherburne (b. Irving), 1779–1854, edu. Valladolid, where he was r. 1822–5. He built the church at Kirkham and had a reputation for charitable works; see Milburn, *History of Ushaw College*, 216–17 for biography and legal troubles, which involved appeals to Rome; see APF, *Anglia*, 10 (1842–45), fols 219–20, 235–7.
[29] Thomas Youens, 1790–1848, of the Northern District, third President of Ushaw; see Milburn, *History of Ushaw College*, 127–31 and *passim*.

in a court case, claiming that Youens had given him the money as a gift. Youens and his executors claimed the money had been a loan and demanded its repayment. When Sherburne died in 1854 without any money, the executors claimed the money from Ushaw where so much of Sherburnes's money had gone. The College authorities refused to acknowledge the claim, arguing that they were not Sherburne's heirs. As already stated, when both sides appealed to Propaganda the verdict eventually (after considerable delay caused by Wiseman's failure to convene the arbitrators) went against the college and it was ordered to pay £8,000 with interest to the northern bishops.[30]

While Goss's main concerns about Ushaw were financial, including the way in which he and the other co-interested bishops had no control over how their money was spent by the authorities there, it was not his only worry. He believed Mgr Newsham had the wrong priorities in seeking to extend the college buildings in as grand a manner as possible instead of spending what money there was on the provision of much-needed priests to serve the swelling numbers of Catholics. He also believed that the quality of the education provided there (and in the other colleges as well) was being seriously neglected. He condemned the system by which students of average ability, once ordained (or even sometimes before ordination) were appointed to teach when their only experience had been Ushaw itself, where they might have been since their early teens; he felt there was something incestuous about the arrangement, even suicidal, for degeneracy such as 'results from frequent intermarriages' would naturally follow; an educational establishment, just like the human body, needed an 'infusion of new blood' from time to time. He thought the colleges could not stand comparison with secular institutions of learning and were rightly criticised for their low standards.[31] There are links in all this to his wish to have a better-educated clergy and to encourage habits of serious study among them.[32] Mention may also be made here of two letters that tell us something of Goss's views on the basic issue of vocations to the priesthood. One deals with the possible temptations that might lead a student to give up his vocation without serious attention to what was at stake. The other suggests a fairly practical approach to determining whether a student had a vocation or not: spiritual directors should not be too ready to judge in these cases. Goss claimed some of the 'new lights' acted 'queerly' about the matter, for if a boy was good and wanted

[30]   Milburn, *History of Ushaw College*, esp. 244–52.
[31]   Letter 1, to Lingard; there is also a very long memorial written by Goss to Wiseman in 1854 (UC/P42/245), which details all that he thought wrong with the teaching and curriculum; Wiseman ignored it and the college authorities dismissed it as 'impertinent'.
[32]   See letters 103, 105, and P. Doyle, 'Education and Training', at 214.

to be a priest, that was enough evidence of a vocation: even if not there to begin with, God would give it.[33]

A further cause of discord between the cardinal and some of the bishops, especially Goss, was Wiseman's treatment of Archbishop Errington, his coadjutor.[34] The two men were clearly incompatible, and after drawn-out efforts by both Wiseman and Propaganda to get Errington to resign, he eventually did so on the orders of the pope; it is clear that Wiseman and others had manoeuvred the dismissal. Goss felt he had been unjustly dismissed and so deprived of his right to succeed to Westminster when the cardinal died in 1865. When Manning succeeded, Goss's relations were affected by what had happened: the new archbishop was in a false position since Errington had been 'shoved out' to make way for him.[35] While there were no longer complaints about poor administration, Goss had taken objection to what he saw as Manning's backstairs, even underhand, influence earlier in Rome in support of Wiseman in the various disputes between the cardinal and the bishops, and had even claimed that if Manning became a bishop it would be 'adieu to fair and upright dealing'.[36] He was later very critical of Manning's manoeuvrings in the lead up to the Vatican Council, especially his refusal to appoint Newman as a theological adviser, and what he saw as Manning's ultra-papalist policies after the council.[37] Overall, he felt that Manning was continuing Wiseman's policy of interference in matters that were properly the concern of individual bishops and of acting as though he was their representative without consulting them first. To Goss's mind, while uniformity might be desirable, it must not be bought at the expense of episcopal autonomy.

Relations with Rome

From the start of his coadjutorship, Goss was necessarily involved in dealings with Propaganda. In general he had a low opinion of the abilities of Roman clerical officials and objected strongly to what he saw as undue interference by them in English matters, which they did not understand, and the ways in which ill-founded rumours were used to destroy the credibility of individual bishops. There was a serious danger, he feared, that Catholicism in England would be dominated and fashioned by curial thinking, that Italian solutions would be found for English

---

[33] Letters 88 and 393.
[34] On Errington: Plumb, *Arundel*; Schiefen, *Nicholas Wiseman*, 298–302; Beck, *The English Catholics*, 199–200, 204–9.
[35] See letter 435 to Newman, March 1870.
[36] Goss to the bishop of Shrewsbury, 9 January 1862.
[37] See letters 429, 432, 435, 436.

problems and that, in the process, the Church would lose its Englishness and its ability to appeal to English people. At the same time, in common with the rest of the hierarchy, he was only too ready to appeal to Rome when it suited him, on national issues and even in his dealings with individual members of his clergy.

Generally, Goss was a rigorist in cases where canon law was involved; indeed, at times he seemed to need the psychological support of knowing that what he was doing was laid down for him by the Church's laws. There were, however, instances where, in the bishop's eyes, local pastoral necessity demanded non-compliance with Roman directives. The most important of these concerned mixed marriages. For some reason, Brown had not published an earlier Roman decree insisting on a strict observance of the law against them and Goss did not hurry to do so when he became bishop; furthermore, he also ignored a decree of 1858 that reinforced the earlier ruling and stressed the Church's horror of mixed marriages;[38] he seems not to have been alone among the bishops in doing so. It is true that he spoke very strongly against the practice in his visitation sermons, and in a pastoral letter of 1863,[39] but priests continued to seek dispensations for mixed couples to marry and he continued to apply to Rome for them to be granted. While the bishops were in Rome in 1862 (Goss was not with them) they had been ordered to take a stricter line and this might have been the reason for the pastoral letter, but it was only in 1864 that Goss considered action. He consulted his clergy through their conferences, asking whether they thought it appropriate to enforce a stricter line. Most of the clergy counselled against doing so: some claimed such a regulation would be 'obnoxious', others that it would cause more harm than good without reducing the number of such marriages, which were 'inevitable' in a country like England; some even claimed the Church gained considerably from them.[40] Goss followed their advice. He continued to speak out against mixed marriages in the strongest terms: they were, he claimed, seldom happy even under the most favourable circumstances and were 'often miserable beyond the conception of those who engaged in them'. He supported the publication by one of his clergy of a sermon against them; the author put heresy alongside adultery as the twin enemies of marriage and made the point that the partners could have no 'sure hope of meeting each other in the next life'.[41] It is interesting to read what his secretary wrote after summarising Goss's visitation sermon at Southport in 1864: 'The Bishop himself the son of a mixed marriage, therefore he did not speak from

[38] See *Decreta*, 315–16, for extracts from this severe 1858 letter.
[39] PL, Sexagesima Sunday, 1863.
[40] RCLv Conference Reports, 1863–64 and 1864–65. See letter 372.
[41] J. Swarbrick, *Marriage: A Sermon Preached at St Augustine's* (Preston, 1858).

feeling but from duty.'[42] He had no alternative but to impose the law even though it ran counter to the situation in which most of his flock lived, but at least he did it less rigorously than Rome desired.

Goss and the papacy

During Pius IX's pontificate there was a positive drive towards centralisation in Rome, with an increasing tendency to interfere directly in diocesan affairs and to impose an all-embracing uniformity. Many Catholic bishops accepted and even welcomed these developments, and the pope used his charm and personal popularity to win over waverers and dissidents; the two great gatherings of bishops in Rome in 1862 and 1867 had a clearly triumphalist and emotional atmosphere.[43] These developments were accompanied by easy accusations that those who questioned what was happening were Gallican, un-Roman, 'cold' and 'Anglican', and all of these labels were attached to Bishop Goss at different times. Wiseman complained to Propaganda that the bishop was always boasting about his Englishness and claiming 'I am English, I am a real John Bull, indeed I am a Lancashire man', and Manning thought this extreme patriotism meant that Goss could never be truly Roman in outlook.[44]

Goss, however, for all his criticism of Roman centralisation, was not anti-papal. He believed that the pope held the primacy over the whole Church, that his person was 'august and sacred' and that the Catholics of Lancashire, as his devoted children, owed him 'profound respect, veneration and dutiful obedience'; the pope was the supreme visible head of the Church in matters of faith and morals.[45] In 1859 he arranged for a diocesan collection to be taken to help the pope in his difficulties against the Italian nationalists and for an address to be circulated for signatures; the collection raised the staggering sum of almost £8,000. In 1867 he issued a pastoral letter on the subject of the pope's temporal power. His views were very straightforward: Garibaldi was a pest to society, and governments that had failed to stop him were unfaithful and untruthful. It was puerile to say that the pope would have more respect without his temporal possessions: they were a necessary guarantee of his independence. Moreover, it was hypocritical of Englishmen to claim that the

---

[42]   RCLv Visitation Diaries, 3/B/114.

[43]   1862: the canonisation of the Japanese Martyrs; 1867: the eighteenth centenary of the martyrdoms of SS Peter and Paul. For Bd Pius IX's pontificate, Paul Burns, *Butler's Lives of the Saints. The Third Millennium* (London, 2005), 44–52 with bibliography (Pius was beatified in 2000). See also P. Doyle, 'Bishop Goss of Liverpool (1856–72) and the Importance of Being English', *SCH* 18 (1982), 433–47.

[44]   See references in Doyle, 'Bishop Goss of Liverpool', 442.

[45]   Ibid., 443.

spiritual and temporal powers were incompatible in one person, or that Rome belonged to Italy; what about Queen Victoria, and Gibraltar? The pastoral ended with arrangements for a triduum of prayer for the pope and another collection, which raised £1,945.[46]

The great issue, of course, in these latter years was that of the definition of papal infallibility at the First Vatican Council in 1870. If Goss had been at the council he would have been among those who opposed the definition on inopportunist grounds (he was too ill to attend). He described his position in a long letter to Newman, in which he claimed there was no general acceptance amongst English Catholics that a definition was appropriate, and a bishop had to be a witness to the beliefs of his diocese and not just give his own theological opinion.[47] The council provided another opportunity for an attack on Manning and the ultra-papalists for their manipulation of events at the council and in Rome in general:

> Rome is only Manning in Italian. It learns all from him and acts by his suggestion ... Rome lives in an ideal world, in a cloud of incense offered by the nauseous Tablet, Univers, Civiltà & Osservatore. Who is Herbert Vaughan or Veuillot to dictate a Catholic policy to the world? When will men cease to allow weight to what appears in big print in a newspaper when you would not listen to the writer for five minutes?[48]

For their part this was all evidence of Goss's un-Roman spirit, evidence that was strengthened by accusations that he would not allow his people to express their opinions on the Italian invasion of Rome in 1870.[49] Goss wrote another pastoral in 1871, upholding the temporal power and calling on the British government to defend the right of its Catholic citizens to claim independence for their spiritual ruler. In a perhaps more balanced view, Goss admitted that the temporal power was in no way essential to the papacy but was in practice intended by God. He did not go as far as the extreme papalists: the temporal power was not necessary for the political health of Europe nor did its downfall spell ruin for the state or the family, as some of them had claimed. Goss included in the letter a balanced refutation of what he called the old 'divided allegiance' accusation against English Catholics.[50]

---

[46]   Ad clerum letters, 3 and 25 December 1859; 13 March 1860. Also, PL, 11 December 1867.

[47]   Letters 435, to Newman, and 436, to Clifford.

[48]   Letter in AAA, Misc. Box, to Brown OSB of Newport and Menevia, 19 December 1870. Vaughan edited *The Tablet*, Veuillot *L'Univers*.

[49]   See the Dolman affair: letters 440, 442, 445, 446, 448.

[50]   PL, 14 February 1871. In 1868 Fisher had sent almost £1, 300 in February and a further £650 in May.

The religion of the people

While Goss's letters give some evidence of his attitude to lay spirituality, most of the evidence is to be found in his pastoral letters and visitation sermons. There is no doubting that for all his involvement in national issues, Goss's fundamental interest was the advancement of religion in his own diocese. His model of lay spirituality was essentially a sacramental one: 'practising Catholics' were those who attended church regularly on Sundays, received the sacraments regularly and performed some practical works of mercy, at least by giving what they could to support good causes, which included church and school building or maintenance. A 'good Catholic' would add attendance at extra-liturgical devotions, membership of a confraternity and some attempt at family prayers. It followed that an important step in providing a church that parishioners would want to attend would be the development of a rich sacramental life, with opportunities for attending attractive devotions and joining like-minded Catholics in friendly sodalities and societies. All the evidence shows that the Lancashire clergy as a body were keen to encourage strong Eucharistic devotion among their people, with a general encouragement of frequent Communion (without defining what 'frequent' meant).[51]

From several points of view Bishop Goss was a rigorist and in the matter of devotions he lamented that the tried and trusted ways of *The Garden of the Soul* were giving away to what he called a 'multiplicity of prayer books', leading to a lessening of the habit of prayer 'as a multiplicity of dainties destroys healthy appetite'; elsewhere he referred to 'the more flippant style of modern devotions'.[52] He had no doubts at all, however, of the value of devotions to the Blessed Sacrament. Some of his warmest approval went to the practice of the *Quarant'Ore* or Forty Hours Exposition of the Blessed Sacrament: he urged it as most beneficial, laying down careful rules for its proper celebration. The Liverpool town churches celebrated it in turn during Lent, so that there was a continuous daytime rota across nineteen churches; in his early years as bishop, Goss tried to attend the opening and closing ceremonies of this remarkable devotional celebration. In this context he spoke of the sacramental presence of Christ as 'the dearest token of God's love', and continued,

> We exhort you to come and fall down before the Lamb that was slain and has redeemed us in his blood ... Do not limit your devotion to the Exposition in

---

[51] RCLv Conference Reports, 1863–64 and 1864–65.
[52] PLs, Lent 1868 and Lent 1872.

the church of your own district, but follow Jesus, if you wish to be healed, to every church in which his presence is manifest.

He recommended a Preston priest to advertise the times of the *Quarant'Ore* in the local secular press, so that as many people as possible would be able to visit the church.[53]

In line with this, Goss also urged the importance of Benediction of the Blessed Sacrament: it was, he claimed, 'an attractive service' that would bear fruit in greater frequentation of the Sacraments; there was no other service that so effectively 'warms the devotion of the people'. He willingly gave priests permission to have it weekly, and even twice a week on special occasions; during parish missions and the annual May Devotions it might take place every evening. Undoubtedly it became the most popular form of 'optional extra', being colourful, concise, convenient, theatrical and mysterious all at once. If, however, one compares the numbers attending it with those attending Mass, it seems never to have become more than a minority interest; at the very most, even during Lent, it attracted less than a third of those who attended Mass and the percentage was normally well below a quarter.[54]

The highlighting of the importance of the Blessed Sacrament should not hide the fact that the Sacrament of Penance loomed so large in the preaching and practice of the day that one could be forgiven for thinking that it, and not Holy Communion, dominated clerical thinking. If one looks at the hours that priests were expected to spend in their confessionals it is easy to understand why the training of expert confessors played such a large role in clerical training. A few examples will suffice. At Barrow-in-Furness confessions were heard every morning from 6.30 am to 8 am; on the eve of holydays and feasts of devotion from 5 pm to 10 pm; every Friday and Saturday from 5 pm to 10 pm, and in Lent every evening. At Leigh, the confessional was manned every morning, every Friday evening, the whole of Saturday and on Sunday before the two Masses (there were two priests attached to the mission). At Great Crosby, confessions were heard every Saturday from 3.30 pm to 10 pm, every Sunday and weekday before Mass if people requested it, and on alternate Fridays for children from 2.30 pm to 6 pm; before special feast-days and during the whole of Lent they were held on two weekdays and on Saturdays from 2.30 pm to 10 pm. A final example of the importance

---

[53] The quotation is from the PL of Lent 1857. For Preston, see letter 111 below. M. Heimann, *Catholic Devotion in Victorian England* (Oxford, 1995) seriously underestimates the occurrence of this devotion (44, 176–8). See AAL, *Guide to the Catholic Church Services and Quarant'Ore in Liverpool for 1861* (Liverpool, 1861) for an example of the rota of churches.

[54] See P. Doyle, *Mitres and Missions in Lancashire: A History of the Roman Catholic Diocese of Liverpool 1850–2000* (Liverpool, 2005) 113; letters 34, 45, 121, below.

attached to confession is a circular to schools of 1864: every child over the age of seven had to answer five questions on Monday mornings. Three questions concerned attendance at Mass, two asked about confession, and none asked about reception of Holy Communion. Overall, this great stress on the provision of confession must have been matched in preaching and catechetics by a stress on sin and the ever-present dangers of losing one's soul. It also affected the theological discussions at the clergy's regular conferences which were heavily weighted towards confessional practice.[55]

When a priest asked Goss to make it compulsory for people to attend their own parish church rather than a neighbouring one, he refused, saying that it was up to the priest to make his church attractive enough for the people to want to attend it. For, in the end, people voted with their feet and 'no power or authority in the Church' could make them attend where they felt uncomfortable or where they judged the priest to be negligent or slovenly. The priest had to keep his church clean and well kept, had to be punctual at Mass times, and in the pulpit should not scold or talk instead of preaching properly. The bishop ended his exhortation by saying, tellingly, 'Ordinarily, it is through the confessional that the church is filled'.[56]

Goss shared with Victorian social and religious reformers a belief that central to any improvement in society was the upholding of family life. Liverpool's social observers and commentators presented a picture as damning as Mayhew's uncovering of London's attitudes and habits. Much could be blamed on the terrible living conditions in courts and cellars: privacy was impossible because of multi-family occupation of inadequate accommodation, and promiscuity and sexual immorality were accepted as commonplace where adults and children shared not just the same room but often the same bed. Goss spoke openly about these evils in his pastoral letters and sermons, constantly stressing the need for moral improvement among the poorer members of his congregations. It was not that he did not see the causal connection between bad living conditions and grinding poverty on the one hand, and immorality and crime on the other: he spoke of the temptations that faced those who had 'to fight in the battle of life for a crust to eat and a rag to cover them', and from which the better-off were exempt through no efforts of their own. On a number of occasions he attacked a 'double standard' approach to morality, most strongly in the case of prostitution and of the fashionable wrong-doer who was acceptable to society because he was cleverer

---

[55] P. Doyle, 'Missed Opportunities: Clerical Conferences in the Nineteenth Century', *The Downside Review* (October 1982), 263–73.
[56] Letter 399.

than the uneducated at concealing his crimes. He excused in public the large number of Catholics in prison on the grounds of the poverty in which they were forced to live and wrote with understanding of the pressures that drove women and young girls to prostitution. Despite this, he was outspoken in his condemnation of vice, believing and teaching that the faithful exercise of one's religious duties would bring from God sufficient grace to overcome all temptations.[57] Such public utterances on what we tend to think of as 'delicate' issues for the Victorians illustrate a directness in Goss that supports Manning's statement that, in an age of refinement, he 'spoke out like a man where he saw vice to denounce or follies to extinguish'.[58]

When it came to parental duties, Goss's most frequent target was their neglect of their children, with both rich and poor at fault. Children depended on their parents to be taught their responsibilities; while gentleness would achieve more than severity, corporal punishment had its place when all else had failed. The large number of children roaming the streets and learning habits of crime and bad behaviour showed how wretchedly parents were fulfilling their duties. Particular parental sins included abortion, infanticide and encouraging their children to turn to prostitution, but his greatest concern seemed to be the practice of parents and children sleeping together. He apologised for raising these topics in public, but his sense of duty and the terrible results of the practice left him no option.[59] Another area of grave concern was that of company-keeping, for parental carelessness here could lead to a number of evils, including mixed marriages and illegitimate births; moreover, the practice failed to achieve the advantages alleged to flow from it, for the parties failed to learn each other's true motives and suitability for each other: only 'indifferent wives were obtained in this way'.[60] One had even to be careful of children who went to Sunday evening services, for this was often just an excuse to meet friends, and their hearts were 'full of other thoughts than prayer', while, especially in country areas, children would hear and see much on a Sunday evening that would 'undo the spiritual advantage'.[61]

Very shortly after becoming bishop Goss issued a circular to the clergy to express his regret that in several churches there was no separation of the sexes in the 'free' parts of the church (i.e. those parts of a church provided for the use of the poor). He considered this to be a great evil and ordered separation to be maintained wherever people were

57 See various PLs: March 1859; February 1866, 1869 and 1870; and letters 95 and 100.
58 Manning, *The Good Soldier's Death*, 12.
59 See PLs listed in n. 57.
60 The topic featured regularly in visitation sermons: see for example RCLv 3/B, 1–4.
61 PL, Sexagesima Sunday 1863.

admitted 'indiscriminately'. Especially on 'occasions of great pressure' in smaller churches, the priest should take care that the stairs and aisles were not occupied by 'a miscellaneous crowd'. Clergy should also take care to keep schoolgirls and boys apart: communicating doors between the separate playgrounds should be kept locked, with the priest holding the only key.[62] Other dangers could exist in school, too: one of the unfortunate provisions of the 1870 Education Act was the recommendation that the Old Testament be used as a class reader; Goss believed this was likely to stimulate prurient curiosity.[63]

As one would expect, Goss was outspoken in his sermons and pastoral letters on the evils of drunkenness and funeral wakes.[64] Perhaps more surprising was his attitude to dancing, an activity that Bishop Brown had forbidden in Catholic schoolrooms. Some priests were keen to have the ban lifted so they could hold fund-raising dances in the only suitable space available in most missions. Goss, however, reissued the ban, although he did lift the penalty of suspension which Brown had threatened for any priest who attended such a gathering. He explained that he did not think dancing in itself was sinful, but 'evils of the gravest consequence' could result from it, and he knew of several cases where Catholic mothers mourned for the loss of their daughters' virtue after Catholic dances. He added that dancing of either sex apart was acceptable and was, indeed, a healthy exercise.

Finally, he lectured the people on the need for them to engage in good works and in particular to be as generous as possible in supporting the main annual collections for the Ecclesiastical Education Fund and the Diocesan Mission Fund. The amounts collected for these key funds remained steady throughout Goss's years and he frequently commented on what he thought was a lack of generosity: when talking about the Diocesan Mission Fund, for example, in 1865, he analysed the subscriptions from across the diocese and claimed they worked out at between ½d and ¾d a head: he then referred to the relatively well-to-do parishioners of St Francis Xavier's, 'Why, they would give twenty times that amount to witness an execution at Kirkdale!'[65] In a rare instance of feedback on a visitation sermon a parishioner was heard to remark, 'Didn't his Lordship come out on the penny a head! My word, he did give it us!'[66]

[62] The Second Synod decreed that such separation was to safeguard reverence in church and the sanctity of morals (*Synodi*, 28, §VIII.). For school playgrounds, see letter 319.
[63] PL, September 1870.
[64] In a sermon at Preston in September 1857 he said that wakes led to the 'grossest indecencies', of which smoking (!) and drinking were the least objectionable; RCLv Visitation Diaries, 3/B, 1/163–9.
[65] Quoted in E. Tenbus, *English Catholics and the Education of the Poor, 1847–1902* (London, 2010), 36.
[66] RCLv, Visitation Diaries, 3/B, 3/90–5, at The Willows, 1864.

The numbers and quality of the clergy

A strongly sacramentalist approach to lay spirituality brought with it an obvious need for a constant, indeed in the circumstances a growing, supply of priests. In 1856 Goss wrote that he did not know where to look for priests and that every year increased the demand; he believed that there was not a mission in the town of Liverpool that would not benefit from having an extra priest. There were then throughout the whole diocese ninety-four churches and chapels to be served by his clergy; this increased to 110 by 1865 and to 121 by 1872 (not including nineteen chapels belonging to religious communities). The number of priests also rose: from 137 (Seculars and Regulars) in 1856 to 202 in 1865, and to 215 by the end of his episcopate, an overall increase of almost 57 per cent. Over the same period, the number of Regular priests rose from sixty-six to eighty-eight, while the Seculars went from seventy-one to 127. While the increase in Regular clergy was, of course, welcome, it did not help the bishop staff new missions, for, with the exception of Holy Cross, St Helens, the Regulars took on none of the newly established ones; indeed, during these years they gave up six missions that the bishop then had to find priests for. It is no wonder that Goss said he was 'well-nigh in despair' at the impossibility of meeting the demands for priests, not just for missions but for 'convents, gaols, workhouses and industrial schools'. He might have added ordinary parochial schools: he insisted that priests should spend as much time in local schools as possible and recommended that, where there was more than one priest attached to a mission, one of them should be in the school every morning.[67]

Where could the bishop expect to recruit priests? The primary source was, of course, the seminaries: Ushaw first of all, then the English colleges abroad – Rome, Lisbon, Valladolid and Bruges – and the Irish seminaries. Between 1856 and 1872 there were ninety ordinations for the diocese, of whom seventeen were from Ireland; in the same period, forty Secular priests died. In his first six years as bishop Goss lost nine priests through death and gained only six newly ordained ones. The outstanding year for ordinations was 1869: there were eighteen new priests, all of them from the various English colleges. Something should be said here about the number of Irish priests working in the diocese. There is, first of all, the issue of definition. Was a priest who had been born in Ireland but had undertaken his major studies in an English college, an 'Irish priest'? Was the same true of a first-generation Irish person, born and educated in England but in tune with the culture and feelings of the Irish immigrant community? The figure of seventeen given above refers to Irish-born

---

67   For numbers see *Directories* 1855, 1865, 1873.

priests trained and ordained in Ireland and having no pastoral experience before coming to England. Their number increased slowly over Goss's years, but at no stage did either type of Irish-born priest account for more than a third of the Secular clergy in the diocese.

There is, secondly, the matter of how Goss regarded his Irish-born priests. There is no doubt that he wanted to build up a native English clergy. In 1857 he wrote,

> Now if we are to preserve the vantage ground gained by those who have preceded us ... it can only be by having a regular supply of native clergy, educated from the people amongst whom they have to labour.

He continued by saying that if 'altogether English' priests were not available, then at least they should be 'bred up in England and formed in (English) habits'. The previous year he had told the dean in Chorley that he did not have a priest to fill a vacancy there as he did not want to appoint another Irish priest to the town. Furthermore, he saw no particular reason to appoint Irish priests to overwhelmingly Irish missions: when the parish priest of St Anthony's, Liverpool, asked for permission to write to Ireland for a priest, Goss refused and said he would appoint a 'highly recommended' Belgian priest instead!

The provision of sufficient clergy to serve a rapidly expanding Catholic population was of obvious importance. It is clear from his correspondence that the quality of the priests employed was of equal concern, and he turned down requests for transfer to his diocese from priests who were disaffected or in trouble elsewhere. He did accept some ex-religious, though not always with happy results. It must be said that the majority of his priests carried out their duties faithfully, visiting the sick, providing the sacraments, instructing their people, building churches and schools, keeping to their rule of life and working where they were sent, though Goss complained several times of daintiness and a desire for 'self-appointment' and on a number of occasions could not make the appointments he wanted because one of the parties involved did not want to move. Occasionally a priest could cause more serious trouble by refusing in effect to accept the bishop's authority. The most serious example was Canon Thomas Newsham, rector of St Anthony's, Liverpool, from 1844 to 1858, who had taken full advantage of the laxer regime under Bishop Brown as Vicar Apostolic and had made a name for himself as an active missioner in the north end of the city, founding missions and schools and opening a Catholic cemetery at Ford.[68] Brown made him a canon but almost immediately regretted it; Goss tried unsuccessfully to get him to resign from the Chapter and eventually moved him out of Liverpool.

---

[68] See letter 126 and n. 311 for a fuller picture and the appeals to Propaganda. On ex-religious see, e.g., letters 36, 94, 167 and n. 293.

There were financial irregularities, serious accusations of priestly and personal misconduct, and a constant sniping at the bishop's authority. Bishop and priest both appealed to Propaganda and an uneasy peace was arrived at, though Newsham continued to attack Goss's officials.

Although individual priests could cause trouble, the bishop was more worried when a major row developed over the Cathedraticum, a tax on the clergy to help the bishop's maintenance.[69] In this case, a small number of clergy, led by Fr John Worthy, questioned the bishop's right to decide the level of the tax and tried to use a diocesan synod to air their grievance; again, the case eventually went to Rome and, again, was settled in Goss's favour: he had no intention of allowing any form of clerical democracy to develop, and saw it, along with what he regarded as remnants of former clerical independence, as inimical to the exercise of proper episcopal control. He exaggerated the effect of the supposed threat and took it personally when he found that some of his friends had signed the petition. But, as Cardinal Manning later acknowledged, Goss bore no grudges: once disputes were settled they were over, and he later appointed Worthy a canon.

There were, of course, some priests who failed and left the diocese and the priesthood. A very small number of these caused public scandal and Goss advised them to go, while others just disappeared. Some reformed and moved to other dioceses, sometimes overseas. There are hints that Liverpool as a busy and crowded port attracted some imposters and failed priests who traded on people's good will: Goss wrote of 'a number of unknown priests, many of them suspended, lurking in the by-ways of the town'. He warned a parish priest that the town had a hostile press and so the clergy needed to be extra cautious with regard to 'strange priests': the people could not 'decide nicely, and if they see a priest at the altar they will trust him with unbounded confidence'.[70]

Not surprisingly, the bishop had clear views about the style of life he expected from his clergy: as a circular letter of January 1859 put it,

> Absence from home, a love of dining out, and a desire to go into society, are marks of an inconstant and frivolous mind, that neither loves study nor the duties of the Sacred Ministry.

There could also be problems within the presbytery. The increase in missions served by more than a single priest obviously meant more of the Secular clergy living communally and there is strong evidence from

---

[69] See P. Doyle, 'Episcopal Authority and Clerical Democracy: Diocesan Synods in Liverpool in the 1850s', *RH* 23 (May 1997), 418–33.

[70] Letter 41, to Bulbeck OSB; he also warned Vandepitte, who had asked for leave to employ a German priest, and said that Gibson had 'burned his fingers' with a Pole at the CI.

Goss's letters that a number of junior priests were unwilling to accept the authority of the priest-in-charge. He had to remind such priests that they were not on an equal footing with the senior; indeed, he expected them to show 'due honour and obedience' to whoever was in charge. Nor was this just a question of respect for one's elders. In practice there was often very little difference in age between the two, and Goss made it clear that the whole governance of the mission, including the running of the presbytery and relations with the people, belonged only to the senior priest, as the bishop's delegate. Sometimes, he felt, troubles between priests in the same house could be bad enough to scandalise the laity, and in 1867 he found it necessary to set up a commission to establish regulations for the proper running of presbyteries. Laws were not the answer: as he wrote to a senior priest, a bishop could no more prevent priests living together from disagreeing than a priest could man and wife.[71]

The bishop and the Regulars

Mention has already been made of the relatively large number of Regulars among the clergy of the diocese – Goss claimed they formed a higher percentage there than in any other diocese in the country. When he became bishop there were five Orders or Congregations working there: the Benedictines and Jesuits were both of very long standing and ran a number of missions throughout the diocese; the Oblates of Mary Immaculate, the Passionists and the Redemptorists (who did not run a mission) had been introduced during Brown's years. Other groups wanted to work in the diocese, but Goss would not allow them to open houses there. While he admired the Regulars' way of life he was convinced that there was a fundamental conflict between the religious ideal and the life of an active missionary priest. He was especially opposed to Regulars living alone in one-man missions, something that both Jesuits and Benedictines had developed for sound historical reasons, but which Goss believed was an unacceptable anomaly and which the Jesuits were themselves keen to end. It is clear from these letters that there were other, more immediate, sources of friction between the bishop and the Regulars. These included the question of the visitation and inspection of regular missions and their accounts; the ownership of mission property, and the right to divide existing missions when new missions were needed. These were major issues and caused trouble in a number of dioceses; they were not resolved until the Bull *Romanos Pontifices* of 1881.[72] Comparatively

---

[71] For the commission, see p. 322 below; the senior priest was Brown of Lancaster (letter of 2 March 1863). See also letter 246.

[72] See *Decreta*, 345–65. See also Martin John Broadley, *Bishop Herbert Vaughan and the Jesuits* (CRS 82, London, 2010).

minor, though occasionally very annoying, was an apparent refusal on the part of some Regular clergy in Lancashire to carry out routine episcopal regulations (especially those concerning marriage) and to attend clerical conferences. Goss readily acknowledged that he had no right to interfere with the appointment or removal of their priests by religious superiors, but he believed that the superiors should inform him when such moves were taking place. He was not out to pick quarrels with the Regulars but found it difficult to understand how they could claim to be missioners and yet try to avoid ordinary missionary duties and stand apart from the rest of the missionary clergy.[73]

Goss and education

Throughout his episcopate Goss was involved in debates about education at various levels. Although, as we will see, he was doubtful about some of its supposed benefits, there is no doubting his commitment to the greater provision of schools for Catholic children, if for no other reasons than it was essential to prevent proselytising in Protestant schools and helped to get the children off the streets and away from the worst temptations to crime and immorality. He often urged priests to build schools before building chapels in new missions; he corresponded on the question of suitable books for use in these schools, on the training of pupil teachers and on the problems likely to arise from proposed national legislation. He advised priests about government grants and corresponded with the Catholic Poor Schools Committee. Before the end of his episcopate he was caught up in the national debates about education and in 1870 spoke strongly in public on the need for increased Catholic provision of schools for the poor. It was not enough to hope that religion could be taught at home and in Sunday schools: if secular learning and religious learning did not go hand-in-hand throughout the week, then the religion learned would be 'of the scantiest description', while education without religion was 'secular and godless' and a great evil.[74]

For all his efforts in this regard there is also in his writings and sermons a questioning of some of the supposed benefits of education in itself and even praise for what might be termed 'holy ignorance'. In two of his pastoral letters he spoke about ignorance being 'a great preservative of innocence' and a 'safeguard of virtue'.[75] Education, he wrote, might just make people cleverer villains: sin was not the result of ignorance but of a lack of moral restraint found in the educated and unedu-

---

[73] See Doyle, *Mitres and Missions*, 143–7, for some particular cases.
[74] It is a frequent topic in his PLs; see especially those of June 1856, November 1857 and September 1870.
[75] PLs, February 1865 and September 1870.

cated alike: the Apostles were ignorant of secular knowledge but had the advantage over Pliny and Tacitus. Goss was always to some extent a *laudator temporis acti*[76] and for him the inventions and discoveries of the age, whether it was travelling quickly by steam power or conversing by electricity, did not improve a person's moral sense nor 'throw light and peace into the dark and troubled conscience'.[77] The ability to read brought with it a craving for news; the press and books only introduced the young to 'fashionable vice' and it would be better to remain ignorant than to expose one's virtue to shipwreck; the 'quiet old times' had gone, however, when Catholics had been content 'because they were forced to be so'. The effect of education on the children of the poor was not always beneficial since it often seemed to make them 'both saucy and indifferent'.[78]

In the context of the lead up to the 1870 Education Act, Goss stressed that education was basically the parents' right and duty, not the state's, and in Liverpool, as elsewhere, there was considerable public opposition by Catholics to the idea of non-denominational schools. Goss had already spoken against mixed (i.e. inter-denominational) schools, a far bigger pastoral danger, he believed, in his diocese than the possible attendance of a small number of wealthy Catholics at mixed universities. Once passed, however, Catholics had to respond to the Act, which put enormous financial pressures on the Catholic community. Goss convened and presided over a national meeting in Liverpool in October 1870, attended by several members of the aristocracy. A general fund to help with the building of new schools was established, to which over £46,000 was pledged on the night.[79] Whatever he thought of some of the effects of education, the 'fight for the schools' had begun and was to become increasingly a defining element in the constitution of English and Welsh Catholicism.

Goss's socio-political attitudes

Goss's attitudes to the social and political issues of his time are more evident in his pastoral letters and visitation sermons than in his day-to-day correspondence; one can only regret the lack of feedback from his congregations as they listened to his frequent diatribes against the supposed evils of the day. The bishop exhibited a strong distaste for democracy in any of its forms and was willing to tell his people so.

---

[76] Trans: 'one who praises bygone times'.
[77] PL, June 1856.
[78] PL, Sexagesima Sunday, 1863; letter to Stokes 5/1/441, March 1857.
[79] See Tenbus, *English Catholics and the Education of the Poor*, ch. 5; Burke, *Catholic Liverpool*, 190–2; PL, February 1867.

Agitation for universal suffrage earned a comment in a pastoral letter: certainly all men were equal in having a common human origin and a common supernatural salvation, but that was all. He continued,

> It shocks our common sense ... that a man who was yesterday discharged from ... Kirkdale gaol, should tomorrow have the same weight in the ... nation as the head of the House of Stanley or Cavendish; and that he who has nothing to lose but the coat on his back should ... have a vote of equal weight with one who has an income equal to ... a kingdom.[80]

Furthermore, democracy introduced into society a levelling process just as tyrannical as despotism: imperial Russia did not crush its people more than Abraham Lincoln was doing.[81] Once make the will of the people into the supreme law, he believed, and one was heading for all the evils of the French Revolution.[82]

Appeals to liberty and liberalism, he believed, were equally suspect. The banner of liberty crushed others in raising itself on high and was responsible for the evils and atrocities being committed in Italy. Liberalism was no more than sentimentality and the sort of mawkish philanthropy that would soften the penal code. It also led to indiscriminate charity, which supported tramps 'in their idle, indolent and pilfering habits'. It would appear that behind these sentiments was a distrust of the people and a fear that they would misuse any power or freedom that might be given them. This is evident, for example, when he was talking about trade unions: they interfered with individual liberty and reduced the skilful worker to the level of the most incompetent by the equalisation of wages. But it is most evident in the following passage:

> Parents who on a moderate allowance brought up their children decently, give themselves up to drink on an increase of wages ... Their furniture, bedding and clothes are pawned, fever and loathsome disease are invited to these miserable dwellings, and death remorsefully carries off the innocent as well as the guilty.[83]

This has the air of the more extreme temperance preachers of the day or of an urban myth put forward to ease the consciences of the better off; yet Goss knew his clergy and they knew their people well.

It was not only the poor who could not be trusted. Emancipation had opened to Catholics the way to 'honours and preferments', but with it had come new opportunities for them 'to feel the world at every turn' and to give up their faith; the liberality of the nineteenth century could,

---

[80] PL February 1865.
[81] Visitation sermon at Euxton reported in the *Preston Chronicle*, 3 September 1864.
[82] PLs, February 1862 and September 1866.
[83] PL, February 1866.

he believed, be more dangerous than the persecution of the eighteenth.[84] Goss was also uneasy about the effect of Catholics' increasing prosperity and social status. Too many 'middling' Catholics, he believed, excused themselves from helping the poor on grounds of not being able to afford it, yet it was just as much a duty as marrying off their daughters and setting up their sons in business. To leave money in one's will was not enough, he claimed, for it was no 'great act of charity to leave to God what one could not take away'. 'Do not people dress, dine, entertain and furnish their houses in a style far beyond their present or probable means? Are there not hundreds of middle-class families who have learned to sneer with vulgar contempt at the simplicity that becomes a modest fortune?'[85] Another reason, the bishop claimed, why not enough was given to the poor was a tendency to 'glorify what is unknown': people closed their eyes to

> The Irish or the Highlander, driven from their wrecked cabins to seek a home in a foreign land … Tears are shed over the exiles of Siberia and the Wanderings of Evangeline,[86] whilst men behold with dry eyes thousands of exiles … yearly leaving for America or Australia … Men would rather scratch their names on the great pyramids of Egypt than engrave them in the hearts of the suffering poor.

Goss's deeply conservative outlook coloured his attitude to the politics of the day but he was careful to avoid any commitment to political parties and did not vote in elections (it was still a time of open voting). He judged governments by what they did for Catholic concerns (e.g. the right to have Catholic chaplains in prisons and workhouses) and their foreign policy with regard to Italian nationalism. Locally it was more difficult to remain neutral and he became caught up in disputes with the Select Vestry and Poor Law Guardians over their anti-Catholic attitudes.[87] As expected, the local Protestant press attacked him quite openly; what is interesting is that he could not rely on the *Daily Post*, edited by an Irish Catholic, Michael Whitty, not to criticise him either. In particular it attacked what it saw as his anti-liberal social views as expressed in his pastoral letters and sermons, his stance on the temporal power of the papacy and what Whitty claimed was a strong anti-Irish attitude.[88]

---

[84] PL, Sexagesima Sunday 1863.

[85] PL, February 1857.

[86] The reference is to Longfellow's very popular epic poem, *Evangeline, A Tale of Acadie*, published in 1847 and dealing with an exiled Acadian woman's lifelong search for her love, also driven into exile. The passage is from the PL of November 1857.

[87] See Burke, *Catholic Liverpool*, *passim*.

[88] Burke, *Catholic Liverpool*, 157–9 and 197–8, gives excellent extracts illustrating these quarrels.

On this last point the bishop found himself in a difficult position. He accepted that the Irish had little cause to look favourably on English rule, admitting that after centuries of government of a kind 'which could hardly be paralleled in Russia, England had failed to win the affection of the Irish or even reconcile them to its rule'; indeed, in a statement quite out of line with his normal attitude, he said that the injustices suffered by the Irish had been so great as to justify rebellion.[89] What, then, were they to make of a sermon (printed in a local paper) in which he stated that his co-religionists had been 'born on the soil', had all the feelings of Englishmen and believed that England had the 'most perfect government in the world', adding 'in heart we are English, in purpose we are loyal'?[90] It is little wonder that some people criticised him and believed he had no sympathy with the feelings of so many of his people, especially when he claimed that the Irish had as much chance of preferment as the English if only they would give up drink and other vices and so benefit from 'their natural ability and the fertility of their mental resources'.[91] It would seem that, in his efforts to stress that Catholics were not 'foreign' in any way, he was prepared to allow a large number of his people to feel let down by his attitude to them. He was aware of the charges of indifference and even hostility but attached greater importance to persuading Protestants that Catholics could be fully English.

The bishop as historian

There are several references in the bishop's letters to his intention to write a history of Lancashire Catholicism. For this purpose he put together a large collection of transcripts of documents from public sources and private family papers which he employed various people, clerical and lay, to copy.[92] He also encouraged members of his clergy to undertake the history of their missions and of the episcopate of Bishop Brown, as 'great things had been done under him' and they should be remembered.[93] Unfortunately, these projects were not realised, but the bishop did publish a few works. His first was *A Sacred History, comprising the leading facts of the Old and New Testaments: From the French of the Abbé Drioux* (London and Derby, 1856). A group of students at St

---

[89] PLs of February and September 1866.

[90] See the *Preston Chronicle*, 3 September 1864.

[91] Burke, *Catholic Liverpool*, 185–6; see letters 44, 206. On Goss's Englishness, see Doyle, 'Bishop Goss of Liverpool'.

[92] Most are in fine copperplate hands and bound in folders in AAL. Joseph Gillow was one of his scribes.

[93] See P. Doyle, 'An Episcopal Historian: Alexander Goss of Liverpool (1856–1872)', *NWCH* 15 (1988), 6–15, at 6. See also letters 141, 310, 314.

Edward's worked on this, perhaps doing the translation under Goss's direction; he lists their names in his introduction to the work, a copy of which is in AAL.[94] In 1863 he was approached by the officers of the Chetham Society of Manchester to work on something much closer to his historical interests; they asked him to prepare for publication an account of the Manchester treason trials of 1694 involving leading Catholics; to this Goss added Richard Abbott's account of his arrest as a Stuart spy in 1689. *The Manchester Trials* (Chetham Society, Manchester) appeared in 1864. Then, in the Chetham Society's volume for 1867, he published a document of rather doubtful authenticity: the supposed conversion to Catholicism of the seventh Earl of Derby, executed in 1657; the editor attacked the authenticity of the document but added that he did not wish to show any disrespect to the 'learned and eminent' ecclesiastic who had produced it. Finally, Goss published a revised edition of the important *Chronicle of Man and the Sudreys*, published by the Manx Society in two volumes; it did not appear until 1874, when Errington added a glowing appreciation of Goss as part of the introduction.

In addition, he wrote the introduction to one of T. E. Gibson's publications, *Crosby Records: a chapter of Lancashire recusancy*, published by the Chetham Society in 1887. The introduction was twenty pages long, a summary of events in King James I's reign (drawing on a range of primary and secondary sources) as the background to Gibson's work on the Harkirke cemetery and the Blundells. All his historical publications are marked by a concern for textual accuracy that must have involved very detailed and painstaking work. This is particularly noticeable in the *Chronicle* volumes, for which he consulted Stubbs on the orthography of some of the additional Latin manuscripts for the appendices, and a British Museum Cottonian manuscript to check variants in the text. He annotated and corrected some of the notes by the original Swedish editor, tracing proper names, comparing the views of different historians and filling out events referred to in the originals.[95] Occasionally he slips from the objectivity perhaps expected of a historian, attacking, for example,

---

[94]   The six students he named are listed in the Student Register of St Edward's College (AAL, SJC/S4/11/B/5) and would have been in their mid-teens in 1856; three went on to ordination.

[95]   The original *DNB* credited him with having contributed to the Holbein Society but I have found no evidence of this. Gibson said that the bishop had intended to write a history of the cemetery and was particularly interested in the Saxon coins unearthed there. Perhaps it is worth mentioning here that Goss was himself the subject of an anti-Catholic work: Charles Hastings Collette, *The Novelties of Romanism: Addressed to the Right Rev. Dr. Goss ... in three parts* (London, 1860; pp. x, 177); the author was moved to write the book by Goss's public claim that he was the representative 'of no new system of religion, the teacher of no new doctrines'. Collette duly rose to the bait. Goss did not mention the work as far as I can see.

the venality of the politicians who invited William of Orange to become king, and the unjust legal and penal systems of the seventeenth century; many an innocent life had to be sacrificed before the country could enjoy the liberty 'of which it is so justly proud' – a whiff of the Whig historian, perhaps?

In this context it is worth saying something about Goss's views on architecture. Here he adopted a practical approach, far removed from some of the Gothic ideals of the day. This was partly on the grounds of finance, but mainly, it seems, because of the people's opposition to having too many pillars in their churches which prevented them seeing the altar. Commenting to E. W. Pugin on the plans for a new church at Westby, he said that the country people would 'consider it heaven after the pillars of The Willows'. If he had to replace the chapel at St Edward's (intended as the Lady Chapel of Pugin's projected Gothic cathedral), he would not, he continued, have a pillar in it, while in another letter to the architect he claimed that words could not express the aversion people had to pillars. Unless Gothic were adapted to modern needs, there would be a return to the old 'barn style'; 'we must cease to be antiquarians', he added.[96] He worked closely with E. W. Pugin on the plans for churches, getting involved on occasions in a surprising amount of detail.[97]

Conclusion

Goss's correspondence shows that he was successful in establishing firm control and in having his authority accepted throughout his diocese. Along with the other bishops, he established his independence from Westminster and, as far as was possible in the circumstances of increasing papal centralisation, he fought against undue interference from Rome. In practice, he was left little room for initiative, and the sixteenth- and seventeenth-century ideal of the diocesan bishop as the key to local reform and growth was in danger of losing out to the nine-teenth-century ideal of subordination to central control. In some ways, perhaps, this may have suited Goss's temperament: while arguing for his independence he seemed to need the psychological support of knowing that he was carrying out the Church's law and doing his duty as laid down for him.

He claimed that he knew best what his diocese required; extensive and conscientious visitation, and use of the network of deans, meant that his searching eye explored every aspect of diocesan life. He could direct decrees to erring missioners rather than just issue general exhortations;

---

96   Letters to E. W. Pugin, October 1858; 5/2/374 and 378.
97   See, for example, letters 129, 226, 236, 240, 251.

when general decrees were called for, his clergy and people knew they were based on sound knowledge. He deployed his clergy to cope with expansion and fought any move on their part to control their appointments; he regularised diocesan finances and used what resources he had to help that expansion. He expected others to be as meticulous as himself and was outspoken in condemning abuses of any kind.

It was necessary for him to be as strict as possible at the beginning of his episcopate to put right the carelessness of Brown's declining years and to put an end to what he saw, exaggeratedly, as the threat of clerical radicalism. He soon knew, however, that he could count on the co-operation of the great majority of his clergy, but caution continued to win out over originality. Just as he knew his diocese, his priests were to know their missions and districts: his insistence on their keeping a detailed *status animarum* meant that they were in touch with their people, knowing them as individuals through regular home visiting, and knowing their children through daily work in the mission schools. His clergy deserve credit for the relatively high levels of religious practice throughout the diocese, but they were not encouraged to use their initiative beyond carefully laid out limits. It may be unfair to Goss but the impression remains in the mind that the steady plodder was preferable to the man of ideas.[98]

For his people, Goss was a dedicated pastor and a man of his times. He urged a strong and positive sacramentalism, with the people being largely passive supporters of the Church. They were to be involved in their individual salvation, which would be best attained by avoiding sin, being good parents and doing a limited range of good works. Again, it was far from being a lowly ideal, but was perhaps more aimed at holding the fort than extending boundaries; he battled to keep the world at bay. The year 1850 was not so much seen as a new beginning as allowing the implementation and strengthening of what was thought to have been lacking or ineffective in the past: firm episcopal control and an acceptance of clearly defined roles for both clergy and people. He was a busy Victorian administrator, deploying his resources as efficiently as possible, preaching an ideal of devotion to duty and ensuring that his authority was accepted unquestioningly, all in the interests of the defence and recognition of the rights of the Church. If we are looking for a Victorian label to attach to him, he was obviously no ultramontane, but perhaps he had a touch of the utilitarian about him.

---

[98] The prime example here is his attitude to Mgr Nugent, the founder of the Catholic Institute, prison chaplain, social reformer and a man with too many ideas for his own good according to Goss; see n. 190 below.

EDITORIAL PROCEDURES

The letters reproduced here are set out chronologically and numbered sequentially. Each letter carries its number, original addressee (in square brackets if not stated in the original) and date of writing, followed by the archival source in italics. As the great majority of the letters were sent from St Edward's College, Everton, Liverpool, where Goss lived from 1843 until his death in 1872, this has not been included in the heading; if a letter was written elsewhere this is shown after the date; the style of dating has been standardised. He sent a small number of letters from missions when he was on visitation and, in later years, from Scarisbrick Hall, Ormskirk, home of his friend Lady Anne Scarisbrick, where he stayed when ill or recuperating. Some letters carry a note of their main contents and this has been included in the heading. Most of the headings and endings have been compressed in order to save space. Two of the letters date from before Goss became coadjutor bishop in 1853; they have been included because they show his early interest in some of the issues that taxed him later as bishop. Letters referred to in the notes but not reproduced in the text are referred to by the letter-book reference without a sequential number.

Throughout the letters footnotes are numbered sequentially and are to be found at the end of the letter to which they refer. References to 'n.' and a number are to these footnotes.

Where underlining for emphasis occurs in the original this has been kept in the text. Foreign languages are reproduced in italics and translated in a footnote (introduced by Trans: followed by single inverted commas). Where brackets occur in the letters they are kept in the text. If words have obviously been omitted by accident in the original they are supplied in normal type in square brackets; where words are illegible, this is noted in italics in square brackets and conjectural words are also given in italics in square brackets, with a question mark; [*sic*] has been inserted to show the correctness of a particular transcription.

There are chronological gaps in the sequence of the letters, some of them covering a few months at a time. Some letters may not have been copied; some of the copies are too faint or too blurred to be legible and, anyway, the letter-books cease in December 1868. At times Goss was away in Rome or on visitation or, in later years, was too ill to write. The gaps were sometimes covered by letters from secretaries or officials such as the vicar general; a few of these have been included here where they seem to be relevant.

Some punctuation has been altered or added to make the letters easier to read, but on the whole Goss's abbreviations (and idiosyncrasies) have been kept. His signature varies considerably and has been standardised here: it can be the full 'Alexander Goss' (with or without the episcopal '+'), or 'A. Goss' or occasionally 'AG'. He almost always used '&' for 'and', and usually Lpool for Liverpool; frequently he used 'Bp' for Bishop and ended his letters 'Yrs in Xt'. More oddly, he used 'mass' instead of the usual Mass and quite often spelt Irish names beginning with O' as a single word, for example, Oreilly and Omeara. 'Diocess' sometimes appears instead of 'diocese'. Capital letters in the originals have generally been retained. Goss is inconsistent in his spelling of words such as 'everything', 'anything', 'whatever', sometimes splitting them and sometimes not.

Goss addressed his clergy as 'Rev. Mr' or just plain 'Mr', only using 'Fr' when addressing Regulars (and that not consistently). As was customary at the time, the style of address and farewell tended to be formal, even when he was writing to friends among the clergy; occasionally he used Christian names and, throughout, he addresses Bishop Grant of Southwark as 'friend' or 'dear friend'. His exasperated 'Jimmy, Jimmy' in a letter to Nugent (letter 366) is uniquely expressive.

The Letters

1. *Dr. John Lingard*   *26 May 1850*   *RCLv Box 76*

My dear Dr. Lingard,[1]

I have no doubt you will be heartily weary of receiving circulars & letters on questions of ecclesiastical politics, from all share in which you have so long retired; but still it is right that you should know what is going on, in order that you may not be tricked into giving an opinion on any partial statement that may be submitted to you.

There are in the Lancashire District 112 secular Priests, of whom 45 have been educated at Ushaw; 24 partly at Ushaw & partly elsewhere; 13 at our foreign Colleges; & 24 are derived from alien sources, principally Ireland. Thus you see that Ushaw has educated little more than half of the Clergy now serving this District. The number of Priests in the 3 Northern Districts at present is <u>three</u> times greater than at the period when Ushaw College was built; in fact, in the Lancashire District alone, our number is double that of the Old Northern District at the same period of the foundation of Ushaw. And yet even with this immense increase in our numbers, our large manufacturing towns are not half supplied.

To remedy this deficiency in our numbers & to increase the funds for ecclesiastical education, the Bishop[2] purposes, in union with his Clergy, to establish a Seminary for the education of youth up to the end of Syntax,[3] so that they will be ready to study Poetry, Rhetoric, Philosophy & Theology at Ushaw, or Rome, or elsewhere; but mainly, if not entirely at Ushaw. If this preparatory Seminary be placed in Lancashire, it is thought that funds will be raised for its support more easily than if placed at a distance; for people do not like their money to go away, they like to see the fruits of their charity in the midst of them. The Bishop purposes to support his Seminary by funds raised for the purpose. He has no desire to interfere with existing funds beyond the wish to add to them. And if the funds already existing at Ushaw are not sufficient to carry to the end of their course those educated in the Preparatory Seminary, the Bishop will be obliged to supply the deficiency from the funds collected.

It is thought also by those interested in education that the status of Ushaw will be greatly improved by the exclusion or rather removal of the Junior Classes. The College has too much the appearance of a school, & too little that of a University. As at present constituted it will never send forth a single scholar in any brand of learning. Nay, we are held up in one of the Periodicals of the day,[4] as being worse educated than any sect or sector of the Community.

To carry out the plan effectually, it will be necessary that Yorkshire & the North should establish Preparatory Seminaries within their respective Districts. In fact, Dr. Briggs[5] has a place already built, the labour of 11 years, though it will probably require 11 years more before he can bring his mind to any determination on the subject. In the North there is St. Ninian's at Wooller,[6] destined to be the seat of the new Oratory, & Cornsay house,[7] both suitable for the purpose.

The present scheme has been long in agitation. Dr. Newsham urged it strongly on Dr. Penswick,[8] &, for a time, Dodden Green [*sic*][9] was thought of. Your friend, the late Vicar Thompson,[10] was an enthusiastic advocate for it, &, at Manchester, soon after Dr. Brown's consecration, he proposed success to it at a dinner given to the Clergy. Dr. Youens,[11] too, who, though slow to act, was far seeing and comprehensive in his views, declared the scheme to be as inevitable as it was necessary. The wish of the Clergy has been long & loudly expressed on the subject, particularly since the establishment of St. Edward's. We were said to have alienated it from its original destination, to have appropriated to lay students a place meant for ecclesiastics; but we always returned the same answer, that we were following the instructions of our reputed founder Dr. Youens: I say reputed founder, for he is denied to have been the founder. Like a bastard we have been fathered on one & another, & no body will own us.

So late as March 14, 1850, the Rev. W. Brown[12] of Crosby, the supposed mouthpiece of Dr. Newsham on most occasions, wrote as follows to Rev. Mr. Fisher, the President of St. Edward's,[13] "If St. Edward's had been an ecclesiastical College, or nursery for ecclesiastical students, as originally contemplated, it would have commanded the active support of the Clergy, & then you & Mr. Goss would have been in order & in your right sphere." Again he writes in another letter, "Let St. Edward's be an ecclesiastical Seminary, & then you are in a right position." St. Edward's is now an Ecclesiastical Seminary, & we, therefore, expect the promised support of the Brethren.

Well, you will ask, what is all this to me? Why am I at the age of seventy-nine to be troubled with this youngster's letters, as interminable as those of a woman? Because I know that the minds of some men – men too occupying high positions – are so warped & prejudiced that an effort will be made to stir up angry feelings & to thwart the good work. And I know, too, that as you are a pillar in the Church, they will attempt to pin their paltry opposition to you, & then proclaim to the world that faction has your support.

Of one thing I am certain that this is the only scheme that will raise Ushaw to its proper position & save it to this District; & this opinion

I expressed to Mr. Sherburne[14] 5 or 6 years ago; for I have long been convinced that unless a gigantic effort were made, the District would fall into the hands of an alien priesthood, & Ushaw would sink down into mediocrity. It is deplorable to learn the state of education in our Catholic colleges, which is worse than as set forth by the Rambler. The professors are taken from the ranks, & after serving for a few years, retire or are dismissed, so that the students are trained by new & ever-varying officers. Were a controversy to arise with any University Professor, where could a champion be found to enter the lists? We have men of talent on the mission, but their laziness outweighs their abilities, & they have sunk down into readers of Newspapers, Magazines, & Reviews. Unless something be done to scourge the lazy elements of our Colleges into activity, we shall fall into a state of pestilential stagnation.[15]

The Sectarians are making the most gigantic exertions. A new College is to be erected at Birkenhead, at a cost of £60,000, & £100,000 has been left for the Endowment of a Collegiate Establishment in Manchester: Oxford & Cambridge have to be reformed & are to be compelled to give a more extensive & complete course of education. We are the only ones standing still. Our examination papers may deceive the world; but they are but puffs, for the manufacture of which the Professor's brain is racked & his energies taxed. Is no effort required to rescue us – I mean our entire body throughout the land – from this state of degradation? And why should not Ushaw take the lead & be the first to cast off the slough of the Junior Classes, that now cramps its energies & fetters its advance?

I must apologise for this long letter, for I know that your eye-sight is not good; though I am glad to learn that you are otherwise better than usual.

Believe me, Revd. & dear Sir, with great respect, Your obedt. Sert. [*sic*] Alexander Goss.

---

1   John Lingard, 1771–1851, the famous historian; he had taught Goss at Ushaw and was currently in charge of the mission at Hornby. See Peter Phillips, *John Lingard, Priest and Historian* (Leominster, 2008), at 399–400, and his *Lingard Remembered* (ed., CRS Monograph 6, London, 2004); also John Trappes-Lomax (ed.), *The Lingard–Lomax Letters* (CRS 77, London, 2000). On St Edward's, see Introduction pp. xxii–iii.

2   George Hilary Brown, 1786–1856. VA of the Lancashire District 1840–50, first bishop of Liverpool 1850–56. See Introduction, p. xxiv, Appendix 2, and correspondence between him and Goss below. For biographical details see J. A. Hilton in *ODNB*.

3   Roughly the equivalent of the present-day Year 11 or Fifth Form; the terminology was inherited from Douai and remained in use down to the 1970s: Underlow, the first, entrance year, followed by Low and High Figures, Grammar, Syntax, Poetry, and Rhetoric.

4   Probably *The Rambler*; see vol. 3, December 1848, 235–41: 'Catholic and Protestant Collegiate Education'. See Introduction, p. xxviii.

5   Bishop John Briggs, 1789–1861; VA of the Northern District, 1836–40 and the York-

shire District 1840–50; Bp of Beverley, 1850–60. See Plumb, *Arundel*; Beck, *The English Catholics*, 70–1.

6   St Ninian's, Wooller, Northumberland; the mission opened 1847; see Michael Morris and Leo Gooch, *Down Your Aisles. The Diocese of Hexham and Newcastle 1850–2000* (Hartlepool, 2000), 261–2, for Hogarth's plans for it as a centre for missionary work.

7   One of the Ushaw farms, about 4 miles from the college, used as a short-stay recreational centre; Milburn, *History of Ushaw College*, 236–8.

8   Thomas Penswick, 1772–1836, Coadj. VA of the Northern District, 1824, VA 1831–36.

9   Dodding Green, near Kendal in Westmorland: see B. W. Kelly, *Historical Notes on English Catholic Missions* (London, 1907; repr. Michael Gandy, 1995), 154–5. Both Goss's uncles had served the mission there; see Leo Gooch, *The Revival of English Catholicism 1777–1807* (Wigan, 1995).

10   Richard Thompson, 1772–1841, grand vicar of Lancashire. See Milburn, *History of Ushaw College*, 185–7.

11   Thomas Youens, 1790–1848; see Introduction, p. xxvii.

12   William Brown, o. 1824, first priest at Great Crosby from 1826; died 1850.

13   John Henry Fisher, 1812–89, first president of St Edward's College, Liverpool, 1842–84; Goss's VG from 1868.

14   Thomas Sherburne, 1779–1854; his true name was Irving, but he adopted his mother's maiden name. He served as rector of the English College, Valladolid, where he had been educated, 1822–24, before becoming rector of The Willows, Kirkham, until his death. See Introduction, p. xxvii.

15   In a very long letter to Wiseman of 26 July 1854 Goss repeated these concerns about the standard of teaching at Ushaw; among his targets was the practice of appointing teachers: 'Our present system of selecting professors is suicidal; we are ever living on ourselves, working in a vicious circle. If a student reaches the average standard, & acquits himself creditably in the ordinary routine of his studies, he has reached the goal, & is thought fit for a Professor's chair. Degeneracy, like that which results from frequent inter-marriages, will naturally follow such a system. An infusion of new blood is from time [to time] necessary, as in the human body.' Goss reported that the letter was dismissed at Ushaw as 'impertinent'; Wiseman did not acknowledge its receipt (UC/P42/245).

2.   *Mr. Sherburne*   *18 June 1850*   *Barmouth, North Wales*[16]
UC/PA/J59

My dear Mr. Sherburne,

I dare say you have no great desire to hear from me, yet I am induced to write to you in hopes of doing good. You probably care little what my opinions are or may have been, but you know that for years I have been, wisely or unwisely, an advocate for a preparatory Seminary, having no idea at the time of St. Edward's ever becoming thus. I have never made any secret of my opinion; for, years ago, I spoke with you on the subject. I act openly & straightforwardly: I do not put forth one thing while aiming at another. I would scorn to wear a mask. I have said this much about myself, in order to give weight to what I am going to state. I have been told that you are afraid there is at the bottom of the present movement regarding a Seminary, a design to interfere with the funds at Ushaw. Now I do assure you that no such thing is contemplated by any mover in the scheme, at least to my knowledge. If I had any such design in view, if I intended to agitate the question, I would at once state my determination & fearlessly carry the thing before the only tribunal capable of deciding it, i.e. Rome. I would not like the Northern Gallicans appeal either to clergy or laity. The Blue book [*sic*] controversy[17] does not furnish a more Gallican act, nor can Wilkes or Berrington [*sic*][18] be taxed with Gallican notions ever again if a like censure has not to fall on those whose names have appeared to the two Northern documents, or who have been concerned in their production. It is a strange thing to see the name of an Ushaw Professor attached to these documents, & yet not to hear of his expulsion or suspension from his duties of Professor. The Bishop of Arras would not have tolerated, nor did he tolerate such principles.[19]

If Dr. Newsham – as in duty bound as head of an Episcopal Seminary – had waited on the Bp. to learn his views in the steps he was taking, every thing would have been rightly arranged. But instead of doing this, a manifesto is issued for the purpose of terrifying our Bishop by an appeal to the clergy & laity, a proceeding which a layman – no friend to St. Edward's – characterised as Presbyterian. He considered the appeal as tantamount to constituting the laity & clergy [*into an*] Archbishop over the Lancashire Bishop, & summoning him to judgment before so motley a court.

What ever may be the opinions of a man regarding the prudence or imprudence of Dr. Brown's recent step, he can form only one opinion of the Northern manifesto & condemn it as utterly & thoroughly as he does the Gallican Convention. For myself, I meddle not in these matters beyond what I am bound to do. I follow the advice of an aged & discreet priest, & I am determined to work in a spirit of peace. If Dr. Newsham would only open his eyes, it is not yet too late [to] arrange matters amicably; but he will be led into error irretrievable if he consult no other counsellors but the Northern Brethren. They want not only to consult for themselves but also for us. If Ushaw can be exalted, they care not how Lancashire be depressed.

I still think a Preparatory Seminary a desideratum, & so does Dr. Newsham, & so he has done for the last 15 years. He does not approve of Dr. Brown's proceeding, because he suspects ulterior views; but his suspicions are groundless. Yet as all men are made of flesh & blood, he may drive the matter too far; he may compel the Bishop to do that which he never had any intention of doing. If the clergy are afraid of being trampled on by a Bp, they will not like to be dragooned or bullied by a conventicle of priests.

You are now getting an old man, you cannot expect to live long. Pardon me, then, if I exhort you to crown a long life of meritorious labour by reconciling the jarring elements now let loose, & by urging

Dr. Newsham to the only course which can be productive of any good, i.e. to ascertain what the Bp's views are, & to act cordially with him.

I hope you will pardon this intrusion: it has been dictated by a love of peace & a desire to correct an erroneous impression or fear. Believe me to remain, Yours very truly A. Goss.

[16] Goss (and Fisher) often holidayed in North Wales; the letter is on St Edward's College headed notepaper.

[17] Blue Books: the name given to the official publications of the Catholic Committee of the 1780s–1790s, involved in the often acrimonious debates about the oaths of allegiance and the Relief Acts. The Committee was predominantly lay, but had some strong clerical support, and was staunchly Cisalpine in outlook. See Bernard Ward, *The Dawn of the Catholic Revival in England 1781–1803*, 2 vols (London, 1909).

[18] Joseph Wilkes OSB, 1748–1829, one of the leaders of the Catholic Committee, see Ward, *Dawn of the Catholic Revival*, I, 124–5 and *passim*; Rev. Joseph Berington, 1743–1827, likewise, see Ward, *Dawn of the Catholic Revival*, I, 7–9 and *passim*.

[19] The Bishop of Arras, Louis-François de Conzie, 1769–1804, instigated the examination of Berington's teachings as Professor of Philosophy at Douai, after the publication in 1771 of Berington's 'Theses on Philosophy and Logic'. While no definite charges were made, the bishop recommended Berington's removal from the staff. See Ward, *Dawn of the Catholic Revival*, and Eamon Duffy, 'Ecclesiastical Democracy Detected I: 1779–87', *RH* 10:4 (January, 1970), 193–210, and his 'Doctor Douglass and Mister Berington: An Eighteenth-Century Retraction', *The Downside Review* 88 (July 1970), 246–69.

3. *Cardinal Wiseman*   *19 August 1853*   AAW:Wiseman & Bps, Goss Folder, n. 55

My Dear Lord Cardinal,

To your Eminence I am indebted for many kindnesses, particularly when studying under you in Rome; for to your teaching, during hours of recreation, I owe the eradication of many erroneous notions & the inculcation of sound principles which, though perhaps, slowly & grudgingly adopted, have influenced, & I hope will continue to influence my actions & opinions. I write now to ask you for another favour, though I am otherwise reluctant to trouble you in your present state of health, viz. that you will consecrate me; for by the Apostolic Rescript, the Holy See has granted me the favour of being consecrated *'a quocumque quem malueris Catholico Antistite' etc.*[20] The Clergy & laity of the Diocese are very anxious that the solemn rite should take place among them. Many of them are unable to leave home, &, were I consecrated in Nottingham, few could be present, whereas at Liverpool, I doubt not the Church would be crowded particularly on a Sunday: for in our mercantile community the gentlemen cannot, or fancy they cannot leave the office till a late hour on week days. If your Eminence has a Sunday at liberty & your health will allow you, I should feel it as a favour done to myself & the Diocese in which I am appointed Coadjutor, if you would consent to officiate. The Catholics of Liverpool are zealous in the good cause, & the presence of your Eminence would tend to inflame their zeal & encourage their piety.

Believe me, my Dear Lord Cardinal, Ever Yours sincerely & affectionately in Xt. Alexander Goss.

---

[20] Trans: 'by whichever Catholic Bishop you would prefer'. Wiseman consecrated Goss titular bishop of Gerra at the Pro-cathedral, 25 September 1853. The event made the national Catholic press because Faber preached at it and, rather impolitically, at least, chose to compare the Secular and the Regular clergy: the Seculars, he claimed, were the 'life' of the Church, the Regulars only its 'ornament': Christ had founded the Secular clergy and had himself been a member of it. See *The Tablet* for 1 October and 10 December 1853, and Dessain, XV, 507, for Newman's reaction.

4. *Cardinal Wiseman   25 November 1853   AAW: Wiseman & Bps, Goss Folder (R.79/6)*

My dear Lord Cardinal,

I do not know whether Your Eminence intended that I should answer the Circular addressed by you to the Bps on the subject of the Charitable Trusts Act:[21] but I venture now to do so, as it may be that it is now engrossing your Eminence's attention. If any Bill be brought in under Catholic auspices, I think it would be well for the Bishops to stand aloof in order that they may be free in evading its provisions if found detrimental, which they could hardly do if the Bill was supposed to have their sanction.

In our diocess of Liverpool, property has been left either absolutely, or with secret instructions, sometimes oral, sometimes written, or in form of Trust registered in Chancery. Nearly all the property is in the hands of the Clergy either as reputed owners or as Trustees, & hence may be more easily dealt with. There is, however, at the present time, a strong feeling against the Bp possessing unlimited control over charitable funds, owing, as your Eminence is already aware, to late mismanagement. Whilst the Bp has complete control over the interest of ecclesiastical funds, they do not think that he should be able to absorb the Principal for purposes other than those for which it was bequeathed, unless such absorption is sanctioned by Canon law or the licence of the Holy See. Now to prevent this, they think there should be some legal security, as otherwise the deficit might not be discovered till too late for remedy. This feeling is strong with those who have become acquainted with the misappropriation of certain monies in this Diocess for some years past, that is, under Dr. Sharples[22] and Dr. Brown. I do not mean to impute blame, but merely to state the fact: for I am not acquainted with the grounds on which they acted.

With regard to property held absolutely, with or without secret instructions, I think the holders would willingly comply with any change in the manner of holding suggested by the Bps; that is, if any authorized form were recommended, by which property could be secured, they would cheerfully consent to the remodelling of the deeds. I must, however, except one class of the absolute holders – Mr Sherburne's school: for I am told that he denies the right of any authority, civil or eccelsiastical, to interfere. He is now selling some large properties, held in Trust for charitable purposes, without, or rather, against the wishes of two out of four of the Trustees, because he has the opinion of his lawyers that he can do so. To the Bp's remonstrances or protest or command – for I do not know how the letter was worded – he pleads his legal right.[23]

I think the whole subject of obligations or masses to be said at particular places on account of bequests to those places, requires a thorough revision; for obligations have been incurred on insufficient grounds, & have been cancelled with perhaps insufficient authority: I speak under correction, as I am not able to say what powers the Vicars Apostolic may have had to diminish obligations. I conceive the English Law about superstitious purposes might be got rid of, by the Holy See cancelling all obligations attached to bequests, so that the parties holding the property might be able to say it was free from any obligation. The same obligations might be subsequently reimposed, but not in connection with any specified bequest. But your Eminence will see your way through the difficulty without any suggestion from me. I am satisfied to have stated the feeling on the question of church property in this Diocess, & the causes which have led to that feeling, in order that your Eminence, knowing the elements to be dealt with, may see your way more clearly.

Does your Eminence think it would be advisable for me to petition the Holy Father for a continuance of my Canonry? You know Dr. Brown. He has no confidence in me, his Chapter, or his Clergy. He will indeed consult all; but as soon as he finds you do not agree with his views, he will seek other advisors. He never lets any set of advisors fully into the real state of a question. He generally acts from himself & then tells you what he has done. He seems to have a rooted objection to consult [*sic*] his Chapter. During the two years of its existence he has never consulted it except on the appointment of a Coadjutor, &, I am told, that, the week after, he undid what he had done. He would use his Coadjutor as a Secretary or a Chaplain, or as one among many advisers [*sic*], & not as one exercising, or ready to exercise jurisdiction delegated to him by his Principal. He looks upon him as one granted for his own personal comfort, rather than for the benefit of the Diocese. Knowing, as your Eminence does, that this is Dr. Brown's way of acting, do you think it would be advisable to petition the Holy Father to allow me to retain my stall? I may otherwise never know what is going on. If your Eminence recommends this course, & it is not too late, I am sure my friend Monsig. Searle[24] would be kind enough to draw up a petition to that effect, if your Eminence were to mention it to him.

I hope soon to see your Eminence back, & I hope we will see you restored in health; for the times require a steady hand at the helm. Believe me, Ever your affte Br in Xt +Alexander Goss.

---

[21] The Charitable Trusts Act of 1853 was intended to regularise the national maze of charitable trusts. Some Catholics suggested a separate Bill for Catholic trusts. Most of the bishops were suspicious about its possible application to bequests for Masses, for so long regarded as invalid because they were for 'superstitious practices'. Propaganda ruled that each bishop should act as he thought best for his diocese: AAL, S1/3/A/2. The issue returned in 1861 when bequests for Masses were again ruled by the English courts to be illegal because superstitious. See Edward Norman, *The English Catholic Church in the Nineteenth Century* (Oxford, 1984), 188–91. Goss later raised a related question: he asked Propaganda whether a Catholic heir could accept an inheritance that came to him because the testator's request for Masses had been ruled invalid; could he even use the money to build a church without mentioning the original bequest for Masses? See APF, *Anglia*, 17, fol. 982, of 1 May 1866. Propagnda replied (in April 1867) that the case would have to go to the Sacred Penitentiary.

[22] James Sharples, 1797–1850, became coadj. VA of the Lancashire District, in 1843. Described as 'confident, fearless and forthright' (quoted in Brian Plumb, *Arundel to Zabi: A Biographical Dictionary of the Catholic Bishops of England and Wales (Deceased), 1623–1987* (Warrington, 1987)), he took part in the negotiations in Rome for the restoration of a hierarchy.

[23] For this very complex issue, see Milburn, *History of Ushaw College*, 230–5, and Introduction, p. XXX.

[24] Francis Searle, 1817–89, Wiseman's secretary. He and Wiseman were in Rome in the autumn of 1853.

5. *Cardinal Wiseman*   *18 March 1855*   *AAL, S1/ 3/ C/7*[25]

My dear Lord Cardinal,

There are two points in my relations with Dr. Brown on which your Eminence seeks for information: 1o. my continued refusal to accept faculties; 2o. my refusal to go over to him to confer, so as to proceed to Visitation. I will endeavour to put your Eminence in possession of the truth on both these points, & to offer such explanations of my conduct as it may seem to require.

[*The first section of this letter is printed as part of Appendix 2*]

2o. I will now pass to the second point, my refusal to go over to him to confer, so as to proceed to visitation.

On the same day on which he offered me the faculties, September 29, I find the following memorandum, "I recommended him to appoint one day in the week for the transaction of business, when Dr. Crooke [*sic*], as well as myself, could be present." Dr. Brown approved of this suggestion; but seldom – not more than once or twice – acted on it. Though he was writing to me every day, & tho' he saw Dr. Crook [*sic*] every week, & sometimes oftener in the week, & tho' he was himself frequently in Liverpool, yet he did not seem to want to see me with others, & I was determined not to meet him alone for many reasons. 1st. At our said interview he spoke so disparagingly & unkindly of Dr. Crooke, who had sacrificed & was still sacrificing his health, peace of mind, & private fortune in his service, that I could not bring myself to risk a repetition of it. He even hinted that his mind was affected. 2nd. I was assured that Dr. Brown would betray me. A canon – not Mr. Fisher – said that he had brought out at a dinner table & in his pastoral secret information which he had given him on conscientious grounds; I know several other instances, one of which, if true, is atrocious. A priest was my informant & his informant, who stated that he had it from Dr. Brown, was also a priest. 3rd. I knew Dr. Brown's memory to be defective, & I knew of many mistakes he had made by misapprehending or forgetting conversations. 4th. I knew our interviews would be useless, as he talked away from the subject by the hour, when he had summoned upwards of 20 priests to meet him from a distance for purposes of consultation. 5th. I believed it to be a slipshod way of doing business, & I knew it would end in nothing, as the first person that went to him after I had left would be able to upset every arrangement made: at least this is the impression among the clergy. I tried to impress upon him that the Diocese wanted action rather than consultation. I will, however, quote passages from my letters to show that I did not decline to go out to confer with him. I find the following memorandum of a letter addressed to him Oct 19, for unfortunately I have not a copy of it. "Professed my willingness to do all in my power to lighten his anxieties; suggested that he should consult his Vic. Gen., such of his Chapter within reach, & myself, when needful; but collectively not individually, as misunderstandings arose from consulting persons apart." Intentionally or unintentionally he seems to play one person off against another, & it was to prevent this that I wrote as above. Nov 18. I again write: "I am surprised that, in spite of what I have so frequently written to the contrary, you should still persist in your assertion that I keep aloof from you. I do not wish to do so: on the contrary, I am desirous to assist you in whatever will tend to the benefit of religion in the Diocese, & even in cases which do not, in any manner, fall within the scope of my duty, provided that religion can in any way be benefitted. I have, however, made one request, a request which I consider myself bound in duty to insist on, that our interviews be conducted in an official manner. I have been appointed by the H.S. to assist you in the administration & government of the Diocese, & I am bound, under pain of disobedience to the H.S. to execute whatever your Lordship may delegate to me, & it will ever be my pleasure & delight, faithfully, & punctually, to carry out the instructions of the Holy Father. Though bound in duty only to act for & not to advise with your Lordship, yet with the hope of doing good,

&, in order to please God by sacrificing my own will, I will carefully & readily give you my counsel at any time, provided it be sought in an official manner. I request, however, that your Lordship be attended by the V.G. or by some canon, or Secretary, otherwise our interviews will degenerate into mere chit-chat, a fault greatly to be avoided in the administration of ecclesiastical matters. The Synod of Oscott,[26] as you will find in several decrees, is very anxious on this point, in order to secure due formality, & I may add that the Bps. even in their private sittings were attended by at least one, often more secretaries." Again Nov 25, "I will, as I have so often stated, come over to your Lordship at any time, but officially, as stated in my last, for in no other way can I be useful to you."

If it should seem to your Eminence that I push a principle too far, yet allowance must be made for the circumstances in which I am placed. Dr. Brown is not, or certainly was not then, always himself. Had I gone out to him alone, violent altercations & scandals must have necessarily resulted. Even written intercourse is liable to misinterpretation, how much more then verbal. Feb. 1st 1854, he wrote to say that some canonist had written to him that a Coadj. ought to be *particeps consilii*.[27] I answered that I was of the same opinion, "I do not think that he has a right to command this, I said Feb 16. [*sic*] tho', I doubt not, the H.F. would give him the right if applied for, particularly in cases affecting the future, as the establishment of missionary rectories,[28] appointment of canons, &, in fact, in all cases which have more than a passing interest, & bear on the future." In his reply to this, March 6. he said, "I have not failed to notice your observation that if Propaganda was asked to give you powers to confer confirmation, it would grant them. Possibly: I will only add, not without communicating with me & giving me an opportunity of saying something. I am not afraid." As your Eminence will observe, I had never hinted at Confirmations, but he wrote his letter after I had written to him about my contemplated journey to Rome, of which I now come to speak. It had been mooted as early as the month of January, but on Feb 2. I wrote to him, saying, amongst other things, "I should not like to absent myself, if my services are required. I shall, therefore, feel obliged if your Lordship will state whether it is your intention to delegate to me any jurisdiction during the three months of Ap, May & June, not that I shall be absent the whole of that time, but I do not wish to restrict myself. Should your Lordship have made up your mind to delegate to me any jurisdiction within that time I will be obliged if you will state the nature & extent of it, in order that I may make arrangements accordingly." In his answer he says "Feb. & March have been the most trying months to me for more than 20 years, but if I find myself at the end of March as well as I am now I shall think the crisis over. I know of no work at present except the Confirmations at Warrington which I fixt [*sic*] for Sexagesima Sunday & the meeting for the settlement of the Coll. funds, which I look upon as the most important affair of all & at which I certainly most earnestly desire to have your presence for the good of the Diocese." In my reply Feb 6. I asked him whether it would not be better for me to give confirmations in certain localities where it had not been given for 8 years & which had been prepared for it since last Autumn. I suggested that he would find ample occupation in the summer if well, by making the visitation & enforcing the decrees of the Synod of Oscott. I further stated that I had had nothing to do since the 20th of Nov. I believe this letter contained the first & last allusion ever made on the subject of visitation.

Feb. 11. he wrote to say that he had no fears about himself after March, in fact that he should consider he had nothing to fear if he was as well after his return from Warrington as he then was. In another letter he speaks of Conferences,[29] which I assured him in reply were all mapped out & published, & only required his order to begin to work. March 14 he writes, "I have no idea of any public business before the month of May, i.e. in present circumstances I mean it may be deferred until your return with Mr. Powell from your continental trip". May 11th just five days before I set out for Rome, he again wrote & enumerated the public business of the Diocese, 1. Conferences, 2. the issuing of documents connected with the late Synod[30] & preparing for another before Winter. 3. the most important, to meet your Eminence at Ushaw.

I believe I have now given your Eminence true & faithful information on the points sought. It is long, & to your Eminence, wearied with many cares, must prove very tiresome, but, at the risk of being tedious, I have thought it best to give the very words of our letters so as to prevent mistake.

[*no signature; Goss added at the end*]: I made some slight changes in the actual letter, particularly towards the end.

---

25   This is in draft form; the letter seems to have been sent but is not in AAW.

26   The first Provincial Synod (or Westminster Provincial Council) had met at Oscott in July 1852; see *Decreta*.

27   Trans: 'a sharer in one's deliberations'; an echo, perhaps, of Cicero's *consilii particeps* of one who shared in the deliberations of state (1st Catiline Oration, c. 1).

28   As parish priests Missionary Rectors enjoyed certain additional rights in Canon Law, mainly concerning their movability; in England and Wales their existence was anomalous since parishes were still canonically only missions; see Introduction, p. xviii; *Decreta*, 11–12, 60–3.

29   *Decreta*, 30, and see Doyle, 'Missed Opportunities', 263–73.

30   The first diocesan synod had been held in December 1853; the second (Goss's first) was held in September 1856.

6. *Cardinal Wiseman*   *19 March 1855*   *AAL, S1/ 3/ C/8*

My dear Lord Cardinal,

In my long &, I fear, tiresome letter of yesterday I confined myself in my answer to written documents. I now wish to offer a few remarks thereon. Your Eminence may think that I ought to have accepted the faculties offered, whatever I might have believed them to be. Had Dr. Brown pressed this acceptance, which he certainly did not, I might have been obnoxious to blame; but for myself I considered it a matter of gratulation ['con' *crossed out*] to be free from them: for one of the Bps. whose opinion your Eminence prizes had observed, the day after my consecration, that being made vicar was a rock to be avoided. Poor Dr. Youens, Dr. Turner, Dr. Sharples, Dr. Crook all experienced the sad truth of this remark. Dr. Crook's position is rather that of an errand boy or a hired clerk than of Vicar, & I find that the Bp. has spoken of him as disparagingly to others as he has to me. He has spoken of myself no better, tho', at present, the false rumour that I am in possession of certain powers makes him treat me with courtesy. But had I accepted the faculties, the result would have been the same, if we may judge from what actually occurred with regard to what he did delegate to me. I was consecrated on Sep. 25, & shortly after was desired to give confirmations in the Fylde. On 7th of October, he wrote to ask if it would not be advisable to defer them till Spring, owing to the approach of Winter with its long dark nights, & the necessity of preparing for the Diocesan Synod. Oct 26 he wrote to the same effect & Nov 10 he wrote the letter which I inclosed yesterday, which peremptorily silenced all further allusion to them till a few days before my setting out for Rome, when he wished me to [? *illegible*] them. It is dangerous to attribute motives, but his conduct & remarks at that time made it apparent to all that jealousy was the real cause for his wishing them to be suspended, for even in lay company he spoke of the acclamations with which I was welcomed as being called forth by a novelty which would soon wear away. Some notice had appeared in the Preston paper about me, probably from the pen of the agent Mr. Buller.[31] He expressed his [*illegible*] that no notice was taken of the Bp. of the D. [*sic*] in the account of the opening of the Institute. Whenever we met at dinner, just after my consecration, he could not conceal his annoyance at any attention shown me, nor at my receiving presents of a few articles of Pontificals, & when our health was proposed in common, he seldom even alluded to me. These are little things, but as commentaries on our correspondence they show that my declining to accept faculties was not the reason I was not employed.[32] To country people weather could have formed no bar to their coming to chapel for confirmations, & as for the Synod I engaged to prepare everything in two days.

Nor must your Eminence imagine from my correspondence that I refuse to advise with him. Scarcely a day in the week passed without my hearing from him up to the time of the Diocesan Synod in December, & afterwards whenever he required help. He not only did not invite me to the Synod, but he expressed surprise in no becoming terms at my being there. With regard to Conferences too, I arranged every thing, but he never would give the order for them to commence. I do not think I do him an injustice when I say that, feeling himself unable to be present at them, he did not want me to meet the clergy. When pressed about them, in my absence, he said he must wait my return; but he has never mentioned them to me.

If I am told my duty, I will do it. I am quite willing to work in the Diocese, if a fixed definite task is set me, or I am content to live retired either in the Diocese or out of it. I do not court one iota of Dr. Brown's jurisdiction, but am content for him to rule uncontrolled. To act with him is impossible, for even where he delegates a fixed work, he interferes with its exercise, owing to his memory being defective or his mind inattentive. He desired me, the other day, to ordain a subdeacon. I wrote to mention about his examination, retreat, etc. He then wrote to tell me to order two persons, whom he named, to examine him, & if I could say when I would ordain him, he would write to him to go into his retreat. Subsequently he desired me to attend to the retreat also, which I did. When I wrote to tell him that the young man had passed his examination, he wrote to say that he would write to Rev. Mr. Clerk at Hodder[33] about his retreat. Every little affair necessitates a quire of paper. In this case I had an interview besides. But so it will ever be: he is no exception to the effects produced by stimulants. He cannot act himself: & he will not let others act, but just throws the blame on them because nothing is done.

I inclose your Eminence [*sic*] a paper he has sent to the Catholic Club[34] about buying a house & raising him a maintenance. They are perplexed how to act. He has never offered me a shilling since my appointment. Some months after my consecration, the Chap. [*sic*] seeing that no provision was made for me, undertook to raise a certain sum by voluntary subscription. This gave him great umbrage & he wrote to them an ill tempered letter on the subject. He has again brought the matter before the Chap. & refused to retire during its discussion. He wants a sum to be raised & paid over to him, & then, I suppose, he will pay me, which is equivalent to my not being paid at all. For in the disbursement of the district fund, he has refused to sign the cheques when presented to him by the treasurer, after the money had been voted by the Board, & had been paid into the bank for disbursement.

At the last meeting of the Chap. they passed a resolution, the Bishop being present & approving, to invite me to be present at their meetings.

I thus have become acquainted with their minutes, and there are two papers from the Bp. of which I should very much like to forward a copy for your Eminence, as they will show Dr. Brown's frame of mind better than all the letters I could write. Does your Eminence consider that I have a right, with the consent of the Secretary, to send you a copy of these documents?

[*The draft ends here with no signature.*]

---

31 Mr E. Buller, journalist/agent, of Fishergate, Preston; see letters 110, 161, 216.

32 For Brown's view of Goss, and especially of his youth and inexperience compared with his own, see Appendix 2.

33 Thomas Tracy Clarke SJ, 1802–62, was at Hodder Place, Whalley, in the early 1850s (*Directory*; Fitz-L).

34 The Catholic Club was founded in Liverpool in 1844 by prominent laymen 'to promote unity of purpose, energy in practical charity, and good fellowship in principle' while also working politically for the protection of Catholic interests (Burke, *Catholic Liverpool*, 80 and *passim*).

7. *Right Revd. the Bishop of Liverpool*   17 April 1855   *Add.Lttrs 1*

My dear Lord,

I am in receipt this morning of your two favours. I will attend with pleasure to the consecration of the altar at Bp. Eton,[35] as desired by your Lordship. I do not quite understand the drift of Your Lordship's other letter, or I would carry out its provisions with like pleasure & fidelity. I wish therefore to ascertain from your Lordship, 1o. whether you renew or withdraw the offer of the faculties frequently alluded to, viz. those granted by Dr. Walsh[36] to Dr. now Card. Wiseman? 2o. Am I to consider that your Lordship wishes me to make the canonical visitation of the Diocess, & that you grant me the necessary & suitable faculties for such visitation?[37] 3o. Am I to understand that your Lordship refuses to allow me the exercise within the Diocess of the faculties for the erection of the Way of the Cross & of Confraternities, granted to me by the Holy See?[38]

I hope your Lordship will enjoy the promised return of fine weather. Believe me, my dear Lord,

Your affectionate Brother in Xt. Alexander Goss.

---

35 Eton Lodge, in Woolton Road, Liverpool, a former school run by an old Etonian, was purchased in 1844 as a residence for Bishops Brown and Sharples. It changed its name to Bishop Eton and Brown invited the Redemptorists to take it over as their house in 1851, which it still is. See Burke, *Catholic Liverpool*, 76, 123.

36 Thomas Walsh 1776–1849; VA of the Midland District 1826–48, and of the London District 1848–9.

37 Brown replied on 23 April, delegating to Goss the faculties enjoyed formerly by Wiseman as coadjutor and telling him to proceed with the canonical visitation; he asked to see Goss who then wrote on 25, 27, 30 April trying to tie Brown down to a definite meeting, but to no effect.

38   On the Way of the Cross, in a later letter (31 August 1855) Goss refers to a rescript
that Brown had obtained from Rome to legalise instances where he had uncanonically
delegated such erections across the diocese; it should have been reserved to the Franciscans. The hierarchy successfully petitioned for the privilege in 1857 and 1862; *Decreta*,
146–7, 195–6.

8.   *Right Rev. Dr. Brown*   *4 May 1855*   *Add.Lttrs 5–6*

My dear Lord,

I am sorry your Lordship had so rude a day for the opening of Bedford
Leigh Church:[39] it could not well have been more unpropitious, for it
was both cold & wet.

I cannot express to your Lordship the pain I have experienced in the
perusal of the inclosed letter from Dr. Newsham to your Lordship. Had
he been writing to the Archbishop of Paris, or to Dr. Gillis[40] or to any
Bishop, who was comparatively uninterested in the College, he could
hardly have written in a different style. No one, to judge from that
letter, would conceive that your Lordship had any jurisdiction over the
College, or that you had any pecuniary interest in its success or failure.
He neither asks your sanction nor consent for the new building, nor does
he vouchsafe to state by whose authority he is acting. Surely some other
more definite sanction than that of Dr. Smith[41] & Dr. Gillow,[42] both of
whom died more than 25 years ago, is requisite. If Dr. Smith, the then
Bishop, was an authority for the undertaking, your Lordship is surely
an equal authority now, & if his consent or authority could sanction the
undertaking then, I should think the sanction of your Lordship & that
of your Confreres is no less requisite now. I strongly recommend you
to write a short civil note to Dr. Newsham to ask by whose sanction or
authority he is acting in the erection of the new wing. In the first letter
I would use no argument against the undertaking, but would simply ask
by whose authority he is acting. I have written to ask Dr. Turner[43] & Dr.
Briggs to do the same. Nothing could be lost, but much might be gained
by such a letter. In the first letter I would not manifest any disapproval,
nor would I make any inquiry as to where the funds come from: all that
would form matter for other letters on the subject. I think it will be quite
necessary, on the receipt of another letter from Dr. Newsham or in the
absence of an answer to your inquiry, to protest against the proposed
erection, notwithstanding the sanction that might be alleged for it; for
I am satisfied that no sanction except that of the Bishops can authorize
such an undertaking. The Holy See would never allow it to go on, if the
Bishops protested against it.

Believe me, my dear Lord, Your affte Br. in Xt. Alexander Goss.

39   Bedford Leigh (usually known as Leigh): St Joseph's was built in 1855; Kelly, *English*

Catholic Missions, says it was designed by Hampden, but the current *Liverpool Directory* says Joseph Hansom.

[40]   Presumably Bp James Gillis, VA of the Eastern District, Scotland, 1852–64.

[41]   Bp Thomas Smith, VA of the Northern District, 1821–31.

[42]   John Gillow 1753–1828, second President of Ushaw 1811–28; see Milburn, *History of Ushaw College*, 116 ff. The Gillow family were prominent members of Lancaster's mercantile elite in the eighteenth century both as shipowners and furniture-makers, and were important members of the emerging Catholic middle class. They had ceased to have an active part in the furniture business by 1830 though it retained their name; it has been said that by the mid-nineteenth century they were producing more priests than pieces of furniture. See D. J Pope, 'Lancaster's Late Eighteenth-Century Catholic Shipowners and Merchants – the Gillows and Worswicks', Part One, *NWCH* 31 (2004), 21–50; Part Two, *NWCH* 32 (2005), 21–35.

[43]   William Turner 1799–1872, first bishop of Salford 1851–72.

9.   *Mr. Guest of Valladolid*   *4 May 1855*   *Add.Lttrs 7*
Dear Revd. Sir,
A letter addressed by you to Mr. Billington of Kirkham[44] has just been put into my hands, in which you make inquiry about the future payment of the pensions of 12 boys. I know of no provision made for the purpose, but still it is possible that something may, as it is certain that something ought to, be done in their behalf. I wish, however, to know the names, ages, school or class, & native places of the said students; also to what Bishop or Bishops they are supposed to belong. Are you or are the boys themselves aware of any arrangement having been entered into with <u>any</u> Bishop in their regard. It is necessary to have this information before any thing can even be thought of respecting them. I should like also to hear something further regarding their respective characters & proficiency in their studies, & the probability of their continuing their studies.

Believe me, my dear Sir, Very sincerely Yours in Xt. Alexander Goss.

[44]   The Billington family of Kirkham were generous supporters of the Church; the reference here might be to William who was later to pay for the chancel of the new church opened in 1860.

10.   *The Bishop of Liverpool*   *19 May 1855*   *Add.Lttrs 8–9*
<u>Confidential</u>
My dear Lord,
You will be surprised to learn that the Bishops finished all business on the Tuesday, the only day of meeting. All were present except your Lordship & the Bp of Newport, said to be detained at Rome by the government.[45]

The Bishops wrote a joint letter to Propaganda, signed by all present, expressing their opinions of the three candidates nominated to Plymouth; I will give your Lordship the names etc. when I see you.[46]

A joint letter was also addressed to the Pope, congratulating him on his escape at St. Agnes.[47]

A joint letter was also written to the Poor School Committee, regarding the addition of a secular department to the Training School at Brook Green, sanctioning also the proposed school for Pupil Teachers by the nuns of Notre Dame, & renewing their promise to appoint a Clerical Inspection of the Poor Schools in their respective Dioceses.[48] A joint letter was also written in recommendation of Dr. English's errand from the Holy Father about the Collegio Pio.[49] Officers, such as Secretaries, Masters of Ceremonies, etc. were appointed for the approaching Provincial Synod.[50]

Subjects for discussion were also proposed by various Bishops, but they were of a very anomalous character, & were not digested or put in any form.

At his soirée, in the evening, the Cardinal fell over a piece of carpet, & hurt his shoulder, but there was no dislocation. He was doing well when I left on Thursday, & it was expected he would be able to preach on Sunday next.

I preach at Blackbrook[51] on Sunday, but hope to get back for the meeting of the Chapter, when I hope to have the pleasure of seeing you.

Believe me, my dear Lord, Your affte Br. in Xt. Alexander Goss.

[*PS on page 9*] Cardinal Wiseman desired me to request Canon Walmsley & Dr. Crook, the executors of Dr. Youens,[52] to furnish a list of 12 priests unconnected with Ushaw or the Diocese of Liverpool, from whom, & from 12 others furnished by Dr. Newsham, he would select four or five for the settlement of the claims on Mr. Sherburne's executors or others. He told me that he could himself appoint the arbitrators absolutely, but that he preferred, owing to his connection with Ushaw, to select them from lists furnished by the respective litigants. I hope your Lordship will notify the receipt of this decision to Propaganda, or they may think we are very clamorous, for a second remonstrance or memorial was forwarded to them, which they would hardly have received when they last wrote to your Lordship. The Cardinal suggests the time of the Provincial Synod as suitable for the discussion of the Claims of Dr. Youens's Executors before the arbitrators. I think the arrangement satisfactory: I regret, however, that it has been so tardy.

---

45   The Bishop of Newport and Menevia was Thomas Joseph Brown OSB, 1798–1880; see Plumb, *Arundel.*

46   In March 1855 Bp Errington left Plymouth to become coadjutor to Wiseman. His successor in Plymouth was William Vaughan, 1855–1902, uncle of the future cardinal.

47   On 21 April 1855 the Pope had escaped unharmed from a building collapse at the

ancient convent of St Agnes after visiting the catacombs with a group of pilgrims and others (including the Bishop of Nottingham); the escape was regarded as miraculous and news of it spread very quickly and was celebrated widely. See G. S. Pelczar, *Pio IX e il suo pontificato*, 3 vols (Turin 1910), II, 44–6.

[48] On the Poor Schools Committee and Pupil Teacher Training Colleges: see J. P. Marmion, 'The Beginnings of the Catholic Poor Schools in England', *RH* 17:1 (May 1984), 67–83; and Tenbus, *English Catholics and the Education of the Poor*.

[49] Collegio Pio: later, the Beda, for older candidates to the priesthood and converts. Dr Louis Bernard English, 1826–63, of Clifton Diocese, was rector of the English College, Rome, 1857–63.

[50] Second Synod of Oscott (2nd Provincial Synod of Westminster), July 1855; both Brown and Goss attended.

[51] On Blackbrook see n. 223.

[52] See Introduction, p. xxvii, for the Sherburne–Youens dispute.

11. *Right Revd. Dr. Brown, Bishop of Liverpool*   25 *May 1855*
Add.Lttrs 10–13

My dear Lord,

According to my promise of yesterday I write for your Lordship's consideration the draft of a letter to Mgr. Newsham, & should you still be afflicted with rheumatic gout in the hands, I doubt not that Dr. Crook will transcribe or rewrite it, making such alterations as you may deem necessary. It would be quite sufficient for your Lordship to sign it, for even if you were not impeded in your writing by rheumatism, it is by no means necessary that letters of this description should be in your own hand writing. The more I consider this painful question, the more convinced I am that a great effort is necessary to prevent Dr. Newsham putting the College of Ushaw into a false position with reference to the Bishops, & to arrest the mania of brick & mortar, which will ultimately prove the ruin of the College, in whose welfare we have so large a stake. I say nothing of the impropriety & impolicy of endeavouring to make your Lordship joint owner in an Establishment which, if not designed to supplant, may at least injure your own Seminary.[53] It may suit the views of the President of Ushaw, but it can hardly suit a Bishop's interest to cripple, by raising up an antagonist, an establishment over which he holds undivided jurisdiction, whilst over the building about to be erected at Ushaw he will have no control, & will be expected to interfere no further than by contributing to its support.

Draft of a letter to Mgr. Newsham

I am in receipt of your favour by which I am informed that the Bishops of Beverley, Hexham, & Salford approve of the Little School, about to be built in connection with Ushaw, & hence am left to infer that it is in consequence of their approval & under their sanction that you are acting. I am quite unable to reconcile this statement with the tenor of your first letter to me, for in it you ask for no sanction, nor do you in any manner intimate that you were anxious for any expression of opinion from me, & I was distinctly informed by the Vice President, whom you instructed to call on me, that I was not expected to reply to your letter. Now if you wrote to the other Bishops for their sanction & approval, why, may I ask, was it thought unnecessary to elicit mine, who am most interested in the welfare of Ushaw from the extent of involvement of my Diocese, from the resources of which Ushaw has drawn so hugely both in past & present times? Where all are interested, it is not too much to expect that the approval of all should be equally sought. If any exception was made in my regard, it might have been in allowing additional weight to my opinion in consideration of the greater interests that I have at stake.

I must, however, candidly assure you that I consider the approbation or rather the alleged approbation of the Bishops an afterthought, for I am assured by Dr. Turner, that he pointedly asked Dr. Gibson[54] whether he had come to solicit his approbation or merely to convey to him information of the contemplated erection, & he was answered by Dr. Gibson that his errand was simply to inform him of the fact. If I am not wrongly informed, plans for the new building had been ordered before the Bishops were spoken to about the matter, a proceeding hardly reconciled with the assurance that you are acting on the Bishops' sanction & approval. Besides I do not think that the very qualified approbation of Dr. Turner can be pleaded in sanction of so gigantic an undertaking, fraught with so much danger to the future interests of Ushaw, for he assures me that what he said was 'that if the money was given for that special purpose it must of course be so applied, but he thought it a pity that it did not go for burses'.

I beg therefore to enter my formal protest against the proposed erection if it has to be considered in any way connected with Ushaw, & I shall never allow any of my subjects to be employed as teachers or superiors of it. It is unnecessary for me to assign any reasons for this protest, but I am prepared with them in case the question be brought before the Bishops who are interested in the welfare of Ushaw. My protest extends not only to the uncanonical & unconstitutional way in which the thing is being done, but to its being done at all.

I cannot conclude without expressing my deep regret that any thing should be done to the prejudice of an establishment with which my earliest & fondest associations are connected, for I feel assured that the foundation stone of the new building will be the first stone laid for the ruin of Ushaw. A President may be flattered by the extent & the splendour of his College halls, but a Bishop can only sit down & weep at the contemplation of new buildings instead of fresh priests. Two hundred thousand souls from this diocese alone look to Ushaw for priests, & I cannot but regret that less should be done in the cause of missionary education by Ushaw in its prosperity than was done by Ushaw in its poverty. If President Gillow impoverished the College, he enriched the mission, whilst now we behold the sad spectacle of an enrichment of the College at the expense of the Mission. The education of a student costs more now than it cost 20 years ago, & yet how much improved is the College in its circumstances!

On second consideration I have thought it better to send your Lordship a copy of this letter already written, so that in case Dr. Crooke [*sic*] is prevented from coming out, you may have the letter at hand in case you should approve of its contents; it is certainly temperate, & perhaps hardly strong enough for the occasion, but it is better to err on the side of gentleness.

I send your Lordship a copy of the announcement of the visitation commenced under your auspices; it is a near transcript of Gavant.[55] As your Lordship is prevented from making the visitation in person, I hope you will pray for its success, & beg that it may lead to an increase of piety & the advancement of religion. Believe me, my dear Lord, Your affte Br in Xt. Alexander Goss.

---

53   See letter 1 to Lingard. On the dispute, see David Milburn, 'The Origins of the Junior House at Ushaw', *The Ushaw Magazine* 69:206 (July 1959), 65–77; Brown used Goss's draft; see Appendix 2.

54   Michael Gibson, 1816–56; vice-president of Ushaw 1849–56.

55   B. Gavanti, 1569–1638, a prolific writer on liturgical matters whose works were frequently re-published; his *Praxis synodi dioecesanae celebrandae* and *Praxis visitationis episcopalis* were both published in Rome in 1628. Goss used *Praxis synodi dioecesanae celebrandae ex opere D. B. Gavanti redacta* (London, Dublin, Derby, 1853); AAL also has two copies of a pocket-sized edition of this, one that belonged to J. H. Fisher, the other to his brother James Fisher. See R. Aubert (ed.), *Dictionnaire d'histoire et de géographie ecclésiastiques* (Paris, 1984), vol. XX, col. 130–4.

12.   *Dr. Briggs*   *25 May 1855*   *Add.Lttrs 14–15*
                               <u>Confidential</u>

My dear Lord,

I know not whether you have heard from the Cardinal in answer to your joint letter, but I understand that he promised a reply. He says that on mentioning to Barnabò[56] his intention to send in his Report & saying that then his visitation would cease,[57] Barnabò replied, No, you are to continue being Visitor. Now I distinctly remember Barnabò saying, in answer to our complaint about the Visitorship, that if the Card. wanted to cease, he had only to send in his report. My impression is that the Card. or Bp. Hogarth, perhaps both, petitioned for a continuance of the Visitorial powers. I feel assured that if you were to draw up a memorial, signed by yourself, Dr. Brown,[58] & Dr. Turner, petitioning for the cessation of the Visitorship, you would carry your point, for, if you remember, you had not only great attention shown to you personally, but great weight was also attached to your opinions on the various subjects opened for discussion. Barnabò certainly seemed to feel & admit the position of the Bishops. He conveyed to me the impression that it was the Cardinal's own wish to continue in his office of Visitor, nor do I think it probable that he would wish to lay it down voluntarily, for he is de facto supreme rector of Ushaw, & Dr. Newsham does not care straw [sic] for the Bishops as long as he has the Card. with him. In fact as Dr. Errington assured Dr. Turner in London the Card. is the only superior of Ushaw & the Bishops have nothing to do with affairs, their duty being simply to send students & to vote for a new President in case of Dr. Newsham's death. With such opinions, our position is not likely to be improved, should the Card. leave England. I do not, however, wish any use to be made of this opinion; I mention it that you may know what to expect, unless you make an effort to recover your rights. The decree appointing Card. Wiseman Visitor, a copy of which is now before me, is dated Dec. 13, 1850, nearly five years ago, & the object of the Visitation was to recommend a constitution in conjunction with the Bishops concerned, owing to difficulties that might arise from the College being situated in one Diocese, whilst it belonged to several others. Now every other Secular College is similarly circumstanced, & yet they have no Visitor, but the Bishops meet together & settle the matter among themselves. The North alone is put under a Visitor, for Prior Park cannot be quoted as being under a Visitor, since it was so placed for very different reasons.[59] Visitors are generally appointed to remedy abuses; & the appointment of them is an unusual exercise of jurisdiction by the Holy See, seldom enforced except to remedy proved abuses. The continuance of it is a reflection on the Bishops as being incapable of managing their affairs either from incapacity or internal dissensions. It was on this ground that the Irish Bishops, when in Rome, are said to have petitioned for the cessation of Dr. Cullen's legatine powers.[60] I feel sure that if you would draw up a petition to the Holy [See] to pray that Card. Wiseman's might now cease, that Dr. Brown & I imagine Dr. Turner, would sign it. I would mention the length of time it had lasted, the slur its continuance cast on the Bishops, their dissatisfaction, the injury it inflicted on the College by leaving the President to act as he liked without consulting the Bishops, etc. Dr. Newsham has just gone up to London. With the Card. he has more influence than all the Bishops together in whatever concerns the College. You are mere ciphers, serving only to increase the value of the figure on to which you are appended.

The Card. has ordered the Executors of Dr. Youens & Dr. Newsham to choose each 12 priests, & from this list, he will select 4 or 5 arbitrators to try the cases at issue with this Diocese.

Unless your Lordship takes up this matter of the College promptly you may reckon on things going on as they are till death, for I doubt whether the Card's absence would improve matters. You have as little actual power at Ushaw as at Oscott; you serve to grace the pageant of an Exhibition or the Defensions[61] & then you have played your part. Believe me sincerely Yrs <u>A. Goss</u>.

I need not add how necessary it is that you should consider this letter strictly confidential & private.

---

[56] Alessandro Barnabò, 1801–74; secretary of Propaganda under Cardinal Fransoni; became cardinal and Prefect of Propaganda in 1856. On Fransoni see n. 87 below.

[57] Wiseman was Apostolic Visitor of Ushaw College, appointed in 1850 at Newsham's request; Milburn, *History of Ushaw College*, 203–4, and 208–9 for the particular 1854 visitation mentioned here.

[58] James Brown, 1812–81; first bp of Shrewsbury from 1851.

[59] Prior Park, Bath, had been opened in 1830 by Bishop Baines, VA of the Western District, who saw it as a seminary-cum-college and, he hoped, a future Catholic university. It had a very troubled and contentious history, and in 1855 Archbishop Errington was appointed apostolic administrator *sede vacante*, to sort out the financial problems of Clifton Diocese, especially those connected with and caused by the college; he decided that it should close and be sold. See J. S. Roche, *A History of Prior Park College and Its Founder Bishop Baines* (London, 1931); Pamela J. Gilbert, *This Restless Prelate: Bishop Peter Baines 1786–1843* (Gracewing, 2006). For Wiseman's involvement, see Schiefen, *Nicholas Wiseman*, 40–6, 54–64, 246–7.

[60] For Cullen and the Irish bishops, see *DIB*. Cullen was appointed Archbishop of Armagh and Apostolic Delegate in 1849, with the task of reforming the Church in Ireland and settling the bitter disputes among the bishops; he was made perpetual delegate in 1852 and became Archbishop of Dublin that same year.

[61] Exhibition Week was held at the end of each academic year at Ushaw to celebrate its achievements, academic and otherwise. Defensions were public oral examinations in which students defended a number of set, printed theses in theology, philosophy or science, before external clerical examiners. See Milburn, *History of Ushaw College*, 141–2, 230.

---

13. *To the Very Reverend, the Chapter of Liverpool* 24 August 1855
5/1/9–10

Very Reverend Brethren,
I am now drawing to the close of the second year of my Episcopacy as Coadjutor of Liverpool. To your kind exertions I was indebted for my first year's income; on the subject of a provision for the outgoing year I shall be glad of your advice.

By the canons he who is assisted by a Coadjutor is bound to provide the Coadjutor with a suitable residence for himself & <u>household</u>, with every requisite for exercising Pontifical rites, with a proper maintenance, & income to defray all expenses of administration. These have not been offered to me, nor have I demanded them, nor made any representation to the Holy See in order to enforce them. The Bishop of Liverpool is an old man, & is suffering from infirmities other than those incident to his age, & he has a right to expect such comforts, conveniences & even luxuries as are deemed requisite for his position & condition. This is my feeling now, & it was my opinion before any rumour of my appointment to the Episcopacy. It was this feeling that prevented me at first, & still prevents me from making any demand upon him; & it was this feeling, if I mistake not, which induced you to raise a voluntary subscription for my maintenance, in order that he might not be called upon to make any division of his revenue. This subscription, I am told, you [are unwilling *crossed out*] hesitate to renew, as you have been told that it is uncanonical; but this, surely, must be a mistake. The canons may not empower you to <u>levy a rate</u>, no more than the laws of England empower government to levy contributions of warm clothing for the army in the Crimea; but they certainly do not forbid you to solicit or receive voluntary contributions, any more than the law of England forbids such to be forwarded to our soldiers. My object, however, in this letter is to apply for advice & not to give it. I do not, therefore, wish to make any suggestion or to offer any opinion, tho' I have very strong feelings on the subject, as any honourable man must have under the circumstances.

If you are in doubt about how to act, you may either decline to tender me advice or to entertain my letter, or you may apply to the Holy See for counsel. To me either course will be acceptable. If you refuse me aid, the canons point out to me the course to be pursued; if you apply to the Holy See, the result of such application must be satisfactory to us all. If a rate has to be levied, I feel sure that application will ultimately have to be made to the Holy See for that purpose, because I doubt, & others doubt whether, under existing circumstances in Eng. such a rate can be enforced without its sanction, & if enforced, even if found that it could be lawfully enforced, the attempt would most likely lead to reclamation & appeal; for the public mind is still sore on the past administration of the Temporalities of this Diocese. I would not have made this observation, had I not known that you were all conversant with it. Believe me sincerely Yrs in Xt. Alexander Goss.

14.   *Rt. Rev. Dr. Brown, Bp. of Liverpool   30 August 1855   Add.Lttrs*
18–19

My dear Lord,
I am glad to find that your Lordship is issuing written faculties to the Clergy, as I shall thereby be freed from much embarrassment & many of the Clergy will be freed from grievous, & by no means groundless, scruples; for hitherto few had duly authenticated copies of faculties; many thought they had received them *usque ad revocationem*;[62] others for the period of 6 years, long since elapsed, whilst they were unable to say whether they had ever been renewed, & not a few were exer-

cising them by mere verbal commission, & possessed only a very vague recollection of the period for which they had been granted, or of any subsequent confirmation of them since the original grant. Under these circumstances, so grave from the high interests at stake, the step which your Lordship has taken cannot be too highly commended.

There is another subject to which I now wish to call your Lordship's attention. Perhaps I ought to apologize for troubling you so often regarding it; for, I believe, this is the fourth time, since my return from Rome, that I have brought it under your notice. I promise you, however, that I shall not again recur to it, nor should I do so now had not circumstances, with which it is unnecessary to trouble your Lordship, compelled me to do so. In my letter of April 17, 1855, I asked your Lordship whether you renewed or withdrew the offer of faculties of the same tenor as those formerly granted by Dr. Walsh to Dr. Wiseman. Your Lordship in your answer, April 23, replied that it was your intention to grant them, but you first solicited an interview. That interview took place on the 1st of May following. Receiving no further communication from your Lordship, I again addressed you on the subject on the 16th of June; but neither that letter nor a subsequent one received any answer.

Faculties cannot be delegated without a written commission, at least, such is the injunction of the Synod of Oscott.[63] I cannot, therefore, consider what has passed between us on this subject, as tantamount to a grant of the said faculties; but on the contrary, should your Lordship decline to answer this letter, I must consider it equivalent to a withdrawal of the offer made in the letter of April 23.

[*Crossed out paragraph*: I must candidly confess that I am unable to explain your Lordship's hesitation in this matter, after the bitter complaints which you have made to the Holy See,[64] ere I left Rome, & to your clergy, both formerly & recently regarding my supposed <u>refusal</u> of them at our interview, Sep. 29, 1853.]

I hope your Lordship will be comfortable in your new house, & that you will find it warm & dry for the winter.[65] You will be surprised to learn that Mr. & Mrs. Powell & Son have gone to the continent, & even hope to reach Rome. They have some thoughts of leaving Edward, but I think he will return with them.[66] Perhaps he may accompany me when I go to lay before the Holy Father, [*crossed out*: whose solicitude for ['your' *crossed out*] this Diocese is great] the details of the Visitation. Believe me, my dear Lord, Your affte Br. in Xt.   Alex. Goss.

---

62 Trans: 'until revoked'.

63 *Decreta*, 12.

64 Brown wrote several times to Propaganda in 1854 and 1855, detailing his accusations against Goss; Propaganda replied with a number of letters criticising his treatment of his coadjutor, ordering him to give Goss proper faculties and allow him to carry out the

visitation of the diocese; Wiseman was also involved in the dispute. See Introduction, pp.
xxiv–v and Appendix 2.

[65]   Brown moved to 17 Catharine Street, Liverpool; see also n. 80 for a later move.

[66]   Edward Powell, 1837–1901; he did study at the English College; o.1862, and was
secretary to Goss 1862–65.

15.   *Dr. Brown of Liverpool*   *1 September 1855*   *Add.Lttrs 21–3*

My dear Lord,

I am duly in receipt of your esteemed favour of yesterday, promisimg
a reply to mine of Aug. 30. I shall be glad to call on your Lordship at
your new house as soon as I find a little leisure: at present I am seldom
at home, as duty summons me elsewhere.

I beg now to solicit your Lordship's attention to the following statement on the subject of Coniston, regarding which I shall be glad to hear
from you at your earliest convenience.

Coniston, as your Lordship is aware, is situated at a distance of 16
miles from Ulverston, on which it has to depend for spiritual help. There
are at present residing there 258 souls, consisting of 101 males & 57
females over the age of 15: of 20 males & 13 females below 15, but
over 8: & of 31 males & 36 females, under the age of 8 years.

These poor forlorn creatures are very desirous of spiritual help, &
the rather, as they are engaged in the dangerous occupation of mining.
Until Mr. Morris's[67] recent indisposition, he visited them every month,
latterly more seldom; but to men, compelled, in order to earn a live-
lihood, to expose their lives in prosecution of their labour, such rare
visitation is unsatisfactory. They are quiet, diligent & zealous, & are
willing to contribute to the support of a priest, if one is sent to them. In
order to prepare them for Confirmation & to give them an opportunity of
frequenting the sacraments, I deputed the Rev. T. Gibson[68] of Fleetwood
to labour amongst them. He found them most attentive to his instructions, & most obliging in their intercourse with him, & most liberal in
their contributions to his support. He found himself most comfortable
in one of their cottages in which he dwelt during his sojourn amongst
them, in order to be more frequently with them & in order to save the
expenses of an hotel. Besides the families at Coniston there are also Mr.
& Mrs. Wilcock[69] & servant, & several families at Ambleside, but the
latter are not in the diocese of Liverpool.

During Mr. Gibson's stay about 100 persons received the sacrament
of Penance & the Blessed Eucharist, among whom were three converts,
& about 40 were confirmed. Owing to the absence of any large room,
even of a barn at Coniston, I administered the sacrament of Confirmation at Lake Bank, the residence of Thomas Wilcock Esq.

The mining company have shown themselves very liberal, not only
in the free employment of Irish Catholics, in their protecting them from

insult on the part of the English, but also in the promise of a plot of land sufficient for a chapel & a priest's house, a promise made in answer to a memorial addressed to them by the Catholics of Coniston, & by a resolution of the Directors, Mr. Barratt, the acting manager, was directed to set out the same to such extent as he should think proper.

Of all the priests in the diocese of Liverpool, I do not think there is one better qualified to begin this infant mission than the Rev. T. Gibson of Fleetwood. He is young & zealous, self-denying & pious; he is fond of the people & they are fond of him. No doubt Mr. Wilcock would assist the infant mission tho' his house is about 5½ miles distant from Coniston.

Fleetwood is now in good working order & might safely be entrusted to other hands. Could it not be entrusted to Revd. Mr. Lynch, late of Leeds, who for some time worked the abandoned vineyard of Blackpool, & who, if report be correct, has petitioned for leave to secularize.[70] I hope your Lordship will not refuse his services, for the diocese will be reduced to a wilderness if some vigorous effort is not made, not only to retain, but also to procure fresh priests. The Oblates who have already joined us are highly spoken of; & those who have since gone from this Diocese elsewhere enjoy the good opinion of the Bishops whom they are serving.

If your Lordship has other views with regard to Lynch, might not one of the St. Patrick's priests, say Mr. P. Power,[71] be deputed to Fleetwood? Canon Kenrick is a man of great personal piety, & I should think one every way able to train up young men, & if Mr. Power were withdrawn, another might be obtained from Waterford[72] & sent to be trained in the same school. It might happen that Mr. Power would not like to accept Fleetwood, but generally priests in a second place are glad to occupy a mission alone, & very often they work with more zeal when they feel greater responsibility, tho' such a remark can hardly apply to Mr. Power, who has the reputation of zeal & untiring energy.

I have reason to know that Mr. Gibson would not object to the appointment to Coniston. If the Jesuits abandon Ulverston – as report states they are going to do – Mr. Gibson might, for a term, work both missions.[73]

My suggestions as to these missionary changes, I beg your Lordship will consider private & confidential.

Believe me, my dear Lord, Your affte Br in Xt.   Alexander Goss

---

67 John George Morris, o. 1808, d. 1855. He was at Ulverston 1844–55; while he served a number of Jesuit missions he was not a professed Jesuit (see Fitz-L, 63).

68 Thomas E. Gibson, 1822–91; at Fleetwood 1848–55. He moved to Croft and then to Lydiate in 1859. He published *Lydiate Hall and Its Associations, in Two Parts, Antiquarian and Religious* (n.p., 1876), *A Cavalier's Note Book* (London, 1880), *Crosby Records* (Manchester, 1887), and *Catholicity in Liverpool* (reprinted in *The Cathedral Record*, May 1935).

[69]   Thomas Wilcock, of Lake Bank, Esthwaite Water. Kelly (*English Catholic Missions*) says that the want of a church in Coniston was advertised in *The Tablet* in 1859 and met by Queen Amélie (Marie-Amélie de Bourbon of the Kingdom of Naples, granddaughter of Maria-Theresa of Austria, in exile in Surrey from 1848 until her death in 1866); a very devout lady who had spent the autumn of 1859 in Coniston. See later letters of 1859 and ff. below, including those to Pugin. In the end, Goss did not open a church there until 1872, a week before he died. *VCH* follows Kelly with the Amélie story. Perhaps she gave some money, but the real benefactor was Miss Elizabeth Aglionby of Wigton Hall, a convert, who left £2,000; the total cost of land, church and presbytery was about £2,300. She had been helping earlier as well: in a letter of 28 May 1866 Goss asks if she was ready to receive an extra priest 'for the Lake District' (5/5/121). There is picture of her in a centenary pamphlet that has a brief history of the parish written by Rev. E. McCartan in 1972, *Centenary Year 1872–1972. Short History of the Parish* (copy in The Talbot Library, Preston). See also P. Conlan OFM, *St Cuthbert's, Wigton* (*c*. 1990), p. 13.

[70]   Francis Joseph Lynch, 1818–99, was at the OMI mission of St Mary's, Leeds, in 1858; at Holy Cross, Liverpool, 1868, and then moved to the Shrewsbury Diocese; there are some gaps in his *Directory* listings.

[71]   Pierse Power, 1823–95, edu. Waterford; at St Patrick's, 1847–59, r. St Anthony's, 1859–68; see Michael O'Neill, *St Anthony's, Scotland Road, Liverpool* (Leominster, 2010), 106–30.

[72]   St John's College, Waterford, a fruitful source of priests for the English Mission.

[73]   The Jesuits gave up the Ulverston mission in 1863; see Anne C. Parkinson, *A History of Catholicism in the Furness Peninsula, 1127–1997* (Lancaster, 1998), 60. Ulverston was the 'mother mission' of Barrow.

16.   *Dr. Brown of Lpool*   *11 September 1855*   *Add.Lttrs 24–6*
My dear Lord,
Continued absence from home since the receipt of your Lordship's favour of Sep. 6. has prevented me from replying. Last week I was paying a visit of inspection to the Conferences, which, your Lordship will be glad to hear, are progressing favourably.

My inquiries about the Sanatorium were <u>not</u> for the purpose of commenting on those erected by you since 1843; but to enable me to give a canonical certificate of the one erected by me at Preston by your Lordship's delegation.

Your Lordship's allusion to faculties I am unable to understand as an answer to my letter of Aug. 30. I hope your Lordship will, therefore, excuse me if, to make the matter clear, I again repeat my question: Am I to understand that <u>I possess</u> or <u>do not possess</u> the faculties so often alluded to, viz., the same as were enjoyed by Card. Wiseman under Bishop Walsh? I shall feel obliged if your Lordship will give me a direct answer to this question.

The only faculties that I at present actually hold from your Lordship, if I except those held by me when a priest, are those of Visitation held, as your correspndence with the Holy See between the months of Dec. 1854 & May last make you aware, under very peculiar circumstances.

I am glad to find that some of the Visitation questions meet with your kind approval, & I have only to add that if your Lordship were acquainted with the anxiety of the Holy See on the various details embraced under the head of *Status animarum* you would hardly under-value the information sought, or strive to throw discouragement on the attempt to obtain it. I am, however, persuaded that your correct notion of the canonical status of a Coadjutor who is, as you rightly state, *quid unum et idem*[74] with his Principal, will prevent you from lending the sanction of your name to any attempt to evade the difficulties it presents.

Your Lordship, I am sorry to perceive, <u>seems</u> to feel that any attempt to get things into more canonical shape is somewhat of a reflection on yourself. Now I beg to assure [you] that such is not the case, & no one can give your Lordship more willing credit than I do, for every attempt made in this direction. The difficulties are many & great, & have been greater & your Lordship may rest assured that full credit shall be given to you for your exertions in the historical account of your administration which will have to be compiled for the Archivium.

Your Lordship more than insinuates that I have shown myself unfriendly to you, yet I am at a loss to conceive in what this unfriend-liness has been exhibited. You seem to think that I am changed from what I was; but is not the change rather in your Lordship than in me? It is indeed gratifying to me to find that you remember with pleasure the efforts I made in your behalf when an attempt was made to talk you down. By whom was that attempt made, my Lord? What is now, in your Lordship's feelings & the frequent & open expression of them, the relative position of your assailant & defenders?[75]

My dear Lord, it is painful to find matters of trifling import & refer-ences to wretched gossip distorted by the malice or sycophancy of the retailer, occupying your thoughts & your pen, when there are matters of such grave importance to occupy as well your own mind as the anxious solicitude of every good & zealous man in your Diocese. If much has been done, my Lord, much more remains to be done. Coniston, the Industrial Schools, the Isle of Man – to which even newspapers advert – & the insufficient manning of many chapels demand prompt & serious attention.

Believe me, my dear Lord, Your affte Br in Xt.   Alexander Goss.

---

[74] Trans:'one and the same'.
[75] It is unclear to what event Goss is referring here.

17. *Mr. Guest, Valladolid*   *5 October 1855*   *Add.Lttrs 27–9*
Very Revd. & dear Sir,
When the Bps met in London, they remained together only one day, & hence there was no time to discuss the question of Valladolid, nor

do I remember it to have been mentioned. At the close of the Synod, a day or rather a morning was set aside for the discussion of the questions which might, well nigh, have occupied a week. Amongst the rest, Valladolid was introduced. As it was seen that I was in possession of the latest information from you, I was entrusted with the matter, i.e., as far as I understood, to examine the papers presented & to report to the Bps as to the best mode to be adopted in its regard. It was thought advisable to make no application to the Spanish Government on the subject of Rector, as it might give them a pretext for immediate interference. The Bps all gratefully acknowledged your efforts in [*sic*] behalf of the College, & I think that you may consider yourself as de facto Rector, & hence possessed of all the rights & prerogatives of that office.

One thing is clear, that, whatever the Bps may ultimately determine, you cannot take students in small numbers to be divided into various classes. Either young or old you may take them, but you must have & exercise the right of refusing admittance to such as could not be associated with any existing class. Meanwhile you must follow your own discretion &, until something be definitely arranged, write to each Bp. to say you have vacancies at such pensions & for such boys, specifying the class they must be fit for.

If I do not assist you as efficiently as you could wish, it is not for want of will, but of power. I am bound hand & foot on every side, &, as things now stand in the Dioceses composing the Old Northern District, the Bp. [*sic*] are crippled in their rights of superintendence over ecclesiastical education. Had I the power I would secure for you an efficient Professor; but meanwhile you must retain any one you like: for your first duty is the College. Should any Bp. protest against you keeping his subject as a Professor, it will be a means of bringing the matter to an issue, which would be for the mutual advantage of both the Bps & the College: for the interests of the two cannot be antagonistic.

I will take care that Mr. Laverty's[76] pension is paid, & that you are reimbursed for the money advanced to him for his return.

Canon Carter[77] is now engaged in getting up a class of <u>young</u> boys. I will lend him what aid & cooperation I can in this matter, as far as this Diocese is concerned.

With regard to Mr. Chas. Gillow as Exec. of Mr. Sherburne, you should first supply Can. Carter with every scrap of information you possess, & then leave him to bring the matter to an issue. I shall be happy to be of any aid to him or you. Leave the matter entirely in his hands, but meanwhile you must <u>insist</u> on the pensions being paid by the Diocese to which the young men belong, & leave them to be reimbursed by Mr. C. Gillow, if the money can be got. But if he refuses to be responsible for Mr. Sherburne's promises, that is no reason why Valladolid should not be paid. If neither Mr. C. Gillow nor the Bps will pay the arrears, you are in a difficulty; but with regard to the future payment of the pension, you have no difficulty; for if the Bps to whom the said students belong, refuse to pay for the current expenses of their students, you must at once give them notice that after a date named you will send the said students home, as you cannot incur liabilities on their account. Even if you have to pay their passage to England, you will find the first loss the least, & you must subsequently decline to take any students for the Dioceses so acting, until you have been reimbursed for the outlay.

I have suggested to Can. Carter the propriety, I might say the necessity of allotting each Bp one or more places in the College, to which he can send students at a small pension. If he has only one such place it will give him a stake in the College. At Rome each Diocese has one free place & a half, to which we can present free of cost; for any others sent, each Diocese has to pay full pension.

You must excuse this hasty letter: I am so little at home that it is with difficulty I can find time or opportunity to attend to distant matters, but towards Xmas I hope to give my undivided attention to this subject. Meanwhile I shall be glad to learn in what you may deem my letter unsatisfactory in order that I may, as far as in me lies, apply a suitable remedy.

Ever sincerely Yours in Xt. A. Goss.

---

[76] Peter Laverty, 1818–1904, ed. Carlow and Valladolid; o. September 1855; taught at the CI 1856–63, then at Ulverston to 1877. See E. Henson (ed.), *Registers of the English College at Valladolid 1589–1862* (CRS 30, London, 1930), 237.

[77] Edmund Carter, 1816–75; edu. Valladolid for the Salford Diocese. See Henson, *Registers*, 229–30. He was parish priest in Bolton and official agent for the college in England; he took his first group of boys to the college in May 1856.

18. *Rt. Revd. Dr. Brown, Bp. of Liverpool   21 October 1855*
Add.Lttrs 31

My dear Lord,

I am duly in receipt of your Lordship's favour of Oct. 14th, forwarded to me from Preston. I am greatly pleased to see the kind solicitude which your Lordship expresses therein for the happiness & comfort of your clergy, as I am satisfied that no Bishop can command the zealous cooperation of his priests who insults their feelings, turns a deaf ear to their just complaints, or endeavours to ride rough shod over them. Your Lordship, however, need be under no alarm on their account from me. The Visitation Questions have not been <u>hastily</u> framed, nor have they been <u>rashly</u> put forth. I will however seriously weigh the contents of your Lordship's letter which, together with other still graver matters connected therewith, though not contained therein, I shall take an early opportunity of laying before the Committee of Visitation,[78] by whose advice in this matter I shall be guided.

I am sure that your Lordship will share the general grief for the sudden & premature demise of our worthy friend Mr. Powell.[79] The poor have lost in him a generous friend, & religion a liberal benefactor. Believe me, my dear Lord, your affte Br. in Xt. Alexander Goss.

---

[78] No other reference to this body has been found.

[79] Mr Daniel Powell of Duke Street, Liverpool, father of Fr Edward Powell (n. 66); corn merchant and prominent Catholic, see Burke, *Catholic Liverpool*, 113.

19. *To the Right Revd. The Bishop of Liverpool*   *9 November 1855*
Add.Lttrs 32–3

My dear Lord,

The fact of my having been for more than two years the Coadjutor of your Lordship without ever having written to you on the subject of money, will form a sufficient apology, if any be needed, for inviting your Lordship's serious & immediate attention to the following particulars.

On the 25th of August, 1853, I visited by invitation on [*sic*] your Lordship at your residence in Sandfield Park,[80] when your Lordship stated, as appears from the minutes of that conversation, that you saw no objection to my living at St. Edward's, but you rightly observed that I must have something to live on.

During the first year of my Coadjutorship, the Chapter voluntarily undertook, without any invitation on my part, but with a kind & charitable desire to spare your Lordship's funds owing to your increasing infirmities, to raise a voluntary contribution for my support.

Instead of thanking them, as they had reason to expect, for their considerate kindness towards you, Your Lordship, on the 24th of October, 1854 denounced their proceedings as uncanonical, springing from inordinate attachment, against which by virtue of your sacred office, your Lordship prescribed the admonitions in the Garden of the Soul. In the same letter, your Lordship claims the sole right of providing a maintenance, a residence, & all things necessary for the exercise of *pontificalia* for the Coadjutor. From that day to this I have waited for the fulfilment of these provisions of canon law; for whatever right such law gives me to look to your Lordship, is greatly increased & strengthened by the fact that you prevented any body else from from [*sic*] doing any thing for me; but as your Lordship knows I have waited in vain.

I beg, therefore, now to claim & to receive from your Lordship a sufficient sum to defray both my residence & maintenance for the year ending Sep. 25th 1855, and I beg that your Lordship will consider this as a formal, & <u>in the eyes of the Church</u>, a legal claim to the same. Fortunately I do not require from your Lordship any thing for the exercise of *Pontificalia* [*sic*], as the munificence of private friends has supplied me, as your Lordship was originally supplied by the Lancashire Clergy. Your Lordship must, however, remember that the Canon Law expressly states that all administration must be at the expense of the Ordinary.

I hope your Lordship continues to improve, & I trust for your sake that we shall not have a damp winter. You are fortunate in having Dr. Eager[81] so near a neighbour, as, I doubt not, you will feel the benefit of his medical skill. Believe me, my dear Lord, Your affte. Br. in Xt. Alexander Goss.

---

80 Bishop's Court, Sandfield Park, Brown's impressive residence in West Derby; it was close to the later site of St Edward's College under the Irish Christian Brothers; the house is still in use, see pictures in Doyle and McLoughlin, *The Edwardian Story*, 119, 136.

81 Dr James Eager, MD, lived in Mount Pleasant and then Chatham Street, off Brownlow Hill (see *Gore's Directory of Liverpool 1859, 1860*); perhaps the father of Fr James Eager, 1850–1914, of the diocese, and Fr William (Alexius) Eager OSB, 1852–1900.

20. [*Dr. Cornthwaite*] *10 November 1855* *5/1/28–31*

My dear Dr. Cornthwaite,[82]

This is a weary world of toil & trouble, I am again on a stormy sea with breakers ahead. You are already aware that, after much haggling, Dr. Brown wrote to me on the 11th of May. "By these presents I delegate you to make the canonical Visitation of the Diocese & grant you all the faculties & powers for that purpose." This document was, as you know, wrung from him by the Holy See, but yet it is most ample. On the 19th May I issued my Edict of Visitation. He took exception to the phrase 'Apostolic Visitor' adopted from Crispino[83] who makes the Bp. say *"noi non solamente in virtù dell' autorità ordinaria, ma anche come delegati della sedia apostolica"*;[84] for he has never been able to shake off the fear of some mystic document that he had been told I was the bearer of. My next step was to issue a series of Visitation Questions, mostly prepared by Dr. Grant & myself from Crispino, during our sojourn in the dear, quiet old Venerabile, & copies of which will, ere this, have reached you.[85] In general these were well received by the Clergy, tho' some, particularly of the laxer & lazier sort, considered them rather searching. Dr. Brown himself wrote to me that he considered those on property very good, but some others he considered useless & unnecessary, whilst he pronounced it impossible to procure a return of the *Status Animarum*, particularly in towns, for that he had himself tried & failed.

Meanwhile, whilst awaiting the answers to the Visitation Questions, I arranged, drew out & published Moral Cases, & set in full operation seven distinct Conferences in the Diocess, all of which I visited in person. During the same time I have preached more than 50 times, have confirmed more than 8000 persons, & communicated over 2360. In the interval whilst I was thus employed, an enemy was sowing zizar in the field of my labours. Dr. Corless,[86] who has made as much mischief as most men & who, since he left the Diocess of Hexham, has threatened to bring William before a court of law about some furniture, went amongst the clergy, endeavouring to induce them to request him to call a meeting in order to condemn the Questions, & seek the protection of Dr. Brown, who, he assured them, disapproved of them. Dr. Brown also wrote to one, perhaps more priests, in the same strain, saying that I & my two Canons were pushing matters too far. Who the two canons are I know not, unless he means Cookson & Fisher, neither of whom have had anything to do with the matter. Oct 14. Dr. Brown wrote to request me to forbear to exact answers to the Questions, & stating further that Card. Fransoni[87] had written him that our Visitation must be made not only by virtue of faculties delegated by him, but also in subordination to him. Feeling confident that the great bulk of the Clergy considered the 'questions' very beneficial to the general interests of religion, & feeling sure that Dr. Brown was swayed by no higher feeling than jealousy, I summoned the 'Deans Forani' [sic] to ascertain from them the feelings of the Clergy & their own on the subject; for you must know that these Deans are of Dr. Brown's appointment & not mine, having received their appointment, with one exception, 18 months before the Visitation. After mature deliberation, they returned me the following answer, Oct. 29. "They are of opinion that the Questions issued by the Rt. Rev. Dr. Goss will be beneficial in placing the Diocess in better ecclesiastical organization, & will be productive of great advantage to the spiritual & temporal state of the Missions. The Deans can also declare that our Clergy in general acknowledge that the step taken by the Rt. Rev. Dr. Goss was called for by the altered circumstances in which the Hierarchy & the Decrees of the Synod of Oscott have placed them, & tho' there may be some who consider the Questions too minute, yet it is generally acknowledged that they are such as should be put, & they doubt not that the result will be highly beneficial to the first interests of religion. They have, however, deeply to regret that any attempt is being made by the Vicar of North Lancashire to excite a spirit of dissatisfaction against the Visitation Questions, who declares that in his condemnation of them he is only proclaiming the sentiments of the Rt. Rev. Dr. Brown, Bishop of Liverpool." There the matter stands at present between us. I am daily expecting his recall of the Visitation faculties, for, with such advisers as Corless & Newsham, no man can tell what may be expected next.

Dr. Brown makes no secret of his determination to destroy St Edward's.[88] He has written twice to Dr. Fisher, within the last few days, to say that he intends to withdraw the education funds from it, & to sever all connection with it. He assigns no reason whatever for this step, but he demands to know by whose authority a Church is being built there. Except to decry me he never mentions my name. Some time ago, a nun was to be professed: in his absence, Dr. Crook performed the service. He deputed Can. Cookson to bless the Preston Cemetery, tho' I was Visitor at the time & frequently in Preston. He also appointed a Commission to look into the state of Great Eccleston,[89] overlooking therein both myself & the Forane Vicar. When I & Dr. Fisher called on him the other day, he said he could not see us as he was expecting some gentlemen about that time. He, however, wrote to me afterwards to apologize. If things go on thus, we must suffer shipwreck. After keeping a canonry vacant for some months, he has recently appointed Gillet,[90] a creature of Newsham's, having previously offered it to Philip Orrell,[91] another friend of Newsham, but he had the good sense to decline it, for he had previously written to me to be dispensed from Conference on the score of deafness. Newsham also boasts that he appointed the rectories. Dr. Brown acts as if his great aim was to embarrass me in my future government of the Diocess. Meanwhile he is utterly incapable of any thing except letter writing. He will probably be unable to leave the house for the whole of winter.

Will you be good enough to bring these facts under the consideration of Mgr. Barnabò, & write me [sic] what has to be done. Believe me ever sincerely Yours in Xt.   Alexander Goss.

---

[82] Robert Cornthwaite, 1818–90, rector of the English College and Roman agent of the hierarchy; bishop of Beverley 1861; first bishop of Leeds 1878. See R. Finnigan and J. Hagerty, *The Bishops of Leeds 1878–1985* (Leeds, 2005), 29–49.

[83] Giuseppe Crispino, *c.* 1635–1721, bishop of Bisceglie and Amelia. Amongst his works was *Trattato della visità pastorale* (1711). (See *Dizionario Enciclopedico Italiano*, Rome, 1956.)

[84] Trans: 'we, not only by virtue of our ordinary authority, but also as delegates of the apostolic see'.

[85] The questions were published: *Questions Addressed to the Clergy of the Diocese of Liverpool at the Visitation of 1855* (Liverpool, 1855); there were about 350 questions in all, though Brown complained to Wiseman that they numbered 1,000 and derided Goss for having copied them from 'some old book in Rome': AAW, R79/6, Brown to Wiseman, November 1855; the same questions were used for later visitations as well. Goss was obviously a little nervous about them; he asked Clifford, about to go to Rome, to get some opinions about them there (letter 5/1/24, 8 November 1855). He also spoke about Brown's views on town *status animarum*: even if difficult, it had to be tried because otherwise nothing could be done about the hundreds of Catholic children not at school and the thousands of adults who never went to church: 'a mass of crime & ignorance' for the clergy to deal with.

[86] George Corless, 1794–1865, moved from Hexham and Newcastle Diocese in 1852 to Cottam, where he stayed until his death. He was a constant source of trouble; see Add. Lttrs 45: Goss to James Fisher, 10.5.62: 'Dr Corless, whose insolence is past bearing with,

seems to consider himself authorised from his age to spend what money he likes, fixing it as a debt on the Mission or Diocese.' See letters 237, 343–4. Corless had been Vicar of North Lancashire under Brown as VA. Zizar: Latin *zizania*: tares, darnel.

87 Jacques-Phillippe Fransoni, 1775–1856, from Genoa; cardinal 1826 and Prefect of Propaganda, with a reputation for sagacity and generosity to the poor. The *Directory* for 1857 has a good portrait of him as its frontispiece.

88 This is a strange claim: St Edward's had been founded by Brown and it was his decision to make it into a junior seminary in 1850; see letter 1 to Lingard and Introduction p. xxiii.

89 Great Eccleston is a village in the Fylde, about ten miles east of Fleetwood. See Kelly, *English Catholic Missions*, 192.

90 William Gillett, 1822–November 1855; o. 1848, he served in Manchester, St Anthony's Liverpool, and the Isle of Man, before going to Croft in 1855; Plumb (*'Found Worthy'*) questions his being made a canon, but this letter is definitive.

91 Philip Orrell, 1800–66, member of the Orrell family of Blackbrook (see n. 223); r. at Poulton-le-Fylde 1834–62, he retired to Ushaw until his death.

21. *Right Revd. The Bishop of Liverpool   14 November 1855*
Add.Lttrs 34–5

My dear Lord,

I beg to acknowledge the receipt of your Lordship's favour, with which I was honoured yesterday. I am sorry that any thing in my letter should have induced your Lordship to stray from the main point at issue. I am not the apologist of the Chapter, nor do I consider that their conduct requires any apology; but, however the case may be, I leave them to answer for themselves. One thing, however, is certain that, after the receipt of your Lordship's letter in October 1854, they, at once, discontinued any collection for me: they deferred to your Lordship's declaration that it belonged to you to raise a support for the Coadjutor. Now as your Lordship signified your disapproval of any collection being raised by them for me, & as they deferred to your Lordship's assertion that the duty was yours, I have now to claim the fulfilment of this duty, & this is the only question that I wish your Lordship to answer: Does your Lordship intend or not to comply with the dictates of Canon Law as laid down by yourself to the Chapter in October 1854. It is for that year, the year ending September 25, 1855, that I now make application to you, & with all courtesy & respect, I beg to solicit a direct answer. The other matters discussed in your Lordship's letter, we can argue at any time. I beg, however, to observe that your Lordship cannot shake off the responsibility of the Isle of Man by trying to throw the blame on me.[92] I rather deserve your Lordship's gratitude for getting you out of a dilemma, &, with all due submission to your Lordship, I beg to observe that I consider your neglect to provide for your Coadjutor & your evasion of a direct reply to his inquiries on the subject to be a far greater violation of Church law, than the liberty accorded by the

Chapter & exercised by myself of expressing my opinion on the subject proposed for deliberation. The right of free & temperate discussion the Chapter enjoys from the kind concession of Holy Church & not by any special tolerance from your Lordship.

I am sorry that your Lordship is again troubled with rheumatism, but I hope a little care will see you better. Believe me, my dear Lord, Your affte Br in Xt.   Alexander Goss.

---

[92] The only issue about the Isle of Man raised in the Chapter at this time was whether its pastoral care should be entrusted to Religious: both the Capuchins and the Oblates of Mary had offered to accept it (June 1854 and March 1855 respectively) but the Chapter turned them down. Brown was generally in favour of inviting Religious into the diocese; perhaps he blamed Goss for the canons' attitude. The Chapter minutes are generally fairly terse and discussions are rarely detailed (see AAL, S4/ 1/ A/1).

22.   *E. Challoner, Oak Hill*   *20 November 1855*   *5/1/33*

My dear Mr. Challoner,

If this my letter should have the misfortune to be delivered at your office, I beg you will put [it] into your pocket until you get home to Oak Hill, for its voice will be drowned in the noise & rattle of Queen's Dock.[93] Though I cannot claim to be as welcome as a Christmas box, yet I hope I shall escape the censure of a Christmas bill.

We are building a new Church.[94] The first part is small but beautiful, an offering mostly if not altogether of one family, in honour of the Immaculate Conception of Our Blessed Lady. In due time we hope to be able to erect another part in honour of our good patron, the Blessed St. Edward, which towering aloft on this protestant hill, that has lost its vegetation but not its heresy by the smoke of Muspratt's chimney,[95] may be invoked by the mariner on his outward voyage, & receive the tribute of his thanksgiving on his happy return to port.

We know that a business man observes a rule & method even in his charities, & we fear, therefore, that we are too late to find a place in the donation account of this year, but we hope good St. Edward may figure as a recipient, in the person of his Church, at the head of the account for 1856. Yet if you deem other demands more pressing or other charities more deserving, I shall not complain; for I know that, whilst not refusing to Caesar the things that are Caesar's, you give to God the things that are God's, & that, therefore, Religion will, in every case, be benefitted.

Many masses are now said daily in the College, but, for want of a Church, they are not available to the people. We have, in fact, a large stock in trade, a capital lying idle, & we are anxious to bring it into the market. We also have land large enough for a Church of any dimensions without encroaching on its usefulness for all College purposes. For a dozen years I have been regretting this spiritual waste, & I think the time has now come for breaking the clay vessels in which the lamps of St. Edward's have been so long concealed, in order that their glare may bring our enemies to nought, as Gideon brought the Medianites.

Hoping that you will make my letter the subject of a Sunday's meditation, & begging the blessing of good St. Edward on you & yours, as well as on us & ours, I remain, Very sincerely & truly Yours, Alexander Goss.

---

93 Edward Challoner, 1799–1874, timber merchant; a leading Catholic layman and philanthropist, built St Vincent's and St Oswald's schools; he resided in Old Swan, Liverpool. See Burke, *Catholic Liverpool*, 101, 128, 232.

94 New church: Our Lady Immaculate, Everton, planned as the Lady Chapel of a cathedral to be dedicated to St Edward; Goss laid the foundation stone in November 1855. It became a parish church until replaced by a new building in 1986. See Doyle and McLoughlin, *The Edwardian Story*, 19, for E. W. Pugin's magnificent vision of the proposed cathedral, and Doyle, *Mitres and Missions*, 292, for the church.

95 James Muspratt, 1793–1886, born in Dublin but not a Catholic. A pioneer in the chemical industry, he introduced the commercial production of alkali using the Leblanc process; he was taken to court on a number of occasions because of the pollution caused by his works – a 'noxious cloud of hydrochloric acid'. He was well disposed to his Irish workers. He developed the chemical industry in St Helens and Widnes. See *ODNB* and T. C. Barker and J. R. Harris, *A Merseyside Town in the Industrial Revolution. St Helens 1750–1900* (London, 1959), 225–30. His son Max was a Liberal MP and strong supporter of Catholic education. Everton was a strongly Protestant area.

23.   *Rt. Revd. The Bishop of Liverpool   23 November 1855*
Add.Lttrs 36–8

My dear Lord,

I am glad to learn from your letter of the 21st that your Lorship is better, & I hope you may suffer no further relapse during the winter. Your Lordship did not need to have offered any apology for your delay in writing what you facetiously call an answer to my letter; as I assure you that I consider no letter an answer to mine of the 9th or 14th current, unless containing a cheque for such a sum as is sufficient to cover my current expenses for the year ending Sep. 25. 1855. I should hope that your Lordship has never thought me mean enough to live at St. Edward's at free quarters.

Though pained at the contents of your last letter, I cannot but admire the ingenious, if not ingenuous shifts to which your Lordship condescends in order to evade giving a direct answer to a plain question, but I assure you that I am not to be turned from my purpose either by cunning or sophistry. Does your Lordship intend or not to make me any allowance for the year ending Sep. 25, 1855, as well as for the present year? Your Lordship must excuse me for requesting a direct & unevasive answer to this simple question. Unless I receive a satisfactory answer within a week, I shall conclude that your Lordship declines my just demand, & your Lordship must then excuse me if I feel it my duty to take such steps as must bring the matter to a speedy issue. Rome is our common Mother, & to Rome the case must be referred.

Your Lordship admits my claim, but you endeavour to evade it by mixing up irrelevant matter in your letters. I presume not to offer an opinion on the motives that have guided your Lordship in your splenetic letters to & cruel treatment of Canon Fisher, nor do I consider your Lordship any more able to judge of the motives which led to my opinions in Chapter on the Isle of Man. Neither one case nor the other have any thing to do with my claims on your Lordship. Nor do the reputed uncanonical acts of the Chapter, or their fond love for me, affect the question. Neither will your Lordship's gratuitous charge of party spirit against me, nor the further charge of mendacity provoke me to a controversy. I wish to limit all I have to say to the one question alone, & I shall be glad for your Lordship's sake, if you give it such an answer as can alone be deemed satisfactory.

Your Lordship assures me that you are praying for peace, but I fear it is that peace which the Scrip [*sic*] calls no peace, & which the Roman Historian describes when he says *solitudinem faciunt & pacem appellant*.[96] I beg to add that your Lordship has been more warmly than discreetly seconded in your pacific endeavours by your judicious Vicar of North Ribble.

Believe me your affte Br in Xt.   Alexander Goss.

---

[96] The quotation is from Tacitus, *Agricola*, 30:4: 'they create a wasteland and call it peace'. (The Latin text normally does not have 'et'.)

24. [*Edward Swarbrick*]   *24 November 1855*   *5/1/36–7*
My dear Mr. Swarbrick,[97]
I must first thank you for the box which so suitably & conveniently has been made to encase my chrismatory.

With regard to the guild, there are two distinct points to be considered, 1o. its temporal, 2o. its spiritual bearing. 1o. You cannot do better than take the Weld Bank[98] scale which has been approved by an Actuary, tho' to be really accurate, a scale should be drawn up for each locality, as owing to variety of occupations, casualties vary, so that what would suit an agricultural district, might not suit a coal or manufacturing district. If, as Can. Cookson[99] avers, the average life of man in Preston is not more than 20 years, you must take care that your burial scale be nicely adjusted, or truly the living may not suffice to bury the dead. Yet, whilst taking the Weld Bank scale of fees & payments, it is not necessary to take all its details of management, as you will have to allow for changes of circumstances in the respective places. I do not like the diminished rate of allowances followed by the Jesuits, for, as Canon Greenhalgh observes, the longer a man is sick, the more he will stand in need of assistance. Besides the usual auditing of accounts at the end of the year, I think it very desirable to have a general overhauling every fifth year, as provided for by the Weld Bank Rules, but I would allow of no diminution in the yearly contributions of members, however flourishing the state of affairs might be found, as an epidemic, such as cholera or the famine fever might cause a great run on your capital.

2o. You are at complete liberty to adopt any regulations you think proper. I would not recommend any great quantity of obligatory prayers, but I would try to select such as are indulgenced, & tho' I did not increase the number of general communion days, I would add to the number of reunions, for being in a town you have your people more in hand than they are at Weld Bank, & much good results from their being brought together either for works of piety or amusement on a Sunday evening. Should not spurious parentage be visited more severely? I should think so, unless you merge the confraternity character of the Guild into a mere benefit society.

If Can. Cookson be consulted about a selection of rules, I think he will recommend, & not without reason, greater <u>brevity</u> in the compilation, tho' take care that he does not use the scissors too freely.

Commend me to him & to Robert,[100] & believe me, Very truly & sincerely Yours in Xt A. Goss.

---

[97]   Edward Swarbrick, 1824–93, at St Augustine's, Preston, as curate and rector 1856–60.

[98]   Weld Bank: St Gregory's, in Chorley, a mill town near Preston; Canon Henry Greenhalgh, 1807–70, was parish priest and Dean there 1842–70.

[99]   Canon Thomas Cookson, 1803–78, first parish priest of St Augustine's, Preston (1840–56); Dean and VG from 1856. For later quarrels with Wiseman see n. 592.

[100]   Robert Gradwell, 1825–1906, curate at St Augustine's to 1856; succeeded his uncle, Henry, at Claughton-on-Brock, 1860–1906. See n. 388 below.

25.   *Very Revd. Dr. Cornthwaite*   *26 November 1855*   *5/1/38–40*
My dear Dr.

I know not when our troubles will end. Poor Dr. Crook is now lying on his death bed from an attack of pleurisy or congestion of the liver. The hardships he has undergone not only in his missionary capacity, but in unravelling the finances thrown into hopeless confusion by Dr. Brown, & the cruel indignities & rebuffs he has, more particularly of late, had to endure from him & the younger priests at Copperas Hill,[101] have completely worn him out; yet he has never complained. At all hours & in all weathers he has walked out to Sandfield Park, a distance of four miles from Liverpool, in obedience to the Bishop's summons who, by the time he had reached [him], had forgotten for what purpose he had sent for him. This is the third occasion of his receiving the last sacraments. The doctors say he is completely worn out. He has rallied once or twice, but again fallen back. Poor Mrs. Powell nurses him by day, & a Belgian nun from her lace schools by night,[102] & Mr Jas. Fisher of Crosby[103] is with him day & night, snatching a little sleep, when he can, on a sofa in the sitting room which opens into his bed room. On Saturday night at 11 we left him with the conviction, Doctors & all, that he could not see the morning: he has, however, rallied, & is again a little better this morning, Monday. He eagerly inquires if any thing has been heard from Rome, & he rejoices that his last act before taking [to] his bed was to write to Card. Fransoni an account of the state of things. We are praying that God may spare him yet a little longer to us, for, were he to die, it is impossible to say whom Dr. Brown would appoint in his place. It is not at all improbable that he would name Can. Newsham his vicar. I shudder to think of the state to which we should be reduced under so reckless an administration.

Dr. Brown went to his present house, 17 Catharine St. in the month of August, & up to this time he has been out only once or twice, at least so his servant man told Dr. Fisher yesterday. He has never said mass, nor has mass been said by any body else for him during that time, tho' Father Sumner[104] has administered to him Communion or Viaticum. His doctors say that his irritability of body & mind are such as to render him totally unfit for any business. They say that he ought to retire, but they know him so well that, they feel sure, were they to tell him so, he would bid them good morning & see them no more. His servant sleeps in the same room, for he is quite unable to move about, yet from his letters you would take him to be quite well. I had myself no idea of his state, nor had Dr. Fisher till he learned it yesterday from his servant Thomas who volunteered the above facts, for he knew that, in times past, no one had shown himself a truer friend to his master than Dr. Fisher.

As from the time of my appointment as Coadjutor, I have not received even the offer of a single shilling from Dr. Brown, & as he prevented the Chapter from continuing a voluntary collection for me by denouncing it as uncanonical, & as he has just set on foot a collection for himself, I have written to him to ask for an allowance. In his answer he evades the question, & tries to provoke a controversy on all sorts of irrelevant matters; but I have written to say that I am not to be turned aside from my purpose in that way, & that, unless he gives me a satisfactory answer within seven days, I shall refer the matter to the Holy See. He is damaging himself by the collection he is making, for it has been the means of making known, what was never suspected, that I am left unprovided for. No doubt many thought that his alleged poverty arose from the allowance he was bound to make me.

I have given you the above details that you may, in due season, make them known at Propaganda, & that you may be able to satisfy inquiries.

Since I wrote last to you, poor Gillet, the recently appointed Can. died suddenly during the night, having been previously long ill.[105] To day's post brings tidings of the death at Torquay of the Rev. George Gradwell, the youngest of the Gradwells.[106] What we should do for priests I know not, but we are in the hands of God, who has been signally good in other respects to this diocese.

Mr. R. Smith purposes leaving Preston on the 28. & hopes to be in Rome before the feast of the Immaculate Conception. I believe he is of Pian age.[107] Dr. Fisher & Walker[108] & Teebay[109] unite in kind regards to yourself, English, & Morris.[110] Dr. F. desires his thanks for your kindness.

Ever Yours, A. Goss.

---

101   St Nicholas's, Copperas Hill, Liverpool, the pro-cathedral.

102   The Institute of St Elizabeth of Hungary, or Lace School, founded 1854 (Burke, *Catholic Liverpool*, 124, 185). *Gore's Directory 1859* lists a Mrs Amelia Powell as patroness of the Catholic Industrial Schools in Everton Crescent.

103   James Fisher, 1814–83, Canon and Dean, was at Great Crosby 1850–71 and served as diocesan treasurer. He was the brother of Canon John Henry Fisher of St Edward's, 1812–89, and of Dean George Fisher, 1810–97.

104   Richard Sumner SJ, 1801–77.

105   William Gillett, see note 90.

106   George Gradwell, 1827–55, nephew of Henry; only ordained 1852; seems not to have served in a parish.

107   Robert Smith: to go to the Collegio Pio; o. 1859, he applied to enter religion in February 1863 but Goss refused because of a shortage of priests. Eventually he left the diocese in 1864 to become vice-rector in Rome; he later became a Camaldolese monk.

108   John Walker (later canon), 1821–73, Goss's successor as vice-president of St Edward's, 1853–66.

109   Charles Teebay, 1824–92, at St Edward's 1854–67; Goss's secretary and first rector of Upholland, 1883–86.

110   Louis Bernard English, o. 1850; see n. 49 above, and John Morris, 1826–93 (o. 1849). English became rector of the English College, Rome, in 1857; Morris became secretary to both Wiseman and Manning before joining the Jesuits in 1867; he is best known for his *The Troubles of Our Catholic Forefathers* (London, 1872).

---

26. *E. Challoner Esq.*   *26 November 1855*   5/1/41

My dear Mr. Challoner,

Though not a recipient of your munificence, at least in my recent application, still I am satisfied because I know you to be a generous benefactor to Religion. St. Oswald's tells of your good deeds, & future generations will be taught to bless the liberal hand which has done so much for the education of their children.

No doubt the property you possess in your native county has claims upon you; but still I hope you will not forget a city in which God has blessed a clear head & kind heart, seconded by untiring industry, with more than moderate competency. I cannot think that, as time goes on, you will allow a Church to be raised to your patron Saint without adding a stone to its walls. As it is not necessary to raise the Church in a day or a year, I purpose to procure <u>annual</u> subscribers, so that the work may be ever progressing, even tho' slowly. It was thus our ancestors raised all their great buildings. The plan was suggested to me by the Bishop of Nottingham[111] & hence will have your approbation: he has himself promised to be an annual subscriber.

In my last I pleaded for a Sunday's meditation on its contents, but was disappointed. May I hope for that privilege for this? Believe me ever sincerely Yours in Xt. A. Goss

---

[111]   The Bishop of Nottingham was Richard Butler Roskell (1853–74), from a prominent Liverpool Catholic family of scientific instrument-makers; Burke, *Catholic Liverpool*, 48–9, 134.

27.   *Right Revd. The Bishop of Liverpool   3 December 1855*
Add.Lttrs 39–40

My dear Lord,

I am sorry to find that some expressions in my last letter have given your Lordship pain, for I have no desire to wound your feelings, & I, at once, withdraw them, & express my regret for the use of them. Yet in justice to myself I am bound to say that if your Lordship's acts, letters & speeches in my regard be taken as a commentary on my letter, that the most fastidious will hardly venture to condemn it, albeit it contains the enforcement of just claims in strong language. I commit my character to the keeping of posterity which will have an opportunity of reading our letters side by side, accompanied by an exposition of circumstances as may render them intelligible.

Whilst, however, withdrawing every discourteous expression from my last or from any previous letter, I do not withdraw my just claim on your Lordship for a maintenance for the second & third years of my coadjutorship. People say that your Lordship cannot have had less than £600 during the year 1855, & yet you have not only not offered, but decline to give me a penny & you have even taken to task some who have offered me relief.

Your Lordship has twice referred me to the life of St. Francis de Sales. I am sorry that, in obedience to your direction, I have read the parts designated, as I am filled with sorrow afresh, my old grief is reopened, when I contrast his reception with that which I have met with, beginning with the manner of your Lordship's first announcement of my appointment, whilst I was still in Scotland. *"L'évêque surtout ne savait comment lui dire son bonheur; et il le serrait dans ses bras avec une affection inexprimable, en remerciant le Signeur de lui avoir donné un tel secours pour le gouvernement de son vaste diocese. Après les premiers éparchements de son amitié, il lui declara qu'à dater de ce jour tous les revenus de l'évêché seraient repartés entre eux deux en portions égales; la justice voulant que, dès qu'il entrait en partage des peines, il entrait aussi en partage des émoluments qui d'ailleurs devaient nécessaires à son entretien et à sa position."*[112]

Believe me, my dear Lord, Your affte Br in Xt. Alexander Goss.

---

[112] St Francis de Sales, 1567–1622: Goss did not add that the coadjutor was his brother, Jean François! Trans: 'The bishop above all did not know how to tell him of his happiness, and embraced him with inexpressible affection, thanking the Lord for having given him such help for the government of his huge diocese. After the first outpourings of his friendship, he told him that dating from that day all the revenues of the bishopric would be shared equally between the two of them, justice demanding that since he was accepting a share in the troubles he should also share the benefits, which anyway was necessary for his upkeep and his position.' In a final short letter of 5 January Goss thanked Brown for £10 and hoped he was well – wherever he (Goss) went there were 'many kind inquiries after you'.

28.   [*Fr Leonard*[113]]   *14 December 1855*   *5/1/44*
My dear Father Leonard,
The bearer of this note has a doubt about her baptism, which it is impossible to clear up, as the parish priest of the place is unable to give any satisfactory information about it. Under these circustances you will have to deal with her as you would with a convert.
1o.   You hear her <u>general</u> Confession by way of exciting her contrition for all <u>actual</u> sin, but you do not give absolution, for baptism being the gate of the other sacraments, she must first receive that before she can receive any other sacrament.
2o.   You must baptize her conditionally & privately.
3o.   You desire her to repeat *in globo* the confession already made, after which you absolve her.
    This I believe to be the general practice, & in following it you cannot err.
    By confession *in globo* I mean such a declaration as the following: I now desire to confess again & I do hereby confess again all the sins of my past life, which I have already confessed to you, for which I now ask pardon of Almighty God, & penance & absolution of you my ghostly Father." [*sic*] The Confession, Conditional baptism & absolution should be gone through conscientiously.
    Ever sincerely Yrs in Xt. A. Goss

---

[113] Presumably Fr Alfred (Leonard) Fryer CP, 1821–89, o. for Westminster Diocese in 1847, but joined the Passionists in 1851.

29.   [*Sr Superioress*]   *14 December 1855*   *5/1/45*
My dear Sister Superioress,[114]
As the faculties which I hold in the Diocese of Liverpool are those of
Visitation, I can hardly say whether I have power to accede to your
request. I will, however, examine the subject, & will communicate with
you in a few days.

As Visitor, I am bound, at some period, to visit the Convent. Give
access to every sister, hear, as if under the seal of Confession, whatever she has to say regarding the state of the Convent, advise with the
Superioress as to the best methods to be adopted for remedying any
just complaint or abuse, speak either to individual nuns or to the whole
sisterhood about the reformation of any irregularity that may have crept
in; but yet so as not to betray either to the superioress herself, or to any
of the sisterhood, the source of my information. At the conclusion of the
Visitation I have to burn in the presence of the sisterhood, the notes or
depositions which I take down, so that they may see that I carry away
with me no document which can violate the confidentiality they have
reposed in me & no memorial of any complaint which for conscience
sake may have been made to me. Could the exercise of this power bring
you the relief you seek from me?

Believe me ever sincerely Your affte Father in Xt. Alexander Goss.
[*Written across the page*] I beg to thank you for your very kind present.

---

114   The convent has not been identified.

30.   [*Dr. Cornthwaite*]   *16 (9 crossed out) December 1855*   *5/1/46–8*
My dear Dr. Cornthwaite,
Tom Bennett[115] was here yesterday, making some inquiry about the
admission into the Diocess of Lpool of O'Brien, who is anxious to
leave Clifton on account, I believe, of some family matters, probably
the convent business.[116] Having no power in the matter, I counselled him
to apply to Dr. Brown. Meanwhile I thought it well to write to you to
inquire if there was any other cause for his leaving Rome besides the
alleged, viz. ill health. I presume that, in the present lamentable want of
priests in this Diocess, Dr. Brown will have no difficulty in receiving
him, tho' it is not yet certain whether his own Bp, at present the administrator, will let him go.

Affairs here are in statu quo. I am glad, however, to be able to say,
that Dr. Crook, contrary to universal expectation, has recovered so far as
to be able to say mass in a quiet way. At present he is rusticating with
Mrs. Powell at Eaton House.

Some days ago, a deputation waited on Dr. Brown to enforce upon
him the necessity of providing a priest for the Industrial Schools,[117]

where there are 400 Catholic children, more if we had our due, who have been left for three months without any instruction, so that the Protestant Chaplain says we are like the dog in the manger, for as much as we neglect to instruct the children ourselves & object to Protestants instructing them. John Yates,[118] an attorney, was one of the deputation, & he told me that they could make nothing of the Bishop, as he began to tell them old tales.

A few days ago Dr. Turner called on him & advised him to retire or leave Crook & myself to do the work, but he said that he saw no sufficient reason for retiring. As long as he can raise money, he will never retire. Fortunately he is now too well known to do me much damage, otherwise he would greatly prejudice me, but still tho' ever talking & writing about peace & unity he has done everything he could to damage me.

I have written to him several times for a maintenance, but he always returns me a shuffling & evasive answer. For the first year of my episcopacy the Chapter collected by voluntary subscriptions wherewith to support me; but the second year, ending Sep. 25. 1855, they forbore to do anything in consequence of his writing to them to say that they were outstepping their duty, as it belonged to him to raise funds for the support of his Coadjutor. Finding however, that he was doing nothing except proclaiming every where his own poverty, I wrote to the Chap. to ask what they counselled me to do. The case was discussed in his presence, & he promised to apply to the Holy See. Whether he has done so or not, I cannot say, but in the interim a lay & clerical committee has been established by his means for the purpose of collecting subscriptions for him. Those who are ignorant of the circumstances of the case give, but those who know that I have nothing, refuse; but all join in saying that he ought to retire. He has a fixed income of £320 or 330 per an. Can. Kenrick[119] gives him £30, Sir Rob. Gerard[120] has subscribed £50: I believe Newsham gave him last year £60. Mr. Jos. Brown[121] £20: R. Shiel[122] on his marriage £25. An unknown person, probably Chaloner, £25, besides many other sums. I believe he applies to his own use the money resulting from licenses or dispensations of banns, which all say exceed a £100;[123] so that he has a fair sum at his disposal; but not one penny will he give to me. I hope you will bring this matter before Monsig. Barnabò. I pay for living at the College, as I am of no service to it, & therefore cannot live out of its resources. During my professorship I never drew my full salary, & on my appointment as Bp. I began life with the few pounds that happened to be in my purse, & I drew my pen through whatever arrears of salary might be owing to me. The people would not let me want, if they knew my circumstances; I do not want to be a burden to my friends, & I want to have something, as long as Dr. Brown has it to give, for the charities of the town.

Please to write & let me know how matters are. I imagine Prop. has written to the Card., as he applied to me for a copy of my Visitation Questions, but said nothing further. Dr. Fisher & other Profs[124] join me in kind regards to yourself, Morris & English. Ever Yours A. Goss.

115 Thomas Bennett, 1832–67, o. Rome 1854; Canon in 1865; died of fever.

116 No appropriate O'Brien is listed. The convent business: there had been scandal and a court case concerning the Franciscan Convent, Taunton, which was accused of holding a Miss Talbot, wealthy heir of the Earls of Shrewsbury, against her will; see J. A. Harding, *The Diocese of Clifton 1850–2000* (Bristol, 1999), 259–60.

117 Industrial schools: for juveniles in danger of becoming criminals but not convicted (e.g. vagrants), and an alternative to reformatory schools that were for juveniles convicted of crime. The Lace Schools qualified as such.

118 John Yates, 1807–87; convert; solicitor and a leading Catholic layman: town councillor, magistrate and School Board member (Burke, *Catholic Liverpool*, 241 and *passim*).

119 Canon Edward Kenrick, 1818–60; c. at St Patrick's 1847–51, r. 1851–60; he had also been c. at St Anthony's, see O'Neill, *St Anthony's*, 101–2, 107.

120 Sir Robert Tolver Gerard, 1808–87, of Bryn, a very generous benefactor to the Church. He was ADC to the Queen and in 1876 was created Baron Gerard of Bryn. J. A. Hilton, *Catholic Lancashire. From Reformation to Renewal 1559–1991* (Chichester, 1994), 20, says of the family, 'well-connected, politically active, and loyal to the Stuarts, the Gerards were typical members of the Lancashire Catholic gentry'. See also his 'Our Lady's, Bryn, 1903–2003: Coal and Catholicism', *NWCH* 32 (2005), 69–76, and J. F. Giblin, 'The Gerard Family of Bryn and Ince and the Parish of SS Oswald & Edmund in Ashton in Makerfield', *NWCH* 17 (1990), 1–17. They had built Garswood New Hall in 1788. Birchley Hall was part of their estate at this time; see John Giblin, 'The History of Birchley Hall and the Mission of Birchley', *NWCH* 4 (1972–73), 1–26. For the family's pedigree, see Edward Baines, *History of the County Palatine and Duchy of Lancaster*, 4 vols (London, Paris, New York, 1836; new edn, 1868–70), III, 641.

121 Mr Joseph Brown: *Gore's Directory* lists several of this name, of differing occupations.

122 R. Shiel, 1790–1871; Dublin born, he became a leading Liverpool businessman, first Catholic councillor and alderman; a public park was named after him. Burke, *Catholic Liverpool*, 201–2 and *passim*.

123 Goss was at pains later to point out that he always applied the fees for dispensations etc. to Catholic charitable causes and that none of the money went into the 'Episcopal treasury' (letter to O'Reilly, 30 January 1856).

124 Profs: the ordained teaching staff at English seminaries were known as professors; non-ordained students who taught or were responsible for discipline were minor professors or just 'minors'.

31. *Revd. Leo Vanderstichele, Bp. Eton*[125]   *Feast of St. Thomas*
Cantuar, 1855   5/1/51

Dear Revd. Sir,

I am sorry that my badinage at Revd. B. Oreilly's [*sic*] regarding an account, or the furnishing of an account of your mission at St. Vincent of Paul's, should have placed you in a dilemma. I wish for no further information than is asked for in a letter addressed by Secretary Walker to your worthy confrere, Revd. John Gibson.[126] As I felt desirous of keeping in a volume apart the reports of the missions in the Diocese of Lpool I was anxious that the reports should be full & readable. The idea was suggested to me by a very interesting & useful account, furnished to me in a letter by Father Furniss,[127] of the mission among the children of Blackstock Street. As, however, my views & motives are not understood, or are explained by the practice of countries in which the lives of the clergy are a scourge to a corrupt people, I must abandon the idea I had formed. From the first of January I expected the said information to be furnished by the clergy themselves, so as to avoid all injurious suspicions, tho' I cannot expect the same happy results as would have followed from the suggestive reports of the Missionaries. If I live, perhaps God will give me a far more favourable opportunity of carrying out a plan which, I think, would be productive of much good.

Commending myself to your pious prayers, & desiring my kind & affectionate wishes for all blessings, spiritual & temporal, to Father Lans,[128] I remain very sincerely Yrs in Xt. A. Goss.

---

125   Leo Van Der Stichele CSSR, 1825–87, Belgian. For details of individual Redemptorists see John Sharp, *Reapers of the Harvest* (London, 1989); the *Directory* (under Vanderstichele) lists another, Bruno, in Newcastle, not listed in Fitz-L.

126   John Gibson, 1822–1902; joined the Redemptorists in 1852 after ordination in 1849 for the Northern District.

127   John Joseph Furniss, 1809–65; joined the Redemptorists in 1851 from Beverley Diocese.

128   John Baptist Lans, 1808–86; a Belgian, he joined the Redemptorists in 1843, ten years after ordination.

32. *[Dr. Cornthwaite]*   *15 January 1856*   *5/1/53–4*

My dear Dr. Cornthwaite,

Many thanks for your letter. About OBrien [*sic*] I may have led you into a mistake, a mistake I had myself made, for I learned on Sunday that his going to another Diocess bears with it the condition that he be allowed to return to Rome. If Dr. Errington will let him go from Clifton to Lpool, I could arrange, I think, to pay for a student of the Clifton Diocese at Prior Park or elsewhere, during the time that OBrien might continue on the Clifton funds. No arrangement can, of course, be made till he has his exeat from Clifton.

Dr. Brown has never, up to this, breathed a syllable about his having had a letter from Propaganda,[129] nor do I think he will let any one know about it: these are matters he usually keeps secret. He has not the heart to resign either power or money. Poor man! from my heart I pity him. He lives by stimulants, I am sorry to hear to day, but I know not if it be true, that he has begun to loathe brandy, if so, he cannot live long. The statement came from Newsham, & may be a ruse, as Dr. Brown will probably know or suspect that complaints have been made to Rome about it. He certainly seems to be shrinking. He sent me £10 the other day, & spoke kindly when I called, as well as to Dr. Fisher: but it was under the influence of the letter from Prop. for he would be as ready as ever to ride me down into the dust, if it were not for fear of the Holy See.

Dr. Crook has gone to Torquay, & can be of no use to us till well on in the Spring, even if then. Meanwhile we are in the hands of God. I am continuing my visitation, & have little leisure at my disposal. As the Chapter has written on the subject of maintenance, it will be unnecessary to say anything on that score. I think it would be well, however, to tell Mgr. Barnabò that up to this time Dr. Brown has conferred on me no further power or jurisdiction, nor am I in any manner consulted or even made acquainted with missionary changes & appointments. Any body may influence the Bp. but his Coadjutor. Tom Bennett is rapidly achieving himself a reputation as a hard working, zealous missionary: I wish we had some more like him. Hines,[130] Wallwork,[131] & he are a credit to the Venerabile. I find from Mr. Teebay that I did not pay him, as I thought, the £4 for you: I will therefore pay it to Dr. Grant for you. All here join in kind regards to yourself, Morris, & English.

Ever sincerely & truly Yrs in Xt. Alexander Goss.

---

[129] See n. 64 and Introduction p. xxv.
[130] Frederick Hines, 1824–1906; o. Rome in 1853; at St John's, Kirkham (The Willows) at this time, where he stayed until 1895; appointed a canon 1889.
[131] John Wallwork, 1825–91; o. Rome in 1849; at the pro-cathedral, and Brown's secretary, at this time.

33. *Cardinal Wiseman*   *25 January 1856*   *AAW: Wiseman & Bps: Goss Folder*[132]

My dear Lord Cardinal,

Poor Dr. Brown is dead. His man servant, who has latterly slept in his room, left him as usual at 6 o'clock this morning. He got up to the night chair about 8. On such occasions it was his custom to rest a little by the side of his bed, until he recovered a little from his exhaustion. His house keeper left him thus sitting on the edge of the bed, whilst she went to stir the fire. She was recalled to him by his falling down, which had often happened before. To her inquiry whether he was hurt, he replied, not at all. The two servants then lifted him into bed, but in a state of exhaustion, from which he did not recover. They, at once, sent for a priest, but he was dead before the priest reached the house.

Yesterday he was as usual, transacting business & showing no symptoms of being particularly indisposed, nor had he had any attack during the night. Office will be said for him at the Pro-cathedral on Monday night at 7 p.m. & High Mass on Tuesday at 10.

I shall feel obliged if your Eminence can drop me a line to say what I must do with regard to the dispensations for Lent, as I presume that I succeed only to the ordinary & not to the delegated powers of Dr. Brown. He had forwarded a copy of the Lenten dispensations to the printer only yesterday or the day previously: it bears date January 23. Must I allow that docuument to stand, & forward it to the Clergy with a few words from myself?

I am completely at a loss, for I had so little anticipated the sudden death of Dr. Brown, that I had made no provision for such an emergency.

I remain, my dear Lord Cardinal, Your obedt Servt in Xt, Alexander Goss.

---

132   There is a similar letter (5/1/59–60) of the same date to Cornthwaite in Rome, asking him to apply for Goss to receive the faculties granted to the other bishops. Goss adds: 'Poor bishop. How much happier he would have died, if he had only admitted his sickness, but to the end he maintained that he was quite well.'

34.   *Rev. R. Cooper S.J.*[133]   *7 February 1856*   *5/1/80*

My dear Mr. Cooper,

I have very great pleasure in giving my sanction for benediction at St. Ignatius's [*Preston*] on Tuesday & Thursday nights of this Lent, & I hope that your services in the Church will be productive of the good results you have reason to anticipate, for I know that your zeal for your children & the soldiers is untiring.

Accept my thanks for your kind wishes in my regard. Commending myself to your good prayers, as well as to those of your Confreres & your faithful flock, I remain Very sincerely Yrs in Xt.
Alexander Goss.

---

133   Richard Cooper SJ, 1816–79, at St Ignatius's, Preston; the town had a large barracks. (There are a number of similar letters about Benediction.)

35.   *Rev. Mr. Oreilly [sic]*[134]   *12 February 1856, Douglas, Isle of
                                         Man*   *5/1/86*

Revd. & Dear Sir,

Understanding that you speak the Irish language, an acquirement of comparatively little use in the Isle of Man, but invaluable in Liverpool, I have thought it well to remove you from Douglas & appoint you to assist the Rev. Mr. Vandepitte of Blackstock St.[135] He has a wretched church, but a large & flourishing congregation, & is anxious to have more masses, as his temporary Chapel is too small to accommodate the people. His residence is No. 6 Juvenal St. Liverpool. There is a large field for your zeal, & I hope that before long it will be possible to purchase land & erect a more suitable Chapel. I have directed the Rev. Mr. Bond[136] to take your place at Douglas, but you had better not leave until he arrives, lest something should prevent him reaching the Isle of Man for Sunday.

Wishing you every success in your new mission, & praying that God may bless your labours & zeal, I remain Sincerely Yours in Xt. Alexander Goss

---

134   Rev. Gerald O'Reilly 1828–96, brother of the future bishop (Plumb (*'Found Worthy'*) and Fitz-L give o. date as (September) 1856, which is clearly too late). His removal upset the people and Goss wrote a special letter in response: 'Pastoral to the Isle of Man on the removal of Rev. Mr Oreilly': this did not mention the priest by name but urged them not to spoil the good effects of their recent mission by listening to the voice of the devil; the letter is full of scriptural quotations on the theme of 'a house divided against itself', etc. (AAL, S1/ 2/ C/2). See letter 40.

135   Vandepitte: the only one listed is Richard, of Middlesbrough Diocese, who left for Nottingham Diocese in 1883 and died 1888. Kelly says he founded Blackstock Street mission in 1854, which became Our Lady's Eldon Street in 1859, with a new church in 1860 (*English Catholic Missions*). Burke calls him Vanderspitte (123), Fitz-L, Vandepitte; he does not feature in Plumb but is the subject of several letters; see 226, 240.

136   Joseph Bond, a former Jesuit, b. 1818, o. 1847; see following letter. The 1856 *Directory* has him at St Walburge's, Preston; no Bond is listed as serving on the island but he was there for some time before moving to the pro-cathedral in Liverpool. For later serious troubles see letters 94, 167; Goss eventually advised him to leave the diocese. He is listed at St Barnabas's, Nottingham, in 1860, but then disappears.

---

36.   *Rev. Mr. Bond*   *12 February 1856*   *5/1/87*

My dear Mr. Bond,

I hope your soul has found tranquility & rest during your retreat at Bp. Eton, & that under the enlightened guidance of my valued friend Father Lans you have formed or laid down a plan of future life, such as to secure your happiness here & hereafter. You have great powers and great zeal that if rightly applied will achieve great good to religion & will tend to the salvation of many souls. You have before you a noble future if you do not abuse God's gifts to you. Throw off whatever of the laic in dress, bearing, or manner that persons may previously have noticed in you: whilst you do not defer to, yet do not set at defiance the opinion & censure of the world. If it is censorious & rash in its judgments, it entails on you & on us all greater circumspection in our conduct.

In hopes that you will take this advice, kindly meant, in good part, & act up to your good resolutions & promises contained in your letter to me, I appoint you for the next three months to assist the Rev. Mr. Fairhurst in the Isle of Man.[137] He is an old neighbour, & you will find him a pleasant & edifying companion. At the end of that time I hope to be able to continue your appointment there or perhaps at some other place. Wishing you every success & happiness I remain sincerely Yrs in Xt. A. Goss.

---

[137] Patrick Fairhurst, b.1824, died of sunstroke as CF in India, 1858. There is some confusion about his postings before he left to become a chaplain; he spent some time in the Isle of Man, at St Anthony's, Liverpool, and at St Alban's, Liverpool, after being at Birchley for a few years after ordination in 1848. See Goss's letter to him of May 1857 (no. 117).

37. [*Mr. James Whitty*[138]]   20 February 1856   5/1/93
My dear Mr. Whitty,
I beg to give you my most sincere thanks, not only on my own behalf, but also on behalf of the Catholics of Liverpool, for your able advocacy, before the Select Vestry, of the cause of the youths Thomas & John Rice. Though unsuccessful in winning them back to the Church, yet your temperate & argumentative speech wrung from Rector Campbell[139] an enunciation of impartiality from which he will find it difficult hereafter to recoil. It also shewed that the opinion of the poor, the "dock-labourers & all labourers in this great Community", constitute a tribunal before which Rector Campbell did not disdain to plead, & whose censure he shewed himself unwilling to incur. Tho' the loss of the Case is injurious to the religious interests of the boys concerned, yet, in other respects, I think that you have gained more than if you had been successful. You have secured the reluctant respect of those who differed from you in the Select Vestry, you have supported your well earned reputation with the public at large, & you have shewn yourself worthy of the confidence of your co-religionists. May God long preserve you to be the advocate of His friendless poor.
    Believe me, very truly & sincerely Yours in Christ, Alexander Goss.

---

[138] James Whitty, prosperous wool merchant; member of the Select Vestry, Town Council and School Board; president of the Irish Catholic Club in the 1850s; he died 1876. See Burke, *Catholic Liverpool, passim.*

[139] Rector Campbell: Rev Augustus Campbell, Protestant rector and surrogate of St Nicholas, Liverpool, and hence chairman of the Select Vestry; he was also vicar of All Saints, Childwall. He was strongly anti-Catholic and anti-Irish. See, e.g., Burke, *Catholic Liverpool*, 130–1.

38. [*Mr. James Fairhurst*[140]]   *20 February 1856*   *5/1/94*
My dear Mr. Fairhurst,
In the name of the Catholics of Liverpool, rich as well as poor, I beg to thank you for your able advocacy of Catholic rights in the Select Vestry on Tuesday, the 12th of February. Notwithstanding the indignation of the Chairman at our impugning, as he called it, the partiality & honesty of the Committee, you were clearly right in the principle laid down. Mr. Crawford's fussy charge of unfairness shewed that he winced under the justice of your remarks, & gave you an opportunity of enforcing the principle whilst disclaiming a reference to individuals. You ably supported the reputation you have long earned, & which I trust you will continue to maintain. What will become of the religious interests of our poor children, if God had not given them such fearless, independent, & untiring advocates as yourself & Mr. Whitty? I hope that God will long spare you, & grant you health to support the Catholic cause in the Select Vestry. It demands a great sacrifice of time at your hands, but it produces its reward, here in the esteem & confidence of your fellow Catholics, & hereafter from him who has promised a reward to the orphan's friend.

Believe me, Very sincerely & truly Your's [*sic*] in Christ, Alexander Goss.

---

[140] James Fairhurst, of 45–49 St Anne Street, Liverpool, a pawnbroker by profession; *Gore's Directory*, 1859, and Burke, *Catholic Liverpool*, 119.

39.   *Rev. R. Arrowsmith*[141]   *21 February 1856*   *5/1/96*
Dear Revd. Sir,
I have not yet received from the Holy See the faculties about which you make inquiry, nor if I had could I grant the dispensation sought on the reasons addressed in your letter. The Holy See will not be satisfied with the mere statement or assertion that a Confessor thinks the parties ought to be married. If I am furnished with a full statement of all particulars either by yourself or Can. Kenrick, I will forward <u>it</u> to Rome. They will, of course, decide on the merits of the case as submitted; it must, therefore, be drawn up theologically & no reasons which have not theological weight ought to be set down.

Never having been previously acquainted with the actual applications for dispensations, I must say that I am utterly amazed at the way in which they come before me. Were I to forward them to Rome, as I receive them, they would hardly fail to throw the officials of Propaganda into convulsions.

Commending myself to your prayers, I remain Very sincerely Yours in Xt. Alexander Goss.

40. *Rev. H. Newsham*[142]   *27 February 1856*   *5/1/104*

My dear Mr. Henry,

I am sorry to hear that Sir Robt. is laid up.

You must have an uncommon number of sick, if you could not manage to leave even for the short interval of a Conference. I had expected that you would have been one of the most valuable members of Conference, as belonging to the new school or the go aheads. Now there is no going ahead unless we rest first on a solid basis.

I cannot conceal from you how grieved I am to receive no return of a collection from Ashton for the Ecclesiastical Education fund: I am sure Sir Robt. & Lady Gerard will not be pleased at the omission, an omission, however, which I trust will not again occur.

I have not written to your Canonical Brother, but will write by this post: I hope to be able to bring the matter to a peaceful solution.

I hope you are getting on with the answers to the Visitation Questions, as they must be in by Easter: your brother's have been in my possession four months.

I am sorry to inform you that the people in the Isle of Man have wrongly persuaded themselves that Mr. Fairhurst, your late neighbour, has procured the removal of Mr. Oreilly, who has joined Mr. Vandepitte. Commending myself to your prayers, I remain sincerely Yours A. Goss.

41. *Rev. Mr. Bulbeck*[143]   *27 February 1856*   *5/1/106*

My dear Mr. Bulbeck,

I forwarded by last night's post the petition for a relaxation of the vow of your penitent: it may be three weeks or a month, probably more, before I receive an answer.

With regard to the Exposition of the B.S. it was quite understood that the Church doors had to be closed at the hour on [*sic*] which they are closed on Confession nights, leaving a certain number of Confraternity men during the night, sufficient to relieve each other. I heard accidentally, after the fact, that Blackstock St. had been open.

I am greatly grieved & distressed at the other information contained in your letter: what remedy can you suggest? I believe there are some persons who go from town to town, taxing priests falsely with solicitation in the Confessional. Of our own Clergy, I mean the entire Clergy of the Diocess, I have a good opinion; but in a town, like Lpool, there are always a number of unknown priests, many of them suspended, lurking in the by-ways of the town. I shall be at all times glad of any suggestions from you either on this or any other subject, for God knows, I am keenly aware of the weight of responsibility upon my shoulders. Believe me, Very sincerely Yrs in Xt. A. Goss.

---

[143]   William Antony Bulbeck OSB, 1822–1903, was at St Augustine's, Liverpool, in the 1850s.

42.   *Rev. M. Hickey, Garstang*[144]   *7 March 1856*   *5/1/129*
My dear Mr. Hickey,
The Church has a horror of vagabond marriages, for soldiers & sailors are like Mahomitans, indulging in a plurality of wives. There must be some Catholics in his regiment if not in his division. Let him give the names of some of these, non-commissioned officers if possible, as they know most about their men. You might write to two of such to make inquiries about him. There are plenty of English both at St. Helena & the West Indies, so that it is natural to suppose that, if a few months residence at Garstang has awakened his amorous propensities, they cannot have been dead during his ten years residence elsewhere. I would advise you also to write to the <u>parson</u> of his native village: it would only cost a stamp, & he would most likely answer. There are few chapels in Bedfordshire,[145] & so it would be as little bother to write also to the priest, by whom also according to our law, the proclamation of Banns ought to be made. There are so many of these double marriage cases coming before me that we cannot be too cautious. The fact of his being a Protestant [*illegible word underlined*] requires a dispensation, but as he makes fair promises, which you should get him to sign in writing, & as he promises to himself, I am willing to dispense from that impediment & hereby do dispense, if you can convince yourself that it is the only demand.
    Ever sincerely Yours in Xt. Alexr. Goss.

---

[144]   Michael Hickey, 1801–71, studied and was ordained at Maynooth. Rector at Garstang 1825–71, he built the present church of SS Mary & Michael.

[145]   The only Catholic mission in Bedfordshire was in the small market town of Shefford; served initially from Weston Underwood, Bucks (home of the Throckmortons), it had its own resident priest from the mid-eighteenth century; see R. Atkinson, *The Shefford Catholic Mission, 1728–1823* (Shefford, 1973), pp. 1–11.

43.   *Revd. John Dawber*[146]   *18 March 1856*   *5/1/140*

Dear John,

I am sorry to hear such a poor account of you, & I am still more sorry that my inability to assist you on Sunday helped to worsen your complaint. Knowing that a letter written on Saturday could not reach you on Sunday, Dr. Fisher made it up into the form of a parcel & sent it by the train that you directed the expected help to come by, with instructions that it should be given to your man. It seems that these were not fulfilled & hence the delay. I can provide for you on Easter Sunday. Mr. Teebay will be with you on Saturday for dinner, leaving here by the 12.25 o clock train. I think it would be well for a few weeks, if I cannot procure you help, to say mass on the Sundays, hearing no confesions <u>before</u> mass but after; for you can communicate them out of mass, up to twelve o clock, as is commonly done in Italy. This <u>they</u> would find equally convenient, & it would be a great relief to you. I would myself have come to help you with pleasure, but I am fast at the Cathedral & the clergy are worked to death with Confessions. They have asked leave to duplicate at Sutton, & the Bp. Eton priests are engaged with retreats.[147] Please to desire your sister to write & let me know how you are getting on. Believe me your sincere & attached friend, Alexr. Goss.

Meet the train at Rufford, if it stops there, if not at Croston.

---

[146]   John Dawber, 1812–70; chaplain to the public institutions in Liverpool where he was accused of 'popish aggrandisement'; r. at Mawdesley 1843–70.

[147]   The Passionists were at Sutton, St Helens, the Redemptorists at Bishop Eton; both were engaged in giving missions.

44.   *James Whitty Esq., Liverpool*   *19 March 1856*   *5/1/141*

Dear Sir,

I beg to thank you, as well as the other gentlemen of the Committee of the Irish Club, for having kindly changed the day of your annual dinner, in order that I might have the pleasure of being present.

It is gratifying to me, as it must be to you, to find that the Irish people in Liverpool are becoming, every year, more alive to the importance of their position. Nothing will evidence it better than the peaceable manner in which the festival day of their patron Saint was observed in Liverpool. In a town like this, still imbued with the old Tory principles, respectability is power, & if we can only induce the people to be peaceable & sober, I have no doubt that they will rise, as many have already risen, by their natural ability & the fertility of their mental resources, to the first positions in this once orange ridden town.

Believe me to remain, Very truly & sincerely Your's [*sic*] in Christ. +Alexander Goss.

45. *Rev. C. Walker, Lea*[148] *19 March 1856* *5/1/143*

My dear Sir,

I am glad to learn from your letter of the 7th that your people have [*word illegible*] come forward to provide you with requisites for Benediction, & that you have succeeded in forming a suitable Choir. I feel sure that Benediction will be to them an attractive service, & that you will find the fruits of it in an increased frequentation of the Sacraments & in more generous contributions to the exigencies of religion. I have great pleasure, therefore, in giving you permission to have Benediction on the first Sunday of every month, as well as on the principal festivals of the year, which fall on Sundays, & on Holydays of Obligation.

Canon Walker[149] will, no doubt, attend to the Demarcation of Boundaries of your mission as well as of the others within his Deanery, as soon as he is relieved from the pressure of the Easter Indulgences.

I hope your people have not forgotten my address to them, & that they have provided a suitable Cross for the Burial Ground, & that it now bears unmistakeable evidence of containing the temples of the Holy Ghost awaiting the Resurrection. I hope also that you have been able to keep your promise of having a font ready for Easter Saturday.

Commending myself to your prayers, I remain sincerely Yours in Christ, +Alexander Goss.

---

[148] Charles Walker, 1806–64; edu. Valladolid; r. at Lea, Preston, 1837–64.

[149] No Canon Walker fits this date or place and no Walker is listed as dean in the *Directory*; the Dean of Preston (including Lea) was either Canon Cookson or Canon Richard Gillow (they changed over sometime in 1856–57). Goss seems to have written 'Canon Walker' by mistake.

46. *Circular to Liverpool Clergy* [*added in pencil*] *28 March 1856*
5/1/162

Dear Rev. Sir,

It has lately been brought under my notice that in several Chapels in Liverpool there is no separation of the sexes in that portion which is accounted free. This I consider a great evil, & contrary to the spirit of the Church. Without wishing to interfere with the present arrangement of bench-letting which secures the same object as was intended by the Church in its enforcement of the separation of the sexes, I feel it a duty to require that this separation take place in that portion of the Church to which the faithful are indiscriminately admitted. I do not, however, wish to interfere with those ordinary regulations by which strangers are accommodated in churches in which they are not bench-holders, but I enjoin separation in those portions of the Church which is altogether set aside for all comers. On occasions of great pressure not unusual in small churches, you will take care that the aisles & stairs are not occupied by a miscellaneous crowd, but that if it be necessary to occupy them, the sexes must be separated.

Believe me, Very sincerely Yours in Christ, Alexander Goss

47.   [*Dr. Cornthwaite*]   *8 April 1856*   5/1/167
My dear Dr. Cornthwaite,
Last night, on my return from London, I found these two letters awaiting my arrival: one is from the finance committee, the other is from Mr. Power,[150] whom you knew in Rome, both on the same subject. When I was in Rome, Mgr. Barnabò told me, & the Cardinal also told me that it had been decided by Propaganda that the case should be referred to arbitration. In the May following (1855) the Card. desired the parties to select arbitrators. Some little difficulties subsequently arose, & eventually the arbitrators were appointed. The Rev. John Canon Walker of Scarborough, Yorkshire[151] is the senior. Up to this time he has not been able to bring them together; for Mr. Glover, one of the arbitrators representing Mr. Sherburne's executors, says it is necessary to wait further instructions from Rome. I believe the truth is that Mr. Sherburne's executors, or Dr. Newsham, have petitioned to have the Sherb. Heatley Trust tried at the same time by the same arbitrators. Now the two cases have no connection with each other: one does not depend on the other, so there is no need of delay, by which nothing is gained, but by which I shall lose a useful missionary, & the charities of the Diocese are suffering, & anniversary masses are remaining unsaid.

I feel the case the more, as it is going now for 18 months since the Holy See decided that the matter should go to arbitration. It is really too bad, for it shakes confidence in Propaganda to which the delay is unjustly attributed. I am now off to lay [the] foundation stone of St. Vincent of Paul's new church for B. Oreilly [*sic*]. All the Bps remained in London over Sunday for a Te Deum in thanksgiving for peace.[152] Tell Dr. English to send me Omeara[153] without delay. Yrs truly, A. Goss.

---

150   Edmund Power 1804–78; Irish, o. in Rome 1847, r. at St Mary's, Aughton. He retired in 1869 to Ince Blundell Hall and later Moor Hall, one of the seats of the Stanley family. See letters 64 and 283.

151   John Walker, 1801–73, of Scarborough, friend of Cardinal Wiseman; see Schiefen, *Nicholas Wiseman*, 296–7.

152   The Crimean War ended with the Treaty of Paris, March 1856.

153   John O'Meara, 1832–1911; Irish, o. Rome 1856 and immediately appointed to Eldon Street for two years before going to St Mary's, Chorley. See nn. 216, 670.

48. *Rev. Mr. Davey*[154]   *9 April [1856]*   *5/1/169*

Dear Rev. Sir,

When you called this morning I was too much engaged to give much attention to the nature of the case submitted through Dr. Fisher. I believe that one of the parties was Protestant, & if so, the Council of Trent does not affect the marriage. The Church is satisfied with forbidding the union of Catholics & Protestants, & does not trouble herself further about the matter, so that they cannot be said to have come to this country to avoid the law or *in fraudem legis*, tho' there is no doubt they have come to escape the law which forbids the marriage of Catholics & Protestants. It was a marriage in Liverpool of the kind that brought the prohibition upon us regarding such marriages; but that prohibition has not been published in this Diocese, so you are at liberty to use your own discretion in the matter. The marriage of the parties will, no doubt, bring a reclamation from the Parish Priest. I beg to remain, Sincerely Yours in Xt. Alexr. Goss.

---

[154] William Austin Davey OSB, 1824–1914, was at St Peter's, Seel Street, Liverpool, at this time. On mixed marriages, see Introduction p. xxx.

49. *Rev. Mr. Weston, St. Walburga's*[155]   *16 April 1856*   *5/1/187*

My dear Mr. Weston,

Inclosed I send you two dispensations, one of which you applied for yesterday, the other on the 22nd of March, which I presume you have already executed. Please to return them to me as soon as you have executed the second, & write at the foot of the page that on such a day the said parties were married by you, &, in each case, write the real names of the parties, as the said document, to be kept in the archives of the Diocese, will be the proof of the marriage.

With regard to the infanticide, you have power to absolve by your ordinary faculties; it is only in the case of irregularity incurred by a cleric that the case is reserved.

Owing to great abuses, much complained of in Lpool, about the defective way in which the bans [*sic*] were published, when parties belonged to different churches, I issued an order that all persons, on coming to be married, must present a certificate that the bans had been published in the church or churches of the respective districts of the parties. So that if a man in your congregation wanted to marry in your church a woman of St. Wilfrid's Congregation, she must present a certificate of the publication of the banns in St. Wilfrid's & vice versa.

Believe me sincerely Yours in Xt. Alexander Goss.

---

[155] Thomas Weston SJ, 1804–67, at St Walburge's, Preston, until 1863; he had earlier been at St Wilfrid's in the 1840s; the spelling Walburga was also used, as here.

50.   *Revd. Mr. Bond, Isle of Man*   *16 April 1856*   5/1/188
My dear Mr. Bond,
I am glad to see that your friends at Preston are grateful for your long
& laborious services amongst them. I beg to thank you for having made
me a sharer in their generosity, though, by no means, deserving of this
act of kindness from you. As it was so totally unexpected I look upon
it as 'treasure trove' or windfall from Providence, & I have accordingly
handed it over as a contribution towards the Church of St. Vincent of
Paul, the foundation stone of which has just been laid.

From the activity of the heterodox in the Isle of Man, I conjecture
that you have awakened the Manx, & I am glad to hear from another
source that your sermons are well attended by Protestants. I hope you
will labour hard to instruct the people, both in the Church & at the
Confessional, for I am told that they are very ignorant.

Commending myself to the prayers of yourself & flock, & desiring
my kind regards to your worthy but over timid fellow labourer,[156] I
remain sincerely Yours in Xt. +Alexander Goss.

---

[156]   On Bond, see n. 136. The *Directory* for 1857 gives James Carr and John Hawksworth
as the resident clergy on the Island; in September 1857 they were joined by John Coll,
'the over timid' curate; see letters 130, 181.

51.   *Rev. Mr. Phelan,*[157] *St. Patrick's*   *16 April 1856*   5/1/191
Dear Revd. Sir,
I have written to Dr. Woodlock regarding Mr. Fortune[158] & hope my
inquiries will be answered satisfactorily.

We are peculiarly circumstanced with regard to our ecclesiastical
funds, & therefore you must use great delicacy & accuracy in your
correspondence with Mgr. Newsham.
1o.   You must specify that the boy is to be for the Diocese of Liverpool, as, owing to the omission of this being stated, he may be put on
the funds of some other Diocese, & thus we shall lose him.
2o.   Of many funds belonging to this Diocese Dr. Newsham has the
sole right of management, you must therefore make your bargain with
him. Dr Newsham has no connection with the Ecclesiastical Education Fund collected in this Diocese, that is under a separate Board of
management.
3o.   Write to Dr. Newsham what you have written to me, viz what the
parents are prepared to pay, & ask that, at the end of four or five years,
he will transfer the boy to a full fund. You need not mention my name,
but communicate to me his answer & I will direct you how to act.

Ever sincerely & truly Yours in Xt. Alexander Goss.

157 Patrick Joseph Phelan, 1825–90, edu. at All Hallows, Dublin; incardinated into Liverpool Diocese from Nottingham in 1852, at St Patrick's, Liverpool, 1852–64; retired through ill health in 1867.
158 William Fortune was at All Hallows College, Dublin, 1854 to o. 1859 for Liverpool. Goss released him to work at the college, where he served as president from 1866 to 1892; d. 1917. I am grateful to Greg Harkin of All Hallows Archives for this information. See also Kevin Condon CM, *The Missionary College of All Hallows, 1842–1891* (Dublin, 1986), 131–40, 167–8. For Dr. Woodlock, r. All Hallows, see *DIB* IX.

52. *Rev. R. Gradwell, Preston   17 April 1856*   5/1/192
<u>Confidential</u>

My dear Mr. Gradwell,

As part solution of your difficulty I beg to supply you with a commentary on the teaching of Bp. Hogarth & Mgr. Newsham drawn from their own practice.

About 10 years ago, Rev. Mr. Sherburne made a Trust of some of the monies given to him by Mr. Heatley, for certain specified purposes, schools, chapels, education. The Deed was enrolled in Chancery, & for 8 or 7 [9 *crossed out*] years was administered by the Trustees, Mr. Sherburne disclaiming all right to any thing but a casting vote as chairman. Mr. Sherburne tried, before his death, to alienate this Trust by selling it to a Darlington man, but he failed. Bp. Hogarth & Mgr. Newsham have now petitioned the Holy See with success to have the Deed submitted to a Commission of 5 priests, that they may decide how & where the money has to be expended. The difference between this case & yours is, that Mr. Sherburne had by a Trust Deed, enrolled in Chancery, made over the property to certain Trustees, whereas you have <u>not</u> done so; yet they teach that he could upset a deed made, but that you cannot alter your mind with reference to a Deed not made. The Will is nothing, as it does not take effect till after death, & can always be altered during life. In 1846, I believe, there was a large personal property of the late Mr. Heatley, held in the joint names of Mr. Sherburne & another. Of this Mr. S. wrote to Dr. Youens[159] in the Dec. of 1846: When I cease to act, this personal property will fall, in the same manner as the other property, under the disposal of the Sherb. Heat. Trust Board. This was a <u>promise stronger</u> than yours, for it was made as an excuse for not repaying the sum of £12000 to Dr. Youens, whereas your promise was made under no such circumstances. How was it fulfilled? The property was <u>not</u> put under the Sherb. Heat. Trust, but was handed over to <u>Chas. Gillow</u> & <u>others</u> for <u>different</u> purposes than those specified in that Trust. Is not the lesson given to you at variance with their own practice?

Yrs truly in Xt. A. Goss.

159 Thomas Youens, 1790–1848; see Burke, *Catholic Liverpool*: he founded the School

for the Blind; was r. of St Nicholas's, Liverpool and was largely responsible for inviting the Sisters of Mercy into Liverpool in the 1840s; bought Domingo House for St Edward's. He was the third president of Ushaw, 1828–33 and 1836–7; Milburn, *History of Ushaw College*, 126–31, with portrait. Introduction, p. xxvii.

53. *James Whiteside Esq., Lancaster*[160] *17 April 1856*   *5/1/193*
My dear Sir,
A private letter received some time ago from the Revd. Mr. Brown informs me that it is your intention to do something towards the education of priests, & that hereafter you may make some permanent provision for the education of a student for the Priesthood. Long before I was Bishop I had come to the conclusion that the education of students for the Priesthood was the greatest charity of the day: schools & churches are alike valueless unless we have a zealous, laborious, & learned clergy to man them. At the moment I know not where to look for priests, & every year increases the demand: there is not a church in Liverpool which would not be benefitted by an additional priest. On the 6th of May I hope to be able to send 8 students to Valladolid for this Diocese, & I have now under instruction a young Protestant, the son of a parson, who is anxious, after he has made his profession of faith, to study for the Church. I beg, therefore, to thank you, on behalf of the Diocese, for your good intentions, & I assure you that there is no work of charity on which your alms could better be bestowed, than on the education of students for the Church.
Believe me to remain very sincerely Yours in Christ, +Alexander Goss.

---

160   James Whiteside: presumanly of the firm of Whiteside and Leeming, Lancaster.

54. *Rev. Mr. Dowding, Clayton Green*[161] *30 April 1856*   *5/1/213*
My dear Mr. Dowding,
The late Bp. of Lpool issued the order against dances in School rooms, not only after the most mature reflection, but after taking advice there on from his Chapter. I believe there had come to his knowledge evils of the gravest consequence. I am told that many mothers had need to mourn over the loss of their daughters' virtue. I heard of two cases of bastardy in one congregation as the result of a dance in the school room of the neighbouring mission. Under these circumstances I should not feel justified in setting aside the decree of my late venerable Predecessor, as I am sure that I should thereby render myself obnoxious to just censure.
I have great pleasure in giving my sanction to the establishment of the Archconfraternity for the Conversion of sinners, in your mission.
As it is quite uncertain when I shall be able to make the visitation of

your mission, I would encourage you to have a mission as soon as you can make convenient arrangements for it. In country places you require to be guided by the weather, & therefore I would counsel you to make your arrangements irrespective of the visitation.

Commending myself to the prayers of yourself & people, I remain very sincerely Yours in Xt.

+Alexander Goss.

---

161 Clayton Green was a Benedictine mission, served by the Rev. James Vincent Dowding OSB, 1809–77; listed as 'Junior' in the *Directory* to distinguish him from Rev. James Hilary Dowding OSB, 1793–1864.

55. *Rev. Mr. Vandepitte*   *10 May 1856*   *5/1/228*
Dear Rev. Sir,

I have long been afflicted by the miserable accommodation afforded to your poor but decent people in the Blackstock Street Chapel. It is unworthy of the solemn services which take place within it & it does not afford accommodation to the vast population living within your district. I am anxious, therefore, that you should organise a system of Collection for the purchase of a plot of ground & the erection of a Church either in that or in some other convenient situation. It may take time to accomplish this object, but your people are zealous tho' not rich; & they are mostly composed of those faithful Irish who, banished from their own country by poverty & persecution, can hardly find a home except in the temple of God, & who, therefore, take a pride in providing for God & themselves a suitable dwelling place on earth. No outlay could make the Blackstock St. Church worthy either of the religion or zeal of your people. It would be better, therefore, to economise in its management & let the Charity & generosity of your people be turned to the erection of a new Church. If you engage in this work with your usual energy, & arouse your people to its necessity, I am sure you will soon have funds in hand, for the purchase of land & the erection of a Church, & I trust that the year which sees the solemn opening of St. Vincent of Paul, may witness also the laying of the foundation stone of Our Lady of Reconciliation.162 The work has my cordial approbation & my Blessing & shall receive my encouragement. Let the money collected be deposited in some Bank in the joint names of you & myself. Believe me to remain very truly & sincerely Yrs in Christ, Alexander Goss

---

162 St Vincent de Paul's was opened in August 1857; the foundation stone of the new Eldon Street church, Our Lady of Reconciliation, was laid in February 1858, and it opened in 1860 to replace a wooden building in Blackstock Street, opened in 1854 by Vandepitte himself (see Kelly, *English Catholic Missions*).

56.   *Poor School Committee*[163]   *12 May 1856*   *5/1/229–32*

My dear Mr. Allies,

I am duly in receipt of your two favours.

1. I will give due notice of the collection, & I will write also to the parties named in your letter; I will request also that the collection be forwarded within the month; but you have had a sufficient experience of the clergy to know the difficulty of securing uniformity except in sacramental ordinances; however, I will do my best. No collections are ever made at Wrightington & Scarisbrick[164] as these two chapels are entirely at the mercy of Mr. Scarisbrick who has expressed his opposition to <u>any</u> collection being made therein, & he has both the power & the will to enforce obedience to his wishes. St. Mary's Preston is united with St. Wilfrid's: it is now a union; Douglas & Castletown are also united.[165]

2. Dr. Manning, as you are aware, was good enough to consent to prepare a scheme for the Religious Examination of pupil teachers: this he has done with the aid of Mr. Glenmire.[166] From the copy I enclose, you will see that it contains only the heads, leaving each Inspector to prepare yearly a series of questions under these heads, suited to the capacity of those to be examined. Were a series of questions to be stereotyped, it would lead to cram; as it is, the scale may be made sliding, as circumstances demand; for pupil teachers in towns are to be expected to reach a higher level than is attainable by those in country schools.

I have sent copies of these questions to the Convents of Notre Dame & the Sisters of Mercy who have great numbers of pupil teachers under them, with a request that they would favour me with the benefit of their experience. I have not yet received any return, owing probably to a shyness to offer suggestions; but I have again sent to them & will also write, as soon as I am in receipt of their answers. I will transmit to each Bishop a copy of this schedule, in order that they may commission their Inspectors to draw up a series of questions based on it for use in their diocese. The questions will have to be varied every year, as at University examinations, the substratum & schedule always remaining the same. It would facilitate the labour by the Inspectors interchanging copies of their questions at the end of the year, so that in successive years the questions used in one Diocese might be serviceable in another.

In those Dioceses in which there are training schools for Queen's Scholars[167] it will be desirable that they should not be excluded from examination & award, for it is more necessary to inspect these than pupil teachers, who are but the raw material out of which Queen's Scholars are manufactured. I am indebted to Mr. Stokes[168] for this suggestion, as also for another, that a knowledge by rote of the common or ordinary

Catechism should be required from every candidate for admission to apprenticeship.

With regard to prizes, though some small reward may be given to the children, yet I suppose the main object of the Poor Schools Committee is to counteract the effect of government influence, & that therefore they will be mainly given to pupil teachers. When the pupil teachers of a <u>school</u> distinguish themselves, I think it would be well that the Inspector should be empowered to give some sort of certificate to the master or mistress of that school under whom the distinction was earned & the excellence could be traced to their teaching. Whatever rewards are given, I think they ought to be for the two classes of males & females both as regards the scholars and the pupil teachers, so that the competition, except in infant schools, should be amongst persons of the same sex, so that there would be one set of rewards for boys, one for girls. It is thought by some that it would be well to limit the silver medal to the fifth or last year of apprenticeship, & the metal medal to scholars, giving other awards & certificates to the intermediate years, whilst to Queen's Scholars a certificate would be the passport to employment as master or mistress. There are more pupil teachers in this Diocese than there were a short time ago in the whole of England. As a matter of economy I have appointed 6 Inspectors & I suppose that each will have to have rewards at his disposal as otherwise the numbers of pupil teachers would be too great as compared with other Dioceses for competition, & being examined by different Inspectors, it would be found difficult to establish a scale of comparison.

I think it will be nearly impossible to lay down any canon on the subject of prizes, until we have some actual experience of the workings of the new system of Inspection. The various dioceses are so differently circumstanced that it will be difficult to forecast the exigencies that may arise; but after each Bp. has tried his plan of inspection for a year, & when the Poor School Committee are in possession of the returns of the Inspectors in a tabulated form, they will be better able to come to some practical conclusions. The actual giving of prizes will not affect either the manner or the results of Inspection, as they can be announced for the subsequent year, or, in fact, they might be awarded for the past year, for each Inspector will preserve the notes of his inspection, whereon, at the close of his year's labour, he will have to award the prizes.

I have explained myself very crudely, & shall be glad of any remarks. I have perhaps exceeded my commission in throwing out these remarks, for *stricte loquendo* my duty was to determine on the amount of knowledge to be required from the pupil teachers at each year's examination. Very sincerely Yrs in Xt. +A. Goss

163   The Catholic Poor School Committee: set up in 1847 to deal with the Committee of the Privy Council on Education about grants to Catholic schools; Thomas William Allies, 1813–1903, a convert clergyman, was its secretary from 1853–90; see *ODNB* (article revised by Martin Murphy); described as 'one of the most influential laymen' in the development of Catholic education (Tenbus, *English Catholics and the Education of the Poor*, 24).

164   Wrightington and Scarisbrick: see J. A. Hilton, *St Joseph's Wrightington, A History* (Wrightington, 1994), 6–7.

165   St Mary's, Preston, was the original seventeenth-century Jesuit mission; its chapel dated from 1761; the new church of St Wilfrid was opened in 1793 and St Mary's became a chapel-of-ease to it in 1814. See Leo Warren, *Through Twenty Preston Guilds: The Catholic Congregation of St Wilfrid's* (Preston, 1993). In the Isle of Man, Castletown (or Castleton) had its own church from 1826; by the 1850s it was being served from Douglas; see *Directory* and letter 374 below.

166   Mr Glenmire has not been identified.

167   Queen's Scholars: scholarships were available for pupil teachers to cover the costs of their going on to a full training school or normal college for two years. Initially the colleges were paid more for those who had passed the examination as first class scholars (and more for males than for females). The individual scholars were paid a small personal amount. The Sisters of Notre Dame opened a school for pupil teachers soon after their arrival in Liverpool in 1851, and in 1856 a teacher training college for the successful pupil teachers to go on to; see Anne-Marie Pennington, *Celebrating 150 Years: A History of Mount Pleasant Teacher Training College* (Liverpool Hope University, 2006).

168   Scott Nasmyth Stokes: 1821–91, first secretary of the Catholic Poor School Committee; from 1853 to 1891 HM Inspector of Schools; see J. P. Marmion, 'The Beginnings of the Catholic Poor Schools in England', *RH* 17:1 |(1984), 67–83; Burke, *Catholic Liverpool*, 93, 117; Tenbus, *English Catholics and the Education of the Poor*, 42–3, 64–5.

57.   *Rt. Rev. Dr. Turner* [*added in pencil at top*]   *16 May 1856*
5/1/235

My dear Lord,

I know that you are so disgusted with our position at Ushaw that you do not like to think about it, but still I think that we ought to take some active steps in the matter. At present we not only have no jurisdiction in the College said to belong to us, but we are losing control over our funds & should we ever live to resume our lost jurisdiction we shall find the College a very different affair to what we left it. Many may think it improved, & so it may be as long as it is full of students, but should a reverse come who will keep it in repair? We must look to the time when some or all of us have our own Colleges, for such seems to be the mind of the Church, & hence it seems folly to me to complicate matters by adding to the College which is already too large for the Diocese in which it stands. I imagine it is the Cornsay house estate[169] which has mainly taken Dr Gibson to Rome, tho' no doubt advantage will be taken of his presence to discuss other matters. He was closeted with Harting[170] as he passed thro' London. I think Dr Briggs ought to send somebody to Rome, & if he will not, that we ought all three to join in sending someone from one or other of the three Dioceses.

Believe me very sincerely Yrs in Xt. Alexander Goss.

---

[169]   Cornsay House Estate: Milburn, *History of Ushaw College*, 236–8, for the dispute between Bp Briggs and Ushaw over its ownership.

[170]   Mr Vincent Harting was Wiseman's solicitor; see Milburn, *History of Ushaw College*, 246.

58.   *T. W. Allies, Esq.*   *22 May 1856*   *5/1/237*

My dear Mr. Allies,

In a Trust Deed for Scholes Schools, the names of one layman & three Priests were inserted as the legal holders of the property. To this the Counsel of the Lords of the Committee of Council on Education objects, 'as priests can have no direct heirs, & are themselves not necessarily fixed to the district'. My Lords suggest that the point should be submitted to the Catholic Poor School Committee, as being one of general importance. They point out the difference between the legal owners of the property & the managers of a school, & suggest that the owners should be readily accessible, which some nephew or cousin of a priest, who might have been the last surviving Trustee, would not be, & hence inconvenience & delay might arise.

I have myself no opinions on the matter, but wish to do what is done by others. If it is customary to have lay trustees only, I have no wish, nor have my clergy, to be different to others or to interfere with the regular practice: perhaps you will drop me a line on the subject. I did not see till this morning, a reference to the Kemerton model Deed.[171] If you will kindly inform me of what is done & has been done with the sanction of the Poor School Committee, the same shall be done in this & all similar cases.

Did the Committee of the Poor School at their meeting make any remarks about the scheme of Inspection? I shall be glad to have the benefit of any remarks. Ever truly Yrs in Xt.   Alexander Goss.

---

[171]   Harding, *Diocese of Clifton*, 139–40: the school in Gloucestershire, founded in 1850, was one of the first to receive a government grant; its trust deeds were 'a roll-call of local Catholic gentry' (140).

59.   *Can. Cookson*   [*n.d.; presumably 22/23 May 1856*]   *5/1/238*

My dear Canon,

Mr. Glover's[172] letter is utterly unworthy of a boy in figures.[173] I am surprised that he should have dared to insult any man by sending it to him. When I was in Rome in the summer of '54, two years ago, the case stood for arbitration & was all but settled. How then can he say that his principal is not prepared, or that you do not know your powers? Why, Propaganda's letter to the Card. last Xmas but one would state the extent of your powers. Walker[174] is not the man he seems to be, or he would not have stood it: he would have written to the Card. when he found himself fooled by Glover, in a style not to be mistaken, & as a man writes when he finds he is being trifled with.

I have told Mr. Taylor[175] to appear before you for examination preparatory to receiving faculties as a Confessor. I wanted him for Crosby while Joh. Fisher came to assist me: but more of this when we meet.

Mr. Orrell, Yourself, & the existing Bp. are the Trustees to look into the state of St. Anthony's accounts: the sooner it is done the better. It will take time too. Wednesday is Chap[ter] day. Shall we begin the accounts Monday or Tuesday? Say on which day, & I will summon the parties to St. Edward's. I intend to go into Wales with Dr. Fisher: in Sep. we shall have the Synod; then I want to finish the Visitation of the North, so that if nothing is done now, it will be put off till Xtmas. Please to write by return. I want it before Chap. meeting. We can then put it in train.

Ever sincerely Yours in Xt. Alex. Goss.

---

172   John Glover, 1802–78, of the Beverley Diocese; see Milburn, *History of Ushaw College*, 170.

173   Figures: see n. 3 about classes at Ushaw.

174   Canon John Walker: see n. 151.

175   Roger Taylor, 1828–85; o. May 1856, at Crosby until 1857. See letter 135.

60.   *Dr. Ullathorne [added later in pencil]*   *23 May 23 1856   5/1/239*
My dear Lord,

I beg to offer you my welcome back to your Diocese, & I hope you have returned in good health, & that you have brought to a successful issue whatever you had on [sic] hand.[176]

My immediate object in writing to you is to state that a Monsieur Du Jardin,[177] a Belgian Priest employed in this Diocese, has put into my hands a Catechism, & has solicited permission to print it. I have, however, informed him that the Synod of Oscott has given its attention to the subject, & has appointed a Commission to superintend it.[178] He seems anxious that I should transmit it to the Commissioners, & as you are likely to have most to do with it, I send it under cover to you. It may contain some useful suggestions, & may be returned to him after perusal. If it contains nothing suggestive, no harm can be done by allowing it the benefit of a perusal.

I think it is high time we should come to some settlement about the decision of contested points in England. In the January of 1855. there were certain instructions given to our Cardinal about the appointment of an arbitration [*sic*] to settle certain matters in dispute in this Diocese, & I am sorry to say we are in statu quo. A crisis must come, & there will be a Bleak house [*sic*] show up.[179] Is there no remedy? Ever sincerely Yrs in Xt. Alexander Goss.

---

[176] William Bernard Ullathorne OSB, 1806–89, bishop of Birmingham, 1850–88; he had been in Rome to present his first *relatio status*; Champ, *William Bernard Ullathorne*, 235–6.

[177] F. du Jardin was at St Anthony's 1855–57 (O'Neill, *St Anthony's*, 107, 125, 480–1); 'St Mary's', September 1857 (letter 127); he had left the diocese by December of the same year (letter 143).

[178] On the complex history of English catechisms for the people see Heimann, *Catholic Devotion*, 105–10.

[179] Dickens's novel began to appear 1852–3; in it a Chancery case goes on for so long that no money is left for the successful appellants.

61. *Rev. T. Seed S.J.*[180]   *24 May 1856*   *5/1/240*

Revd. & dear Sir,

If the late venerable Bishop of Liverpool gave leave to the nuns at Wigan to have a private Oratory, they, of course, retain the privilege, tho' they remove their dwelling. But if he gave them leave to have mass only in a certain house or room, then the privilege is lost by a change of residence. I have no power, nor has any Bishop power to grant the privileges of a private oratory: it is the prerogative of the Pope. Dr. Brown did grant such privilege, & I presume therefore that he held special powers for that purpose from the Holy See, & consequently I shall in all cases respect his act. Though I cannot grant them an oratory I can grant any priest leave to say mass there, but I cannot grant leave indiscriminately for mass to be said there by any body, but only by such priests as I specify in writing, & I am willing to specify any you name; but I cannot grant leave for the Blessed Sacrament to be kept there: nor do I see any great necessity, with a church so convenient to them, to borrow the Irish use of the word.

Can. Greenhalgh wrote to me about burials but not about sharing the cemetery, & I gave him my notion on the subject. No doubt the matter will be discussed at some future Provincial Synod. Ever sincerely & truly Yours in Xt. +Alexander Goss.

---

[180] Thomas Seed SJ, 1807–74; at St John's, Wigan, 1852–60 (Kelly, *English Catholic Missions*); presumably the nuns were the SNDs.

62. *[Abbot Burder CSO]*   *24 May 1856*   *5/1/241*

My dear Lord Abbot,[181]

We are endeavouring to raise Reformatories in Liverpool, first for girls, & secondly for boys; but meanwhile our boys are being sent to the Akbar,[182] a ship moored in the river, to which a Catholic priest has no access. To day, however, I have received a communication from the Protestant Chaplain of the borough gaol who wants an interview with me on the subject of our boys. I imagine they find themselves incapable of reforming them, & think they had best hand them over to us. He mentioned Mt. St. Bernard, & asked if they could be received. I have appointed Tuesday for an interview with him, & meanwhile will be obliged if you will state whether you could receive boys sent from Liverpool, & on what conditions. Perhaps you will be good enough to drop me a line, giving me such information & forwarding me such papers as you may think will be useful. It is not often that the Prot. Clergy are disposed to help us; but I think this one is more anxious for the reformation of criminals than for their apostasy to Protestantism.

Commending myself to the prayers of your good community I remain With unfeigned respect, Very truly Yours in Xt.   + Alexr. Goss.

---

181   The abbot of the Cistercian Mount St Bernard's Abbey, Leicestershire, was Very Rev. Fr Bernard (George) Burder, 1814–81. The reformatory had opened in February 1856. Goss reluctantly put up £2,000 to help the Cistercians; a long struggle to retrieve the money ended only in 1878 when the diocese recovered £500. See letter 322.

182   The *Akbar* was a reformatory ship. On the reformatory movement in general in Liverpool, the ships and the farm schools, see Bob Evans, *The Training Ships of Liverpool* (Birkenhead, 2002) and Joan Rimmer, *Yesterday's Naughty Children: Training Ships, Girls' Reformatory and Farm School: A History of the Liverpool Reformatory Association, Founded 1855* (Manchester, 1986). For the reformatory movement and the Diocese, see John Furnival, *Children of the Second Spring: Father James Nugent and the Work of Child Care in Liverpool* (Leominster, 2005), ch. 8; Canon Bennett, *Father Nugent of Liverpool* (Liverpool, 1949; 2nd edn, 1993), 50 ff.

63. *[Dr. Errington added in pencil]*   *27 May 1856*   *5/1/244*

My dear Grace,

I am happy to inform you that the Protestant Chaplain of our Borough Gaol has applied to me through Mr. Aspinwall[183] to learn whether the institution near Bristol will consent to take girls committed to a Reformatory from Liverpool. He probably finds that Catholics are beyond the reach of Protestant remedies & hence is anxious that they should be handed over to ourselves for reformation. I believe there are some funds available for travelling expenses & thro' the influence of this Protestant Chaplain, I doubt not that we should receive a portion of them. Next week he is going to call upon me, & meanwhile, I shall be glad to learn whether children from Liverpool would be admitted, whether any thing beyond the government payment could be demanded, & whether there is any rule as to the amount of clothing required from the candidates for admission. I shall feel obliged if you can secure me this information whether in printed or written documents, & also please to inform me by what name the institution is known, so that I may make the committing magistrates acquainted with it. The Chaplain is one of those men, whose religion is philanthropy, & he is more anxious for the reformation of those consigned to his care, than for their profession of faith.

Believe me to remain, Very truly & sincerely your's [sic] in Christ, +Alexander Goss.

---

183   J. B. Aspinwall was a Catholic lawyer and Recorder; his name was more usually spelt Aspinall. Errington was Apostolic Administrator of Clifton, 1855–57; see n. 59. The letter is in an unusual hand but signed by Goss.

64.   [*Dr. Cornthwaite added in pencil*]   *30 May 1856*   *5/1/247*
My dear Doctor,
I fear I shall be thought troublesome, but what can I do? The Priest at Aughton, who is not a native of this Diocess,[184] & who was educated on his own means, threatens that he will leave his mission unless his claims are satisfied, which cannot be till the arbitration between the Executors of Sherburne & Youens has taken place. It has no connection with any other case. It was in Rome for adjudication two years ago, & so no pretence can be alleged for delay on the ground of want of preparation. The arbitrators chosen by Mr. Sherburne's Executors refuse to act on the ground that their principals have not authorised them & that they know not what they have to arbitrate upon: this is thought to be a mere pretence. The state of Power's affairs (he is priest at Aughton) are well known; some of the monies involved are known to the township, Catholic & Protestant; Power is influentially connected & his friends cannot but know something of his position, & this with other matters will induce Catholics to place their property – I mean property left for the Church – under the care of the civil rather than the ecclesiastical law, an event very much to be deplored. I have no love for civil law administration, but in a mixed country like this, when the eyes of the government & the country are peering into the secrets of our administration, this delay is most unfortunate. If Dr. Gibson's advent to Rome is connected with this Diocess or business, I trust you will, as agent for the absent, protect its interests.

                    Ever sincerely Yours in Xt.   Alex. Goss.

---

184   For Edmund Power, see n. 150.

65. [*Dr. Manning*]   *30 May 1856*   *5/1/248*

My dear Mr. Manning,

I beg to forward to you the remarks of Mr. Stokes, the Convent of Mercy, Notre Dame, the Holy Child Jesus, Miss Bowles,[185] Liverpool, on the scheme of religious knowledge prepared by you. As these different Orders are largely engaged with female pupil teachers, I thought they would be of value. If you think it advisable to make any modifications, I shall feel obliged if you will do so. I will then forward a copy to each Bishop, as I was delegated by them to look after the matter, & leave them or their Inspectors to draw up each year a series of questions based on the Scheme furnished. As they will probably have the questions printed, it will be easy to make an interchange, or to forward copies to each Diocese, as the Bishops now do with their Pastorals. I think Mr. Stokes' suggestion very good, that a knowledge by rote of the First Catechism[186] should be required from every candidate to the office of pupil teacher, male & female.

I should scruple to trouble you so much, did I not know the lively interest you take in the religious education of the young, & the confidence which is so justly placed in you by the Bishops & the Poor Schools Committee. Believe me ever sincerely Yours in Xt. Alexander Goss.

---

185   The Holy Child Jesus Sisters had a Pupil Teacher Centre in Preston; see Warren, *Through Twenty Preston Guilds*, 55. Miss Bowles was presumably Henrietta Bowles, author of *Extracts from the Bible ... for lower classes in the national schools* (4th edition, London, 1862). She was keenly interested in the training of pupil teachers, but no biographical information about her has been found except that she died in the very early 1860s. See letter 56 for Manning's scheme.
186   First Catechism: see n. 178. This would seem to refer to the 1836 edition.

66.   *Canon Cookson*   *31 May 1856*   *5/1/250*

My dear Canon,

I addressed a letter on the day of our meeeting, regretting Can. N's absence, & requesting him to furnish, & say when he could furnish an account, year by year, of the income & expenditure of St. Anthony's, at the same time disclaiming any wish to see his <u>private</u> memoranda. In answer he says that in keeping private memoranda & not public books, he has acted as the rest of the clergy; that Bp. Brown was aware of the fact, & pronounced them ample enough for any purpose; that they are sufficiently carefully drawn up to satisfy any one the Chancellor may depute to examine them; that he ought not to be blamed for what the Bp. in power at the time, deemed to be right; that in face of such sanction he denies any one's right to force him to draw up public books; that he is prepared to exhibit these private memoranda to me, but that he declines to let others see them; & in conclusion he asks why he is to be dealt with differently to others!

What is your idea of the present state of the question? I have slept on it, & don't think I shall return any answer, but put in an administrator for the future administration – if I can find one able & willing to undertake it – & then compel him to exhibit to the trustees as such a statement of his accounts, whether drawn up from his private memoranda or other sources. I am at a loss to conceive how he can call the memoranda of the income & receipts of his mission <u>private</u> <u>memoranda</u>. I should consider his private accounts to be the manner in which he expended his salary.

Ever sincerely Yours in Xt. Alex. Goss.

67. *Revd. Mr. Carter*[187]   *4 June 1856*   5/1/252

Revd. & dear Sir,

During my visitation of Woolston I have learned, for the first time, the extent of service performed by you at Lymm. It is quite necessary that priests in border missions should cheerfully & willingly give their services to those who, tho' living beyond the limits of their diocese, have no other priest appointed to attend them, & hence such priests hold faculties from the bishop bordering on their mission. The practice at Woolston, however, seems to me exceptional, for you not only attend the people, but you serve a chapel, & give the people at Lymm greater advantages than you give your own congregation, viz, mass at 10½, & afternoon prayers at 3, whereas your own people have mass at 9 & evening service at 6. Besides, you attend them when sick, & administer to them the sacraments the same as you do to your own people. Under these circumstances I think that they or the Diocese of Shrewsbury, ought to contribute a moiety of your maintenance. You are soliciting aid from the Lpool Diocesan Fund, but I feel sure that the Committee will reject your claim, unless you receive a maintenance grant from the Diocese of Shrewsbury which now enjoys fully one half of your services. Again you are not now a young man, & I feel sure that you cannot long endure your present fatigue, & you ought at once to discontinue the saying of afternoon services at Lymm. Were both missions in my own Diocese, I should not think it right to allow you, at your age, to continue your present labours. During the summer the hardships are less; but you ought to receive such a stipend as will help to free you from the embarrassments which so poor a mission have brought on you.

Believe me very sincerely Yours in Xt. Alexander Goss.

---

[187] John Carter, 1801–75; at Woolston 1837–75. Woolston is NE of Warrington; Lymm, SE in Cheshire, became a parish in 1902.

68. *Very Rev. Can. Maddocks*[188]   *4 June 1856*   5/1/253

My dear Canon,

Though I have frequently been at St. Oswald's, I am not well acquainted with the cemetery of the Convent, for I generally limit my observation to the object in hand.

You are probably aware that the Cemetery cannot be consecrated or rather solemnly blessed, unless it be separated by a wall from all unconsecrated ground. Now I hardly think this is the case, nor should I think that they would like it to be so; for being small, it would look a dismal hole if wholly surrounded with walls. However, they must please themselves in that matter, or arrange it with you, for I have no opinion formed about it. One thing only I know, that the laws of the Church are so severe on the subject of burials & burial grounds, that I dare not lend myself to their transgression, though the good sisters will hardly credit me; for, whilst it is one of the perfections of Religious to attach great importance to their own rules, it is one of their imperfections to set slight value on general regulations, imagining probably in their charity & good nature, that a Bp. can dispense with them. Believe me very sincerely Yours in Xt.   +Alexander Goss.

---

188   John Maddocks: 1801–65; first rector Old Swan 1840–65. The convent was that of the Sisters of Mercy, St Oswald Street. The name was sometimes spelt Maddox. See n. 440.

69. *Rev. G. Fisher*[189] *[added in pencil]*   *4 June 1856*   5/1/257

My dear George,

I have written to Mr. Carter on the subject of his serving Lymm, & I have written him so that he can forward the letter to the Bp. of Shrewsbury as a basis of operation. Contrary to his expectation, he tells me that his sister has arrived from the Convent & is now at his house.

As you will be near Croft, would it not be well to call & see the place where Mr. Gibson keeps the B.S. whilst the tabernacle in the Church is damp. It ought to be lined with silk & a light burning. See also his pyx for the sick, his holy oils & the place where he keeps them, his altar linen, Registers for Bap. Marr. Confirm. Bur. Deaths. *Status animarum.* Ritual, burse & stole for the sick, & any thing else that was omitted. He must get sound cruets, as humble as his means compel him to get, but they must be whole & not broken, & his vestry should be kept in a more tidy state. For the ordinary appliances of divine service, I have seen no church so deficient. His means may be cramped, but I would have soon as seen a *pot du chambre* as an empty Char pot [*sic*] brought for me to wash my hands. Mr. Carter's ciborium ought to have a veil.

Wishing my kind regards to Mr. Brown, & hoping you will succeed in your mission on Thursday, I remain truly Yours. A. Goss.

---

[189] George Fisher, 1810–97, brother of Canon J. Fisher and Mgr Canon J. H. Fisher; at St Bede's, Widnes, 1849–75.

70. [*Rev. J. Nugent*] *13 June 1856* *5/1/260*
My dear Mr. Nugent,[190]
I am sorry to receive from you so indifferent an account of your health; but I hope that during the warm weather you may be able to throw off your cough, tho' I know from experience that the throat may be affected in summer as well as winter. Your return, that is the time of your return I leave entirely to yourself. Be not influenced in your movements by any idea that you may be wanted, for I take it to be the best step to take a long rest with the hope of being ultimately restored, rather than to rest for a time with the certainty of a relapse. I leave you entirely to yourself in the matter. Do not what you think may be best for the Diocese, but what may be best for your health. That, at present, is the first consideration. God will take care of the Diocese, but he leaves you the duty of taking care of yourself. You are therefore completely free to do what is most conducive to your restoration, & to extend your leave of absence as long as is necessary. If the Doctors think well of the Isle of Man, I will let you go as a supernumerary or to take Castletown cum Peel. I had just returned from it with Walmsley when I got your letter. When you return you may go back to the Institute, or if unfortunately you should no longer be able for it, I will give you any place in the Diocese at my disposal, for which you & your medical advisers think your strength equal. I cannot say more, & God forbid that I should say less. Ever truly Yours in Xt. A. Goss.

---

[190] James Nugent, 1822–1905; the best known of the Liverpool clergy, with a public statue of him still standing in the city centre; clearly a close friend of Goss, though also at times a thorn in his side, with 'too many ideas' and a tendency to flit between them; Brown had supported him but thought 'his soul was too big for his body' (Brown to Newman, Dessain, XV, 336). The standard biography is by Canon Bennett (*Father Nugent*); for more recent studies see Furnival, *Children of the Second Spring* and J. Davies, 'Father James Nugent, Prison Chaplain', *NWCH* 22 (1995), 15–24; there is some very good material on him in Belchem, *Irish, Catholic and Scouse*.

71. [*Rev. James Swarbrick*[191]] *13 June 1856* *5/1/262–3*
Confidential [*heavily underlined and on second page too*]
My dear Mr. Swarbrick,
I have hardly a moment at my disposal. I hurried home from the Isle of

Man yesterday, in order to lay the foundation stone of Mr. de Trafford's Church at Croston,[192] tomorrow I have a meeting about the Reformatory, on Saturday I have several engagements, on Sunday I am at Formby. And so week after week it goes on. Not only have I no acting V.G. owing to Dr. Crook's illness, but the Diocesan accounts &c are all at Crosby, so that I am sorely pressed & unable, at once, to give answers. I purpose going into Wales with Dr. Fisher, for I have much desk work, which I cannot do in town. On my return, I purpose finishing my visitation of the Northern portion of the Diocese, leaving this neighbourhood to the back end of winter.

1o.   I have no objection to your hearing Confessions for the winter in the house, but I should like Mr. Hines[193] to hear them in the Church; but I shall be with you before winter, so that we can settle then. It can cause no great inconvenience to leave the house vestry [sic] in statu quo, as inside painting is little more than a question of look or appearance.

2o.   I will settle the Westby monies[194] at the same time, but if you consider the case urgent, I will depute the Dean, who is near the spot. Where many interests are concerned it is necessary that all come and should have a hearing. If the monies were being spent, the case would be more urgent.

3o.   I am distressed at the account you give of yourself, & at the account I hear from others. I must urge upon you the necessity of keeping good hours: I do not think you should ever be out later than 9 oclock, even in summer, & not out of bed later than 10. This may seem twaddle, but I assure you I consider it most important, & particularly for you.

Is there any other mission that you think would suit you better? If so, I will give it you with pleasure, if I can make it vacant. I have just returned from the Isle of Man which is, in my opinion, one of the most promising, as it is one of the most varied & beautiful in the Diocese. I purpose keeping two priests at Douglas, & one at Castletown, which is ten miles from Douglas. There is a fair Church at Douglas, but land is bought for a new one & I hope to be able to lay the foundation stone next year. There are, I believe, about 1100 Catholics in Douglas, & it has been arranged that a room be taken in Ramsey, 16 miles to the North, in order that the people there, about 100, may meet for prayers every Sunday, & may be visited by a priest once a month. I do not know whom I could put in your place, unless Fairhurst if you took his place at Douglas. I should then place Mr. Hines at St. Anthony's, & let you take Mr. Walton to Douglas where under your Deanship & guidance he would be formed into a valuable missionary. Cooke,[195] now at Lancaster, I would put at Castletown, for I hear Lancaster is too cold & hard for him.[196]

You will see how confidential all this is, & how necessary to keep it entirely to yourself, beyond the privilege of consulting your Doctor &

your brother or some friend on <u>your own</u> taking the Isle of Man, but not farther. I hope in this you will see the desire that I have to remember in my prosperity those who shared Joseph's captivity. If you like, visit the Island before you decide: a return ticket is only 8/–.

   Ever sincerely Yours in Xt.   A. Goss.

[191] James Swarbrick, 1822–98, taught at St Edward's to 1855; after illness, r. of St John's, Kirkham, 1855/6–7, then Thurnham.

[192] The de Trafford family owned Croston Hall, near Chorley. Staunchly Catholic, they had built a chapel in the grounds which later became Holy Cross chapel-of-ease to the Mawdesley mission.

[193] Frederick Hines, 1824–1906, curate at St John's, Kirkham, then rector from 1857–95; canon 1889.

[194] Various donors had given money for a new church to replace the old one in Westby Hall, closed in 1845; these included Miss Dalton of Thurnham Hall, Miss Ann Orrell of Blackbrook, and Mr Billington of Kirkham. See Hewitson, *Our Country Churches*, 345–52. The church was eventually opened in 1860.

[195] Henry Cooke, 1829–90, St Peter's, Lancaster 1856–7, r. at Fleetwood 1857–9, then c. and r. St Marie's, Southport.

[196] For a far less rosy picture of the state of religion on the island, see letter 181, of December 1858; see also Doyle, *Mitres and Missions*, 54, 89.

72. *Very Rev. R. Brown*[197] *13 June 1856*   *5/1/264*
My dear Mr. Brown,
Many thanks for your communication from Mr. Whiteside. I will now make immediate arrangements for Mr. Cranmer's[198] going to Rome, tho' I think it would be prudent for him not to set off till after the warm weather. I am sorry to hear so indifferent an account of our little friend Mr. Cooke, for I had hoped that he would have soon grown into an able & valuable missionary under your ecclesiastical training. I know not whom I can offer you in return. Ball[199] has, I fear, lost his respectability in Lancaster, otherwise there is stuff in him that might be yet fashioned into something stirling [*sic*]. He began life too early alone, after an indifferent training at St. Anthony's. There is a Mr. O'Meara from the Collegio Pio. He is an Irishman, but has been in Rome about 3 years, & Dr. English gives an excellent character of him as an amiable, pious, & well disposed young man. He is virgin soil, & I believe that you could mould him, so as to fall into your habits better than one trained in an English College. At all events you could give him a fair trial. He could have no allies in the neighbourhood & would stand a better chance with you than elsewhere. I have spent half an hour in looking for Dr. English's letter, but cannot find it. I am glad the Woolston matter ended so well: Mr. Fisher says he was greatly indebted to you. Ever sincerely Yrs in Xt. A. Goss.

[197] Richard Melchiades Brown, 1806–68, at Lancaster from 1839; canon in 1851 but resigned 1854; nephew of Bp. Brown. Responsible for building St Peter's, Lancaster, 1857–9.

[198] Untraced.

[199] William Ball, 1826–80, curate at St Anthony's 1851–2, r. Thurnham, nr Lancaster, 1852–57; subsequently at Kirkham and Westby; see letter 84 and n. 451.

73.   *[Fr Vincent CP]*   *14 June 1856*   *5/1/267*

My dear Fr. Vincent,[200]

The Retreat or Mission at St. Anthony's is given by my direction, but not, at all, contrary to the will of the Senior Priest, as he had himself previously tried to make arrangements for one. I beg, however, that you will arrange all matters as is your wont or custom, both as to the services & the hours of the services. Do exactly as you have done in other places, & if you think it advisable to have Holy Benediction every night, you have my full sanction & permission for it. I am particularly anxious that you should give every facility in the Confessional, & that there, at least, you should have as many Fathers as you can command to assist you. I am deputing Can. Walmsley: but I am desiring the other priests not to hear confessions, as I wish the people to have the benefit of other than the usual confessors. I greatly fear that I shall not be able to be present, but I will do my best, for my time is fully employed. I am leaving home for some weeks on Friday next, & find myself fully engaged previous to my departure. Commending myself to your good prayers, I remain very sincerely Yrs in Xt. +Alexander Goss.

[200] Vincent Grotti CP, 1820–83; priest of Viterbo Diocese before joining CPs; sometime provincial at St Joseph's, London, before returning to Rome.

74.   *Rev. H. Gibson,*[201] *Catholic Institute*   *17 June 1856*   *5/1/272*

My dear Gibson,

I am in receipt of your favour containing an invitation to the Examinations at the Institute, & a statement of its present liabilities. The funeral of Dr. Crook on the Thursday will prevent my being present on that day, & I shall not be in town on Friday.

With regard to my signing the recommendation you include, I cannot consistently do so, till I know more both of the management & of the state & prospects of the Institute. I am in no hurry & can easily wait till the return of Father Nugent; but I think I should ill deserve the trust which the public place in my honesty if I signed a paper which, headed [*not clear*] by the statement that accompanies it, is something more than the approbation or affirmation of a principle. When Father Nugent returns I purpose making an inspection of the accounts, as in duty bound, & should circumstances warrant it, I shall have great pleasure in recommending an appeal to the public in the most cordial manner possible. We have all of us only one object in view, the advancement of religion, & whatever secures that shall have my most strenuous support, & being fallible I shall in all such matters seek the advice of my chapter, or of other prudent & discreet counsellors. Commending myself to your prayers, I remain very sincerely Yrs in Xt. A. Goss.

---

201   Henry Gibson 1827–1907, at CI until 1858; see later letters.

75.   [*Mr. Bonney OSB*]   [*n.d.; summer 1856*]   *5/1/273*
My dear Mr. Bonney,[202]
It seems to me that the case, about which you write, is precisely one that requires the security of the publication of banns. It is not enough to know of no impediment, but to know that there is no impediment. Only last week I saw a case of a sea captain who, having taken an affectionate leave of his wife in the North of England, landed in the South & married a second wife. Nothing is more common. The case of sea faring men as well as of soldiers comes under the regulation for vagabonds or *vagantes*, & inquiry is obliged to be made in the locality from which they come. What guarantee is there that he has not a wife in Italy? More inquiry must necessarily be made than the mere publication of banns, which could only be proof of the unmarried state of the woman, but certainly not of the man who is a stranger about whom inquiry ought to be made in his own habitat.
       Ever sincerely Yours in Christ   +Alexander Goss.

---

202   Thomas (Benedict) Bonney OSB, 1813–64; Kelly (*English Catholic Missions*) puts him at St Peter's, Seel Street, Liverpool 1847–64.

76.   [*Abbess?*]   *Feast of the Assumption* [*1856*]   *5/1/274*
My dear Abbess,
I have great pleasure in giving you the permission you ask, but, at the same [time], I feel sure that a lay sister, though a native of Liverpool, will feel lost in this large town. I think it would be much better to make application by letter. Were you to inclose a package of letters to the Messrs Lynch,[203] accompanied by a letter, I doubt not they would direct them to such persons in the town as were likely to help you. Priests, though accompanied by men, find it difficult to beg satisfactorily in this mercantile Babylon, & I feel sure that a lay sister would be frequently made to feel the disagreeableness of such a position, in itself hardly reputable for a female, much less one accustomed to the seclusion of a

convent. Commending myself to your prayers, I remain sincerely Yours in Xt.

+Alexander Goss.

---

203 Messrs Lynch: Burke, *Catholic Liverpool*, 44, mentions a Lynch among 'Irishmen of standing' in the town but there are too many of that name in *Gore's Directory* (1859) to identify this firm.

77. [*no addressee*]   *23 August 1856*   *5/1/278*

Revd. & dear Sir,

I have considered the subject of your note of the 5th but have not taken thereon the opinion of my Chapter as I should have to do, in case I thought it advisable to act in the matter. I fear that at present the good brothers would have no field for their labours in this country, for 1o. I think the bigotry is too great to admit them into our public hospitals or Infirmaries: it is difficult for a Priest to gain access, & never unless expressly sent for; 2o. we have no means of building or supporting a hospital exclusively Catholic; 3o. Old infirm priests are difficult to control. We have a fund for their support, which would go much farther if they could be induced to live together; but any such attempt they would view as an infringement of their liberty. These seem to me the difficulties. Unless the Brothers have ample means for establishing a house, as also for their support, I think it would be difficult to accomplish any thing in the face of the clamour for Reformatories for boys & girls. With many thanks for your kind note, Believe me very truly Yours in Xt. +Alexander Goss.

78. [*Rev. Mr. Carter*]   *25 August 1856*   *5/1/280*

My dear Mr. Carter,

I have carefully considered the circumstances of your attending Lymm, & have taken advice thereon, & I do not see how you can be offered less than £25 per annum. I have nothing to do with Mr. Brigham, & have no wish to dictate to him, but as a professional man himself I do not think that he can offer you less than £20, leaving you to receive whatever may be made by the offertory. He would not as a medical man attend any family at that distance in all weathers, & for that length of time without receiving a much higher fee. If he does not wish to give it, I have no power & no desire to exact it; but I consider it my duty to prevent your risking your health for the convenience of any private individual, wherever such individual may reside & much more when he resides out of my Diocese. I think you had better claim the intervention of the Bp. of Shrewsbury, for he will never sanction or countenance so shabby a proceeding. In my own Diocese I would not sanction any priests undergoing such fatigues & risks for such a remuneration.

Believe me very truly Yours in Xt. Alexander Goss.

79. [*Rev. J. Nugent*]   [*n.d., but late August 1856*]   *5/1/283*

My dear Mr. Nugent,

I have no wish to interfere with your remaining at the Institute, if your health will stand it, still less have I any intention of putting you at the still more arduous post of Copperas Hill. I want you to be where you will do most good. Yet if your health is not restored, it will be madness to return to the Institute, for nursing & quiet are incompatible with the bustle of Lpool. Similar reasons have led to the retirement of Mr. Carr to [*sic.* ? *from*] Copperas Hill. Dr. Roskell[204] takes his place, as Mr. Hawksworth [*sic*] place will be subsequently taken by the Vic. Gen: [*sic*] tho' this fact is not yet known. Mr. Carr[205] is pleased with the Isle of Man, &, in all probability, will be appointed to it. It is a great field for both energy & zeal, yet not so killing as Liverpool. My anxiety to have the matters of the Institute settled arose from the difficulty of making changes after the new appointments are announced. I was anxious that nothing should remain to be done after the Synod:[206] for the retirement of Mr. Oreilly [*sic*] from Blackstock St. & the advent of many fresh priests necessitates some changes, & I need not add that the matter had engaged my attention for many weeks past.[207] The reports about the finances of the Institute certainly require prompt attention, or your credit will be gone.[208]

[*written across letter*] I have been greatly pained, as well as others of your good friends, at the rumours in circulation. If you had come over for a few days, you might have returned, for I am sure that, as far as I am concerned, I will do every thing in my power to facilitate your recovery.

Praying God that you may continue to improve I remain very truly Yours.   Alexander Goss.

---

204   Thomas Tasker Roskell, 1831; o. 1855; died 1862 from typhus caught while ministering in the workhouse.

205   James Carr, 1826–1913, canon (1867) and VG (1884), at Douglas 1856–62, then Formby until his death.

206   Goss held his first synod in November 1856.

207   In a letter to the Vicar General Goss wrote in exasperation, 'What a time it will take before the system of self-constituted appointments is eradicated!' (5/1/282, 28 August 1856).

208   Finances of the Institute: the records referred to have not been identified.

80.   *Rev. J. B. Spencer*[209]   *29 August 1856*   *5/1/286*

Revd. & dear Sir,

As I stated in my conversation with you, I have this year received so great an increase of clergy that I have no further vacancies, nay I have received five or six applications from priests, soliciting employment in this Diocese, whose offer of service I have been obliged to decline. Should you wish a prolongation of your *licentia celebrandi*, you will receive it on application to Canon Walmsley, 53 Ashton St. who may be found also at Copperas Hill, on the nights of Friday & Saturday & at the Convent of Mercy every morning. Wishing you every blessing & commending myself to your prayers, I remain truly Yrs in Xt. Alexander Goss.

---

[209]   J. B. Spencer is not listed; there is a Thomas Spencer among Plumb's 'unexplained departures' (*'Found Worthy'*), who may be Fitz-L's Plymouth priest, Thomas, 1826–96, who transferred from Liverpool about 1865 and was in Dorset from 1868 onwards; there are gaps in his *Directory* listings. (The name has been added later in a different hand, and may read 'Spenser'.)

81.   *The Rev R. Sumner S.J., St Francis Xavier's, Lpool*[210]
                    31 August 1856   *5/1/287*

Dear Rev Sir,

The Bishop desires me to acknowledge your note of yesterday. A correspondence between the late Vicar, Dr Crook and Father Collyns,[211] on the subject of attendance at Conference, has been placed in his hands, but it does not contain any claim of exemption as granted by the late Bishop. [*inserted*: Probably this may have been given afterwards] His Lordship would therefore feel obliged if you would forward him a copy of Dr. Brown's leave of exemption, that it may be placed among the minutes of the Conference.

The reasons assigned for Father Carroll's[212] absence will be laid before the proper Officers at the Synod: but as notice of its being held on the 3rd was formally given some time ago, & as it takes precedence of all other duties, there will be a great difficulty in allowing such cause of absence as sufficient.

          I remain Yours very truly, Charles Teebay, Notary.

---

[210]   Richard Sumner SJ, 1801–77; in Liverpool 1851–66. This is one of a small number of letters to priests who had requested leave of absence from the Synod; the tone is the same in all of them.

[211]   Charles Henry Collyns SJ, 1820–84.

[212]   Presumably Richard O'Carroll SJ, 1807–58.

82.   [*C. Newsham – in pencil*]   5 September 1856   5/1/293
Very Revd. & Dear Sir,

His Lordship has caught a severe cold, & hence will be unable to sing Mass at S. [*sic*] Anthony's on Sunday. Canon Fisher however has consented to sing Mass, & nothing but a real impossibility of attendance will prevent His Lordship from being present – so that the Mass will be *coram Episcopo* – a more solemn & imposing ceremony than a Pontifical Mass. – It is a subject of deep regret to His Lordship that his letter regarding districts has given rise to insubordination & dissension; that letter was called for from the continued perseverance in the injudicious & injurious practice of Sick weeks, – the grave reasons which demanded it form its justification. – As far as His Lordship's acquaintance with the enactments of the Provincial Synod & of other Councils goes, it is laid down that Catechism & other Parochial duties belong mainly to the Rectors of Churches, not only for their superintendence, but also for the actual discharge of those duties, – & your own long Missionary experience must have proved to you the necessity & importance of personal inspection, & much more of personal administration in these matters. – Mr. Walsh[213] has very widely erred in considering himself as the Rector of his district, & His Lordship will take an early opportunity of speaking to him on the subject.

Meanwhile His Lordship feels most anxious that concord & harmony should be restored, as he is convinced that little good can be done for the cause of Religion, where misunderstandings & dissension divide the energies of those who are devoted to works of charity for God & for man. –

I am, Very Revd. & Dear Sir, Yours truly in Xt Thos. T. Roskell [*secretary*].

---

[213] Samuel J. Walsh, 1822–93, at St Anthony's 1855–59; for biographical details, O'Neill, *St Anthony's*, 110–11. Born in Ireland, he had been educated in Marseilles; he left the diocese in 1867 for the USA and died as a priest in New Jersey. See later letters.

83.   [*Whiteside Trust*[214]]   [*n.d.; presumably August or September 1856*]   5/1/298
These presents are to signify that the sum of £1000 held by us Richard Brown, Thomas Cookson, James Fisher and Alexander Goss as a gift from Mr. James Whiteside of Lancaster, is held on trust for the education of a youth for the priesthood of the Roman Catholic Religion, as long as such purpose be allowed by the laws of England; but should such purpose be declared unlawful, we the said Trustees are empowered to spend it in any other way we may in our discretion think best. The youth to be educated on the interest of this sum of £1000, to be called

the Whiteside Fund, must be selected & approved of under the rules & regulations laid down in the Diocese; but we declare it to be one of the conditions of this Trust that preference be given to a youth from Lancaster, provided he be in other respects eligible; & should one or all the Trustees die without appointing a successor or successors, we declare the Roman Catholic Bishop, or the Spiritual Superior of the Roman Catholics of the part of Lancashire in which Lancaster is situated, to be empowered to appoint other Trustees.

---

214   In the light of the on-going rows about funds for training students, it is interesting this new fund says nothing about their place of education.

84.   *Very Rev. Canon Greenhalgh   3 September 1856*   *5/1/303*
"In re Chorley"

My dear Canon,
I know not how to fill up Chorley. You would not like Mr. Ball, & Mr. Ball would not, I am told, like it: what then must be done? I do not wish to send another Irish priest, yet Mr. Aylward's[215] touchiness about a senior makes it difficult to act.

Mr. Gerald OReilly[216] [*sic*] is a young active man & might push the place on, yet things would languish & he might be prevented from acting, if Mr. Aylward were the head. How can the matter be arranged? Is there any one that you or he can suggest? I fear Gerald has been too long a master at Ushaw to have the disposition to work under another, unless that other had in him a certain power of command. It is very desirable that my name should not be mentioned in this matter to Mr. Aylward; but you might ascertain his sentiments in an 'accidental' conversation. If Gerald had been ordained in his course, he would not be thought young. Ask Mr. Aylward himself to make a suggestion: let him take a Directory & go thro' the names, so that he may see what I have at my disposal. Begging my kind regards to your niece & wishing you both every blessing, I remain truly Yrs. A. Goss.

---

215   John Aylward *c.* 1824–84; at St Mary's, Chorley, 1856 to 1865; see n. 671.
216   Gerald O'Reilly, brother of the future bishop. In the end it was another Irish priest, John O'Meara (n. 153), who served at St Mary's, but he was not appointed until September 1858 (5/2/333). In his letter of appointment Goss described Aylward to him as 'one of the most amiable of men' and hoped O'Meara would bring 'the Roman school of theology' to the Chorley conferences.

85.   [*Rev. Wm. Henderson*]   *11 September 1856*   *5/1/306*
My dear Mr. Henderson,
I think you may safely act in reference to the B.S. being kept at

Leighton,[217] seeing, however, that the conditions of the Indult as to saying Mass or any other [service] are observed.

I grant what you ask about Benediction, & you can at once act upon this grant, but I will make out a more suitable document on the receipt of my formula from the printer. I am glad you are going to have Benediction: there is no rite that so effectually warms the devotion of the people. The *Ritus servandus*[218] contains every information you will want.

Wishing you every success, Believe me,   Very truly Yrs in Xt. +Alexander Goss.

---

[217]   Leighton Hall, Yealand, home of the Gillow family and one of only two houses with a proper Indult for a private chapel (see P. Doyle, 'Bishop Goss and the Gentry', *NWCH* 12 (1985), 6–13).

[218]   See *Decreta*, 18–19, for the regulations laid down by the First Provincial Synod in 1852.

86.   *Very Revd. Canon Maddocks*   *19 September 1856*   *5/1/313*

My dear Canon,

It is now generally admitted that the *contrahentes* are the ministers of matrimony, & hence, if the marriage takes place in the Protestant Church first, the parties are really married, & to repeat the service in the Catholic church would be the equivalent to rebaptizing one confessedly baptized. Besides to receive the sacrament of marriage in a Prot. Church – & they would receive the sacrament if married there first – would be a *communicatio cum hereticis in religione*,[219] & therefore sinful. Whereas if they received the sacrament of marriage in the Cath. Church, the service in the Prot. Church might perhaps be winked at as a mere civil service done to gratify the husband, tho' in Dr. Errington's Diocese, even this much is strictly forbidden, & he would refuse to marry them if he knew they intended afterwards to go to the Church. Our Synod has only one passage about it, page 74 no.6.[220] The parties cannot of course receive the nuptial blessing.

Believe me, Very truly Yours in Xt. +Alexander Goss.

---

[219]   Trans: 'co-operation with heretics in matters of religion'.

[220]   The page reference is unclear; the only §6 that is relevant is in *Decreta*, 26, dealing with the usual promises about the children of mixed marriages and the conversion of the non-Catholic party. The stricter regulation was adopted in 1864; see *Synodi*, 55–6, for the relevant Visitation Decree.

87. *Mr. H. OBryen*[221] *24 September 1856* *5/1/319*

My dear Mr. OBryen,

I regret that your Father will not assist you by furnishing the means to pay for your expenses to Rome. I had hoped that he would have done so, & so I did not calculate amongst the anticipated Educational expenses your journey. You are probably aware that the main part of [the] money belonging to the Diocess for the education of students for the priesthood is not under the say or conrol of the Bp. He may approve or disapprove of a student; but he cannot appoint him to be placed on a burse. Since accepting you I have sent to College, or adopted students already at College, to the number of 8 or 10, so that I fear that I may be brought to a dead halt. For myself I have literally nothing. Up to this moment £10 is all that I have received from the funds of the Diocese for the last two years. But for rigid economy I should have been on the parish. I daily wear my professors [*sic*] gown which is 10 years old, & I say mass in the cassock I wore in Rome, which was an old one when I was made Bishop. I hope therefore you will study economy. Inclosed I forward half notes for £15 & to Mr. Ford I forward the corresponding halves. Your Father will relent later if not now.

　　Believe me truly Yours in Xt.　　+Alexander Goss.

---

[221]　On O'Bryen see letters 397, 441, 443, 444; he was ordained in Rome in 1858.

88. *[John Baker, student]*　*30 September 1856*　*5/1/323–6*

My dear John Baker,

As you are one of my flock, whether you study for the Church or live in the world as a layman, for whom I shall have to give an account to God, I feel it a duty to write this letter to you.

You have ever been taught that no one, whatsoever his talents or piety, can be raised to the dignity of the Priesthood, unless he be called by Almighty God, & that were anyone without such call, to aspire to it, it would be at the peril of his own salvation. You have been taught also that if anyone, conscious of the call, refuses to obey it, he does so at the risk of eternal damnation. You know, therefore, the greatness of the interests at stake in the decision of this question, viz. the salvation or damnation of your own immortal soul. Since, therefore, so much is at stake, & since your eternal welfare or perdition depends, in all probablity, on the step you now take, it is necessary that you omit nothing which prudence can suggest, that can guide you, or enable you to take this important step aright. Have you done so? Do you feel that you have done so?

You have been for many years an inmate of St. Edward's College as an ecclesiastical student, &, during that time, you have had, no doubt, your spiritual trials. Year after year the sincerity or reality of your vocation must have engaged your thoughts, & you will have felt it doubtful or certain, strong or weak, according to the graces granted to you thro' prayer & the sacraments & according to the severity of interior trials from passion, or of exterior circumstances affecting on [*sic*] them, companions, & vacation times & its dissipation, [*three words illegible*] & impatience of control etc. These are trials which all have to undergo, & from which there is no reason to believe you to have been exempt. Whatever temporary influence, however, these various assaults on your vocation may have produced, they did not, up to Midsummer, make you reverse from the intention avowed on your admission as an ecclesiastical student & repeated frequently to me & your superiors. Knowing the importance of prayer in the settlement of this great question, & knowing that God usually speaks to the soul at the time of Retreat, I desired you especially to open your heart to him & to beg his enlightenment at that time, & I desired you, as well as others thus similarly circumstanced, to make known to me freely, without fear or guile, the result to which God had brought you. This you did at the end of your retreat. Sharrock fell off; but you answered unhesitatingly that your intention was fixed to go on, nay, that you had never doubted. Now can this resolution, confirmed in you by prayer at the foot of your Crucifix when speaking alone with God, & strengthened by holy communion so often & so piously received; can this resolution persevered in through so many years amid so many trials, which remained unshaken when one of your dearest friends fell away, can this resolution, John, secured by prayer & the sacraments & strengthened by retreats, year after year, have been a mere suggestion & temptation of the devil who was anxious to coax you to be consecrated a priest in order that he might accomplish your damnation? Ordinarily, John, it is the voice of God, & not of the devil, that is heard in prayer, at communion & during retreats. The devil usually speaks to the soul by temptations & allurements to vice: at dances & parties, pleasure trips & feasting, at music & singing, drinking & carousing, through the voice of singing women & the smiles of laughing girls, rather than at communion will his whispers be heard in the soul. Now, my dear boy, if up to the vacation, you believed God to have called you to serve his Church as one of his ministers, when did you hear his voice, calling you to another state of life? Was it at prayer or in light reading? Was it after communion, or after being in the company of gay companions? Was it when you felt grace to be working in your soul, or when your passions were awakened, & soft feelings engendered in body & soul, by the indolent or enervating pursuits & pleasures of vacation time? These are questions, John, which you will one day have to answer to God, & which it will be well to answer now.

When you stand before God the time for change will have past: you will be judged by what you have done & not by what you might have been or would wish to have been. Now, however, you have still power & I trust grace to regulate your future life according to what you, in your conscience, believe to be the will of God in your regard; for I sincerely hope that neither in feeling nor in thought have you given way to those debasing temptations that so often seduce the young from virtue, happiness, & God both here & hereafter. If God is by your side, & you feel by increased spiritual favours, & you know by actual improvements in virtue, by greater frequency & increased fervour at communion that God is guiding & directing you in your present course, then, John, I say to you persevere, walk boldly, & may God's blessing attend your steps. But if, my dear boy, this is not the case, if you do not feel yourself to be better, if you are less pious than you were, if feelings you would have fled from crowd for admittance into your heart; if you can hear, without horror, hints or words of suspicious meaning, then, John, I say to you in God's name, stand & pause. Do not follow the new path you have selected, but return to God & to me. God will receive you, & as his servant, I will receive you as kindly as ever. I will again enable you to continue your studies, where, as before, you shall want for nothing. At least, John, let me implore of you as a duty you owe to God & to the Diocese, not to decide on the future without first making a Retreat. Go to Stonyhurst or to Bishop Eton for a week or ten days: you can do it unknown to any one. You will gain admittance at either place if you say that I advised it. Justice to the Diocese, which has borne so large a share in the expenses of your education, demands this from you. And now, my dear John, may God guide you in your choice.[222] I feel I have done my duty & at the last day I hope to be held guiltless of your soul.

Your affectionate Bishop, A. Goss.

---

[222] He did not go on to ordination; strangely, he does not feature in the student register of St Edward's.

89. [*Miss Elizabeth Orrell of Blackbrook*[223]]   *20 October 1856*
5/1/354–5

My dear Miss Eliza,
I trust that by this time you know me sufficiently well to believe, that I am not disposed to refuse you any favour which I can grant conscientiously. You say that Oratories are going to be placed under more stringent rules, but this is not correct, nor does the priest, whoever he may be, that told you communion could be given without the Bp's leave know much of his theology. The Church forbids a Bp. to allow Mass to be said except in <u>public</u> oratories or churches, & it is only by his

extraordinary faculties granted him for 6 years, that he can do so. When, however, as in your case, the privilege is held by Papal Indult, Mass can be allowed according to the terms of the Indult, & I have never seen one more ample, because it does not except holidays & Sundays as is usually the case in such Indults.

I do not think any Indulgence can be gained by communicating in a private oratory, at least, as far as my reading extends, there is usually a clause which says that Communion must be received in a church or public oratory, an exemption, however, being made for Religious, for except in cases of sickness, the Church seems to dislike communion out of the public church or chapel. Moreover the people have a right to the edification of seeing those placed above them in station, frequently approach Holy Communion, which would not be the case, if it were made in private chapels. Mind, I am not influenced by scruple in these matters, for I have studied the subject for days together, & have consulted the very best authors, & the best living authorites both in England & Rome, so that I consider myself entitled to form an opinion, at least, for my own guidance. The faculties issued by the Cardinal contain exactly the same clause as my own, word for word.

Miss Ann already enjoys the privilege of receiving holy communion in the private chapel, whenever Mass is said therein, if she be so disposed. I am willing to allow you & Miss Orrell, & one servant, necessary to attend on you or on any one of you, the same privilege, excepting, however, Sundays & holidays of obligation, except in case of sickness, when I withdraw the exception. This letter will suffice for this permision for the present, but when I receive my papers from the printer, I will write it in a more formal manner. There are more than twenty private oratories in this Diocese, & yours & Leighton are the only two I know of that are held by Papal Indult. In past times the Church found them to be the origin of great abuses, & once prohibited even Bps from saying Mass in them unless sanctioned by the H. See, & even now, except by special grant a Bp. could not say Mass out of his own house, i.e. in any other house, unless he had spent the night there.

I am glad to hear that Miss Ann has, occasionally at least, been some-what easier than when I last saw you, & I hope she may now steadily improve.

I expect that when I visit you I shall have to bring a folio vol. of theology with me to answer all objections. If you could only occupy my weary post & sit, as many hours as I do, bent over my desk, I am sure you would be gentle with me.

Wishing my kind regards to Miss Orrell & Miss Ann & begging every blessing on you all, I remain very sincerely Yours in Xt. +A. Goss.

223   The Orrell family of Blackbrook, Parr, St Helens: James and Anne (née Corne, of Staffs.) Orrell had seven surviving children. The eldest, Charles, inherited the estate but died unmarried in 1843; Fr James died at Blackbrook in 1825; Fr Philip died in 1866 (see n. 91), and four daughters, none of whom married. The estate passed to the diocese on the death of the last daughter and the house became a convent of the Sisters of Mercy, who ran a girls' reformatory there. See T. A. Orrell, *A History of the House of Orrell* (privately published, Bolton, 1990), at 252–5; also, J. Giblin, 'The Orrell Family and the Mission of St Mary's, Blackbrook in Parr, St Helens', *NWCH* 7 (1980), 6–19.

90.   *Very Revd Canon Morris*[224]   *22 October 1856*   *5/1/358*

My dear Canon,

If I had known that you were disengaged when I last heard from you, I should certainly have given you a warm invitation to the Diocese of Liverpool, but now St. Thomas has you as his own,[225] but I am glad that you are once more amongst us, & hope you will have leisure not to forget your books.

I am, as you know, a plain man without any pretensions except an honest will to do my duty, & hence am not a good authority on difficult matters. Punctators, it seems to me, are a species of canonical police, who mark delinquent as well those absent with just cause, as those who, tho' present, do not satisfactorily do their work; & hence the Synod Fulgense[226] directs those to be punctured amongst the absent who were seen talking, [or who] said office, read, omitted to sing etc. when in choir. Barbosa[227] says that Canons absent from the Church to which they are attached *ex Pontificis privilegio*, can gain the daily distributions & hence would not be punctured, because it was from the punctuation book that it was ascertained who were present, or rather who were absent, & if their names had occurred there, they would not have received the distributions.

I rather incline to hold with your opinion about the Titular of the Pro-Cathedral. The Cathedral itself seems to be spiritually & temporally beyond the administration of the Chapter, tho' that would not affect the right of the Titular, as they are allowed *ibi divina officia peragens*,[228] but to say the truth, I cannot speak on the matter, for I have not had time to examine it, as for three days I have had my Finance Committee, Chapter, Deans.

On Friday I go North for 12 days on a visitation tour. I find things generally in very good order, spiritually & temporally, & I find that God has blessed a pious diocese with exemplary priests & an indifferent Bishop. You used to think me unRoman: here I am thought to be an out & outer. I have only one wish, honestly & without sham or falseness to carry out the law of the Church, enforcing my own rights & respecting those of others. Ever sincerely & affectionately Yrs in Xt Alexander Goss.

224 Canon Morris: see nn. 110, 515.

225 Thomas Grant, 1816–70, Bp of Southwark, Goss's 'Dear Friend'.

226 One of the *fontes* of the 1917 Code was 'Fulginatensis' (of Foligno, in Umbria) of February 1639.

227 Agostino Barbosa, 1589–1649, Portuguese; he was the premier canonist of his age, working in Rome and Madrid; he wrote on the duties of the episcopal office. *DDC*, II, 203. Trans: 'by privilege of the Pontiff'.

228 Trans: 'while performing divine services there'.

91. [*Sir Robert Gerard of Garswood*] *8 November 1856*   *5/1/365–7*

My dear Sir Robert

I was sorry that I was from home, on the visitation of the Diocese, when you were so kind as to call upon me a few days ago, & I am again leaving home for a fortnight's absence on Thursday next.

From a letter lately received from the Revd. Mr. Penswick,[229] I am sorry to find that he communicated to you the contents of a private letter, addressed to him by me previous to the meeting of the Synod, & has thus prematurely forced on the discussion of a subject which I had hoped to have treated of in a personal interview at the time of my visitation of Ashton. From what Mr. Penswick writes I conjecture that he has led you to suppose, that I have authority to sanction the reservation of the Blessed Sacrament in a domestic oratory; but this is quite a mistake, I have no such authority. Were Garswood my own place of residence, I could not keep the B.S. there without leave of the Holy See. Mr Penswick is an old man, & began his missionary labours under very different circumstances to those in which we are now placed by the re-establishment of the Hierarchy, & hence he is unable fully to realise the change. Formerly Bishops were Vicars Apostolic, & as representatives of the pope, had very extensive powers; but by the resoration of the Hierarchy these powers were abolished, & the government of the bishops was reduced to a more constitutional form, & hence the bishops do not now possess the extensive authority enjoyed by their predecessors. During persecution also the laws of the Church were in abeyance, & hence many things were allowed which are now prohibited.

Mr. Penswick wrongly imagines that I have succeeded to the powers of my predecessors, & hence I feel that my inability to dispense with the law of the Church will be construed into an unwillingness to oblige, or to an inclination to sacrifice the liberties of the English Church to Italian notions acquired by a Roman education, than which nothing could be more untrue. A Bishop cannot even grant permission for a private oratory, tho' I doubt not, that Mr. Penswick imagines that any gentleman who chooses to keep a priest, may have the luxury of a domestic chapel; but this is a mistake, for the Holy See reserves to itself the granting of such privilege. Then, you may ask, why have I made no objection to your domestic oratory? I answer, because I hold, by special grant from the Holy See authority to allow a priest to say Mass wherever I may deem proper, & hence, tho' I cannot grant you the right of having Mass said in your house, I can grant him leave to say Mass there, & thus I secure to you what you desire without violating the laws of the Church. The case, however, is widely different with reference to the Sacrament. I have not only no power, but there is a positive prohibition against the usurpation or exercise of such power by any Bishop. The circumstances of the prohibition were these: an old Catholic gentleman, of great piety, large property & living four miles distant from a Church, applied for permission to keep the B. Sacrament; but this permission was refused, & the Bishops were told that the Holy See alone, & not they had power to grant such permission. Mr. Penswick has written me a long letter to show that the Oratory at Garswood partakes of a sort of public character, because his servant, & the friends of the hall servants are allowed to attend; but I considered the reasons as frivolous & so unworthy of your honoured name, that I felt sure you would scorn to allow them to be advanced, & I shrank with dread from the idea of trifling in a matter concerning God's visible presence on earth.

Miss Dalton of Thurnham has recently built a beautiful chapel[230] & furnished it in a most expensive manner, with all the requisites for keeping the B.S., yet I was compelled, to my great grief, to assure her that I had no authority to concede the privilege, & I felt it the more because the state of her health does not allow her to visit the B.S. in the Church which her magnificence has erected.

I shall be truly grieved if what I have written fails to convince you, whatever may be said by ill-informed persons to the contrary, that I was influenced in this matter by the most conscientious motives, & I assure you that nothing will ever give me greater pleasure than to oblige you or Lady Gerard whenever in my power to do so. Towards Mr. Penswick I am influenced by the sincerest feelings of regard, & I have dispensed with his observance of new laws as far as I could. There is no other priest in the Diocese, except himself, dispensed with the use of a Confessional. In the matter of keeping the B.S. at Garswood, he has made a false step, & I shall be surprised to learn that it did not originate with him, for Lady Monica assures me that it was not reserved there whilst she was resident.

Wishing yourself, Lady Gerard & family every blessing, I remain very sincerely Yours in Christ, Alexander Goss.

---

[229]   John Penswick, 1778–1864, last of the 'Douai Collegians' and one of the 'Trente-deux' who escaped at the time of the French Revolution. He was at Birchley 1803–49, then retired to be chaplain at Garswood in 1849, to d. in 1864. He built the present church at Birchley.

230 Miss Elizabeth Dalton had inherited the Thurnham estate in 1837 and built a domestic chapel at Thurnham Hall in 1854–5: see A. J. Noble, 'Thurnham Hall Chapel'(with illustration), *NWCH* 36 (2009), 100–1, 104; she died unmarried in 1861 and the estate passed to a cousin, Sir James George Fitzgerald, who added Dalton to his name; he died aged thirty-six in 1867; *VCH, Lancashire*, VIII, 103.

92.   [*Mr. Parkinson*[231]]   *18 November 1856*   *5/2/10*
<u>Most Confidential</u>

My dear Mr. Parkinson,

I need not urge upon you the necessity of treating this communication as most strictly confidential, seeing that it involves the character of a Priest.

During the time that you remained at St. Anthony's, do you remember being in company with Can. Newsham & others, when he received a letter from the Redemptorists about giving a mission there, & do you remember whether he shewed, in his attempt to read that letter or in his remarks thereon, that he was in liquor? Do you think that he was on that occasion, or have you seen him on any other occasion, the worse for drink? Do you remember whether in your presence he ever spoke of the doctrine or dogma of the Immaculate Conception in an unbecoming manner, & can you give me the substance of any such remarks?

This is a strictly conscientious matter, on which I think you are bound to speak according to the extent of your knowledge. Your answer shall be treated as confidentially as I expect this letter to be, so that I trust you will have no difficulty in freeing your conscience & mine by a plain declaration of facts.

I am sorry that our first communication after so many years should be on so unpleasant a business. Ever truly & sincerely Yrs in Xt. Alexander Goss.

231 Thomas Parkinson, 1818–79, priest of the Westminster Diocese, originally from Lancashire.

93.   *A. M. McDonnell Esq.,*[232] *Clarendon Rooms, North John St.*
          18 November 1856   *5/2/11*
<u>Most Confidential</u>

My dear Mr. McDonnell,

I need not urge to you the necessity of treating this communication as <u>most strictly confidential</u>, seeing that it involves the character of a Priest.

You have been, I believe, on various occasions in company with the Very Rev. Can. Newsham of St. Anthony's, & I am given to understand that you have seen him on some of those occasions the worse for liquor.

I wish to learn from yourself whether this be true or not; & if true, how often or in what state of drink you may have seen him. I put the question for conscience's sake, & much may depend on the issue, for there is a priest's character, on the one hand, & the spiritual welfare of thousands of poor Catholics, on the other. Whatever you know, I think you are bound to speak: for I make this appeal to you in God's name.

It is hardly necessary to add that your answer will be considered as strictly confidential, so that I trust you will have no difficulty in freeing your conscience & mine by a plain declaration of facts.

Believe me to remain, Very truly & sincerely Yrs in Xt. Alexander Goss.

---

232 The chambers of J. B. Aspinall, Catholic barrister, were in the Clarendon Rooms; but *Gore's Directory* (1859 and 1860) gives them as being at 1 South John Street; perhaps McDonnell was a solicitor working there.

94. [*Mr. Bond*]   *12 January 1857*   *5/2/13*
                              Confidential

My dear Mr. Bond,

In consequence of communications made to me, some time ago, at the command of a penitent's confessor, I feel it a duty again to urge upon you the necessity, & propriety, of not outraging the feelings of the world, tho' you may afford to despise them. I am told that you often call at the house at which Miss Clarkson resides, & that great scandal is thereby caused amongst persons who are conversant with the tittle-tattle of Preston. It is quite possible that jealousy rather than religion may have been the motive which has impelled this disclosure; but that only affects the informer. My duty is to deal with facts, however made known. I make no inquiry as to motive: that must remain between the informer & God; but what I have to determine is fact or no fact? Something also has been said of a trip across the water, & of your having been seated alone with the girl Clarkson as evening set in, & of an objection having been made to the introduction of lights, but that Mrs. Alty [?Athy] would bring lights into the room, alleging the impropriety of a gentleman & a lady being left alone in a room without lights at such an hour, after whiskey & water.

Now, my dear Mr. Bond, it may be that these statements are coloured; it may be that they are false. I do not make, nor purpose to make, nor have I made any inquiry. I only repeat, what I have before implied, that you should not frequent the company & the lodging of this singing girl. Of her I know nothing; I never saw her that I know of; but after what has been said, tho' falsely said even, it is my duty to see that the faithful be not scandalized & that no ground be given, even tho' innocently, for the world's censures by your gratifying the vanity [of] the girl by your company.

Believe me ever sincerely & affectionately Yours in Xt. Alexander Goss.

95. *Miss E. Clements*[233]   *18 January 1857*   *5/2/14*[234]

My dear Child in Jesus Christ,

I am glad to find that your soul is at rest under the guidance of the Revd. Mr. O'Carroll & that you feel that your steps have been guided to him by God's special assistance. I should be glad if I have been distantly instrumental in rescuing you from a perilous state.

Your letter may posssibly be read in a sense not condemned by the Church, but the natural interpretation of it would argue a state of mind, or a practice condemned by the Church. You are therefore on the verge of a precipice, if you have not already thrown yourself down. This alone would convince me, – tho' I have formed my opinion on other data, – that unless God mercifully interfere, your mind will become a prey to habitual delusion. God never could guide or lead any of his children into pastures which lie beyond the pale of his Church; yet into such pastures your soul seems to have strayed. It is not for me to interfere with your actual director, but I should strongly recommend the active practice of vocal prayer, & escape from the state of quietude into which you throw yourself.

Praying that God may guide you through your present dire straits into healthy pastures, I remain very sincerely Yrs in Xt. +Alexander Goss.

---

[233] The *femme fatale* in the Gibson case. Fr Henry Gibson of the Catholic Institute became infatuated with a local woman who was running a hostel for fallen women set up by Gibson. There was public scandal and after several warnings Goss removed him from duty and suspended his faculties. Gibson, guilty at least of naïve waywardness, appealed to Rome and went there in 1858 to defend himself but made the serious mistake of taking his lady friend with him. He saw the error of his ways (as did she) and returned to work in the diocese until his death in 1907, doing pioneering work for homeless children. Goss's efforts to save him are striking. The case takes up over 150 pages in APF, *Anglia*, 15. See letter 128 and for his later work Doyle, *Mitres and Missions*, 186–7.

[234] This letter is out of place: it should be in 5/1, according to the date.

96. *Rev. Mr. Hickey*[235] *[added in pencil]*   *21 January 1857*   *5/1/399*

Dear Rev. Sir,

In answer to your letter to the Bishop of the 20th inst: I would recommend you to consult with Dean Brown & Rev. J. Doherty[236] who have had experience in building schools, & in correspondence with Government. Secondly I would recommend you to consult with the respectables of the congregation about the land to be appropriated for the schools; about raising the money, etc. I would do this without formally appointing them a Committee, & without putting any proposition to a vote, & after the school is built it would die a natural death. Thirdly I would recommend you to correspond with the Government yourself & be cautious of shewing the correspondence to others. Fourthly, I would say to [the] Government correspndent as little on the subject as I could, & absolutely nothing until I was forced. He will require some of the laity to be Trustees, but the Bp will name these, & not of your congregation. You might use the following expression if you have to say anything about management: that the same respectable persons of your congregation form with yourself a Committee of management.

His lordship desires his kind regards. I remain Dear Revd. Sir, Yours ever truly, Thos. Cookson.

---

235   Michael Hickey, see n. 144. This letter was written by Cookson VG, and is interesting for his (and presumably Goss's) attitude to the laity and lay committees, as well as its attitude to the government over grants.
236   John Doherty, 1826–76; at Chorley 1854–58.

97.   *Mrs Anderton,*[237] *Haighton House*   *24 January 1857*   *5/1/405*
Private Chapel
My dear Mrs. Anderton,
Almighty God has visited you severely, & whilst ready to bow with submission to his holy will, we must hope that in his mercy he will spare your surviving family. Should he, however, afflict them or yourself with sickness, or should he call any of them to himself, I will do what lies in my power to soothe your affliction by allowing mass to be said on an application being made to me. I may grant in a particular case, what I cannot grant generally. It is not necessary that you should be actually present in the private chapel, but such presence would suffice as would be sufficient for the hearing of mass, that is an uninterrupted communication between your room & the chapel.

If you will procure for me, as I have no doubt you can, a written opinion from your medical adviser according to the tenor of your letter, I will grant you permission to receive holy Communion during the next three months in your private chapel. I should wish, however, that, if convenient, it should be administered by the Rev. R. Gillow the resident priest, but, if not convenient, if the priest who says mass should have his sanction to administer communion to you, which I doubt not he will, under the circumstances, cheerfully give.

Wishing every blessing on yourself & family, I remain very sincerely Yours in Xt. +Alexander Goss.

237 Anderton of Haighton Hall: a recusant family with several branches; see J. Gillow, *A Bibliographical Dictionary of the English Catholics*, 5 vols (London, 1885–1902), I. Goss complained of receiving a 'cool reception' when he insisted on inspecting their private chapel; see Doyle, 'Bishop Goss and the Gentry', 10.

98. *Very Rev. Canon Newsham, St.Anthony's*   *24 January 1857*
5/2/16[238]

Very Rev. & dear Canon,

I never sat down to address a priest with more pain than I do now to address you. For the last nine months I have had in my hands an Indictment of 15 counts against you: but a feeling of delicacy & a hope of better things have hitherto kept it within my portfolio & I would not allude to it except to show my reluctance to give you pain. In November, however, a fresh charge from a different quarter was brought against you. Witnesses appeared before a priest, driven by motives of duty, as explained, I believe, in the Confessional, & requested him to convey to the Bishop a charge of your having been seen by several witnesses in an unbecoming state from the effects of drink on the evening of the 17th November 1856. Various circumstances were stated & taken down in writing in corroboration of this charge.

Nothing but an imperative sense of duty could have urged me to write this letter: but my convictions that a charge, supported on the evidence adduced, formally laid before me against a Canon of the Diocese, could not conscientiously be passed by, have compelled me most reluctantly to seek an explanation from you.

You may think that your complaints against the Rev. Mr. Walsh have been received slightingly, but what I have stated above will show the reason of my silence. You will see the necessity of giving an answer in writing rather than a verbal explanation.

I remain very sincerely Yrs in Xt. Alexander Goss.

238 This and other letters on the subject are printed in O'Neill, *St Anthony's*, 325–30.

99. *Very Rev. Canon Newsham*   *27 January 1857*   5/2/17

Very Rev. & dear Canon,

I hardly expected that my forbearance in pressing the heavy charges that have from time to time been made against you should be construed into an act of injustice, as it is in your characteristic letter of yesterday. I regret that an error should have been made; but it is no doubt an error of the priest who took down the deposition & has put Oct. for Nov.: for the charge was brought the day after it is said to have occurred & was taken down from the statements of the parties again repeated a few days after. My duty was to copy the statement in my hands: for I am not in the habit of doctoring documents. I am not your accuser, nor do I intend to be your judge; for though not being a missionary rector, you have no claim to be tried by the Commission of Investigation,[239] yet, in case I judge it necessary to bring the matter to an issue, I shall send it before that Commission. Though I use the words accuser & judge, yet you are aware that the Commission of Investigation lays no claim to legal powers; it is a voluntary court as arbitration courts are. Should the charge be pressed against you, and you rebut it, to no-one will your triumph be a greater subject of joy than myself; but I am at a loss to know what you refer to when you say you will prove this charge is as idle as others that have been brought. You surely do not mean the charge of kissing young girls in the confessional, for though you <u>denied</u> you did not <u>disprove</u> that charge: no man's denial is held to be a disproval of a charge.

You say that no man is bound to answer a charge of 4 months standing: pray, in what *carnot* did you find that dictum? Are no civil charges pressed after 4 months? Is there not usually a longer interval? If the case goes for a disproval: the Synod of Oscott has settled the method of procedure, which will be strictly adhered to. You say you do not expect your word to be worth more than the accusers': but on what are you relying when you tell us that you have not spent out of your own house more than 6 evenings since September? You expect that to be believed as proven & then you will prove your innocence on those days, but the first assertion will require proof. Your hundred witnesses will serve no purpose unless they can testify to your state on the day, hour & place named by your accusers. I shall not, however, interfere in the matter, nor shall I be present. My duty will be to do what the Church ordains under such circumstances. Do you solicit an investigation before the Committee?[240]

I remain very sincerely Yrs in Xt. Alexander Goss

---

239   *Decreta* explains the make-up and role of such a commission with regard to missionary rectors; see 11, 61–2, 176.
240   In another letter, of 28 January, Goss explained to Newsham that some of the witnesses claimed to have followed him to St Anthony's: 'They were not more than 2 or 3 yards, at times, distant from you & they heard persons remark as you stumbled along – "What a sight! That is a Catholic Priest! He is going to fall!"'

100.   *Very Rev. Can. Walmsley*   *3 February 1857*   *5/1/411*
My dear Canon,
I am informed that there are certain sums of money devised by the late Mr. Thos. Coulston[241] for charitable purposes. My opinion has been sought as to whether a portion would be well applied to the protection of young women of virtuous character. To this I answer that the object

is very deserving of your consideration: for the city of Liverpool, on account of its nearness to Ireland, is especially liable to be the receptacle for this class of our fellow Catholics. It is too an emigration port, & many flock to it who are unable to forward their journey, & who, after a few nights lodging in covered passages & by door steps, at length take to the streets & swell the great crowd of Catholic prostitutes that now invest this town. Many, no doubt, could be saved if at the first pressure of want when these poor creatures are thrown desolate on the streets there was a home of refuge to receive them. No inland town of the same Catholic population has the same claims upon it, for it is deluged with a population that was not born in it, but which flows into it from other parts, & hence one great cause of its wickedness.

Believe me very sincerely Yours in Xt. +Alexander Goss.

---

[241] Thomas Coulston, possibly father of Rev Gabriel Coulston DD, born Lancaster 1829, of the diocese but never served there; a man of means himself.

101. *Rev. T. Gibson*   *3 February 1857*   *5/1/412*

My dear Mr. Gibson,

You are not obliged to publish the banns between a Catholic & a Protestant, because the church does not allow, & hence does not legislate for such marriages; but the law forbidding such marriages in this country without the dispensation of the Ordinary, is not published in this Diocese, tho' I obtain from time to time a renewal of my power to grant dispensation. Seeing then that there need be no publication of banns, you must contrive to have them married in the Catholic Church, & tell the wife, according to the Synod, to procure a written consent from her husband to allow the children to be brought up Catholics. You must satisfy yourself before the marriage that there is no impediment. Notwithstanding the decision in the case of the parson remarrying persons previously married by a dissenter, the Cardinal said, when I was in London, that it would not be well to imitate the practice, as a jury or judge might give a very different decision in the case of the Established Church versus a Catholic priest. Let the parson remarry them, if he likes, but I think it would be a dangerous experiment for you to do it, & the wife might afterwards greatly irritate the husband if she were to tell him she had been advised so to act, i.e. to withold her consent.

Believe me very sincerely Yours in Christ. +A. Goss.

102.   *Rev. J. Gosford,*[242] *St. Wilfrid's, Preston   27 February 1857*

5/1/433

Dear Revd. Sir,

I am directed by the Bishop to acknowledge the receipt of your favour, & to say that he has great pleasure in allowing you to defer the reading of the Pastoral on the Exposition of the Blessed Sacrament, to another Sunday; but he regrets that you should have fixed your Charity Sermons for St. Mary's on the Sunday previous to the Collection for Ecclesastical Education. As that Collection is of some standing, & is advertised in the ordinary Directory, he is at a loss to conceive why some other of the 52 Sundays of the year should not have been selected in preference to that which precedes the said Collection. He hardly likes to glean upon a well reaped field, as he fears that he will not enjoy the privilege of Ruth, who was allowed to glean amongst the sheaves without reproach, nay, who had handfuls purposely dropped for her to gather. He thinks, therefore, that you had better defer the Collection for Ecclesiastical Education to some later Sunday.

I am, Very truly Your's [*sic*] in Xt. John Walker, Sec.

---

[242]   John Gosford SJ, 1818–1904.

103.   *Rev. R. Turpin*[243]   *7 March 1857*   *5/1/440*

My dear Mr. Turpin,

I have just returned from the erection of the Stations or Via Crucis at Lytham, & hasten to acknowledge the receipt of the sum of £10.9.6 by cheque, being the yearly dividend from the Jenkinson Trust for Ecclesiastical Education.[244]

I beg also to thank you for your own subscription of £1 to the Ecclesiastical Education fund of this Diocese, one of the most important, if not the most important charity of the day. You have ever given it your warm support. It has ever been my wish & it will be the aim of my episcopate to educate a native clergy for our wants, & to educate them well; for I am one of those who think that the Catholic clergy should stand at the head of education. Hence I would wish to have some at least amongst us who are acquainted with the various languages of Europe, as well also as with the biblical languages. The clergy of Lancashire have long been pre-eminent for their zeal, & I am anxious that they should be pre-eminent also for their learning.[245]

All unite in kind regards to you. Believe me, Very sincerely Yrs in Xt. +Alexander Goss.

---

[243]   Robert Turpin, 1806–63, r. at Scorton 1838–63.

[244]   The Jenkinson Trust produced just over £10 per annum; see AAL, FDC/S4/2/B/1–.

104.   [*Mr. Nasmyth Stokes*[246]]   *8 March 1857*   *5/1/441*
My dear Mr. Stokes,
I beg to thank you for your two communications which shall receive immediate attention. I am surprised at what you state about the spiritual state of the lace schools; for I was given to understand that one of the Jesuit fathers was in constant attendance. I will however confer with the Vicar in order to consider what can be done to carry out your suggestions. There seems to be great difficulty in keeping the children of the poor at school, whether industrial or other. The facilities of education seem to make them both saucy & indifferent. I am not so surprised at the state of St. Helen's schools,[247] for Can. Newsham puts himself forward as a cheap manager, & he acts & talks among all classes as if he believed himself to be the only efficient manager, & hence he is not open to advice.

I am greatly obliged to you for bringing this matter at once under my notice, & I will do what lies in my power to apply a suitable remedy. I have appointed Clerical Inspectors, but they are excessively slow in their movements.

With many thanks for calling attention to both cases, & wishing you every blessing, I remain truly Yrs in Xt. +Alexander Goss.

---

246   Scott Nasmyth Stokes, see n. 168.

247   St Helen's school was in Eldon Street. Interestingly, Newsham was highly praised by H.M. Inspector in 1852; see glowing report in Burke, *Catholic Liverpool*, 103. In 1870, only 144 of the 500 places available in the school were regularly filled; Burke, *Catholic Liverpool*, 190; see O'Neill, *St Anthony's*, 84–5, 122–4.

105.   *Rev. Dr. Corless*   *9 March 1857*   *5/1/446*
Education Fund
My dear Dr. Corless,
I write to thank you for your subscription to the Ecclesiastical Education fund during the past year. The collections also in your church are such as to shame many more pretending places, another proof of the importance which you deservedly attach to this charity. My aim is to educate not only a native clergy, but an ample supply of such clergy, & to educate them well. I am desirous that the Catholic Clergy of the Diocese should take the lead & stand preeminent in the county not only for their theological, but also for their secular knowledge. Should I be spared to carry out my views & should I be seconded therein by the clergy, I hope to see priests of the Diocese acquainted as well with the

languages of Europe as with the Eastern tongues necessary for biblical scholars. I do not mean to say all the clergy, but I trust there will be at least some. Nor ought the sciences to be forgotten. If a priest, particularly a country priest, has no literary resources, how will he spend the many vacant hours which remain to him after the faithful discharge of his duty? Do not isolation & want of occupation expose him to many temptations?

I have written at some length in thanking you, as I feel convinced that you fully appreciate the importance of the subject. Wishing you every blessing I remain sincerely yrs in Xt.

+Alexander Goss.

106. [*Mrs. Bennett*[248]]   *9 March 1857*   *5/1/447*

My dear Mrs. Bennett,

I regret that absence from home on business in North Lancashire, has prevented me answering your letter sooner. The treatment you have experienced at the hands of your late servant is cruel & inhuman. I could not have thought it possible for any servant to forget herself so far & to betray the trust placed in her, & to treat with such insolence one who had been so kind to her, & whose long sickness ought to have earned her sympathy; but you must forgive & forget, & it will be another jewel in the crown which I trust your long & patient suffeing will earn for you.

Dr. Fisher has succeeded to day in hearing of a girl, who is said to be clean & tidy & well behaved, & who, I hope, will suit you in the present emergency. He has desired her, thro' our housekeeper, to wait on you tomorrow, Tuesday. It is impossible to give an opinion of an untried person, but she has been well recommended as being clean & well behaved. I hope she will suit, & that she will never show the ingratitude which your late servant has exhibited. I am sorry to hear that you do not improve, but still even not to get worse, is sometimes an improvement. I do not fail to pray for you, & I hope God will preserve you in his holy keeping. Believe me your sincere & affectionate friend, Alexander Goss

---

248   It is clear from letter 258 that she was a generous benefactor to the Church; see AAL, FDC/S4/2/B/1-.

107. [*John Yates, Esq.*]   *11 March 1857*   *5/1/449*

My dear Mr. Yates,

I beg to call your attention to V. page 3 of the Industrial Schools Bill.[246] This clause is corrected by XI: but when we recollect how parents disown their children to relieve themselves from the burden of their maintenance, & how difficult it is to make them or the childrens' guardians to come forward when there is a question of their religion at the Kirkdale Industrial Schools, we may calculate the damage & ruin this will be to our poor Irish children in Lpool, Preston & Wigan. There is an impression in the House of Commons that we in Liverpool support this Bill. I suppose this arises from the public meeting held in the Town Hall by the Mayor, Jan. 26. 1857, which we attended. Now tho' pressed to second this resolution I refused on two grounds, 1o. that it would empower the police to kidnap our children, 2o. because I did not think that the State has a right to take children from the care of their parents. Both Mr. Pollock & Mr. Carter pressed me to second the resolution, but I refused & even threatened to oppose it, tho' for the sake of peace I refrained from doing so. Mr. Carter then seconded it in a temperate speech, & I consented to second the resolution which had been assigned to Mr. Carter. They are passing the Bill rapidly in the Commons. It was committed pro forma on the 6th & stands over for <u>to night</u>. I think we should lose no time in petitioning against it in the three towns enumerated above. Believe me sincerely Yours in Xt. +Alexander Goss.

---

[249] The Industrial Schools Act of 1857: children aged seven to fourteen could be forced to attend an industrial school if they were found to be homeless or otherwise in danger of falling into crime; it was extended in 1861 to include children found begging or guilty of minor offences otherwise punishable by imprisonment. See P. Horn, *The Victorian Town Child* (Stroud, 1997), 204; J. Duckworth, *Fagin's Children: Criminal Children in Victorian England* (London, 2002).

108. *Rev. J. Penswick*   *13 March 1857*   *5/1/452*

Rev. & dear Sir,

I write to thank you for your subscription to the Fund for the Education of Ecclesiastical Students during the last year. It is, I consider, the greatest charity of the Diocese, & the most important want of the day. Our numbers are yearly increasing, particularly in the towns, whilst our means of education are nearly stationary. Now if we have to preserve the vantage ground gained by those who have preceded us, if the future has to keep what the past & the present have gained, it can only be by having a regular supply of native clergy, educated from the people amongst whom they have to labour. The supply of priests from Ireland has very much diminished, whilst Australia & N. America, but ill supplied, are competing with us in the Irish market. Besides it is found that fewer youths are now offering themselves in Ireland so that already in some parts they are unable to supply their own wants. It is to ourselves, therefore, & to our own resources of lads & money that we must look, independent of any other consideration that might be urged.[250] There is nothing more beautiful than to see the old contributing to the education of the young: for having served God in the ministry to a good old age, they show themselves anxious to leave a race of spiritual children to take their place. Wishing you every blessing and praying that God may long preserve you amongst us, I remain Yours truly, +A. Goss.

---

250   In a similar letter to Rev. Mr. Crowe of Formby of 9 March, 1857, Goss spoke of the need for a native clergy, adding that the shortage could lead to the employment of 'external dubious characters'.

109.   [*John Yates Esq.*]   *14 March 1857*   5/1/454
My dear Mr. Yates,
I am informed by the Rev. Mr. Bradshaw of Holy Cross,[251] that there is now in the ragged school, Soho St., an Irish girl whom they refuse to deliver up to the mother. She has been there about 4 years with her brother. The boy has come out, but the girl refuses to go with the dirty Irish Catholics, & to her face she called her mother a liar in the presence of the Matron. The latter told Mr. Bradshaw that she got into the school 18 Catholic boys on the very day that he & the mother withdrew the brother of this refractory girl. The boy, who is, Mr. B. says, very intelligent tells him that the school master daily lectures them on the horrors & abominations of Catholics. If he is to be believed, there is only one Protestant boy in the establishment. Cannot the woman demand her daughter by a writ of habeas corpus, or is the girl's age, about 14, an impediment? Mr. B. has written to Ireland for her register, but has not yet received it.

Mr. Baines, who is a poor law guardian, says that some effort should be made to return more Catholics for the W.D. Union.[252] I am going to write to Major Blundell & Mr. Weld Blundell on the subject. Would it not be possible to have Mr. Corbally[253] – a gentleman at large – elected for W. Derby, & could he not be induced to stand? We are building churches & schools, & meanwhile our poor, young & old, are being devoured. Believe me very sincerely Yrs in Xt. +Alexander Goss.

---

251   Edward Joseph Bradshaw OMI, 1821–92. Holy Cross Mission, Liverpool, had been founded in 1849 and was run by the Oblates of Mary Immaculate.
252   The West Derby Poor Law Union: there were constant troubles over anti-Catholic attitudes; see, e.g., Burke, *Catholic Liverpool*, 132–3.
253   C. J. Corbally: prominent Irish councillor, see Burke, *Catholic Liverpool*, *passim* and 241–2. *Extracts*, 137, gives his obituary.

110.   [*Printed circular to clergy*[254]]   *16 March 1857*   UC/PA/U53
Dear Rev. Sir,
[*The diocesan visitation was opened on 27 May 1855; a detailed questionnaire accompanied this announcement, to be returned within twenty*

days of this present notice.] We have only further to add a request, that you will not answer the queries by yes or no, but that you will insert in the answer the substance of the question, so that your returns will be intelligible without necessitating recourse to the queries. To discharge this duty satisfactorily, you will find a tiresome labour; but you will be rewarded by the consciousness of having achieved a useful work, that will be handed down in the Archives of the Diocese for the information and guidance of posterity; and we need hardly add, that we feel assured, from the consoling zeal displayed by those to whom the questions were first addressed, that they will meet with a ready attention also from you.

We beg particularly to impress upon you the necessity of a faithful and speedy compilation of the Status animarum in the district assigned to you. The Council of Trent observes that it is an injunction by Divine precept on those who have the care of souls to know their own sheep; and the first Synod of Oscott enjoins all Rectors of Churches to draw up an exact account of the state of their respective Missions. No pastor, Barbosa observes, should be satisfied with knowing merely the number of his flock; he ought <u>himself</u>, personally, to know each family and each person in a family, their respective ages, the Sacraments they have received, and whatever else will enable him to provide for their salvation. [*There is reference here to the Visitation Questions already published.*]

Strictly speaking, as Baruffaldi notes,[255] the census ought to be taken yearly during Lent; or, at least, says Monacelli,[256] every third year, and two copies ought to be made out, one for the Missioner's own use, and the other to be deposited with the Bishop within fifteen days after Easter. This, with the heavy pressure, mental and physical, incident to Missionary life, it would be unreasonable to ask for, and we shall be satisfied with the sum of your labours as specified in No. VIII of the Visitation Questions, with the further addition of the number of Easter Communicants.

[*St. Charles Borromeo advises leaving room after each family for additions re births, First Communions, etc.*] The servants, male and female, should be entered immediately after, but in connection with the families in whose service they are living. [All this] will be of essential service to those who succeed, when you have been called to receive the reward of your labours. To benefit from the experience of the past, is one of the highest attributes of civilization, whilst to neglect it, is one of the most hopeless features of savage life.

As erroneous statements have been put forth regarding the numbers who attend service in our Churches, as compared with sectarians, we request that you will take steps to ascertain the numbers who attend the various services in the Church under your charge next Easter Sunday. [*To be done for all services*] by persons appointed to count the people as they go in and come out, to secure greater accuracy. In country Missions this will not be difficult, whilst in towns the labour will be greatly facilitated by the members of the Young Men's Societies. Doorkeepers, who have to take the pence of the people as they enter, cannot be relied on for this purpose, as the discharge of one duty is incompatible with the other. [*Returns to be made at the close of the Easter Indulgence. Missions are also to keep a Liber Defunctorum, and a Liber Sepultorum where appropriate.*]

Wishing you the mercies of this penitential season, and commending ourselves to the prayers of yourself and people, We remain affectionately Yours in Christ, +ALEXANDER, Bishop of Liverpool.

---

254 Parts of this long document have been omitted and summarised in brackets, keeping the original tenses.
255 Hieronimo Baruffaldi, 1675–1753/5, *Ad Rituale Romanum commentaria* (Venice, 1763 and later edns).
256 See n. 263.

111. [*Dean Richard Gillow*] *1 April* [*1857*]   5/1/461
My dear Dean,
I am sorry to hear that you have not been well: something, perhaps, may be owing to Lenten fare, something to the Spring season & changeable weather; but I hope the change of visiting the schools, if you do not over-fatigue yourself, will prove beneficial.

This morning's post has brought Father Weston's appeal.[257] He gives you credit for having taken every pain to come to a fair decision, & he says that the boundary laid down pleases neither party; but he does not draw the natural conclusion from that fact, that what limits the pretensions of both claimants has a prima facie appearance of justice & impartiality. He proposes what F[r]. Etheridge proposed, a commission of a Secular & Regular with a chairman selected by the two. Such an arrangement hardly seems to admit that the decision lies with the Bp. I shall not be in a hurry to answer his letter, as it is a matter that requires every deliberation.

Would it not be well to publish the arrangement for the Quarant'ore in the Preston Guardian: I dare say Mr. Buller could get it inserted, for it will be an important announcement for many of his readers.

Dr. Fisher is very busy with his Secretary, examining schools: he gives them a five hour dose at one spell, taking the boys one day & the girls another. Ever sincerely Yours in Xt. +Alexander Goss.

---

257 Thomas Weston SJ, 1804–67, superior at St Wilfrid's, Preston 1845–49, continued to serve in the town until 1863; James Etheridge SJ (1808–77), rector of the College of St Aloysius, was based at St Wilfrid's 1855–57. The boundary question in Preston was a

long-standing cause of dissension between Seculars and Jesuits. The unnamed dean was Richard Gillow, 1794–1864.

112.   *Rev. Mr. Callaghan*[258] [*added in pencil*]   *17 April 1857*   *5/1/471*
Dear Revd. Sir,
I shall require some time to examine the petition addressed to me for leave to have procession of the B.S. on certain days, in which the boys' & girls' guilds take part. No cause is assigned for such procession, which the crowded state of our churches renders it any thing but a devotion or honour to the B.S. & the presence of the gild girls renders it, to my mind, very objectionable. The presence of females, or rather their prominent presence in processions of the Bl. Sacrament appears to me to be one of the abominations imported from France: for as far as my reading goes it is prohibitory of their prominent presence on such occasions. I have seen them joining processions en masse, but never as a distinctive or attractive part of the procession, except in convents. I will however give the matter mature consideration & careful examination. Meanwhile I leave it to your discretion whether to have a procession or not on Low Sunday; but if you have it, do not allow girls to take part in it except in the body of the congregation. I remain, Very sincerely Yrs in Xt. +Alexander Goss.

---

[258]   Patrick Ignatius Callaghan OSB, 1829–59; o. 1854; listed in the *Directory* as being at St Mary's, Edmund Street, Liverpool, in 1857. Burke, *Catholic Liverpool*, 142, calls him O'Callaghan.

113.   *Rev. Mr. Holmes*[259]   *8 May 1857*   *5/1/476*
Rev. & Dear Sir,
I am appalled at the magnitude of the debt which encumbers the Church of St. Vincent of Paul, & at the certainty of its future income being adequate to do more than barely keep the clergy & pay its working expenses if it can even do so much. You will see then the necessity of making a united effort to collect additional subscriptions, for after the opening, public attention will be directed to other charities & the erection of other Churches.[260] My predecessor placed three priests at St. Vincent's in order that one at least, might be left at liberty to collect or aid in the collection of the funds. This duty has mainly fallen on one, though it was common to all. You will see, therefore, the necessity of carrying out the compact made with my predecessor. Whether the senior priest himself will undertake that duty, wholly or in part, or whether he will depute it to you or your confrere, must depend on himself; but it is imperative that one should be devoted mainly, if not exclusively, to that object, while he should receive every assistance from his brethren

either in accompanying or meeting the collectors as circumstances may permit. The work requires the active & energetic cooperation of all three, for it is a common not an individual duty.

Commending myself to your prayers, I remain very sincerely Yrs in Christ. +Alexander Goss.

---

[259] Peter Holmes, 1828–82; o. 1854, at St Vincent's 1854–60; he died of typhus fever caught during a sick call.

[260] It was opened in August that year; see Kelly, *English Catholic Missions*, 256. See also Introduction, p. xxii, for the 'pennies of the poor' tradition.

114. *The Ford Cemetery Commissioners*[261] *12 May 1857*   *5/2/27*
Very Rev. Brethren,
Since the receipt of your two resolutions dated April 17. & 24. complaining of the studied absence of the Very Rev. Canon Newsham, of his ignoring the authority of your very Rev. Board, & of his usurpation of all jurisdiction over the Cemetery, I have had an interview with the said Canon, in which he expressed his willingness to act in unison with the Board in the spirit of the principles laid down in the Diocesan Synod.[262] I trust therefore that you will experience no further difficulty in bringing matters to a satisfactory issue. I wish you, therefore, to meet speedily & require of you to forward me a Report on the subject:– stating all particulars regarding the purchase, the cost, the tenure on which it is held, the expense of management up to this period & probable weekly outlay; income & all other particulars that usually enter into a report, & I wish such official report, uniform in the size of the paper etc to be provided half yearly in June & December. I recommend also that you should draw up a code of laws or bye laws for its future management, which, if necessary, I will sign & sanction, so as to give them a binding power. Bear in mind, that the dead are placed especially under the Bp's care, so that they cannot be moved from grave to grave without his license [*sic*], under pain of censures, & that in giving authority to the Board, he gives it to it in its united or corporate capacity, so that none of its members can act without its delegation.

Given at St. Edward's, May 12. 1857. Alexander Goss. John Walker. Sec.

---

[261] On Ford Cemetery and Newsham, see O'Neill, *St Anthony's*, especially 87–9 and 342–3.

[262] The Second Synod (September 1856) issued a decree, 'On Fees Received for Burials': the priest performing the funeral should not keep the fees for himself but put them towards the maintenance of the mission; *Synodi*, 23, §III.

115. *The Archbishop of Trebizond   15 May 1857*   *5/2/29*
My dear Grace,

We are <u>daily</u> expecting to find a house for a Reformatory. We had fixed on one in Kirkham, were negotiating with the agent when a Prot. Gentleman at the request of the Prot. Vic. bought the house over our heads by electric Telegraph. Foiled there, we determined on the Isle of Man, but found from the Sec. of State that the Act did not extend to the Kingdom of Man. We are making every inquiry, & diligently, &, as soon as provided, we are promised a staff of Notre Dame nuns for the working of it. The delay has not arisen from any fault of ours, or from any want of energy; but from the difficulty of being suited.

I do not think there is any doubt about the Card. making the visitation in his own name if he be deputed. There is in Monacelli[263] a long formula for that purpose, delegating to him by special mention powers to visit what his principal has power to visit, & requesting him at the end to forward to the principal a report of his visitation, which would not be if the act ran in the name of the Principal. I think the fact of delegation should be rehearsed in your announcement, as we rehearse delegation by the Holy See in our Lenten Dispensations, because the visited might otherwise deny your authority. I made no laws or regulations, as the office of lawgiver belongs to [the] ordinary, but I enforced existing laws & regulations. I was received at door, etc; but I should think everything will depend on the extent of the powers deputed; if unlimited, you exercise them unlimited. Ever truly Yours. A. Goss. President [*sic*] joins me in kind regards. A. Goss

---

[263] Monacelli, F., *Formularium legale practicum fori ecclesiastici* (Venice, 1732).

116. *Rev. R. Gillow*   *20 May 1857*   *5/2/34*
My dear Dean,

The Vicar doubts whether government will allow you two hundred pounds towards enlarging your school unless you also raise two hundred; but I think it would be well to ascertain from the Privy Council what you are likely to receive. With a compact property like Fernyhalgh, it seems a pity to give government a hold for a slight consideration. The sacrifice on the part of the Church – viz. the land & existing schools – ought to be met by a corresponding advantage. It would however be well to be very certain, before you have a deed made out. I think government aid should be taken in all isolated or large schools: but in small schools, forming part of compact portions of Church property, I would not take government aid without an almost absolutely [*sic*] necessity; but I would take it if necessary. My fears are not so much for the property we give up, as for what we retain, the nature of the tenure of which they can learn from the release of that portion whereon the schools are built. Do, however, what your own prudence suggests.

I send Mr. Sidgreaves'[264] altar stone to Mr. Sharples,[265] as being consecrated & having to be fitted in the wooden altar, it ought not to be entrusted entirely to lay hands.

I suppose we shall meet on the 15th at Mr. Brockholes[266] if not earlier, as it is understood he is inviting his neighbours, & I suppose Fernyhalgh is not wide of Clayton.

Ever truly & sincerely Yours in Xt. A. Goss.

---

264 There was a Sidgreaves family who were important cotton merchants in Preston; a later letter (28 May 1866) gives their address as Ribbledale Place. They had a private chapel, though there was some doubt about their right to have one; see Doyle, 'Bishop Goss and the Gentry'.

265 Henry Sharples, 1812–74, brother of former coadj. Bp Sharples; at Alston Lane, Preston, 1849–74.

266 The Brockholes family of Claughton: Gillow (*Bibliographical Dictionary*) says the original recusant family ended in 1759 and in the nineteenth century was represented by William Fitzherbert-Brockholes. (Goss's 'Clayton' was the phonetic form of Claughton.)

117. *Rev. P. Fairhurst*   *30 May 1857*   *5/2/39*

Dear Revd. Sir,

I am at a loss to imagine what grounds you can have for not considering your present position at St. Alban's an appointment. It is not usual (I believe, for some technical reasons) to appoint except for a time, tho' such appointments are seldom cancelled except at the request of the person appointed. It was not my intention to have removed you from St. Anthony's, but I was told that you felt so strongly on your remaining there (tho' to me you spoke not unfavourably of the matter) that I allowed you to leave it. Since your appointment to St. Alban's, I refused to nominate you to assist Can. Walmsley; but after repeated entreaty on his part, I promised to allow you to go, if you wished, but I declined doing any thing more than giving my sanction to your own expressed wish.

I believe your own predilection – as it is my own – is for a country mission, but I have none at my disposal, nor if I had, should I feel justified in putting you at it; for you are now in the prime of life & it is very desirable that you should fit yourself for the charge of a town mission in due course. You cannot sigh for the country more ardently than I have done, or than my Vicar General has done, but our life in the sacred ministry is a life of sacrifices, & having set our hand to the plough, we must not look back. There is a wide field before you, in which your labours will be gratefully appreciated by the people you serve.

Regretting that you should have been in uncertainty without adopting the simple expedient of writing earlier, & wishing God's blessing on your labours, I remain very sincerely Yours in Xt.

+Alexr. Goss.

118. *Rev. Mr. Seed S.J.*   *30 May 1857*   *5/2/40*
Dear Revd. Sir,

Some time ago Can. Greenhalgh mentioned to me that you had expressed a wish that I should do something for the part of Wigan, mentioned in your letter of the 28th & that you had offered to lend every assistance. This, I imagine, was with a view to freeing the upper part of the town from the unseemly spectacle of two churches, standing so near as St. Mary's & St. John's.[267] As this seemed to involve the abandonment of St. Mary's, if I undertook the work, I desired Can. Greenhalgh to make some further enquiries, which resulted in his informing me that you had no authority for making any definite proposition, but that you had concluded by renewing the expression of your wish that I should at once establish a mission there, & divide the town into districts, as the rest of the Diocese is divided. I shall be glad to see you at any hour on Wednesday next.

Commending myself to your prayers & desiring my remembrance to Mr. Selby,[268] I remain very sincerely Yours in Xt. +Alexander Goss.

---

[267] A bitter public quarrel between the Jesuits and the Seculars had resulted in 1817 in two new churches being opened in Wigan, less than a hundred yards apart: St John's, staffed by Jesuits, and St Mary's, staffed by Seculars; no agreement had been reached about the districts to be served by each and this was still the case down to the 1870s. In December 1858 Goss wrote to the Secular priest at St Patrick's, Wigan, claiming that he should have a curate to 'hold his own' against the Jesuits' appropriation of the outlying districts of the town (5/2/421, to Rev. H. McCormick). See Introduction pp. xix, xli.
[268] Thomas Selby SJ, 1824–90.

119. *[Fr Lans CSSR]*   *30 May 1857*   *5/2/41*
My dear Father Lans,

With reference to the screens & stalls at Bp. Eton, what took place between Mr. Baines & myself was this. He said they were advertised in the Tablet for sale, but you wished me to have the first offer in case I were disposed to purchase. I replied that I had nothing to say to their being offered for sale: but with reference to my purchasing them, I could not think of buying what my Predecessor had bought & had not sold, as the Diocese, through the Bp., would thus be paying twice for the same thing. You are no doubt aware that at the sale of Bp. Eton by the Bp. to the Redemptorist Fathers, no charge was made for the Church & its fittings. Before the sale, the Bp. had empowered me to remove whatever I wished, but I declined to do so. It is not from this offer that I made the remark, but from the fact that the Bp. did not sell the Church & its fittings to the Fathers. I forebore to say that their having been given was a reason why they should not be sold; but I simply said, which I repeat, that being on sale I could not, as Bp. of Liverpool, feel justified in buying property which had been bought by my predecessor, & had not been sold by him. Beyond that, I did not then, nor do I now, offer any remark. I know that your duty is to do the will of your superiors, & you need have no fear of any unpleasantness arising. Wishing every success to your new church I beg to remain

 Ever most sincerely Yrs in Xt. +Alexr. Goss.

120. [*Rev. T. Crowe*[269]] *2 June 1857*   *5/2/44*
My dear Mr. Crowe,
I beg to thank you for your kind donation to my maintenance & expenses. I hope that eventually some charitable body will relieve the Bp. of the reputed wealthiest diocese in England from the hard condition of seeking outdoor relief from the parish.

 I have spoken to the Vicar about Mr. Comberbach[270] & he fears that, at his age, he will take badly to the fag of an English mission. One Belgian priest left us before he had been here six weeks. Tho' an Englishman, yet Mr. Comberbach has been more accustomed to the amenities of society than fall to the lot of most of our priests, & unless he retains a practical remembrance of the wear & tear of an English mission, I say this to prevent the possibility of his thinking himself deceived; for from his letters last year, he seemed to me a man who would shrink from the hard reality & depravity of Liverpool life, which appals the Vicar, tho' accustomed to a town. There is plenty of work & great need of workers: but it is impossible for a man past middle life to buckle on his armour to encounter the mudlarks of an abandoned town. I should like Mr. Comberbach clearly to understand our position. In Belgium I believe the clergy do not live in community as here.

 The trio desire their affectionate regards: on Saturday we hope to add a fourth in the person of Mr. Ray.[271] Ever most truly Yrs in Xt. Alexr. Goss.

---

269 Thomas Crowe, 1792–1862; he was at Formby 1851–62.

270 Fitz-L gives a Charles Comberbach, 1801–91, in Southwark and also in Birmingham for a short time; a convert, ordained in 1825.

271 James Ray, 1829–78, the first student from St Edward's to be ordained; he taught there 1857–66. He was revered as a saint; see Plumb, *'Found Worthy'*.

121. *Rev. J. Grant S.J.,*[272] *St. Francis Xavier's, Lpool*   *3 June 1857*
5/2/45

My dear Fr. Grant,

I have great pleasure in granting you leave for Benediction one day in each month, in addition to those already ceded to St. Francis Xavier's, for the benefit of the Sodality of young men, over whom you are Director, & I hope this privilege will be found conducive to the interests of religion & the increase of piety amongst those who are the flower of the Church, wherever they can avoid the seductive influences employed for their spiritual destruction.

Wishing you every blessing on your labours, I remain Very sincerely Yrs in Xt. +Alexander Goss.

---

[272] Ignatius Grant SJ, 1820–1904.

122. *Very Rev. R. Brown, Lancaster*   *8 June 1857*   5/2/49

My dear Dean,

1o. When at Cottam on visitation, we examined the question of the Eaves [?*Eames*] property & I think Dr. Corless admitted that he had no further say in the matter. I spoke to the V.G. & I understood him to say that he proposed to confer with you & Newhouse on the occasion of the Clergy meeting. 2o. I think you might remove the bodies <u>now</u> from [*lost word*] without any opposition from any quarter, tho' opposition might be made by bigotry after you had sold it. If you fear, the Inspector, I conceive, could authorise it: if not, the Secretary of State would on being told that the chapel in D.S.[273] was crowded, & that you had a cemetery out of town to which they could be removed during the night. After what the Inspector has said I think you could safely remove them, & the sooner the better. 3o. I shall be on Visitation in the North after the Assumption, & can then consecrate the Cath. portion of the gen. Cem. if you think they are not likely to disturb our possession of it, owing to so few being buried there in consequence of having already an ample & beautiful cemetery for Catholics. 4o. Mr. Holland[274] wants a month in Ireland, where he has some business. You need have no fear about Mr. Cooke now the warm weather has set in. At the end of the month I will give Mr. Cooke leave of absence for 6 or 8 weeks, & will appoint Mr. H. to supply for him in his absence: but I will say nothing to either about a permanency. You will thus see how Mr. H. suits & whether Mr. Lenon[275] [*sic*] is likely to come out of College. I am pleased with what I have seen of Mr. H. & I think you will find him a worker. He is new material & therefore his formation must depend on yourself. But I shall see you before he comes to you, so that we can talk the matter over in <u>seasonable</u> time.

Plymouth Cathedral, you will have learnt, is a ruin:[276] but it was not built on a rock nor *super fundamentum apostolorum*. Its fall will make Mr. Hickey[277] very nervous. He must have been hard up for an ally when he discarded the Master & was content with his men. The fable of the man & his ass is applicable to all. Ever truly & sincerely Yours in Xt. Alexander Goss.

---

273   Dalton Square, Lancaster; the church was opened in 1799, with a burial vault; a new plot was bought outside the town in 1847 and a cemetery opened there 1849–50; the foundation stone of a new church was laid April 1857. Presumably this letter refers to the removal of remains from the vault to this new cemetery; or it could be to the new town cemetery opened in 1855, with a section reserved for Catholic burials. See R. N. Billington and J. Brownbill, *St Peter's, Lancaster. A History* (London 1910), 103. The Dalton Square church was sold to the Total Temperance Society in 1859 and later became the Hippodrome Theatre.

274   Jeremiah Holland, 1829–88; o. 1857, c. at Lancaster to 1858, then Eldon Street, Liverpool.

275   James Lennon, 1828–1900, o. 1859 but stayed on the staff at Ushaw, becoming president 1886–88.

276   Architects for the cathedral were the Hansom brothers. Building started in 1856 but 'construction problems' and the firing of heavy guns in Plymouth Sound (!) caused a collapse in 1857, before completion (see www.plymouthcathedral.co.uk, accessed October 2013). It is not clear why the Latin tag (not built 'on the foundation of the apostles') is relevant here.

277   Michael Hickey built a new church at Garstang 1857–58; the reference to 'the Master' is not clear, perhaps the builder. The fable is, presumably, Aesop's 'The man, the boy and the donkey', with the moral 'try to please all and you please none'.

123.   *Very Rev. Can. Greenhalgh*   *8 June 1857*   *5/2/50*

My dear Canon,

I fear we shall have to put off the blessing of the Cemetery till after the Assumption, for there is hardly suitable time before the 15th as the people have had no notice.[278] Whenever done, it should be advertised to the people on the previous Sunday. Meanwhile, it would be well to see the document prepared, as was the case at Preston; for the laws of the Church are very stringent & I believe that all the Bps are not prepared to consecrate the Catholic portion of public cemeteries, unless they be separated by wall fence [*sic*]. This I do not require but only that the Catholic portion should be made over to us, as free from the control, & as irrevocably, as the Prot. portion is made over to Prots. In answer to Mr. Walmsley apply for the document already made out, as it will have to be kept in the archives of the Deanery of Wigan & I shall have to preserve a copy of it in the Epis: Archives. The same would be done with the Bp. of Chester.

As far as myself am concerned, I could have come any day this week as I am quite disengaged except on Thursday, but I think the people would reasonably complain at not having had notice. Besides, the document should be previously examined, as upon its wording rests the lawfulness of the consecration. Ever truly Yrs in Xt. +A. Goss.

[*Two postscripts*:]

The new *Casus Morales* leaves by this post.[279]

Poor Plymouth Cathedral!

---

[278]   Presumably Goss was not going to be in the area before 15 August, but the gap seems unnecessarily long.

[279]   The cases to be discussed at the clergy conferences: *Questiones Morales de Quibus Deliberabitur in Conventibus sub Praesidentia V. F. Dioeceseos Liverpolitanae* (Liverpool, 1855–62); copy in AAL.

124.   *Very Rev. Can. Bagnall*[280]   *8 June 1857*   *5/2/51*

My dear Canon,

I send you by this post a copy of my Visitation Questions & of my last *Casus Morales*. The Vic. Gen. has already sent Dr. Weedal[281] copies of the previous *Casus*.

With regard to the Visitation questions, I must remind you that, when they were issued, I was not a member of any administration Board, & that consequently I had no means of obtaining any information except as Visitor: I did not exist in any other capacity to [*sic*] the Diocese.

Again I designed the questions to act as hints, so that knowing for a considerable time beforehand what would be required, the clergy might prepare accordingly & thus be found watching.

Further I was desirous to have <u>on paper</u> the actual state of each mission after the restoration of the hierarchy, in order that it might be bound up & put into the archives of the Diocese: for, as you will see, much of the information sought could have been more easily obtained by actual inspection; but this would have thrown on myself the labour of describing the actual state of things. I mention these views to excuse the apparently useless minuteness of many of the questions. This, however, I say without fear of contradiction, that they do not trench [*sic*] on the rights or liberties of the clergy: for tho' I ask the amount of fees, it was not with the intention of legislating on them. Retributions for masses are perhaps the most inviolable fees that a priest can claim, yet you will find in Monacelli. Form. Leg. [*word illegible*] Pars III. Tit. II. Form. IX & X. [*added,* vid. this & vol. II in append.] that Innocent XII orders under pain of suspension that books should be kept in the Sacristy for their entry.[282] I have chap. & verse for every thing I have set down. The clergy of Eng. are an honour to the Church for the care they take of God's house. The answers to the Visitation Questions chronicle that care for the edification of posterity. Ever truly Yrs in Xt. A. Goss.

280   Rudolphus Bagnall, of the Birmingham Diocese, 1801–83.

281   Henry Weedall, 1788–1859, president of Oscott 1825–40; Provost and VG.

282   Innocent XII, 1691–1700. His constitution '*Nuper*', December 1697, dealt with the proper recording of Mass stipends. For Monacelli see n. 263.

125.   *Very Rev. P. Greenough Prov. Ebor. O.S.B.*[283]   *29 August 1857*
5/2/57

My dear Provincial,

I am grieved to hear that there is likely to be some unpleasantness at Wrightington[284] in consequence of the removal of the Rev. Mr. Margison;[285] & I am surprised that you should have proceeded to such removal without even mentioning the matter to me. Wrightington is a sort of chaplaincy with care of souls, & tho' Mr. Scarisbrick may not dispute your right to move one of your Religious, yet he may refuse to sanction or admit a new appointment. May God grant that no future evil may result from the course you have adopted.

Wishing you every blessing I remain, Sincerely Yrs in Xt. +Alexander Goss.

283   Peter (Ignatius) Greenough OSB, 1801–70.

284   Wrightington Hall, near Standish; originally the seat of the Dicconsons, then of the Scarisbricks. See V. Marsh, *St Joseph's, Wrightington: A History* (Chorley, 1969). For troubles re. appointing family chaplains, see letters 287, 304.

285   Thomas (Maurus) Margison OSB, 1814–91.

126.   *Very Rev. Can. Newsham   1 September 1857*   *5/2/58*

Very Revd. & dear Sir,

Your soul will never enjoy peace if you allow it to be disquieted by what is said against you, or if you allow yourself to endeavour to find out the authors of such reports. You teach your people to bear wrongs patiently & to forgive the injury; is it not your duty to do likewise?

Though provoked, I have previously declined to name the source of the accusations against you, & must still decline to do so; but allow me to ask in what letter I said that they emanated from the congregation? If I wrote it, I wrote it not without evidence of its truth. In reference, apparently, to a decree of visitation, you single out two facts – the having offered up the holy sacrifice in fifteen minutes, & the having heard from 30 to 40 confessions in an hour – & you demand the restoration of your character – I suppose by the cancellation of the decree – on the grounds that a female, the supposed source of information, has given you a certificate of the falsehood of these charges. Now if my decree be referred to, allow me to say that it was not based on that evidence. I am not responsible for what your Reverend Confreres may say or be reported to say; but I am responsible for the accuracy of the facts recorded in my decree. With regard to their removal, I consider that neglect of duty & not personal feeling ought to form the ground for such a step. If that exists & be proved to exist to an extent to warrant their removal, you may rely on my doing my duty, though I might not in such act deem it necessary to allege such neglect. I remain very sincerely Yours in Xt. A. Goss.

127.   *Rev. Mr. Dujardin*[286]   *2 September 1857*   *5/2/59*
Rev dear Sir,
I am informed by the Vicar that Mrs. Picavance placed money in yr [*sic*] hands for the journey & pension of her daughter in Belgium, & that much less has been paid for her maintenance than, Mrs. Picavance thinks, should have been paid by you; & that other people have, or had pecuniary claims on you, for which they have or had difficulty in procuring a settlement from you:– & moreover, he, the Vicar, has written three times to you, & has received no answer, & that up to a late date, you had given no satisfaction to Mrs. Picavance. I consider that in future you shd. live with the other Clergy of St. Mary's, that yr expenses may be curtailed, & thus, no further disedification be given to the faithful. I give you however a month for the completion of yr arrangements: but, if you have not complied with this instruction by the 1st of October next, you must consider yr Missionary faculties in this Diocese to be withdrawn.

Wishing you every blessing, I remain very sincerely Yrs in Xt.
+Alexander Goss.

---

[286] According to O'Neill (*St Anthony's*, 125, 480–1) there was a Rev. F. du Jardin (a Belgian) at St Anthony's, Liverpool, 1855–57; see n. 319.

128.   *Rev. Bulbeck O.S.B.*[287]   *4 September 1857*   *5/2/60–1*
Dear Rev. Sir,
I did not understand your letter in the sense you suppose; but my doubts as to the identity of the two persons arose from her having presented herself to you, when to me she expressed herself so satisfied with the Jesuit Father. I have never implied, nor, in fact, thought that she possessed any undue affection for Mr. Gibson. You may rest assured that I am not acting without knowing her case, yea knowing it more fully than Mr. G. Grace does not bring persons to the danger of suicide, or despair, tho' its extraordinary workings may earn for those in whom it works the epithet of cracked from the world; nor does God lead souls in whom he is working extraordinarily to the youngest Confessors, nor does love of him make persons weak minded.

Wishing you every blessing I remain sincerely Yrs in Xt. +Alexander Goss.

---

287 William Bulbeck, as above, n. 143. The letter concerns Miss Clements and Fr Henry Gibson; see n. 233.

129. *E. W. Pugin Esq.*[288]   *24 September 1857*   *5/2/73*

My dear Pugin,

I have received the working drawings for the Eldon St. Church.[289] The tower, however, must not diminish the nave or increase the width of the aisles; for it is most important that the original features of the church be preserved in that respect. I don't suppose the tower will ever be built, but if built, it must stand at the end of the aisles on a distinct foundation, but must not be allowed to interfere with the erection on the original plan. I did not wish my suggestions to go farther than a little change in the doors & a sketch of a tower. I hope that the drawings sent down will be serviceable for the original plan. One door for each aisle, & one door for [the] centre of the church: there must be a passage down [the] centre, as in last plan. The side chapel must be retained. There must be no door by the apse leading to church & sacristy, but only a door into the sacristy.

Now for Westby.[290] I fear I have misled you as to size. It should seat 350, & will require no standing room, & no font outside, as baptisms will be rare. Could not the organ loft be above porch so as not to damage W. window? I send a rough tracing for house & church, compounded of yours minus the long passage &, of course, picturesqueness. There should be privy & latrine outside the yard, for the people, as it is a country place. The décor must be plain, but with a pretty belfry. The whole church will be exposed to strong West winds. I am sorry to have given such a [? *word illegible*] of this church. I shall be from home till Nov. except for a day occasionally. They will know at St. Edward's where I am. Yrs truly A. Goss.

---

288 E. W. Pugin, 1834–75, son of the famous A. W. Pugin; this is one of many letters. See R. O'Donnell, in *ODNB*.

289 Eldon Street: Our Lady of Reconciliation: the foundation stone was laid by Goss on 2 February 1859 and the church opened the following year; Kelly, *English Catholic Missions*, 257, calls it 'French gothic'. See letter 226 and Sharples, *Liverpool*, 255; the photo shows Goss did not always get his way.

290 Westby: Kirkham, Lancs, St Anne's; see Kelly, *English Catholic Missions*, p. 423: 'Early English Gothic'. Now served from Kirkham.

130. *Rev. Mr. Coll*[291]   *25 September 1857*   5/2/74

My dear Mr. Coll,

I beg to congratulate you on your elevation to the holy order of priesthood, & I pray that God may grant you many years of health & strength for the display of your zeal in his service. The work is great & the labourers, I regret to say, few; still by his blessing much has been achieved, & much still remains to be done.

I am anxious that you should have a fair chance of regaining your strength, & hence I write by today's post to the Rev. Mr. Carr of the Isle of Man, to say that you will be with him for Sunday, October 4th. I know of no place likely to prove as beneficial; for the climate is healthy & the scenery beautiful, & the work light; for you will be a third priest where previously there have been only two. This arrangement will last till the meeting of Synod, Nov. 4. when I shall have an opportunity of seeing you & learning how you are. You will also be examined about the same time;[292] but meanwhile you may exercise the usual missionary faculties of this diocese, copies of which you will find in the Island. Wishing you every blessing & success in your new sphere of action, I remain truly Yrs in Xt. +Alexander Goss.

---

[291] John Coll, b. 1829 and educated at Ushaw. See letter 182 and n. 374.

[292] Examinations for faculties for junior clergy, they became known irreverently as the 'November handicaps'.

131. *Rev. J. Nugent, Catholic Institute*   *10 October 1857*   5/2/77

My dear Mr. Nugent,

I am in receipt of your favour on the subject of Father Honorius,[293] & will give it my attentive consideration before the close of next week: for it is now too late to remove a priest from Blackstock St. without being able to send another in his place. It is rather hard on Mr. Vandepitte to remove a priest from so crowded a district in order to send him to another where the necessity is less urgent. I have every desire to give you rest & help; but, at the same time, I have ever felt that you are too anxious to have a larger staff than necessary about you. Neither do I underrate either the advantages or importance of the Institute, but I think that its strength lies in working out its legitimate objects. This is what I have always acted on at St. Edward's, so that beyond our own walls we are unknown. If we had done otherwise, we should have been bankrupt. We have worked the place without the aid of collections or grants of public money: for the money collected for Ecclesiastical Education does not come to us, but goes to pay for the education of boys at any College at which they are studying for this Diocese, when existing funds cannot meet the pension usually paid. The questions addressed to you, most of which the Vicar wrote, were not altogether financial: I gave them to you the very last time you were here. Beyond the day & night school, there is an indefiniteness in your views, which I have never been able to comprehend either from your conversation or letters, or from those of Mr. Gibson. I will do what I can for you, so as to give you that rest which I believe to be necessary for you; for I am sorry to have from the Vicar a very indifferent account of your health.

Wishing you a speedy recovery & every blessing, I remain sincerely Yours in Xt. A. Goss.

---

293   Fr Honorius Magini, a former CP, is given as being at the CI in the 1858 *Directory*, but by December 1858 Nugent was asking Goss to remove him, whether there was a replacement for him or not (letter 5/2/422). Magini had previously been in London; the 1861 *Directory* has him at Broadway. See letter 264 of June 1860 to him there: he has been in serious trouble and Goss refuses to have him back in the diocese. No biographical details are available.

132. *Rev. J. Nugent*   *14 October 1857*   *5/2/83*

My dear Mr. Nugent,

I write by to day's post to Fr. Honorius to request him to proceed to your aid at the Institute during your indisposition. I hope, however, that God will so far protect you that you will not long require his services. I hope you will have more satisfaction in him than you lately had in your previous helpmate, who, notwithstanding his goodness will soon come to a dead halt unless he practically learns to obey some other guidance than that in Nile St.[294]

I am glad to learn that you are working your day & night schools well, as in that, by universal acknowledgement, lies the strength of the Institute. By aiming at a multiplicity of objects you weary your spirit, & do not achieve that good which follows from a steady adherence to one plan. Excitable men, like yourself, who are ever sighing for quiet yet cannot live out of bustle, win by a dash; but yet it is the steady untiring plodder that does the abiding good. I fervently trust that the rest, to a certain extent at your disposal, will prove beneficial to you. Entire rest no one can have that has the solicitude of a large establishment, even tho' he were bodily absent.

Wishing you every blessing I remain truly Yours in Xt. +Alexander Goss.

---

294   The 'helpmate' was Henry Gibson; Nile Street, the site of the house run by Miss Clements: see n. 233.

133. *Deanery of St. Oswald's*   *19 October 1857*   *5/2/85*

My dear Dean,[295]

I am informed that in St. Mary's Southport, in the Deanery of St. Oswald's, there took place a religious service on a day, known as the fast day, appointed by authority of the Crown or by the Queen as Head of the Church in England:[296] & that on that day there was read the Pastoral of some Bishop or Archbishop, enjoining a collection & that a collection was made in obedience to such injunction. It is your duty as Dean to make inquiry & to report on the matter: for it is heretical to recognise the authority of the crown in spirituals: & no Episcopal letter, except that of the Ordinary, can without his sanction or authority, be read in any public chapel or church of a Diocese. The Ordinary is the fons et origo of jurisdiction in a Diocese, so that nothing that affects the cure of souls can be done, even by Regulars, without his sanction & delegation.

In a Deanery which, I am told, is especially jealous of the rights of the clergy, & puts forth, for the imitation of its brethren a manifesto against Episcopal encroachment, it is important that in the advocacy of their own, the clergy should not tread on the rights of others. The Dean is the 'eye' of the Bishop & represents him in all ecclesiastical matters placed under his jurisdiction, & hence is bound to watch over & protect the rights of the Ordinary within the limits of his Deanery.

Wishing you every blessing, I remain sincerely Yours in Xt. +Alexander Goss.

---

[295] Richard Hodgson, 1798–1879; canon, VF and MR at Burscough 1850–71. It was in his deanery that the clergy objected to the cathedraticum tax, causing major trouble at the synod that month; see the following letters and 152 to Errington (7 January 1858, 5/2/149–54).

[296] A day of national fast and humiliation was declared by the Queen for 7 October 1857 in connection with the Indian Mutiny; in a pastoral letter Wiseman called for a collection to help priests working as CFs in India, dispossessed religious there, and to relieve distress (see *The Tablet*, 10 and 17 October 1857). He asked Catholics to observe Rosary Sunday in this cause. He was strongly attacked by *The Times* in one of its bitter anti-Catholic outbursts.

134. *Rev. Mr. Walker*[297]   *9 November 1857*   *5/2/92*

My dear William,

When I heard that your name was attached to the Bill of Indictment[298] against me for the levying of the Cathedraticum, an imprescriptible right, I could not but feel *Et tu Brute*. When I called to mind our early friendship, the frequent intercourse & the many letters, that had passed, I could not but feel, perhaps too bitterly feel, that I was alone in friendship, as well as dignity. Your letter has removed this unpleasant impression, & I efface from my mind the recollection of a false step, so handsomely withdrawn.

I am assured by a Jesuit that not one of their body signed the Indictment, & furthermore that I shall find them to be the firmest support of my Episcopacy.[299] Yet if there was amongst them any not-right-minded man, he must, on the day of Synod, have received value for his money, when he beheld the Bishop baited by the Secular Clergy, who ought to be the firmest supports of his See, for the amusement of the Regulars, [*three words unclear*] as they leaned forward with ill concealed glee to watch the gladiatorial show.

Seeing the use – the unauthorised use – made of the Burscough Resolutions, I think you ought to write to the mischievous author of the agitation to withdraw your name from the Indictment.

Wishing you every blessing, I remain sincerely Yrs in Xt. +Alexander Goss.

---

297   William Walker, 1820–93, at this time curate at St Augustine's, Preston.

298   'Bill of Indictment': Goss's name for the petition against him at the Synod on the subject of the cathedraticum.

299   There is a certain irony here: the Jesuits constantly sniped at Goss's authority; see Peter Doyle, 'Jesuit Reactions to the Restoration of the Hierarchy: The Diocese of Liverpool, 1850–1880', *RH* 26:1 (May 2002), 210–28.

135.   *Rev. R. Taylor*[300]   *9 November 1857*   *5/2/94*

Dear Mr. Taylor,

However much I may have felt disposed to yield to a feeling of displeasure on learning that you had signed a protest against the legality of an Episcopal enactment, yet the frank way in which you have atoned for an unintended mistake, banishes every unpleasant feeling from my mind, & I freely forgive & forget the share which you unwittingly had in this matter. I had flattered myself that, whatever might be the failings of my clergy, they were at least free from the taint of radicalism in their notions of church government: am I mistaken? Even in <u>political</u> matters I do not know any scene to parallel the exhibition on St. Charles' day, unless it be when Charles I was arraigned at Whitehall to be tried by <u>his own subjects</u> for having laid illegal imposts on his people. It is competent for the clergy to seek a mitigation of an enactment that presses heavily on them, & any Bp. as in duty bound would receive their petition with kindness, if urged with becoming modesty & reverence; but the clergy violate all ecclesiastical propriety when they claim to be allowed to set forth arguments before the Bishop's own subjects, against the legality of his acts. I think you ought to write summarily & unconditionally to the mischievous author of this agitation, to require your name to be erased from the Bill. Wishing you every blessing, I remain sincerely Yrs in Xt. +Alexander Goss.

300   See n. 175. A similar letter of the same date to Rev. E. Swarbrick (5/2/93) argued that such conduct 'could not be tolerated even in England where liberty verges on licentiousness'. See also letter 137.

136.   [*Rev. Mr. Brown*]   *20 November 1857*   *5/2/99*
My dear Mr. Brown

I do not think that Mr. Holland's case offers any difficulty, as regards the nuns. He is not the Confessor of the house, & if he were, he would have no authority to see any of the community except in the Confessional. It is clearly therefore the Superior's duty to deny him, basing her denial upon rule. Her fear of his not saying mass for them at extra times can afford her no excuse for neglect of duty, & mass said under such circumstances can be of very little spiritual profit, because it is a privilege purchased at the expense of duty. She has no right to expect you to interfere, unless either Mr. Holland or the nun refuse compliance with her commands.

I am glad that Mr. H. has become more attentive to some branches of his work & that he is trying to make himself more amiable. You should not, however, let him neglect the schools: for that is the great fault of the rising generation of priests.

The Burscough Conference, not as Conference but in the Dean's house, have resolved to print & circulate & bring before the H. See, Mr. Worthy's essay on the Cathedraticum. It is the most pitiable of all our Conferences, & yet destined, I think, to arouse feelings that will not be allayed for years. Printing is a dangerous experiment: they may burn their fingers.

I <u>fear</u> Swarbrick's policy will be to monopolise Miss Dalton for Thurnham.[301]

Ever sincerely Yours in Xt. A. Goss.

301   Miss Dalton of Thurnham was a very generous benefactor, see n. 230 above; James Swarbrick (1822–98) had become rector there in 1857. Richard Brown of Lancaster was dean. See n. 398 below.

137.   *Rev. B. Oreilly*[302]   *21 November 1857*   *5/2/106*
Dear Revd. Sir,

I beg to thank you for your favour of the 20th. It contains the expression of sentiments for which, up to a late period, I had ever given you credit & had endeavoured by my acts & words in your regard to show that such was my belief in you. If you, however, feel so deeply a certain pain [*word not clear*], as implying the possibility of your lending yourself to an act you condemn, do you think that I could feel unmoved the degradation of being made by a body of the secular clergy, acting together & by concert, a spectacle for the amusement of the Regulars? You will search the whole of ecclesiastical history in vain for a precedent of the treatment to which I was subjected. The right to petition does not give a right to catechise the Bishop, much less to lecture him or to attempt to show that his acts are unconstitutional & against law. A synod is not the tribunal before which to bring the Bishop to answer for the reasonableness or legality of his administration, but it is an assembly of clergy called together to receive from the Bishop, modestly & reverently, words of reproof or encouragement, according as he is satisfied or not with their discharge of the duties he has entrusted to them during the last year. Neither the levying of Cathedraticum nor the passing of decrees requires by law the consent of the clergy: in these matters the Bp. acts jure suo.

Wishing you very blessing I remain sincerely Yrs. in Xt. +Alexander Goss

---

302   Bernard O'Reilly, 1824–94, succeeded Goss as Bishop of Liverpool in 1873. At this time r. of St Vincent de Paul's, Liverpool, he was a cousin of John Worthy who began the cathedraticum agitation.

138.   *Right Rev. Dr. Wareing,*[303] *Bp of Northampton*
               7 December 1857   *5/2/110*

My dear Lord,

You are aware, from the discussions that have taken place at our meetings, of the deplorable state in which Valladolid has been for many years, & of the efforts of Mr. Guest to set matters to right. For some time back he has written to me the most imploring letters for a Professor. I have written to the Cardinal to ask if he could suggest anyone; but I have received no answer. Mr. Guest has again written to say that his health cannot much longer stand the harass [*sic*] & isolation of his position, & he has begged of me to apply to your Lordship for the loan of Canon Dalton[304] for one year & a half. I hope you will consent to spare him; for you will thereby be deprived of his services for a time, yet he will more than compensate for his absence on his return by the additional knowledge & stimulus he will acquire in a foreign & a Catholic country. Your consent to allow him to go will confer a favour on every Diocese, & on the College, & will be beneficial to religion.

Tho' you may not be able to fill his place as efficiently, yet I trust you will be able to manage so as not greatly to feel his loss. You could easily recall one or other of the subjects you have lent to other Bishops. I am myself bankrupt in men, or I would have lent you one.

When shall we again have the pleasure of seeing you here? The Superiors unite in kind regard to you. Ever sincerely Yours in Xt. +Alexander Goss.

---

[303] William Wareing, 1791–1865, bishop 1850–58; his was the largest diocese, but contained only *c.* 10,000 Catholics and *c.* thirty priests.

[304] John Dalton, 1815–74. He wrote to Goss, 24 May 1859 (AAL, *S1/3/E/1*): he had done his eighteen months and was returning to the diocese, mainly to look after his mother; he claimed Guest had serious problems and a bishop should visit the college.

139. [*Abp. Errington*]   *7 December 1857*   *5/2/111–14*
My dear Grace,
I have not as yet returned any official answer to the Benedictine claim of exemption, though in practice I have visited them & the other Regulars as exempt, tho' I do not think that the Benedictines can claim it under the Apos. Minis;[305] as they do not observe its provisions, e.g. going at certain periods to a house for regular observance in order to rub off the rust contracted in [*?illegible; perhaps* mission] observance.

1.   The limitation to section V. in cap. VIII. of the 2nd Synod[306] sadly cripples us, for as it makes the measure applicable to <u>new</u> foundations only, we have no means of settling what is, and what is not missionary property, & the people, who alone could tell us how existing churches were raised & to whom & for what existing funds were left, are fast dying out. Besides, we have no guarantee that they will not pawn missionary property to carry out Religious schemes: they might re-enact what Dr. Baines is said to have enacted in the foundation of Prior Park.[307]

    Unless you have decisive information on XVII & XVIII (page 29, 2nd Synod)[308] I do not think you can deduce therefrom that they are bound to show these books to the <u>Bishop</u>; for they are equally bound to keep in the Sacristy a book for the entrance & fulfilment of both perpetual & casual obligations; but the Bishop is not allowed to inspect that book. Nor can he examine Confessionals in <u>exempt</u> Churches to see whether the Synodal regulations regarding them are carried out, tho' the Synodal regulations may apply to the Confessionals of exempt as much as to those of the Secular Clergy. The whole position of Regulars holding missionary faculties is anomalous; they are less priestly in their dress, habits & amusements than the seculars. More than one half of my Diocese is in their hands, so that I speak feelingly.

    If you have had answers from C??? [*sic*] I should like to know their exact tenour: for I shall act up to them in the next Visitation; but I don't like venturing alone, as their name is legion in my Diocese.

2. Regulars claim exemption on the ground that they are serving the mission: but where they do not exercise missionary faculties, they cannot put forward such claims, & hence must be visited as *parva monasteria.* Yet if they have a community of six, I believe they are exempted. The first law said 12, & six for those existing before the Council of Trent; but my impression is that a subsequent law exempted them if they had six, the greater part of whom were priests. Now, has not Farm St. this number, lay brothers included? Bishop Eton is the only place in this Diocese at which there is no quasi-parochial church. Salisbury St.[309] had normal missionary faculties before I was Bp. of Lpool. I suspect that there is a strong pressure on them from Rome, & that they believe that it is the Cardinal who turns the screw. I believe Rome wants them to concentrate men in towns where they hold many missions as in Preston: they once spoke to me on the subject.

3. I will ascertain the status of Mary Sothern [? *page torn here*], the who & the what.

I shall be glad for a word of advice, for the Ghost at St. Anthony's, after being long laid, has again appeared. Can. Newsham declares his inability to pay his interest, i.e. the int[erest] due on St. Anthony's. He has not paid it for the last year: it is something better than £400, all trust money, i.e. having different obligations attached to it. If it is not paid, my finance Committee cannot meet their obligations. The mission is wretchedly worked, & he has made no effort to meet his int[erest], not even having had, till quite lately, an offertory. His accounts are recently written, being compiled from papers or extracts from the original books, which he burnt, because they contained the priests' accounts as well as those of the mission, & he did not wish Dr. Brown's administration to see them. These accounts Can. Jas. Fisher has examined, & he pronounces them to be 'worthless'; in fact, he says that, as they stand, St. Anthony's would owe Can. N. £2000, a fact of which the said Canon has no suspicion. He has also pawned or mortgaged the Eldon St. schools, in order to raise money for the new Cemetery at Ford, on the verbal permission, he states, of Dr. Brown. This he did in April 1857, more than a year after Dr. Brown's death & more than 6 months after a Diocesan Synodal decree had abrogated "*privilegia sive exemptiones sive concessiones*"[310] which did not bear Dr. B's signature.[311]

The Chapter, consulted by me, advised Can. N. to resign; but this he declined to do; he has the title of Mis[sionary] Rector, but there is a flaw in his appointment, yet I would deal with him as such. My own notion is to appoint an Administrator, leaving him still there; for the Interest due must be raised or we are bankrupt. I could then let him go before a commission to examine his accounts & pronounce on the extent of the exercise to raise the interest.

His schools are neglected, & he is slovenly in the administration of the sacrament of penance & holy communion. He is reported to have said that he can retire on his own property, tho' he did not get a copper from his relatives, & that he is tired of priesting. Miss Saunderson on her death bed confided to Can. Walker & desired him to tell me, that Can. N. had called me & those at St. Edward's 'damned scoundrels' etc. His most illegal act, however, is I think the mortgaging of the Eldon St. schools without the sanction of me, the existing Bp., after the revocation of Dr. Brown's verbal grants mentioned above.

I have been so long absent to & fro that I have yet done nothing in the matter beyond consulting the Chapter, so that now another half year's interest is nearly due. He will no doubt resist any attempt either to appoint an administrator or a successor, & will carry the case to Rome. He will also plentifully bespatter me with mud, as he did Dr. Brown, thro' the length & breadth of the land. I shall be glad if you would talk the matter over with the Card. as it will be referred from Rome to him, if entertained: & I do not want to move unless I feel that I am on safe ground.

Ever sincerely Yours in Xt. A. Goss.

305 Pope Benedict XIV's constitution *Apostolicum Ministerium* of 1753 had regulated the role of the Regulars serving English or Welsh missions apart from their monasteries.

306 *Decreta*, p. 101: Chapter VIII deals with 'Ecclesiastical Property'.

307 Peter Augustine Baines OSB, VA of the Western District 1829–43; for Prior Park, see Schiefen, *Nicholas Wiseman*, 24–33, 40–5, 54–64.

308 Printed in *Decreta*, 104–5, dealing with parochial account books.

309 The house of the Jesuits serving St Francis Xavier's parish, Liverpool.

310 Trans: 'privileges, whether (arising from) exemptions or concessions'.

311 Burke (*Catholic Liverpool*) calls Newsham (at St Anthony's 1844–59) 'a man of extraordinary energy and capacity' and praises his work for the development of Catholicism in the north end of the city (see, e.g., 80). O'Neill, *St Anthony's*, 81–105, is more guarded and gives a detailed account of the financial problems and of the Commission of Investigation of 1858. The case did go to Rome: see APF, *Anglia*, 15, fols 184–7, 193, 459, 482–3. O'Neill, *St Anthony's*, 98–100, gives Goss's defence of his actions. See later letters for the relations between the two and Newsham's eventual move to Fleetwood.

140. *Mrs. Anderton, Haighton House* *7 December 1857* *5/2/115*
My dear Mrs. Anderton,
I have great pleasure in renewing the permission to communicate in your private chapel during the winter months & until the end of May, sought on the grounds of ill-health, at mass celebrated by the Revd. Fathers Bateman & Cardwell.

And furthermore I license the priests herein named to say mass in the said Oratory, till 10 days after the next Diocesan Synod, to wit: Dinmore, Gradwell, Cook, Walker, Taylor, Swarbrick, Bateman, Weston, Cooper, Grimston, Corr, Hill, J. Corry, Knight, Jenkins, admonishing them to adhere to the regulations & conditions laid down in my schedule.[312] May I beg that you will exhibit this or forward a copy of it to the Revd. Mr. Gillow, the Rural Dean.

Wishing yourself & family every blessing, I remain sincerely Yours in Xt. +Alexander Goss.

---

312   Bateman, James SJ: 1805–79; Cardwell SJ, prob Wm: 1817–99; Dinmore, Edward OSB, 1805–79; Gradwell, Cook, Walker, Taylor, Swarbrick – all Seculars of the Diocese; Thomas Weston SJ: 1804–67; three possible Coopers, all SJ; John Grimston SJ, 1819–82; Richard Corr SJ, 1816–76; Thomas Hill SJ, 1825–1909; James Corry SJ, 1826–74; William Knight SJ, 1813–59; George Jenkins SJ: 1799–61. The large number of Jesuits no doubt reflects the propinquity of Preston and Stonyhurst.

141. *Rev. Thos. Gibson*[313]   *9 December 1857*   *5/2/116*

My dear Mr. Gibson,

Mr. Maddox[314] has not permanently resigned the mission of Gt. Eccleston, as he hopes, at the close of six months, to be able to resume missionary duties. I fear, however, that he will not be able to do so; still I think it due to him to keep the mission open, not only on account of his age & long services, but because I think it would be hard to fill up any mission vacated for ill-health by any priest, unless it was patent that even on his recovery he would be unequal to his duties.

I have no intention & never have had of appointing Henry to it: & should Mr. Maddox vacate it, I shall be glad favourably to entertain the consideration of your claims. I have had another application since yours, to which I replied that in case of change there were prior claims to be considered.

I hope you are beginning, even at Croft, the compilation of a history of the Missions. Open an account in a large master ledger with each mission, & put down regarding it whatever you hear from any quarter, specifying the authority. You can afterwards sift, arrange & digest the information so collected, so as to preserve yourself from Oliverism.[315] Think less, act more. Have you put in order & indexed the late Bishop's pastorals & circulars? Ever sincerely Yours in Xt. +Alexander Goss.

---

313   Thomas Ellison Gibson: see n. 68.

314   Walter Saunders Maddocks, 1799–1869, at Great Eccleston, 1846–60; then r. at Lea.

315   Oliverism: V. Rev George Oliver, DD, canon of Plymouth Diocese: published *Collections, illustrating the History of the Catholic Religion in the Counties of Cornwall, Devon, Dorset, Somerset, Wilts and Gloucester* (London, 1857). Goss implies his writings were voluminous and rather undigested, and few would disagree. See letter 314 for a more favourable mention.

142. *W. Gillow Esq.*[316]   *10 December 1857*   5/2/118

My dear Mr. Gillow,

We have had a meeting of the Reformatory Committee, & being mostly business men present, we came to no practical conclusion, for one & all declared it to be visionary to attempt to raise money at present.

Myself & the Vicar have, however, taken the matter over, & I am disposed to do what lies in my power. Previously, however, I wish to know in whose hands the property at Arno's Court[317] is legally invested, & whether it be held absolutely or in trust; for whatever agreement is come to between you & us, must be ratified & signed by the holders of the property, so as to give a definite position, otherwise the agreement may hereafter be legally or ecclesiastically disowned, when you have ceased to act or interest yourself further in the matter.

I must also again remind you of the understanding on which I agreed to furnish the money. I mentioned to you confidentially, which I again do, that a sum of money out of this Diocese would probably be paid to Arno's Court for what had been done for Lpool & London. If this sum did not reach £500 I undertook to make it into that sum, or if it were not paid at all, I undertook to furnish it; but if it were paid, then it had to stand for the £500, of which we are now treating. If therefore I now raise that £500, it must be on the understanding that it be repaid when the other £500, of which I have spoken confidentially is paid over.

Wishing you every blessing I remain sincerely Yrs in Xt. +A. Goss.

---

316 William Gillow, Esq., share broker of Gillow & Pyke, 16 Lord Street, Liverpool; he lived at 55 Shaw Street.

317 Arno's Court was established by the Clifton Diocese at Arno's Vale, near Bristol; certified in April 1856 for ninety girls, run by Good Shepherd nuns (see www.missing-ancestors.com, accessed February 2013). Harding, *Diocese of Clifton*, says it was not opened until 1861, but an earlier date fits with Goss's letter better.

143. *Very Rev. Canon Carter*   *10 December 1857*   5/2/119

My dear Canon,

Dr. Wareing consents to allow Canon Dalton to go to Valladolid to the assistance of Mr. Guest, provided that he can find some body to supply the deficiency, which will be caused by the supplying of Mr. Dalton's place. I write by to-day's post to ask Dr. Turner if he can spare a priest. Dr. Wareing says that an elderly man, or even an invalid, may do, as the place he wants him for is not large, the town in which it is not numbering more than 2000 inhabitants; but it is comfortable & has an income of beyond £90 per an.

If you can do any thing to back my recommendation with Dr. Turner, it may help to facilitate arrangements. I cannot possibly do any thing; for one priest has gone to the Indies,[318] another is on the fund, Mr.

Maddox; & a third *abiit, evasit, erupit*, Mr. Dujardin;[319] so that you see clearly I cannot spare one. I hope this venture may succeed, but if you have any suggestions to offer to Dr. Turner, pray do not neglect the opportunity.

Wishing yoy every blessing I remain sincerely Yours in Xt. +A. Goss.

---

318   This could be Patrick Fairhurst; see n. 137 above.

319   This is a partial quotation from Cicero's Second Catiline Oration of 63 BC; the original has four verbs, with *excessit* as the third (§1). Catiline had fled after planning to destroy the Republic; presumably Goss was only accusing Dujardin of having left in a great hurry. Trans: 'has left, has escaped, has broken out'; see n. 286 above.

144. [*Cookson, Esq.*]   *12 December 1857*   *5/2/121*
                            Confidential

My dear Mr. Cookson,[320]

I write to you on the subject of Singleton,[321] to see if you can be of any help to us. I believe we have <u>now</u> no <u>legal</u> claim to any thing but the chapel, which we hold by Deed. I cannot, however, learn whether rent was ever paid for <u>all</u> the other property held by the priest there: Mr Pemberton, formerly incumbent says not, tho', at the advice of Mr. Sherburne, it was paid for some portion. Yet until Mr. Miller purchased the property, the rent was only nominal. It is not desirable at present to continue the performance of regular services there, as the income is not sufficient for a priest & the population is too small & too near other chapels to justify me in keeping a priest out of Diocesan funds; yet I will endeavour to arrange for occasional services & the instruction of the children.

Mr. Fair is, I believe, Mr. Miller's agent & will have maps of the estate purchased by him. Now what I want to learn is, how much of the chapel house property at Singleton was sold by Mr. Hornby to Mr. Miller? Did Mr. Miller purchase all except the chapel, or what is down on his maps of the estate as belonging to him? I want you, if possible, to ascertain this from Mr. Fair. It would not do to let him know that the inquiry comes from me, as I do not wish him to know that I am in any uncertainty. Mr. Miller's Attorney (Wilson of Preston) saw our Deed in Mr. Sherburne's days, & will therefore know that that Deed covers nothing more than the chapel & a road round it; but Mr. Pemberton declares that he did not pay rent for the outhouses & a portion of ground, tho' he did pay for the house & garden. As soon as I see my way I will order the key to be given up & will wall up the communication between the house & chapel. Hoping that Mrs. Cookson is better, & wishing yourself & family every blessing, I remain sincerely Yours in Xt. +Alexander Goss.

[320] Cookson, Esq: obviously a layman.

[321] Singleton, in the Fylde, was the only mission to close altogether in Goss's time, due to a falling population and lack of endowment. The only Mr Pemberton that fits is James Pemberton, 1808–81, at this date serving in the Shrewsbury Diocese but presumably earlier in the Northern and Lancashire Districts.

145.   *Rev. F Hines*[322]   *18 December 1857*   *5/2/124*

My dear Mr. Hines,

I have consulted with the Vic. Gen. on the subject of your memorial, & however anxious we both are that your children should have the blessings of Benediction of the B.S. yet we are both agreed on the undesirableness of having a late service for the children. Benediction is an attractive service, yet Sunday is the only free day at their disposal, & if they be worked too hard even attractive services lose their charm, & they might be induced to sacrifice instructions for Benediction. Again evening services have been forced on the church by Dissenters, but the church does not like them on account of the dangers to which the faithful are thereby exposed, which become doubly great for the young. Though your people might be kept out of harm's way, yet those from the country could not but hear & see much on Sunday evenings on their way from Church, that would be calculated to undo the spiritual advantages derived from Benediction. I think, therefore, that it would not be wise to introduce an evening service on their account.

Wishing you by anticipation the blessings of this holy season, I remain sincerely yours in Xt.

+Alexander Goss.

[322] Frederick Hines, 1824–1906; at Kirkham in the Fylde 1854–95.

146.   *Rev. Mr. Swarbrick, Thurnham*   *18 December 1857*   *5/2/125*

My dear Mr. Swarbrick,[323]

In accordance with my promise, I have discussed with the Vicar the proposed plan of heating the Thurnham Church with hot water. He was more than astonished to hear that its walls were so damp, & he thought it most desirable that something should be done to remedy it. Yet we are both of opinion that to take up money for the purpose, unless with the sure prospect or determination to repay it in a few years, would be inexpedient in itself & would justly expose us to the animadversion of posterity. The Congregation must be able to do something & it is not too much to expect that, if Mr. Crowe[324] raised nearly a thousand pounds for the building of a Church, the people should contribute what is necessary to keep that Church in suitable repair. It is obligatory on them, as a duty which they are bound to discharge. With a little patience you will, I think, carry them along with you; but you may rest assured that if you begin, they will expect you to aid every good work, & eventually they will do nothing. I know from bitter experience how the matter is even in my own case. When I was first appointed Bishop, I was urged to take a house in Abercromby Square;[325] why, what I received during my Coadjutorship would have hardly paid the rent of a <u>little</u> house. So people say now, take a house, don't be a lodger, you ought to have £800 a year: yes, but they would fall by the way as to the principle on which it should be raised, & I should be left in the hands of a sheriff's officer! There are splendid exceptions, but as a mass the Catholics do nothing; they may be worse at Thurnham than elsewhere; but they are but part of a general practice.

Wishing you by anticipation the blessings of the season, I reamin sincerely Yours in Xt. +A. Goss.

---

323   James Swarbrick, 1822–98, r. at Thurnham, near Lancaster 1857–82.
324   Thomas Crowe, c. 1800–62, r. at Thurnham 1824–48. The new church was built in 1847–48; Miss Elizabeth Dalton of Thurnham Hall (see n. 230 above) provided the rest of the money.
325   Abercromby Square: one of Liverpool's finest and wealthiest areas, developed in the late Georgian period; see Joseph Sharples, *Liverpool* (Pevsner Architectural Guides, London, 2004), 216–17.

147. *Rt. Rev. the Bishop of Beverley   19 December 1857*   *5/2/126*
My dear Lord,
I have not as yet decided any thing on the subject of fees. I consulted my Chapter on the subject, & laid before them the respective rules of Dr. Brown of Salop & Dr. Turner. They almost unanimously recommended the rule of Dr. Brown, of which you have a copy in his last Pastoral.

I have discountenanced dispensations from banns & do not grant them except to avoid scandal. In such cases, the parties are poor, & unable to afford any offering, but before I had made known my determination not to grant dispensations, they were granted, & the parties dispensed paid from one to five pounds. This I uniformly handed over to some charitable institution. All such applications are now sent to the Vicar.

It seems to me to be the mind of the Church that, or rather of the Synod of Oscott, that [*sic*] fees, as distinct from retributions for mass, should go to the general fund for paying the working expenses of the churches, & considering how strongly the Church discountenances fees for administration of the Sacraments, I would never sanction this exaction, if they had to swell the private income of the clergy, not that I think they have got too much, but I think the Church has too little, for their debts remain almost undiminished. Fees, it seems to me, are sanctioned on the same principle as admission charges, in the want of other adequate sources of income.

I am glad to see your hand writing is once more itself, & I sincerely hope that you have taken out a fresh lease, & I pray God to grant that it may have many years to run. Wishing you the joys of the coming season, I remain sincerely Yours, +Alexander Goss.

148. *Very Rev. Can. Hodgson*   *21 December 1857*   *5/2/129*
Confidential

My dear Canon,

I am sorry that my manner betrayed a feeling which did not exist at the last Chapter dinner. I do not think, nor have I ever thought that you entertained towards me any but the most cordial feelings, & I am sure that no one more sincerely regrets than yourself, the conduct of the Rev. Jn. Worthy.[326] He is said to be a man of principle, but I fear it is such principle as makes a man impracticable. Even Dawber[327] tho' he inherits his father's wisdom, will find it difficult to reconcile his present mode of acting with that which caused his exclusion from the board of Ushaw rulers: it looks rather Palmerstonian. No one can blame him for entertaining his own views on a subject open to inquiry: but I think he must be thought to have tested Episcopal forbearance to the utmost by not only himself <u>protesting</u>, but endeavouring to enlist the members of Conference & the clergy generally to join in a public protest. The Church allows the right of <u>petition</u>, but not of <u>protest</u>, & my act on Cathedraticum is no more a subject for inquiry & protest & agitation among the clergy than my removal of Mr. Ball from Thurnham or, if it took place, my removal of Can. Newsham from St. Anthony's. A bishop's acts can be canvassed only at the Holy See.

I certainly feel what has been done; for I have never shown a love of money. I have served the Church for as little money as any priest in this Diocese. [*next nine lines difficult to decipher – packed in at end of the page*] No other priest has had harder work, none as little salary & perquisites, & even that little I never fully drew. During the years of my coadjutorship I had next to nothing. From none of the clergy did I ever receive less than from those comprising the Burscough Conference. But think no more about the matter: let it be forgotten. Yet I cannot forget that even for the paltry sum that had to be paid to the Bp's mensa from Ormskirk, they applied to my own sister, so that my own blood might be made to feel that I was a public pauper. If I kept a carriage or dressed expensively or bought luxuries, they might have had a place for their acts; but as it is they have none.

Believe me as ever most sincerely Yours, A. Goss.

326 John Worthy, 1815–93, cousin of Bishop O'Reilly; r. of St Mary's, Euxton, 1851–93; Introduction p. xl on the cathedraticum dispute. See Milburn, *History of Ushaw College*, 171 ff. for a riot at Ushaw under Worthy.

327 John Dawber, see n. 146.

149. *Capt. John Thomas RN (St. Vincent of Paul's)* [*sic*]
          22 December 1857   *5/2/131*

Dear Sir,

I beg to acknowledge with many thanks the receipt of a P.O. order for £1 to be paid over to the Church of St. Vincent of Paul, due to your kindness & charity.

The new church is now up,[328] & the clergy have migrated from the wretched shed; but the head priest, Mr. Oreilly, brings with him a shattered constitution, being, at times, incapacitated from rheumatism, brought on by exposure to street cold after stove heat. Yet he bears with him also much zeal & great confidence in God & the poor, & he stands greatly in need of them, for he has a heavy debt & a very poor congregation. The kind sympathy expressed in your letter makes the gift doubly dear, & I beg you will accept my thanks on behalf of him & his poor congregation, as well as on behalf of myself & diocese. Wishing you the blessings of this holy time as well also as its festive joys,

I remain Sincerely yours in Xt. +Alexander Goss.

328 On the new church see Burke, *Catholic Liverpool*, 126–8, the origin of the 'pennies of the poor' myth. It is unclear who Captain Thomas was; *Gore's Directory* has half-a-dozen mariners or master mariners of that name.

150. *Rt. Rev. Dr. Grant   4 January 1858   5/2/142*
          (Chapter Dress)

My dear Friend,

Your letters are all the same & always full of kindness to myself & to all about me. How warmly I reciprocate your kind expressions in wishing God to bless you & your diocese, you at least know for you – & you are nearly the only one – have stood by my mind, seen its growth & know its strength & its weakness.

The Chapter here seem to think that they look frights when habited *in sacris* over their canonical habit, as the black cassock refuses to harmonize with the rich colours of the chasuble. They certainly do look like men who had plundered a vestment depot & had arrayed themselves in the spoils, without due regard to appearance. They would like purple instead of black & a close rochet instead of the wide sleeves which hook everything in their way.[329]

There is one sore in my diocese: it was there in Dr. Brown's time,

& to that source may be traced every unkind feeling in my regard. He can no longer say of me what he said of my predecessor, that he had the Bp. in his pocket. I am amongst my clergy when duty calls, & I have not spared myself, for I have given Confirmation at times in three, often in two churches on the same day, after communicating great numbers, & each time at confirmation, addressing the people, but I decline to do important business except in writing, & don't drop in after dinner to hear what rude men may have to say when their tongue is loosed. My only great cross has been the attempt of Jn. Worthy & Jn. Dawber, but mainly the former, to excite the clergy to petition me in Synod against or rather protest against the exorbitant Cathedraticum of one pound, which is really below the value of the *Solidus*; but I will write you again on this subject, & send you the Chapter notes. Ever sincerely Yours +A. Goss

---

[329] On capitular dress, see *Decreta*, 54, 74; 193–4 gives the papal brief of May 1858 on the topic.

151. *His Grace The Archbishop of Trebizond*   *7 January 1858*
5/2/149–54

"Cathedraticum"[330]

My dear Grace,

Before holding my <u>first</u> Synod,[331] the Secretaries sent round a notice to the clergy, what they had to bring &c, & also that a cathedraticum of two *solidi*[332] would have to be received from each priest, which sum by the advice of the Chapter was declared to be one pound. Before holding my <u>second</u> Synod the Notary sent round a similar notice but, on the subject of the cathedraticum, wrote, "It has been fixed by the Chapter at one pound".

This gave umbrage to the Burscough Conference, consisting of Revv. Jn. Worthy, Jn. Dawber, Jas. Abraham, Wm. Wells, Seculars, Hoole, Abram, Greenough, Shann, Dowding, Benedictines, & Spackman, Jesuit.[333] The Rev. Jn. Worthy, therefore, addressed a note to the Provost of the Chapter, containing the following resolution "The members of this Conference protest against the interpretation of two *solidi* by the Chap. to mean <u>one pound</u>, whereas it really means <u>two shillings</u>, & if the one pound is to be looked upon not exactly as a cathedraticum, but as a voluntary contribution for the support of the Bp. it is an objectionable way of raising the money & ought not to be tolerated lest it become a precedent for future Synods. The practice of Italy, Oxford (?) &c confirm this their view of the subject. They also object to the chapter, through their private interpretation of a latin [*sic*] word, assuming authority to impose such a tax upon the Clergy."

He sent a similar note to the Deans, begging them to submit the resolution to the consideration of their respective Conferences. The Deans returned for answer, "that Conferences were an episcopal organization for the consideration of cases of conscience submitted to them by the Bp. & that without his authority they were not competent to discuss extraneous matters["]. The Provost returned for answer that they were not answerable to the Burscough Conference for any advice which they gave to the Bp. & therefore he returned the resolution, refusing to lay it before the Chap.

Mr. Worthy then sent round to the clergy an essay against the one pound cathedraticum desiring them to sign it in order that at the approaching synod it might be read to the Bp. How many signed it I do not know; but I am told that the Jesuits returned for answer that their principle was, to stand by the Bp. & his Chapter. Three of the Seculars who signed it have since written to me to express their regret.

Mr. Worthy came to the Synod with a variety of petitions, all in his hand writing, but presented by different priests. Mr. Kelly presented the first, asking for the appointment of Rev. Jn. Worthy as a second *procurator cleri*, for, after the example of Baptistelli,[334] I had appointed one of the Canons. He based his petition on certain words in the *Praxis Synodi* cap. XVI. P.14.[335] On reading the passage, I answered that he put a false interpretation on the words, which did not recognise two procurators, but only one who might transact other than Synodal matters for the clergy, if the Bp. thought fit. Mr. B. Oreilly then asked whether the one pound Cathedrat. was to be perpetual & to be levied without the consent of the Clergy: I answered that the Bp. levied a cathedrat. de jure suo, & therefore did not require the consent of the Clergy, & that as the synod was dealing only with the present, I could not undertake to say what either I or my successors might do on future occasions.

Mr. Worthy then petitioned to be allowed to read his expostulation against the one pound Cathedrat., he having ascertained the feelings of the Clergy upon the point. This I refused on the grounds that there was no evidence before me that he was authorised to speak in the name of the Clergy. He made several attempts to be allowed to state his arguments against the Cathedraticum, & eventually petitioned that I would join in a common reference of the matter to the Holy See. I answered that being satisfied of the legality of my acts, I had no need to seek advice from Rome; that if he believed my acts to be illegal, it was for him to bring the matter before the Holy See. He eventually petitioned for time to amend his petition, i.e. to leave out of it all phrases that identified it with the clergy, but this I refused to allow, on the grounds that he had already had a considerable time allotted to him.

At the next meeting of the Burscough Conference, it was resolved, I am told, after the conference was over, to print & circulate his arguments against the Cathedrat. to collect signatures, & then appeal to ['the clergy' *crossed out*] Rome.

Meanwhile, as the Procurator Cleri had not deposited with the Notary the petitions presented, the latter wrote to him for them, & he applied for them to Mr. Worthy, in whose handwriting they were. Mr. Worthy returned the inclosed answers, addressed to Mr. Teebay, Dec. 18. Mr. Teebay was from home & hence no answer was returned. Today I have received the inclosed letter from Mr. Worthy.

He has, I am told, written to every Diocese, as also to Belgium, to learn what the Cathedraticum is & contends that *consuetudo* [custom] is against the cathedrat. of one pound.

In order that you may understand his letter, I should observe that I stated in Synod that the advice of the Chapter which had been given to me, had been given after mature deliberation, & I left the Chapter at liberty to state or read the notes which they had drawn up; but they very properly declined to avail themselves of it.

What answer must my Notary make to his letter, what answer must I make? He writes as if himself & those who act with him, on the one side, & the Bp. & Chapter on the other, were equal authorities, contending on equal ground about a matter which rested on the value of arguments employed by either party, whereas the Cathedrat. de jure belongs to the Bp. alone, & he might as well put any others of his rights up for discussion as this.

I declined to allow a protest or petition from the clergy as a body, for I found a decision of the Cong. of Con. Trid. on the subject.[336] The clergy had caused a protest to be read or put in at Synod, the Bp. suspended them unless they withdrew it; they refused, he suspended them: they applied to Rome, which desired him to remove the suspension on their publicly begging pardon.

Mr. Worthy seems to consider that the Clergy at Synod have a right to argue: now this cannot be considered, for the right to petition does not include a right to question the legality of the Bp's acts, but only the right to appeal to his mercy, or to beg the repeal of certain enactments on account of particular circumstances, &c. The legality of the Bp's acts can only be questioned or discussed before his superior, viz. the Holy See.

I have never seen a copy of Mr. Worthy's Essay, but I am told that every succeeding copy improves in its tone of civility, as do his letters on the subject. I believe that his first effort was to arouse the clergy to protest against the Cathedrat; now he styles it a protestation, but No. 8 of his petition, as in his letter to Mr. Teebay, was for his arguments against the one pound Cathedraticum to be heard; and another in its preamble proposed a plan to reconcile the differences between the Bp. & his clergy. As a body, the Clergy are, I believe, with me.

By tomorrow's post I will forward you the Chapter's notes on the value of the Cathedrat.

The Bp's mensa is worth £150 per. ann. The Chapter proposed to increase it to £500 on condition that the Cathedrat. should form part of it. To this I consented, & they advised its being fixed at one pound. They have received authority from the Holy See to levy a rate on the different missions for the Episcopal mensa. On condition that it was raised to £500 I was to receive no offerings on occasions of Confirmations &c.

Have you yet seen the Cardinal about Newsham's case.[337] I should like to act soon. I fear my hands will be feeble, what with him & with Worthy & Co. & shall probably in both cases be brought before the Propaganda. I hope I shall be backed on the Cathedraticum by the other Bps. The principles embodied in Mr. Worthy's letters seem to me to be the very essence of ecclesiastical radicalism. Please to return Mr. Worthy's <u>two letters</u> & let me have your opinion soon. Ever truly Yours A. Goss.

---

330   The fullest statement we have of Goss's version of the cathedraticum dispute; see Introduction p. xl. (Page 150 is missing.)

331   Dates of the Liverpool synods: first (under Brown), 1853; second (Goss's first): November 1856; third, November 1857; then 1865, 1866, 1867, 1868 and 1869. See AAL, *Synodi Liverpolitanae I–VIII* (Liverpool, n.d.).

332   There appeared to be no way to establish what exactly a *solidus* was; at their third synod the bishops agreed that the tax should be fixed at ten shillings, though they thought one pound was a reasonable interpretation and had been customary in England (*Decreta*, 174–5).

333   Presumably Thomas Speakman SJ, 1811–89.

334   Presumably Josaphat Battistelli, Bishop of Foligno, author of *Diocesana synodus* (Modena, 1724).

335   See n. 57. The section referred to says it is is usual for the bishop to appoint a Procurator of the Clergy, to whom the clergy have access to raise matters of concern; if the clergy should elect such a person then the bishop may choose him as Procurator. There is no mention of two Procurators and the initiative clearly lies with the bishop.

336   The Congregation of the Council of Trent: the Roman congregation with responsibility for the interpretation of the Tridentine decrees and disputed canonical issues.

337   i.e. Canon Newsham of St Anthony's, Liverpool.

152. *Rev. Jn. Worthy*   *22 January 1858*   *5/2/171*
"Cathedraticum"

Revd. & dear Sir,

In acknowledging your favour of the 6th I beg to say that I give you full credit for the spirit of peace & charity which it breathes, & I will meet it in the same spirit. I shall be glad, therefore, to receive any arguments which you may have to advance against the amount of the Cathedraticum & promise to give them both a careful & impartial examination. I cannot, however, agree to refer the discussion of the question to a mixed commission of canons & clergy, as such a tribunal is unknown in the Church for the settlement of disputes that arise out of canon law. Neither clergy nor canons are judges, nor can they be constituted judges, of the legality of the Bishop's acts: both are subjects & cannot therefore sit in judgement on their Superior. Your mistake has arisen from your considering the settlement of the amount of the Cathedraticum to be a question between the Chapter & the Clergy, whereas it is between the Bp. & Clergy, amongst whom in this matter the canons are numbered. Your mistake arose, no doubt, from the loose announcement of the Notary who said the Chapter had fixed, instead of the Bp. with the advice of the Chapter had fixed. The mistake would be further strengthened by my consenting to the reading of the grounds on which the Chap. had based their advice, but this I did, as it had been currently rumoured that the Chap. had decided off hand. I was not bound to consult the Chapter unless the one pound had to be considered as both Cathedrat. & a *donum charitativum*, but I did so, as the H. See had commissioned them to raise a suitable revenue, & I agreed to let it stand as a portion of the sum to be raised. To me personally it is immaterial whether it be one pound or one farthing.

Wishing you every blessing I remain sincerely Yours in Xt. Alexander Goss.

I will mention to the Chap. your proposition for an interchange of papers, tho' I cannot do so officially.

153. *Rev. Jno. Penswick, Ashton Cross 2 March 1858   5/2/195*
'Commission of Investigation'[338] Confidential
My dear Mr. Penswick,
It is become necessary for me to summon the members of the Commission of Investigation to decide on the propriety of removing the Very Rev. Canon Newsham from the incumbency of St. Anthony's, as he has paid no interest on its debt for the last eighteen months, & there is now due the sum of £600, of which the Bp. is only the administrator; for the money belongs to various missions or charities. You are one of the members of this Commission. It is important, if not necessary, for all to attend, as two thirds are requisite for a decision, tho' I do not see what number constitutes two thirds of five. The meeting will be convened for Tuesday, March 16; for unless something be done speedily, we shall be bankrupt. You shall have a bed at St. Edward's, with a fire in your room, & nothing shall be neglected to make you comfortable. Please to let me hear by return of Post, as time presses, & if you should feel yourself unable to come & resign in consequence, I should have to seek another, tho' I should much prefer your attendance.

Wishing you every blessing, I remain sincerely Yrs in Xt. +A. Goss.

154.   *Rt. Rev. Dr. Grant*   *8 April 1858*   *5/2/234*
My dear Friend,
A truth is none the less valuable for being stated, & I hope therefore that you will profit by the acknowledged fact that a bow cannot be always bent without losing its pliancy. I am no advocate for a man being too chary of himself; but your work is incessant even in recreation time. Be advised, & give yourself a holiday. Run away from letters & business.

Many thanks for your kind interest in the great case of Youens versus Sherburne, which, if the Card. perseveres in his inertness, is destined to damage clerical honesty in public opinion beyond the hope of redemption. After the spendthrift administration of Dr. B. & his first coadjutor,[339] it will require a generation of Bps to redress the character of Ep[iscopal] Honesty, & I may say the same about the other case with regard to the clergy, when the matter becomes more fully known to the laity. It would endorse the dicta of F. Trappes & Riddell on the subject of clerical honesty & competency.

Mgr. N. wants the Sherb.–Heat. Trust to be arbitrated upon, not for the purpose of settling how far it is liable for claims on Mr. Sherb's estate, but to make it compulsory on the Trustees to spend a <u>fixed</u> sum on education at <u>Ushaw</u>, whereas by the Deed both the amount to be spent, & the place whereat it has to be spent, is left to their unfettered discretion. At the time Dr. Y. made the declaration of which you speak, if made, the £12000 – the money in dispute – stood in his own name, & whilst he denied having property in Mr. S.'s money, he equally denied that Mr. S. had any property in his money. At the time the Sherb. Heat. Trust Deed was made, & for long afterwards Mr. S. had more than £15000 in his possession, standing originally in the name of Cookson, but possessed in addition to the property of the Sherb. Heat. Trust. I believe that money passed to Mr. C. Gillow, but I cannot speak positively, tho' Mr. Cookson will know. There are plenty of assets without interfering with the Trust. Ever sincerely Yours, A. Goss.
Have you read the Rambler's character of the Card. put as a companion to the Card's of Dr. Baines?[340]

339   Bishop Sharples.
340   *The Rambler* 9 (n.s.) (April 1858), pp. 273–80, carried a review notice of Wiseman's book, *Recollections of the Last Four Popes and of Rome in their Times* (1858); it was rather critical, claiming the account was all too 'sunny', with no critical analysis or 'dark' episodes, and omitting the weak sides of Bp Baines; but the review is not too severe in tone. A later issue (June, 425–32) carries a long, stringent attack on Wiseman as a historian by Mark Tierney over the Lingard as cardinal *in petto* affair; Tierney claims Wiseman accused him of lacking veracity, but this is in the form of a letter from Tierney, not a *Rambler* review or editorial.

155. *Rev. Mr. Fayre, Salmesbury*[341]   *14 April 1858*   *5/2/241*
"Mr. Jas. Taylor"[342]

My dear Mr. Fayre,

I fear it is impossible to send your nephew to any College for the completion of his theological studies under a professor; for it would be next to impossible to find classes studying the treatises which are necessary to complete his course, as it is not usual, except abroad, to have more than one theological class. I have therefore made arrangements for him to come to St. Edward's for a year; for tho' I cannot provide him any active help, yet he will have every facility for study, & fewer opportunities of distraction than would be offered by a country mission. He will have his own room, & Dr. Fisher will see to his having suitable diet. I trust also that he will have his health; for tho' we lie high, yet it is not cold & we have no damp.

I will desire Mr. Jas. Fisher to write to your brother regarding the payment of the £50 & I will also desire the Vicar to write to Dr. Newsham – if the Fair [*sic*] fund be under his administration – to desire him to allow your brother's son to have the benefit of it. Your nephew, Mr. Taylor, can come at any time; the sooner, the better.

Wishing you the paschal joys & every other blessing, I remain sincerely Yours in Xt. A. Goss.

---

[341]   William Fayer, 1814–83; o.1840; served in Salford Diocese after 1850.

[342]   James Taylor, 1831–1908, was o. for Liverpool 1858; later Monsignor Canon. Brother of Rev. Roger Taylor, uncle of Rev. John Taylor. Dr Newsham, president of Ushaw, where Taylor had hitherto been educated.

156. *Mr. Buller. Preston*   *7 May 1858*   *5/2/260*

My dear Mr Buller,

I think the Diocese of Liverpool has no ground of complaint against the P.S. Committee; for if we have received little the fault is mainly at our own door. Few applications, comparatively speaking, have been made from this Diocese, & some that have been made, have been rejected as informal. This year, however, the applications have been more numerous, & the grants will consequently be more numerous, but at the same time, of less amount. In some cases, where great efforts have been made, & great sacrifices incurred, in order to erect suitable schools, very little encouragement has been given, because they have supposed from what has been done, more could be done. This mistake would be remedied by the applicant making the Clerical Representative acquainted with the real facts of the case. In many instances I have made the suggestion, but the applications are usually forwarded to me at so late an hour, that I have neither the opportunity of writing nor of verifying the statements, the accuracy of which I am called on to guarantee by my signature. I have not yet received the printed report of the grants or I could have supplied the information you ask. Preceding reports would show the comparative grants in previous years.

Wishing you every blessing, I remain sincerely Yrs in Xt, +A. Goss.

157.   *His Eminence Card. Wiseman   Ascension Day 1858   5/2/270–3*
My dear Lord Cardinal,
According to the rule laid down by the Bps, with your Eminence's sanction, at their last meeting, I hasten to forward to you my views on the plan proposed to our consideration by a circular from the Secretary of the Cath. Poor School Committee. The Committee proposes taking steps to cheapen certain books named; but there is no guarantee to the appropriateness of the selection, & consequently a country priest, unacquainted with their contents may fill his school library at a cheap rate with worthless books, which bear no Imprimatur as a warrant for their orthodoxy & no recommendation of their appropriateness. I think that every book on the list of the P.S. Comm. should have the Imprimatur of the Ordinary where it is published, and that the recommendation of the P.S.C. should be based on such Imprimatur as far as concerns orthodoxy. But leaving to the bishops the province of orthodoxy in faith & morals, I think that they are competent to pronounce on the suitableness of such books for schools; for mere absence of evil, though a great thing in these times, does not give a positive value to a book: it can give, at best, only a negative recommendation.

Hoping that your Eminence continues well I beg to remain, Your sincere & devoted servt. in Xt.

+Alexander Goss

158.   *Right Revd. Dr. Briggs, Bp. of Beverley 15 May 1858   5/2/281*
My dear Lord,
I have examined the passage to which you refer page 55, no 5 1st Prov. Synod,[343] & am of opinion that having consulted your Chapter, you can act as you like, always supposing that you have reasons that would stand a scrutiny at Rome, to which we are liable to have to give an account of the reasonableness as well as the legality of our acts. The same phrase, *de consilio*, is used higher up no 1o. [*sic*] where it implies consulting: for to take & to follow advice are two very different things. Now in changing the investments, according to written faculties forwarded by the Card. from Rome, we must have the consent of the Chap., a word which would not have been used if *de consilio* meant the same. I do not think there is any doubt, & I could refer you to Barbosa,[344] for it was under my notice a short time ago.

People have always access to the Bp: & he can, according to his judgment, act or send the complainant to another tribunal. When I was coadjutor, a complaint, overlooking Dr. Brown, was taken to the Pope, & was referred to me for adjudication, Dr. Brown knowing nothing of it: surely then a person can apply directly to the Bp: access to him must not be in the hands of a Missionary Rector. – I am going into Retreat for a week, but shall be glad to be of any further use. Believe me afftely Yrs A. Goss.

---

[343] The reference is to Decree XVIII, *De Regimine Congregationum seu Missionum*; no. 5 deals with the setting up of new missions and the definition of their boundaries, irrespective of whether the original mission came under a Missionary Rector or not. See *Decreta*, 11–12.

[344] Barbosa: see n. 227.

159. *Rev. W. Henderson, Yealand   31 May 1858*   5/2/285
"Thos. Atkinson & Valladolid"

My dear Mr. Henderson,

I am sorry to say that I take a different view of the letter of Thos. Atkinson[345] to that taken by yourself. My belief is that the boy has no vocation, & that his letter is an indirect way of making known what his selflove dare not honestly avow. His letter travels over much ground & advances many charges, most of which are general, only ten, I may say, particular. 1o. he says they have milk or chocolate for breakfast, but the milk is mixed with water. Now any one who has been abroad knows that goat's milk is more frequently used than cow's milk, which latter is by no means as rich as in England. 2o. I see no hardship in his being asked to fix what he will take for a month: it is a practice <u>universal</u> in Colleges for obvious reasons. 3o. What he says about dinner, I do not believe. Neither Can. Carter nor any other Valladolid priest would lend himself to upholding such diet. Write to Can. Carter & make the inquiry. 4o. There are no female servants in foreign Colleges, & it is the practice at Lisbon as well as Valladolid to perform for themselves certain household duties. For some years after I went to Ushaw, I cleaned not only my own shoes, but those of my pedagogue. From this his humility does not shrink, but it is not his business: true, but it is part of his business which cannot occupy very much of his time. When I was at Rome, my neighbour brushed out his room daily. 5o. He complains of having to sweep the church on account of the fleas etc. Why in Rome, any man of ordinary skill may catch 10 fleas daily. 6o. His scheme of studying with Mr. Clark[346] is visionary & the connexion smacks to me of petting; for on what grounds could Mr. C. ask him, if he would like to be with him on his mission? 7o. He says the College was empty in former times because boys did not like it; now we know that it was empty because the Spanish government had swept away its revenues.

8o. He complains of the severity of the prefect, yet he had no complaint to make regarding the treatment of himself. 9o. He says that if he stays twelve years there, his father & mother may be dead: such consideration might have prevented him going abroad, but surely it does not justify his reflections on the College. 10o. He complains of his clothes; but I question whether they are of coarser material than we wore in Rome. Every body knows that cloth is coarse & dear abroad. The clothing is no worse for him than it was for the many priests who have studied at Valladolid. Mr. Guest has a character for kindness, & I am sure that Can. Dalton, who has recently gone over, is very kind in both manner & disposition.

My experience has proved to me that the boys of poor parents are the sauciest about their diet & the more extravagant in the spending of money, than the children of wealthy parents. I augur no good of the boy & should be sorry to see a priest made out of such material. I should recommend the letter to be sent to the Rector; were a similar letter sent to me about a priest, I should send it to him: for he has no right to make the complaints & shrink from the responsibility of them. I have read his letter several times, & I think that when your first burst of indignation is over, you will come to the same conclusion as myself. Wishing you every blessing, I remain sincerely Yrs in Xt. A. Goss.

---

345 No Atkinson fits in the lists of ordained.
346 No Clark with appropriate dates is listed.

160. [*George Bowyer, Esq.*347]   *4 June 1858*   5/2/291348
My dear Mr. Bowyer,
In answer to your kind favour, I forward the inclosed papers as I received them. It is difficult, without application to the authorities, which I wished to avoid, to obtain accurate information about the gaols. I am told that the writer of Liverpool Life349 states the number in the Borough jails, when he visited it [*sic*], to be one thousand, one half of whom he set down as Catholics. During the year ending Sep. 29. 1857, there were in Lpool 3295 apprehensions for indictable offences, 1334 of which were committed by persons from Ireland, mostly, no doubt, Catholics, & of the 989 committed by persons belonging to Lpool, many no doubt would be Catholics, so that we may safely set down one half of the prisoners in the Borough gaol as Catholics: probably rather less than one half in the County gaol.

There is now more accuracy in the registration of the religion of children sent to the Industrial Schools, in consequence of the watchfulness of a Catholic member of the Vestry, of the Chaplain, & of attention being called to it by a Placard set up in the churches.

We have two paid Chaplains set aside entirely for the public Institutions, & the Clergy of St. Francis Xavier's do the work of a third; not one of whom receives a farthing from the authorities. We have collections in the churches to pay their salaries; but it presses on us as a heavy burden. I hope you may be able to help us or to suggest what we must do to press forward the matter.

With many thanks for your kindly [*sic*], I remain sincerely Yrs in Xt. +Alexander Goss.

---

347   Bowyer: after 1860, Sir George, 7th baronet; lawyer and Whig politician. He had become a Catholic in 1850 and written in favour of the pope's right to restore the hierarchy. He lobbied government for the proper religious instruction of Catholic workhouse children (*ODNB* and see Ward, *The Life and Times of Cardinal Wiseman*, II, 451–2, for a brief account of the legislation, 1858–62; also, J. M. Feheney, 'The Poor Law Board August Order, 1859', *RH* 17:1 (May 1984), 84–91). Bowyer was the notary at three of the provincial synods (*Decreta*, 106, 178, 255).

348   Pages 292, 293 are missing.

349   H. Shimmin, *Liverpool Life: Its Pleasures, Practices and Pastimes* (Liverpool, 1857). For prison statistics and Catholics, see Burke, *Catholic Liverpool*, 89, 90, 94; Bennett, *Father Nugent*, chap. 4; Neal, *Sectarian Violence*, 110–15; Belchem, *Irish, Catholic and Scouse*, 82–5.

161.   *Rev. Mr. OMeara [sic], Blackstock St.*   *12 June 1858*   *5/2/294*
My dear Mr. OMeara,
I am in receipt of your two favours, which have caused me considerable pain, for absence of peace among brethren cannot be the work of God, since his spirit has said, *quam bonum & jucundum fratres habitare in unum*,[350] & he has declared that love for one another should be the mark of his disciples.

In whatever situation or state of life a man may be, his life must be a warfare; neither the episcopal nor the sacerdotal character free a man from this hard condition. Every man, too, must have his special cross, & if it were otherwise, there would be no need of Bps or Priests; for their life is spent in exhorting men to bear their cross patiently & in administering the sacraments to help them to fight the battle of life successfully. No two men can live together without having to bear & forbear, & if a quarrel arises it is as likely to occur from a too great touchiness on one side, as from too great exaction on the other. I do not speak without experience, for I have lived for thirty years in community, & mostly in a secondary position. Even now, I never so much as order a cup of tea: I live as the rest, & never interfere with the procurator's office. The consequence of this exactness is that Dr. Fisher & myself have grown up with mutual respect, & have never exchanged an angry word for the 16 years that we have lived together. How can priests exhort married people to bear their trials, if they cannot themselves bear their own? Thousands of married people will rise up in judgment against you. I do not deny the existence of crosses in Everton Crescent;[351] but I am sure that if you will review your resolutions made during Retreat, you will be sorry, on second thought [sic], to be freed from them.

Wishing you peace & every other blessing, I remain sincerely Yurs in Xt. +A. Goss.

---

350   Trans: 'how good and pleasant it is for brothers to live in unity' (Ps. 133, v. 1).
351   John O'Meara (n. 153) was at Eldon Street at this time.

162.   *Mgr Talbot   5 August 1858, Aberdovey, N. Wales   VEC: Tal 338*
My dear Mgr Talbot
I am exceedingly sorry that I happen to be from home at the time of your visit to Liverpool, as it deprives me alike of the honour of entertaining you & of the pleasure of showing you what is being done in Lpool proper as well as in other parts of the Diocese.

Like other English Dioceses, we are crippled for means, but we have taken advantage of government aid for our schools, & if we can buy land for a church, we do not hesitate to build one trusting to the pence of the poor to enable us to keep it open. Unlike London we have no gentry or even wealthy people living in the town: most reside in the vicinity, & hence they support the suburban rather than the town churches. Again their absence places us under serious disadvantage for the efficient working of the Society of St. Vincent of Paul. The Magdalen Asylum is likely to prove a favourite charity.

Though we do not receive any special notice from the authorities of the town, yet I believe that we enjoy their respect, & in the commitment of criminals to Reformatories we have met with marked favour.

I hope that on your return your own observation will have enabled you to report favourably to the Holy Father & beg that you will present to him the profound & affectionate homage of myself & Diocese to his sacred person & beg his apostolic benediction on the labours of myself & clergy. I need not add that I shall be glad to receive from you any suggestions founded on what you see deficient & remediable amongst. [sic]

Believe me ever to remain, Most sincerely Yours in Xt. +Alexander Goss

163.   *The Sister Superior, Convent, St. Helens[352]   16 August 1858*
                                                                  5/2/298

My dear Superioress,
In your letter of the 10th you desire to have in writing a permission given verbally to the Superioress of the Convent Mt. Pleasant [sic] for benediction of the B.S. at St. Helen's, for the satisfaction of the Jesuit

Fathers who serve the Mission. I can hardly give to this request the definite reply you seek, unless I know what services the Jesuit Fathers are prepared to render. Already Father Ullathorne[353] has certain engagements at Ditton,[354] & the mission of St. Helen's is large & straggling, has many schools, & hence severely taxes the energies of the clergy. You must remember that what is given to you is snatched from the poor or from scanty leisure which hardly suffices for the discharge of their religious or private duties. Amongst us the supply of priests is so inadequate to the duties they have to discharge, that you should not look for distinct services which can be so easily provided abroad. Not being an inclosed order, you can always attend benediction in the Church, & the graces it brings are as great there, as they would be in your private oratory. Every individual in a crowd of 2000 receives as many spiritual graces at Benediction of the B.S. as he would do if the benediction were given in his presence only: nay, as benediction is but the finish of Exposition, & as Exposition is but a more open manifestation of that presence, which exists always in the Tabernacle, for the purpose of doing it honour, private benediction seems somewhat of an anomaly. I await yr. answer.

Wishing yourself & community every blessing, I remain afftely Yrs in Xt. A. Goss.

---

[352] North Road, St Helens: site of an SND convent and school: see John Bridge, *The Lowe House Story 1743–1993* (St Helens, 1993); a new church (Holy Cross and St Helen) was opened in 1862.

[353] Thomas Ullathorne SJ, 1817–1900, at St Helens 1854–86.

[354] Ditton, Widnes: the mission of St Michael was established about 1875 and run by German Jesuits expelled from Prussia; the church was opened in 1879 on land given by the Stapleton-Bretherton family (Kelly, *English Catholic Missions*). Clearly the Jesuits from St Helens were staffing some sort of Mass centre there for several years beforehand.

164. *Rev. Father Bampton S.J.,*[355] *Blackpool   4 September 1858*
5/2/306

"Confraternity of the Sacred Heart of Jesus"

My dear Father Bampton,

I am glad to learn that you have received from the proper authorities letters of aggretation [*sic*] to the Confraternities of the Bona Mors & the Heart of Mary. And I now give you the necessary consent & canonical sanction for the establishment of the Confraternity of the Sacred Heart of Jesus, which seems to me almost a necessity in a church dedicated to the Hearts of Jesus & Mary.

I hope that your people will derive from these Confraternities those spiritual blessings which they usually bring with them, & which are no where more needed than in a mission whose people had previously to the building of the Church at Blackpool lain at a great distance from chapel.

Wishing you every blessing, I remain Sincerely Yrs in Xt. +Alexander Goss.

---

355   George Leopold Bampton SJ, 1816–68, was the first resident priest in Blackpool. The church, dedicated to the Sacred Hearts of Jesus and Mary, was opened in December 1857; designed by E. W. Pugin, it was the gift of Miss Monica Tempest, sister of Sir Charles Tempest of Broughton Hall (Kelly, *English Catholic Missions*).

165. *Rt. Rev. Bp. of Shrewsbury* 14 *September 1858*   *5/2/314*
"Questions"[356]

My dear Lord,

At the time I was made visitor, I was only Coadjutor, & was not a member of any of the boards of administration, & hence had no means of coming at knowledge except thro' questions. Again, being only a subordinate, if I had gone hat in hand, I should have been kicked out, hence it was necessary to knock with a ran-tan to secure admittance. I had paper ruled & supplied by the Diocese so as to secure uniformity for the purpose of having them bound up afterwards. The clergy should be instructed to embody the question in their answers, so that when you examine them you will not have to hold a copy of the questions in one hand. Do not be content with yes or no: you will find it the easiest plan to supply to each Dean an example of the way in which each Quest. ought to be answered, otherwise they won't understand. I delayed the furnishing of maps, plans, etc. till I had settled on some uniform plan. Ever sincerely Yrs in Xt. A. Goss.

---

356   Bishop James Brown had written to ask how to go about organising visitation returns for his diocese.

166. *Rt. Rev. Dr. Grant*   16 *September 1858*   *5/2/322*[357]
Confidential

My dear Friend,

You will think that I am always in hot water; but what you write about is the old affair – the Opposition having failed to compel me to allow them to impugn my arguments in Synod [on] the Cathedrat. of one pound; & having failed by negotiation to induce me to allow certain members of Chapter to meet certain members of the clergy to meet together to compare arguments, & so make me the victim of a middle term, & having farther failed in their efforts to induce me to meet Rev. J. Worthy & two others for the purpose of framing a joint petition to the H.S. against my own acts, they have at length, thro' a Roman Priest, Romagnoli, brought the matter before Propaganda.

They say they had 60 names on the petition originally; but some of the signees withdrew, & most were obtained on false pretences. The whole affair originated with jealousy against my Chapter, & there is not on the document one man of standing, tho' there are names of some good, simple men. Mr. Worthy, <u>probably</u> aided by Mrs. [*sic, read* Messrs] Wells & Dawber, concocted the matter at Burscough. You must bear in mind that the H.S. commissioned my Chapter to raise a maintenance. Thinking themselves as good as the chap. they grumbled that they should be taxed, & hence the encounter. Mr. Worthy you know: he is good, but awkward. At Ushaw, when prefect, he succeeded in causing a rebellion.[358] Mr. Wells is a sample of a man who is not made into a thorough Catholic by having abjured heresy & recited the creed of Pope Pius.[359] Every thing that interferes with him he calls Red tapism: he considers himself a gentleman amongst boors.

Ever sincerely Yours. A. Goss.

With one exception – Newsham – my Chapter are sound & devoted, tho' Worthy has rather made a tool of Hodgson. Mr. Wells actually one day sang mass while a musicless priest said mass & went thro' the manipulations to correspond with the singing at the foot-board. Yet he sets up for a doctor in Israel.

---

[357]   The letter is unclear and difficult to read in parts.
[358]   See n. 326 above.
[359]   William Wells, 1810–75; o. Rome 1848, r. St Mary's, Wigan to 1859, then Croft to 1875.

167. *Rev. J. J. Bond*[360]   *6 October 1858*   *5/2/341*
                             "Confidential"

Dear Rev. Sir,

It is now several weeks since you craved from me the indulgence of a week before adopting further proceedings with reference to the charges which had been made against you. I regret to say that the interval has aggravated rather than lessened them. At that time there were three or only four charges, two of solicitation, said to have occurred in Preston, before you came to Lpool; the others of your having exposed your person in your room at Copperas Hill, & of having elsewhere taken liberties with females. In the solicitation cases, I have ascertained that one of the persons enjoys a reputation for veracity: on the other, perhaps little reliance can be placed, tho' the statement is very circumstantial. The depositions in the two cases, said to have occurred in Lpool, were made before two priests & have been persisted in. No depositions have as yet been taken in the two other cases recently brought before me; but I will have them taken, if you require it, &, after due consultation, I deem it necessary. You stand charged then by four different individuals of having exposed your person to them etc. in Copperas Hill, or of having taken liberties with at least one of them elsewhere. These are out of Confession, & hence allow of investigation; there are besides two other charges, as I said, of *solicitatio*. Now considering the charges brought against you previously at various times, all of which would be considered presumptive evidence against you, I put it to you whether it would not be better for you to retire voluntarily at once from the Diocese of Lpool, than to face an investigation which would not be kept secret by the females who would appear to testify against you. Bear in mind that two have already given evidence most circumstantially before two priests. I had hoped that in the long delay I have accorded you, I should have been freed by your voluntary retirement from the disagreableness of having had to write this letter; but I pray you not to force on the catastrophe such a weight of evidence can hardly fail to bring. Believe me very sincerely Yours in Xt. A. Goss

The girl Ion or [*sic*] Kirk is not one of your accusers.

---

360 See n. 136 above.

168. *His Grace The Archbp. of Trebizond*   *9 October 1858*   *5/2/347*

My dear Grace,

You will of course see my answer to the Cardinal's circular, & I hope that my views are sufficiently explicit as to render my presence unnecessary. Do have compassion on us poor provincials. I do not think that our interests could be better represented than by those whom Providence has placed together: there is the honey of Southwark, the pepper of Trebizond & the salt of Westminster: the gentle, the firm, & the conciliatory are all there.

Inclosed I send you a copy of a note I addressed to the Cardinal on the subject of the reference to you of Newsham's appeal. I cannot account for the delay, which is most serious. My finances will soon be £1000 to the bad, & meanwhile Can. N. is spending every shilling of income, whilst his schools are in such an utter state of neglect that the Government Inspector has told me that all government allowances will be cut off. He has further just helped himself to £100 from the New Cemetery for fees, tho' the Cemetery is not paying int[erest] on borrowed capital. He has also served the Trustees of St. Anthony's with a notice that he shall claim a maintenance from them in case of ejection; but meanwhile he has circulated a report amongst clergy & laity that he has beaten the Bishop, for he has got the matter referred to the Cardinal.

Money transactions to the extent involved in his mission will not admit of such delay. It is 6 months since the appeal was made. I do not think that an appeal against removal from a Mis[sionary] Rector suspends sentence: the laws on appeals refer mostly to censures; where there is a *damnum imminens* they allow you to act.

Ever most sincerely Yrs. Alex. Goss.

169.   *Very Rev. Can. Bamber,*[361] *Sunderland 9 October 1858   5/2/348*
My dear Canon,
I am the last man in the world to attempt to preach an opening sermon. I do not do it, or I should say attempt it, even in my own Diocese. I am a rough & ready speaker & can tell my mind to plain homely Lancashire folks, who are glad to be addressed by one of themselves in their own tongue; but I should be quite at a loss out of my own county on such an occasion. I assure you I have written only one sermon since I came to St. Edward's some sixteen years ago.

Again I cannot at the present time be even absent from home. I have been playing truant like the grasshopper all summer, & now winter is coming I find my work before me. I assure you I seldom leave my room & hardly ever the College inclosure except to some church & back, & yet I have great arrears of work. I try to do things in a right way & this multiplies my work; for I am single handed & tho' all about me are kind in lending a helping hand, yet there are many things which a Bp. must work out for himself. I have just written two letters to deprecate a meeting of Bps in London, so I am sure you will hold me excused – yet I wish you every success & hope you will allow me to subscribe myself. Ever sincerely Yrs. A. Goss.

---

361   John Bamber, 1819–1902, of Hexham and Newcastle Diocese; from Lancashire, edu. at Lisbon.

170.   *Rt. Rev. Bishop of Salford   9 October 1858*   *5/2/349–50*
"Confidential"
My dear Lord,
Mgr. Newsham is again moving to disturb the Sherb. Heatley Trust. He wishes to have an order from the Holy See to compel the Trustees to spend the money not according to their discretion on certain objects specified by the Deed, but according to what he declares to have been Mr. Sherburne's last intentions. He may probably have some paper drawn up by himself & signed by Mr. Sherburne; for some of Mr. Sherburne's letters were written at Ushaw & forwarded under cover to his housekeeper that they might be posted at Kirkham to elude suspicion of the authorship.

The Cardinal, while at Sir. R. Gerard's, desired me to tell the Trustees

that Mgr. Newsham had forwarded his statement to Rome, & wished
them to do the same. Now they do not know what to forward; for they
have never had any information of what is wanted from them, & they
cannot answer statements which they have never seen. At the end of '54
the Card. was empowered to order an arbitration about Youens versus
Sherburne. Arbitrators were chosen, but were never told to act, & now
after 4 years' delay for which no cause has ever been assigned, the Card.
has sent the whole case back to Rome & Mgr. Newsham has already
made his statements, translated them into Italian & forwarded them to
Rome, before Dr. Youens' executors know what they are called on to do.
If you will sign the inclosed, I think it will be of service to the Trustees.
Please to send it back by Sunday's Post, as I shall have an opportunity
of forwarding it, if I receive it from you on Monday morning. Ever truly
Yrs in Xt. A. Goss.

[*Statement to be signed*]
We, the undersigned, judging from the Instructions in the hand writing
of the late Mr. Heatley, found side by side with his Will, believe the
Sherburne-Heatly Trust Deed, as at present constituted, to express his
intentions with regard to the disposal of his money: We believe also
that this was Mr. Sherburne's conviction when he established that Trust
& we know that he has, since then, had no further means of judging of
Mr. Heatley's intention: We believe also that this Deed expresses Mr.
Sherburne's views on the matter, for it was made after mature deliberation & consultation with his Legal Adviser, & after being made was long
in his hands before it was signed; & when signed, was for many years
acted on by Mr. Sherburne & the other Trustees: We know that this Deed
was drawn up by Mr. Sherburne, when the memory of Mr. Heatley's
intentions was fresh in his mind, & when his own faculties were in their
prime, whereas his attempts to change it took place when his memory
was failing & his faculties were weakened: We believe that the opinions
of Counsel against the disturbance of the Deed have been conscientiously given on accurate data for they are good men & good lawyers:
And we fear, with them, that any interference with the discretionary
powers of the Trustees may have the effect of taking the administration
out of Catholic hands, & may also endanger other Catholic Trusts by
accelerating Parliamentary legislation thereon, and We think that Mr.
Sherburne having resigned all dominion over the said Trust Property
ought not to be allowed to resume it by himself or others, further than
he has reserved to himself in the Terms of the said Deed.

171. *Rt. Rev. Bishop of Clifton*[362]   *11 October 1858*   *5/2/351*
My dear Lord,
There is going to be held here a great meetings [*sic*] or rather a series
of meetings for three days for the promotion of Social Science.[363] Mr.

Nugent has no paper, but he wants, I apprehend, to have information to offer on papers read. I think what the nuns have sent may be safely intrusted to him: I wish the good sister had dwelt more on the necessity of the Religious element for the Reformation of the juvenile criminals, as, at present, universal Christianity, as distinct from any belief in special dogma, is held to be the panacea for all ills.

Is not the Bp. of Northampton going to Rome soon?[364] If you can jot me down a few memorabilia on the case in hand, I might forward them to him & ask him to push the question at Prop: for there is nothing like viva voce agency. The Pres. Gen.of the Benedictines is also going at the end of the week.[365]

I dont [*sic*] want to hold my Synod till I know something defnite from Rome about Cathedraticum & the right of petition; for if every priest have a right to have read aloud in Synod what he chooses to call a petition, the Bp. may be compelled to listen to a Disraeli summing up of all the obnoxious acts during the session. Ever sincerely Yours in Xt. Alexr. Goss.

---

362 William Joseph Hugh Clifford, 1823–93; appointed bishop of Clifton in 1857.

363 The National Association for the Promotion of Social Science, founded in 1857, held its second AGM in Liverpool, 11–15 October 1858, in St George's Hall; speakers included Edwin Chadwick, Florence Nightingale and Charles Kingsley. Nugent did not present a paper. See George Hastings (ed.), *Transactions of the National Society for the Promotion of Social Science 1858* (London, 1859). The Liverpool branch had asked Goss to join the planning committee for the conference, but he had turned down 'the honour' on the grounds of being too often absent on business (Secretary's letter book, 5/6/1/305, 3 May 1858). Presumably the unknown nuns were from the community at Arno's Court reformatory, near Bristol. Goss later used statistics given at the conference to put pressure on the government to establish paid Catholic chaplains; see letters 176, 177.

364 Bp of Northampton: Francis Kerril Amherst, 1819–82; appointed to Northampton May 1858, retired 1879.

365 See the following letters.

172.   *Very Rev. Dr. Burchall, Pres. Gen. O.S.B.*[366]   *11 October 1858*
5/2/352

My dear President General,

I take advantage of your visit to the *limina Apostolorum* to beg that you will earnestly press on the attention of the Card. Prefect of Propaganda the necessity of a speedy settlement of the case Youens versus Sherburne & of the desirableness of that settlement taking place in England in consequence of the multitude of documents & the technical difficulties of the case which you will be able to explain to him. In a commercial country, nothing secures the confidence or elicits the alms of the faithful more abundantly than a conviction of the honesty & integrity of those who administer the temporalities of the Diocese, & nothing weakens this confidence more than the loss of public charitable funds & delay in bringing to a settlement doubtful questions. The faithful are aroused to suspicion by delay, & they take more than an ordinary interest in funds from which they or their children may derive benefit. Monies of this sort are involved in the said dispute of Youens versus Sherburne.

Of the attempt of Mgr. Newsham to unsettle the Sherburne Trust Deed I shall say nothing, as your own experience of the dangers to be apprehended from the hostile legislature of a Protestant country make you fully aware of the consequences to be apprehended from interfering with a document which has its highest sanction.

With every best wish, believe me sincerely Yrs. +Alexander Goss.

---

366   Richard Placid Burchall, OSB, 1812–1885; President General 1854–83. Served at St Mary's, Woolton, near Liverpool, and was responsible for building the present church there in 1860. For *limina Apostolorum* see n. 475.

173.   *Very Rev. Dr. Burchall, P.G.O.S.B.* (*sic*)   *Woolton Priory,*
                                    13 October 1858   *5/2/354*

My dear President General,
It is to me a great source of pleasure to be able to say that I have ever found in my brethren of the Benedictine Order in England, both in town & country, zealous fellow labourers in the vineyard of the Lord. At my Visitation I found religion flourishing under their care & I found them, not only anxious to carry out the regulations of the Provincial Synod, but desirous also to follow my suggestions in whatever concerned the spiritual interests of the faithful. On all subjects which came under my notice as Visitor, they unreservedly gave me every information asked for, & even invited inspection for the sake of asking advice in the little difficulties inseparable from Missionary life.

My intercourse with them was entirely as Missionaries, being confined to those matters only which regard the cure of souls. I studiously abstained from making any inquiries or even receiving information in what regarded them as religious, knowing that in whatever regarded religious observance they were answerable only to their Superior in Religion. Peace, good feeling, & kindly intercourse have resulted from this discretion.

Wishing you a prosperous journey & a safe return, I remain, my dear Pres.

Ever sincerely Yrs in Xt. +Alexander Goss.

174.   *Most Rev. Dr. Errington   13 October 1858*   *5/2/355–6 [very*
                                                       faint in places]

My dear Grace,
I send you a copy of my letter to the Card. but, as the matter was

discussed in his absence, I thought you were having the entire management of it. You will see from it that I go altogether with your views, & that I am not so adverse to a meeting, if a majority of the Bps think it requisite, as to decline to be present.

In re Can. News. acting on my own conviction that, pending an appeal, the Bp. not only could, but was bound, to see that Eccles. Property received no harm, I ordered him to transmit to a person named the administration; subsequently I allowed him to remain on condition of his paying into court securities for the payment of int[erest]. This I did in ignorance of the powers of the Mortgagees, which are not civil law powers only, but _ecclesiastical_, as the Bp. of the time was a willing party. The trustees have no other sanction. If the mortgagees had not had the sanction of both civil & eccles. law, they could not have lent money of which they were Trustees for charitable purposes. Taught by this lesson, it only remains for me with the advice of my Chap. to call in for their investment all monies lent to Missionary Rectories, or in fact to chapels; for if non-payment of int[erest] does not constitute a valid ground of removal in case of a Rector Mis. it will not in case of a simple Rector or Pt: for he is no more _amovibilis_ than a Mis. Rector, after the Court has pronounced its sentence.[367] Perhaps an appeal to Rome might upset an _amovibilis_, but if bound to respect his appeal where would a Bp. be with arrears of int[erest] meanwhile. As far as I can see a Rector Mis. who kept a mistress might hold you at bay, if he chose to appeal. As removal is not a censure, I do not think in _any_ case it admits of appeal, any more than the withdrawal of faculties, tho', no doubt, a Bp. doing it irrationally could have his knuckles rapt. I think removal of Rector Mis. would be unlawful, against the command of Synod, an infringement of another's rights; but I do not think that an appeal against an act of injustice, would suspend judgment. There is no law about it & a Rector Mis. has no powers or rights except those _specified_; if it is allowed that he has rights, where are they defined, where do they end? Already there is a disposition to graft Parochus rights on Rectorships, & a stand must be made soemwhere.

Please to refer to Zallinger lib. II, sect. xxviii & xxix _De appellat._ §425. viii, where it is said that appeals in matters of food, salaries, wages, repairing dykes, bridges, &c, cannot delay execution: _ac executio sententiae, maxime ubi de retinenda possessione certatur, non suspendatur_.[368] Tho' I may not act on my impression, yet my belief is, that the Bp. ought to issue a document allowing the mortgages to take possession to prevent loss of funds, but warning them that by granting such permission he does not wish to give any advantage, nor should any advantage be taken by such permission to the rights of the very Rev. Can. News. in quality of Rect. Miss. But that such concession does not affect his claims, but merely puts them in a position to secure from loss of funds for which they are responsible, for the rights of the Church are as much compromised by the breach of trust on the part of the Trustees as by any threatened invasion of the rights of appeal, & they are liable to be called to account both by civil & eccles. law for not having fulfilled their duty. Again I do not think the Card. should allow himself to be considered an adviser in cases between a Bp. & priest, or in cases that may subsequently come before him as judge. Ever truly Yrs A. Goss.

---

367   The status of 'amovability' was attached to certain missions and thence to the rector of such a mission. He could still be removed for certain actions that were thought to render his rectorship inefficient or illegal, but only after formal examination of the case by the bishop and three synodal consultors; the rector had a right of appeal. See *Decreta*, 11, 60–1. For a summary of the rather complex issues involved, see T. L. Bouscaren and A. C. Ellis, *Canon Law: A Text and Commentary* (3rd edn, Milwaukee, 1957), 191–3 (although this refers to the post-1917 Code situation).

368   Trans: 'and the execution of the sentence is not suspended, especially where there is a dispute over keeping possession'. Zallinger: Jacques-Antoine Zallinger Zum Thurm SJ, 1735–1813, professor of canon law at Augsburg and Rome, wrote a number of important works on ecclesiastical law. See *DDC* VII, 1668.

175.   *Rt. Rev. Dr. Grant*   14 October 1858   *5/2/358*
                          Most Confidential

My dear Friend
When at Sir R. Gerard's the Card. told me that he was referring back to Rome the questions which, when we were in Rome together, were ordered by Prop. to be referred to arbitration, each side selecting their own arbitrators. The Card. refused Bps. & ordered 12 priests to be chosen from which he would select two. An appeal was made to Rome & during the second Synod he received a letter, allowing the parties to select their own arbitrators. After some little delay that was done, but from that day to this, they have never met. No official reason has been assigned, & now the case has to be sent to where it was four years ago. Meanwhile Dr Newsham has had such information of what was intended as to enable him actually to have already translated his statement before Prop. I don't say who does the injustice, but this way of acting is not just, measured by English standards. As there is a sum at stake of something like 30 or £40,000, it is thought advisable that a priest should go to Rome, accredited in what refers to our Dioceses by Salford, Shrewsbury & Lpool: the Sherb. Heat. Trustees stand on their own bottom, as the trust is not applicable to any special diocese. I cannot spare a pt. beyond Xmas: could he manage in that time? How often does Prop. meet? once a month? Is December a working meeting or merely for mass? I want to keep the whole matter at present secret. Could my envoy, probably Dr Fisher, be of service to you? Dr Cullen[369] you know is there. If I can bring Dr Briggs to any thing I shall propose a

move about the College, for the present system is an intolerable tyranny on the part of H.E. For six years we have been ciphers: our opinion is never asked: the whole system is revolutionised, education is dearer, & with 36 in a school cannot be better, whilst they are building & spending to a fabulous extent. Speak out in your reply & say what you think would be best.   A. Goss.

[*Added in space at top of the page as a postscript*]
I think the Trustees could fight their own battle better than I could: their Deed is registered in Chancery & I think they will resign their trust rather than be compelled to act against the Deed.

I have calmed the mind of the Superioress.[370] How often she must regret the little Bp. of Southwark. I am too distant with them.

---

[369]   Dr Cullen was Archbishop of Dublin; see n. 60 above.

[370]   This probably refers to letter 163 above; the Notre Dame nuns had opened a house in Southwark in 1854.

---

176.   *Rev. R. Doyle, St. Anthony's*[371]   *25 October 1858*   *5/2/368*
"Institutions. Statistics"

My dear Mr. Doyle,
You have made a mistake about Mr. Carter's paper read at the meeting of Social Science. His statistics are taken from the Police Reports, & he speaks not only of those who have passed thro' the Boro' gaol, but of the general criminal population. I have referred both to his paper & the Police Reports.

In the letter to Mr. Bowyer I think it would be wise to limit yourself to a simple statement of facts as they come under your cognisance or knowledge: I would recommend therefore the omission of all conjectural statistics.

The account should be written on folio. I propose writing in a few days to him, as soon as I can get the returns from the Workhouses. I will send them also on folio, so that he can more readily file them for reference. In all probability he will lay them before the Home Secretary as he receives them, hence it is desirable to omit all feeling, as tho' it may relieve us of a part of our indignation, it damages our cause with those who are endowed with marble senses.

Wishing you every blessing I remain sincerely Yours in Xt. +Alexander Goss.

---

[371]   Richard Doyle, 1819–87, worked in India and Shrewsbury before moving to Liverpool in 1856 where he was chaplain to the prisons and public institutions until 1859; he served at The Willows and at Lea, where he was described as 'stern, mysterious, coldly grandiose, eccentric, determined and inflexible' and as keeping his eyes shut while he preached; Hewitson, *Our Country Churches*, 304.

177.   *Rev. J. Nugent*   *25 October 1858*   *5/2/369*
                        "Workhouse statistics"

My dear Mr. Nugent,

As I am anxious again to bring under the consideration of Government thro' Mr. Bowyer, our unremunerated services at Public Institutions, I shall feel obliged if you will ascertain for me: 1o. the total number of persons in the Workhouse, say during last month, or average number in a year. 2o. What numbers of these totals are Catholics? 3o. What amount of Sunday service do you give to them? Do you give services at any other time? 4o. How often does Mr. Fleetwood visit the Workhouse, & how long does he remain? This you may have some diffculty in ascertaining, as he may possibly keep no account: but yet an approximation to accuracy may be obtained from him. I write to you, tho' it is a matter that regards him, as I do not like bothering him with questions, the drift of which he may misunderstand. I shall be glad of this nformation as soon as you can conveniently procure it.

Wishing you every blessing, I remain sincerely Yrs in Xt. Alexander Goss.

178.   *Most Rev. Archbishop of Trebizond*   *4 November 1858*   *5/2/381*

My dear Grace

Many thanks for your letter. I will be at my post to sustain the freedom of education, yet on other counts, I am most averse to the meeting. I cannot disguise from myself that the Card. is, in more than one case where this Diocese is concerned, both judge and advocate. My Finance Committee tell me that I am at a dead lock, that I cannot furnish interest on the £9,000 invested at St Anthony's. I have, therefore, no remedy but to announce a smash, which I will do if I hear nothing from Rome before December. Either I must be content to be posted as a rogue, who has lived on others [*sic*] money, or I must explain how I am unable to meet my engagements. Clergy & laity alike yearn for government security for our monies; &, if I mistake not, Dr Hogarth makes all his Deeds trusts; & if so, he has an object.

Inclosed is a letter from Mr H. Vaughan[372] which please to return. I wrote to him, as I was told he had some decisions of Rome on the case on which I wrote to you: it appears to be a cognate case. I believe with you that the *cura animarum* gives the right to have Mass; but I believe also, that the benefit of that Mass will go, tho' nominally *pro popolo*, to the person who pays for the support of the Church. People have no right to a priest, if they cant [*sic*] or wont [*sic*] support him & consequently can have no right to a mass: but I have not studied the question. I don't exactly like the bargaining which your solution involves.

Ever most sincerely Yours A. Goss.

It is hardly a sound state of things when a priest of a diocese can boast among the laity as Canon N. has done, that he has beaten the Bp. because he has got his case referred to the Card.

---

372 H. Vaughan: presumably the future cardinal, 1832–1903, o. 1854 and on the staff at St Edmund's, Ware, and vice-president there in 1855.

179. [*Cardinal Wiseman*] *19 November 1858*   *5/2/390*

My dear Lord Cardinal,

At the risk of being thought importunate duty compels me to draw the attention of your Eminence to my letter of the 13th. At Xmas my Finance Committee must suspend payment, for my Diocese cannot stand the abdication of a capital of £20,000 or more, under which it now groans. In July I signified to Prop. my consent to the hearing of the case in England. In August, three months ago, your Eminence, consulted by Card. Barnabò, signified your approval, but up to this time I have not heard one word further.

The financial ruin, however, is nothing compared with the spiritual ruin. Hithero, to spare Canon Newsham's character, I have forbourne [*sic*] to make it a matter of enquiry; but when the sick are allowed to die without the Sacraments further forbearance would be guilt.

I have the honour to remain, my dear Eminence, Your obedt. Servt. in Xt. +Alexander Goss

180. *Rev. Mr. Bridges,*[373] *17 Everton Crescent*   *13 December 1858*
                                                                   5/2/405

"Indian Chaplaincy"

Dear Rev. Sir,

If your object in seeking an Indian chaplaincy be to save your soul by work, you need not go so far for this purpose. There is more work to be done, greater good to be achieved, & more souls to be saved in the Blackstock St. Mission than in India. If your letter on the subject has not received earlier attention, the reason has been that I consider your project visionary & I cannot for one moment entertain it whether by letter or interview. I transact no business by interviews, because they are open to misunderstanding & are a great waste of time.

This letter gives me an opportunity of saying how much I have been grieved at the list of miserable trifles which you brought under the notice of the Vic. General as grievances. You have fallen amongst evil counsellors who have abused your inexperience. Let me entreat of you to retrace your steps, to take the advice of a prudent director, to study, as the model for your missionary labours, the lives of St. Francis of Sales, St. Philip, St. Vincent of Paul, or, believe me, your labours in the

Lord's vineyard will be without fruit, if not positively injurious. You are too young to be thinking of saving yourself labour by restricting services for the poor. If the people desire your presence in the Confessional every day, & not merely three days a week, you are bound to attend. Your recreation & your work should lie amongst your people. Think, I beseech you, if you want either to save your own soul or be instrumental in saving the souls of others. Praying that God may give you an apostolic spirit, I remain truly Yrs in Xt. +Alexander Goss.

---

373 Thomas Bridges 1832–1916, o. December 1857; at Eldon Street to 1860; served in the diocese until his death but see letters 245, 250.

181. *Rev. J. Carr, Isle of Man*   *27 December 1858*   *5/2/411*
                      "Wayward helpers"

My dear Mr. Carr,
You have now discovered by experience the waywardness of youth in your two coadjutors. I know nothing of Mr. Coll's spiritual difficulties: they must have been laid before the Vicar.[374] Nor can I act upon them without knowing them; for were I to admit the authority of Confessors in the conduct of affairs, I should cease to be pastor of the Diocese tho' retaining the responsibility. I cannot think that <u>duty</u> has been discharged in the Island till I learn that there is a complete written status animarum for the four towns, the mines, &, as far as practicable, the bye ways of the Island. Again, when this has been done, it will reveal much ignorance & neglect of sacraments & so open the way for additional work. Then I think it is very desirable for a young man to have time for <u>hard</u> study: it is one of the most discouraging features of the day that, as a rule, there is <u>no study</u> amongst the clergy: a newspaper, the Rambler or a Review seems the extent of their reading. The exceptions are few. I shall have to advertise for a race of coadjutors for missions, as most of the present ones have vocations to be head priests. I have no present intention of making any change in the Island: but if I do will communicate with you & bear your wishes in mind.

Wishing yourself & Confreres every blessing, I remain, Sincerely Yrs in Xt. +Alexander Goss.

---

374 After the Isle of Man Coll went to Eldon Place, Liverpool; in 1862 he asked for a transfer on health grounds to Hexham and Newcastle, where his brother was a priest. Goss claimed it was his own fault that he found the diocese uncongenial: 'you know (and God knows) this is not the result of hard work but —' [*sic*]. Goss also demanded that Coll repay the cost of his education or get his new bishop to do so, just as Goss himself had had to pay a bishop £200–£300 when a student transferred late in his studies to Liverpool. Failing this payment, Goss would settle for a Mr Smith, a Chorley man newly ordained for Hexham and Newcastle, in exchange! Not surprisingly, Bp Hogarth rejected these transfer

arrangements, but accepted Coll, and Goss seems to have let him go without further ado. We do not have Coll's date of death. (Letters 5/4/324, 326 and 335, all of June 1862.)

182.   *Very Rev. H. Greenhalgh, Weld Bank   30 December 1858*
                                                                   5/2/418
                                "Adlington"[375]

My dear Canon,
We ought to increase the number of our country missions, for many of these in the Diocese are not available for a weak or an elderly priest, as they belong to the Regulars. The Diocese is deceptive, for few give themselves leisure or trouble to consider, or they would find that the Secular clergy are in a minority in this Diocese.[376] With every best wish, Truly Yrs in Xt. A. Goss.

---

[375]   Adlington: a mill and pit village near Chorley.
[376]   An odd claim for Goss to make: in 1856 there were 137 priests in the diocese, sixty-six of whom were Regulars, seventy-one Seculars, but it was a close run thing.

183.   *H. W. Lloyd Esq.*[377]   *31 December 1858*   *5/2/427*
       Sec. of Association for publishing Cath. Books [*sic*]
Dear Sir,
I write to thank you for the copies of the books already issued by the Association, & to give also my cordial approval of the plan for providing a series of Class books for Schools. I can offer no useful suggestion to gentlemen so well up to the task they have undertaken. In the execution of the task I think it would be well for the writers & compilers to bear in mind the necessity of counteracting the tendency of uncatholic books, which are objectionable on the score of omission more than commission. God & his providence & prayer are studiously kept back as agents in human affairs, & youth are taught that everything depends on self-reliance and their own determination to get on. The whole education movement, if not intended, is calculated to impress youth with a desire to rise above their sphere, not in their sphere of action, and wealth is set before them as the guerdon of mental culture. Extracts, minute and circumstantial in detail, are better than summaries, for giving an accurate summary of the various periods of history. Views of history whether sacred or profane, & scenes from lives rather than continuous biographies should be given: for they strike & remain, while methodical abridgements pass bodily away from the memory. The every day struggles of heroes whether in profane or sacred biography should be given if the reader is to derive any advantage. We cannot learn to work miracles, by reading of them; but we can learn how to fight the

battle of life in city, town, & country, by seeing how men like ourselves fought it with success & achieved holiness.

Praying you to excuse this hurried note & wishing the undertaking every success & yourself every blessing, I remain sincerely Yrs in Xt, A. Goss.

---

377   Howell William Lloyd, 1816–93. A convert clergyman, archaeologist, historian and author, he was later appointed external lecturer to University College, Kensington.

184.   *His Grace The Archbishop of Trebizond   31 January 1859*
5/2/458

My dear Grace,
There is great discrepancy between your account & the Cardinal's of the proceedings of the Westminster Chap. On Wednesday he called together Drs. Brown, Roskell & myself at Mr. Challoner's. He told us there was to be a Synod not later than July for the settling of divers matters, as Prop. now seemed to refer every difficulty to a future Synod. He said that his Chap. assumed the right not only to <u>give advice</u>, but to have their advice followed in what regarded the Seminary:[378] that they pretended also to have a right to advise the Bp. in other matters, in which their advice was not sought, & in cases in which the Bp. was not bound to seek it; that in order to give advice they claimed a right to institute inquiry, & that his Chap. had even summoned witnesses before it for the purpose; that, when he had annulled their acts, they had, without obtaining his consent – an official requisite – sent off their papers to Rome, which were of that character that Card. Barnabò told the Pope he could not touch such parchments without soiling his fingers. All this had taken place, he said, simultaneously with the letter of Drs. Brown, Turner, Briggs & myself. This letter, he said, opened up a new subject, viz. the amount of jurisdiction possessed by Bishops over a common Seminary. Dr. Roskell said he thought the question of funds ought to be considered: but the Card. answered that such an inquiry would open a *mare magnum*: in fact that we could not legislate about Colleges in the form of decrees, but only in the way of suggestions to the H.S. Lunch was announced & our conversation terminated as abruptly as my letter. Ever truly Yrs. +A. Goss.

---

378   For Wiseman's major rows over the role of the chapter, the Oblates and the seminaries, see Schiefen, *Nicholas Wiseman*, esp. chapter 6. Goss wrote in similar terms to Bp Turner on 1/2/59. See also the next letter to Briggs and letter 190.

185. *Rt. Rev. Dr. Briggs*   *1 February 1859*   *5/2/461*
Confidential

My dear Lord,

I quite agree with you as to the necessity of our Clergy & Canons & also of the Bishops having their due say as to the administering of our Seminaries. Now the question of the rights of the Clergy & Chap. are the very ones that have been mooted at Westminster & which have been ordered by the Pope to be referred to the Synod, which, Talbot[379] writes to the Cardinal, ought to be held not later than July. Our chance – & Archbp. Errington strongly urges this view – lies in having our affairs referred also to the Synod. They are in fact identical: for as the Chapter & clergy are only advisers, tho' necessary advisers to the Bishop, a discussion on their rights must necessarily be based on an admission of these our rights. At a meeting of Drs. Brown, Roskell & myself, convened by the Card. he said we had started a new question, viz. the rights or jurisdiction of the Bishops over a College held in common: now that question was raised by Dr. Hogarth in his petition to the Holy See, & not by us. The Card. has put us off for 8 years, & may put us off for 8 years more, if we contend for our rights apart: now if we get the whole matter referred to Synod we shall have the support of the Chapters & of most Bishops who have shares in Colleges <u>out</u> of their dioceses. Dr. Newsham is only one at a Synod, without a decisive vote, whereas at the Ushaw meeting he had an equal vote with the Bishops. On learning your adhesion to this view, in which we are all agreed, I will write to Card. Barnabò in answer to his letter.

    Ever most sincerely Yrs. in Xt. A. Goss.

The Card. was 4 whole days in Liverpool, arriving on Monday & leaving on Friday, without calling at St. Edward's.

---

[379] The Hon. Mgr George Talbot, 1816–86, son of the third Baron de Malahide, a convert, spent almost all his priestly life in Rome. He had too much influence there and interfered too much in English matters, making himself unofficial agent for the English bishops. Manning, for whom he worked tirelessly, described him as 'the most imprudent man who ever lived'; he was completely opposed to Newman. See J. Champ, *ODNB*.

186. *Rt. Rev. Bishop of Shrewsbury*   *1 February 1859*   *5/2/462*
Confidential

My dear Lord,

Inclosed I forward Dr. Briggs's draft of a letter to the Card. of which I spoke. Dr. Briggs agrees that it is better that you should write in our name, than that we should write a joint letter. It is much less formal, & his own letter acknowledges the receipt of the copy of our letter to Card. Barnabò, is addressed only to you. I think you might further add that, as you gathered from what he said at our little meeting, of College questions having to form the burden of our deliberations in the future Synod, a copy of what had already been done might guide us in our views. None of us have ever seen the scheme he drew up, & none of us, till the receipt of his letter, was aware that the scheme was now being acted on at Ushaw. If it gives us no more jurisdiction than we at present exercise, it is a delusion.

Either the Card. or Archbishop Errington must have grievously misunderstood the nature of the proceedings of the Chap. at Westminster: for they differ *toto caelo*.[380] Is it right that having to settle the questions at Synod, we should be summoned together to hear a one-sided statement? Would the Card. think it right if the Chap. were to do by a circular what he did by word of mouth? I like a fair game. Ever sincerely Yrs in Xt. Alexander Goss.

---

[380]   Trans: 'totally'.

187. *Rev. Jas. Carr*   *1 February 1859*   *5/2/463*

My dear Mr. Carr,

Mr. Holmes[381] declines to go to the Isle of Man, as a matter of preference, & as the only object of change was to have willing workers, nothing would be gained by substituting one ego for another.

The only remedy for Mr. Singleton's[382] doubts about the salvation of his soul, is daily morning meditation, a day's retreat monthly, & a ten days retreat annually. This will remove uneasiness, if really felt, of conscience, better than the dissipation of Liverpool which offers quite as many inducements to indulgence as to work. Bid him meditate on the words of our Lord to St. Peter that when he was young he guided himself & went where he would; but now that he is older & has exchanged his liberty for the guidance of Christ, another will guide & direct him. If he claims the position of gentleman from his clerical office he must needs fulfil its duties. With regard to food, bid them not to be solicitous. The Senior priest has to provide the house, as well as to exercise the *cura animarum*, & no one gives orders to servants except him. I never ask a servant to do for me what I can do myself, nor do I ring a bell twice a year. For the 16 years I have lived here, I have never ordered a dish, & when I have not liked a dish on the table, I have not ordered another, tho' I knew it was in the house. Consult no one's fancies as to food, but provide what is sufficient & wholesome. With the exception of bacon at breakfast in lieu of butter, we have at St. Edward's flesh meat only once in the day, i.e. at dinner, & we have no lack of work. Ever truly Yrs in Xt. A. Goss

Push your collection in & out of the Island.

381 Peter Holmes, 1828–82; at St Vincent's, Liverpool at this time, he died from typhus caught while visiting the sick.

382 James Singleton, 1831–72; he was in the Isle of Man from ordination in 1858 until 1860.

188. *His Grace The Archbishop of Trebizond   4 February 1859*
5/2/466

Private

My dear Grace,

Dr Fisher's last letter bears date Jan. 29, & announces that the Westminster business will not again occupy attention till after the Synod. He says that Card. W's letters to Patterson[383] & one for Barnabò during the present year, remained at the Post Office till the 25th when they were all given at once to Patterson. Patterson could do nothing, & could make no change on any point. The matter is left to the Synod & there it must be, a decision which has mortified our Card. Dr. F. says that P. Cullen's views do not differ from yours, & he says you might write to him on any subject with the greatest safety. Dr. F. promises to speak to Barnabò about referring our College matters to Synod: he says it would be best for us to address a petition to the Pope: he knows it would please B. & not displease the Pope. It is said that Card. W. will be very amenable & manageable before the Synod, but that after it he will rely on the chances of delay & getting the decrees buried for a while: a fortiori, if he gets our labours put in the form of suggestions only. Passaglia has left the Jesuits.[384]

Dr. Briggs has at length agreed with the other Bps that I should write to Barnabò to ask him to refer our matter to the Synod & I am doing so & am asking him to give specific instructions, as our labours last Synod on the subject, under the instructions of Fransoni,[385] ended in nothing.

I hear that the Tory paper commented on the fact that the Bp of Lpool had nowhere appeared in public with the Card. I do not think that the lad who threw the stone at the carriage was hired, but I will enquire.[386] On Feb. 2nd I laid the stone at Eldon St, with the whole street crowded & banners across it: at night there was a sermon on the ground, but there was no manifestation of any kind on either occasion. It is only when we put on the lion's skin that we are laughed at. I dined with the Card. on both state days: there was neither mayor nor corporation: how silly announcements of what is to be & is not, make us appear: yet they will reach the Vatican as they appear in print.

Ever Yours, A. Goss.

383 James Laird Patterson, 1822–1902; a convert, educated in Rome and ordained 1855. He was frequently used by Wiseman on Roman business; he was president of St Edmund's 1869–80, when he was appointed auxiliary bishop of Westminster (Plumb, *Arundel*).

³⁸⁴   Carlo Passaglia, 1812–87, professor of dogmatic theology at Collegio Romano in 1845 and said to be one of the finest theologians of his age; after 1848 he lived for a time in England, France and Louvain. He fell out with his Jesuit superiors and left the Order 'noisily' in 1858. Pope Pius appointed him Professor of Philosophy at La Sapienza; he became an apostle of reconciliation between the Vatican and the new Italian state, but pleased neither side. See *DTC* XI, cols. 2007–10.

³⁸⁵   Cardinal Fransoni, Prefect of Propaganda, see n. 87 above.

³⁸⁶   For the stone-throwing incident, see Burke, *Catholic Liverpool*, 137–8; Neal, *Sectarian Violence*, 167, and letter 190.

189.   *Rt. Rev. Dr. Turner*   *4 February 1859*   *5/2/467*
Confidential

My dear Lord,

Dr. Briggs has written to say that he is willing that the subject of our letter to Card. Barnabò should be referred to the approaching Synod, & I will write accordingly by to-morrow's post to that effect. In the extract which you forwarded to me Card. Wiseman clearly indicates that we were acting irregularly in pressing for a decision in our case, when the general question of which ours was a part had been referred to Synod. [*added here between lines*] I will cite the passage in my letter to Barnabò.

When he spoke about our letter coming at the same time as the petition of the Westminster Chap. I told him that the coincidence was accidental, as our meeting had been partially arranged at least 6 weeks previously. In his letter I see he states that we must be prepared after combatting for the Chap. to find a new conflict arise against the exaggerated views they may take about their rights, so that in his own mind he views in a similar light our proceedings & those of his Chapter. His letter, however, is much more cautiously worded than he chose to express himself to us at Mr. Challoner's. I do not think he fully realises the position taken by the Chapter: I should think Dr. Errington's statement more likely to represent their views. No letters have passed between the Chap. of Westminster & mine, nor do I think they have sought support elsewhere.

Believe me very sincerely Yours in Xt. +A. Goss.

190.   *Rt. Rev. Dr. Briggs*   *5 February 1859*   *5/2/468*

My dear Lord,

Many thanks for your note. I write by today's post to Card. Barnabò as follows. "I write to thank your Eminence for your kind favour of the 7th of Jan. a copy of which I have sent to the Bps of Beverley, Salford & Shrewsbury, by whom the letter addressed to your Eminence from Lpool, on the 15th of Dec. 1858 was signed, & I have been directed by them to convey to your Eminence their united thanks for the kindness of

your letter & the information which it gives, thus furnishing a new proof
of your knowledge of our affairs & your solicitude for whatever concerns
the education of ecclesiastical students. We have communicated with his
Eminence, the Archp of Westminster, & he gives us to understand that a
Synod has to be held immediately, & that one of its duties will be to take
into consideration what relates to Seminaries, according to the instructions of Card. Fransoni June 25, 1855,[387] especially in what relates to
deputies of chaps [*sic*] & clergy, & the discussion of what modification
might be necessary in regard to the character of those institutions & the
condition of the country. (I then quote the words of Card. W.'s letters)
I am instructed by the Bps of Beverley, Salford & Shrewsbury to say
that they do not wish for themselves any exceptional legislation & that
they are quite content to yield to the views of Card. W. in this matter, &
therefore authorise me to petition your Eminence to refer to the Synod
the consideration of the jurisdiction to be held by Bps over seminaries
which are the joint property of several Bps." I then give it as my own
opinion that the jurisdiction of the Bps must be defined before the Synod
can assign how far the chapter & clergy have a right to advise him on
its exercise.

When you have read this please to send it to Dr. Turner as it saves
me writing.

Believe me ever most sincerely Yrs A. Goss.
The mob so far damaged Mr Chaloner's carriage, which was supposed
to contain the Card., by throwing brickbats that it has had to be sold &
only realised £15.

---

[387] Date changed from 6; the true date of Fransoni's letter was 27 June 1855; see
Decreta, 161.

191. *Very Rev. Mr. Gradwell,*[388] *Claughton   7 February 1859*
                                                              5/2/474

My dear Mr. Gradwell,
I send you a rough draft of a balance sheet, which I think will be found to
contain all necessary items, without entering into unnnecessary particulars. If all priests worked their missions & kept their books as you do,
it would be quite unnecessary for any Bp. to make any inquiries about
income or expenditure; but such is not the case & general returns, both
in Church & parliament, are often called for in order to get at a single
particular. Recently I had to pay £10 of a tailor's bill for a priest, & I am
still paying something ever & anon to lessen the debts of another. The
continuance of Can. N. at St. Anthony's, after my efforts to remove him,
was effected at a cost of £1000: for he paid no int[erest] for those two
years; & yet the very priests whose money was jeopardised are the first

to cry out against his removal. Neither St. Anthony's, nor St. Joseph's, nor St. Alban's have paid off any debt for years, & yet the erection of every new church in their neighbourhood diminishes their means. We are hurrying on to a universal bankruptcy, & should ere this have been bankrupt, if God had not sent us a chancellor of the Exchequer in the person of Can. Jas. Fisher. I had hoped that the returns in the balance sheets would have enabled me to legislate on the subject of fees, but the letters & remarks that reach me from an irascible & cloud capt [*sic*] Doctor, & a talkative do-nothing, have more than disgusted me: but it was ever so. To borrow the indignant expression of the Latin Poet: a bp. is a common —— post [*sic*] for every dog. Begging my kind remembrance & hoping the new year will treat you better than the old, I remain sincerely Yrs in Xt. A. Goss.

Robert will be surprised to hear that Passaglia has left the Jesuits. Sir Jas. Sutton has established at Bruges an Anglo-Belgian College: we have each one place & shall have more.[389]

---

[388]   Henry Gradwell, cousin of Bp Brown, 1792–1860; succeeded his brother Robert (later VA in London) at Claughton-on-Brock; canon 1851–4 but resigned; after his death in 1860 he was succeeded by his nephew Robert who had been his curate there and who stayed there to d. in 1906: author, and donor of the Gradwell Library at Upholland College (now part of Liverpool Hope University library).

[389]   Actually Sir John Sutton. On the college in Bruges, see Stewart Foster: 'The Life and Death of a Victorian Seminary: the English College, Bruges' *RH* 20:2 (October 1990), 272–90.

---

192.   *Circular*[390]   *12 February 1859*   *5/2/476*

Dear Rev. Sir,

I have been exceedingly pained to learn that several instances have occurred in which persons have died without the sacraments. I hope, therefore, that you will take efficient steps to prevent this in your mission, or if it have [*sic*] occurred already, to prevent, at least, its recurrence. The law of residence is exceedingly strict, & no mission ought to be left without due provision being made for the attendance of casual sick calls. As the junior priests are immediately responsible to the Senior priest for the fulfilment of the duties assigned to them, they ought not to absent themselves for "*notabilem diei partem*" without his knowledge, nor as a matter of courtesy & economy ought they to dine out, without advertising him of the fact. I have myself always observed, & still observe this practice. They should, moreover, leave word with the servant where they may be found, when not out of town. "*Ne contingat seniorem & juniores sacerdotes eodem tempore extra missionis fines versari, horum neuter limitibus egredietur, nisi altero praemonito. Cura quoque sit, ut quotiescumque, breviori etiam tempore, domo quis abesse voluerit, de eo saltem domesticos moneat, eosque informat, ubi, pro casus exigentia, adiri ac inveniri possit.*"[391] What an excellent regulation for our guidance! I never grudge a priest his vacation, but I like to see him mind his work at other times. Absence from home, a love of dining out, & a desire to go into society are a mark of an inconstant & frivolous mind, that neither loves study nor the duties of the sacred ministry.

Wishing you every blessing, I remain sincerely Yours in Xt. A. Goss

Please to read this to your clergy & then forward it to the priest whose name follows yours on the back of this note. I shall be glad of the experience of yourself & brother clergy to enable me to lay down some more permanent regulations on these matters.

---

[390] No names of missions or priests are given. The following individual letter of the same day is interesting in this context. A fair hand-written copy of the circular is bound in at the end of the volume.

[391] Translation: 'Lest it happen that the senior and junior priests are outside the bounds of the parish at the same time, neither should leave the limits of the parish without alerting the other. Care should also be taken that whenever anyone has planned to be away from the house, even for a shorter time, he should at least alert the servants and inform them where he is going and can be found in case of an emergency'. Quotation from Synod of Ireland; see n. 394.

193.   *Rev. J. Holland,*[392] *Blackstock St.   12 February 1859   5/2/477*
Dear Rev. Sir,
I have now before me a letter in which you are stated to have designated some members of the choir in Black Stock St. Chapel impertinent <u>sluts</u> for daring to sing the benediction service without an organ, & that you called them fools for singing at all, when they told you that they lost much time in coming to sing. Without stopping to inquire whether you applied the unbecoming epithet as stated, I cannot but think that you do not clearly understand the nature of your position at Blackstock St, for I was more than surprised on the occasion of my visit to that church to have you continuing the mass quite irrespective of the choir. Now all matters concerning church services are under the jurisdiction of the Senior priest, *nec licet aliis sacerdotibus illi in ministerii adjutorium adjunctis aliquid aggendi [sic] praeter illius voluntatem.*[393] Instead of manifesting your disapproval either before one of the people of the singing of the choir, & thereby indirectly of what had the sanction of the Senior priest, you ought, on the contrary, to remember that in what concerns the discharge of your pastoral duties, you ought openly to testify to him, what your duty compels you to give him, honour & obedience. *Meminerint Coadjutores* – enacts the Synod of Ireland[394] – *Parochum esse rectorem parociae, & proinde erga parochos rever-*

entiam et subjectionem exhibeant, illos semper consulant de rebus in parochia ordinandi & nihil ipsis invitis innovent. The teaching of other Churches is the same, *quum repugnat legibus ecclesiae pluribus sacerdotibus simul ex aequo concedere auctoritatem pastoralem regendi eamdem ecclesiam.*

Wishing you every blessing I remain sincerely Yrs in Xt. +Alexander Goss.

---

392   Jeremiah Holland, 1829–88; Irish born. At Eldon Street 1858–60. Blackstock Street: see Kelly, *English Catholic Missions*, 257.

393   Trans: 'nor is it allowed to other priests, his helpers in the ministry, to do anything unless he wills it'.

394   Synod of Ireland: the major reforming synod held in Thurles, 1850; see *Decreta synodi plenariae episcoporum Hiberniae apud Thurles habitae, anno MDCCCL* (Dublin, 1851), pp. xvi and 79. The quotation is from the section *De Coadjutoribus Parochorum*, n. 4: 'Let Curates remember that the Parish Priest is the rector of the church, and therefore let them show reverence and obedience to parish priests, always consulting them about the arrangements for parochial matters and not introducing anything new against their wishes.' [*then*:] 'since it is repugnant to the laws of the church for several priests to have at the same time equal pastoral authority to rule the same church'.

---

194.   *Rev. S. Walsh, Southport   12 February 1859*   *5/2/478*
'Southport & St. Alban's'

Dear Rev. Sir,

Anxious to oblige you & to give you a chance of establishing for yourself a character for missionary zeal, I am induced to appoint you, which I hereby do, to assist Rev. Mr. Kelly at St. Alban's Lpool, on your being relieved at Southport by the Rev. Mr. Cooke. I feel it, however, a duty to give you some admonitions, yet without thereby wishing to endorse as true the various reports which have from time to time reached me. Make the mission house your home: do not accept, much less seek invitations out, whether for dinner or supper. All Synods discountenance lay society, as being inimical to a priest's discharge of duty, & to be ill at ease at home, to spend the day or the evening out, & to love parties are the signs of a want of a proper vocation. I do not grudge a priest a suitable vacation: but I like him to mind his work for the other part of the year. Even when you do go out, do not return later than 11 o'clock. Be careful in the use of spirits, at home or abroad: for disparaging reports have reached me. Above all keep a guard over your tongue, particularly re ecclesiastical matters. Remember that to the Senior Priest you are bound to yield both due honour & obedience in all matters re the discharge of the pastoral office: for to him alone belongs the government of the Church & congregation: you are not *ex aequo*, but you exercise your faculties with dependence on him. You have much to make you a useful missionary, but you have also some things to avoid or amend. These remarks are not based on any thing I have heard from Can. Newsham.

Wishing you every blessing, I remain sincerely Yrs, A. Goss.

195. *The Sister Superior, Convent of Notre Dame, Mt. Pleasant,*
   Lpool 11 March 1859 5/3/19
   "Her Majesty's Inspectors"

My dear Sister Superior,

The letter to Mr. Stokes of which you speak in your letter of the 6th, was a private letter in answer to a question addressed to me by him. If it conveyed an impression or insinuation that you had sought his advice when you ought to have sought mine, it did what it was not meant to do. I never had a doubt that you would consult me directly or indirectly; yet that need not prevent you from taking the opinion, or asking the opinion of other persons supposed to possess special means of acquiring information. You are, in fact, supposed to take steps to acquire the best information in order that you may lay it before the Bp. to aid him in giving advice. I know that if you wanted my opinion at any stage of the matter, you would have applied for it directly or thro' the Vicar & not thro' Mr. Stokes; hence in my answer to him I pointed this out, viz. that it was his opinion, as Inspector, & not mine as Bp. that you wanted. You suppose that he consulted me as to the grounds for the view he took; but I could give no information on that point, for he must have had grounds, which to him seemed good, upon which he based his opinion; he did not first take a view & then seek about for grounds; but he took his view from his knowledge of government action. I did not wish to discuss the question or state my opinion, because I was convinced that if you wanted Mr. Stokes's opinion, it was as Inspector, & consequently his own opinion, unmodified by any expression from me. I hope Mr. Stokes saw it in that light.

Wishing yourself & Community every blessing, I remain sincerely Yrs in Xt. A. Goss.

196. *To the Very Rev. Can. Wallwork, Sec. of Boys' Orphanage* [395]
   11 March 1859 5/3/20

My dear Canon,

As your letter has no date, I cannot tell how long it has lain unanswered; but I hope my reply will be considered within a reasonable time, tho' it is certainly not by return of post.

All the information that I have about the Boys' Orphanage is comprised in a note dated Nov. 12 1855 from Dr. Brown to Rev. J. Nugent, nominating that gentleman & Rev. P. Power & Very Revd. Cans. Walmsley & Kenrick to form a Committee; I see also by a blue book lately issued from the Press of E. Travis,[396] that it is situated in Everton Crescent;

but how many boys it contains, what are their names & ages, what their occupations; what the rules & constitution by which they are governed; how they are supported & what is the cost of their support; what the treasurer has in hand, are matters of which I know nothing, nor can I find any official document to give me information. Your previous note informed me of the difficulty in which you were placed, & I presume if it had not been for such difficulty, my aid would not have been invoked. I cannot form any opinion without data. It seems to me that the Institution cannot support a priest, & that the Diocese cannot afford to educate a priest for the purpose. Why should the orphanage require a priest more than St. Elizabeth's Institute or the lace schools, or the Blind Asylum, or the Girls' Orphanage? You will I am sure see the necessity of an Official Report being regularly furnished to the Bp. particularly if you look to him for advice or guidance. Wishing you every blessing I remain, my dear Canon, sincerely Yrs in Xt. A. Goss.

---

395   John Wallwork, 1825–91, Goss's first appointment as canon. Goss could be frustratingly official at times!

396   Evan Travis was a printer and bookseller, with premises at 88 Scotland Road, Liverpool.

197. *[E. W. Pugin]*   *12 March 1859*   *5/3/22*

My dear Mr. Pugin,

I hope you settled dates, particularly with Sir R. Gerard about the Birchley Schools.

I have yielded to Father Vandepitte's request to have a panelled roof, but on the condition that its cost does not exceed £150, for which there will be a special contract.

With regard to Westby, let the stairs to the gallery be shown in the plans & drawings made for it, as in contract, but mark at foot that it is not to be constructed at present. The window will be a separate job. I should like it to be like one I saw in Conway, about 4 foot high & one foot each side, thus so as to enable you to see each way; let it be between the chimney & the other window, so as to be convenient for study for a person sitting with his back to the main window. Let Mr. Cattermole have the plans soon, as he wants the masons & joiners to be ready with this work; for he will soon have the brick work in place.[397] Ever truly Yrs. A. Goss.

---

397   The church at Westby opened in 1860 (Kelly, *English Catholic Missions*), on a site donated by Miss Dalton; presumably Cattermole was the builder.

198. *Rev. R. Turpin,*[398] *Scorton   12 March 1859*   5/3/23
"New Church"

My dear Mr. Turpin,

Major Stapleton has come forward in gallant style; but you ask from me an impossibility as regards application to Miss Dalton.[399] You know she is dead against it & hence would not be accessible to any appplication that I could make. Without benefitting you, I might injure other charities. I think, as I have always thought, that your best plan is to rely on your old connection & friendship with her. Appeal to that, to the many years that you have known her, have placed your services at her command, the benefit she will do to religion by enabling you to build a more suitable house for God, the glory of leaving her name associated with the neighbourhood by good works, that the poor will pray for her & remember her when others have forgotten her, & the benefit that will come to her own soul by storing up treasures where neither rust nor moth can consume. I need not suggest to you arguments. You are losing heart in your old age: make the trial. Meanwhile I am pressed for a church at Fleetwood, where the land will be lost unless [taken] soon: Dr. Corless[400] too sleeps in daily or nightly fear of having his place blown down or crumbling away with rot. Take heart now: make a lenten job of it & let me know the results. If you succeed it will be worth a journey to come & relate it; you know you will meet with a hearty welcome. The weather still [*illegible*], but I will attend to it. Ever Yours truly, A. Goss.

---

[398] Robert Turpin, 1807–63. He was responsible for the new church that opened in 1861, designed by Charles Hansom and Son. See Kelly, *English Catholic Missions*, and J. Dunleavy, 'Mr Hansom of Coventry' *NWCH* 37 (2010), 10–19 and *ODNB*.

[399] Major Stapleton has not been identified. For Miss Dalton see n. 301.

[400] Dr Corless was at Cottam; see n. 86 above.

199. *Rev. R. Gillow, Newsham   12 March 1859*   5/3/24
"Site for schools"

My dear Mr. Gillow,

I have spoken with your cousin, the Dean, about the site proposed by you for your schools, & have carefully considered your own letter. I must confess that I have ever felt reluctant to allow for a Trust for school land lying in the middle of Church property; for we know not how soon we may be inconvenienced thereby. We must consider the Trust a reality, & we must expect that the Trustees will eventually exercise all the powers given them by the deed. It is therefore very desirable that you should place them in a corner, & I think that by inviting over your own Dean & your good natured cousin, you could come to a satisfactory arrangement. I will sanction whatever they recommend. Schools have become very dear appendages to Missions & unless required I do not think it wise to erect them. An effective school in an indifferent building is better than an indifferent school in an effective school-house. You are not as young as you used to be, & I would have you consider well before you embark in [*sic*] a new undertaking. I have no view in the matter, but will cheerfully sanction whatever those on the spot who represent me counsel me to do; can I do more?

Wishing you every blessing I remain sincerely yrs in Xt. A. Goss.

200. *The Religious of Notre Dame on the death of the Sister Superior*[401]   *14 March 1859*   *5/3/25*

My dear children in J.C.,

It has pleased God, at this penitential time, to afflict both you & me by the severe loss of your sister superior, but we must bow with submission to his holy will. Her loss is not only that of the Community, over which she presided with so much prudence & edification, but of the whole Congregation of which she was so devoted & exemplary a member. Her loss also will be mourned by all Liverpool that owes so much to the efficient & successful labours of the sisters under her care. Her spirit animated you all, &, in the hour of trial, she was a prudent adviser, & in time of trouble a rock of defence. "She has proved herself to be the valiant woman whose price is of things brought from afar off. She hath looked to the paths of her house & hath not eaten her bread idle", & we may rest assured that God, according to his promise, will not let her lamp be put out. She was at peace with God: she received the holy unction, & we may without presumption hope that instead of allowing her to wait till Sunday morning to receive him at holy mass, our sweet Lord took her earlier to himself & communicated her in heaven where he will evermore abide in her & she in him. If you mourn, mourn with hope, if you pray, pray with confidence. The first in every duty, it was fitting that she should first go to her reward, & show to her dear children of whom she was the guide, the way to heaven.

Rest assured that you will continue to receive my fatherly protection, & that I shall ever love you as my dear children in Jesus Christ. +Alexander Goss.

---

[401]   Sister Jeanne SND was an early Sister Superior at Mt Pleasant, Liverpool, who died suddenly in 1859. See Anon., *Centenary Memoir, Convent of Notre Dame Mount Pleasant* (Liverpool, 1956), 22.

201. *Rt. Rev. Dr. Brown, Bp of Shrewsbury* 14 March 1859

5/3/26[402]

"Visitation Questions"

My dear Lord,

I believe that when my Visitation Questions were first issued, they produced a sensation, which was fomented by the late Bp. whose Vicar over Ribble was most vehement; but with few exceptions the clergy accepted them, & at [?*subsequent*] Visitation I found no difficulty in obtaining any information. With one exception I met with a hearty reception [*one illegible line*] but that arose from an idea that an account was demanded of the household expenditure of all missions; but when I explained that I wanted it only of missions served by more than one priest, I heard of no further remarks, beyond a dread of the trouble it entailed. The Clergy, like all Englishmen, dislike what they call prying into their private affairs, & hence their objections to balance sheets or returns of any kind. There are, no doubt, a certain number of radicals in every diocese who dislike all control; a certain number who grumble loudly but yet do as requested. Some [? *like*] to cite opinions & remarks of other Bps, perhaps falsely, but still they work mischief. I cannot think that the practice of the Card. of giving advice calculated to foment a bad spirit, for having, as Archbp. to act as judge, he should not give advice as counsel [*illegible*] I know that after Canon Newsham had appealed to the H.S. the Card. received letters from him & made those letters the ground of remarks disadvantageous to members of my temporal administration.

I am told that the Cathed. Dispute excited more attention out of my diocese, particularly in the North, than in it, & some time ago I received a fiery letter, but was told that its principles were not advocated in my Diocese, but that the writer had just returned from the North. I should not be surprised if the opponents of [the] Cathed. in my diocese were to form a permanent radical clique in consequence of their defeat. The reputed hostility of the Card. to the leading men of my diocese & myself, strengthened by his not having called on me during his late visit contrived by Mr. Nugent without my knowledge, will ever lend encouragement to discontents, who will rely on his [*illegible word*] support at Rome. Some days ago, it was current that the Oratorians were coming to the Institute to give a mission,[403] but I wrote to Mr. Nugent in answer to his application to say that I considered it inexpedient. I received in reply a lecture regarding the duty of the Bp. to answer the correspondence of his clergy, whether high or low, within a reasonable time, whilst for himself, considering his position, [*three words illegible*], he demanded an answer by return of post. If you read his speeches you will see that he ignores the existence of any authority except his own & seems to act as the [*two words illegible*] leader & organ of the Catholic body in the town. He may have some little support in the lay element, but not much among the clergy. [*Two illegible lines*]. A. Goss.

---

402   The letter is very difficult to read; some of it is written across the text.

403   Nugent originally had asked Newman to open a branch of the Oratory in Liverpool in connection with his Catholic Institute, opened in 1853 and dedicated to St Philip Neri. Newman was interested enough to have it discussed officially by the members of the Oratory; he advised Nugent about the steps to be taken, and mentioned the idea to the pope, who was in favour. When Goss became bishop in 1856 Newman's support lessened as he thought the new bishop was opposed to 'assemblages of priests'. He thought, however, that it might still be possible to send an Oratory priest to help at the CI. See correspondence in Dessain, XV, 336–7; XVI, 206–7, 247, 337; XVII, 147, 154. See also Doyle and McLoughlin, *The Edwardian Story*, 15–16, for the founding of the CI.

202.   *Rev. T. Spenser,*[404] *Bootle   14 March 1859*   *5/3/27*
'Litherland Schools'

My dear Mr. Spenser,
I hope that by increased activity on your part, seconded by the Committee, you will be able to make all ends meet; the difficulties of the case should stimulate the Committee to solicit aid among their Liverpool & even Protestant friends, for schools are looked on by them as neutral ground.

I am given to understand that members of the Crosby congregation have been firm annual subscribers or have made contributions, & I believe that Canon Fisher & others of his congregation contributed to the erection of the schools, & that he promised to continue his subscription, if needful, but that it has not been asked for.

I feel sure that by a little management, a little of the *sauviter in modo*, as well as *fortiter in re*,[405] you will command the support of your own people & neighbours so as to preserve the schools in an efficient state. If in course of time it be found necessary to have a school near the Church at Bootle & there be a reasonable prospect of success, you may rely not only on my sanction, but warm recommendation.

Could you not induce the Committee to take the entire responsibility as in former times, leaving you the management, as is the case with all our schools built by the aid of government?

Wishing you every blessing I remain sincerely Yrs in Xt. +A. Goss.

---

404   Thomas Spencer/Spenser: see note 209.

405   'Gently in manner, strongly in purpose', a saying attributed to Claudio Acquaviva, Superior General of the Jesuits in the 1580s.

203. *Rev. P. Malone P.P. V.F. Belmullet, Co. Mayo*
                    22 March 1859   *5/3/31*

Dear Rev. Sir,

I beg to acknowledge the receipt of your favour & am obliged for its contents. There is no subject that gives me more trouble than that of marriage, & I have repeatedly called the attention of the Clergy to its difficulties. Parties living [in] one district of Liverpool, frequently get married in another by falsely representing themselves as dwelling in that district, which they do to avoid having the banns proclaimed in what is usually their own Church. With us this is only an irregularity, but in the case of persons coming from Ireland, it is fatal to the validity of the marriage, as they come over *in fraudem legis* & do not acquire even a quasi domicilium.[406] You would naturally suppose that the clergy would know the people of their district, but this is not possible, for the people frequently shift their place of residence, & in the last year the number of persons, mostly poor persons, coming from Ireland to Liverpool, was more than 81 thousand; in other years it had exceeded 200,000. Oftentimes the persons are living in a state of concubinage, or represent themselves as on the point of sailing. Where it is known that the parties come from Ireland, application is made to learn if they are free; but such applications frequently meet with no reply. I inclose a portion of a letter from Can. Kenrick on this subject.

Thanking you for having called my attention to this matter, & wishing you every blessing, I remain sincerely Yrs in Xt. +Alexander Goss.

---

[406] The decrees of Trent about marriage were not in force in England; see next letter. *In fraudem legis* – 'in contempt of the law'.

204. *Very Rev. Provost Cookson V.G.*   *26 March 1859*   *5/3/35*
                    "Banns & Marriages"

My dear Vicar,

I think it will be quite necessary to insist on persons who are not personally known giving the number of their houses, as well as the street, when putting up the askings.[407] Furthermore I think it very desirable that the priest in whose district they are supposed to dwell, should visit their houses in order to verify the fact of their residence. It would be no great hardship, as he would have three weeks for it & is or ought to be in his district nearly every day. I have had, as I told you, a complaint from Ireland of insufficient residence & consequently of a null marriage as they come from Ireland where the law of Trent is promulgated, *in fraudem legis*. I shall be obliged if you will examine the Register at the procathedral to see if on <u>Quinquagesima</u> Sunday there were married

Ann Dolan & – O'Brien [*sic*], & if so where they represented them-selves as living at the time, & to let me know the result.

The Pastoral on Magdalens is printed & will be out for next Sunday.[408]

If you think well of what I have said about marriages, I will call the attention of the town clergy to the matter thro' the Conferences. Ever truly Yrs. A. Goss.

---

[407] 'Askings': a popular term for the banns.

[408] Pastoral on the Magdalen asylum: March 1859 (AAL, S1/2/C/5), one of Goss's outspoken pastorals, dealing with the evil of prostitution but also attacking the 'double standards' of the day. Introduction, p. xxxv.

205. [*Lord Campbell*]   *1 April 1859*   *5/3/58–9*

My Dear Lord Campbell,[409]

My sentiments are quite in accordance with those expressed in your letter: under every form of government Catholics are the natural allies of Conservatives. Whether for us or against us, the Conservatives are honourable in their dealings, whilst Liberals are too often profuse in their promises, but faithless in their Execution. Should the present government remain in office I hope they will do something for the Catholic poor in Workhouses.

I will endeavour to secure the good offices of my clergy, but like myself they do not interfere in politics. If however I can do anything, you may rely on my cooperation. With every kind wish,

I am yours sincerely in Christ, +Alexander Goss.

---

[409] John, first Baron Campbell, 1779–1861; he had been the judge at Newman's Achilli trial and it is odd that he should be writing for Catholic support, but see Schiefen, *Nicholas Wiseman*, 337, for a possible change of heart.

206. *Rev. Father Lans. Bp. Eton*   *15 April 1859*   *5/3/64*
                    "Can. Thrower"

My dear Father Lans,

I will confer with the Vic. Gen. on the subject of granting faculties to Can. Thrower.[410] Unfortunately when a priest makes a mistake, it is industriously circulated among his brethren & sometimes amongst the laity. When such a priest is employed where the thing is known, the Clergy think that the Bp. readily pardons such offences, & hence the restraint of public opinion is thrown off, & the laity are led to believe that the priests against whom they know nothing may be as bad as has been the other, since they see them employed indifferently.

I have seen Mr. Nugent. I think he is all right. I have banished from my mind what he wrote. There is however more of restlessness than of useful activity about him: he seems ever straining at new things, instead of consolidating the old ones, & thus keeps up an unhealthy excitement. In a mixed community like L'pool, we should endeavour to keep down and not keep up a spirit of nationality: we should make men forget that they are Irish or English in the fact that they are Catholic. Now [h]is whole policy – I do not say intentionally – heads in the opposite direction. It is impossible to say what are his real honest views: to me they seem so diverse at different times that I can only explain them on the supposition that he is inconstant & changeable.

It is good news what you mention about the Good Shepherd. I am greatly consoled with the prospects of that Charity.[411] With many thanks for your letter & wishing you every blessing, I remain sincerely Yours in Xt. Alexander Goss.

---

[410] Henry J. Thrower DD, 1824–91; something of a wanderer: Canon of Northampton Diocese, but resigned; taught at Oscott; CF; served in Newcastle-on-Tyne; Shefford, Beds (Northampton Diocese); taught at CI, Liverpool, to 1867. Remained in the diocese until his death.

[411] Presumably the Good Shepherd Sisters: Goss invited them into the diocese in 1857; they opened a Magdalen asylum in Netherfield Road, then moved (1861) to Mason Street and eventually to Ford.

207. *Rev. Mr. Walker, St Augustine's, Preston   19 April 1859   5/3/73*
      "The Elections"[412]   Confidential

My dear Mr Walker

I have never voted but once for an election, & I am no advocate for clerical interference in elections beyond the exercise of their own right, yet I think the circumstances of the time require consideration. What are the views of the present Ministry on foreign politics we know, what may be those of Lord John or Palmerston we do not know, beyond the fact that both are fond of meddling & hate Catholics & the Holy See.

The present government has been favourable to us in sanctioning the appointment & payment of army chaplains; I am confidentially informed that it will remove our Reformatories from Protestant inspection in religious matters, & I have <u>good</u> reasons for believing that it will facilitate our intercourse with prisons & workhouses & sanction the payment of chaplains. This we can never get from the local guardians, & the Poor Law Board in London advises me to invoke the legislature. Under these circumstances will it not be wise to support, as far as we can effectually, but inostensibly, the government candidates? I have written to Mr Jn. Turner, & authorised him to send my letter to Mr. Gillow. If you take the same view as myself, you can probably do more with Mr. Gillow than either Mr. Turner or myself. Having submitted to your consideration these particulars, the rest is left to your own discretion: for I have no wish to interfere with any man's independence. I hope the mission is helping you over the Easter week.

Ever truly Yrs A. Goss.

---

[412] With the defeat of the Tory government over parliamentary reform, Parliament was dissolved in April 1859. Elections were held in the first week of May. In Preston, the Catholic candidate Clifton was defeated by forty votes – sitting members, Cross (C) and Grenfell (L, who had brought in the Ecclesiastical Titles Bill) were re-elected. Clifton had not been the first choice of Preston Catholics – they had offered it to Robert Townley Parker of Cuerdon Hall, but he had declined; a letter from Preston Catholics to *The Tablet* (23 April) makes this clear and calls Parker a 'Liberal Conservative'. South Lancs went to Lord Derby, according to *The Tablet*; in fact, one Liberal and one Conservative were returned for that division. Tom Smith, '"Let Justice Be Done and We Will Be Silent": A Study of Preston's Catholic Voters and their Parliamentary Election Campaigns, 1832 to 1867', *NWCH* 38 (2001), 5–54; also, 'Religion or Party? Attitudes of Catholic Electors in Mid-Victorian Preston', *NWCH* 33 (2006), 19–35. See also letters 209–13.

208.   *Convent of the Faithful Comps. of J.[sic]   20 April 1859   5/3/74*
   St. George's Square   "Confraternity of the Children of Mary"
My dear Sister Superior,
I have great pleasure in sanctioning the erection of the Confraternity of the Children of Mary amongst your pupils: for whatever tends to increase devotion to the Immaculate Mother of God is especially dear to me, as she is the Patroness of the Diocese, in which religion has increased & prospered under her fostering care. I have, however, serious doubts whether the Indulgences cited as belonging to the societies of the Children of Mary will be applicable to your Confraternity, for tho' I can sanction the erection of any Confraternity in my Diocese, I cannot attach thereto any Indulgences, but I can allow it to share the Indulgences granted to the parent Society, provided it be <u>canonically</u> erected. I have also the power of erecting canonically all confraternities approved of by the Holy See, but in order to do so, I must see the regulations of the parent society, in order to know how to erect it canonically. There are many associations in honour of our B. Lady, some local, some general, & if you will state the name of the parent society after which you wish to be modelled, I will see that it is done in a canonical way. You will find them all mentioned & described in Bouvier's treatise on Indulgences.[413]

Wishing yourself & Community every blessing, I remain truly Yrs in Xt. +Alexander Goss.

---

[413] Jean Baptiste Bouvier, 1783–1854: *Traité dogmatique et pratique des indulgences, des confrèries et du jubilé, à l'usage des ecclésiastiques* (?Paris, 1826 and later edns); also … *à l'usage des fidèles* (1826).

209. *E. Ryley Esq.*,[414] *26 Poultry, London E.C. 25 April 1859 5/3/76*
My dear Mr. Ryley,
As early as the 19th of April, I wrote to one of our most influential Catholic electioneering agents in Preston to use his influence on behalf of the government candidates. I wrote also on the same day to one of the Clergy to support effectually but inostensibly the government candidates. I find that my friend Colonel Talbot Clifton is putting up for Preston, & I have written to him to wish him success & to say that if the Catholics of Preston knew him as well as I did, there would not be one who would not vote for him. I have written also to Lancaster to the same effect. You know Catholics in England are jealous of clerical interference in political matters, & know whatever has to be done must be done with discretion. All Catholics that I have met with, both lay & clerical, are sincere & hearty in their wishes for the success of the present government. There is an honesty about the Conservatives that you look for in vain among the Whigs.[415]

At present our leading Catholics, who have no fear & no want of spirit, think that a public meeting would be injudicious on the subject of the Workhouses etc; but we are taking steps to have the matter brought before the legislature, & we shall back our move either by meeting or petition. Lpool will not be wanting to itself & the cause on the day of battle.

Wishing you the Paschal joys I remain Sincerely Yrs in Xt, A. Goss. Sir R. Gerard's interest, not small, in S. Lancashire, will be with the Conservatives.

---

[414] Edward Ryley 1812–96, sculptor and actuary; he was an active campaigner in London for the rights of Catholics in prisons and workhouses; Wiseman praised him for this in *The Tablet* (14/5/59). Also, he tried to wean Catholics from their traditional allegiance to the Whigs/Liberals. See F. Boase *Modern English Biography*, 3 vols (Truro, 1901), III, 24. He also helped to run *The Tablet* (Michael Walsh, *The Tablet 1840–1990. A Commemorative History* (London, 1990), pp. 13–14).

[415] In a letter a few days later Goss claimed he had 'positive but confidential assurance' from Lord Derby's cabinet that they would make every legal effort to get payment for Catholic priests serving workhouses and jails (5/3/80, 29 April 1859, to J. Scarisbrick).

---

210. *Mr. E. Buller, Fishergate Preston 25 April 1859 5/3/77*
My dear Mr. Buller,
Many thanks for your Election intelligence. I admire the spirit of the Preston Catholics evinced in their determination to be rid of Grenfell of the Titles Bill, & I admire their decision & judgement in determining to support a liberal Conservative, & I am glad that that gentleman is my friend Colonel Talbot Clifton. Persecution is part of our inheritance & therefore we must not expect to shake it off entirely: but I feel satisfied

that we shall have less of it under the Conservatives than under the
Whigs. Lord Derby has always been fair, if not favourable to Catholics
in the Colonies, & I have no doubt that he will be so at home, if we can
make our power sufficiently felt, which, in the present state of political
parties, we can do.

I may truly to [*sic*] say that I take a personal interest in Colonel
Clifton's success: for in addition to possessing his friendship, I believe
that he will be found both honest & honourable in his public capacity,
which is not always the case with men, as those who are known to be
men of private worth, sometimes turn out to be worthless in their public
capacity. I feel sure that my friend Colonel Clifton would scorn to be
different as a public man from what he is as a private gentleman. I need
not say, do your best for him. Wishing you the Paschal joys, I remain
sincerely Yrs A. Goss.

211.   *Rev. R. Taylor, St. Augustine's Preston   29 April 1859   5/3/79*
"Hibernian Society"[416]

My dear Mr. Taylor,

In the faculties conceded in the Diocese of Lpool, there was reservation
made of the Hibernians because such reservation had been made in the
faculties granted by my predecessor. After they had once been expressed
by name, they could not be omitted without leading to an impression
that I had withdrawn the prohibition to admit them. The Bishops themselves have not powers to admit the members of <u>secret</u> societies as that
word is understood in Rome. This includes, I believe, a secret oath,
secret sign, & that their principles should be inimical to religion & the
state. If any one of these conditions are [*sic*] absent, they do not fall
into the category of secret societies as defined by the Holy Office: tho',
mind, it may still be unlawful to admit them to the sacraments. The
Holy See allowed no discretion in the matter with respect to what it
defined to be secret societies, but it left the admission of other societies
to the discretion of the Bp. The late Bp. following the example of the
Irish Bps excluded the Hibernians: I have done the same. I am assured
that where Hibernians have been admitted, it has been by deceiving the
Bp. or clergy by holding back part of the rules. I never saw their rules
till you forwarded me the form of oath, & if I have referred to Father
Weston[417] or others, it has been simply to explain what the Holy Office
meant by a secret society, but I could not express an opinion about
the admission of a society of whose regulations I knew nothing. Mr
Marsland of Newcastle[418] can give you information about them as the
Bp. of Hexham has published enactments about them. Mr. Sheridan of
St. Mary's Lpool is, I believe, conversant with them. The Rev. Messrs.
Kelly of the Hexham Diocese are, I am assured, in error about their

principles, & have advocated their admission. I do not see how men taking such an oath can be admitted.

Ever truly Yrs A. Goss.

---

416 The Hibernian Society: Burke, *Catholic Liverpool*, 38, refers to various Hibernian societies in the 1820s, all 'respectable'. The rise of a more active Irish nationalism in the 1850s and 1860s raised suspicions; Goss could even think that the CYMS might be a cover for Fenian activity, as he wrote to its national chairman, Lord Edward Howard in 1865 (5/6/2/65–6).

417 Thomas Weston SJ, 1804–67, was at St Walburge's, Preston, at this time.

418 Mr Marsland of Newcastle: Henry, Secular priest 1822–59. James (Joseph) Sheridan OSB, 1801–60; Kelly, *English Catholic Missions*: Hexham had two Irish priests that might fit the bill here: Edmund Joseph, 1794–1866, b. Kilkenny; and John, 1807–83, b. Waterford.

212. *V. Rev. Dean Gillow*   *30 April 1859*   *5/3/82*

"Newhouse School Plans"

My dear Dean,

I think the change of plan is an improvement which would be still greater if above the transom there were two panes instead of one, so that each window would contain 20 panes instead of 16 as now, i.e. 8 above the transom, & 12 below in each window. The windows of the house would look better if the moulding were continued all round, instead of being broken by the spout & the string course; at least that is the opinion here, but we judge by the look.

On Monday I set out for London to the meeting of the Bps usually held at this time.

I suppose you will have been all astir this last week with the Preston elections. The Catholics deserve all praise for the spirit they have shown: both parties will respect them the more, because they will see that they have a will of their own.[419] There is no contest in Lpool, tho' there is in South Lancashire: Catholics will be the gainers if Lord Derby can hold his place.

Wishing you the Paschal joys I remain truly Yrs. A. Goss.

---

419 But see n. 412 above. Goss was being over-simplistic here as it is clear that the Catholics in Preston were divided. In general, Catholics exaggerated their influence in national elections; see Smith, n. 412, and Dermot Quinn, *Patronage and Piety: the Politics of Roman Catholicism, 1850–1900* (Basingstoke, 1993), 234.

213. *John Turner Esq. Preston*   *9 May 1859*   *5/3/85*

My dear Mr. Turner,

I write to thank you for your letter containing the Preston election news, which I would have answered sooner had I not been from home. I feel convinced that Mr. Talbot Clifton's election was lost by bad generalship amongst the Conservatives, for there could not otherwise have been so large a discrepancy between the votes for Cross & Clifton.

The Daily Post here, edited by a half renegade,[420] has devoted two columns of abuse to me, but the only effect it will produce on me will be to make [me] more decisive & energetic at the next opportunity. He also gravely informs his readers that the Bps have every where been throwing their influence into the scales of the Conservatives, & he particularly mentions the Rt. Rev. Dr. Turner's efforts & exertions at Preston! So you see the Daily Post has elevated you to a bishopric notwithstanding your having a wife & children. The Liverpool Catholics have acted basely as well as foolishly, for having failed to secure my influence for the wretched Whig interest they must have put Whitty of the Post into possession of things which he could learn from no Tory else. In their weakness they thought themselves entitled to dictate to the electors of South Lancashire. Well we must keep up heart & be determined to act independently of all parties so as to secure the greatest advantages to the Church. Wishing you every blessing I remain truly Yrs. A. Goss.

---

420   Michael Whitty *c.* 1795–1873, Irish journalist and editor; he was a frequent critic of Goss and Irish politics in Liverpool. See Burke, *Catholic Liverpool*, 232–3 and *passim*.

214.   *Mr. Robt. Catterall,*[421] *Kirkham   17 May 1859*   *5/3/92*
                                "Westby Church"
Dear Sir,
You can get in the foundations before the stone is laid. I will arrange with Mr. Hines to have the stone laid on the 30th or 31st. We will place it in the <u>centre</u> of the <u>West end</u>, about or just above the floor line. As we move in procession round the walls – either inside or outside – you must have the space free. It is not necessary to have the foundations of the same height all round: it will be enough for the blessing, if you have dug out, tho' it will be all the better to have them built up to the level of the ground. The stone should be a yard square <u>through</u> stone,[422] with outer surface dressed & a small cross cut in the centre of about two inches, i.e. each arm of the cross to be one inch.

I will arrange with Mr. Hines to lay the stone on Tuesday 31st, & I will come down to the ground to see that all is right some time on the Monday.

Hoping you are getting on satisfactorily, I remain Yrs etc. +A. Goss.

---

421   Could Catterall the builder be the earlier Cattermole of letter 197?
422   The meaning is not clear.

215.   *Very Rev. Dean Gillow. Lea School*   *8 June 1859*   *5/3/111*
<u>Confidential</u>

My dear Dean,

Inclosed I forward Mr. Walker's application about a new school, & shall be glad if you will report thereon. Mr. Stokes is ever urging improvements in school buildings without considering how such enlargements impoverish poor missions. When I saw Mr. Walker's school it was only <u>half</u> occupied, the other half seemed to be used as a granary. He says that he has 78 on the books; but what of that if not more than 50 attend? He had only 105 persons at mass on the day he took the census. He does not sustain his school but by the help of the P.S. Committee & Lea is a bye word amongst them. He speaks of help from the District Fund, but helping schools is not one of the objects of that collection.

The Bps have consented to give government certain information about schools, & in a short time I will forward you the circulars for distribution & shall be glad if you take steps to have them returnd <u>soon, properly filled up</u>. If you will keep an account of expenses, the government will refund them. I hope you will see that the School Schedules are properly filled up before you send them in; I cannot conceive why so many of the Clergy fill up Schedules in so slovenly a way.

You have many valuable papers at Fernyhalgh, of which I want copies. Will you send them to Mr. Jas. Taylor[423] of Lancaster that he may take copies, or will you have him at your house for a week that he may make them under your own eyes, or will you send them here, that I may see what to have copied, or will you have copies made by a competent person that you may have at your command? I have not spoken to Mr. Taylor, but will do so when I hear from you. Properly authenticated copies will be valuable to have in the Archives. I saw an abridgement of one at Mr. Swarbrick's. Ever Yours truly, A. Goss.

---

[423]   James Taylor, 1831–1908, o. June 1858; see letter 248.

216.   *James Trees Esq.,*[424] *19 New St. Worcester*   *20 June 1859*
5/3/139
"St. Patrick's Burial Society"

Dear Sir,

I can give you no information regarding St. Patrick's Burial Society, for my Patronage extends no further than that of her majesty, which is placed over half the shops in the kingdom. It is, however, my intention, at my next visitation, to go into the working of the Society & examine its accounts. I am careful not to sanction the monetary arrangements of any guilds in my Diocese till they have been subjected to the examination of an Actuary: but this Society was in existence under my

Predecessor, & my name was naturally added, tho', no doubt, with my knowledge, as Patron. I have, however, meanwhile sent your letter to Can. Kenrick, the Senior Priest at St. Patrick's, & have desired him to obtain the necessary information from the Chaplain & communicate it to you. I hope you will find it satisfactory.

Regretting that it is not in my power to give you more complete information, & wishing you every blessing, I remain truly Yrs in Xt. +Alexander Goss.

---

424   The letter is indexed under 'Tree' but the addressee here clearly has the 's'. For the Burial Society, see letters 388 and 389 below.

217. *Rt. Rev. Dr. Briggs*   *22 June 1859*   *5/3/140*
        "Ushaw – Dr. Errington"   Confidential

My dear Lord,

I have this morning received a letter from Dr. E. in which he says "I have just heard from Dr. Grant a circumstance which I quite agree with him in thinking makes it advisable not to stir in the way of writing to Rome for the present". He does not mention what the circumstance is, but I suppose it will be something which Dr. G. has picked up in London. As nothing will be done in the matter at once, we shall have an opportunity at Synod[425] of looking over the whole subject. Rev. Mr. Rogerson[426] has returned from Rome & reports, I am told, the contemplated removal of Dr. E. from Westminster to Trinidad. Dr. D. Lee is in Dublin & is to be married on Monday.[427] Dr. E. asks if any thing has yet been heard of the details to be proposed to Synod: is it not curious that we have heard nothing of them? Is it not part of the policy which in London put off the mention of the College question to the last hour of the last day of our meeting? Ought we not to ask for the suggestions, prepared at last Synod, to be produced at the next Synod? Why are there to be no Defensions at Ushaw? How can the Synod interfere with them? Is it necessary to have the Cardinal at them? I think that both the Chapters & the clergy of the Dioceses interested in Ushaw would petition against the College being made into a Pontifical one,[428] if they knew of it, & understood the bearings of the question: it is a pity that we did not propose something for circulation. Dr. Errington's address is 10 Rutland Square, Dublin.[429] Hoping to find you well at Synod, I remain sincerely Yrs A. Goss.

---

425   The second Provincial Synod had been held in July 1855; the third was planned for July 1859, also at Oscott.
426   Rogerson: there are two possibilities: John, 1830–93, o. 1854 for Shrewsbury, or John S., 1817–84, o. 1841, served in Hexham and Newcastle.

427 Dr Lee has not been identified.
428 Pontifical Colleges: Milburn, *History of Ushaw College*, 202, 237–42. Goss wrote in very similar terms to Errington on the same day (letter 5/3/142).
429 See n. 492 below.

218. *Rev. Jn. Worthy, Euxton 25 June 1859*   *5/3/147*
"New Church"[430]

Dear Rev. Sir,

If a fund be left for a specified purpose, I do not think that I can, by my own authority, divert it from that purpose; but, if the reasons for diverting it be sound, there will be no difficulty in procuring the sanction of the Holy See. Such a reason would be the existence of a church, particularly if it were likely to be a permanency: for if it were not so, the Catholics of Euxton would be no better off than they are now, except that they would have a fairer Church. If I remember rightly, Mr. Crooke of Chorley told me that the origin of the building fund was a sum of money given by the present Mr. Anderton's grandfather or father, or other ancestor, when at Ince, on his making up his mind not [*sic*] longer to have the chapel in the house. If I have not canonical power to alter the destination of the building fund, I cannot of course of myself guarantee that the interest shall be paid to the priest; but if Mr. Anderton's [*sic*] grants the use of the New Church on the condition that such should be the case, I suspect that there will be no difficulty in having such arrangement sanctioned. When it comes to the point, when the matter is complete, I will make a necessary application to the H. See. I will not apply to the H.S. unnecessarily and will take advice before doing so; but if it should turn out that I am bound to do so, that will, in no way, interfere with or interrupt Mr. Anderton's plans: it will but change the source from which the act comes. So far from putting any obstacle in the way I am anxious to expedite the measure; but I should not be acting in a manner worthy of my position if I were to do by my own authority what requires the sanction of my superior. Wishing you every blessing I remain truly Yrs in Xt. A. Goss.

430 Euxton is near Chorley; a new church was opened in 1865, to replace the old one of 1817 (Kelly, *English Catholic Missions*).

219. *Rev. Mr. Jarrett, Ulverston   27 June 1859*   *5/3/149*
"Coniston Church"

My dear Mr. Jarrett,

Enclosed I send you a letter from Mr. Jas. Whiteside of Lancaster whom I have engaged to sound Mr. Coulston, as he is in the Lancaster Bank of which Mr. Coulston is manager. I fear we shall not stand much chance in that quarter, for Mr. Coulston, beyond having been baptised, is no Catholic: I don't suppose he was ever taken into the Church & has no Catholic sympathies.

As Mr. Whiteside says, there seems to be a screw loose; for things do not seem sweet between Mr. Barrett & the railway Proprietors, if we may judge from the notice in the Weekly Register.[431]

I have not yet written my letter to the miners but I would at once do so, if Mr. Barrett could be induced to set aside a piece of ground for us, tho' even in the absence of an allotment they may organise a system of collections.

Wishing you every blessing, I remain sincerely Yrs in Xt. +Alexander Goss.

---

[431]   *Weekly Register*, 20 June 1859. On Coniston, see letters 15, 236, 252. In a letter to Jarrett of 8 April 1861 (5/4/72) Goss said he had full confidence in him and the local dean to settle things at Coniston; in a letter of the same time (5/4/77) to Dean Brown of Lancaster, Goss told him to see the proposed site at Coniston before agreeing to any conveyance of land.

220.   *Very Rev. Dean Gillow   28 June 1859*   5/3/151
"Fernyhalgh Schools"

My dear Dean,
Theodosius is said to have been greatly flattered when Ambrose, one of his judges, was made Bishop of Milan:[432] may not a Bishop feel also flattered when he reads the following notice of one of his Deans from the pen of her Majesty's Inspector of Schools?

"I may specify the enlargement of the rural school of Fernyhalgh, which in the paternal solicitude of the manager, no less than the steady, but not overstrained zeal of the teacher, and the kindly feelings of the children, forms a model for country schools. I observe with particular pleasure that the simple minded, persevering, pious apprentice from this little school has gained a Queen's Scholarship of the first class."

Thanking you for the good example given to your Deanery, as well as for the zeal & kindliness by which you have made yourself beloved & your office respected, & wishing you every blessing,

I remain sincerely Yrs in Xt. +Alexander Goss.

---

[432]   St Ambrose, c. 340–97, became bishop in 374 after being provincial governor; Valentinian was the emperor at the time and Butler's *Lives* attributes the remark to him and not to Theodosius, who became emperor in 379 – a rare historical error by Goss?

221. *Rt. Rev. Dr. Briggs* 6 July 1859 5/3/155
"Synod" Confidential

My dear Lord,

I think the four Bps are prepared to resist the attempt to make Ushaw a Pontifical College. The Card. I am told, argues that our Colleges are not Seminaries & cannot therefore be legislated for as Seminaries: their history will disprove this view. Is he bringing Chaillot to Synod to aid him in support of this view?[433]

The Archbp. thinks that the Co[llege] Congregation ought to be appointed first, as being most important, whereas at London it was discussed last, or rather was not discussed at all. Dr. Grant & Dr. Errington ought both to be upon it, & if they are not named or proposed by the Card. the Senior Bp. should propose them. Each Bp. has the same voice as the Card. in the formation of the Congregation. The notes of the last Synod on the Colleges ought to be brought to Oscott.

If the Card. has not proposed any decrees, we ought to – i.e. you, the Senior – ought to [*sic*] propose the decrees we have prepared: Dr. Grant has made a Latin copy of what I sent you in English, with modifications & additions.

Can you tell me what changes or arrangements were made about Ushaw on the increase in the number of Vicars Apostolic? Did the Vicars meet at York or elsewhere to arrange for the altered circumstances? If they did, I wish you could let me have a copy of what they did.[434]

I have sent Dr. Errington a copy of Fr. Caccia's letter.[435] He went to Manchester yesterday & had to go to London today. I hope you will come on Saturday. If it is impossible, be at Oscott early, for <u>every</u> thing depends on the <u>Monday</u> arrangements. Ever faithfully Yrs. A. Goss.

---

[433] Schiefen, *Nicholas Wiseman*, 277–81, for the Cardinal's preparations for the Synod; and his chap. 15 on the Synod itself. Chaillot was Abbé Ludovic Chaillot from Rome, editor of the *Analecta Juris Pontificii* and Wiseman's theologian at the Synod.

[434] On the troublesome meetings of the post-1840 VAs about the College, see Milburn, *History of Ushaw College*, 183–6 and 193–6.

[435] Francesco Caccia, an Italian Rosminian, 1807–82, had been in England 1851–6 (Fitz-L); the *Directories* list only a Charles Caccia, at St Mary's, Rugby, and then Market Weighton Reformatory School.

---

222. *Very Rev. Mgr. Searle* 24 August 1859 5/3/163
"Chap. Min. Book"

My dear Mgr. Searle,

At the risk of being thought to be intrusive, I venture to tender you my advice on a subject arising out of a transaction to which I was invited to become a party at the request of your Synodal Deputy.

Whether the Card. presses or does not press his request for the destruction of the Min. Book of the Chap. of West., I would advise you to destroy it, because by doing so you will cement more firmly the peace between you & him, you will prevent the necessity of an appeal to Rome, & the mortification of a defeat. If the Bps condemned the addenda to the petition, they must a fortiori have condemned the inquisition on which the addenda were based, had their opinion been asked thereon. Your right to petition was never questioned by the Bps, nor was any opinion expressed on the substance of your petition, but disapprobation was expressed at the addition of extraneous matter that did not fall within the cognisance of the Chap. It must be left to the publication of the Synod to see whether the substance of your petition has been granted or rejected: my mouth is sealed thereon.

Your resolution book will of course contain your petition to the Card. in extenso, the Card's answer, the resolutions & petition to Rome, the answer from Rome, & the Apology. I do not think you can claim the insertion of more, & if you do, you will be lost in case of further appeal. Peace is within reach without the sacrifice of honour, why not accept it? If you do not accept, begging you will appreciate the motive that has dictated the advice, I remain truly Yrs. +A. Goss.

223. *Rev. J. Nugent. Catholic Institute*   *26 August 1859*   *5/3/165*
"Gibson"

My dear Mr. Nugent,
I have neglected to fill up the vacancy at the Industrial Schools with the hope of being able to make such arrangements as might place Mr. Gibson at your service. Had you not made application for him, I should on the retirement of Mr. Doyle at once have appointed him to that charge.[436] My desire to oblige you has laid me open to the odium of having neglected that important place: for few people see with both eyes.

After all, I fear that I shall not be able to place Mr. Gibson at your disposal. Tho' I am sorry for this, yet I do not anticipate that it will cause you any difficulty. You are & will be still at the helm, & tho' you may not have them to aid you who will at all times pull to your satisfaction, yet you have the guidance of them, & are more fortunate than most others placed under similar circumstances.

I hope that a few weeks at Moore's port[437] will set you all right. If doctors had to be implicitly followed Dr. Fisher & myself would have rusticated for two years in Greece & one half of my clergy and 2/3 of the merchants of Lpool might ship their oars. They don't know our metal. I have written to Mr. Carr not to expect you. Begging my remembrance to Mrs. Moore & family & wishing you speedy restoration to health I remain truly Yrs AG.

[*Written across the page*] I will leave Gibson unplaced for another fortnight in the chance, faint however, of placing him at the service of the
Institute.

---

[436] Henry Gibson became chaplain to the prisons and industrial schools in 1859.

[437] Presumably 'Moore's port' was Bank Hall, home of the recusant Moore family. See
Robert J. Stonor OSB, *Liverpool's Hidden Story* (Birchley, 1957).

224. *Rt. Rev. Dr. Grant*   *26 August 1859*   5/3/167
My dear Friend,
In the Necrology for the Diocese of Bruges edited by command of Mgr.
Malon, I find the following entry for 1859. *R.P. Joan. Bap. Verkist* [*sic*;
?*surname*] *in Wynghem Prov. S.J., antea per 6 annos Professor S. Theol.
et Praeses Seminarii Provincialis in Universitate Catholica primum
Mechliniae diu Lovanii, ob. Namurcii 6 Aug. 1858."* [*sic*] From this
it seems, as Mr. Vandepitte argued, that there is in connexion with the
University of Louvain a <u>Provincial </u>Seminary, under the joint administration of the Belgian Bps.[438]

I think Dr. Errington's presence in Rome would be a security against
any sudden impulse on your part in the face of the gigantic interests at
stake.

What salary do your priests receive at churches served by more than
one priest? Is that salary over & above what they receive for masses?
Do they receive fees? or do the fees go to the Church? Is the salary a
fixed sum or is it supplementary of what has already been received in
fees or for masses? In some churches the retributions amount to £40 or
50 each; in others it is less. My churches are so fearfully in debt, & the
emoluments of the Lpool churches make priests so anxious to get into
Lpool in preference to other places, that I want to equalise matters if I
can in town churches.

Dr. Fisher joins in kind regards. Ever truly Yrs A. Goss.

---

[438] Trans: 'R. P. John Baptist Verkist (?), of the Wynghem Province of the Jesuits,
formerly for six years Professor of Sacred Theology and President of the Provincial
Seminary in the Catholic University that was first at Mechlin then for a long time since
at Louvain, died at Namur, 6 August 1858'.

225. *Rev. Mr. Lynass O.S.B.,*[439] *Leyland   26 August 1859*   5/3/170
                        "Living Rosary – Scapular"
Dear Rev. Sir,
In answer to your letter of the 18th, praying to establish the Living
Rosary in your congregation & furthermore asking for faculties to enrol

members in the Confraternity of the Brown Scapular, I write to say I grant both petitions.

1.   By this letter I establish & hereby declare to be established the Living Rosary at our mission of Leyland, & I attach thereunto all the spiritual favours that have been awarded to it by the Holy See & by powers derived from the Holy See. Furthermore I grant you permission to enrol members therein & constitute you Director thereof until Feb.10.1862.

2.   For the same period I grant you also faculties to bless & to invest with the Brown Scapular, requiring you, however, to take down & enter into a suitable Book the names of those so invested.

Eventually I hope to be able to give you a printed formula.

Wishing you every blessing, I remain sincerely Yrs in Xt. +Alexander Goss.

---

439   Edward (Benedict) Lynass OSB, 1823–83; Leyland was served from Ampleforth Abbey.

226.   *E.W. Pugin Esq., 5 Gordon Square   10 September 1859   5/3/172*
"Eldon St. Church Sacristy"

My dear Pugin,

I am heartily sick of my endeavours to make the Eldon St. Church creditable to you & to me. Tho' a round sacristy will please Mr. Vandepitte, it will, I am sure, disappoint every body else & bring blame both on you & me. If it stood to the church it might exteriorly look tolerably well; but as it has to be fenced from the street, I don't see how it can be such.

[*L-hand plan*] 'A' door into street. 'B' door into sacristy. 'C' chest for boys caps & coats etc. 'D' cupboard for vestments. 'E' Lavatory or piscina. 'F' water closet. 'G' Priests sacristy. 'H' boys sacristy. 'I' door from sacristy to Lavabo on left & water closet with another door on right [*sic, 'I' not on plan*]. 'K' door to shut off boys sacristy from the rest.

[*R-hand plan*] How will the boundary wall A & B look, impinging on the semi-circular wall? What can be made of the nooks C & D? There then will have to be a wall at E for the [?]room, for whatever purpose that may hereafter have to serve. I have given you my ideas & shall be glad to see how you can work them out & how the others can be worked out. Mr. Vandepitte does not seem to like the other idea of prolonging the aisles or side chapels & the making of a square sacristy in the centre. I was an hour with him yesterday. A. Goss

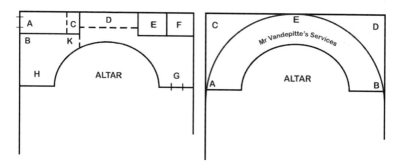

227. *Very Rev. Can. Maddox [sic]*[440]   *12 September 1859*   *5/3/179*
                         "St. Oswald's debt"
My dear Canon,

Among the many anxieties that press on me day & night, there is none
greater than the financial difficulties of the Diocese, which prevent me
making more ample provision for the spiritual wants of the faithful.
Nothing can surpass the zeal of the clergy at their respective churches,
but they are deficient in earnest endeavour to pay off existing debts,
being content to meet the interest due on their respective establishments.
St. Oswald's has been open for many years – 14 or 15 I suppose – & yet
the debt is between £2 & 3000, too large a sum on a suburban church
of only moderate dimensions. I am aware that much has been done, but
yet, as long as the debt remains, a Bishop's anxieties must remain. An
ecclesiastical property is unlike a lay property, in as much as it does
not increase in value by what is done for it; hence what is done does
not enable it to pay off debt, unless it be an increase of the building,
which by giving increased accommodation, affords greater opportunity
for increasing the revenue. The addition of schools & convent do not
increase the value of the property, whilst the filling up of the burial
ground is fast diminishing an important source of revenue. If that ceases,
hope ceases: for if the ordinary revenue sufficed to pay off the debt, it
must have long since been discharged. I had hoped that, ere this, you
would have paid off a considerable sum. I trust soon to hear a favourable account, or otherwise posterity will not speak well of either of us.
Commending myself to your prayers & wishing you every blessing I
remain sincerely Yrs in Xt. +A. Goss.

---

[440] Maddocks: John (brother of Rev.Walter Saunders Maddocks), 1801–1865; first r. St
Oswald's, Old Swan, from 1840 until his death. He had a reputation locally as a 'saintly
priest' and had a local street named after him. The church, opened in 1842, had cost
£5,000 in all; a presbytery had been added in 1858.

228.   *Very Rev. Can. Walmsley   15 September 1859*   *5/3/180*
"Educational Returns to Government"

My dear Dean,

I hope you will attempt to procure from the Clergy of your Deanery the returns mentioned in my last. It is impossible for me to undertake the task for any of the Deaneries, much less for all, & I shall not attempt it.

The interests of the Diocese now at issue in the case of the Executors of Mr. Sherburne & Dr. Youens are so immense that I trust you will see the necessity of making diligent search for all papers that may throw light thereon. Dr. F. has spent & is spending hours in poring over old letters & accounts, in hopes of finding something to the purpose, & he is satisfied, if after hours of search, he can find only a word. It is a question of justice, & hence a grave duty, which cannot be neglected without grievous sin, lies upon all who are able to do it, to furnish information. As Dr. Youens, Mr. Sherburne & Dr. Brown were all official men, the papers & letters which came into their hands as such, ought to have been placed into the hands of their successors in office. Had it not been for the good sense of Can. Wallwork, the papers of the Diocese, thro' the officiousness of the Rev. J. Nugent, would have fallen into the hands of the Very Rev. Dr. Corless, who, on the death of Dr. Brown, held no office beyond the incumbency of Cottam. It is time that such irregularities ceased. Pray leave nothing undone & no place unsearched where you are likely to find any help: much often depends on what looks as [*sic*] trifles. – Wishing you every blessing, I remain truly Yrs in Xt. +A. Goss

229.   *Miss Elizabeth Lord, The Warren House near Ashby de la*
         Zouche Leicestershire   15 September 1859   5/3/181
"St. Bernard's Colony"[441]

My dear Madam,

I beg to acknowledge the receipt of your letter of the 12th on the subject of the disorders or rather immorality among the boys & brothers at St. Bernard's Colony, praying for a searching inquiry to be made into the same. It is very shocking to contemplate the possibility of such crimes amongst them, &, no doubt, the matter should be speedily, rigorously & impartially sifted. It is however beyond my jurisdiction; for tho' many of the boys are my subjects, I have no authority beyond the limits of my own Diocese. I am further unable to say whether, at the present moment, the place is under Cardinal Wiseman as Apostolic Visitor, or whether it is under the Ordinary of Nottingham.

To prevent delay or mistakes, I have sent a copy of your letter to both of them, & no doubt one or other of them, whose duty it may be, will promptly attend to the matter.

Wishing you every blessing, & regretting that so painful a subject should have been forced on your notice, I remain truly Yrs in Xt. +Alexander Goss.

---

[441] St Bernard's Reformatory: see n. 577: Elliot says three lay brothers were convicted of sexual abuse of some of the boys; this was reported on by the government inspector (Bernard Elliot, 'Mount St Bernard's Reformatory, Leicestershire, 1856–81', *RH* 15:1 (May 1979), 15–22 at pp. 15, n. 1, 17.

230. *Rt. Rev. Dr. Roskell, Bp of Nottingham*   15 September 1859
5/3/182
"Mt. St. Bernard's Colony & Elizabeth Long"

My dear Lord,

As I do not know who at present exercises jurisdiction over the Colony of Mt. St. Bernard, I send to both you & the Cardinal copies of the inclosed addressed to me by a Lady, with the hope of securing attention to its contents. I know nothing of the writer or any thing of the allegations beyond what the letter itself contains. If true, it reveals a sad state of things; but I am in hope that the charges are exaggerated, for the writer seems to possess a fervid mind. Yet even so, it will not be well to postpone examination, as she threatens to bring the matter under the notice of government in order to obtain permission to remove the boy, unless there be an alteration in the management.

Believe me very truly Yrs. Alexander Goss.

231. *Very Rev. Canon Kenrick, St. Patrick's*   14 September 1859
5/3/188
"Cathedral Campaign"[442]

My dear Canon,

Mr. Kelly has arranged to have the erection of the Via Crucis at the Ford Cemetery on the 25th in the afternoon. If you can make arrangements, I think it would be well, if I were in the morning of that day to open the Cathedral Campaign at St. Patrick's, for on the two following Sundays, Oct. 2 & 9, I shall be North of Ribble. I will, however, be entirely guided by you in the matter. In order to keep up the agitation for a month, I think you ought to follow the Sunday after, & I could ask Dr. Fisher or Mr. Teebay or both to take up the strain on the two other Sundays so as to complete the 4 weeks. You will of course have to expound the matter previously to your people & exhort them to come with something in hand, & you will also have to act as Master of Ceremonies: for I do not know how the Bp. of Limerick managed the matter, & we must be careful not to shock the feelings of our critical – I might say cynical – English. I shall be glad to have a line from you or to see you. I shall be from home on Monday, but at home every other day. However you had best drop me a line. I would have the Collectors call at <u>every</u> house, Cath: or not Cath: This would involve the status animarum. The Collectors should be many, but each with a small district, taking in back, front, courts, villas, & cellars, docks, ships, work yards, & offices. Ever truly Yrs. AG.

---

442   The Lady Chapel of the proposed cathedral had been opened by Goss in December 1856 (see n. 94 and letter 22). In a later letter to Canon Greenhalgh (10 November 1859; 5/3/257) he proposed to appeal in Chorley for the cathedral, as he 'has been doing in Liverpool'; the appeal would be followed 'by a month's collection in Church and out from door to door'. I have found no other mention of the appeal. The reference to Bishop John Ryan of Limerick is unclear; he was in the middle of building his own cathedral; had he run a successful fund-raising campaign that Goss might follow? See Peter Galloway, *The Cathedrals of Ireland* (Belfast, 1992), 161–4.

232.   *Mr. Mercer,*[443] *Newton   26 September 1859*   *5/3/193*
"Land for Chapel"

My dear Mr. Mercer,
The spiritual destitution of the Catholics of Newton & Warrington junction have [*sic*] been frequently brought under my notice, & it is to me a matter of regret that I have not earlier sought a remedy. The good may go to Ashton to service; but those who stand most in need of the active superintendence of a pastor, will only be too ready to sieze on the excuse of distance for neglect of duty, & experience shows that where the chapel is empty the public house is full. If I had had the honour of Mr. Legh's acquaintance I would have made direct application to him; but I doubt not that he will prefer it to come through you. I feel sure that he will not decline to accede to the request, both because the late Mr. Legh had signified his willingness to do it, & because there has ever existed a kindly feeling between Catholics & the Leghs. In 1694 when a number of Catholic families – the Gerards, Standishes, Molineuxes, Blundells etc were arraigned for high treason, I find also Mr. Legh included, tho' the family was, I believe, even then Protestant. I shall feel obliged if you will take a favourable opportunity of bringing the matter under Mr. Legh's notice. Mr. Newsham has the best acquaintance with the district, but I believe that a plot of ground between Newton & the junction would be best suited for the purpose.

Wishing you every blessing I remain sincerely Yrs in Xt. +Alexander Goss.

---

443   The mission at Newton-le-Willows started in 1861; Kelly says the church opened 1863–64 with help from the Gerard family (*English Catholic Missions*).

233. *Very Rev. H. Gradwell,*[444] *Claughton   26 September 1859*
                                                                    5/3/194
          "Ushaw Contributions"   Confidential
My dear Mr. Gradwell,
I have headed this letter confidential, but I leave it to your own discretion to make what use of its contents you find necessary. I cannot tell you now the object of my inquiries further than that it is essential for the maintenance of our right position at Ushaw that I should be able to show, as far as can now be ascertained,

1o. what were the benefactions from Lancashire for the <u>building</u> of Ushaw;

2o. for the <u>endowment,</u> under which latter would of course come funds. Dr. Newsham will, of course, try to show that all educational funds, which are assigned to Lancashire, are inalienably attached to Ushaw, & that, when not specified to the contrary, the right of presentation belongs to the Pres; [*sic*] he has exerted every influence at [his] command to have it made a Pontifical College, not so much that it may be under the immediate control of the H. See, but that it may be exempt from the jurisdiction of the Bps. My aim is that each Diocese should retain an equal share in the property & administration of the College, a promise made in print to the public when Dr. Brown first announced his intention of taking ecclesiastical students at St. Edward's. Can you aid me either by documents or recollection as to the sums collected from this Diocese for the above purposes? It is not impossible that the defence of the common interests may take me to Rome.

[*Written across letter:*] Begging to be remembered to Robert & wishing you every blessing I remain truly Yrs, Alex Goss.

---

[444] Henry Gradwell, 1792–1860; see n. 388. Goss wrote in a similar vein to Richard Gillow on same day.

234. *Rt. Rev. Dr. Briggs, Bp of Beverley 26 September 1859 5/3/196*
                          "Ushaw Statistics"

My dear Lord,
Dr. Grant writes me that it is necessary for the success of our cause that we should be able to show

1o. What Lancashire & Yorkshire & Cheshire contributed towards the erection of Ushaw or the purchase of the farm.[445]

2o. What they have contributed to its endowment in the way of funds or property for Eccles. Education.

3o. What are the instructions of the founders of burses, i.e. did they irrevocably attach their property to Ushaw & under whose management did they place them, & to whom did they assign the right of presentation.

4o. The number of Ecclesiastical students belonging to the Beverley Diocese.

Other information which Dr. Grant thinks necessary, I already possess; but I shall be glad of any information on the points named above. Are any of your educational funds in the hands of the College or of persons in the Hexham Diocese? If so, to what sums. Has the President of the College de jure or de facto the privilege of presenting to your funds & to what number? Our aim must be to show that our respective Dioceses have larger interests at stake in Ushaw than Hexham has.

Hoping you continue well I remain sincerely Yrs in Xt. +A. Goss.

---

[445]   Cornsay; see nn. 7, 169.

235.   *Rt. Rev. Dr. Briggs, Bp of Beverley*   *26 September 1859*
5/3/197
"Banister or other letters"

My dear Lord,

I find that my uncle Mr. Banister[446] of Mowbreck wrote many letters to Bp. Gibson & to Mr. Gillow, when resident at York, about the establishment of a College in England, on the suppression of Douay College. Do you think these or similar letters exist, either among the Bishop's papers or at the old Chapel in York? Barrow of Claughton[447] also corresponded with them both, & Mr. Eyre[448] too. If those letters could be found, they would add greatly to my information on these subjects. I have read hundreds of letters, & I hope to be able to make good the view we advocated at Synod. I am anxious to preserve the collection of the letters of Banister & Rutter,[449] both my relatives, & the more so, as both played an important part in public affairs particularly at this very time. Can you either furnish me with any such letters, or can you tell me where I am likely to find them. The Bp. was often at York or Stella. Banister, Rutter, Gillow, Eyre, Smith, Story, Barrow, Orrell[450] were the principal correspondents on these important subjects. Please to let me hear from you soon. Believe me ever sincerely Yrs. A. Goss.

---

[446]   Robert Banister, 1725–1812, great uncle of Goss; see Gooch, *Revival*.

[447]   John Barrow, 1751–1811; known as the 'Old Tar' after his press-ganged years in the navy; see Gooch, *Revival*.

[448]   Thomas Eyre, 1748–1810, see Gooch, *Revival*; he was the first president of Crook Hall/Ushaw; see Milburn, *History of Ushaw College*, 37, 108 ff. The old domestic chapel at Stella Hall, on the banks of the Tyne, where Eyre had been chaplain for a time, was replaced by a new building in 1832 (Kelly, *English Catholic Missions*).

[449]   Henry Rutter, 1755–1838; nephew of Banister and Goss's uncle; see Gooch, *Revival*.

450   All these names feature in Gooch, *Revival.*

236.   *E.W. Pugin Esq., 5 Gordon Square, London 27 September 1859*
                                                              5/3/199
                          "Coniston. Eldon St."
My dear Pugin,
I have received the drawings for Coniston which are not very unlike a
set which I had prepared that I now forward. The roof must be simple,
for timber is dear. There must be no mouldings or any dressed stone
except the slightest bits to mark the windows, a style adopted with effect
in the old churches, Isle of Man. I have no prospect of building yet.
     The Eldon St. Sacristy still keeps up the fallacious notion of an even-
tual continuation of the aisles, which has so dissatisfied me that I have
not for some time been near the church, nor shall I probably go near it
again till it is finished. The wall that supports the galleries at the end of
the aisles, renders completely useless the space beyond, so that all that
is gained by a gallery is to render useless the space below it, in order to
accommodate the same number above it: nothing more was needed than
a gallery in the centre for the organ. Every body says that it disfigures
the church. I think the sacristy in the tracing preferable to the plan sent
down, & cannot see why it cannot be adopted. Eventually I doubt not
we shall have to open a central doorway, blocking up that in Eldon St.
& supporting the gallery on a beam instead of a wall. Mr. Vandepitte's
fancies have not improved the church, whilst I feel greatly mortified that
they should have been gratified. Ever truly Yrs in Xt.
     A. Goss.

237.   *Very Rev. Dean Gillow   14 October 1859   5/3/200*
                          "Cottam Repairs"
My dear Dean,
You have rightly conjectured that I was not likely to give a verbal
commission for the repairing of the roof of Cottam, & equally right
are you in the supposition that I had given no such commission at all. I
required Millar to inspect the roof & report to me thro' Mr. Ball.451 He
reported thro' Mr. Swarbrick that the roof was positively unsafe. I then
desired Mr. Tom452 or your cousin or both to desire you to see Millar &
to give instructions for the dangerous plaster to be removed, so that we
might be then able to judge both of the extent & nature of the repairs
required; in fact we should be able to judge whether it was better to
repair the old place or give Dr. Corless leave to rebuild. There is no
order from me, written or unwritten to repair any thing, nor any permission to pay for the repairs, nor have I any intention of doing so. You had
better therefore order the plaster that threatens to fall to be removed;

but <u>stop at once & entirely</u> any other act, no matter at whose expense it is supposed to be done. I have not forgotten that Dr. Corless actually began his schools without any authorisation. No instruction of mine has ever gone further than the removal of the plaster, to prevent its falling on the people, & this I desired to be done thro' you: tho' it is possible the order may have been misunderstood. Ever sincerely Yrs in Xt. A. Goss.

---

451   William Ball, 1826–80; r. Thurnham 1852–57, c. Kirkham 1857–61, r. Westby to 1877. A real Fylde priest!

452   Mr Tom has not been identified.

238.   *Most Rev. Archbp. Errington   15 October 1859*   *5/3/201*
"Roman journey"

My dear Grace,

Dr. Grant has called here on his way home from Lord Ed. Howard's Glossop.[453] He tells me that the Card has been suffering from angina pectoris, & was thought on Sunday to be in danger. He desires me to tell you that he wrote to Dr. Cullen according to your directions, but has received no answer. He thinks some months will pass over before we could be of use in Rome on the subject of the Synod, as, after the Cardinal's arrival with it, it will have to be read, placed in the hands of a Consultor who will take his time, & then be printed to be placed in the hands of the Cardinals, at which juncture only could we be of assistance; for any representations on the subject would be unintelligible, until they had the matter before them.

If you will tell me the <u>exact week when you will be over</u>, I will invite the Bps. of Bev. Salf & Shrews to meet you & Dr. Grant will also join us in order that we may deliberate on what has to be done.

Dr. Hogarth has promised to send to Dr. Fisher the additional matter which he is inserting in the case, so that I do not know that it will be necessary for him to go. Dr. Grant's view is, that you should watch events, let us know if we be wanted & when: for as the Card. is staying till Easter he would weary us out.

I was <u>not</u> mobbed as stated by one of the papers. I saw no disturbance, & no body was brought up by the police who were there. Ever truly Yrs. A. Goss.

Dr. Grant & all join in kind regards.

---

453   Lord Edward George Fitzalan Howard, 1818–83; Liberal MP for Horsham 1848–53 and Arundel 1853–68. Created first Baron Howard of Glossop (Derbyshire) in 1869; chairman of CPSC 1869–77. See *ODNB* and Smith, 'Religion or Party?' 27.

239. *Very Rev. Can. Newsham"   15 October 1859*   *5/3/202*
"Lydiate – Fleetwood"

Very Rev. & dear Sir,

I am in receipt of your letter of Sunday last in which you inform me that Lydiate[454] has to be given to the Seculars, that you presume it will be in my gift, & that you wish to be presented to it. In reply I beg to say that I have not the presentation to Lydiate, & that, with my approbation, it has already been filled up by Mr. W. Blundell.

I am pained & startled by a further announcement in your letter, – 'that you have no intention of settling down at Fleetwood & that you do not think you ever will have'. I cannot recognise in any priest the right of choosing his own mission, as by the College oath[455] he has sworn to serve the mission, an obligation which equally binds him tho' he may not have taken his oath, & at his ordination he has promised to obey the Bp. & his successors. In the face of such an obligation I cannot understand how any priest can write to his Bp. to say that he has no intention of settling down at a particular place. To a zealous man Fleetwood offers greater scope than Lydiate. Surely no priest is any more free to choose his Diocese than his mission. The avowal of such principles by one of his clergy cannot produce a favourable impression on the mind of any Bp.

On receiving from you some details about the obligation of building within a certain time at Fleetwood, & about the new wants created by the purchase of the hotel for a barracks, I will furnish you with an authorisation to seek the alms of the faithful.

Wishing you peace with God & man, from which all blessings flow, I remain sincerely Yrs in Xt. Alexander Goss.

---

[454] Lydiate had been a Jesuit mission. The site of the new church (1854) was given by the Weld Blundell family and its endowment had come from Charles Blundell. Thomas Gibson was the first Secular incumbent (Kelly, *English Catholic Missions*); see n. 68.

[455] College oath: Newsham had been educated at Douai and Ushaw. Goss, however, did offer some a choice.

240. *E. W. Pugin Esq., 5 Gordon Square, London   16 October 1859*
5/3/204
"Eldon St. Church"

My dear Pugin,

Yesterday I visited Eldon St. Church with the Bp. of Southwark. He was much pleased with it, but felt the same objection as myself to the arrangements at the West end. It is too much subdivided by walls, which only provide lurking places for those disposed to seek concealment. No gain is effected by the gallery, except by the centre portion to serve as an organ loft: the two portions over the aisles would not hold a dozen people whilst the walls that support them render the lower part useless.

At the altar too he suggested what I think a desirable change. At present, as at St. Vincent's, those going to communion would have to mount several steps. Now this could be avoided, without diminishing the height of the Sanctuary, by placing the altar rail at the first step, which would have to be prolonged about three feet: thus

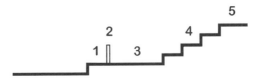

1 step for communicants to kneel on, not wider than 10 or 12 inches. 2 communion rail. 3 space for the priest to stand & walk on whilst communicating the people. 4 steps leading to 5 the plane of the Sanctuary. You know I want Eldon St. to be a model Church as well in ecclesiastical propriety as in architecture. The arrangement would necessitate the widening of the present spaces between the benches & the altar rails, & hence the flags now down would have to be put a yard lower down the Church & the step (1 & 3) would have to be advanced a yard which would form its entire width, i.e. a narrow flag could be inserted to form a plane between the 1st & 2nd steps. I think you had better give orders for the West end & loft [*two illegible words*], & the flooring from the Altar to the steps – pillars not to be proceeded with till you come down. I should like to be with you when you go over the Church. Truly Yrs AG.

241. *Rt. Rev. Dr. Briggs, Bp. of Beverley   21 October 1859   5/3/224*
"Missionary Coadjutors"

My dear Lord,
One of the great omissions at our last two Synods has been the consideration of the position & pay of Missionary Coadjutors. At present, there is, I think, no difference in their stipend in this Diocese; tho' I have said that I consider the Senior priest to have a claim for an extra £10 for expenses of management. Our large missions you will remember are heavily burdened. I think it would be an excellent plan to make a difference, to have a graduated scale: for as things are now, a pert, flippant youth, fresh from his ordination, receives equal pay with a gray headed missionary whom accident has placed in a second position. All my young priests have an itching to get into Liverpool, where they find or make good pay & plenty of amusement, knocking thro' their work in a brisk cavalier way. I see a change since I have been Bp. & I intend to

grapple with it. There is a general complaint amongst the senior priests, & I think not without reason. The apostolic spirit that founded missions is gone: must not much of this be attributed to education? It requires something more than the use of silver forks, & large Gothic halls to turn out men of the right sort of stuff. Several of the Bps. have ordered prayers for the Pope. I am corresponding with Archbp. E. about the journey to Rome. I think that he & Dr. Grant ought to go first & that I ought to follow, if needed, as deputy of the Northern Bps. Sincerely Yrs AG.

242. *Very Rev. Canon Greenhalgh   10 November 1859   5/3/257*
"Conference: absence. Wigan"

My dear Dean,

Conference, as such, has no power of any kind. It meets for a special purpose & has no duties beyond that. The obligation of attendance results from the law of the Church, & consequently the Executive of the law – the Bp. & in his place, the Dean – must decide on the sufficiency of excusing causes. Mr. Lynass[456] cannot seriously have maintained any other opinion.

I do not think that any student would suit us who would not suit the Benedictines, for our duties are so much alike, that the clergy of both are required to have similar qualifications.

As the Adlington Church scheme is not yet launched,[457] I have intended to propose to you that I should address your people on behalf of a Cathedral, as I have been doing in Lpool: which is followed by a month's collection in church & out from door to door. I will be guided by you: but whatever you decide, should be announced on Sunday. I think Mr. Seed's promises about Wigan will end like his last, in smoke; for, when pressed, if you remember, he would do nothing.[458] Begging my remembrance to Maria & wishing both every blessing, I remain truly Yrs AG.

---

[456] Edward (Benedict) Lynass, OSB, 1823–83, was in charge of the Leyland mission at this time.
[457] See letter 182.
[458] Thomas Seed SJ, 1807–74, was in charge of the Jesuit church of St John; see n. 267.

243. *Rev. J. Adamson,[459] Orrell   22 November 1859   5/3/272*
"Burial of a Protestant"

My dear Mr. Adamson,

I fear this letter will reach you too late to be of any advantage; but I have been giving Confirmations at Chorley & had yesterday a profession at the Convent of Mercy, so that I did not get home in time to answer your letter.

It is not the practice in Germany or other countries of mixed religion to bury non Catholics in Catholic burial grounds, tho' such burial would not desecrate the ground. Yet if the right of burial were conceded, there must also be conceded the right to have the service, which would shock the piety of the faithful; & however soothing to the feelings of the relatives, would diminish the horror of heresy which it is our duty to inculcate. I have consulted a number of theologians, but they are all against it on one ground or another. When I tell you that my own father was a Protestant, your disconsolate people will feel that I should have been willing to stretch a point in their regard, if I could have conscientiously done so.

I am sorry to have so poor an account of your health: the weather has certainly been trying. I have myself suffered a whole week from tic, but am better, & I hope a few days will set you all right.

Ever truly Yrs A. Goss.

---

459   Thomas Adamson, 1817–1869; at Orrell from 1848 until his death.

244.   *Rt. Rev. Dr. Briggs, Bp of Beverley*   25 November 1859
5/3/274

          "Dr. Grant – Rome"   Confidential
My dear Lord,
I think it will need all your influence to induce Dr. Grant to go to Rome. Dr. Errington is very strong as to the necessity of his going, in order to sustain the acts of Synod; for no one understands better the style of action necessary at Rome in such circumstances, & no other Bp. has the ear of Card. Barnabò to the same extent. Dr. Grant has written to Rome to ask if he must go this year or he may postpone his visit, for he is due *ad limina*. He has received for answer that he may postpone his visit, but that answer only exonerates him from visiting the *limina* this year, & ought not to be pleaded as an excuse for not going to sustain the Synod, of which Card. Barnabò as yet knows nothing. I hope, therefore, you will use your influence with him to go, in order to complete our work at the Synod; for otherwise our labours will have been in vain, & what we have laboured so long & so hard to accomplish, even before Synod, will fail. The Card. is bent on leaving at the end of the month. He is going to try for a week, if lying in a horizontal position will reduce his pulse. He might yet live & be happy, if he would resign himself to circumstances & not strive, for the sake of gratifying Dr. Newsham & carrying out his views about Ushaw, to trample on the rights of the Northern Bishops. I partly expect the Archbp. [Errington] on Sunday,

who purposes setting off soon to Rome. I have been suffering from your enemy, the tic; but am better & hope you keep pretty well. Believe me ever sincerely Yrs A. Goss.

245.   *Rev. T. Bridges,*[460] *17 Everton Crescent   25 November 1859*
5/3/275
"Retreat – Sick call"

Dear Rev. Sir,

I write to acknowledge receipt of your letter of the 18th written from Bp. Eton, & to express the satisfaction I feel at the manifestation of a somewhat better spirit. Yet I cannot but feel that under whatever circumstances a priest is placed, if lawfully or canonically so placed, it is his duty to conform himself thereto & to fulfil his obligations therein. I was so taught & have so acted: for on having a choice given me, I declined to express any opinion, tho' I had very strong predilections in the matter; but I answered that I would do as I was bid, as I had come on the mission not to do my own will, but the will of others. I think a priest should no more seek to be released from a particular mission to which he has been duly appointed, than a husband, lawfully married, should seek to be released *a mensa & toro.*[461]

I wish to know if you have had, during the week, a sick call to a cellar 22 Cherry Lane, & 1o. at what time the sick call was first brought to you? 2o. how often that sick call was brought & at what hours? 3o. How often you visited the sick person after the first call? 4o. What sacraments you administered to him? I beg an early attention to these enquiries.

Wishing you meanwhile every blessing I remain truly Yrs in Xt. Alexr. Goss.

---

[460]   Thomas Bridges; see letter 180 of the previous year and 250.
[461]   Trans: 'from board and bed'.

246.   *Rev. R. Doyle, St. Patrick's Wigan 26 November 1859   5/3/277*
"Hardship of position"

Rev. & dear Sir,

I am much pained by the contents of your letter, for yours is the seventh case of a similar kind now before me. If the only remedy be change, then if I change one, I must change all, so that at the present moment I should have to make no less than 14 changes, the responsibility of which before the Diocese would fall upon me. This convinces me, even if many other considerations had not already convinced me, that there must be some other remedy for this unfortunate & deplorable state of things. It is not a trivial thing that should mar the harmony of priests, who are saints by profession & gentlemen by position & education, & whom duty has placed in a common field of labour in the interest of a common Master, J.C. Allowance must be made for temper; for all senior priests are not equally gentle in the exercise of authority; yet your senior priest has been ever noted amongst his brethren for his amiability. After making every allowance for the various cases that have come under my notice, I am bound to believe that differences most frequently occur from the erroneous belief that all priests are equal, which, if ever true, is true only in the sense that all men are equal. The cura animarum is vested in the senior priest & the junior priests exercise even their faculties dependently on him. They have no share of authority in the administration of the mission except so far as the senior commits it to them. To him they owe respect & submission, & should cooperate with him, even tho' his conduct be not irreproachable. As to him belongs the care of the household, let all things belonging to the house be done thro' him. I have never acted in any other way myself. I have lived here since 1843 & have never ordered a meal, not even since I have been Bp. If such principles regulate your conduct, peace will reign in the house.

[*From here on lines are written across the letter and somewhat difficult to read:*] As you have already spoken to the Vicar on the subject of local circumstances & he has corresponded with Mr. McCormick,[462] you had better write to him on any thing that may further arise, which I pray God to avert. Wishing you peace & every other blessing, I remain very truly Yrs Alexander Goss.

---

[462] Hugh Nugent McCormick, 1805–77; first rector of St Patrick's, Wigan, 1847–75. Another letter of the same date (5/3/278) to Rev. J. Holland covers the same ground, with added recommendation to read Dubois on zeal (see n. 464). See also letter 241.

247. *Rev. T. Walton,*[463] *St. Anthony's Liverpool* [*added later*]
                    26 November 1859   5/3/279
                         "Conduct"

Rev. & dear Sir,

I am sorry to say that for some time remarks about your conduct have reached me, that have caused considerable pain. I wish therefore to have from you in writing a categoric reply to the following statements by to day's post.

1o. On the Sunday after notice had been given in the church that funerals must be reported by 10 o'clock in the morning, you announced that you must have notice on the night before, or you would not perform the service; & you have acted on this announcement, for during the week funerals have left St. Anthony's without the service being read over the bodies.

2o. The vestry hours at St. Anthony's are from 4½ till 10; you usually attend from 5½ till 8½ or 9 oclock?

3o. You usually, if not always, spend the evening out of your own house, not returning till 11 oclock & on Sunday & Monday last, not till ¼ to 12?

4o. You do not retire to rest till one oclock, & often rise late, at times omitting the morning mass without making provision for its being said? On two occasions you did not rise till 11 oclock; on one occasion till one oclock in the day, you being well enough to spend the evening out?

5o. That you keep in your room or had conveyed there two jars of spirits, notwithstanding my letter to you of March 12, 1856, & that you have ordered, on one occasion, a kettle to be taken to your room, as you alleged for shaving water, tho' you have hot & cold water in your bed room?

Praying God to keep you in his holy keeping, I remain sincerely Yrs in Xt.

   Alexander Goss.

---

463   Thomas Walton, 1829–97, at St Anthony's, 1856–60. See letters 249, 302.

248.   *Rev. Jas. Taylor,*[464] *St. Peter's Lancaster   26 November 1859*
5/3/280
"Appointment"

My dear Mr. Taylor,

I have a distinct recollection of the circumstance mentioned in your letter of yesterday, on the occasion of my going to bless the hall at Garstang some four months ago, & of your having spoken to me in the railway on the subject of your removal from Lancaster. I feel more disposed to accede to your request on account of the grounds on which you base your application, – want of mutual harmony, association or confidence – than I should have done, had you urged some of the trivialities which form the staple of complaints. You will however be content to bide your time when I inform you that yours is only one of seven cases now under my notice, that this is actually the fourth letter I have written to day, besides an interview, & one yesterday on this most painful subject. Tho' I am quite willing to concede that every senior priest is not irreproach-able or free from foibles, yet I cannot but believe that the juniors or some of them are too impatient of control, & yield themselves captive too readily to a criticising & disdainful spirit, notwithstanding a certain amiable character in other respects. Let me recommend for your perusal a work I am now reading with profit, entitled Zeal, price 10/6, which treats most fully of this very question. Dubois, the author, is French, but the book has been well translated into English.

Wishing you peace & contentment of spirit, I remain truly Yrs. A. Goss.

---

464   James Taylor, 1831–1908; later Mgr. Canon and Dean; he left Lancaster in 1860. The recommended book was Henri Dubois, *Zeal in the Work of the Ministry, or the Means by which Every Priest May Render His Ministry Honourable and Fruitful* (London, 1859; trans by C. A. Comes de G. Liancourt from the French 5th edn, *Pratique du zèle ecclésiastique*).

249.   *Rev. T. Walton, St. Anthony's Lpool   28 November 1859   5/3/281*
"Conduct"

Rev. & Dear Sir,

The case mooted in my letter of the 26th is not between you & Mr. Power, but between you & me, & it matters not, as to the facts inquired into, by whom the charge is made. My letter of inquiry & your answer to it are the only official papers in the matter.

1o. You appeal to an announcement by the Cemetery Board for a justification of your declaration in the Church, that you would not perform the Burial Service unless you had 24 hours notice. Now as regards St. Anthony's it is to the Rector & not to the Burial Board that you must look for instructions to guide you. In this matter, therefore, you must conform to the regulations laid down by Mr. Power, for he, being Rector, has supreme authority both in the church & mission in whatever concerns the cura animarum.

2o. What I have said of funerals, applies to the Confessional. The Rector has the cura animarum. He considers a certain time necessary for the use of the faithful, & lays down rules accordingly. It will require time to gather a vestry[465] & must demand from you a sacrifice of time & comfort, but you will be amply repaid by the good you will see effected by it.

I am most anxious for the peace & happiness of all who are working with me in the great work of saving souls, & hence you must know how greatly pained I am at the misunderstandings & differences that occur among brethren. Mr. Power was by no means prejudiced against you: on the contrary it was his own wish to retain you there. You are young & strong, able & talented, & throw yourself heart & soul into your work. I do not not [*sic*] wish to deprive you of relaxation, but always bear in mind that thousands are looking to you for the bread of life. Thro' you hundreds, probably thousands will be saved or damned. Gird up your loins, then: work with a cheerful spirit & you will enjoy peace & get on with Mr. Power, tho' you have not the essence of 20 saints distilled into you.

Sincerely Yrs in Xt. A. Goss

465 In the sense, perhaps, of a group of regular parishioners.

250. *Rev. T. Bridges, Our Lady of Reconciliation*
                        28 November 1859   *5/3/282*
                        "Sick calls"

Rev. & Dear Sir,

Few saints pass away with the prospect of eternity & judgment before them, who do not feel, whatever may be the grounds of confidence, some alarm at that dread hour. Now if this be the case with saints, what must be the feelings of sinners, of those who have had to struggle through a long life amidst the temptations which beset the poor in this country & in these times. Had not our Blessed Lord thought the sacraments necessary, he would not have instituted them, nor would the Church have ordered them to be gratuitously administered, or enjoined the priest to go at all times, whatever the nature of the disease, to bear consolation & salvation to the dying. I regret much that you did not think it your duty to go when twice called at night to a case which you had visited during the day, specially as you knew you had neithered [*sic*] administered Holy Viaticum nor Extreme Unction, & had not taken the trouble to refer to your note book about the case. I hope the same will not occur again. If the Senior Priest had directed you to go instead of going himself, & had you then refused, it would have been a very serious matter for you. Let the fear of dying yourself without all the consolations of religion, too often the misfortune of priests, be a continual stimulus to your charity. Wishing you every blessing I remain sincerely Yrs in Xt. Alexander Goss.

251. *Very Rev. Can. Greenhalgh   28 November 1859*   *5/3/283*
                        "Adlington"

My dear Canon,

I think it better to build a school than to rent an indifferent cottage; but the building should be a school without any pretensions. I would have no gable windows, not even at the altar end; & for altar & sanctuary would have no different construction from the rest, but simply dividing or folding doors. The old square-headed window with a transom looks very well, such as often are found in grammar schools. I should think Fairclough could sketch & give estimate with no architect. The roof I would have very simple [*sketch of large* A *shape here*], plastered or in [*illegible*] at the cross piece. The schools should be build [*sic*] on one end of the land, tho' not quite at the extremity: sufficient land for protection should be left.

Can. Newsham is fencing: he does not want to abandon his canonry, & I shall not grant him an exeat otherwise. He is doing much mischief in the Willows Congregation, spreading a report that attempts are being made to propose Mr. Sherburne insane, in order to upset his Will. I have no memorandum about Mr. Parkinson's legacy to Weld Bank & have not got a copy of his Will, but will refer to it, if you will remind me, when the matters come into my hands. Between us, Mr. Lynass is leaving Leyland, so I hope things will mend.

The answer given to Mr. G. Oreilly[466] comes from the Superioress in Namur: I don't think they would purchase St. Mary's, as the premises are not suited for conventual residence, tho' they might do for a school. I will give £10 towards the Adlington school: apply to James Fisher for it. Ever truly Yrs in Xt. A. Goss.

---

466   Gerald O'Reilly, 1828–96, brother of the future bishop, at St Mary's, Wigan, 1859–73. See n. 267; was Goss actively pursuing the sale of St Mary's? The Sisters of Notre Dame de Namur (SND) had begun teaching in the town in 1854 'in a small and beautifully fitted out house'; see Jennifer Worrall SND (ed.), *Jubilee: Sisters of Notre Dame de Namur celebrate 150 years in Britain* (n.p., 1995), 28.

252.   *Rev. T. Gibson Croft*   5 December 1859   5/3/286
             "Fleetwood. Coniston. Collections. Ledger"
My dear Mr. Gibson,
Can. Newsham has abandoned all idea of change of land or building a church, in consequence of my not having given an immediate sanction to his proceedings, which I could not do either legally or conscientiously till I had taken the advice of yourself & my Chapter.

2o. You know Coniston. I want you to draw up for me the draft of a Pastoral to them, exhorting them to attend mass at Ulverston, now that the railway is open, instead of taking advantage of it for excursions, & also to make weekly collections towards a chapel, each person in work paying monthly so much, the unmarried more than the married. I send you Mr. Jarrett's letter which please to return with draft.[467]

I think it would be well to prepare for the two Diocesan collections a resume [*sic*] of the collections, not so detailed as the one I drew up, but adding all the years together, headed thus: Contributions to the Fund of the various Missions for the last … years, from its commencement in … to the year ending 1859.

Many thanks for the Ledger with the additional particulars. I am now trying to complete my Status from the Papers you drew up, having sent to the parties for the particulars omitted.

Wishing you every blessing I remain sincerely Yrs in Xt. AG.
I shall have two good maps, showing Churches & also their distances from one another.

467 Pastoral Letter: Goss had already written an 'Open Letter to the Irish Colony in Coniston' in August 1855 (AAL, S1/2/C/2): until they had a resident priest they were to gather on Sundays in one of the cottages to say the Rosary and other prayers, listen to some pious reading and take a collection. I have not found a copy of any letter resulting from Goss's appeal to Gibson. Mr Jarrett was the Jesuit at Ulverston; see letters 15, 219.

253. *Sister Vincent, The Lace Schools*[468] *5 December 1859 5/3/287*
My dear Child in J.C.

I have been greatly pained at the letter of Nov. 30, in which you make known to me the sorrow which has overflowed your soul, for I cannot but be afflicted with grief at the anxieties that oppress my spiritual children. It is the misfortune of our country to possess few directors that are conversant with the spiritual obligations of religious, & your adviser is not one of them. You left your Convent in Belgium with the consent of your Bishop, & you are in your present position with the sanction of the Bp. under whom you are living: I do not see what more is needed, or how any director, knowing this, should say that you cannot conscientiously remain. All religious men in this country – & there are as many in this Diocese as there are secular priests – can plead no higher sanction for dwelling in communities that do not contain 12 inmates. You can fulfil your vows where you are as well as if you were in community, with the exception of that encouragement which numbers & example afford. Work therefore peaceably & cheerfully in God's name. Strive after perfection in your present circumstances & let not your mind be teased with regret for the past or anxiety for the future.

Wishing yourself & companions every blessing I remain sincerely Yrs A. Goss.

468 The Lace Schools (industrial schools) were run by the Augustinian nuns; see Burke, *Catholic Liverpool*, 185, and Bennett, *Father Nugent*, 83; Sr Mary Vincent was Superior. – listed in *Kelly's Directory for Lancashire*, 1858, p. 793, as Miss Vincent Page. A later letter, 5/3/299, shows she was happy with Goss's reply, but gives no further details.

254. *V. Rev. Dean Gillow 8 December 1859 5/3/290*
Statistics. Address
My dear Dean,

I write on Sat. for leave to appear at Rome with my status animarum either in person or by deputy, so that there is a prospect of my not troubling you so much for some time. I send you the returns from your Deanery as I have been able to compile them from the papers hitherto furnished to me; but I want you to get them filled up. For this purpose it will be best to fix an early day – say within a week – for the next conference, write to them & tell them to bring their status, as you wish to fill up the details: you might state the heads on which you will want information – I think also it would be well for the Conference to sign an address to the Pope in his present difficulties[469] – I have written to Wm. Walker to prepare the draft of an address, so that [at] Conference it can be adopted & signed without further ado; for I should like to have it here in 10 days or so. I know that it is very troublesome having to furnish these details, but Rome requires them of me, & if we want to stand well, they must be supplied, otherwise they will give us a character for negligence which we by no means deserve. Wishing you every blessing I remain sincerely Yrs in Xt. A. Goss.

---

[469]   The defeat of Austrian forces by Piedmont in 1859 was followed by a number of popular uprisings in some of the papal states and saw the beginning of the final, decisive, stage in the struggle for Italian unification, against papal wishes.

255.   *Very Rev. Can. Walmsley*   *9 December 1859*   *5/3/291*
"Statistics. Petition for Convent"

Dear Canon,

1o. Tell Mr. Allies that when the Royal Commission was issued, I was told that each school, as Boys, Girls, Infants, Mixed, would require a separate paper, hence 200 were applied for. On perusal, managers of schools thought that one paper would suffice; hence little more than ¼ were required. If he will refer to the returns, he will find that few that were worth returning, have omitted to do so.

2o. I think it would be well for all the Sisters of Mercy in my Diocese to sign a letter of sympathy with his Holiness, saying that they not only pray for him themselves, but that they teach … thousand [*sic*] children who are confided to their care to do so also. Thus they have an indirect way of stating to His Holiness how many children they are educating.

3o. I want Rev. Mother[470] to return to me the names of the Convents of Mercy in my Diocese, the number of Sisters, whether choir, lay or novices in each, & the number of schools in which they teach & the number of children in each of the schools, whether girls or infants, the distinction being observed when they are in separate schools.

4o. I think it best for each Deanery to sign & write a letter of sympathy, as a general letter would not get signed. Will you look to this? You might summon the Conference for next week, giving due notice to the Proponent, so that you would not need to bring the Brethren together for this object alone.

5o. I send you a list of the returns from your deanery, please to see that they are returned properly filled: you could do it at Conference, if you give notice. Yours truly A. Goss.

470 Canon John Walmsley, 1812–68, was chaplain to the Convent of Mercy in Mt
Vernon, Liverpool, from 1849 to death; the Mother Superior there was Mother Mary
Liguori – see *Extracts*, 1.

256.   *Rt. Rev. Dr. Turner, Bp. of Salford 15 December 1859   5/3/296*
                         "Delegate to Rome"471

My dear Lord,

Dr. Errington was in Paris on the 11th with Dr. Roskell & Mr. Thompson,
who had missed the Card. & was to sail with them on the 12th. So that
I suppose he would arrive in Rome yesterday.

He seems to think we shall lose everything by not having one of our
number on the spot, for he says that if he & the Card. be reconciled,
he cannot assist us against the Card. & if he be dismissed, he will be
considered to be out of court, as having no longer an interest in affairs.
I hear from both Rome & Paris – on undoubted authority, that Dr. Cornthwaite & Mr. Jn. Gillow are going to Rome & from Ushaw I hear that
Mr. Gillow is not attending class, as he is busy drawing up a document.
Now he is the great Ushaw historiographer, & has drawn up, years ago,
an account to show that Ushaw is the veritable successor of Douai &
is in fact a Pontifical College. It seems passing strange that all who are
against our views & interests are off to Rome, whereas we have not one
Bp., Canon or Priest to advocate our side. Dr. Fisher could do little, for
he was not at the Synod and could not therefore be a witness. What
might be done? Will you please to send me the list of students furnished
to you last Midsummer, as I want to collect our numbers by way of
showing the interests we have at stake in Ushaw as compared with Dr.
Hogarth. I cannot but think we are too supine, when the last cast of the
dice is being thrown. Ever most truly Yrs in Xt. Alex. Goss.

471 In a very similar letter of the same date to Briggs (5/3/298) Goss says he 'has become
more distrustful since Synod'.

257.   *The Hon. C. Longdale*472 *[in pencil]*   *17 December 1859*
                                                              5/3/301

Dear Mr. Langdale,

When I saw my name quoted in the newspaper in favour of holding
a public meeting in London, I had some thoughts of writing to you
to explain the matter. The fact is I was invited to attend a meeting &
not asked my opinion as to the propriety of holding it. In my reply
I stated that a meeting would probably be held in Liverpool & that
therefore I declined to go up to London for the purpose, but wished
them every success. I do not think that meetings in England, considering
our numbers etc. would be a success, whilst they might rekindle the

feelings of the so called Papal Aggression. I think the plan you have adopted decidedly the best: I have recommended it to the Gentlemen in Liverpool, as a substitute for a public meeting. You will easily understand how unpleasantly the Bishop of a large diocese is situated when meetings are being held in other dioceses, for if he declines to hold a meeting, he is suspected, particularly by strangers, of being lukewarm in a cause which he has at heart just as much as those who are clamorous in the expression of their feelings. The clergy of this diocese are signing addresses in their respective Conferences. Begging this may be treated as a private Communication & wishing you every blessing, I remain, my dear Mr. Langdale, very truly Yrs. +Alexander Goss.

---

472   Charles Langdale, 1787–1868, son of Lord Stourton, but took his mother's name; one of the first Catholic MPs after 1829 and remained very active in Catholic causes – Norman (*The English Catholic Church in the Nineteenth Century*, 167) calls him 'the most important Catholic educationalist of the century' (quoted by Rosemary Mitchell in *ODNB*); he chaired the Poor School Committee 1847–68.

258. *Rt. Rev. Dr. Briggs*   *19 December 1859*   5/3/302
Delegate to Rome

My dear Lord,
Dr. Cornthwaite & Mr. Jn. Gillow, I hear, are already in Rome, & a letter from Dr. Grant says that the temporal questions now pending before Prop. have to be decided to day: but whether he means his case only or Dr. Fisher's also, I cannot tell. In order to avoid delay, Dr. Hogarth promised to send to Dr. Fisher the Ushaw case, as soon as prepared. Dr. Fisher has made three applications & is informed that it is not ready as yet. Surely he cannot have sent it by Dr. Cornthwaite & Mr. Gillow to Rome, & they cannot be undertaking to decide it without hearing his reply. My Diocese is now reaping the fruit of the delay in this case: for an old lady – Mrs. Bennett[473] – having left some thousands of pounds for Catholic charities has made it obligatory that one of her trustees for ever should be a member of the Established Church, & another is threatening to do the same. Unless justice is done, I fear it will be put into Chancery.
    I have not yet received leave to go to Rome: but if it comes this week I purpose setting off the day after Xmas; & depend upon it, if I have been over reached I shall not be mealy-mouthed.
    Can you tell me what sum of money, i.e. what amount of funds are under Ushaw management, that belong to your Diocese, including the Taylor estate,[474] which they partially or conditionally wrested from us? I want to show that each of our Dioceses has at stake as large a sum as the Bp. of Hexham. I will write again as soon as I get leave to go.
    Believe me, my dear Lord, ever most sincerely Yrs in Xt. A. Goss.

473 See Goss to her, letter 106.
474 On the Taylor estate see Milburn, *History of Ushaw College*, 236–7.

259. V*ery Rev. Canon Morris   19 December 1859   5/3/303*
                  "Sectional Notes of Synod"
My dear Canon,
Foreseeing that some instruments of the Synod of Oscott might lead
to future discussion elewhere, I applied to Mr. McSweeney for a copy
of his résumé of the arguments used in Congregation. He had already
surrendered them to one of the Promoters who told me that I should
have a copy furnished me after the hurry consequent on Synod was
over. The tide of Eminent & Rt. Reverend & Reverend doctors that
has lately set in for Rome, has again drawn my attention to the Synod
and on writing to Dr. Clifford, the Promoter, he says, "All the Synodal
papers were given in charge to Can. Morris the Sec. at the close of the
Synod. I have had nothing further to do with them. I remember that
it was decided that you or any of the Bps. might have a copy of F.
McSweeney's or the other Secretaries' notes on applying for them. I
do not know whether Can. Morris still has charge of them or whether
they have been deposited by him at York Place: but you will no doubt
be able to learn from him." Is it possible as things stand to obtain this
promised copy?
     It augurs well for the devotion of the Eng. Church to the H. See that
so many bishops, canons, & clergy should be hastening at the present
moment to the *limina sancta Apostolorum*.[475]
     Believe me, dear Canon, very sincerely Yrs in Xt. +Alexander Goss.

475 *limina sancta Apostolorum*: 'the holy threshold of the Apostles', commonly used
with reference to the bishops' regular *ad limina* visits to Rome to report on the state of
their dioceses.

260.   *Rt. Rev. Dr. Briggs, Bishop of Beverley   23 December 1859*
                                                          3/3/304[476]
My dear Lord,
I am off on Monday in company with Dr. Fisher.
     Mr. John Gillow, I am told, is charged with a commission, to petition
to have Ushaw made into a Pontifical College. Now I think it would be
well if the Chapters of our respective Dioceses were to send up petitions against this: for 1o. such was not the design of Dr. Gibson;[477] 2o.
Colleges were made Pontifical to shield them from a hierarchy to which
they did not belong, tho' in whose territory they were placed; but this
is not the case with Ushaw. 3o. They were made Pontifical when there
was somebody residing as a nuncio who could exercise the power as he

represented the person of his holiness. 4o. Dr. N. originally urged that it should be made a Pontif. Col. in order to shield it from the irresponsible control of the Vic. Ap.; but the case is now reversed: for a Bp. governs by a Constitution whereas the Pontifical representative would be irresponsible, as no body but the Pope, his superior, could call him to order – I will have forwarded to you a short statement of our case in a few days – My address will be at the Minerva Hotel – The Card. is much better & in good spirits. He, Roskell, Searle & Thompson are at the College: Dr. E. is at the Minerva – Wishing you the blessings of this holy Season & praying God to preserve you, I remain sincerely Yrs in Xt. Alexander Goss.

---

476   There are similar letters of the same date to other bishops. Number 5/3/305, to Brown of Shrewsbury, repeats the above, and asks him to appoint Fisher his official procurator in Rome, as he says Briggs has done. Number 5/3/306, to Turner, adds Goss's fear of Gallicanism if the clergy were to be educated outside their bishops' control, just as Belgian bishops argued against Pontifical Colleges there.

477   Dr Gibson: Bishop Matthew Gibson, VA of the Northern District 1790–1821, founder of Ushaw.

261.   *[Copy headed in English] Correspondence between Rt. Rev: Dr. Goss and Propaganda.*

H.E. Cardinal Barnabò Pref:, Rome 18 February 1860 UCH/123(a)[478]

Most Eminent and Reverend President

In the last Provincial Synod of Westminster, whose Acta and Decrees the Most Eminent and Reverend Archbishop himself took to Rome, he worked very hard so that the decrees on the Colleges would not be approved. It is, therefore, to be feared that, in any account that might be given along with the Acta, he would oppose those matters which to the majority of the Bishops seemed to have been approved: it is indeed scarcely credible that he should be part of the meeting of the Sacred Congregation when it is dealing with the Synod, because in that case he would be attending as both judge and party.

Therefore I beg you, Most Eminent President, that in my own name and that of the Bishops whose letters of proxy I have shown you,[479] I be informed of anything affecting the decrees, whether in writing or otherwise, so that I may put forward in writing to the Sacred Congegation whatever will lead to a greater clarification of the issue.

Your Most Reverend Eminence's Humble and Devoted servant Alexander, Bishop of Liverpool.[480]

---

478   Copy of Latin letter from Goss to Propaganda; my translation.

479   In the margin in English: 'Bps of Beverley, Newport, Salford, Southwark, Salop'.

480 Answer from Propaganda: UCH/123 (b), 23 April 1860: they reject Goss's appeal because at the meeting to discuss the matter Cardinal Wiseman had the 'natural delicacy' to absent himself and took no part in the proceedings.

262. *Mgr Talbot* *Minerva [Rome] 3 April 1860* *VEC: Tal 340*
My dear Mgr Talbot,
I beg to thank you on behalf of myself & Can. Fisher for your kind favour & to say that we shall both deem it a high privilege to receive communion from the hands of the Holy Father.

I hope on that occasion, after the H. Father has made His thanksgiving, to have an opportunity of making an offering of £1,000 from one of my Diocese, who desires that I should myself present it.[481] Believe me Very truly yrs in Xt. Alexr. Goss.

481 The £1,000 was included in the £8,000 that Goss presented in person and for which felt he was inadequately thanked; see n. 605.

263. *Very Rev. Dr. Maguire*[482] *26 June 1860* *5/3/307*
"Old Hall Green" <u>Private</u>
My dear Dr. Maguire,
It was a great mortification to me that I could not wait on you as I passed thro' London; but I was unfit to appear in public from having my face scorched & blistered with travel, & not finding Dr. G. at home, I was anxious to communicate with my northern brethren. Lest Dr. G. should not see you at once, I write to ask you to furnish some information for the furtherance of the late Synod. I want an account of the foundation or erection of Old Hall Green.[483] As far as possible the account should be drawn up from original documents, which, referred to in the text, should be copied or put in extenso in the Appendix. The account should consist of a simple statement of facts, & <u>not</u> of such facts only as go to prove a particular point of view. It should begin with the purchase of the property, from what means or funds the purchase was made, by whom made, in whose names or by whom the property has been successfully held, what appeals have been made by Pastorals for the aid & contributions of the faithful & what donations have been made, whence the funds for education come, what conditions etc. are attached to such funds, who now holds them, thro' what hands, & by what process or deeds or legal instruments they have been transferred etc. All this will require research, but you must call in aid. Unless we make a determined & sustained effort, based on <u>facts</u> that nothing can shatter, we shall be thrown back into chaos or relapse into ciphers at the right hand of a unit. Can you find a copy of a general Pastoral, issued by the 4 Vics. Ap. for the erection of a common Seminary? Have you any [*some illegible words*;

presumably, information relating to] old Douay funds at Old Hall? Can you learn whether, when application was made to government for the restoration of the Douay funds & compensation for property – called Mr. Daniel's claims[484] – it was on the understanding that such property was common to the different vicariates & that if the application was successful the money would have been divided.

Believe me ever sincerely Yrs A. Goss.

---

482   John Maguire, 1801–65; canon and VG; Schiefen, *Nicholas Wiseman*, 255–6 and elsewhere; he was thought to be a Gallican.

483   Old Hall Green: St Edmund's, Ware, the southern continuation of Douai, founded in 1793.

484   On Bishop Poynter's attempts to obtain compensation from the government, see P. Phillips (ed.), *The Diaries of Bishop William Poynter, VA (1815–1824)* (CRS 79, London, 2006), *passim*.

264.   *Rev. Jn. [Honorius] Magini,*[485] *Woodchester*   *26 June 1860*
5/3/309

"St. Patrick's"

Dear Rev. Sir,

Since my return from Rome, the Vicar General has made me acquainted with the circumstances that have led to your absence from the Mission of St. Patrick's, in order to make a Retreat of fifteen days. It is hardly necessary to express to you the pain which this manifestation has caused, as since I was appointed as Bishop, I have known nothing more distressing.

The Vicar General tells me that you have written to him, expressing a hope that God may again call you to a religious life. I sincerely hope that he will vouchsafe you that grace, for I must candidly own that an ex-religious is exposed to great peril when living free from the restraints which religion had imposed. In any case, I trust that you will see the expediency of not returning to the Diocese of Liverpool, as your further continuance in it could not be but very trying to you. – I shall be glad to transfer to any other Bp. the obedience which you have hitherto rendered to me.

With every sincere wish for God's blessing on the future, I remain truly yrs in Xt. A. Goss.

---

485   See n. 293 above.

265. *Rev. J. Swarbrick*   *12 July 1860*   *5/3/332*
"Elston Fund"[486]

My dear Mr. Swarbrick,

Forgetting that you were bound south, I was writing to you the day I got your letter to ask you to come down to St. Edward's for a week, partly for work, partly for amusement.

The Elston Fund was left for the education of a Priest <u>at Douay</u> for England, a preference to be shown to the issue of his sister Mary Newsham. By the destruction of Douai, the first clause falls to the ground: by the division of funds by the Vic. Ap. in 1840 & by the Bps in 1850, the application of the fund was narrowed from Eng. to the Diocese of Lpool; yet both Dr. Newsham & the authorities of the Beverley Diocese contend that it belongs to Yorkshire. <u>If</u> such were the case, either the Lancashire issue of M. Newsham would lose their right or Beverley would lose its right in case a Newsham were educated on it, because the Bp. of the Diocese of which Newsham was a native would not surrender his right to those born in this Diocese. I don't, however, fear the issue being raised. As the representative of a branch of the Newsham family, probably the eldest branch, you, e.g. 1o. Thomas ought to have a <u>full</u> copy of Elston's instructions <u>properly authenticated</u>: otherwise what have you to show? Dr. N. is only one of 3 trustees, & there is no <u>authentic</u> <u>proof</u> that Mr. Williamson's letter expresses even <u>his</u> views. Nothing can claim respect but the founder's intentions, where they exist. 2o. Having a beneficial interest, you have a <u>right</u> to know how the principle of the Fund is invested, & whether the Trustees hold by any legally expressed trust deed, or whether, if they are holders by law, they have given under their hand any declaration that they hold the property on Trust for the intentions specified by Mr. Elston. Card W., if you remember, in his examination before the Mortmain Committee,[487] admitted this right in any body who had a beneficial interest in a property left for church purposes.

Believe me sincerely Yrs in Xt. A. Goss.

---

[486] G. Anstruther, *The Seminary Priests*, 4 vols (Ware and Ushaw, Great Wakering, 1968–77), III, gives a John Philips, alias Elston, who died 1738 and had nephews named Newsham (Swarbrick's mother was a Newsham); Kirk gives John Elston, d. 1737; Anstruther also gives a John Elston, d. 1774 under alias Francis Lacy. AAL, FDC/S4/2/B/1-. No appropriate Williamson is listed.

[487] The Mortmain Committee decided cases where wills appeared to be contrary to the laws of mortmain, especially where property or money was left for religious purposes; Wiseman was involved in a number of these cases and it is not clear which one is being referred to here.

266.   *Very Rev. Prov. Platt Vic. Gen.*[488] *12 July 1860*   *5/3/333*
"Fate of the Synod"

My dear Provost,

Many thanks for the note of Mr. Lodge's death:[489] I wanted it to fix the date of a letter which was somewhat important.

I can hardly credit what you tell me as coming from Ushaw regarding the fate of the Synod; for when I left Rome only three weeks ago, no such result had been announced. The official answer of the Holy See was '*nullum pro nunc ferendum esse judicium*', with the expression of a wish '*ut Archiepus. et Epi. excitentur ad opportunos notitios exhibendos quibus prospecta fiant origo, progressus, fundatio, nec non presentes Collegiorum conditiones*'.[490]

If any body interested in the matter sees in this sentence the triumph of the Cardinal & the downfall of the Synod, I envy his easy content-ment, in the same manner as I do the complacency of French historians who see in the battle of Waterloo the triumph of Napoleon. Unfortu-nately the English did not know that they were beaten & I am stupid enough to be in the same position.

When I consider the acts, the expedients, the slanders that some had recourse to, I am even more amazed that nothing more was done than to arrest defeat by delaying the decision. Believe me ever sincerely Yrs in Xt. AG.

Fortes estato[491]

---

488   Ralph Platt, Provost and VG of Hexham and Newcastle Diocese, 1812–74; at St Cuthbert's, Durham. See Milburn, *History of Ushaw College*, esp. 169–73, for his troubles while on the staff at Ushaw and attempts to reform the curriculum.

489   Probably John Lodge, 1722–95, professor of theology at Douai and prefect of studies; see Anstruther, *Seminary Priests*, IV.

490   Trans: 'No judgement is to be made for the present'; and: 'that the Archbishop and Bishops be urged to put forward in due course relevant notes whereby the origin, develop-ment, founding and also the present condition of the Colleges be made clear'.

491   Presumably, 'Be strong' or 'Take courage' (in poor Portuguese?).

267.   *M. Errington Esq.,*[492] *Bushy Park, Enniskerry, Ireland*
12 July 1860   *5/3/334*

My dear Mr. Errington,

I beg to thank you for your kind invitation to Ireland. I fear, however, that I must forego the pleasure, for I find my hands full of work. I fear much for your brother's healthy [*sic*] during this hot weather, for he will never yield to its influence till it has done its work. I am myself still suffering from its effects, in a complete dearrangement of the digestive organs & in other ways, the result of the heat & relaxing atmosphere.

You will probably have heard from your brother by this mail, & will I trust have received a copy of the last official letter. Since then he has had another audience of the H.F., who has repeated all his former promises of preferment if he will only resign. This offer, made after the Card's Commissioners have examined the case, tho' in a very one sided way, is a proof positive that they find no ground for his dismissal; yet from the fact of their having laid before the Pope all the previous instances in which Pontiffs have acted <u>beyond</u> the law in the matter of dismissal, I fear that, as he stated at the beginning, he had made up his mind & the officials have made an easy bed of supposed precedents on which his conscience may safely repose.

I am told that all the working clergy are strongly in favour of your brother. The whole affair is a basic conspiracy to upset a man too honest for the atmosphere in which he was destined to move. My kind regards to Mr. J. O'Farrel [*sic*]. Dr. Fisher is suffering from gout in Wales. Ever sincerely Yrs in Xt. A. Goss.

---

492 Michael Errington, the archbishop's brother. Enniskerry is a village in Co. Wicklow, fifteen miles south of Dublin; the family also had a town house in Rutland Square, Dublin. Michael's wife was Rosanna O'Ferrall; presumably the Mr O'Farrel mentioned at the end of the letter was her brother John, a QC, sometime Commissioner of the Dublin Metropolitan Police. I am grateful to Dr Serenhedd James for this information.

268. *Very Rev. Can. Walker. Scarbro.* [*sic*]   *14 July 1860*   *5/3/335*
"Rome & rumours"

My dear Can. Walker,

I know not how it is, but every statement affecting certain parties, is tinted with couleur de rose. The North as well as London seems to be provided with this charming dye. It is stated on authority, not surmised, that Dr. E. has been condemned, that the Synod has been upset, that Rome has decided that Ushaw has to be under the Ordinary & that the other Bps have no rights beyond that of receiving a general statement of the receipt & expenditure of their own funds, & that the great money case has been as good as settled for Ushaw.[493] De facto Dr. N. refuses to give us any but a general account: he will not state to what boy's education each fund is applied, he will not say how or where or in whose names the funds are invested, nor will he furnish any copy of instructions that accompany them: he declines any information even to those who have the right of nomination to the funds. Yet they say the longest lane has a turn!

Dr. E is still in Rome. Address, Archbp. E. Rev. J. Mulhooly, San Clemente, Roma. If no sentence can be come to <u>after</u> the delivery in court of the Card's charges against him, is it not proof that there is no case? & is not the offer of honour elsewhere an admission of competency? Bad advisers – be they internal or external – will make his E's

[*sic*] sun set in clouds whenever the evening comes. Ever Yours truly
AG

How Athelstan[494] will fidget when he gets your letter! It will fill up the
cup of his displeasure against foreign parts & particularly Italy.

---

493   In a letter to Briggs of the same date Goss was more outspoken: 'How wildly somebody is lying about the issue of events in Rome' regarding these matters, 'for the whole
country is filled with false rumours' (5/3/336).

494   Athelstan: 895–939, king of the West Saxons and Mercians and later of England;
defeated the Danes and rebels at Brunanburh in 937; he was quite involved in European
politics. Presumably it is Bp Hogarth who is being referred to here, but the reasons for
the name are unclear.

269.   *V. Rev. P. Allanson Prov. Ebor. O.S.B.*[495]   *12 July 1860*   *5/3/337*
"Little Crosby. Money Case"

My dear Father Provincial,

Many thanks for your kind letter of congratulation on my return home:
I assure you I am rejoiced to be once more in the field of my labours.

Not knowing what was the character of the Mission at Little Crosby,
I naturally declined to sanction its being permanently occupied till I
had received official notice of your intention not to send a successor to
our late worthy friend F. Shann.[496] I have told Major Blundell that both
the Jesuits & the Benedictines have exemption for missionary life in
Eng: but I have expressed my dislike for other religious, who have no
canonical existence in the Diocese, to take charge of an isolated cure
when not demanded by the necessity of the times. I fear he may not feel
the weight of the objection.

The sympathy of the H.F. for Card. W's state of health has led to
delay of all Eng. business in which his E. was thought to be intrusted.
The case with Ushaw is a claim on behalf of the Dioceses of Liverpool,
Salford, & Shrewsbury against Mr. Sherbourne's eatate for the recovery
of a sum of money lent to him by Dr. Youens. By the manoeuvers of
Mgr. Newsham with the connivance of Card. W. the answer has been
delayed for the last 5 yrs. Leave was given for an arbitration in Eng.
in 1854–5: but Mgr. N. again threw the case into Prop; last year it was
ready for settlement when Mgr. N. or Hexham prayed for delay: this
year he has had two envoys at Rome, & again fearing a decision in our
favour a petition was made for further delay; a period of 3 months has
been granted them. The Votum of the Consultor of Prop.[497] communicated to both parties is entirely in our favour. Believe me ever sincerely
Yrs. A. Goss.

---

495   Peter (Athanasius) Allanson OSB, 1804–76; Northern Provincial from 1858 and
Abbot of Glastonbury, he lived as missioner at Swinburne, Northumberland, for forty-

seven years. He was the official historiographer of the English Benedictine Congregation and left a wealth of MSS records (at Ampleforth and Downside). His biographer describes him as a 'careful and critical' historian (Anselm Cramer, *ODNB*).

[496]   Christopher (Augustine) Shann OSB, 1801–60.

[497]   Consultor of Propaganda: one of the specialists chosen to advise the Congregation in complex cases; they were appointed for life by the pope. See *DDC*, vol. IV.

---

270.   *Rev. Jn. Worthy*   *12 July 1860*   *5/3/338*
                              "Rev. R. Hubbersty"

Dear Rev. Sir,

I am sorry to learn from your letter of July 11 that my quondam school fellow, the Rev. R. Hubbersty,[498] is again in trouble. It is very charitable of you under the circumstances of his & your position, to afford him the shelter of a home. He has a good heart but a weak head, & will, I fear, be easily led astray again in a neighbourhood where he is not without acquaintances: yet the fear of a relapse is no cause why he should not receive credit for his present disposition, tho', at the same time, the chances of scandal are great.

In order to give him a *locus standi*, I think a letter should be procured from Dr. Amherst, stating that he is not under censure – I mean censure in the ecclesiastical sense. Then I think he ought to make a Retreat at some religious house for 8 days. On receiving a certificate of the absence of Censure & a testimonial of the spiritual retreat, I will grant him leave to say mass – not the public mass – under the restrictions mentioned in your letter. If you will embody them separately on a sheet of paper, I will sign them on receiving the two certificates specified above. I have known Mr. Hubbersty in happier days & sincerely hope that God will now give him the grace of perseverance.

I inclose a clip from a Newspaper: the subject of the paragraph tried hard to obtain a footing in the Diocese of Liverpool.

With my kind remembrance to Mr. Hubbersty, I remain sincerely Yrs in Xt. A. Goss.

---

[498]   Robert Hubbersty, b. 1816, o. 1839 for the Lancashire District, later of Salford Diocese; he also worked in Northampton 1859–60, where Amherst was Bishop; see n. 759; the absence of a date of death usually means the priest left the priesthood unofficially.

---

271.   *Rev. F. Seraphim O.S.F.,*[499] *Pantasaph, Holywell*
                              12 July 1860   *5/3/339*
                              "Little Crosby Chaplaincy"

Dear Rev. Sir,

I am in receipt of your favour of the 9th & beg to thank you for the kind offers of spiritual help on behalf of the Apostolic order of which you are so worthy a member, yet I cannot but regret that you should have been put to the inconvenience of writing to me in consequence of my letter to Major Blundell, the contents of which he was not authorised to communicate to you. I would myself have written to you had I thought that the circumstances of the case required it.

The object of my letter to Major Blundell was to convey to him my reluctance to be instrumental, directly or indirectly, in sanctioning the anomaly of a religious living out of a community without necessity, when the spirit of the order of which he was a member required that he should live in community; tho' the Fathers were prepared to forego the graces of community life when the good of souls required their labours in isolated positions as in missionary countries. The Franciscans formerly held missions in this Diocese, but they abandoned them when it lost its missionary character: only recently the Jesuits have abandoned 3 missions here from a desire to withdraw from isolated positions in order to concentrate themselves as is required by the spirit of their religious profession. Tho' still called a missionary country, this Diocese is now as completely divided into separate missions with their prospective boundaries as is any Catholic country on the continent. Under these circcumstances I feel that I should be acting wrongly if I yielded to Major Blundell's request tho' made from the best of motives. Believe me sincerely Yrs in Xt. A. Goss.

---

[499]   A new church in Pantasaph, North Wales, was entrusted to the Capuchins in 1852, by its patrons, the Feilding family. Fr Seraphin OFM Cap., from Bruges, was superior there from 1853 to 1866 and was responsible for the first phase of the friary buildings. See M. Swarbrick, *The Story of Pantasaph and the Coming of the Capuchin Friars* (Pantasaph, 1993).

272.   V*ery Rev. Can. Fisher, Gt. Crosby   14 July 1860*   5/3/340
"Can. Newsham's affairs"

My dear Canon,
I have before me two letters of Can. N. one to myself, the other to the Vicar; to both of which, as well as to one addressed to me in July 1859, he requires an answer. Write to him to say, that the Bp. has desired you to reply to his letters, that you cannot do so, as you have hitherto been unable to understand the nature of his claims in the face of all that has been written & decided, that you had understood that he had alleged that his case was in Rome, having been put there by Prov. Cookson, & that nothing can be made out of such varied statements, addressed sometimes to me, sometimes to another, tho' the Bp. had named you as his official to wind up all affairs connected with his bankruptcy, & beg of him in conclusion, if he thinks that he has a suit to press, to make a clear statement on foolscap paper, & to put in the Appendix in extenso

letters, balance sheets, agreements & all other documents, as the Bp.
will not allow documents connected with other cases to be detached
from them. Say that no one – Bp. or other person – can be expected to
go into any case unless proofs are alleged for what is asserted, & that he
cannot expect you to hunt out what he asserts to be proofs of his assertions. Tell him in the second place, that if he has two cases or claims,
they must be kept totally distinct, as it is impossible to disembarrass the
pleadings of extraneous matters. Say that he must know that the issues
of any of these cases are to the Bp. personally immaterial. Ever truly
Yrs, Alexr. Goss.
Get a copying machine if you have not got one, as copies of letters
should be preserved, & it is too laborious to be done by hand.[500]

---

[500] See the Note on Sources.

273. *Rt. Rev. Dr. Brown, Bp. of Shrewsbury*   *25 July 1860*   *5/3/349*
              "College Question"   Confidential
My dear Lord,
No doubt the College authorities are acting in concert or by instruction.
They are acting as if the Synod had been decided in their favour, instead
of observing the status quo, & they will then plead that the existing state
of things should be left undisturbed, as it works well & has created no
difficulties. It is our duty, therefore, to prevent the status quo from being
disturbed & to meet their assumption by acts equally vigorous. I trust
that you will be at the opening of Mr. Vandepitte's Church,[501] in order
that we may take counsel, for if they act as if the Colleges had been
signed over to the Ordinaries & refuse to give us any account of our
funds, we must also decline to let them have the free disposal of our
means whether men or money. I have no doubt they have been advised
to this plan, as the fait accompli is the doctrine of the age. I am going
to spend a fortnight with Dr. Fisher. I shall be glad if you will send me,
at your convenience, a copy of the statement about Oscott in English,
as it helps much to have the various documents within reach. The Prior
Park history is not meant for Prop: but for the lawyer, in order that
thoroughly understanding the case, he may be able to draw up a suitable
paper on the Synod.
    I have just received a remarkable letter giving an account of an inter-
view with one of the Card's chief men. 'The priest being asked about
the Cardinal's health answered that it was excellent. He then went on
to say that the Card. had completely triumphed in everything. Being
asked if this triumph over them would not be distasteful to the Episcopacy & clergy of Eng. he answered that there was nothing to be feared,
as, now that the Coadjutor had <u>resigned</u>,[502] the Card. knew <u>for certain</u>

that the Bps would adhere to him. *Et sane cum Epi. multos offensiones contra illum Romae patraverint, effectus docuit omnia non sine eorum dedecore rejecta fuisse.*'[503] He then said that Prop. had <u>reprobated</u> the Synod, but had answered dilata, *ut Emus. Archiepus. anglos antistites alloquetur, periculum inutilis concertationis demonstret, et negotium cum illis sine judicii strepitu componat.*[504] In fact that the Bps had already begun to see their error! I believe that this is the Card's scheme & that Dr. M[anning] has assured Prop. of its success. I have no doubt that Dr. M. has already got a scheme cut & dried, for no doubt he is expecting Old Hall to fall into the hands of the Oblates.[505] Communicate this information to Minerva, saying that it has just come from Rome: it would be well if you could see him & Amherst, for the Card's agents are very busy, both in Rome & Eng. Truly Yrs A. Goss.

---

501   Eldon Street, Liverpool.

502   i.e. Errington, who eventually resigned unwillingly from his coadjutorship on the Pope's orders in July 1860.

503   Trans: 'And certainly since the Bishops had committed many offences against him in Rome, the result showed that everything had, to their shame, been rejected'.

504   Trans: 'so that his Eminence the Archbishop should address the English bishops, should demonstrate the danger of useless quarrelling, and should settle business with them without noisy disagreements'.

505   On the Oblates and their links with St Edmund's, Ware, see Schiefen, *Nicholas Wiseman*, 254–62.

274.   *Rt. Rev. The Bp. of Salford*   25 July 1860   5/3/351
"Rev. Jn. Gillow's letters"
My dear Lord,   Confidential
I am astonished at the impertinence & perversity of Mr. Gillow's letters. His letter (July 9) reads like a page of a theological lecture given to a class of students in the limina of their course. He bases a justification of himself on the ways of God which are inscrutable.

If he speaks merely in his own name & not on behalf of others, who is he to enter into correspondence with you? Besides, the use of We in a private letter cannot be supposed to represent merely the writer, & I am told that the writer of that letter in his remarks to the students at Ushaw reprobated the use of We by any one individual.

The only answer given by Prop. to the Synod was the one forwarded by the Cardinal: no opinion was expressed by them as to the nature of the government recommended; tho' every effort was made to decry it on account of its supposed Parliamentary character. Throughout the whole of these proceedings Rome has been represented as saying & doing what it never said or did, e.g. the money case, the particulars of which I gave you [are] widely at variance with that given by your correspondent. I am going into Wales tomorrow: my address will be Morannedd, Llandulas, Rhyl. Believe me ever truly Yrs A. Goss.

275. *Rt. Rev. Hogarth, Bishop of Hexham*   *2 August 1860*   *5/3/352*

"The Ushaw Mortgage"

My dear Lord,

I am in receipt of your esteemed favour of July 30, & beg to say in reply that, if my letter conveyed to you the impression that I supposed you were to give information to the Holy See through me, it failed to express my meaning. I have no doubt that I should satisfy my conscience by giving such information to Propaganda that I may be seized of: but I conceived, perhaps erroneously, that filial duty to the Holy Father required me to make myself acquainted with those matters which I did not know, & about which he sought information. As you have more than once openly – shall I say publicly – announced that all the cointerested Bps had an equal interest in the College, I did not conceive it possible for you to refuse the information sought.

I have no wish to discuss the question: but perhaps you will be good enough to state whether I am right in inferring from your letter that you decline to give any information about the actual state of the College & that you do not admit my right, as a cointerested Bishop, to request the information from you.[506]

I have the honour to remain, my dear Lord, Very truly Yrs in Xt. +Alexander Goss.

---

[506] Hogarth's letters to Goss on this issue are in UC/P42, nn. 370, 375, 383; in the last, of 11 August, he declines any further correspondence on the subject.

276. *E.W. Pugin Esq. 5 Gordon Sq.*   *2 August 1860*   *5/3/353*

"Cemetery Church"   <u>Confidential</u>

My dear Pugin,

The permission given to Mr. Kelly to go as far as £1500, was given before I saw you at Mason St.

The Cemetery is under a Committee: that Committee wish the Church to be impressive. Mr. Kelly is the manager of the Cemetery, appointed by the Committee. Now it is clearly for your interest in every way to give satisfaction to the Committee, which you can do by making the plans inexpensive. Let not the size of the Church be interfered with, but let it be simple. You need not allege any instruction either from me or others; but prepare your plans, & if the estimates are below even £1000 the Church will be built accordingly, & you cannot fail to give general satisfaction. If your plans mount up, the Church will still be built, if not over £1500: but the result will be a certain soreness which militates against your interest in several ways. Great efforts have been made to place the Magdalen in Mr. Hansom's hands[507] – I should not have written this letter except in reply to Yrs of July 31.

Truly Yrs. A. Goss

[507]   The Catholic cemetery at Ford. Charles Hansom, 1803–82, was actively seeking commissions in Liverpool. See n. 398; Champ, *William Bernard Ullathorne*, 115–16, and next letter.

277.   *Charles Hansom Esq., Rock House, Belle Vue, Clifton*
              [n.d. but 2 August 1860]   5/3/355
              "Convent of the Good Shepherd"

Dear Sir,
I beg to acknowledge the receipt of your favour of July 31 on the subject of a Convent for the Sisters of the Good Shepherd at Crosby.[508]

I assure you that it was quite unnecessary for you to procure any letter of recommendation from Father Rinolfi,[509] as your name cannot but be well known to all lovers of ecclesiastical architecture. The contemplated Convent had, however, been entrusted to Mr. Pugin a week before the receipt of your letter. I beg to remain very sincerely Yrs. Alexander Goss.

[508]   Crosby: their convent was actually built at Ford; see Burke, *Catholic Liverpool*, 152.
[509]   Fr Angelo Rinolfi IC (Rosminian), 1813–77. Hansom had been responsible, for example, for St Anne's, Liverpool, and SS Thomas and Elizabeth's, Thurnham.

278.   *Rt. Rev. Dr. Brown Bp of Shrewsbury*   2 August 1860   5/3/356
              "College Question"

My dear Lord,
I have heard from Dr. E. date 20 July: he was then at Osimo,[510] on his way home. He had heard nothing official from Prop. after the declaration that it was not the intention of the H.S. to come to any judgement. He had, however, an audience of the H.F. who had in vain exhorted him to resign: Card. B. subsequently made an attempt but with no better success. What may be done next, remains to be seen: he had on leaving Rome given them his address, & will remain at Osimo for 2 or 3 weeks, if they wish to write to him. It is impossible to explain or account for the erroneous statements which are put forth apparently by authority in his case & ours.

1o. He asks for a copy of [the] Oscott arrangement between the Bps cointerested in that College in 1840 & in 1850. Could not this be got from Dr. Wareing or Amherst, as also the agreement between London & Northampton?[511] 2o. He wants the history of Oscott with dates, also the dates of the opening of Prior Park: he again asks for the information about Prior Park about which I wrote before: I hope you are preparing it, for there is nobody else to do it. 3o. Is there any document to show that the 2nd Synod took the same view of the College question as the 3rd Synod? I hope you will get up the Prior Park case from the documents in the possession of Menevia. He wants also a copy of the amount of restitution which each Diocese had to receive from Prior Park had it been able to pay. Every post I have to send large packets that cost me some days of labour to get up: my hand & head are alike weary. Truly Yrs in Xt. A. Goss.

[510] Osimo is on the Adriatic coast of Italy, a few miles south of Ancona.

[511] Presumably settling the rights of the various dioceses vis-à-vis sending students to Oscott and St Edmund's.

279. *Sr. M. Stanislaus, St. Ursula's Priory, Iffley, Oxford*[512]

13 August 1860 5/3/360

My dear Sister in J.C.

I beg to acknowledge the receipt of your favour of the 10th written at the request of Rev. Mother, containing an account of your efforts to establish a school at Oxford & of your wish to transfer it to Liverpool, whose proximity to Ireland seems to promise you success. There are already conventual establishments in every town of the Liverpool Diocese, where there is the least chance of success. In Liverpool itself, we have the Sisters of Mercy, of Notre Dame, of the Holy Infant Jesus, & some time ago we had one also of the Holy Child Jesus, which after struggling for an existence for some years was finally abandoned & all the furniture, including crucifixes etc. sold by public auction. Under these circumstances I do not think there would be any chance of success, particularly as you would have to depend on the public for your establishment. If you had possessed the means to buy a large house in the neighbourhood, you might in time have succeeded; but with an enormous pauper population craving help to save its children from proselytism, I do not think there would be any reasonable hope of success.

Wishing you every blessing I remain sincerely Yrs in Xt. +Alexander Goss.

[512] The 1856–61 *Directories* give the address of the priory as 10 Holywell Street, Oxford; it is not listed in 1862. A notice in the 1856 edition says that the priory in Moorfields, London, would open a school in Oxford 'in the new year'; obviously it was not a success. Goss also turned down applications for the Little Sisters of the Poor (letter 394), but allowed in the Sisters of St Paul to teach at Lydiate (December 1862, 5/4/317), and Les Soeurs de Troyes (May 1866, 5/5/113) on condition they held no collections without his express permission.

280.   *Revd. B. Jarrett,*[513] *Ulverston   13 August 1860*   *5/3/365*
"Coniston"

My dear Mr. Jarrett,

During my absence in Rome I have frequently thought with solicitude of the poor people of Coniston. The fact of the new railway having been opened although it may lessen the amount of evil committed on the spot, yet affords the people greater facility and inducement to leave their home & get into disorder elsewhere. Such being the case I think the sooner you see Mr. Barrett about the land the better – in order that having a Church built amongst them the poor people may be called to spend their Sundays in a more profitable manner.

As it is now some years since the proposal was first made, it looks as if they were putting us off, so I hope you will ascertain Mr. Barrett's intentions on the matter & thus set all to right.

I beg to remain Very truly Yrs. wishing you every blessing, Alexr. Goss.

[513]   Bernard Jarrett SJ, 1805–90; on Coniston, see nn. 431, 467 above.

281.   *C. Hansom Esq.*[514]   *13 August 1860*   *5/3/368*
"Orphanages"

Dear Sir,

On the very day on which I wrote my letter to you I received a note from the committee of the Orphanages to say that they wished to give the building of the new Orphanage to an architect in the Town of Liverpool. I wrote back to the Secretary to desire them to take no further steps till my return and to beg that you might have the work.

Yesterday another architect with a letter from one of the Committee waited upon me with a drawing in order to solicit the work. You see therefore that it was not without reason that I used the qualifying phrase "as far as in me lay". Beyond giving a recommendation I have not either with committees or individuals used any further influence on the appointment of an architect. Where I am myself sole director I use my own liberty of choice, but even then not without the advice of competent persons. Such advice I took & followed on the case of the Magdalene and cannot therefore with honour to myself or justice to others retrace my steps. I will however do what I promised, that is, use my best endeavour with the Committee of the Orphanage.

I beg to remain truly Yrs in Xt. A. Goss.

[514]   See n. 398 above.

282. *Rt. Rev. Canon Morris, 45 Devonshire St. London W.*

14 August 1860   *5/3/370*

My dear Canon,

Last night we had a meeting about the Workhouse question & entered into a subscription & passed various resolutions, having for their object the finding of suitable situations for children leaving the Industrial Schools, in order to diminish the chances of their perversion now great from their being sent not infrequently to Protestant places. I took advantage of the opportunity to commend and recommend the series of Workhouse Papers now in course of circulation.

I should certainly like a commemoration on both anniversaries & shall be obliged by your inserting them as proposed.[515]

I greatly commend the place you suggest: but instead of noting the specialities at the beginning of the <u>day</u>, I would note them at the end of <u>it</u>: for if there be any inconvenience it ought to be incurred by the exceptionalists rather than the regulars. I hope you will restore the fasting cross to the margin as in olden time. To show how much we throw ourselves on the Directory, I may mention that having in Rome only the <u>first</u> copy of Direct: [*sic*] sent for correction, I did not notice my own anniversary day: in the published copies it was differently noted & so I hope I was prayed for, a blessing I have been deprived of for some years.

Excuse these suggestions & believe me truly Yrs A G.

---

[515] Morris edited the *Directory*. Presumably the anniversaries were of Goss's appointments as coadjutor and as bishop. The 1857 edition gives only the 1853 date; the 1862 edition and onwards gives both 1853 and 1856.

283. *Rev. E. Power*[516]   *17 August 1860*   *5/3/371*

"Bastewell Fund"

My dear Mr. Power,

I have ventured to make some changes in your proposed letter. It will not be well to state the <u>extent</u> of your information in your first letter, nor will it be well to refer directly to Mr. Bastewell's Will, which must be the ultimate appeal. Hence it will not be advisable to say that the Will is in <u>your</u> <u>position</u> [*presumably a mistake for* 'possession']: for, if so, they will ask for a <u>copy</u>, which it is not advisable to let them have, as they will not give to my Vicar General copies of the instructions of funds of which he is trustee, & it will naturally be supposed that the original Will will be in the Diocesan Archives.

In the next place you must be careful not to let drop any hint that you will be satisfied with knowing how the fund is invested, by whom the securities are held, & how it is appropriated. It is well to proceed step by step: but the ultimate claim must be for the entire administration of the fund. I am getting the Will copied: but this is the passage from Bord-ley's books. "The Executors for Mr. James Bastwell's [*sic*] spiritual Will are Messrs Bertram Bulmer & Simon Bordley both of Aughton & their successors, each of them for what is left to their respective orders."[517] No time should be lost in making application to Dr. Newsham. I am going to Mr. Weld Blundell on Saturday & shall remain over Monday. Believe me very truly Yrs in Xt. AG.

516   See letters 47 and 64. In September Goss sent Power a final draft of a letter to Gillow of Ushaw, claiming an immediate payment of almost £300 owing to the mission's funds (letter 5/3/393).

517   Simon Bordley, 1709–99, of the old Northern District; Kirk calls him a learned man 'with some oddities'; see Gooch, *Revival*, 72. Bertram (Maurus) Bulmer OSB, 1704–88, was at Ormskirk. On the Bast(e)well Fund, see AAL FDC/S4/2/B/1-; it appears that the majority of the fund was held by the Ushaw authorities, with about £300 being in the bishop's direct control.

284.   *Rt. Rev. Dr. Brown*[518]   *22 August 1860*   *5/3/373*
"Archbp. Errington"

My dear Lord,

I shall not be surprised to learn any day that Archbp. E. is in England on his way to his friends, for his official connection with Westminster terminated on 22 July.

Notwithstanding an official assurance that the H.S. did not intend to pronounce any sentence & notwithstanding a promise that the Cardi-nal's statements about him should be placed in his hands, in case the H.F. should change his mind & proceed to a judicial examination of the affair, a decree of removal has been made out on the ground of incom-patibility; but as a testimonial to his personal worth an offer is made of Trinidad & Haiti: of course he will decline them.

News from Rome reports "that the Card. says that he will easily conciliate the Bps. now that Archbp. E. is removed". What is this but the repetition of the old charge of a complot with an assurance that the plotters will be dismayed by the fate of the supposed ringleader.

I wish you would put together your recollections about Prior Park: for we must have all information required for the presentation of our claims.

After reading this & showing it to Dr. Vaughan,[519] please to forward it to Dr. Brown of Salop.

With best wishes I remain sincerely Yrs AG.

It is said that the Card. is detained in Paris by sickness.

518   Thomas Joseph Brown OSB, bishop of Newport and Menevia 1850–80.

519   William Vaughan, 1814–1902, bishop of Plymouth from 1855; nephew of Cardinal Weld and uncle of the future cardinal.

285. *Rt. Rev. the Bp. of Shrewsbury* [*no day*] *August 1860* *5/3/378*
"Stockport petition in re Youens"

My dear Lord,

Inclosed I send you a petition to be signed by the priest at Stockport to Card. Barnabò, in order to hasten the consideration of the money question. As it is not an ecclesiastical document, I thought the readiest way would be to put it into French. It will be well, if your Lordship will add a sentence below where Mr. Can. Frith[520] signs, commending the petition to the wisdom of Card. Barnabò: perhaps it would be more appropriately done in Latin.

Can. Carter tells me that he has sent one from Bolton, & that Dr. Turner has endorsed it; both places are auditors of the same fund. Will your Lordship kindly forward it with a letter of instruction to Can. Frith?

Letters received from London to-day again speak of the Cardinal's intention to convene us; but I trust the Bps will refuse to be convened. His supposed victory & their supposed defeat have been sufficiently noised about without its being added that they were summoned for a scolding, as my later letter from Rome led me to believe was in contemplation.

By the Ushaw Articles of 1846[521] – the status quo – the President "in the nomination or removal of the Vice President is bound to have the approval of the Vicars Apostolic." Does not the violation of the status quo by them, leave us equally at liberty to disregard it? The very next rule to the one violated is that the Pres: shall have power to retain any subject for teaching! I have just lost by drowning at Rhyl a promising subject, John Livesley.[522] I expect Archbp. E. here on Monday or Tuesday en route for Dublin. Ever Yrs AG.

---

520 Randolph Frith of Shrewsbury Diocese, 1808–93.
521 On the so-called Articles of 1846, see Milburn, *History of Ushaw College*, 193–6, and the 1849 visitation document in his Appendix A, 355, giving the text.
522 See the next letter.

286. *Rev. Mr. Phelan*[523] *24 August 1860* *5/3/379*
"Mrs Livesley"

My dear Mr. Phelan,

If I had known the address of Mrs. Livesley, I should have written to her to express my sympathy with her in the sad bereavement with which it has pleased God to afflict her. No doubt she has been looking forward, as my mother once did, to have one day her son a priest to offer up the adorable sacrifice for her when she was dead & gone; but God has disposed otherwise & she must bow to the affliction. We know not his designs upon us, but we know he deals with us in mercy, & that whatever happens is for his glory & our benefit. Exhort her then to make this sacrifice cheerfully, as She did who offered her only son to death because God, his father wished it, & encourage her to look in her grief at the Mater Dolorosa, in order that by sharing Mary's sorrows, she may also share Mary's joys.

My heart fails me to speak of my own loss & the loss of the Diocese in the death of this promising young man, when I think of that heavy weight of grief which must weigh down the heart of his afflicted mother. But we must bow down with resignation & say Blessed be the will of God: the Lord gave & the Lord has taken away. And let us add: "May he this day be with them in eternal rest." Wishing you every blessing & the poor afflicted mother the gift of resignation to God's holy will, I remain very truly Yrs in Xt. +A. Goss.

---

523   Patrick Joseph Phelan, 1825–1890; r. St Patrick's, Liverpool, 1860–64, c. at St Antony's to retirement in 1867. *Extracts*, 165–6 (from the 1891 *Directory*).

287.   *Major Blundell*   *20 September 1860*   *5/3/399*
                              "Crosby"

My dear Major Blundell,

I am sorry to hear that you have been without mass & particularly at a time when you are visited with family if not domestic trials. You know, however, that the clergy are at all times fully employed & particularly on Sundays, when many of them are compelled to duplicate in order to give the people the benefit of mass. It is quite impossible therefore for me to provide a casual supply; for I have lost three priests by death, two have retired, a third went to join a religious order, & I have opened a new mission at Westby. I shall be glad to learn that you have made or are [on] your way to making satisfactory arrangements. I have done my best both by letter & personal interview to explain my ideas, & I shall be glad to sanction any arrangement that will conduce to the benefit of religion. It is to me a satisfaction to find that all persons to whom I have explained myself, as well in the Diocese as out of it, concur in what I have laid down. Whatever promises or hopes individuals may hold out to you, I am sure that no religious order, except those already in the Diocese as missionaries, would occupy a chaplaincy when there is so wide a field of labour elsewhere. I have only just returned home from the North & start again at 8½ [*sic*] for the Isle of Man.

Begging my kind remembrance to Mrs. Blundell I remain truly Yrs. +Alexr. Goss.

288. *Rt. Rev. Dr. Clifford   17 October 1860*   *5/3/404*
"Rev. Jn. Magini"[524]

My dear Lord,

I write to assure your Lordship that the Rev. John Magini left my Diocese free from every Ecclesiastical censure for the purpose of entering the noviciate of the Order of St. Dominic.

As he has referred you to me on the subject of his leaving I beg further to add that for some scandal which had been laid before him in connexion with his mission at St. Patrick's, the Vicar General desired him to make a retreat. This he did at Woodchester, & there conceived the desire of entering the Dominican order. He did not return to the mission in Liverpool after he had made known this wish; but I am unable to say why he did not persevere in his resolution.

When a Passionist he had been stationed in my Diocese & after he left the order he was employed by me first at the Catholic Institute & subsequently at the Mission of St. Patrick's.

I beg to remain, my dear Lord, Very sincerely Yrs in Xt. Alexander Goss.

---

[524] See n. 293.

289. *Major Blundell, Crosby Hall   26 October 1860*   *5/3/412*

My dear Major,

I am leaving home on Monday for a two months absence north of Ribble, on the duty of Visitation. My Vicar General will possess in my absence all necessary faculties for the government of the Diocese: I write to prevent disappointment as no business letters will be forwarded to me from Liverpool.

As it is my intention to commence my Visitation of Liverpool & the neighbourhood as soon after Xmas as circumstances will allow, I shall feel obliged if you will allow me an office copy of the Trust Deed made by you with reference to Little Crosby, & also of any arrangement or agreement made by your late Father with the late Bishop of Liverpool on the occasion of the consecration of the Church; for I have been told that the Church was consecrated, tho' this may be incorrect, as the opening of a Church site being blessed for service is sometimes called consecration. I am the more solicitous in this matter, as the people at Little Crosby have been left so long without a resident Priest, & in the absence of any other arrangement I shall be compelled to make some provision for their spiritual wants. I am fully sensible of the responsibility incurred somewhere [?] by the existing state of things. I could not leave home without laying before you my solicitude in this matter. Wishing you every blessing I remain very truly Yrs in Xt. A. Goss.

290. *Rev. Jas. Gibson,*[525] *Kendal   26 October 1860*   *5/3/413*
My dear Mr. Gibson,
In my arrangements for the visitation of the North of my Diocese, I had set aside a few days for a visit to Kendal, in order that in the recollection of old times I might leave for a brief space the reality of the present, & forget the many burdens that day & night oppress the most light hearted of Bishops. But these happy dreams have been dispelled by my having to open a new church, & thus being compelled to devote what I thought spare days to the prosecution of the work originally allotted to the day on which I have to open the church.

I am anxious to know the upshot of Doddin Green,[526] as I have neither heard nor seen any thing about it since the letter received from you relative to the sale. I am sorry I did not visit it in the time of Mr. Bingham; for I suspect that many of my papers are still lying there as well as my books, & as the M[ess]rs. Roydons were formerly at Doddin Green I have no doubt that information might have been found to throw light on matters connected with at least the Northern part of Lancashire. Please to drop me a line: I shall be at Lancaster on Nov. 4, & then move southwards in a day or two, but do not return home till near Xmas. Believe me ever truly Yrs. A. Goss.
NB. The Whisker fashion is spreading.

---

[525]   James Gibson of Hexham and Newcastle Diocese, 1816–95.

[526]   Doddin or Dodding Green was near Kendal; the mission dated from 1724; the first priest there was Thomas Roydon, d. 1741; he was succeeded by his nephew Thomas Roydon, who d. 1764; Robert Bannister, Goss's great-uncle, was there 1802–12 and Henry Rutter, Goss's uncle, was there 1834–1838 (see Gooch, *Revival*).

291. *Rev. R. Smith, Lancaster   31 December 1860*   *5/3/417*
"Transcription"
My dear Mr. Smith,
I shall be glad if, by the end of the week, you can find time to make me a fair copy of the inclosed, & then return it to me with the copy, as I want to forward one to Rome & keep the other.

Mr. Brown says that I ought to have a Secretary, so say I: but I ought also to have a house of my own to live in & a sufficient maintenance to enable me to live at it, without having to send round a hat yearly, thereby exposing myself to the insolent remarks of men born on straw; but we must have patience. It is not every one that has a Lancaster & Lancaster purses to draw from. Therefore until better times, we must needs be content to have a helping hand to public works for the public good; for I have no greater stake individually than any body else in the great questions now pending an issue in Rome.

Taking advantage of this opportunity to wish yourself & Mr. Brown the joys of this happy & merry time, I remain sincerely Yours in Christ, +Alexander Goss.

292.   *Right Rev. Dr. Grant   31 December 1860*   *5/3/419*
                    "St.E. other Bps etc. etc." [*sic*]

My dear Friend,

Courage: battles are not won by dispondency. You cannot be shifted from one see to another without your consent, unless the pope chooses to use a power which no one will dare to gainsay, as in Trebizond's case; but yield not except to a command should your name be sent up by the Chapter; refuse to allow it to be discussed on the grounds that you are not eligible. You are married to one See, & until you are divorced from that, cannot receive proposals to marry another. Why a new election? I know the reason alleged, but what is the <u>real</u> reason? I opine that [*name heavily scored out*] knows that <u>his</u> name was sent up & was approved of, & H.E. knows that he knows this. Now, if H.E. wants him to be set aside, it could not be better done than be done by others. Perhaps I am suspicious, but I suspect that that gentleman has lost cast [*sic*]. 2o. If invited to York Place to dinner on the occasion of considering the Beverley appointment, we ought not to accept it, because we have been traduced & we must show that we feel & resent the injury. Personally we may not care a straw, but the independence of our office requires that we should let it be seen that we are not to be trampled on. Prop. could never have seen what it allowed itself be made to do, had Card. B. not been convinced by Rt. Rev. Dr. N. that we should be managed. 3o. We must refuse to discuss any other matter than the Beverley business, not excepting the Trusts Bill, otherwise where will it end? For my part I purpose to return home on the evening – 5 p.m. – of the day of meeting.

Is the Pantomime *ludi scenici*?[527] When does Stonor go to Rome? Why don't you get some body to contradict & ridicule what appears in the Papers about your going to Beverley? They at Ushaw are ruling matters on the basis laid down in the Programme of the last Synod by H.E. & I expect they will petition for that status quo to continue, tho' it is daily become more & more clearly at variance with what had existed up to 1850. We ought to take some great step or both we & our clergy will be held to be satisfied with things.

How often do you require your clergy to renew the B.S? Can't we constitute our Churches trusts and enrol them? The Card: does. Many happy returns of the New Year: keep heart, tho' we have been fighting for a year without result, it is a great deal not to have been defeated. Can nothing tempt you to come & spend a few days or weeks down here? You must always be at work. Ever Yrs, AG.

What of the old altar stones consecrated [*two or three words illeg-ible*] for the relics?

---

527   Goss was asking if pantomimes came under the prohibition of clergy going to the theatre; although *Decreta* does not mention them they would seem to have been included in what was a severe prohibition (p. 29): *Prohibemus districte, ne ecclesiastici sacris ordinibus initiati, scenicis spectaculis in publicis theatris intersint, imponentes transgres-soribus poenam suspensionis ipso facto incurrendam, hactenus ubique in Anglia vigentem, cum reservatione respectivo Ordinario.* The prohibition remained in force until the 1960s.

293.   *Rev. Jn. Dawber*528   *31 December 1860*   5/3/423
"Separation of Man & Wife"

My dear Mr. Dawber,

I am in receipt of your favour on the subject of the separation of Man & Wife, &, in reply to your inquiry about the causes which justify it, beg to make the following observations.

The Church allows husband & wife to live in separate habitations when there is a grave reason for it, but in the absence of such reason she forbids it, even tho' the parties mutually & voluntarily consent to it, unless they enter religion. Diversity of tastes & incompatibility of temper, accompanied with quarrels, do not justify it, unless there be frequent infliction of blows, or danger of life, & in the absence of such excesses confessors are told by theologians they ought not to absolve them living apart. The same duty of self preservation would justify them in case the faith or salvation of one were endangered by the heretical or sinful practices of the other; but in the absence of such danger, such sinful practices, unless opposed to the end & intent of matrimony, would not justify separation. I say opposed to the end of marriage, for tho' adultery or the commission of unnnatural crimes with others might not endanger the salvation of or be accompanied by personal danger, yet such crimes would justify the injured party in separation, as being contrary to the marriage contract by which they are made one flesh. Under all other circumstances a man must remember the teaching of St. Paul. "The husband is the head of the wife, as Christ is the head of the Church. Therefore as the Church is subject to Christ, so also let wives be to their husbands in all things."

I know nothing of the circumstances which have led to the separation of your brother & his wife. I have read the letter addressed to you by Mr. Fisher of Appleton, who states that your brother cruelly denied his wife food & shelter, but I cannot gather whether this expression means that he turned her out of house & home, or that he neglected his business & failed to provide her a competency: if the former, she ought to have a guarantee of better treatment before she consents to return: if the latter, she ought not to have said "I take thee to my wedded husband, to have & to hold, from this day forward, for better, for worse, for richer, for poorer, in sickness & in health, till death do us part, if holy Church will it permit; & thereto I plight thee my troth." It was on the strength of this declaration that the Priest said, *"Ego conjungo vos in matrimonium"*. And is it not written, "What therefore God has joined let no one put asunder". Ever Yrs in Xt. A. Goss.

---

528   John Dawber, n. 146.

---

294.   *Rev. M. Burke, Sheffield*[529]   *3 January 1861*   *5/3/430*
          "Renewal of faculties for the Sisters of Charity"
Dear Rev. Sir.
I have great pleasure in renewing for another year the faculties which expired with 1860, & I hope that on your visit to Crosby you will find the Sisters well & happy.

     I am sorry that you should have thought it necessary to enter into any explanation about Little Crosby; for your former communication had sufficiently explained the matter. The similarity of name had led my Vic. Gen. to believe that you were the gentleman who he had the interview with, tho' I felt it difficult to reconcile the details of the interview with the estimate I had justly formed of you. I must confess that at the time I felt somewhat annoyed at the attempt to dispose of a Mission without my having even been acquainted with it. In fact before I received any official notice that the Benedictines had abandoned it, I learned that it had been offered to the Passionists & Capuchins, & now lastly it has been offered to the Franciscans, tho' neither of these two Orders are established in my Diocese, & I have been assured that the place is considered – wrongly I believe – a chaplaincy & not a mission. I regret the circumstance as it places me in a false position with those zealous & disinterested body [*sic*] of labourers in the common vineyard.

     Wishing you every best wish of this holy season I remain truly Yrs in Xt. Alexander Goss.

---

529   Michael Burke CM, is in the *Directory* (1857–63) as superior of the Vincentian mission in Sheffield; he is not listed in Fitz-L.

---

295.   *Very Rev. Canon Flanagan, Bp's House, Birmingham*[530]
                    12 January 1861   *5/3/432*
               "Bishop Edward Dicconson"[531]
My dear Canon,
In vol II. p. 369 of your history of the English Church, I find Bp. Edward Dicconson named, as having been instrumental, whilst yet a Priest, in

procuring the rules of the Mission: I shall feel obliged if you can refer me to any source, published or unpublished, where I can glean any particulars of the said Bishop; for I am anxious to collect the Ecclesiastical history of my Diocese.

Wishing you every blessing, I reamin sincerely Yrs in Xt. +Alexander Goss

---

530   Thomas Flanagan, 1814–65, of Birmingham Diocese: author of *History of the Church in England: From the Earliest Period to the Re-Establishment of the Hierarchy in 1850* (1857). The work was attacked by Richard Simpson in *The Rambler* for its pro-Catholic bias.

531   Edward Dicconson, 1670–1752, VA of the Northern District and Bishop of Mallus from 1741; he lived at Finch Mill, part of the family's estate at Wrightington. The 'rules of the Mission' refers to the regulations issued by Benedict XIV dealing with the relations between the VAs and the Regulars. This was the brief *Apostolicum ministerium* of 1753, confirming earlier papal briefs of 1698 and 1748; *inter alia*, it laid down that Regulars should have the approval of the VAs before accepting appointments on the English Mission. Before becoming VA Dicconson had been the Roman agent for the Secular clergy. See J. A. Hilton on Dicconson in *ODNB*.

296.   *His Grace, Archbp. Errington*   *13 January 1861*   *5/3/436*
"Dr. Briggs' funeral etc."

My dear Grace
We buried Dr. Briggs on Thursday. The Mass was sung by Dr. Grant, Dr. Ullathorne preached, & Liverpool, Salford, & Hexham assisted. After the absolutions, the body was removed to Hazlewood,[532] but the Bps. did not accompany it.

Dr. U. said that he understood the Pope wished the Card. to make an explanation to the Bps, but he thought the Card. dreaded a scene. I asked why? He replied because you are a [*?hurt*]. Dr. T. then asked me if I should speak in case the Card. explained matters. I replied that I should either walk away before he began, or I should say that he must correct misrepresentations where they had been made & that none had been made in the Bps' meeting, & that if he mentioned your name, I should say that I should repeat every word to you & denounce the cowardice that would speak of the absent. I ended by assuring them that having purchased liberty of speech I meant henceforth to use [it] unreservedly. Dr. U. suggested that the Bps had not always used this liberty, & he said that when the pope's name was used we could never tell what did & what did not come from him. Dr. T. then asked if anything could be done in your case by representation to Rome, asking for you to be employed. Dr. U. said he thought not under the present Pope; Dr. G. thought you would not take office for some years, & I said that I did not see how you could under the present administration, as you could have no security.

There was a general wish for our future meetings to be not at London, but at Oscott. Dr. G. told me that Rome had desired the Card. to make known the decision about the Chapter; he sent down an Eng. translation, which they translated into Italian & sent to Barnabò. Efforts in private are being made to say that the affair had best drop, seeing the state of the Card's health: but how much has temper to do with his ailment? William[533] told me that after seeing me in Lancaster he wrote to say that he had heard from me that *Epi casi*[534] had been decided without exchange of documents. The Card. pronounced that this simulated a calumny & told him to suspend his judgement till he had heard both sides. I am told that U. was disappointed with Walker[535] in Rome because he had a fondness for nothing but pagan antiquities! Did he not visit the Minerva too often? I think we are up to the mark.

Begging my remembrance to your brother & Mr. J. O'Farrell, I remain ever Yrs AG

---

[532] Hazelwood, Tadcaster, the seat of the recusant Vavasour family and a long-established mission, dedicated to St Leonard and established in 1290, according to Kelly, *English Catholic Missions*. Briggs had died on 4 January 1861, having resigned his see on 7 November 1860.

[533] It is unclear who this William was; it could be Bishop Turner but the use of the first name to refer to a bishop is most unusual for Goss.

[534] Trans: 'the cases of the Bishop'.

[535] Presumably Canon John Walker of Scarborough, friend of both Wiseman and Ullathorne.

297. *Rev. Mr. Chadwick   14 January 1861*   *5/3/438*
"Jacobe, ad quid huc venisti"[536]
<u>Confidential</u>

My dear Mr. Chadwick,
We have both of us assisted at the funeral obsequies of the good Bp. of Beverley, & now that he is no more I feel free to write to you on a matter touching your future position, which I did not feel that I could honourably do as long as he whom you had undertaken to serve, was still living. When leaving Ushaw before setting out on your travels I should have written to ask your services had I not been told that you did not consider yourself free to leave the Diocese of Hexham, but that objection is at an end, & I consider that I may now fairly claim a hearing. If not Lancashire born, you are a Lancashire man: for generations your relations have held honourable place among the clergy of this county, & for more than a century have held offices of trust among us. Yorkshire can put forward [no] claim on you, & the personal tie which may have bound you to the late Bishop has been severed by death. The crozier which he wielded may be placed in the hands of a stranger who knows not Joseph.

For years you have studied & laboured to fit yourself for the Mission, & you have promised to serve it: are you doing so efficiently? Does the scattered flock at Stourton afford you employment? Is your zeal satisfied with breaking the bread of life to a scanty population whilst the teeming thousands of Lancashire are crying to heaven for spiritual bread?

The world will say, you are changeful. Do we teach our people to fear what the world will say or does St. Paul bid us to conform to it? Do now what you would wish to have done when you come to die. I know you too well to believe that you can be happy in your forced idleness, or to believe that you will stay in your present place when the depths of your heart are stirred by the cry for labourers. Better make the change now than later; for it will have to come, & the death of Dr. Briggs offers you a suitable occasion.

Only say the word & by return of post you shall receive an appointment to Southport, a healthy spot, where there is plenty of work but not too much, & where you may harvest as many souls for heaven in a year as you will be able to at Stourton in a long life. Some men are born drones, but you are not one of them, & you cannot be happy where you are: *ad quid, Jacobe, huc venisti?* Consult your own conscience & follow its voice: don't dally. Ever Yrs AG

---

536 'James, why have you come to this?' An extraordinary letter! James Chadwick, 1813–82, had been born in Ireland; his father's family came from Standish. Ordained in 1837 for the old Northern District under Bishop Briggs, in 1866 he became second bishop of Hexham and Newcastle. Stourton: Chadwick was chaplain to Lord Stourton at Allerton.

298. *Mrs Whiteside*[537] *16 January 1861* 5/3/440
"Death of Mr. Jas. Whiteside"

My dear Mrs. Whiteside

Little did I think when I last called upon you in Lancaster that God would so soon call himself [*sic*] your brother in law, Mr. James, tho' he was then an invalid. Whilst his relatives lament his loss as a kind & affectionate member of their family circle, the poor will lose in him a generous helper, & Religion a munificent & charitable patron. We must all pray, as we fervently hope, that he has gone to receive the reward for his good works: could his voice now be heard amongst us, it would be to proclaim that what he had done for religion & the poor, God had rewarded as done to himself. Though death makes aching hearts & a desolate fireside, yet it cannot quench the bright cheering ray of hope that hovers over the graves & memory of those who, like our Blessed Lord in the flesh, have gone about doing good.

And now, my dear Mrs. Whiteside, by making you, so to speak, doubly a widow, God shows that he designs to separate you more &

more from the world, that by redoubling your labours & charities among the poor, you may become more & more his spouse.

Praying God to comfort you & your mourning friends, & wishing you every blessing I remain sincerely Yrs in Xt. +Alexander Goss.

---

[537] Presumably Isabella Whiteside of Lancaster, widowed mother of the later archbishop (born in 1857).

299. *Very Rev. Canon Newsham   9 February 1861*   *5/4/4*
'Library at St. Anthony's'

Very Rev. & dear Canon,

For ten days I have hardly been able to hold up my head, & my labours on Monday have neither improved my health nor my Pastoral: yet I shall consider my time & labour well spent, if you returned home with your mind at ease. You certainly throughout the day evinced a sincere desire to have all difficulties brought to an amicable arrangement, & I think we have all reason to thank God for our success. Every one will give you credit for having made what you felt to be a great sacrifice. I am glad to say that Mr. Power has consented to your housing the Library at St. Anthony's & I have great pleasure in giving hereby the necessary sanction for its removal.[538]

Begging yourself & Sister every blessing, I remain sincerely Yrs in Xt. Alexander Goss.

---

[538] Goss's euphoria was premature: on the 13th Teebay wrote to Newsham (5/4/10): he was glad all had been settled, but the Bishop was 'not willing to re-open any part of the controversy, & only the Card. can explain authoritatively his own document'. See Introduction, p. xxxix re Newsham's case and Rome: APF *Anglia*, 15, fols 184, 482–5.

300. *Major Blundell, Crosby Hall, Liverpool 11 February 1861 5/4/5*
"Trust Deed of Churches etc."

My dear Major Blundell,

I beg to acknowledge receipt of yours of the 9th requesting to be informed as soon as possible whether I will allow the Recollect Fathers[539] to take the Mission of Little Crosby, & I have to say in reply that the cause of the delay does not rest with <u>me</u>. In the month of October I applied for an office copy of the Trust Deeds, & on the day following received from you an assurance that you would speak to Mr. Sharman & <u>get me a copy made of it</u>. It is now February & I have not received it, yet without it, it is impossible for me to decide whether the necessary security is provided for Religious, & whether I can decide the question without the intervention of my Chapter.

Wishing you every blessing I remain truly Yrs Alexr. Goss.

⁵³⁹ The Recollect Fathers: a branch of the Franciscan Observants, originating in France in the late sixteenth century and spreading among English exiled Franciscans in the seventeenth; St John Wall, martyred 1679, was a Recollect. By the nineteenth century they were strong in Belgium and northern Germany; an English province was established in 1858 under Belgian influence. See *DIP*, VII, cols 1307–22. Teebay wrote to Blundell on 13 February (5/4/9): Goss very unwell, but as soon as Sharman sends the copy he will decide the issue: 'As yet he has been quite unable to reconcile your views with those of the Recollects.' See letter 320.

301. *Rev. Jas. Nugent*   *11 February 1861*   5/4/6
                 "Application for Removal"

My dear Mr. Nugent,
I am in receipt of yours of Feb. 3. in which you inform me that you have waited for 6 months for an answer to your application for permanent or temporary removal from the Institute, & in which you renew the application of [*sic*] Southport with a demand for a change or from 6–12 months absence.

In reply I beg to condole with you & to express my regret that you should still feel unequal to the duties of your position. I have so often told you both by word & letter that we could not spare your superintendence of the Institute, that I am sure you will not attribute my silence to any other cause than my conviction, & your knowledge of my conviction, of the truth of this assertion. I have never refused to allow you leave of absence when your health demanded it: I gave you six months or so for your journey to Rome; subsequently I gave you three months in Ireland, & the Vicar General, since your application to me in July, has given you leave to be absent for three months. Notwithstanding the changes that have been made by request, I have still seven applications on my list; I despair of satisfying all. Were it not that faith teaches me that there is another world & that hope sustains me in the expectation of it, I would throw down my pen & flee the country, for my head aches as if held in a vice, & my eyes burn & my ears ring: but still I must know no rest, but work, work, work. To be candid, I cannot recognise the right of any priest to demand twelve months absence unless the doctor has admitted him to be enrolled a pensioner on the sick list. However I will see if any arrangement can be made to give you a temporary change: perhaps Can. Walmsley would exchange duties, if I cannot succeed in finding a place in the country.⁵⁴⁰

It may be change or rest that [you] require as well as or more than change of air. It is the retirement of able men in the prime of life that hampers my movements & prevents my being able to afford suitable changes for the invalid. Wishing you better health, the source of every earthly blessing, I remain truly Yrs, A. Goss.

⁵⁴⁰ See n. 470.

302.   *Very Rev. Can. J. Fisher, Great Crosby   11 February 1861 5/4/8*
                     "Propag. of Faith £400"[541]

My dear Canon,

I send you a cheque or order for £400 to be allocated as below. Eldon St.
£200; Douglas £100; Ramsay £50; Peel £50. Don't let Mr. Carr know
of this allocation, but say that if he will furnish a complete account of
Church & house, that you know the Bp. will help him. As I wish funds
to be raised for buildings to be erected at Peel & Ramsay, let an acct. be
opened for these two places,[542] & meanwhile let the money be put out to
profit: it must not be thrown into Douglas Bay. You have left your keys.
What has become of Walton?[543]

Begging my remembrance to your Sister & wishing you every
blessing, I remain truly Yrs. A. Goss.

---

[541] The Association for the Propagation of the Faith, founded in France in 1822, was
active in England from 1837; Goss urged people to support it and overall in his years the
diocese gave more than it received, but on occasion it was a useful source of funding; see
Annals of the Association for the Propagation of the Faith (London).

[542] Peel church opened 1865, that in Ramsey in 1864.

[543] Perhaps Thomas Walton, 1829–97; see letters 247, 249.

303.   *Very Rev. Dean Gillow   16 February 1861*   *5/4/12*
              "Dripping. Gallows Hill. Exam Papers"

My dear Dean,

I am glad to hear that you have got rid of your cold, & I hope that you
will take care of yourself during the Spring, often a trying time.

Tho' dinner & collation only are mentioned in the Lenten Dispensation, yet I conceive that dripping is allowed at every meal that can be
taken. Those <u>not bound</u> to fast can therefore take it for breakfast, for
it is not, like flesh, limited to once in the day: but there is a large class
that <u>do not</u> fast, but yet who by the <u>law</u> are not ipso facto dispensed,
but are dispensed by the Priest. With these I think the P[ries]t can
use his discretion, commuting the fast into alms deeds, or prayer, or
even dispensing with portions of it. This applies to those who are not
exempted by their labour or profession from fasting, but who yet seem
to have good cause for some exemption, e.g. students, & with them the
P[ries]t uses his discretion, partly commuting or partly dispensing. With
labourers whether men or women, whose work is never done, there
is no difficulty: but still I think the confessor, as spiritual physician,
should recommend some abrogation: mortification consists in denying
ourselves what the law allows.

I am glad the matter about the land at Gallows Hill is progressing
favourably: your brother, Mr. Carr, & Mr. Turner are three worthies
deserving of all honour & commendation.[544]

I will attend to the Examination Schedules: have you any changes to suggest in them?[545] For the last fortnight I have hardly been able to hold my head up, but am better today. My head has too much work & I take too little exercise: Visitation duties, so hard to many, are to me a relief.

Ever Yrs. A. Goss.

---

544   Gallows Hill: an area of north Preston, site of the new church of The English Martyrs, eventually opened in 1867. Gillow's brother was Joseph, who gave £1,000 towards the project. Messrs Carr and Turner not identified, but both were local Catholic names. See www.englishmartyrspreston.org.uk/history (accessed 27/10/2013). There were later disputes about the boundaries between the new church and the Jesuit missions in the town; see Doyle, 'Jesuit Reactions', 224.

545   Probably the religious tests for pupil teachers used by the local clergy or inspectors.

304.   *Major Blundell*   *19 February 1861*   *5/4/18–19*
"Little Crosby Presentation"

My dear Major Blundell,

At our time of life, when friends are not easily made, it is not worth our while seriously to disagree, particularly after an acquaintance of 20 years, formed before you had felt the weight of family cares, & I had experienced the prick of the thorns that line the jewelled mitre. No doubt each thinks the other to blame; now what say the facts of the case? You say that you "have been much annoyed at the delay & the little anxiety that seems to have prevailed in the settlement of the affair". Mr. Shann died, I believe, in April; now it was not till June 25 that you wrote to announce the fact to me, & not till July 12 that the Prov. of the Bened. wrote to say that they could not supply you. I was never asked to furnish you with a priest, & am not therefore chargeable for your failure in procuring one. When you asked to appoint a Capuchin as <u>Chaplain</u>, I explained the anomaly of such an arrangement in my letters of July 5, 11 & 21. On the 24 I waited on you at Crosby Hall, explained the matter fully, & left with an assurance, given in the presence of Mr. Ray, that you would make me acquainted with the steps you intended to take. This interview referred especially to the overtures made by the Recollects of Sclerdin.[546] In July & again in Sep. you wrote to propose the Vincentians, still as chaplains;[547] I replied to your communication; moreover the young Mr. Burton who spoke to you on the subject, had not the sanction of his superiors for so doing. On the 26. Oct. I wrote to point out the evils arising from the neglect of a permanent appointment, asking for an office copy of the Trust Deed, & telling you of my absence till Christmas. During my time in the North, there arrived the letter of the Recollects, written 9 November. This convinced [me] still further that nothing could be done till I had a copy of the Deed, & hence my first question on my return home, was to know from my officials whether or not the Deed had arrived; to my surprise I found it had not. You say that it "was most unfortunate that I did not in the first instance forward to you the letter received by me from the Prov. which was couched in terms quite different to the offer you made them". But how was I to know this? You had never communicated to me the terms of your offer, tho' at our interview, July 24, I had been led to believe that you would do so. My only chance of knowing what you really wanted, under such circumstances, was to see the Trust Deed, hence my continued application for the copy, which in your letter of Oct. 27 you had promised to have made for me. As the Deed was registered in Chancery, I knew that it must form the basis of every arrangement, & I naturally hesitated to commit myself to the expression of any view in the absence of that document. I discovered also a letter of your father's to Dr. Brown, saying that he wished to reserve to himself & his heirs the right of presentation, which further increased the difficulty, as such a right seemed to me to be abandoned if the Church was made over to the Recollects, as their letter seemed to contemplate,[548] & I had no reason to doubt that they had correctly understood your wishes, as they had had, & their Prov. had had a personal interview with you, as well as written communications from you.

Now I submit that if you had cited to me, or furnished me with a copy of the provisions of the Trust Deed, & had moreover given me a copy of your proposals to the Recollects, the whole affair might have been settled almost by return of Post, as their letter to me offered the terms on which they were prepared to accept the mission. But instead of this, you referred me to Bp. Eton for information about the Recollects, & to your Agents' office for the provisions of the Trust, indignantly asking my Vic. Gen. whether I supposed that you would part with the possession of the Deed. Now I had only asked for an office copy & that had been promised me. Meanwhile a report has gone out among the gentry that I have refused you a priest, tho' in truth I have never been asked to [do] so. In conclusion I beg to assure [you] that I shall be as ready now, as I was at the beginning, to meet your wishes in this as in every other matter, saving the duty which I owe to God in the person of his Church. Ever sincerely Yrs. A. Goss.

---

[546] In Belgium; see n. 540.

[547] The Vincentians had a mission in Sheffield, founded in 1853 and later handed over to the Rosminians. Burton has not been identified.

[548] Goss thought such a hand-over would be a reasonable stipulation on the part of a religious congregation, to avoid being under 'the influence of a change of circumstances or of Squire' (5/4/17, to Blundell, 16 February 1861).

305.   *Rt. Rev. The Bp. of Shrewsbury   27 February 1861   5/4/22–3*
"Synod Ushaw Accounts. Beverley"

My dear Lord,

No news of Synod. I think all hands are at present employed on the great money case which, it is said, is likely to come off next month. The Ushaw Statement is already in Rome, containing nothing new, unless it be fresh abuse: for their lawyer says – so I hear – that they said 3 years ago all they had to say: then why ask for a *Dilata*?

It is impossible to learn how the Card. really is. I understand that Can. Walker has gone to London this week, but why I know not. Why have we not met for the Beverley election? The Synod provides for the absence or sickness of the Archbp. by empowering the Senior Bp. to act in such cases.[549]

I have directed Can. Jas. Fisher to send back to Dr. Newsham the Balance sheet of account for education at Ushaw. 1o. because it is headed Rt. Rev. Dr. Goss in acct. [*sic*] with St. Cuthbert's College. Now the law does not recognise [the] C. as a corporation, nor can we sue it: we ought therefore to have a real person; it ought to be with the Pres: of St. Cuthbert's. By these little dodges they strive to effect what they failed to accomplish at the Synod: they act as if they had accomplished it, & then they will petition for the status quo to be kept. 2o. because they have again inserted the obnoxious impost of medicine.[550] 3o. because they charge for vacation outfit [*sic*]: now if I have to pay the outfit, I will reserve to myself to decide who ought to go home. I hope you will act as we are doing in this matter. I think we ought to protest against the election of Dr. Gibson as Vic: Pres: it is a violation of the status quo, as it ought by the existing regulations to have had the sanction of the Bishops. I think our first step should be to write to Dr. N. to say that we had heard of Dr. Gibson's appointment, & to ask if it be true. If he writes back to say it is true, we ought then to apply for a copy of the Instrument of his appointment, in order that we may see how & by whom it was done, & then we ought to lodge a formal protest against the same with Dr. Newsham, Dr. Hogarth, & the Cardinal: & at the same time we ought to write a strong joint letter to Rome. Next we ought to inquire from Dr. Hogarth if it be true that the coal from the Cornsay Estate be sold: for if that property were left for the benefit of the College, we ought to have a voice in its disposal. Not to insist on this, is to give up our right to the College & its property. When we get his answer, we can frame our next query; but we ought to ask by whose authority it was done; for it is something more than a change of investment, & we ought to know what has become of the money. It cant [*sic*] have gone to build the new College, for before that was begun they said a friend had given them the money for the purpose. Lastly my lawyer says that we ought to insist on the property of the College being invested in a Bp. & priest of each Diocese: for that was and has been the principle hitherto followed. He gave this opinion after reading Dr. Lingard's letters on the subject, when, being sole legal owner, he made the transfer to a Vic: Apos: & one priest from each Vicariate with the addition of the Pres: of the College. Then at midsummer we ought to remove all our Professors. By our remaining quiet they are consolidating the changes they are gradually introducing, & they are habituating the Clergy to their views: for Dr. Gillow has been frequently down to propagandise. I shall be glad if you & Dr. Turner will give me your views, for we must act together whatever we do. Be good enough to send this letter to Dr. Turner, with your own comments. Our policy should be to keep them employed: a defensive warfare is generally a losing warfare: if we want to succeed, we must be aggressive.

I have been able to do little since Christmas, for I have been very so so. Ever Yrs AG

---

[549] *Decreta*, p. 10, sect. 2. In a letter (5/4/25) to Newport and Menevia, 28 February 1861, Goss claimed. 'We stand before the world as a body of incapables, who cannot or dare not move hand or foot unless H.E. is there with his wand to direct our movements. How long has this to last?'

[550] Elsewhere Goss spoke of the 'strong, hale sons of the yeomanry studying for the Church' not needing medical aid to the extent that 'the more delicate children destined for the world' did (5/4/20–1, same date, to Newsham).

306. *Rt. Rev. the Bp. of Birmingham* 14 March 1861 5/4/26
"Ursulines. Trust Bill"

My dear Lord,

I do not at present see an opening here for the Ursulines from Oxford, though it is possible that there may be one somewhat later. I have no town except Chorley, which is small & very poor, unprovided. Preston has 3 houses of the Infant Jesus & one of the faithful companions, opened for Boarders. Liverpool has two houses of the Sisters of Mercy, one of Notre Dame, another of the faithful companions; at Wigan & St. Helens of Notre Dame, Lancaster of Sisters of Mercy, so that poor Chorley is the only place without, & I doubt if there is a single family that could afford to board a child, hardly to pay the extra charge of a middle school. The Clergy too like an order, like the Sisters of Mercy, that can visit the sick poor.

I am obliged by a copy of Mr. Estcourt's letter forwarded by your direction. It sets the matter in a clear light yet unsatisfactory, as I fear we shall be caught by the succession duty in many instances in which we have hitherto escaped.[551]

I am sorry to hear that the Card. has had another relapse. Can. Walker of Scarboro was telegraphed for last week tho' I know not whether on business or as a private friend. Meanwhile Beverley suffers: surely we ought before this to have availed ourselves of the provision made by the 1st Synod, which authorises the Bps to meet under the Senior Bp *Archiepo impedito.*[552]

With many thanks I remain sincerely Yours. Alexr. Goss.

---

[551]   Edgar Edmund Estcourt, 1816–84, Ullathorne's friend and administrator: see Champ, *William Bernard Ullathorne, passim* and 457–8. 'The succession duty': presumably a type of inheritance tax, as a result of the Trust Bill. (This letter is not in Goss's hand, but signed by him.)

[552]   Trans: 'when the Archbishop is prevented'.

307.   *Very Rev. Dr. Ilsley.*[553] Lisbon   *14 March 1861*   5/4/33

My dear Dr. Ilsley,

I am very sorry to hear that you have been so ill, but am glad to hear that you are better, for we cannot afford to spare you yet, even to go to receive the reward of your labours. Paralysis has been very common this season: Dr. Newsham of Ushaw is now suffering from it.

Mr. Lenon [*sic*][554] has arrived safe & has reported himself: unfortunately I was not at home, but have written to him & hope soon to have him in harness. My present intention is to have him here till he has completed his theological reading, tho' I imagine that will not be a long task; but I shall have an opportunity of becoming somewhat acquainted.

I send by a young gentleman, once a student in our College both this letter & a copy of our Diocesan Synod: he is on his way to Brazil after studying some years in Germany.

I am at present endeavouring to collect the names & scattered notices of the secular clergy who have laboured in that part of Lancashire now comprising the Liverpool Diocese. I shall be glad of any help, & if you can supply me with information from the College Diary shall be much obliged. One of my students could copy it at his leisure time, for I presume you have the names, age, birth place, particulars of ordination etc. from an early date. Begging a remembrance in your prayers & wishing yourself & superiors of the College every blessing I remain truly Yrs. Alexander Goss.

---

[553]   Joseph Ilsley, DD (1805–68); edu. Lisbon and rector there 1853–62; then r. at Scorton.

[554]   Lennon: there were two brothers at Lisbon – this one was John Joseph, 1830–97, o. December 1860; served briefly at Fernyhalgh, then first r. at Newton-le-Willows 1861–70; later at Weld Bank.

308. *Rev. W. Fayer*[555]   *21 March 1861*   5/4/48
                    "Can. Newsham's claims"

My dear Mr. Fayer,
Many thanks for your letter: I would have written sooner, but have been little able to work. I fear I shall be obliged to seek sooner not after Easter [*sic*], for my visit to Rome was a fatigue rather than a pleasure.

Can. N. had over with me what he calls Mr. Fisher's mistake; but the fact is, that he & F. start from two different points, one maintaining that what he did not owe for int[erest] at St. Anthony's was his own; the other contending that all that he had & much more if it had been there, belonged to the Church; in fact, that considering the burials he ought to have had the place out of debt or nearly so. I advised him to let the matter drop as of no practical consequence. I regret that he has not fitted himself for a change of mission; but to change him would be to reward him for what he must acknowledge to be neglect of duty; for he boasts that he is seldom at home, & that he knows no body etc. If he were near Lpool would it not be the same? would he not be always in the town? I assure you those I have spoken to dread it. He cannot help interfering, & his talk does harm in proportion to his sphere of action. Now that all is settled, amicably settled, his best plan would be to retire to some other Diocese, if he cannot be content to be anywhere but near Lpool. With every best wish, truly Yrs A. Goss
All desire their kind remembrance.

---

[555] William Fayer, 1814–83, of the Salford Diocese.

309. *Circular to the Clergy of Liverpool & the Deans*
                    23 March 1861   5/4/53
                    Confidential

Dear Rev. Sir,
I write to say that I have received reliable information that both Propaganda & the Apostolic Delegate of Syria have prohibited collectors to come into these parts, & furthermore I am told to be on my guard against a monk Assa, or Issa, present at the Catholic Club dinner at the Adelphi, pretending to collect for the poor Christians of Syria, but in reality for himself.

Wishing you every blessing, I remain sincerely Yrs in Xt. Alexander Goss.
Act on this, but use it with circumspection.

310.   *Rev. Jn. Dawber*   *4 April 1861*   *5/4/61–2*
                                   "Variorum"

My dear John,

1o. Please to send word to Edward Hatter that I will send him a parcel on <u>Sunday</u> by the Train reaching Rufford at 8.20.

2o. I will send you Gregson's fragments[556] which I have borrowed from the Orrells: go over to Croston on Sunday for them: dont [*sic*] keep them above two weeks.

3o. Write to Mr. F. Taylor of Wigan & ask him if he will allow you to read the Lancashire trials,[557] <u>now in my possession</u>. I have been collating my MS. & am about to return his book, but it may return thro' you with his consent: it will repay perusal. Ask Mr. Taylor for the Norris Papers.[558]

4o. I again revert to my old plan of having a short history of the Diocese from the earliest period till the restoration of the hierarchy: 8 or 10 lines about each Bp. where attainable would be ample. See Gregson's appendix Page lxxvii. Dodd will supply materials.[559] Do I beg you set to this work.

5o. Write to Sir W. Lawson: say you have been asked by the Bp. to collect materials for an ecclesiastical History of the Diocese: that on application to Mr. Townley for information about the Dicconsons of Wrightington, you are referred to him as the best authority on the subject; & then ask for the pedigree of the issue of Hugh Dicconson who died I believe in 1693.[560] Lord Herries has a return of the landowners of Lancashire ordered by Walpole when a tax was levied on recusants. I am going to try to get a copy of this part, but I fear he may object, as diminishing the value of the original MS.[561]

6o. Send me [an] abstract of your application to Dr. Gillow & of his reply about Bp. Dicconson's Will: there is no doubt that this ought to be in our possession, for I have the bill of the payment made for its being transcribed or copied: you had best send me his letter. Some how thro' Brown, Sherburne & others they have contrived to obtain possession of documents which belong by right to the Archives of this Diocese. It is a mistaken notion to suppose, with many of the clergy of North Lancashire, that documents referring to a place ought to be kept at the place, for they are liable to disappear with every new incumbent. I cannot otherwise account for the absence of papers: if it had not been for the West Derby Hundred we should have had nothing. Besides when they are scattered, no one person is master of their contents & thus much valuable information is lost, for they throw light one on another.

7o. Let me have the particulars of Finch's bequest[562] to your school: (a) was the money left by Will to Thomas Finch of Mawdesley by Hen: Finch of Burscough? (b) Did he by verbal or written instruction signify to Thomas that he meant it for the school at Mawdesley? If so, can you furnish a copy of the exact words. (c) Did they put into your hands exactly £100? (d) Was any thing said or ought any thing to be done about an anniversary mass? When I have all particulars I will draw up a proper document to be kept at Mawdesley, in which all these particulars shall be stated. Ever Yrs truly AG.

I have too much on hand to allow me time to correspond with Sir W. Lawson, as you know.

556 Matthew Gregson, *Portfolio of Fragments, Relative to the History and Antiquities of the County Palatine and Duchy of Lancaster, in 3 parts* (Liverpool, 1817). This is a lavish folio production, profusely illustrated, with genealogies, topographical sketches and accounts of some recusant families, as well as detailed lists of official records and documents. See also n. 566 below.

557 Mr Taylor has not been identified. Goss published a Chetham Society volume on the Manchester Trials in 1864; see Introduction p. xlvii.

558 Thomas Heywood (ed.), *The Norris Papers* (Chetham Society, 1846). The recusant Norris family lived at Speke Hall, near Liverpool, an active recusant centre in the seventeenth century, with three hiding holes; see Stonor, *Liverpool's Hidden Story*, 90–6.

559 Charles Dodd, *The Church History of England from the Commencement of the Sixteenth Century to the Revolution of 1688*, 5 vols (Brussels, 1737–42; new edn by Mark Tierney, London, 1839–43). Dodd was the alias of Rev. Hugh Tootell (1671–1743), chaplain at Wrightington in the 1690s.

560 Perhaps Sir Wilfrid Lawson, 1829–1906, Liberal politician and temperance reformer; later MP for Cockermouth. Hugh Dicconson lived at Wrightington Hall; he was the father of Edward Dicconson, VA of the Northern District 1741–52; he died in 1691. See Hilton, *St Joseph's Wrightington, A History*, 6–7.

561 William Constable-Maxwell of Everingham, eleventh Baron Herries of Terregles, 1804–76.

562 The Finch family of Mawdesley and Eccleston, an ancient Catholic family (connected with Bd John Finch, martyred in 1584).

311. *Rev. G. Gillow*[563]   *4 April 1861*   5/4/63
"Alston Lane Mission"

My dear George,

I am glad to find that you have buckled on your armour afresh. I have heard of your achievements in Advent & Lent & thank God that you have been enabled once more to take the field in the good cause. I must leave Mr. Sharples & his confreres to make the best arrangements they can for the occasion as regards the Confessional: we cannot accomplish impossibilities, & hence as far as necessary I dispense with the law. I cannot say how overjoyed I have been at the grace given to & obeyed by the good old Squire. Charles Moore too has been taken into the Church. The death of his boy at Ushaw has been the occasion, so that the wife has lost a son but gained a husband, a great sacrifice but cheerfully & resignedly submitted to.

Wishing every blessing to yourself & on your labours at Alston, I beg to remain ever affectionately Yrs in Xt. Alexr. Goss.

---

563 George Gillow (brother of Mgr Charles Gillow), 1815–1894. A new church was opened at Alston Lane in 1857 by Rev. H. Sharples (brother of the bishop), who was there 1849–74. Plumb places Gillow at Ushaw at this time (*'Found Worthy'*), but see also letter 313 to support his being at Alston Lane.

312. *Rev. A. Watson, Stella*[564]   *20 April 1861*   *5/4/79*
"Archiv. Sec: Sol:" [*sic*]

My dear Mr. Watson,

I have received your letter with its inclosures. From my experience in such matters I am inclined to disbelieve it. That the person named may have adopted an endearing manner, for reasons confined to the secrecy of the Confessional, I am willing to believe & blame in the case of women: but I suspect that whatever there was of harm was in others not in him. I have known similar cases, afterwards disavowed & contradicted, arising from a mawkish jealous feeling. This case is the more suspicious as the accusations are made in concert & one speaks for all, tho' all she says cannot possibly apply to all. It is, I believe, necessary for me to have their names, in order to learn or test if possible their credibility, & lest the same writer should be personating three individuals. Then each should draw up or have drawn up her statement independently of the others. Their names cannot of course be ever made known to the person accused, but there can be no objection to their being made known to me, as the narrative contains nothing to their disparagement, but if true commands our sympathy. I do not & shall not shrink from acting in this matter: but I fear the responsibility of bringing an innocent man to grief.

I am sorry to hear that you are an invalid. I suppose you will visit Valladolid: perhaps Mr. Guest may persuade you to stay. Many thanks for your trouble about the papers: I want to get a history of my diocese & clergy, but fear I shall have to abandon it on account of want of adequate materials. Ever truly Yrs A. Goss.

---

564 Arsenius Watson, 1816–65, o. for the Northern District in 1842; did return to Valladolid in 1861. (Henson, *Registers*, 30, 229) The letter's heading reads 'Secret Archive: Solicitation'.

313. *Rev. G. Gillow*   *8 May 1861*   *5/4/94*
"Mission at Alston Lane. Mission at Goosnargh"

My dear George,

I have great pleasure in sending my blessing on yourself & labours at

Alston & doubt not that you will derive much consolation from a good but simple people.

I grant also all the necessary faculties for Goosnargh, both as regards the Confessional & Confessor. You will meet with a hearty welcome from the Hill folk; but you must bear in mind that they are on the Yorkshire border, & require more brimstone than our Lancashire lads, who are rough but tender hearted. Commend me to all friends. Wishing you every blessing & thanking God that you are once more yourself, I remain truly Yrs A. Goss.

314. *Rev. R. Smith, Lancaster*[565] *14 May 1861* 5/4/98
"Catholicity in Lancashire"
My dear Mr. Smith,
Dean Brown tells me that you are fond, too fond, of study in so far as it keeps you from taking due exercise. Besides studying for your own improvement, I shall be glad if you will direct your studies to some object of general use. We have no Catholic Antiquarian in the county, no body to do for us, which Dr. Oliver did for Exeter or Devon, whilst, meanwhile, the records & traditions of our county are fast passing away. Now the Crown courts at Lancaster must contain a fund of information, & though a fee is required for examining the records, I think you could for a slight consideration obtain a standing leave to work in them.

In the Office of the Clerk of the Crown for the Co. Pal. of Lr. are the proceedings of the Assizes. This should contain the trials of the Priests & other martyrs executed at Lancaster. In the Office of the Dep. Clerk of Peace are Cath. Deeds from George I, also registers of Roman Cath. Estates from 1717 to 1788; Register of Oaths taken by Catholics holding civil or military office. Besides these there are other courts where there may be interesting information. You can copy any documents & I need not say how valuable such copies would be. A fixed time given for a short period would enable you to accomplish much. The information thus obtained would enable us to compile memoirs of our martyrs & priests: it would help us also to trace our property, which, at the present moment would be of great advantage to us.

The plan to proceed on would be to obtain personal introductions to the gentlemen in charge of these offices, which could easily be done in Lancaster. In a short time you would be better informed of the matters in the offices than the gents who have the custody of them. I have thought much & long on this matter.

Truly Yrs A. Goss.
Gregson's Portfolio of Fragments of Lancashire p.124 has a reference to these documents.[566]

565   Robert Smith, see n. 107 above.
566   Gregson, *Portfolio*, see n. 556 above; p. 124 gives detail of the records at Lancaster of the Court of Chancery, the Court of Common Pleas, the Court of the Crown and of the Deputy Clerk of the Peace, with notes on the state of the records, their accessibility and frequency of use.

315.   *Bp.of Southwark*   *20 May 1861*   *5/4/105*
                        "Meeting. Talbot. Amherst"

My dear Friend,

At the meeting be true to yourself & the interests of your Diocese.[567] You know that on money questions Prop. will only echo what it gets from Eng. & that therefore to apply to Rome is only to invest the Card: with its power, as it will not only speak thro' him but he will speak thro' it. If we can conscientiously act, let us act: we have done so hitherto. It is this which has saved our property.

I have it on good authority that it was said in Rome that the Card: wanted Bev: to have been filled up without a meeting of the Bps on the names proposed. I am told that Dr. Amherst has written to Talbot to say that efforts have been made to induce him to take part against the Card: Now this may or may not be true: but I think Salop should know it, & should try to pump him about it or about Talbot, in a way not to excite suspicion, for I should not like him or Talbot to know that the matter is suspected. I fear that on the money case they are not going to hold by the first announcement.[568] I think they will try to explain that by £8000 with interest, they mean interest from the date of settlement, & not from the date of borrowing, which is the proposition made to Dr. F. & accepted by him. Try to ascertain what was the representation made by their Agent to Ushaw & by Ushaw to its friends. Strain, not to send any body to Rome: but if any body does go, it will be dangerous to send Dr. U on account of Synod. I did not think of this when I wrote to him to say that I thought himself & Clifton suitable for the purpose. It won't do to hurt his feeling, but it would be disastrous. The Card: will see the advantage of such an appointment. In haste ever Yrs A. Goss.

---

567   See Introduction p. xxvi: Wiseman had called the 'momentous' meeting at very short notice; Goss felt this over-rode the bishops' rights.
568   Propaganda announced its decision against Ushaw in April/May 1861; see Milburn, *History of Ushaw College*, 244–6. It had already settled the third Synod issue in May 1860, again, against the College; Introduction, pp. xxvi–xxviii. For Ullathorne in Rome at this time, Champ, *William Bernard Ullathorne*, 265–7.

316. *Rt. Rev. Dr. Clifford, Bishop of Clifton* 28 June 1861 5/4/109
"Peter Pence Association"

My dear Lord,

I quite agree with the views expressed by you in your letter to the Pres: & Sec: of the Peter P. Assoc: & I will answer their application to me in the same sense.[569] Unless a check be put to the current of events we should have only one Diocese, one Bishop, & one Parliamentary Representative: Centralization is productive of more evils than unity is of good. I beg to remain my dear Lord, Ever sincerely Yrs. Alexander Goss.

Mr. Shepherd[570] applied to me for letters of <u>excorporation</u> which I did not think he needed as he said that he had never been <u>incorporated.</u>

---

[569] See the following letter.

[570] Shepherd: presumably James, 1814–96 of the Clifton Diocese; a Rosminian who left the Congregation in 1842; wrote *Reminiscences of Prior Park*, where he had been educated.

317. *Sir G. Bowyer, Bart. M.P.,*[571] *Charles John Brett Esq.*
29 June 1861 5/4/112

Gentlemen,

I beg to acknowledge the receipt of your letter of the 21st, & to thank you & the members of the association whom you represent for the obliging offer to forward to the Holy Father the collections made in this Diocese for his assistance in these troublous times: but as I have a paid agent in Rome I find it unnecessary to trespass on your kindness. Wishing you every blessing,

  I remain, Gentlemen, truly Yrs in Xt. Alexander Goss.

---

[571] George Bowyer: see n. 347.

318. *Very Rev. Can. Newsham, Fleetwood*
9 September 1861 5/4/151
"Charges against Can. Jas. Fisher"

My dear Canon Newsham,

I must decline all communication, verbal or personal, on the matters treated of in your letter of yesterday, as I am determined not to reopen any of the questions that have been at issue between you & this Diocese. Since the last settlement I believe that neither my official nor myself have alluded to them, & whatever preceded the last settlement must be supposed to have ended with it, I shall be sorry to hurt your feelings but must repeat my determination not to notice any further communication on the subject.[572]

Wishing you every blessing I remain sincerely Yrs in Xt. A. Goss.

---

572 Later letters on the issue were written by Goss's secretary; Goss only wrote to Newsham if the matter concerned immediate mission business.

319. *Rev. Thos. Walton*   *9 September 1861*   *5/4/154*
"Schools – yard door"

My dear Mr. Walton,

Though I have been at my desk all day & it is now 5 o'clock, I cannot let the day pass without writing to you, so that you see how important I hold the contents of this communication to be.

1o. The yards of the boys & girls school at Widnes communicate with each other by a door, so that they are separated in vain by a wall, & in vain is it for them to leave the school by separate doors as long as that door remains unlocked. You have been too long on the mission with large juvenile populations to attend to, not to know the necessity of keeping the boys & girls separate from each other when out of school. This, therefore, is to command you *sub poena revocationis facultatum*[573] to keep that door locked & to keep the key in your custody.

2o. I noticed two – there are probably more – spouts pouring their contents into the foundations. Now tho' it may be the Contractor's business to run those spouts into the drains, yet I wish you should lose no time in having it done, irrespective of the Contractor.

3o. As I passed an open door in your house I was sorry to see a tobacco jar: I trust you will not smoke in your parlours.

God will never bless your labours unless you are resident. Hoping that your last out will have strengthened you for a year's labour & wishing you every blessing, I remain sincerely Yrs in Xt.

    Alexander Goss.

---

573 Trans: 'under pain of revocation of faculties', a rather severe penalty in the circumstances.

320. *Maurice Hoare Esq.*[574]   *14 September 1861*   *5/4/159*
"Trust Bill & Deeds"

My dear Mr. Hoare,

As an attempt is being made to invoke the intervention of the H. See to prevent our declaring Trusts of ecclesiastical property, it will be well not to <u>execute</u> the new deeds till I see you or you hear from me: yet meanwhile, let them be fully prepared for signature. [*these three lines marked* 'confidential']

The Bp. of Clifton seemed to like the draft prepared by you & Mr.

Turner, as securing every protection. Mr. Harting says that if the Trustees reserve to themselves power to deal with the property as income, the Commissioners will have no ground of interference [*sic*]: he rests on page 1741 of the 1st Act, as I am told. He seems to think that having to register only the 1st Deed of conveyance, gives great protection as it does not enable the Commissioners or others to know the present Trustees, & if the Declaration of Trust executed about the date of enrolment be kept secret, even a hundred years may pass over before it may be imperative to produce it. I apprehend that it does not matter whether a succession of owners has been kept up or not: for if it has not, the only fear will be from heirs who are not likely to molest us. Of course, if the 1st Deed be a trust, & it is not enrolled, it will be advisable not to enrol it, but to make another, as the existing Deed might not sufficiently protect us if enrolled. If therefore the 1st Conveyance to the Jesuits of Missions now held by us from them be enrolled, subsequent Deeds of Trust or declarations of Trust can be executed. I suppose that on the face of the 1st Deed the Jesuits as such will not appear. I do not know how they are acting in this emergency; but the Benedictines have enrolled the 1st Deed & are preparing Declarations of Trusts to be kept secret till called for bearing date about the time of enrolment. Mr. W. Blundell tells me that the Formby Deed is null, being a conveyance of Mr. H. Blundell of entailed land; but I suppose that if enrolled the title would be made good unless he opposed it & I will suggest this to him. I have not seen the Deed. Tho' Aug. has past I presume they would still extend the benefit to us. Perhaps Mr. Turner & you will confirm what I have written & if necessary state an opinion. I will inquire what other Bps. have done. Truly Yrs in Xt. A. Goss.

---

[574] Maurice J. Hore is listed in *Gore's Directory* (1859, 1860) as an attorney, at 32 Castle Street, Liverpool. The letter deals with the Roman Catholic Charities Act of 1860, to come into operation in 1861; hitherto, Catholic charitable trusts had not been recognised as legally valid. Wiseman opposed the Act and plotted with Manning in Rome to get it condemned; most of the bishops supported it. See Cuthbert Butler, *The Life and Times of Bishop Ullathorne 1806–1889* 2 vols (London, 1926), I, 217 ff., for what happened in Rome and Propaganda's decision, which in effect left it to individual bishops.

321. *E.W. Pugin Esq.*   *14 September 1861*   *5/4/160*
                        "Magdalen Plans"[575]
My dear Mr. Pugin,
I write in answer to yours of the 7th to give you my recollections about the preparation or commission to prepare plans for the Mag. Asylum.
1o. Every effort was made to put the work into other hands than yours, & even after you had prepared a draught Mr. Hansom was assured that the question was still open & he applied for the work.

2o. I desired the nuns to place in your hands a sketch which they had prepared as indicative of their wants.

3o. I met you, accompanied by Mr. Sharples,[576] on the occasion of your presenting the draught at the Convent. I was there assured by you that you had had a rough estimate of the cost which was to be £6000. I hesitated, knowing the amount of funds at my disposal, but I eventually consented, on being told by Mr. Sharples that it could hardly be done for less. Some modification was thought advisable in some round headed windows. I believe Mr. Sharples can testify to the accuracy of my recollection so far. Now on that sum I am prepared to pay the charges usual in the profession: but I protest against commission on future extension or on a church: for what could we want with a church in the Ford, the then proposed site of the Magdalen, with a cemetery church on view? Nor can I admit commission on estimate of Surveyor for warming; & I believe the charges for quantities to be an unusual charge with the profession in Lpool.

Any thing further on this matter I must place in other hands as my frequent absence from home does not allow me to attend to all details of local business.

With every best wish sincerely Yrs in Xt. Alexr. Goss [*Written upside down across the top of the page:*] Please to place this before Mr. H. Sharples of Oswald Croft to see if his recollection of the matter agrees with mine.

---

575   The Magdalen Asylum: run by the Good Shepherd nuns; originally a refuge in Netherfield Road, then in Mason Street and eventually in 1861 in Ford. Also in Ford was a new Catholic cemetery: Canon Newsham had bought twenty-four acres there for the purpose and it was opened in September 1859. The church of the Holy Sepulchre was opened there in 1861 – presumably the church Goss refers to here as 'in view' of the convent. A church was eventually added to the convent in 1886; see Burke, *Catholic Liverpool*, and Kelly, *English Catholic Missions*. See earlier letters about Hansom, 277, 281.

576   Mr Henry Sharples: nephew of Bishop Sharples; prominent Catholic business man in the timber trade, town councillor; and one of the first Catholic magistrates. He was very interested in social causes such as the girls' orphanage and the *Clarence* reformatory ship; see Duckworth, *Fagin's Children*, 180–1. He built the Lady Chapel at St Oswald's, Old Swan (Burke, *Catholic Liverpool*, 232).

---

322.   *Rev. Robt. Henry Smith*[577]   *21 September 1861*   *5/4/163*
                                  "The Reformatory"

Dear Rev. Sir,

I am sorry to hear that fresh difficulties have arisen about the management of the Reformatory, as I have great interests in its success. At an earlier period I might have been able to make arrangements for its direction, but now it is impossible. Besides the fact of its being outside of my Diocese could not fail to cause embarrassment, notwithstanding the kind expressions in my regard by my friend the Bp. of Notts. I hope, however, that it will not be allowed to go down, nor do I see how the solemn contract entered into with my Diocese can be set aside. With every best wish to yourself & compassion for you under difficulties of another's creation I remain sincerely Yrs in Xt. Alexander Goss.

577   Robert Smith CSO, 1807–1866, director of the reformatory; see n. 181 above. For an account of its many difficulties, see Bernard Elliot, 'Mount St Bernard's Reformatory'; T. L. G. Tucker, 'Mount St Bernard's Reformatory', *RH* 15:3 (May 1980), 213–17; Bernard Elliot, 'Mount St Bernard's Reformatory: A Reply', *RH*, 15:4 (October 1980), 302–4. The Bishop of Nottingham was Dr Richard Roskell, a native of Liverpool.

323.   *Mrs. James Dawber   26 September 1861*   *5/4/165*
                     "Div: a mensa et toro"578
My dear Mrs. Dawber,
When I was on visitation at Mawdesley, your husband begged of me to bring about a renewal of intercourse between him & you. In reply I stated to him that I understood you to have objections based on his incapability of supporting you. He claimed to be heard in answer. As this is a painful matter, & as both he & you are anxious to do what Religion requires from you under the circumstances, I think it desirable that you should state in writing thro' some friend the grounds on which you object to live with him. I will then submit that statement to him, that he may reply thro' a friend, & I will then submit both documents to my Vicar General for his opinion or decision, as from his age he must have had experience in such cases.
    [*These lines written across letter:*] Hoping that this communication will meet with your approval & wishing you every blessing, I remain sincerely Yrs in Xt. Alexander Goss.

578   'Separation from bed & board'. This is a unique letter indicating that lay people had access to Goss at visitation. See letter 293.

324.   *Very Rev. Can. Newsham   27 September 1861*   *5/4/172*
                     "New Church: Rev. G. Green"
My dear Canon Newsham,
In reply to a very kind note received from Sir Hesketh Fleetwood,579 I wrote to say with reference to a change of site for the future church, that I doubted not that my Council, without the advice of which I could not act, would readily approve of it. As the Chapter meets on the 16 of October, I will bring the matter before it, & I have no doubt that you will be able to return home fully empowered to act in the matter. I have

already told you that I consider the new site preferable to the old one in the existing condition of Fleetwood.

With regard to the new church I said that, if you were willing to undertake the laborious task of raising subscriptions, I would furnish you with suitable letters & aid you to the best of my power. I observed, however, that we have no funds applicable for such purpose except what we could raise annually. Those subscriptions, you know, I have never disbursed except in accordance with the advice of the Board; but I have before assured you that the claims of Fleetwood should receive favourable consideration. The efforts of your people should be met in a liberal spirit as far as I am concerned.

With reference to Mr. Green,[580] I suppose you understood me to require a certificate of his having made a retreat at some suitable place – say Stonyhurst, Bp. Eton, the Passionists or other similar Institution – before I would allow him to say mass, & that I would not concede to him further faculties. Wishing you every blessing I remain sincerely Yrs in Xt. A. Goss.

---

579   Sir Peter Hesketh-Fleetwood (1801–66) of Rossall, founder of the town of Fleetwood, gave the land for a new church, eventually opened in 1867. See letter 328.
580   G. Green does not feature in Plumb, *'Found Worthy'*. Fitz-L gives a George Green in Plymouth: 1815–90, b. in Lancashire, o. 1840.

325.   *Very Rev. Can. Tierney, Arundel, Sussex*[581]   *15 October 1861*
5/4/181

Confidential

My dear Canon Tierney,

I am sorry to hear from our friend the Bishop of Southwark that your health is still very delicate, for these are times when every soldier is wanted at his post to defend the liberties of our infant Church. I should like to have seen the Elenchus submitted by Prop. as a theme for the exercise of Episcopal talent, handled & sifted by your rigorous logic: for it was the most transparent imposition ever attempted to be practised on an unsuspecting Synod. I fear that whilst we are sulkily recovering from our disgust, a certain powerful intellect may be at work to accomplish by intrigue what he failed to accomplish by open discussion.

Having relieved my mind on this Synodal matter, I now turn to the immediate object of my letter. I am endeavouring to compile a history or chronicle of religion in my Diocese in perilous times. This as you know is a slow & difficult work. Prov Allanson O.S.B. tells me that the Doway Diary & a list compiled by Dicconson, *Epus. Mellensis*, & perhaps other papers that you have would be of assistance.[582] I know you cannot write except with extreme pain & difficulty & therefore I do not seek for a reply to my letter; but I can assure you that I would preserve with extreme care & return with fidelity these or any other documents that you could entrust with me. Begging you to excuse my intrusion into your sick room, & wishing you better health, I remain truly Yrs in Xt.

    Alexander Goss

581   Mark Anthony Tierney, 1795–1862, canon of the Southwark Diocese and chaplain to the Duke of Norfolk; noted historian. Schiefen calls him 'one of Wiseman's most vocal opponents' (*Nicholas Wiseman*, 71; and see 270–2).

582   Edward Dicconson, 1670–1752, VA of the Northern District and Bishop of Mallus 1740–52; he listed the clergy of the Northern District and the confirmations he had administered; Anstruther, *Seminary Priests*, III, 48–9. For the Douai Diaries, see *The Douay College Diaries 1598–1654* (CRS 10, London, 1911) and *The Douay College Diaries. The Seventh Diay, 1715–78* (CRS 28, London, 1928); also, P. R. Harris, *Douai College Documents, 1639–1794* (CRS 63, London, 1972).

326.   *Rev. P. Power, St. Anthony's Liverpool*   *26 October 1861*
                                            5/4/195
                    "Chaplain's Salary"

My dear Mr. Power,

I am well aware of the difficulty of raising money for any Cath. object, & so it will be as long as the milliner gets so large a share of Cath. Female support. The Salary of the Chaplain for gaols & workhouse & Industrial Schools should be regarded as part of the working expenses & paid accordingly. It was fixed by the various incumbents or their representatives under my Predecessor. Mr. Walmsley[583] has pressed me again since the receipt of your letter, so that I hope you will remit the Amount. Ever sincerely Yrs in Xt. A. Goss.

583   John Walmsley, 1812–68; see n. 470.

327.   *Can. Walker, Scarbro. [sic; added in pencil later]*
                    5 November 1861   *5/4/199*

My dear Canon,

Shame on the black-coated Pensylvanian of Darlington who repudiates his debt.[584] When applied to for payment of interest by virtue of the decree of Prop: he replies that he will forward to the person whom it concerns the demand upon him. In March 1858 he & Mgr. Newsham wrote to Prop. "We ought again to call the attention of your Eminence to the question pending between the Diocese of Liverpool & the writers, the Bp. of Hex. & the Pres. of St. Cuth: as representing the College". They say that Dr. Y's Executors demand from the Col. £6000 which Sherb: had given it, in payment of the £12500, whereas Dr. Y's Execs.

believed that Sherb: had given them more than twice £12500. They say that they are so sure of the justice of their position, that they had intended to beg of the H.S. to recall the order to have it referred to a Commission: but they desire with all their hearts that this inquiry should be proceeded with, they have nothing to fear from it, nay they demand it, "*lo domandano*". In June he wrote to say that he willingly submitted to the superior judgment of the H.S. as he owed to its wisdom the transference of Cornsay to the Col; & the D. of M. [? *sic*]. They even pray that Dr. Y's Execs may be prohibited from ever more raising the question.

The answer of the head of the Ushaw republic is worthy of Jno. Wesley. Mgr. N., he says, begs to assure the applicant that Mr. Sherburne's Exec. has <u>solemnly</u> assured him that he has not wherewith to pay. More of the other matter in a few days: I have sent for copies but have not received them.

Ever sincerely Yrs AG.

---

584 'Black-coated Pennsylvanian of Darlington': the reference is obviously to Bishop Hogarth, who lived in Darlington; the 'Pennsylvanian' reference is obscure, but may possibly refer to some fraudulent bonds issued in the 1850s by a Pennsylvanian called Biddle (see *OED*). See Milburn, *History of Ushaw College*, esp. 236 ff., on Cornsay and on the resolution of the Youens case in favour of the bishops.

328.   *Very Rev. Can. Newsham   23 November 1861*   *5/4/204*
"Church & Schools at Fleetwood"585

My dear Can. Newsham,
I return by this Post the plans of the new Church at Fleetwood, which, you tell me, you intend to alter by reducing the length, breadth, & height. Interiorly it would be improved by omitting the chancel arch, by bringing the Lady Chapel forward, as at the Old Swan, & by increasing – not diminishing – the width of the nave, also by making a double door into the Sacristy, as at Mawdesley, for the purpose of a Confessional, *ut fideles altare, & sacros ritus qui in eo peraguntur <u>facile</u> discernere valeant*,586 which they cannot do at St. Albans. Exteriorly I think the plan expensive both in the tower & windows, the latter especially would be found costly in the erection & difficult to make water tight.

I shall be glad, however, to hear how you propose to raise funds for the erection, & I should not like any steps to be taken till this is ascertained: to build by day work would be ruinous. With regard to Mr. Ball's £100 on the present Chapel, you must bear in mind that the Diocese has at its disposal no funds except those which belong to Missions, & that it cannot advance money except on suitable security. I do not even know the Trustees of the Chapel, nor did I ever see the Deed, nor did any one connected with my administration.

The cost of the Schools was £649.12.8d, & I do not think that with the present price of material as good schools could be built for the same sum: "the walls are 18 inch & the timber enough to float a 74 gun ship". The old Chapel would not do for schools: this, however, is a matter which I should have to lay before the Chapter, as the existing law of the Church in Eng: requires. Believe me sincerely Yrs in Xt. Alexr Goss.

---

585 See letter 330. The 'old' church had opened in November 1841, the new one in 1867 from an E. W. Pugin design. William Ball, 1826–80, was at nearby St Anne's, Kirkham, and Thurnham, at relevant times.

586 Trans: 'so that the faithful can <u>easily</u> see the altar and the sacred rites performed at it'.

329. — *Vaux Esq.* [*sic*], *Brit: Museum*[587]   *23 November 1861* [*added later*]   5/4/207

"Harkirke coins"[588]

Dear Sir,

My friend, Mr. Leeming of Spring Grove, Richmond, writes me that he placed in your hands a print of some old Saxon coins found in 1611 at a place then called the Harkirke, near Crosby Hall, Lancashire, then as now the seat of the Blundell family, & that you were kind enough to promise that you would give to him or me any information in your power on the subject. I do not believe that any of the coins themselves can be procured; for what were not sold were made into a pyx for carrying the B. Sacrament to the sick. I speak the more confidently as, at my request, Mr. Blundell has been good enough to make a diligent search. I have not found any one who can give me information about the name of the place – Harkirke – in which they were found; but it may have been a chantry or oratory in Saxon times. I shall feel obliged if you can give me any information about the coins, either as to date, or the king or mint master by whom they were coined or the legend or other particular, or if you can refer me to any book where I am likely to find similar coins delineated & explained.

Begging you to excuse my importunity & renewing the expression of my readiness to give you any information in my power, I beg to remain truly Yrs. Alexander Goss.

---

587 William Sandys Wright Vaux, 1818–85, antiquary; he entered the British Museum in 1841 and became first keeper of coins and medals in 1861. He was president of the Numismatic Society 1855–74, but apparently was more interested in Oriental antiquities than coins (*ODNB*).

588 Harkirke – see Stonor, *Liverpool's Hidden Story*, *passim*, but esp. 53–5; he says the coins were made into a chalice 'recently stolen'. It was a burial ground for recusant Catholics from the early seventeeth century: 105 lay people and twenty-six priests were buried there. Also, F. O. Blundell OSB, *Old Catholic Lancashire*, 3 vols (London, 1925–41), I,

34–6. Nicholas Blundell's *Great Diurnal*, I, 86 reports that 300 silver Saxon and other coins had been found on the first burial in 1611; William Blundell had drawn them, had a copperplate made of some of them and prints were taken. The *Diurnal* mentions several burials taking place there; an inventory in III, 239, mentions the 'pixis' made of the silver coins. See Frank Tyrer (ed.), *The Great Diurnal of Nicholas Blundell*, 3 vols. (Record Society of Lancashire and Cheshire, Liverpool, 1968–72). See Introduction, p. xlvii: Gibson used a print of the copperplate as frontispiece to his *Crosby Records*, for which Goss wrote the historical introduction.

330.   *E.W. Pugin Esq., Ramsgate*   28 *November 1861*   5/4/213
My dear Mr. Pugin,
Can. Newsham writes me that he has sent to you the plans of Fleetwood for <u>attention</u>, but whether for alterations suggested by himself or me, he does not say. <u>He</u> proposed to diminish the length, height & breadth: I propose a wider nave, no chancel arch, a side chapel taken from the Church as at St. Edward's, & a double door at the end of the other aisle for access to sacristy & Confessional, as at Westby. He suggests the erection at present of <u>nave, one aisle</u>, & tower as far as gutters. Now, as a vestry & confessional are more wanted than 2 altars, it would be better to raise the vestry aisle rather than the other: but he proposes the reverse. He writes me that stone can be laid down at 4/6 per ton, & that the building will require 1000 tons = £250; that ashlar will cost 1/– per cubic ft & that 1000 cubic feet will suffice = £50; that the timber will cost £350. Omitting glass, plastering & flooring, he calculates the cost of erection, not including slates, will be £800. What is your opinion of the accuracy of these calculations?

Zoological Gardens. This Church will have to stand by the side of an immense building. The land has cost £1020, of which £100 has been paid, but I do not think that a second £100 has been raised. You see therefore what you are likely to have at disposal for building. 1. wide nave, narrow aisles. 2. One roof which will be broken at the W. by tower, at the East by an apse extending beyond the two aisles, so that there will be no clerestory; but you will have the advantage of high aisles: [*two words illegible*] clerestory windows & <u>low</u> aisles would be crushed into the ground by the hospital near. 3. Red stone for the ashlar work. 4. Arches to be all [*illegible*] with brick. 5. Floor of church & sanctuary wood. 6. Roof plain blue slates. 7. Mouldings in stone or wood, <u>nothing</u> beyond a splay. 8. aisles entrance [*illegible*]. No other building can confront that great hospital. With nothing more an imposing effect has been produced at the Isle of Man; but you have the advantage in a W. tower to break the broad gable. Truly Yrs. A. Goss.

331. *[Bp Grant]*   *27 December 1861*   *AAW W.3/37,*
                                                          item 64[589]

My dear Friend,

Dr. E. suggests that we should send to Martini[590] only our proposed corrections, not the body of the work. I am getting them transcribed on foreign paper for the purpose.

If approved of, we shall have to insert them in the copies of the *Votum*, which he says we should all sign. It will conduce to this, if they can see it beforehand, as they will now be able to do, as it may be making the circuit of them whilst the corrections are being subjected to Martini. I will keep his copy at home whilst completing the transcript of the corrections until I see how far they are approved of, when I will transfer the corrections without the explanatory notes meant mostly for him.

I cannot get a copy of the Weekly Register with the Card's address to his clergy.[591] Will you get one & send it to Dr. E. for he has written to ask for it.

Dr. F. joins in kindest wishes of the season. Come down after your festivals & recreate with us. When does Menevia go to Rome? Ever Yrs AG

---

[589]   The letter is filed in correspondence to Wiseman, but is obviously to Bp. Grant; the same applies to the next letter as well.

[590]   Martini was the Roman representative or agent of the *Weekly Register*. He produced a memorial or *votum* on the issues in dispute between Wiseman and the bishops, written mainly by Bp Grant; Goss thought it excellent and urged other bishops to sign it; it had, he said, 'plenty of Roman oil and not a spoonful of vinegar' (letters to Menevia and Shrewsbury of January and March 1862, 5/4/232 and 239); but see also next letter.

[591]   *The Weekly Register* for 8 November 1861.

---

332. *[Bp Grant]*   *15 January 1862*   *AAW W.3/38, item 10*

My dear Friend,

I feel that it is too bad to trespass on your good nature, but I shall be glad in any way to relieve you of any share in the common burden. When this question & the money get settled, I hope to be comparatively at rest.

I send an instalment of my own private letter to Prop: change what you like: add salt, but don't take away what little pepper is left unless an odd grain that is too pungent for the sensitives at Rome.

I have on hand my Vicar's case with his Em:[592] so that my hands are full: & when he has done his, I have another with his Em: on my own account.

Can you find out the names of the two persons now in London: I want to learn if either of them are subjects of mine or of Salford or Salop.

It is hard to be compelled to educate yr. Students at an establishment actually at war with us for years.

Dr. Fisher asks me to thank you for your letter: the information is of service. Ever Yrs AG

---

592   Thomas Cookson, 1803–78, had taught at Ushaw and had been the favourite to become coadj. to Bp Brown in 1853; Wiseman prevented his appointment (Schiefen, *Nicholas Wiseman*, 240) on grounds of his un-Roman spirit. In June 1861 Cookson accused Wiseman of denigrating his character over a number of the disputed issues and asking for written proofs; Wiseman replied to Propaganda, claiming Cookson was a Gallican, an open enemy of Rome, adding that he could not produce proof of all this 'because it's a question of conversations temerarious to the Angels'! Goss became involved; the quarrel appears to have eventually petered out. See APF, *Anglia*, 16, 357–9, 492, 503, 504–10.

333.   [*Mgr Talbot*]   *17 January 1862*   *5/4/251–2*

My dear Mgr. Talbot,

Your letter contains the first intimation I have had that Mr. Tobin[593] was in Rome. At the close of the year I purchased a hospital capable of containing about 14 hundred children, half boys & half girls, for it is a double building. It is meant to meet the provision of a new act of the legislature,[594] by which vagrant children are committed. Adjoining it, I have purchased a plot of land for a church. When I say buy, I mean covenanted to buy: for as yet I have only paid £100, whereas I shall have to find thousands. Until I have means to build, I intend to open one of the large rooms as [a] temporary church wherein to form a congregation, for it is a poor neighbourhood. To this Mission I appointed Mr. Tobin. As the hospital needed airing & cleaning before it could be used, Mr. Tobin obtained leave of the Vicar General, under whom I have placed the vacation absence of the clergy, for a few weeks' absence; but neither the Vicar nor myself had any idea that he was going out of the country. Tho' he may not have exceeded the time given by the Vicar, I certainly expected him home for the new year: his place, however, is not yet fit for use.

With reference to the money question, Dr. Fisher has ever assured me that you were favourable to a settlement, & in fact there is a strong feeling of irritation on the part of those whose missions have suffered so severely by the withholding of the money for so long a time. The report now is that Dr. Gillow, having failed to get a new trial, intends, on the part of Mgr. Newsham, to repudiate the debt. In fact he has written to Dr. Fisher from Rome to that effect. Meanwhile it is current amongst his friends that Cardinals Riesach & Marini[595] have declared that Rev. C. Gillow, the executor & legatee of Mr. Sherburne, & not Mgr. Newsham, is the person affected by the decision. I cannot think this can be true: for Mgr. Newsham & Dr. Hogarth voluntarily came forward in this case, declaring that the College of Ushaw was the real defendant & that they represented it. Letters of Mgr. Newsham, Bp. Hogarth, & Card. Wiseman repeatedly make this declaration. They cannot therefore deny a responsibility which they have admitted for so many years, & on the strength of which they have put this Diocese to the expense of sending a Procurator three times to Rome, & of employing a Roman lawyer. Besides, there is something strangely indecorous in naming individual Cardinals as holding opinions out of court on a matter, which might [be] before them judicially. Tho' allowed to go round to the Cardinals before a trial, to give them information, it has been the practice of their Eminences to withhold the expression of a judgement till the case was really before them. Such rumours are injurious especially to the Cardinals & also to the H. See, & I cannot but regret that such information should be in circulation. Dr. Gillow was not more discreet about the Synod; for he wrote to Bp. Turner that he heard when he was in Rome that the Cong. disapproved of the project of placing the Colleges under the rule of a plurality of heads, & that the Pope approved of the view of the Cardinals, & that as I was well aware of what passed in the Cong. he supposed that I should have reported the matter to him. I need not say that I did not hear one word about it. Can the Bps have much confidence in the Col: when the Pres: is incapable of business, & the Vice Pres: is absent to oppose them. Believe me sincerely Yrs. A. Goss.

---

[593] Thomas Tobin, 1819–88, first r. St Michael's, Liverpool, 1861, where he built the church in 1865.

[594] See n. 249.

[595] Karl August Reisach, 1800–69, archbishop of Munich, cardinal in 1855, rector of Propaganda's Collegio Urbano with a strong interest in seminaries. Pietro Marini, 1794; created cardinal in 1846; in charge of financial matters at Propaganda; see C. Berton (ed.), *Dictionnaire des cardinaux: contenant des notions générales sur le cardinalat* (Paris, 1857; repr. Gregg, 1969). He was known to be a strong supporter of the anti-Ushaw party; see Milburn, *History of Ushaw College*, 247.

334. *Rt. Rev. Dr. Turner* *7 March 1862* *5/4/280*
"Dr. Manning – St. Patrick's Society"

My dear Lord,

I am surprised that Dr. Manning should write to you saying that he hopes that matters in Rome in which you are interested will end in peace, as we all wish. For whether by matters, he means the money question, or the Trusts, or the Synod, he has done & is doing every thing in his power to thwart us. He himself went to Card. Marini & endeavoured to render him favourable to a rehearing of the case this very winter, and it is notorious that Dr. Gillow never showed himself in Rome till Dr. Manning's arrival. I believe that no one has exerted himself more against us than he. Under such circumstances does not his letter smack of hypocrisy? On the Synod & Trusts he is the Cardinal's agent & must be dead against us.

He wrote to me, without any one's knowledge, as he said, to explain a matter about some cards supposed to have been left on Dr. E. & myself by the Card. having been withdrawn; but I desired Dr. Fisher to write & say that I could not on such a matter receive explanations from a person who professed himself that he was not delegated to give them.

What of St. Patrick's Society? Is Lavelle[596] trying to establish it in Manchester? I hear that it is condemned in Ireland. In my Pastoral I mentioned Secret Societies, as one of the Priests told me that they were being introduced; but I named none. The head of the St. Patrick's Society is, I am told, a Presbyterian. If you write to Dr. M. I hope you will say that there can be no peace that is not based on justice. I shall pay no more bills at Ushaw till I see whether they will pay. Dr. Ullathorne had to leave Rome last Sunday. Ever Yrs truly AG.

---

596   Patrick Lavelle of Tuam, o. 1853, was a national figure who was very critical of Cardinal Cullen; he was vice-president of the National Brotherhood of St Patrick (the political wing of the IRB) and toured Britain in 1862 to collect funds for it. Suspended by Rome in 1864 he took refuge in England and turned to constitutional politics. See C. O'Carroll, 'The Pastoral Politics of Paul Cullen' in J. Kelly and D. Keogh (eds), *History of the Catholic Diocese of Dublin* (Dublin, 2000), 294–312, esp. 306–7; also *DIB*, V, 340–2, and Belchem, *Irish, Catholic and Scouse*, 47, 163.

335.   *His Grace The Archbishop of Dublin*   *8 March 1862*   *5/4/282*
"St. Patrick's Society"

My dear Grace,
The Society of St. Patrick has made its appearance in this Diocese. Mr. Lavelle last week wrote in its favour; but I am told that in some parts of Ireland it has been denounced. I shall be glad to know from your Grace whether or not you consider it to come under the class of secret societies condemned by the Church, & also whether the Rev. Mr. Lavelle is allowed to say Mass in your Diocese. I fear his presence bodes no good in Liverpool.

With every best wish I remain truly Yrs in Xt. Alexander Goss.

336.   *Bp. Clifford, Rome [in pencil]*   *21 March 1862*   *5/4/291–2*
My dear Lord,
I have seen Dr. Ullathorne since his return. I sent him a copy of the Card's letter to Mr. Langdale about the school Deed to show how completely he yielded himself to the principle of the Trust Bill. Dr. Ullathorne was desirous to draw up an exposition of our views about the delegating of powers to one or more Bps. to allow application to

be made: this was thought could be productive of little good & would work badly.[597]

Dr. Gillow has returned. He wrote to me from London, saying that he would call upon me in order to inspect the Bastwell papers. Now tho' he had previously rejected this offer as insufficient, & tho' the case is already before a superior tribunal, I allowed him to inspect them. He also took copies, which he subsequently returned on my Archivistor;[598] showing him that to <u>copy</u> documents submitted for perusal was a breach of confidence. It is curious that in his letter he did not use the word <u>Lord</u>, which courtesy in England from time immemorial has assigned to Bps, but he addressed me as Rt. Rev. & dear Sir: yet he is the V. Pres. of the College & has about 50 of my students under his care. If they are similarly brought up it must not be surprising if in youthful heat they occasionally deny to us even the scanty title which his mature age is willing to concede. I was rather suurprised that he asked to see the papers: for it was not <u>my</u> papers, but <u>his</u> own that he told Card. B. he wished to see before giving an answer.

In spite of my longing for peace I seem destined never to obtain it: for I have recently received a letter from Dr. Cornthwaite, informing me that he has made a claim at Rome for the Elston fund, which, to say the least, is [*one word illegible* – ? *factious*], for he has carried the case to Rome without even telling me previously that he had a claim, so that he could not tell whether I was willing to allow it or not.

The division of funds was made on the increase of Vicars Apostolic in 1840, so that it claims a prescription of 20 years. Elston who established the fund was a Lancashire man, & he left the fund for ecclesiastical education with a preference for his family, also Lancashire; but because he died in Yorkshire, Dr. Cornthwaite claims the fund for Beverley. He alleges the case of Crathorne,[599] a Yorkshire man, who established a fund that was adjudged to Lancashire, <u>because</u>, Dr. C. says, he served a Lancashire Mission: but here Dr. C. has committed an error which has led him to advance a false claim: for I have papers to show that the Crathorne fund was adjudged to Lancashire not because he served the Mission there, but because he himself directed that it should be exclusively under the direction of the officials in Lancashire; so that the case of Crathorne offers no parallel. Martini, I believe, has all the papers on the Elston fund: for some years ago, Dr. Newsham as Pres: of Ushaw tried to compel my Vicar General, his co-trustee, to sign a general order for the dividends of the stock composing the Elston fund to be paid over to the College. It was part of Dr. Newsham's general scheme to get control over all educational moneys here, so that he might compel us, even if we had a College of our own, to educate our students at Ushaw.

I fear Barnabò is not with us in the Synod question, notwithstanding his fair promises. Dr. Manning could tell you about his writing to me to explain some matter about the Card: but I could not receive it as he expressly told me that he had no authority to do it, & he is greatly in error if he thinks that such like matters at all affect my line of conduct towards the Cardinal. Our attitude is entirely one of self defense [*sic*]. Will you be good enough to tell Powell Ed: that I don't care about Moroni's Dictionary:[600] if purchased at sale, it can be resold & I will pay [the] difference, for carriage etc. is so heavy that I don't care to incur it for a still incomplete work. I shall be glad to give any information about the larger question you may want. Dr. Vaughan has left for Rome I hear.

With every best wish affectionately Yrs A. Goss.

---

597   Ullathorne was in Rome on behalf of the bishops in early 1862 over the trusts and the bishops' being allowed to act within English law, and Wiseman's primatial authority; see Champ, *William Bernard Ullathorne*, 266–71. During the visit Ullathorne had offered his resignation, which the pope refused to accept; *ibid.*, 267–8.

598   *Decreta* uses *archivista*.

599   Probably Francis Crathorne, of the Northern District, 1762–1822.

600   Moroni's Dictionary: *Dizionario di erudizione storico-ecclesiastica da S. Pietro ai nostri giorni: compilazione di Gaetano Moroni romano*. Moroni (1802–83), published the 103-volume dictionary 1840–61 at Venice, in a compact edition of only fifty-one volumes.

337.   *Circular to several Bishops* [*in pencil*]   *7 April 1862*   *5/4/299*
            "V.G. of Liverpool & Card.W: Copy of correspondence"
My dear Lord,
My Vicar General, Prov. Cookson, has lately had a correspondence with His Eminence Card. Wiseman, which I submit for your perusal, as illustrating the anomalous position which we are made to occupy with reference to Propaganda, from the fact of H.E. acting as one of its S[acred] Cong[regation] & as our Archbp. The letter in which he made the statements complained of was addressed by him to Prop. & referred to a claim of no less a sum than £18,000. In that letter he not only attacked myself, my V.G. & my clergy, but he also prejudiced my claim by assuring the S.C. that he had many documents which would conduce to a speedy decision & that there were irrefragable proofs of matters which, as the issue shows, were incapable of proof. This language was that of a partisan, but Prop. would receive his report as that of an unprejudiced Archbp. who, as a member of their own body & past judge of the case would be naturally considered as beyond the reach of partiality. The effect of his representation was shown in the fact that, tho' we afterwards obtained a verdict in our favour, our agent, on his first arrival, met with anything but an agreeable reception. What is my case today may be your Lordship's tomorrow & I think we ought to have some protection against the secret agency at work in matters connected with

our administration, which, whilst never appearing among the adverse pleadings, may quietly influence the minds of the judges, as emanating from one of their own body unsuspected by his very office of partiality. I remain ever Yrs. Alex. Goss

338. *Rt. Rev. Bp. Ullathorne*[601]   *7 April 1862*   *5/4/300*
                    Meeting of the Bps etc.

My dear Lord,

I am surprised that Card. W. who is capable of sustaining a position on high ground, should condescend to such miserable shifts as he has lately had recourse to. The H.S. is no longer guided in its intercourse with Eng. Bps. by overt acts & statements, but by secret communication at which we cannot get, often on the grounds of privileged documents.[602] Even at our meetings, when H.E. has alleged commission from the H.S. to commit certain matters to the Bps, he has never read such commission. In the dispute with his Chap. we were asked to do one thing at the meeting, another at the Synod. In his dispute with his Coadjutor, Dr. E. was not allowed to see a <u>single statement</u> put forward by him. In his attack on my V.G., on me and on the Clergy of my Diocese he shelters himself under privileged communications. At our last meeting I had an assurance given me by his V.G. that nothing involving my feelings or my D. was to be brought forward, & one day was consumed in a defence against my supposed attacks on him in Rome, during which he alleged a petition, which was <u>not</u> presented. We meet in London away from our advisers & without documents often necessary for the matter under discussion, whereas he has a numerous staff of officials & papers to hand. In fact our liberty is gone, & not only so, but he seems, by the reports mysteriously put in circulation, that he wants to let the world know that he has us under his feet. My opinion is that if again asked to meet we should decline, contenting ourselves with replying 'non expedit'. By today's Post I send to Dr. B. [*of Menevia*] my V.G's case with a request to forward it to you. When read, please to send it to Dr. B. of Salop. If H.E. triumphs over us now, we are obliterated from the hierarchy of the Church & are in a worse position than under the Vicariates: for instead of having 8 independent VV.AA. we shall have 12 VV.GG., under H.E. as representative of Prop. Ever truly Yrs. A.G.

---

[601] This is a particularly strongly worded letter; a month earlier, writing to Bishop Brown of Menevia, Goss had spoken of the Cardinal as a 'certain party who cannot be propitiated but by having the hierarchy prostrate before him' (7 March 1862, 5/4/276).

[602] In fact the attitude of Propaganda towards Wiseman was not at all favourable at this time; see Champ, *William Bernard Ullathorne*, 266.

339. *Rt. Rev. Bp. Cornthwaite   14 April 1862*   *5/4/304*
"Chadwick – Hornby"

My dear Lord,

I have been from home & hence your letter has lain unanswered, for tho' business letters are, under such circumstances, sent to the Vic: Gen: yet when he is not able to deal with them they are reserved till my return unless demanding immediate attention.

When I wrote about Mr. J. Chadwick I was not aware that he had accepted a canonry, otherwise I should have waived my claim till such time as change of circumstances might have made the claim look more seemly. Should his heart ever yearn to his quasi-native county or his friends seek his return to it, I shall hope that the matter will meet with favourable attention, meanwhile let it sleep.

Mr. Garstang seems to have put Mr. Gibson into a bad humour.[603] Every new incumbent seems to turn a wistful eye on Mr. Gibson's farm, from the accident of its being situate in Yorkshire. The donor, however, was Lancashire, & should a mission ever arise between Hornby & Lancaster, I believe it would have a claim to part of the rest. As Mr. Gibson says, the matter was sifted before, & Dr. Briggs, to whom I forwarded Mr. Gibson's statement, was satisfied: it will be somewhere among his papers. With regard to the Cong: [*sic*] it is understood that they go to the nearest or most accessible chapel unless the Bp. shall rule otherwise. If they are far away from any chapel, then the Bps settle by agreement which of the nearest priests shall have care of them, regard being had to facility of access, &c. The Pt. attending them must have faculties from the Bp. in whose Diocese they are, & the people will have to follow the regulations of that D. as to fasting &c.

I hope to see you at Ripon, meanwhile I remain ever Yrs truly Alexr. Goss.

---

603   Rev. George Gibson, 1806–1875, missionary in Africa 1842–46; served at Hornby after Lingard, 1851–75. Rev. Robert Garstang, 1808–69, was of the Beverley Diocese.

340. *Rt. Revd. Bp. Ullathorne, Birmingham   16 April 1862   5/4/308*
"Meeting in Low Week"

My dear Lord,

After the abuse which H.E. has made of our meetings by forcing on us explanations of his conduct, which were, in reality, attacks on our own, & by giving his own colouring of them at Rome, I don't see how we can meet, with due regard to our self respect. Our consenting to meet him would be interpreted at Rome as a submission to his influence & as an augury of our willingness to accept <u>any</u> solution of the Trust question. I believe that after matters have passed the Cong: they are toned down in Prop: so as to be made palatable to Eminent sensibility. Would not our meeting be interpreted as a confirmation of the rumour that we had been beaten? I shall limit my reply to thanking H.E. for the honour of the invitation to dine which I should have accepted had circumstances allowed me to be in London in Low Week; but I will write any answer that may meet with the general approbation.[604] I think it would be well if your Lordship were to see Dr. Brown of Menevia, so that a common form of letter might be agreed upon. I wrote to the other Bps. omitting to them the sentence following approbation.

Ever truly Yrs in Xt. A.G.

---

[604] Goss wrote similar letters to Brown and Clifford on the same day; see also the next letter. Not surprisingly, Wiseman saw through Goss: for Wiseman's comment, see Butler, *Ullathorne*, I, 241. See also letter 342.

341. *Rt. Rev. Bp. Grant* *16 April 1862* *5/4/311*
"Meeting of Bps – Rome – St. Helens Church"

My dear Friend,

Unless compelled by duty to visit Rome, I cannot under existing circumstances make up my mind to undertake the journey from any other motive. I have not yet recovered [from] my last sojourn prolonged too late far into the summer: a repetition of it might prove fatal, & I should not feel justified in undertaking it unless duty demanded the sacrifice. You know the expense my Diocese has been put to by unnecessary delay in settling the claims of various charities on Mr. Sherburns [*sic*] Estate, which they will probably not enforce: you know how the Bps. were treated about the Synod, officially told to answer like school boys the Cardinal's Elenchus, unofficially told not to mind it or to tear it into rags: you know that Archbp. Errington was treated like a dog, & cast forth as a reprobate & is now abroad like a ticket of leave man: & you know that after presenting from my D[iocese] more than £7000 I was hardly thanked & took nothing back to my D. but my independence.[605] I don't like to dwell on these sore subjects, tho' at this sacred time they are not without their moral.

Of course I shall not be in London for Low week: I should think no Bp. will.

How ought I to arrange with the Jesuits about a new Church which they have built out of their own means. It is their own property. They are willing to take cura animarum, but I doubt how far they will want to pledge themselves. I have a claim on them because they opposed the Passionists – their neighbours – building to supply the same district, & by their building I am precluded. I want the basis of a fair, friendly & honourable agreement as recommended by the 2nd Synod.[606]

Wishing you by anticipation the Paschal joys, in which Dr. F. joins me, I remain Ever yrs afftly A.G.

---

605   Goss had visited Rome in person and presented an address of support signed by over 53,000 people and a staggering sum in excess of £7,000 (£1,000 of which came from 'the widow Stapleton'); on his return he wrote to pass on to the people the pope's thanks and blessing, but clearly had been disappointed by his reception. But his support continued: in February 1868 he sent another £1,295 12s 7d; Barnabò sent a fulsome letter of thanks: the Holy Father was most grateful, and it was a clear sign of devotion to the Holy See (AAL, S1/3/A/15). In May of the same year, he sent another £650 (see APF, *Anglia*, 17, fols 638, 670, 746).

606   Holy Cross, St Helens, was built by the Jesuits as a chapel of ease to Lowe House; it opened in May 1862 and became a separate mission in 1866, remaining in Jesuit hands until 1932. The Passionists were at nearby Sutton (St Anne's). See Bridge, *The Lowe House Story*. Lowe House remained a Jesuit parish until 1980. The Second Synod had dealt with the relations between Regulars and the bishops concerning church property and its transfer; see *Decreta*, 101, section 7; this stressed the need for a 'clear agreement' to avoid trouble and possible scandal.

---

342.   [*Card. Wiseman*]   *18 April 1862*   *5/4/316*
My dear Lord Cardinal,
I wish to thank your Eminence for your kind invitation to dine with you in Low week, but as circumstances do not allow me to be in London on that occasion I shall not have the pleasure of meeting my brethren or the honour of dining with your Eminence.[607]

Wishing your Eminence by anticipation the Gaudia Paschalia, I remain
Your devoted Servt. in Xt. Alexander Goss.

---

607   A similar letter of the following year, 28 March 1863, claimed Goss had 'too severely tried an iron constitution, had not said Mass for a week & must rest'.

---

343.   *Very Rev. Dr. Corless, Cottam   4 May 1862   Add.Lttrs, 43–4*
"Biennial Retreat"
Very Rev. dear Sir,
I am in receipt of your letter of May 1st. & regret to find that you allow your feelings to overpower your judgment. It is not my intention to argue with you, nor demand proof of the charges brought in your letter not so much against me, as against persons in every part of my Diocese whom you accuse on what you seem to consider good authority of carrying to me idle & unjust reports as truths, & you call those around me, – placed around me, let me observe, by my Predecessor – sycophants guilty both of giving bad advice & doing evil things. These are weighty accusations & should be sustained by weighty proof to save you from the penalties inflicted by the canons against those guilty of defamation. As far as I am

personally concerned I forgive you all, as I have forgiven much before, therein following the example of my amiable Dean;[608] but I have to request that such like charges & insinuations be not repeated.

As the Synod of Oscott requires that priests should once in two years make a spiritual Retreat,[609] I beg to be informed when, where & under whom you made your last retreat; & if you have not made one within two years I beg to have forwarded to me a copy of the letter or document so exempting. I am aware that you once made application to me; it may be oftener, but duty compels me now to make inquiry.

With every best wish I remain truly Yrs in Xt. Alexander Goss. [cont'd overleaf, p. 44]

Your denial of denouncing the conduct of my Vicar General & Treasurer as that of highwaymen I consider equivalent to withdrawal of the charge; for of your having made it there can be no manner of doubt; for you made it to me at St. Augustine's, & it was your making it that made me display what you considered somewhat of excitement [sic]. If you will again read my letters you will find that they leave no doubt of your having made the charge in my presence: I did not give you to understand that the matter had been brought under my notice by a third party. A.G.

---

[608]   Richard Gillow of Fernyhalgh.

[609]   *Decreta*, 30, section 7: *Cum devotionis fervor facile refrigescat, et de mundano pulvere, ut ait S. Leo, oporteat etiam religiosa corda sordescere, singuli sacerdotes teneantur, quoque saltem biennio, exercitia spiritualia, quae episcopi providebit, adire.* Trans: 'Since the fervour of devotion easily cools and, as St Leo says, even religious hearts are necessarily soiled by the dust of the world, individual priests are bound, at least every two years, to attend spiritual exercises which the bishop will arrange.'

344.   *Very Rev. Can. Fisher, Gt Cosby*   10 May 1862   *Add.Lttrs 45*
St. Augustine's, Preston

My dear James,

Inclosed I send you a letter from Mr. Hines to be laid by you, if the V.G. be absent, before Chap. I have desired him to forward to you fuller information.

Dr. Corless, whose insolence is past bearing with, seems to consider himself authorised from his age, to spend what money he likes, fixing it as a debt on the Mission or Diocese. He has £300 from the Diocese: of this he says – falsely says – that £200 was <u>given</u> him by the V.G: the other £100 he <u>presumes</u> must remain as a debt on Cottam. He says he has spent £53 of his own in building gig house & back kitchen to the school house, intending to <u>give</u> the same at his death to the school, on payment of £1 a year ground rent: he has also borrowed money to complete the outside of the Church. In all this he is acting without any warrant from me.

As he again applies for an order to have paid to him the interest which he says has been witheld [*sic*], I want you to write to him to say that you have been instructed by me to say that, with the exception of what is due to him for masses or obligations, no money or interest will be paid until he has furnished a current account of what has been spent on the repairs & alterations of Cottam, & that such statement must be accompanied by the vouchers, so that the accounts may be audited: moreover that, if he wants a grant from the Diocese or Mission fund, he must make the application in the usual way, omitting from his letter all personalities, as it will have to be laid before the Commissioners whose advice the Bp is accustomed to follow in the distribution of that fund.

He is advising Mr. Jas. Teebay to make over the Dun Cow Rib Estate to the President of Ushaw College.[610] I am going on Monday to Weld Bank for a few days.

With every best wish sincerely Yrs in Xt. Alexr. Goss.

---

610   The intriguingly named Dun Cow Rib was a farm near Preston which became an Ushaw property; see 'College Land', *Ushaw Magazine* 62 (1952), 5–6.

345.   *V. Rev. Fr. Allanson P.O.S.B.[sic]*   *4 June 1862, Belle Isle,*
                                              Bowness   *Add.Lttrs 55*

My dear Fr. Provincial,

I have come here to spend a few days with Mrs. Dunn, a lady from Liverpool, a circumstance which will account for my not having earlier acknowledged the letter in which you acquainted me that Mr. Tyrer & Mr. Corlett[611] have changed places. Tho' I have from time to time had remarks made to me regarding Mr. Tyrer, as he knows, yet I never received any communication from members of the Standish family & did not even know that Mr. Lionel acted in what concerned the Estate.

Considering Mr. Tyrer's age & habits I doubt whether he will be equal to the duty at Hindley; it seems to me that the congregation mostly poor needs a young, active, & systematic priest who will be able to work the new schools effectively. Mr. Tyrer is somewhat excitable, & I should fear that difficulties may arise between him & his new flock, for Mr. Corlett was not without his troubles. Perhaps it may seem premature to make these remarks; but I know that you like me to state frankly my impressions, tho' I should like them to be considered rather private than official, in as much as I should not like them to reach Mr. Tyrer.

Letters from Rome inform me that all is quiet & that the Cardinal & the English Bps had arrived.[612]

With every best wish & many thanks for your obliging letter, I remain ever truly Yrs A. Goss

---

611 Richard (Cyprian) Tyrer OSB, 1799–1871; William (Placid) Corlett OSB, 1807–72. Standish family: the chapel/mission was staffed by OSBs to 1873. There is a note in the registers: Mr Corlett 'took possession of the Mission of Standish 7 June 1862', and 'this book was kept from me for two years by my predecessor' signed W. P. Corlett. See A. J. Mitchinson (ed.), *The Registers of Standish Hall Chapel 1742–1884* (Wigan, 2001), 97.

612 Wiseman and the bishops went to Rome in 1862 for celebrations in connection with the canonisation of the Japanese martyrs, but without Goss, who wrote to Propaganda, 4 June, to explain his absence on grounds of the effect of the summer heat on his health (APF, *Anglia*, 16, fol. 580); and see letters 347, 349.

346. *Rev. Mr. Mulkerns, Widness* [*sic*]   4 June 1862   *Add.Lttrs 56*

Dear Rev. Sir,

As the seventy two disciples were sent forth without purse or scrip to commence their Missionary labours, so also do you go forth to establish a Mission at Widness [*sic*] without a house to live or church to preach in or an endowment to live on. I have, however, no fears about your support: for a faithful people will always do their duty to a zealous priest, who resides amongst them & devotes himself heart & soul to their spiritual welfare. But when they have done that, they have done all that can reasonably be expected of them & more than their limited means can well afford. You will have therefore to look elsewhere for the means to erect an humble church & a modest presbytery; but the Diocese is open to you, & the generosity of the Lancashire people has never been known to fail when they were able to work, for they are always willing to set aside a portion of their earnings for the support of religion. Now, however, they cannot do so, for tho' willing to work they can find no employment, & tho' ashamed to beg they are compelled to live on what they have not earned.[613] All England knows our difficulties & therefore to all England you must appeal, yet appeal in a manly way. Do not whine like some who plead their wants in Catholic Journals, but be mindful of your sacred calling & strive not to influence by other motives than those which God has promised to reward.

And that He, who has promised that even a cup of cold water given in the name of a disciple shall not lose a reward, may bless here & hereafter those who come to your help is the prayer of

Yours affectionately in Xt. +Alexander Goss.

NB: Written from Belle Isle, Windermere, tho' dated from St. Edward's, as my known residence.

---

613 The 'cotton famine' caused by the American Civil War.

347.   *Most Rev. Archbp. Errington   1 July 1862*   *5/4/340*
"Bishops address [*sic*], etc."

My dear Grace,

1o. Will you rusticate in the Isle of Man for a month? I send you Mr. Carr's letter. I purpose going over the 13th or 22nd of July: I should like a week or a fortnight at Port Erin.

2o. Dr. Grant was not telegraphed for to Rome. In addition to the printed summons English wrote to say, when sending dispensation, that at Propag: he found that I was expected: to Dr. Grant he wrote to say that Rinaldini[614] said offence would be given in high quarters if we did not go.

3o. I fear Dr. Grant's officious good nature would originate a document like the inclosed, which I had hoped to escape. In fact one motive – if any were needed besides the heat – why I did not wish to go to Rome was, that I expected an address would be voted, not such an address as the Bps really thought best, but such as the officiousness of a few, who expected by increased influence to reap the fruit of the act, would elaborate; & such, if we may believe statements in the papers seems to have been the fact. Now that Dr. Grant has brought us into this bother I see no remedy but to sign; & if those sign who have ceased connection with the hierarchy of England, or never had it, I dont [*sic*] see why you were not invited. For any thing that has appeared to the contrary, you might have asked to be relieved from a burdensome duty. Not to sign might be used against you, tho' you were not asked; to sign reveals your presence, an unwelcome one to those who must have the consciousness of the wrong they have done. In any case, please to read & post it, not stamping it. I go on the 8th to Everingham[615] for 3 or 4 days.

With every best wish sincerely & affectionately Yrs in Xt. A.G.

---

614   Achille Rinaldini: an 'officialis' at Propaganda. In the event, Barnabò wrote, on 24 July, accepting Goss's excuse and saying the Holy Father was pleased with his letter and its declaration of loyalty, etc. (APF, *Lettere*, 353, 1862).

615   Everingham: home of the recusant Constable family, Yorks; see Kelly, *English Catholic Missions*, 170.

348. [*Circular to the clergy*]   *2 July 1862*   *5/4/341*[616]

Rev. & Dear Sir,

On all sides I am told, that a continuance of ungenial weather will not only injure the prospects of the farmer, but will endanger the produce of the land & raise the price of food. Now, if scarcity of food be added to the absence of employment, I need not tell you that famine & fever may make the land desolate. You will be pleased, therefore, to discontinue the prayer *Pro quacumque necessitate*, & in its stead say the prayers <u>Ad repellendas</u> <u>tempestates</u>: <u>A domo tua</u>: until the harvest is gathered.[617]

I take advantage of this opportunity to remind you of the obligation of attending a Retreat, at least every second year, & to inform you that the Redemptorist Fathers of Bishop Eton have kindly consented to open their home to the Secular clergy from Monday the 28th of July till Saturday the 2nd of August. The erection of commodious apartments enables them to admit twenty-six priests without interference with the convenience of their own congregation. If you intend to avail yourself of the opportunity thus afforded of fulfilling the injunctions of Synod (I Con. Prov. XXIV, 7o) you will please to notify your intention to the Rev. Edmund Vaughan, the Rector of Bishop Eton;[618] if you do not intend to be present, you will be pleased to inform me by letter [when] & where you made your last spiritual Retreat.

Commending myself to the prayers of yourself & flock, I beg to remain

Sincerely & affectionately Yrs in Xt. +Alexander Goss.

---

[616] There are two letters with no. 5/4/341 – the other is to Rockcliff the Liverpool printers, ordering 150 copies of this circular and sending a cheque for £20.

[617] Replace the Occasional Prayer 'For any necessity' with the one 'For driving away tempests' that begins 'From thy house'.

[618] Edmund Vaughan CSSR, 1827–1908; uncle of Cardinal Vaughan and one-time Provincial of the Redemptorists. On clerical retreats see n. 609.

349. *Rt. Rev. Bp. of Shrewsbury*   *14 July 1862*   *5/4/355*

     Rambler – Pope's address.   Confidential

My dear Lord

What next? I suppose you have received Cardinal Barnabò's instructions about pastoralising the Rambler, a sure plan to rekindle the Gallican spirit among Catholics, to alienate the Converts & to bring down the whole Prot. Press upon us. Base as the spirit of the Rambler has been for some time, has it exceeded the freedom of discussion formerly exercised by the Schools on much more serious & holy subjects? Is it sinful to blame the administration of the Pontifical states – *pontificia ditionis administratio*?[619] The Periodical censured is now defunct, dead & buried; why resuscitate it? If it has been bad so long, why did not Card. W. in whose Diocese it was published by a Cath. Publisher, forbid its issue? If Rome has thought it necessary to censure it, why has it not done so in its own name? Why throw the odium & responsibility on us? Is it not unusual to prescribe to Bps to issue pastorals on particular subjects? Does it act so with France & Germany? If not, why are we treated so exceptionally? Prov. Synods are never set aside unless they contain enactments contrary to faith or morals or the admitted discipline of the Church: but ours has been set aside or squashed or questioned;

like a set of school boys we have been ordered to send up our themes to Prop: and now we are ordered to issue pastorals on a given theme within a given time! Verily are we anything better than V.Gs? Does Talbot or Manning or Card. B. govern our dioceses? We certainly do not. Dr Cornthwaite tells me that the Pope <u>commands</u> the Eng. Bps. to oblivion [*sic*] & bury the past, & he <u>wishes</u> them to continue their meetings![620] So we are where we were, unless we make a stand & exercise our rights as Bps. by refusing obedience to any but official acts & commands. I am told that Card. B. says the Prop. can do no more in Sherburne's business if Ushaw will not obey.   Ever Yrs AG.

(*PS at top of letter:*) Let me know what news you have gleaned about the affairs at Rome, i.e. funds or College question, money affairs, the Pope to the Bps. or Card. B. on you & me for absence.

---

619   Trans: 'the papal exercise of authority'.

620   Pius IX had used the occasion of the celebrations in Rome to reprimand the English Bishops over their dissensions and attitude to Wiseman (Butler, *Ullathorne*, I, 247–8).

350.   *Rev. S. Walsh*[621]   *5 August 1862, Douglas*   Add.Lttrs 59

Dear Rev. Sir,

I did not answer the letter addressed to me from Kingstown as I saw no benefit to be gained by writing about home duties to a priest not at home. Your letter of July 31st has taken me by surprise as I understood that you were lying at Kingstown in so precarious a state that your medical advisers thought you unfit to return for Sunday's duty.

As soon as Canon Fisher can dispense with the services of Mr. Davison[622] I will forward you my instructions regarding the new mission. I am utterly at a loss to understand how your present position can be seriously painful and impossible to be longer endured. Your duties are the same as when Mr. Kelly was at St. Alban's and I am much disappointed in Mr. Seed[623] to find that he has rendered the discharge of those duties painful and unbearable. It is what I did not expect, but I will examine into the matter on my return. Meanwhile wishing you every blessing I remain Sincerely Yours in Xt. Alexander Goss.

---

621   See n. 213 above and letter 355.

622   Robert Davison, 1829–96, o. Dublin, June 1862, a few months at Great Crosby, then St Alban's, Liverpool, to 1868.

623   Richard Seed, 1825–77, r. St Alban's, 1862–71. Canon, 1868.

351.   *Rev. Mr. Trappes,*[624] *Hull   7 August 1862, St. Mary's, Douglas,*
                           IoM   Add.Lttrs 59 [sic, but should be 60]

My dear Mr. Trappes,

I beg to acknowledge the receipt of your favour of Aug 2 in which you inform me that St. Cuthbert's Society has resolved to devote £35 per an. to the education of an ecclesiastical student at St. Cuthbert's & that the Council has kindly offered me the first presentation. I beg that you will as their hon. Sec. accept my best thanks & present the same to the members of the Council in the name of myself & my Diocese.

I will forward the resolutions to my Vicar General to whom I have entrusted the department of ecclesiastical education in the Diocese & I doubt not that he will gladly avail himself of the kind offer made by St. Cuthbert's Society.

Wishing you every blessing, I remain with many thanks, Very sincerely Yrs in Xt.

Alexander Goss

---

[624]   Michael Trappes, Beverley Diocese, 1797–1873. For this Old Boys Society, see Milburn, *History of Ushaw College*, 220–1, 315.

352.   *Rev. P. Laverty   8 August 1862, Douglas   Add.Lttrs 61*
                  (Regulations for Deacon Wilson[625])

Dear Rev. Sir,

I have always been of opinion that young ecclesiastics of suitable ability should be employed to teach both at the Institute and St. Edward's, a plan that is followed in all other colleges both at home and abroad, secular as well as regular. I am glad to find that the Vicar has been able to make a commencement with the Institute and I doubt not that Mr. Wilson's labours will be alike beneficial to himself and the Institute.

I feel however that in committing him to your charge I am placing on you a grave responsibility and I therefore deem it my duty to lay down the following regulations for your guidance.

1o. Mr. Wilson must not exercise the office of deacon at any church but the Institute and Pro-Cathedral without leave of the Vicar General.

2o. He may preach at the Institute, but his discourses must be written, and must be submitted to your supervision, a practice always followed at Ushaw with those not in priest's orders.

3o. He will take his walk or exercise at the times allowed by rule, which are I believe from 4 to 6 o'ck: on school days, and the afternoon of play days. In these walks he will be accompanied by one of the other professors or yourself, and on these occasions he cannot take refreshments nor call at any house without your leave. But it must be understood that he is not allowed to dine out without the Vicar's permission.

4o. Anyone who calls to visit him he must see in the common parlour, not in his own room; and the call of such visitor must be announced by the porter to you before it is communicated to him.

5o. He will rise and retire to rest and attend church and schools at the hours fixed by rule.

6o. His salary will be fixed by the Vicar General and must cover all expenses.

I need not say that his position, somewhat isolated, must bespeak for him kind and affectionate treatment. No expense has been spared in his education and I doubt not that he will communicate to others efficiently and zealously some portion of that learning with which in England, Germany and Italy, his mind has been stored.

With every best wish I remain sincerely Yours in Xt. Alexander Goss.

625 Thomas Wilson, b. 1838, edu. St Edward's and Rome; o. May, 1863; chaplain to Brownlow Hill workhouse, where he caught typhus fever and died, April 1864. See Burke, *Catholic Liverpool*, 161; Plumb quotes from Goss about Wilson's overload of work (*'Found Worthy'*) and E. Powell (Goss's sec): 'Poor Wilson, his well-known qualities were marred by a self-will and unalterable conviction that he had a special vocation to restrain superiors within due bounds.'

353. *Thomas Kelly Esqr, Freshfield, Nr. Formby*   [*15 August*
                  1862], *Douglas, IoM*   *Add.Lttrs 62–3*

My Dear Sir,

It is now twelve months since you waited upon me at Ince Blundell to represent the insufficient accommodation of the church at Formby which in summer was so oppressive from the heat and crowd that a person not in robust health, was unable to remain through the service. I promised to communicate with you in writing, but have hitherto not done so, because I could not see my way to the erection of a new church in the absence of means and in the precarious state of health of the Rev. Missionary Rector. God, in his own good time, has come to our aid, and it now only remains for us to co-operate with Him, and take our share of the labour. The health of the Rev. Mr. Crowe has somewhat improved, and Mr. Weld Blundell with the traditionary [*sic*] generosity of his family, has promised a donation of £1000 to be given in the year 1863.626

This sum the congregation must endeavour to equal by subscriptions amongst themselves and friends; and as you were kind enough to offer your services, this is to empower you to solicit their charity for that purpose. We must exonerate the incumbent from all personal labour and anxiety, for, though better, he is unequal to the fatigue incident to the erection of a new church. We must not aim at great things but still we must be mindful of the past glories of Formby. Religion has not only

never died out there but has flourished during the darkest days of persecution; and at the beginning of the last century, when the Rev. Edward Molyneux of the Grange, after a long career of missionary labour was found dead on the sands,[627] he had under his care a larger congregation than attend the present church, though both Ince Blundell and Little Crosby were amply supplied with priests. When the subscriptions raised amount to a sufficient sum to be invested, an account had best be opened with some bank – the Union or any other – in Lpool in the joint names of Thomas Weld Blundell Esqr and the Very Rev. Thomas Cookson. Wishing the undertaking every blessing, I remain sincerely Yours in Xt.
+Alexander Goss
Assumption of B.V.M. 1862

---

626 The new church was opened in 1864 on a site donated by Blundell, as well as the gift of £1,000 (Kelly, *English Catholic Missions*). Goss wrote to Crowe on the same day, asking for his moral and financial support, but unfortunately he died on 24 August.
627 Edward Molyneux 1640–1704, at Alt Grange from 1666 to his death; Stonor, *Liverpool's Hidden Story*, 41–2, gives the story of his death, possibly a murder. See also Anstruther, *Seminary Priests*, III, 151.

355. *Rev. S. Walsh, St. Alban's* [*15 August 1862*] *Douglas,*
Isle of Man Add.Lttrs 67–8[628]

Dear Rev. Sir,
Warned by the extention [*sic*] of the docks in the direction of Bootle and by the transference of the timber trade from the south to the north end of the town with the corresponding encrease [*sic*] of the labouring population, I have for some years been endeavouring to provide for the spiritual wants of this new congregation, and have sought for this purpose the advise [*sic*] of the neighbouring clergy as well as of my Chapter; for while wishing to provide for new wants I have been anxious not to peril [*sic*] existing missions. Up to this moment I have been unable to hear of any suitable plot of land on suitable terms, but I have indirectly learnt that one of your future congregation will be likely to come to your aid. Furthermore I am now able to supply your place at St. Alban's and thus give effect to your appointment made more than twelve months ago. I have instituted a commission to mark out the boundaries of the new district, and my wish is that the future church should be erected, as near as possible, in the centre: meanwhile however a room may be opened in any part of the district as a temporary chapel.[629]

I cannot conceal from you that you will find it difficult to raise funds for the erection of a new church: for unfortunately the charity of the faithful is not always directed to the most necessary or useful objects. Go forth however hopefully, and should anyone question the necessity of the undertaking, bid them take their stand on the great road recently constructed to a district unprovided with Catholic teaching, whilst the sects have set up their tabernacles in every direction. Go forth cheerfully and make your quest from house to house, for you will not gain what you do not strive to earn, and those are striving with much toil to make a living in the general scramble have neither time or [*sic*] inclination to attend to magniloquent appeals reaching them through the columns of a newspaper. You have a hard but a blessed duty before you. Do not shrink from it; but gird up your loins and manfully shew yourself equal to the occasion.

Wishing you God's blessing on yourself and your labours, I remain sincerely Yours in Christ,

+Alexander Goss.   Assumption of the B.V. 1862.

---

628   On Walsh, see n. 213. It is not at all clear why Goss should have written two letters to him on the same day (see letter 356); the second has an undertone of possible rebuke of Walsh's conduct.

629   This was St Alexander's, Bootle, on St John's Road (originally called St John's until 1864; now demolished); Kelly (*English Catholic Missions*) says designed by Pugin and opened in 1867 (an old hay-loft had served as the first chapel).

356.   *Rev. S. Walsh*   [*15 August 1862*], *Douglas. Isle of Man*
Add.Lttrs 70

Dear Rev. Sir,

Herewith I enclose the commission to start a new mission which, however, you will not put in execution till the arrival of Mr. Davison at St. Alban's. For the first time you will soon find yourself alone. New responsibilities will arise. New difficulties will surround you, and in the midst of your trials you will find yourself unsustained by the example of a confrere. You will no longer share with another the duty of being a model to your flock. To you they will look not only for lessons in the pulpit and confessional, but for an example in the discharge of the daily duties of life, at home and abroad. If you wish to win their respect you must be punctual in church, attentive to sick-calls, frequent in the confessional and remember that early rising depends upon going early to rest. A priest is never unobserved, and though reports may not reach him, yet comments are freely made on his conduct. Be careful not to provoke them. Let your place of residence be your home and when wanted do not have to be sought for in the house of strangers or beyond the limits of your own district. The presence of a priest amongst his flock is to them what the sun is to the earth. The blessing of God will surround the house of prayer, and if his mass, his office, and his meditation are offered up amongst them, they will bring down greater blessings than that precarious help which he may fancy he will obtain by visits amongst strangers. Wishing you every blessing in the discharge of your new duties and again reminding you of the injunctions of the xxiv and xxv chapters of the First Synod of Oscott,[630] which I commend to your perusal and observance, I remain sincerely Yours in Xt.

   Alexander Goss. Aug. 15th 1862.

---

[630] *Decreta*, 28–34: xxiv: *De Vita et Honestate Clericorum*; xxv: *De Rectoribus Ecclesiarum*.

357. Rev. *T. Spencer* *15 August 1862, St. Mary's Rectory, Douglas*
Add.Lttrs 71
(New church)

Dear Rev. Sir,

Having carefully weighed the objections urged by you to the opening of a new mission between St. Alban's and St. James', and having on different occasions submitted your reasons to the consideration of my Chapter, I have come to the conclusion, in which they agree, that considering the wants of the district, and the probable encrease [*sic*] of population, such a church is a necessity. In fact I stand reproved indirectly at least by the zealous Fathers of St. Augustine's,[631] who judging from many years' delay that the plan was abandoned, found themselves bound to accept the invitation to occupy the neglected vineyard. I have therefore to request that on Wednesday the 20th at eleven o'clock you will attend a meeting at St. Alban's for the purpose of determining the limits of the new district. Bring a peaceful and conciliatory spirit to the labour enjoined. Wishing you every blessing I remain sincerely Yours in Xt. Alexander Goss

---

[631] St Augustine's: a Benedictine mission, known as the 'martyrs' church' because planned as a memorial to the Benedictines who had died in 1847; opened in 1849; see Burke, *Catholic Liverpool*, 95–6. A later letter (Add.Lttrs 83) of 23 August, to Spencer, praises the spirit of his report but restates Goss's desire that the church should be in the centre of the new district although this is not in the plan of the boundaries.

358. *Rev. T. Kelly*[632] *15 August 1862, St. Mary's Rectory, Douglas*
Add.Lttrs 72
(District of New Church)

Dear Rev. Sir,

I am instructed by the Bishop to request your attendance at eleven o'ck. on Wednesday the 20th at St. Alban's, in order to preside at a commission which His Lordship has named for the purpose of assigning the boundaries of the new mission to be opened between Athol St. and Marsh Lane. Your duty will be to draw up a paper signifying the limits approved of or recommended by the Commission. Allow free discussion, prevent the use of personalities, and let the discussion be confined to the matter in hand, as it is no part of the commissioners' duty to express opinions as to whether it is advisable or not advisable to establish such a mission. Preserve a kind and conciliatory tone whatever observations may be addressed to you: your example cannot fail to command imitation.

I remain Dear Rev. Sir, Yrs. sincerely in Xt. John Wallwork[633]

---

632   Thomas Kelly, 1818–88, r. St James', Bootle, 1861–87.
633   John Wallwork, 1825–91, Goss's first appointment to the Chapter in 1856, currently at the pro-cathedral. He wrote all these Isle of Man letters, mostly signed by Goss.

359.   *Rev. J. Phelan*[634]   *20 August 1862, St. Mary's Rectory,*
Douglas   *Add.Lttrs 75–6*

Dear Rev. Sir,

Some time ago I was much pained to hear it remarked that St. Patrick's had lost its old spirit, as evidenced not only by a less frequentation of the sacraments among the people, but by the manner of life among the clergy. Priests of a spirit widely different from that cherished by the late Canon Kenrick are said to visit at the house, and the clergy of the house are said frequently to spend their evenings with members of the congregation, in whose house Canon Kenrick was never known to eat or drink. I have not heard of any excess, but it has been lamented that St. Patrick's, so long the bulwark of a right clerical spirit, should be fast losing its once eminent position. I must look to you for the correction of this degeneracy and hope that you will not allow St. Patrick's to be considered a party house, or to be the rendesvous [*sic*] of men of exaggerated opinions. Discourage intercourse between your clergy and young persons of the opposite sex, whether school teachers or members of confraternities, lest it degenerate into a familiarity, which may result in scandal or a greater evil. I make these remarks advisedly, with the hope that I may not be compelled to suppress existing associations or confraternities, whose members are not always mindful of the holy object of their institution. I hear with fear of priests being the attraction on gala days of young women's societies when I learn that young men are not always kept sober on their annual excursion. I do not know the custom of St. Patrick's with reference to the street door but in face of chapters xxiv and xxv of the First Synod of Oscott, you ought not to leave the house accessible by a latch-key, after eleven o'clock at night: whoever wishes to enter after that hour should be compelled to ring the bell.

I hope you are pushing the matter of the new mission of Mount

Carmel[635] vigorously forward as it is a cause of complaint, that whilst the north end is yearly founding new missions, the south remains comparatively inactive. Wishing you every blessing I reamin sincerely Yours in Xt.

+Alexander Goss.

---

[634] Patrick Joseph Phelan, Irish, 1825–1890; originally o. for Nottingham, moved to Liverpool in 1852; curate at St Patrick's from 1852 and rector 1860–64; after illness returned as c. at St Anthony's to 1867, then retired. See Add.Lttrs 82 (23.8.62) from Goss's secretary Wallwork (in the Isle of Man with Goss) to him: Goss was very angry that Phelan had taken these criticisms to apply to the clergy of St Patrick's when they were clearly meant for Phelan himself and he recommended its contents to his 'serious meditation'. (O'Neill, *St Anthony's*, has two priests named Phelan at St Anthony's at different times, but they were the same person.)

[635] Our Lady of Mount Carmel, High Park Street, Liverpool; founded in 1865 with a chapel above a schoolroom; the present church was opened in 1878. See M. Hewlett, *Centenary of the Opening of Our Lady of Mount Carmel Church* (Liverpool, 1978).

360. *Rev. W. Johnson*[636] *20 August 1862, St. Mary's Rectory,*
 Douglas   Add.Lttrs 77–9

Dear Rev. Sir,

I fear that you find the mission of Copperas Hill too laborious for your strength, as I cannot otherwise account for your apparent inability to fulfil its duties. The charity of your brethren has forborne to make this manifest, but it has not escaped my own observation. Feeling that it is my duty to watch over the health of my clergy I am anxious that you should for a year try an easier mission, but at the same time I must impress upon you that it is better for us all to die martyrs to our duty, than to prolong an unproductive life by excessive care. We must have a reasonable care for our health, but we must not nurse ourselves as if our only duty was to live – it is better to die in harness than in the stall.

I wish you to try the mission of Poulton in the Fylde,[637] at least for a time: should your health be found equal to its easy duties and your spiritual labours constant and productive, the appointment may become permanent. You will find the house and chapel in excellent repair; and you will find Mr. Orrell reasonable in his proposition for an arrangement about the furniture, for I regret to say that not much belongs to the mission. On this matter you will consult with Dean Gillow, but I see no necessity for purchasing more than is strictly requisite. Mr. Ball at the new mission at Westby may wish to purchase a portion of it. I have promised Mr. Orrell to leave him free by the 6th of September. By this appointment you will soon find yourself alone ... [*Here Goss repeats his letter to Walsh, no. 356 above*] ... frequent in the confessional, which must be arranged for such hours that best suit the occupations of an agricultural population, and remember that early rising depends upon going early to rest, and nothing shocks a regular people more than when a priest is unable to get up for mass which they have walked a considerable distance to hear. A priest is never unobserved ... [*again Goss repeats his letter no. 356*].

Procure a 'Liber status animarum' in which to set down every man, woman, and child of your congregation, and endeavour to win back the issue of mixed marriages, if any have fallen away. Make a point of calling upon your people at least four times in the year, but do not let your calls be burdensome: labouring people can never be detained unemployed without injury and subsequent annoyance; and even to prepare a cup of tea takes them from their household duties. Wishing you every blessing in the discharge of your new duties, and again reminding you of the injunctions of the xxiv and xxv chapters of the first Synod of Oscott, which I commend to your perusal and observance, I remain sincerely Yours in Xt. +Alexander Goss.

---

636 William Johnson 1831–85; at Poulton 1862–79; a composer of some fame. See letter 364.

637 Poulton-le-Fylde: an ancient mission, with a new church in 1814. Johnson remained seventeen years.

361. *Copy of Circular to Committee of Cath. Boys' Orphanage*
20 August 1862, St. Mary's Rectory, Douglas. Isle of Man
Add.Lttrs 80–1

Dear Rev. Sir,

I am sorry to find from a letter from the Rev. N. Molloy,[638] that there exists amongst most members of the Committee great apathy as regards the interests pecuniary and disciplinary of the Boys' Orphanage. The recent erection of the Orphanage with the liabilities of the past and the difficulties of the present, require every care, and I trust that until the establishment be in thorough working order, it will experience the benefit of your exertions, which will not be withheld at ordinary or extraordinary meetings. Let two persons deputed, as I previously requested, to visit it, take down the name and age of its inmates, and the names of the parties, if any, that are responsible for the payment of their pension. The contributions of general subscribers should be applied to diminish the amount of pension for each individual, but not in a partial way to exempt favoured individuals from payment. If the priest who sends a boy to the orphanage cannot raise means to pay his pension, it is not possible for the Committee with so many other claims upon them, to raise sufficient to keep twenty or forty of such individuals. Let those who are old enough be bound apprentice and let efforts be made to get situations as errand boys or any suitable occupation for those thought suitable. Be prepared to give the institution a little more time and labour until it is placed in proper working order. Praying that you will really exert yourself in behalf of this charity, I remain sincerely yours in Christ, +Alexander Goss

---

638 Nicholas Molloy: 1832, o. 1858; Fitz-L says he was laicised in 1873, but instead he was excardinated to Newark, New Jersey, and died in Paterson, New Jersey, in 1880, after building a church and school; see O'Neill, *St Anthony's*, 131–9.

362. *Very Rev. Fr. Seed [added later]*   *6 September 1862, Preston*
Add.Lttrs 86

My Dear Father Provincial,
The Preston Guild will have to plead for me as it will have to plead for many others under similar circumstances for not replying earlier to your letter. I am too well acquainted with the exigencies of missionary & religious life to offer any objections to the clergy you propose, particularly as I know that you will in such cases consult the interests of the missions under your care. You will require an active priest to take the place of Fr. Williams:[639] for he leaves a void at St. Walburge's and few will be found in any part of the town that will not regret his departure.

I quite understand the motives that influence you in the proposed changes at Portico & Prescot;[640] but whilst admitting that the proposed arrangement may be best for the interests of their Reverences, as religious, I cannot but consider it disadvantageous to the mission. Residence brings a special blessing with it: where the holy sacrifice is daily offered & prayer & meditation made, God will not be absent. The presence of a priest, like the sun, fertilizes the spot on which he daily shines & hence the Church enforces with so many penalties the residence of both bishops & clergy. I understand the difficulty of the position, but I think on trial you will ultimately be compelled to abandon it. Those who do not live on the Prescot side of Portico will feel that they are a long way off a priest in case of sickness.

Every thing has gone off quietly at the Guild. With every best wish I remain truly Yrs in Xt.
Alexander Goss.

---

639 Thomas Williams SJ, 1818–89; left Preston in 1862 for Chesterfield.
640 On the closing/amalgamation of Religious missions, see Introduction, p. xli and letter 434.

363. [*Canon Fisher*]   *14 September 1862, St. Augustine's, Preston*
Add.Lttrs 87

My Dear Canon Fisher,

I am sorry to find that after all that has been done for the Institute by the public in the form of subscriptions it should still be in arrears. No doubt credit must be given for what has been done, and all the property belonging to it must be taken as a set off to its debts. But there must be a limit. It is not a concern that must be considered to run on for half a century. Each year ought to stand alone, or least three years – the period of Visitation – otherwise if as Missions, e.g. St. Anthony's fell into arrears of payment we should have to credit the years of deficiency with the amount paid off in years of plenty & thus every place would be kept in a floating uncertainty. If the Institute was solvent when the furniture of house & church was bought years ago, it ought not now to be considered a set off against debts of recent years. Mr. Gibson made out the place to be solvent. Mr. Laverty must understand that he must sign on the accts yearly.

With every best wish I remain truly Yrs in Xt. Alexander Goss.

364. [*Mr. Orrell*]   *15 September 1862, St. Augustine's, Preston*
Add.Lttrs 88

My Dear Mr. Orrell,

When I promised to free you by the close of the Ushaw vacation I by no means wished you to understand that I meant you to leave Poulton at that time. I thought I was consulting your own wishes by that arrangement; for as regards myself I should have been glad if you had continued your services amongst us. When I named Mr. Johnson as your successor, I desired him to consult with Dean Gillow about the furniture. Had he done this he would have been saved the little annoyance of his coming to inspect the place in your absence, a pardonable mistake in a man eager to escape from the heavy duties of a town to the easy quiet of a country mission. When there has been made out a list & valuation of the furniture I shall be glad to see it with the hope of its being purchased at least in part for the mission. In my letter to Mr. Johnson I told him he would find the place in excellent order & yourself prepared to deal with him on reasonable terms, for I have ever had a pleasure in saying that no mission was in better repair than Poulton. I shall be glad to have some days notice before you leave in order that I may communicate with Mr. Johnson. I take leave of you with regret, & shall be sorry if any act of mine at any time in my life has influenced you to separate you from a county in which your family bears & has borne for years an honourable distinction. With every best wish for your present & future happiness

I remain sincerely Yours in Xt. Alexander Goss.

365. *Rev. F.A. Dunham,*[641] *All Hallows, Drumcondra*
                                  27 November 1862   *5/4/371*
                                  "Exeat for Religion"

Dear Rev. Sir,

Could you, as our B. Lord once did, survey the harvest which is white for the sickle, but has few to gather it, you would withdraw the request contained in your letter of Nov. 23. In Missionary Countries the line of demarcation between the Secular & Regular Clergy is not great. Both labor [*sic*] side by side in the same field. Let me exhort you then to persevere in your first Vocation, and do not renew your petition unless after years of labor in the vineyard God shall make you feel that he wants you elsewhere. With every best wish I remain, sincerely Yrs in Christ Alexander Goss

---

[641] Francis Augustus Dunham, 1836–1905, o. for the diocese 1863; in charge of the new mission of All Saints, Golborne, to 1870, then emigrated to Australia in 1871. In a letter 5/4/424 of 31 December 1862: Goss insisted: 'if the call [to Religion] … really conveys to you the will of God in this matter, time & change of circumstance will confirm it rather than weaken it … the faithful discharge of the duties of a secular Priest will be the best preservative of your vocation, should the call really be from God.'

366. *Rev. Jas. Nugent*[642]   *10 December 1862*   *5/4/388*
                          "His letter to Major Blundell"

Jimmy, Jimmy,

Your easy pen will get both you & me into trouble, if you do not check it. Major Blundell has sent me your letter, but, I am glad to say, without any unpleasant comments: he only requires the matter to be settled & promises to call upon me about it.

If you had had as much experience as I have had of the gentry, you would find that they are very impatient of strong language: they do not use it in their intercourse with each other. In any case, but particularly when discussing undefined rights, it is best to do it verbally, not in writing, & it is legitimate for you to fall back upon the Bp, tho' I know that in this case you wanted to spare me & prevent any conflict between me and the Major. I am sorry you alluded to the past management of the Mission, as it would raise against you the whole Benedictine body, if Mr Blundell were to show it to them & there is no knowing what a man may do when you drive him into a corner & require from him categorical answers within a given space of time. The Major is really a good fellow, & we must strive to humour him, if it can be done without a sacrifice of principle. If his Father reserved certain rights when he gave the land & the Bp. of the time accepted the reservation, I am powerless. Sir R. Gerard claims a similar reservation at Ashton. He has not surrendered the place to me, but early converted it from a chaplaincy into a Mission, if I rightly understand; but you will err egregiously if you apply to Missions either the name or the rights of parishes. I like outspoken men, they are the only pals I have ever kept; but Jimmy, you must not be too mettlesome.

With every best wish I remain Yrs. in Christ, Alex. Goss

---

642   Nugent was rector at St Mary's, Little Crosby, 1861–63.

367.   *To Edward Challoner Esq.*[643]   *13 December 1862*   *5/4/393*
"Little Sisters of the Poor"

My dear Mr. Challoner,

I have delayed answering your letter until I could make inquiry from the Vicar who was out of town, regarding the statement in Mr. Vidal's[644] letter that I had declined to give my approbation to the introduction of the Sisters of the Poor into Liverpool: for I knew that no such application had been personally replied to by me. I find that the application was forwarded to the Vicar, & that he deferred his concurrence as many of the Charities of the town were seriously embarrassed & that a new candidate for popular favour had little chance of effective support. It is quite impossible, as Mr. Vidal states, that such an institution can be self supporting: for the inmates are generally old & infirm & often bedridden. It is clear therefore that they cannot support themselves, but must be supported by the contributions of others. Now tho' such an institution is a great charity it is not of an imperative necessity as the Poor house is open: whereas it is of necessity to provide a Catholic Reformatory, as otherwise Catholic children will be committed to Protestant Reformatories with the certain shipwreck of their faith. Mt. St. Bernard has not kept faith with us, & hence the Vicar has had to become responsible to the G[irls?] Reformatory for the payment of boys, & I have had to pay £100 out of my Privy Purse on behalf of girls. Meanwhile we have purchased the West Derby Fever Wards & shall have to depend on the purse of the poor for its payment; & the Boys' Orphanage has been partly erected by borrowed money, whilst it cost £800 of [? *arrears*] for the keep of its inmates. You will agree with me that this is not a very cheering prospect for my Christmas Holidays. The Committee of the Orphanage applies to one of our wealthiest firms, representing, I believe, several partners, & received from the whole a donation of £20. If others contribute in like proportion the building will tumble down before it has been paid for. I think therefore that you will with me agree with the Vicar's opinion, that at present it is inexpedient to introduce the Sisters of the Poor.[645]

I remain with every best wish very sincerely Yrs in Xt. Alexander Goss.

---

[643] For Challoner, see n. 93.

[644] Mr Vidal: this may have been Alexander Thomas Emeric Vidal, who died in Clifton, February 1863, where the Little Sisters had opened their first English convent in 1862.

[645] The Little Sisters of the Poor eventually opened a house for the aged poor in Liverpool in 1874 (Burke, *Catholic Liverpool*, 223), first in Hope Street, then in Belmont Road, until closure in 1989.

368. [*Bishop Hogarth*]   [*n.d., but c. 3 February 1863*]
UCPA/M19[646]

My Dear Lord,

I am sorry to hear of Mgr. Newsham's death & still more sorry that the terms in which the announcement is made to me by your Lordship prevent me assisting at his funeral in order that I may testify my personal respect for one under whom I had studied, & the respect of my Diocese for the President of the Common Seminary of the Seven Northern Counties.

I beg to remain, etc. Alexander Goss

---

[646] This single document contains copies of correspondence made by Bp Hogarth. He had written to Goss on 2 February 1863 to tell him of Newsham's death on the previous day; this is a copy of Goss's reply. I have not found the original. Hogarth attached a note: 'To this I of course gave no reply.' On 7 February he wrote to 'the four bishops' to announce the appointment of Newsham's successor, Canon Tate; a copy of Goss's reply follows.

369. [*Bishop Hogarth*]   *13 February 1863*   UCPA/M19

My Dear Lord

We the undersigned Bishops of Salford, Salop & Liverpool have received a communication dated 7 Feby 1863 from your Lordship stating that you have appointed the Very Rev. Canon Tate D.D. to fill the office of President at St. Cuthbert's College Ushaw.

As your Lordship does not state upon what authority you have assumed this power over our common College, the undersigned Bishops must confine their answer to protesting against the validity of the appointment & inform your Lordship that we have written to Rome about this extraordinary Proceeding.

We remain truly yours in Xt. W. Turner, J. Brown, Alex Goss.[647]

---

[647] Again, Hogarth added a note: 'The above are all the communications which have taken place up to this day 16 Feby with the three Bps on this subject.'

370.   *J.B. Aspinall Esq.,*[648] *64 Queen's Garden's [sic] Bayswater,*
London   27 February 1863   5/4/454

My dear Mr. Aspinall,

I am obliged by your favor [sic] including the letter from Mr. Carter,[649] as it shews that you still take an interest in the Diocese of Liverpool, and that the reformation as well as the committal of offenders engages your consideration. Educated Protestants must see that there is a wide difference between Catholics claiming a right to enter jails & workhouses, & the building of Reformatories at their own cost. They claim the former on the ground that the poor in the workhouses and prisoners in jails do not forfeit, either from poverty or crime, liberty of conscience, tho' they may lose or abridge their civil liberties by confinement. But it is quite another matter to be able to erect large & commodious buildings for the reformation of criminals: that depends on their having the means as well as the will.

You remember the transaction which connected us with St. Bernard's. If my wishes had prevailed, & my advice followed, the £2,000 so hardly raised would have been invested in our own Diocese, & not elsewhere. It would be well, as you are in London, to jog the memory of your friend the Cardinal on this matter, for I believe he is Apostolic Visitor, & if he does not choose to act himself, such power prevents anybody else from acting, & so the sore remains open to the great scandal of the public. To secure a footing in the Girls' Sheffield Reformatory I have had to pay £100 of my own pocket. The Diocese of Salford & my own have tried to purchase an abandoned Workhouse near Bolton, but a person, less liberal than Mr. Carter, outbid us through dread of a popish neighbour. Mr. Sydney Turner proposes a ship, but *timeo Danaeos et dona ferentes*,[650] & sailors & devils have much in common. My Chapter meets on the 4th of March, & I will see if it can help me in this embarrassment. I beg to remain Very truly Yrs. Alexander Goss.

---

648   Aspinall was Recorder in Liverpool (Burke, *Catholic Liverpool*, 60 and *passim*). See n. 232 above.
649   The Rev. Thomas Carter was Anglican chaplain to Liverpool Borough Gaol; he had read a paper, 'The Crime of Liverpool', at the 1858 meeting; see n. 363.
650   'I fear the Greeks even when they are bearing gifts.' See n. 182 on reformatory ships.

371.   *Joseph Pyke Esq. 3 Winckley Sq., Preston   10 May 1863*
5/4/466

"Private Oratory renewed"

My dear Mr. Pyke,

I have great pleasure in allowing the transfer of your privilege of having Mass in your little Oratory, originally granted by my Predecessor, & of confirming to your residence in Winckley Sq. the privilege you enjoyed at Penwortham. A long & valued acquaintance with you has taught me that the enjoyment of private privileges only makes you more zealous in sustaining the public burdens.

Hoping that your change of residence may benefit the health of yourself & family, to each member of which, as well as to yourself, wishing every blessing, I remain truly Yrs in Xt. Alexander Goss.

372.   *Circular to Presidents of Conferences*   *5 February 1864*
                                                                    AAL, S1/3/D/3
[*Copperplate; last three lines in Goss's hand*]
Revd. & dear Sir,
There is much to console me in the manner in which our Conferences have been hitherto managed; but there are also some things which require emendation. The decrees of the Second Synod[651] require 1st that every Member shall ['should' *crossed out*] bring answers in writing to each of the questions, whilst the Proponent solves the whole case at length in writing. 2nd **A gravis causa** is required to justify absence, & notice thereof should be given to the Dean, to whom also should be sent a solution of the case, under penalty of being subjected to examination before the renewal of faculties. Now this will have to be put into effect; for those who absent themselves do not always assign the cause, & when assigned, it is not always causa **gravis**, & they seldom send a solution of the case. I wish therefore that this be exacted [*sic – originally* 'enacted', *but* n *changed to* x], & it should be written for by the Dean when neglected. I wish also that the cause of absence should be inserted in the return.

Having had occasion to apply for further information on matters connected with Conferences, I find that no book is kept in some Conferences; Now this is to require that a Book shall be provided by the Conference in which the names of the present, & the excuses of the absent shall be entered, & the first act of each Conference shall be to read the report forwarded to the Bishop, since instances have been known of the report not embodying the decision of the members but simply that of the Proponent. The report forwarded to the Bishop must therefore be an exact transcript of the one in the Conference Book, & it must be forwarded within a week after the meeting.

I shall be glad to have the opinion of the Conference regarding mixed marriages. Some time ago the Holy See forbade them to be celebrated without the leave of the Ordinary: that Decree was published in most Dioceses of England, but for reasons unknown to me was not published by my Predecessor. Let the votes of the Members of Conference be taken and forwarded to me regarding the advisability of publishing that decree in this Diocese.[652] The Status Animarum of each Priest's district, showing the results of mixed marriages, will form the best basis on which to found this opinion.

Wishing you every blessing, I remain truly Yrs in Xt +Alexander Goss

---

651   This was Goss's first synod, held in September 1856; see *Synodi*, 22–5, *De Collationibus*.

652   Most of the clergy were against any stricter regulation of mixed marriages and Goss accepted their views. See Introduction, p. xxx.

373.   *Sir Thomas Hesketh*[653]   *19 March 1864*   *5/4/525*
"Electioneering"

My dear Sir Thomas Hesketh,

I have only just returned from a visit to Lady Scarisbrick, & my Secretary's Brother, a Major in the Volunteers, has been killed by a fall from his horse, so that I fear your letter has remained unacknowledged.

I will write to Mr Brown of Lancaster; but the clergy are very impatient of any interference on the part of the Bishop in matters lying outside of his jurisdiction. I don't think that Mr Brown has been in the habit of interfering in elections beyond recording his vote, & indeed the people, who in towns are often of a radical turn, are jealous of clerical influence.

I don't know Mr Saunders,[654] but I believe he is thought to entertain extreme views, & voters will not always take the trouble to reflect that extreme opinions are unproductive of evil when controlled by an able statesman of Lord Derby's character.

I beg to remain Very sincerely Yr's [*sic*], (signed) Alexander Goss

---

653   Sir Thomas George Hesketh (1825–72), fifth baronet, of Rufford Hall, near Ormskirk. Conservative MP for Preston 1862–72. In 1867 he changed the family name to Fermor-Hesketh. See Boase, *Modern English Biography*.

654   Presumably William Saunders, 1823–95, newspaper proprietor, politician and pioneer of the syndication of news; he co-founded the Central Press Agency in 1863. Later an MP, described as Gladstonian Liberal, but outspoken re land nationalisation and in support of Henry George and other radical causes; see *ODNB*.

374.   *Rev. Mr. Donnelly,*[655]   *22 July 1864, Douglas IoM*   *5/4/575*
"Removal of Rev. R. Gillow"

My dear Mr. Donnelly

In consequence of the conviction forced upon me, at my recent visitation, by the examination of your accounts, of the inability of Douglas to keep three Priests, I write to say that I remove Mr. Gillow on Aug. 1st & name him to Ramsey.[656] His district will comprise the Parishes of K.

Christ Lazare, K. Jarby, K. Bride, K. Maughold, & K. Michael. I make the division by parishes so as to prevent complication by the marriage act.[657] You will still continue to serve Castle Town & Peel, every other Sunday. To enable this to be done with less fatigue, I think the Masses at Douglas should be reduced to two each Sunday, fixing such hours as may be judged most convenient to your people. The arrangement will, I trust, enable Douglas to meet its engagements. I think one of the two chalices not used at Douglas might be surrendered for use at Ramsey. Hoping that God will bless this new arrangement, I remain very truly Yrs in Xt. Alexander Goss.

---

[655] Michael Donnelly, 1833–1901; first r. of Our Lady of Mount Carmel, Liverpool, to 1881.

[656] Robert Gillow 1831–1900, o. 1860; c. Douglas to 1864, r. of Ramsey to d. in 1900.

[657] Isle of Man parishes: the 'K' stands for Kirk; correct spellings are Jurby; Leyzayre. It was important not to split civil parishes for registration purposes.

375. *Rev. Wilfrid Cooper O.S.B.*[658] *23 July 1864*   *5/4/576*
"Marriage case: Douglas"

My dear Mr. Cooper,

During my visitation of the Church at Douglas, Isle of Man, it was alleged that on Sunday June 19th there were married at St. Augustine's Church, Lpool, John Cowley of Douglas to Annie McTagg. Now the law of the Church requires that when parties from different parishes or districts are about to be married, the banns should be proclaimed in the Church of the parish or district to which each of the said parties belong, & that they should present before marriage to the priest about to marry them a certificate of the proclamation of the said banns, without which he should not presume to marry them. Now I am assured by the Clergy of St. Mary's Douglas to which district or mission John Cowley belongs that no proclamation of banns was ever ordered to be made. If therefore the said parties were married at the Church of St. Augustine, a false certificate must have been produced, or they must have been married, contrary to the law of the Church, without any certificate of the proclamation of banns, a formality necessary to prevent bigamy, which is of very frequent occurrence. I beg you will refer to the marriage Register & let me hear from you.

With every best wish I remain truly Yrs in Xt. Alexr. Goss.

---

[658] Wilfrid Cooper OSB, 1819–77. Introduction, p. xlii on Regulars and marriage regulations.

376.   *Rev. Fr. Cobb S.J.*[659]   *24 December 1864*   *5/4/619*
                    "Mission Fund & St. Wilfrid's"
My dear Fr. Cobb,
I have been pained & surprised to learn that one of the Priests at St.
Wilfrid's, before the last collection of the Mission Fund, "advised
members of the Congregation not to give more than one penny each",
& since the collection he has "expressed himself very glad, very glad
indeed, that it was scarcely as much as last year, for it was quite enough
for the Bishop". This information I have on the evidence not of one,
but several highly respectable individuals. Now a house divided against
itself cannot stand. This Priest holds his right to teach the people from
me to whom is committed the care of Christ's flock. Is he gathering
with me, or is he scattering, if he presumes to strive to undo what I
laboured to do, & discountenance what I recommended? I care not who
is Bishop, but there can be & must be only one, & as I am in possession it is my duty to maintain my position by the use of those weapons
which the Church has placed in my hands. During my epsicopate I have
tried to govern with an even hand: I have made no distinction of race or
profession amongst my clergy & I have been especially careful not to
interfere with the discharge of those duties which a Religious, as such,
owes to his Superior: is it too much to expect from him obedience in
those matters which are under a Bishop's jurisdiction? With every best
wish of the Season I remain truly Yrs in Xt. Alexr. Goss.

---

659   William Cobb SJ, 1804–77. And see letter 380 below, also to Cobb. Introduction
p. xli.

377.   *Rt. Rev. the Bp. of Shrewsbury*   *2 January 1865*   *5/4/624–6*
                    "The Commission of Ushaw"[660]
My dear Lord,
I am very sorry, very, at the contents of your last letter, for I fear, with
Archbp. E. that having gained the victory we shall lose its fruits. By
meeting at Ushaw till the Commission has made its report, we shall
be playing into our enemies' hands. I call them enemies, because they
show themselves to be such in spite of every concession. The great,
nay the only work now on hand is the Commission: <u>our</u> work begins
when it ends. The Archbp. was amazed at what they had done, & at
the perfect way in which it had been done, mainly owing to the very
Commissioner they wanted to set aside. He says that it is, & when
completed will be, invaluable: but they want to prevent its completion.
Before the Synod, the Card. declared that if the Bps cointerested were
admitted to their rights, they must take up the College, as they found

it, that there must be no going back. They are conscious that since the suit began with Rome, they have invested <u>our</u> property in buildings so as to render it <u>irremovable</u>. Before we met at York, Dr. Hogarth had his instructions. Both he & Can. Consitt[661] admitted to me that he had made a mistake in objecting to Dr. Fisher, it was James F. he <u>had</u> to object to; but the good old Bp., he said, was forgetful. This is why they want to have the meeting at Ushaw, that they may prime him, & try to get us instead of the <u>Commissioners</u> to act with Rome: but independently of us, the Commissioners have a work to do, & if we will not force our agents – the College authorities – to give them the necessary facilities they will have to apply to Rome. For the sake of peace, we let them put in thro' Bp. H. Mr Glover,[662] an ex-Procurator, who had been employed by them to back the Commission named, like this, by the Holy See to settle the case of Youens versus Sherburne. He succeeded, <u>& will succeed here</u> I fear, & Archbp. E. fears, because they act compactly, we are many & are not following a common council. At York we were told that Ushaw had £2000 in hand to pay in the Moray case;[663] in their accounts they set that down as a loan from a friend, taken up by command of the H.S. & the £3000 which Dr. Turner & myself had to pay, outstanding accounts, they set down as loans, so that we are to be debited with the College debts, but are not to be credited with its proceeds. It was agreed that they should pay off £500 a year, & that we should continue to pay our accounts to our Receiver, instead of to the College, but we repudiated the attempt to exact a promise to take out the residue in education; yet what has Dr. H. the effrontery to do? He sends for signature a legal instrument drawn up by Harting in which we are made to pledge ourselves to take out the remainder of the debt in education, the College trying to pay £300 a year: we very properly scouted such an imposition. When at York we declined to define the powers of the Commission: what did Dr. H. do? He wrote to Dr. Tate[664] to say that the Bps. had <u>unanimously</u> decided that the Commission had nothing further to do than to report to the H.S. how the funds for Ecclesiastical Education were invested, so that we were not to learn in whose name the College's property is invested, nor what are its liabilities or its income, information which up to this moment has been carefully withheld. Furthermore they endeavoured to make it out that I had bound myself to a declaration to Can. Consitt, that the Commission extended only to Ecclesiastical Education funds, & Dr. Tate actually wrote this & Mr. Glover read it to the Commission, but refused to hear my letter read on the same subject. Mr. Glover also declared that before he was appointed to the Commission, he had the opinion of a civil lawyer to that effect. I mention all this to show how they are scheming & acting in concert. Probably the Card., certainly Harting & the U.C. Professors are at Dr. Hogarth's back, & want to make him their mouthpiece, hence the determination to force us to meet at Ushaw. Even since the Commission has been appointed, consider how Mr. Glover has acted. First he said that the Superiors would present a statement, which they would have to sign and then forward as their report. The Commissioners insisted on doing more than this, then he left them at the end of a week & refused to return during the season at Whitby. Eventually they met again, when he again left them, but returned, & finding them determined to continue left them finally, refusing to press for any further information, tho' the information supplied contains nothing about the state of the College & property, or the value of the assets or liabilities: tho' I have no doubt that Dr. Hogarth knows every one of these matters. Tho' more subdued than formerly, the feeling of the Professors is as hostile as ever, & it cannot be otherwise as long as Dr. Gillow is there. I have now in my possession two of his letters, in one of which he declares it impossible for the College authorities to do business with you or me, & in the other he is instructing a priest how to contest with me the right to certain educational funds. Just consider how Bp. Hogarth has proceeded towards [us] <u>since</u> the Synod, when his conduct was uncivil to the last degree. For the sake of peace, we let him remove one of the Commissioners, then he objects to another, at the instigation of Ushaw to whom he lays open the whole matter. Now he is backing Dr. Tate & Mr. Gillow in their attempt to frustrate the labours of the Commissioners. We sign a joint letter, he keeps it a fortnight before he replies to it. When written to he assigns no reason why he will not forward it, but asks to meet us at Ushaw, & appeals *ad misericordiam* on account of his age, tho' after a long journey by rail, he would have to travel four miles in a cab. He wants to bully us, as he did about the appointment of the President. He claimed it, & has claimed it, in a public speech before Professors, visitors & students, as <u>his</u> act, even since Rome declared that he had no power to make the appointment, & set forth that it was done by the Cardinal.

At present the business on hand is the right of the Commission to gather information, that right is practically denied, the Commission appeals to us, we back them by a letter & Dr. Hogarth snaps his fingers at us, tho' forming a majority, compels us to meet, & is compelling us to meet at Ushaw, where we know that everything is hostile, & where he will be backed by a host of advisers. Now what I propose is to cease to be led by the nose any longer & therefore to resolve, 1st. that the meeting be held on an early day at York or Darlington. 2o. that when we meet, Dr. Turner should propose that the Secretary do send a letter which he will have ready to the President, ordering him to furnish the documents required by the Commission. 3o. that you should propose that Dr. Tate furnish each of us with a list of the students, ecclesiastical & lay, showing their ages, their class, & their Diocese & place of residence, & the Masters who are teaching them. 4o. that I should propose that Dr. Tate forward to each of us a copy of the rules now in force at the College. 5o. that we do meet on a day to be named after Whitsuntide. A meeting under such circumstances would be efficient, but not if held now. We should go unprepared & be baulked as we have been so often before. With every best wish truly Yrs. A. Goss.

---

660 The Third Provincial Council of Westminster of 1859, whose decrees were finally approved by Propaganda in September 1863, set up commissions for the three colleges, to establish their true financial position, including their property, debts and off-site rights and funds, and to meet and report annually thereafter (Decree XV, *Decreta*, 170–2). The disagreement about the commissioners' brief and powers, outlined by Goss here, lasted some time: he wrote a number of letters to Propaganda, the last one dated 30 April 1866; this asked whether the commissioners had to be unanimous in their decisions or whether the absence of one of the three commissioners rendered them inquorate, as the authorities at Ushaw claimed. Additionally, he asked if they had the right to demand all the documentation they thought relevant to the issues or whether they had to be content with what the President offered them. Propaganda replied in November 1866, supporting Goss's position and agreeing that the commissioners could demand to see whatever they thought fit. See APF, *Anglia*, 17, fols 973–5. (Goss wrote a similar long letter on the same day to Clifford, 5/4/627–9).

661 Edward Consitt, 1819–87, canon of Hexham and Newcastle Diocese.

662 John Glover, 1802–78; Beverley Diocese.

663 Moray case: untraced.

664 Robert Tate, 1799–1876, Beverley Diocese; sixth president of Ushaw, appointed by Hogarth 1862–63.

378. *Lord Edward Howard, Glossop*   6 January 1865   5/6/2/65–6

My Lord,

In reply to your kind letter, I beg to say that the Bishop has always encouraged to the utmost of his power the various Young Men's Societies & that his Lordship appointed their Directors. It has been his endeavour in connection with the Clergy to make this as far as possible in the form of a Confraternity, in order to do away with any political organisation or agitation specifically attending their formation in consequence of the large Irish element in them.

The Bishop was absent from home when your valuable letters appeared in the Catholic Newspapers; his Lordship had intended to address a letter to you on the subject. The difference of the state of society in this country to that abroad makes it difficult for lay men to take part in works of mercy corporal & spiritual. Abroad the rich & the poor dwell together: often the Prince & the Beggar under the same roof: but here the wealthy live out of the towns, the middle class – the main instrument in France of these works – live in streets far away from the poor. In consequence of this, it often happens that an entire congregation consists only of the poorest & most depraved, so that no power can be brought to bear upon them in the way of public opinion, & there are absolutely no individuals suited for the Society of St. Vincent of Paul. In Liverpool we suffer under another disdavantage: we have no mills as in Manchester, & the large bulk of our poorer children has only a precarious living such as porters, hundreds of whom are driven out of work by the prevalence of an East wind. It would be a great help to the Clergy could lay persons take their proper share in their work. Hitherto the almost only work of the Young Men's Societies has been that of their own sanctification.

Wishing you many happy returns of the New Year, I beg to remain, my Lord,

Your's [sic] very respectfully, Ed. Powell, Sec.

379. *Rev. M. Hickey,*[665] *Bonds, Garstang*   *7 January 1865*   *5/4/635*
"Masses, etc."

My dear Mr. Hickey,

I thought I had answered yours of November 4th but probably I spoke only of the altar & Walker's Will. When in London I asked Bp. Grant about Mr. Horrabin's Executor.[666] Your safest plan would be to write to him to ask if there was amongst Mr. Horrabin's papers, a copy of Mr. Walker's will, or any instruction about it, stating Mr. Walker's Christian name, & when he is supposed to have died. About the legacy of £100 for 3 masses, I will sanction it, if the money be to be [sic] invested in permanent security. Much the best plan, recommended by the Bps., is not to make obligations permanent, but for a time, say 50 years from the time of death, only granting a greater number of Masses, say 6 or 8. This is quite in accordance with old English Catholic custom & secures a greater number of Masses when the soul is thought most to need them.

I am glad to see the Dean makes complimentary mention of your schools. A happy new year. Truly Yrs ever. Alexander Goss.

---

665   Michael Hickey, 1801–71, r. Garstang 1825–71.
666   Rev. Thomas Horrabin 1747–1801, of the London District; Milburn, *History of Ushaw College, History of Ushaw College,* 81–3.

380. *Rev. Fr. Cobb S.J., St. Wilfrid's, Preston*   *7 January 1865*
5/4/637

"Remarks on Ep: Collections"

My dear Fr. Cobb,

I would willingly investigate thoroughly the charges made against one of your Fathers for indiscreet remarks made about the Diocesan Collection, but I may not do so, as my informant declines to allow his name to be used, & Church law compels me to defer to his wishes, otherwise

I should have prosecuted the inquiry & acted accordingly if the charge had been brought home. Before writing to you I had the matter sifted & was assured that there was no doubt of the fact, tho' the parties did not wish their names to be given up; in fact the name of the Priest was not mentioned in the letter addressed to me, tho' it was given on inquiry. This was the reason that I was obliged to content myself with giving thro' you, as local superior, a caution; for whether spoken seriously or in earnest such remarks disedify, & in this instance several <u>respectable men</u> were greatly shocked.

With every best wish to yourself & brethren for the new year, I remain very truly Yrs in Xt. Alexander Goss.

381.   *Rev. Mr. Gibson, Hornby*   *7 January 1865*   *5/4/638*
                         "School Schedules"
My dear Mr. Gibson,
In the answers to the School Schedules No.1.[667] I am pained to find that you balk [*sic*] the Inquiry. The question 12 asks "<u>How often</u>, & at what stated times do the children, who have not made their first communion, go to Confession". You reply "When I fix a time for them or their parents send them". But how often do you fix a time, or do their parents send them? To question 14, "How often do they communicate", you reply, "Generally as often as their parents". Has not a Bp a right, nay is it not his duty to know the state of his flock, & can he know it if all answer these questions in the way you have done. I must confess that I did not expect it, & must also add that I do not like it.
With every best wish for the New Year I remain Yrs in Xt. Alexander Goss.

---

[667] Questions to be answered as part of the Visitation Returns.

382.   *Rev. Wm. Henderson, Yealand*   *9 January 1865*   *5/4/639*
                         "School Schedule"
My dear Mr. Henderson,
My attention has been recently called to the state of the young in this Diocese, but more especially in the town of Liverpool. On turning to the School Schedules for information, I find that in your answers to the Schedule you do not mention whether any special benches are set aside for children at Mass, nor do you state how often the Children who have not made their 1st Communion, go to Confession, nor how often those communicate who have made their 1st Communion; nor do you mention whether you have any Confraternities or sodalities for keeping the children to their duties – a provision the more necessary as you have no

School. Mr. Dinmore of Goosenargh[668] is similarly circumstanced but he has answered all the questions.

Wishing you every blessing I remain truly Yrs in Xt. Alexander Goss.

---

[668] Edward Dinmore OSB, 1805–79; he was at Goosenargh, nr Preston, from 1834 to 1879.

383. *Rev. Peter Laverty, Ulverston* *9 January 1865*   *5/4/646*
"School Schedules"

My dear Mr. Laverty,

I am surprised to find that out of a population of 1200 you have only 30 at Catechism on Sundays. No doubt that number includes Barrow, Coniston, & other outlying districts, but still I think you ought to have a greater attendance, for I find you have 52 on the Class list, & 46 actually present at the Examination. Under these circumstances, would it not be well for Catechism to be given in the School room on Weekdays, as well as in the Church on Sundays. Your answer to No. 12 I am at a loss to understand. The Question [is] how often, & at what stated times do children not having made their 1st Communion go to Confession? You answer, "monthly on the Saturday afternoon, & weekly on the Friday evenings."

I shall be glad to hear that the prospect of getting land at Coniston is nearing, for I am anxious to begin to build in the spring. It may be six weeks or two months before I shall be able to supply Barrow, tho' the want is daily before my mind.

Wishing you every blessing, I remain truly Yrs. Alexr Goss.

384. *Rev. M. Hickey, Bonds, Garstang* *18 January 1865*   *5/4/649*
"New Altar"

My dear Mr. Hickey,

I am glad to hear of your success in reference to your new altar. I hardly know what advice to give you on the subject, for I have never seen an altar that I liked. Architects seem to ignore the rite of Benediction. I like the altar to stand from the wall, but in such cases the reredos ought not to be brought forward as is the case at Lancaster, but it should allow of a passage, so that if necessary the reredos could be covered with suitable hangings, between which & the altar could be arranged flowers & candles; for when they are placed on the altar hot wax drops & often the water from the vases spills, so that the altar cloth is rendered unfit for Mass. I would recommend you to have a sketch made embodying the ideas in your letter of Nov: 4: so as to be enabled to form a better opinion of the effect of what you design. I would not have a variegated material like Lancaster & St. Vincent's, Lpool, as it does not show the moulding. I don't dislike colour, but it ought to be employed to aid the mouldings. With every best wish I remain truly Yrs in Xt. A. Goss.

385.   *Rev. Mr. McCormick,*[669] *Scholes, Wigan   20 January 1865*
                                                        5/4/655
                                    "Schools"
My dear Hugh,
From your answer to Schedule I, I find that you have attending Catechism 240 children, not infants. Of these 68 have made their first communion; 50 have not, but go to Confession: Now, why do not the others (240 – 118 = 122) go to Confession? Surely if they are not infants there must be out of that number of 122 many who have come to the use of reason.

You say <u>you</u> catechise on Sunday from 10 to 10.45 & on week days from 11½–12 & 3½–3.50 [*sic*]. Now I want to know, 1o. <u>who</u> catechises at these times, & 2o. <u>where</u> he catechises. Do the pupil or assistant teachers receive no special instruction either from you or the Sisters? You say they are instructed on Monday & Thursday evenings – where, by whom, at what hour? I am sorry that the boys' school is named again as unsatisfactory. You are two: why is not one frequently about the schools? Depute your coadjutor, but give him scope & let him feel his responsibility.

With every best wish truly Yrs in Xt. A. Goss

---

[669] Hugh Nugent McCormick, 1805–77; o. Ireland, at St Patrick's, Wigan, 1847–1875; a friend of Goss, despite the tone of this letter.

386.   *Very Rev. H. Greenhalgh, Weld Bank, Chorley 7 February 1865.*
                                                        5/4/672
My dear Canon,
You have your hands full. Tell Mr OM[670] that my mission is to save not to destroy. I have no wish to deal suspensions but only to do what is most conducive to the salvation of souls. The law of fraternal correction is our Lord's, not mine; his declaration that he will not act according to the Gospel does not free him from responsibility. Tell Mr A[671] that I have no wish for his removal, but I must have a guarantee that will justify me in the eyes of God, & prevent the possibility of scandal. 1o. Bind him *verbo sacerdotis*, equivalent to an oath, that he will not take ale, beer, wine or spirits out of his own house except when dinng out. 2o. In his own house, except at the public table, in company with Mr OM. 3o. If you deem it necessary, let Mr OM keep the key. This is not a

question of etiquette, but of the salvaton of souls. If this is not sufficient
[*remaining two lines illegible*]
Alexander Goss.

---

670   John O'Meara, see nn. 153, 216.
671   Probably John Aylward, *c.* 1824–84, rector at St Mary's, Chorley, 1858–65.

---

387.   *Rev. Pierce Power, 144 Gt Homer St.*   *10 August 1865*   *5/5/1*
"Fees"

My dear Mr. Power,
Learning that there was some dissatisfaction among your confreres with
the appropriation of the fees in a way hitherto unusual in this Diocese, I
have been led to peruse the Trust Deed of St. Anthony's made & enroled
[*sic*] in Chancery in 1837. This deed prescribes that all fees & gratuti-
tous emoluments paid in consideration of the services of the Incumbent
& the other clergy shall be paid for the same purpose as the Bench
rents, that is insurance from fire, repairs, clerk's salaries, interest on the
mortgage, maintenance of the clergy, or other uses which the Bishop
may direct by any writing under his hand. It is clearly illegal therefore
for you to claim these or to appropriate them to your own use. They
belong to the Church & must be appropriated for the purposes identified
in the Trust Deed. It is my wish therefore, & I hereby decree that all fees
& emoluments whether derived from Baptisms, marriages, churchings,
proclamation of Banns, or for any other service exclusive of the retribu-
tion for Masses be paid towards the liquidation of the debt, & for this
purpose a separate & distinct account be opened in the Ledger under the
head of "Fees". This decision is not only in accordance with the legal
provisions of the Trust Deed, for the faithful execution of which we are
liable to citation before the Chancellor, but is also in accordance with
the Synod II of Oscott, which speaking of the application of such Fees
decrees "*Anteferenda vero videtur caeteris ea distributio quae magis
ad allevianda onera missionis possit conferre*" (cap VIII #XV).[672] To
prevent any future contravention of this Decree on the score of ignorance, it is my order that this letter be deposited in the archives of the
Mission.
      +Alexander Bishop of Liverpool.

---

672   *Decreta*, 104: 'However, such distribution as can rather alleviate the debt on the
mission seems preferable to any other': not as clear cut, perhaps, as Goss claimed: the
decree said fees should generally go to the priests, but local custom varied and *better* if
… The letter is in copperplate, and is very similar to one sent to on the same day to Rev.
Joseph Duggan of St Joseph's (5/5/3). Power offered his resignation, which Goss refused,
12 August 1865 (5/5/7), asking him to substitute in the archives a formal memorandum
based on the Trust Deed rather than the letter, but it says nothing new. For Power, see n.
71.

388. *Right Rev. Bp. of Salford   10 August 1865* 5/5/4
"St. Patrick's Society"

My dear Lord,

I sent you by yesterday's post a copy of a Liverpool paper containing an account of a meeting of St. Patrick's Burial Society. Bad as that account represents it to be, I am told by those present that it fails to convey an accurate picture of the disgraceful scene. This Society was founded in connection with St. Patrick's Church or at all events the Senior Priest of St. Patrick's had the management of it. Under Mr. Phelan it seems to have fallen under the dominion of Mr. Treacy[673] & during the earlier part of my episcopate I was constantly besieged by poor people complaining of being defrauded. The managers professed to recognize the Bishop & other Bishops as patrons: I suppose at all times it is competent for the Bp. to make the visitation of such a society, especially as the rules contained a provision for having Masses said (no. 12) [*sic*]. On this account I required from Mr. Phelan, the President, a statement of accounts. Eventually the concern has come into court, & Mr. Treacy stands charged with having appropriated more than £7000, which he has been ordered to disgorge. On this revelation I compelled Mr. Phelan to resign the Presidentship. The Meeting in Manchester & the late Meeting in Liverpool was [*sic*] intended to hear the decision of the County Court. Strangers had their expenses paid, & had money given them for drink, in order to aid the carrying out of this scheme. Canon Walmesley's note which I enclose explains the grounds on which my clergy attended. I think I have a right to ask that the Clergy from your Diocese who interfered on this occasion should be punished, for such interference in another Diocese, & in a matter which from the reasons explained above belongs to the Visitation of the Ordinary where the head quarters of such a Society are established. It is said here that after the Manchester Meeting, Canon Ca[well?] & others [*illegible bottom line and six short lines written across the main text*] a protest against the practice.

Hoping you continue well, I remain very truly Yrs Alexander Goss.

---

[673] John Treacy and St Patrick's Burial Society: see Belchem, *Irish, Catholic and Scouse*, 106–13, for a detailed, colourful account. The doings of the society, the largest such friendly society in the country, became a national scandal, with endless legal actions, corruption and intimidation; the local press described the fight at its 1868 AGM as one of the 'most disreputable disturbances' in the 'disreputable history of Liverpool friendly societies'.

389. *Right Rev. Bp. Turner, Bp's House, Salford   14 August 1865*
5/5/11

"St. Patrick's Society"

My dear Lord,

When I wrote to you on the subject of the Salford Clergy attending a Meeting in Liverpool, & frustrating what they considered my protest, I had no wish to ask you to do more than caution them against interference with the jurisdiction of the Bp. of another Diocese, but a reference of the matter to the Holy See might bring them into serious trouble: for it is one of the subjects to which our attention is called in the elenchus of questions that we have to answer in providing our *relatio status*. I was not aware that any Liverpool Priests attended the Manchester Meeting, nor do I know who they are, but if my attention had been directed to the matter, I should not have failed to give an analagous admonition. We are differently circumstanced in the matter for you had repudiated years before all connection, whereas I was supposed by your clergy to be the patron, & to have sent down some edict or other to the Meeting. I believe the judge in the County Court … [*illegible*] to my clergy the necessity of public repudiation, & had no Order been made the interests of thousands of poor in my Diocese would have been left in the hands of Treacy, whom the Judge ordered to disgorge £7000. I had no wish to create for you any embarrassment, much less urge a suspension, which even if it could be sustained would create more harm than good.

With every best wish faithfully Yrs. Alexd. Goss.

390. *Sir Robert Gerard, Garswood, Warrington   16 August 1865*
5/5/15

My dear Sir Robert Gerard

You will be prepared to hear that I find it quite necessary to remove Mr. Hardman[674] from the care of the Birchley flock. His Mission embraces a large district, & a numerous people, much beyond his present strength. I have had some difficulty in making arrangements to fill his place; for being myself a Lancashireman I can well understand your dislike to have one from a country where nationality seems to override every other feeling. I hope you will be pleased with the choice I have made, the Rev. Mr. Walton, formerly of St. Augustine's, Preston.[675] He is Lancashire [*sic*], perhaps a mite too much so, is able, has good common sense, & will I think manage the people well. In order to secure proper visitation of the Schools & attention to the children, I think it would be well to make your annual donation dependent on that fact, & let it be known thro' your agent to the priest; & if he does not do what ought to be done in this respect, let the donation be withheld. Hoping that this change will be beneficial for the interests of religion which you have so much at heart on your estates & in the Diocese, & wishing yourself & family every blessing, I remain Sincerely Yr Alexr. Goss.

---

674 John Hardman, 1820–81, r. at Birchley 1855–65, then c. St Mary's, Wigan.

675 Thomas Walton: see letter 319. Goss wrote to him on 19th August saying he was unhappy with the way he had kept residence in Preston; this must improve. A new house was to be built in Birchley, but nothing should be done without Sir Robert's sanction. Walton was a man of many appointments and left Birchley in 1869 to return as curate to St Augustine's, Preston.

391. *Rev. W. Walker, Preston.*[676] *20 October 1865* *5/5/34*
"Misconceptions"

My dear Mr. Walker,

After an intimacy of a quarter of a century, can you find no other reason why I should feel pained at having to write the letter of 17th, than that you had endorsed it "private"? That is the especial ground of the most ample apology you hasten to tender; but surely, William, you dont [*sic*] expect me to believe that you believe any such thing? You speak of my believing the charge of non-residence whispered against you. Now no charge has been whispered against you; but common rumour, a fair source of information, proclaims it from the house top in every part of the Diocese, & can I in conscience shut my ears? Was not that the basis of the incompatibility between yourself & Mr. Walton?[677] Did you never hear it hinted that he kept a journal of your suspected absences from home? Sit down & between yourself & God, calculate how often you have been from home since the first of the year; & then tell me whether common rumour belies you? Mind, it does not allege that you are absent on Friday, Sat: or Sunday. If in saying that St. Augustine's is the most critically placed mission in the Diocese, you refer to its monetary position, you are mistaken, as a reference to the Lpool Churches will show. You significantly observe that my letter has taught you more lessons than one. Well, if it has the effect of making you a better observer of residence, I am content to take or to leave what is implied or may seemed [*sic*] to be implied in the rest, however I might wish it to have been otherwise. With every best wish I remain truly Yrs in Xt. A. Goss.

---

676 Walker, a friend of Goss, had replied to an official complaint that he was late with his returns, marking his reply 'private'. Goss had queried the use of 'private' and had suggested that it was absence from home rather than overwork that had made Walker unable to meet the eight-month deadline; he had ended by saying Walker 'would never know what it had cost him to write the letter' (AAL, 5/5/30).

677 For Walton, see previous letter.

392.   *J.B. Aspinall Esq. Q.C., Recorder of Liverpool*
                    12 December 1865   5/5/42
                    "Gardner & Pilling"[678]

My dear Recorder

I believe you know Mr. H. Gardner, a solicitor or barrister who has land at Pilling. Now I have some poor Catholics there who are 7 miles from any existing Catholic Chapel, &, if I had land, I could build for them a modest chapel. I am told that the best site for this purpose is where 4 lanes meet near Stackpool, a property belonging to Mr. H. Gardner. Will you be good enough to use your influence on behalf of those poor moss siders at Pilling? If Mr. G. would let us have about two acres at a small cost, I think I could manage the rest by the aid of kind friends. With every best wish for yourself & family I remain very sincerely Yrs in Xt. +Alexander Goss.

678   The Pilling mission was founded only in 1891, from Garstang. Bp O'Reilly in 1875 spoke of 'the wild district of Pilling ... wide tracts of moss land' (AAL, *Liverpolitana, 1873–78*: 1875 'Report on the Diocesan Mission Fund'), so Goss's appeal was obviously unsuccessful.

393.   [*Mr. Fayer*]   *31 December 1865*   5/5/62

My dear Mr. Fayer,[679]

I think the advice you have given to Mr. Howard is unexceptional. If he pay into my administration the £200 I will give him a promissory note, binding on my successors, to give him during his life an annuity of £8 per an.

Young Barker is doing well & is a good lad. The elder seems unsettled, but why I cannot learn.[680] I believe that after the last retreat Fr. Suffield[681] told him that he had no vocation; but why or wherefore I know not. The lad is certainly old enough to know his mind. When at Gt. Eccleston I found Mr. Adamson's nephew, after going back at the end of the vacation, had left under similar advice. Some of the new lights act very queerly about vocations. For my part I believe that if a lad be good, & wants to be a Priest, that is evidence enough of vocation: if not there to begin with, God would give it. I don't think men are predestined to run in one groove, & that out of it is no salvation.

With best wishes of the season I remain truly Yrs A. Goss

P.S. I am keeping Cottam for Mr. Taylor[682] if he returns, as he hopes, able to undertake it.

679   William Fayer, 1814–83; priest of the Salford Diocese, at Samlesbury, near Preston, at this time.
680   Joseph A. Barker, 1850–1926, was ordained for the diocese in 1875.
681   Robert Rudolph Suffield, 1821–91; o. 1850 and joined St Ninian's (see n. 6); became

an OP in 1860. He opposed papal infallibility and came to doubt the authority of the Church; he was laicised in 1870 and became a Unitarian minister, prominent in local politics and civic matters (*ODNB*).

[682] Roger Taylor, 1828–1885; he did return and undertook 'light duties at Cottam to 1872' (Plumb, *'Found Worthy'*).

394. *Sister Lucy, Convent, Fox St., Preston 22 January 1866 5/5/64*
"Live Bambino"

My dear Sister Superioress,

I am told that for the last two years, perhaps longer, there has been exhibited in the Fox St. Schools a live infant, lying in a crib to represent the Birth of the Son of God, & that incense was used on the occasion. I wish to know whether this impiety really occurred, or whether I have been cruelly hoaxed by a false statement. I wish therefore to have from you a full & circumstantial account of what took place; if such account be at variance with what I have heard, I shall feel it my duty to name a Committee to examine into this strange affair.

Wishing you every blessing, I remain Your's [*sic*] truly in Xt. Alexander Goss.

395. *Mother [sic] Lucy, Convent, Fox St., Preston.*[683]

30 January 1866 5/6/2/140
"Live Bambino"

Dear Mother Lucy,

I am instructed by the Bishop to acknowledge receipt of your letter of 26th January & to say that he will be satisfied if the representation of which he speaks is not repeated. In ages of faith a simple people might reasonably do things which may not be repeated in this age. Besides the whole teaching of the Church is against the copying of the features of living persons to represent Saints, & must therefore be against the substitution of living persons for so sacred a character as Our Lord. With every best wish, I remain Ed. Powell, Sec.

[683] See letter 403 of a few months later.

396. *Rev. Mr. Bartley*[684] *15 March 1866 5/5/87*
Week's Retreat

Revd. & dear Sir,

How long will you abuse my forbearance? From no priests under whom you have served, have you come with an unexceptionable character. Besides betraying impatience of control, you have shown weakness for the pleasures of the senses in complaining of the food set before you though your senior sat down [at] the same meal, in keeping for private consumption a supply of drink, in encouraging amongst the flock remarks disparaging to the priest whom you are placed to assist, & in holding long, private conferences with a school-teacher – the scandal of which traversed beyond the limits of your own body & became the subject of letters some of which are now lying before me. Another bishop would have upbraided you for your folly, or have punished this unpriestly conduct. But I was content to speak to you kindly & receive from you a promise of amendment. How have you kept that promise? You have held clandestine interviews with a young lady, your penitent – you have walked out with her, you have taken her home in the evening – her mother's servant having called for her in vain. You have been closeted with her in your private room, having the door fast inside or by equivalent thereto by having no handle outside, & when warned by your superior on the impropriety of your conduct, you have reviled him & repeated the offence. Now this cannot & shall not be tolerated. This therefore is to order, first that you do not take any lady to your private room or allow her to visit there. 2o that you do not take up to your room any lay person without the knowledge & sanction of the senior priest for the time being. 3o that you have the handle of your door repaired so as to make your room accessible. 4o that you do not keep in your room or elsewhere for private consumption – ale – beer – wine or spirits. 5o that you do not attend the confessional or see persons in your confessional except at such times as are approved of by the rector of the Church who has the care of souls, & dependently upon whom you hold the exercise of your faculties – that you do not walk out with that or any other young lady or hold clandestine interviews. 6o that you apologise to Mr. Br[? *unclear*] & the Archbishop whom you have grossly insulted. 7o that you come over to England by Monday's boat & proceed direct to Bishop Eton for the purpose of making a retreat until such hour on Saturday as shall enable you to return to the Island for Sunday's duty.

You must understand that the continuance of your faculties will depend on the faithful discharge of these instructions. I trust that the double warning that you have now received will make you more prudent for the future, & I sincerely hope that you will profit by the advantage of a retreat, & that having thoroughly entered into your self, you may be able to celebrate with an easier conscience the glories of the Resurrection. With every best wish I remain Yrs in Xt. +Alexander Goss.

---

684   Francis Bartley, 1834–96, at Douglas: he left the diocese in 1867, transferring to Clifton Diocese; died in Birmingham. The letter is in a very unusual hand but signed by Goss.

397.   *Rev. Dr. O'Bryen,*[685] *Catholic Institute*   *28 March 1866*   *5/5/91*

"Quis est hic et laudabimus eum"[686]

My dear Dr. O'Bryen,

I am glad you are able to sit up; but am sorry to find that your mind is on business. Rest you want, & rest you should have. Mr. Thrower will, I trust, be equal to the occasion. I am indebted to him for keeping me acquainted with your progress.

As for priests, they cannot be had. I have applications, but all want little work & plenty of pay. Only within a few weeks, one newly ordained refused to go where sent. If one began with 5 hours a day, he would soon abandon it under town influences. When Mr. Thrower came to the Institute, he was thankful to get shelter & offered to take any amount of school work, but shrank from mission duty, or rather declined to qualify himself. I will refer the matter to the Vicar Gen. & Chapter: I feel assured that lay masters are much cheaper than clerical, where board & lodging, as well as salary are concerned. Dr. Fisher is of the same opinion. Where you have boarders, you may require clerical superintendence. Is the inclosed [*sic*] map of your district? If not, clip it or ask Mr. T. to clip it to the proper dimensions. My walking powers are still indifferent, & my side is a constant grief, but I am not otherwise as ill. May God bless you & keep you. Ever Yrs. A. Goss.

PS: I regret that I cannot give a satisfactory answer to your letter. Bear in mind I can only work with the tools I have. Look thro' the Directory, & offer a suggestion.

---

[685]   Henry O'Bryen, 1835–95, b. in Montpellier, edu. Rome, o. 1858; principal of CI 1863–5 and rector of St James's, Orrell, 1869–73. He was a noted linguist and learned speaker. See Bennett, *Father Nugent*, 26.

[686]   'Who is such a one and we shall praise him?' (Ecclesiasticus 31, v. 9); a phrase used in the Office and Mass of Confessors. See n. 414 for Thrower.

398.   [*Archbishop Manning*]   *6 April 1866*   *5/5/97*

My dear Grace,

I think well of the address you propose, but as you ask me to state my opinion, I venture to propose certain changes. Though the Conservative interest has been supported in many quarters on account of Eng: influence having been lent by the Whigs to Revolution in Italy, yet the Eng: Catholics are very Whig, and the Irish Catholics universally so. Extreme caution is therefore requisite or the differences of Blue book notoriety may be resumed.[687] I think therefore our strength lies in laying down & acting on principles universally admitted; but I think we weaken those principles, if we intermix those with others that may be questioned. As an Episcopate, we are neither Whig nor Tory, & when speaking authoritatively to our flocks we ought to avoid the introduction of principles which they can refuse to admit without ceasing to be orthodox Catholics. I know nothing of any Catholics but those in my own Diocese, but those I do know, both rich & middle class & poor, & have felt it a duty to make these observations. Any attempt to control them in matters where the church does not condemn liberty of opinion would have the effect of driving them to the opposite extreme. I should propose to conclude the 2nd paragraph with <u>Christian world</u>. In par: 3 after Sov: Pontiffs, I would omit the words <u>to whom — Society</u>. Between the words any secret Society I would add 'such', otherwise it might include some benefit societies which are secret. In the last paragraph I would omit all between <u>to His Church — to uphold the ....</u> It does not really concern the matter in hand. My reasons for these suggestions I can state more fully when we meet.

I have Mr Powell[688] in my house hovering between life and death from typhus fever.

With every best wish, I remain sincerely Yrs Alex. Goss.

---

[687] 'Blue book notoriety': see n. 17 above.
[688] Edward Powell, 1837–1901; Goss's secretary 1862–65, he caught typhus at Eldon Street while covering for Rev. A. Kelly who had died from the fever in 1865.

399. *Rev. T. Tobin, St. Michael's, West Derby Road*   *6 May 1866*
5/5/105

"Benediction"

My dear Mr. Tobin,

Inclosed I send a licence for Bened. of B.S: let it be deposited in the Archives of the Church. For the present, I think it better not to have procession [*sic*] of the B.S. It is the most solemn of all rites, & requires more than your Church as yet possesses, to be carried out rubrically.

There is no power or authority in the Church to compel people to attend the church of their own district: it can not be done even in Catholic countries: nor does Rome want it to be attempted. If your services are rightly carried out; if you are punctual in observing the hours set down for the services on week days as well as on Sundays, & if you don't scold, & if you preach & don't talk, you will find that your Church will fill. Ordinarily it is thro' the Confessional that the Church is filled. I hope you have your accounts in good order as I shall soon be sending a person to inspect them. If you have not, I would advise you to ask Mr. Lennon of Newton[689] to spend a week with you; he would help you to write up, & he understands it, having been in a mercantile office.

Mind I don't say that you scold or talk; but I am told that both are too often done in our Churches. I want the accompanying sheet returned filled up: the number of Easter communicants, & the number present at Mass, catechism, & evening service. If not already taken, let them be counted next Sunday.

Truly Yrs in Xt. A. Goss.

---

689 John Joseph Lennon, 1830–97; Lisbon; o. 1860. At Newton-le-Willows 1861–70 where he built the house and church.

400. *James Fairhurst Esq.,*[690] *97 Shaw St., Everton*   *9 May 1866*

5/5/107

"Constabulary & Friday"

My dear Mr. Fairhurst,

I should have been glad to have had it in my power to relieve the Catholic members of the Constabulary from the awkwardness in which they are place [*sic*] by having their review on a Friday, but I cannot do so. The abstinence on Friday is a general not a local law, &, except in individual cases dealt with by Spiritual Directors, cannot be suspended. Soldiers in camp, provided for by the Commissariat, are allowed to eat flesh meat, but not soldiers that are billeted or are living at home like the police. In Lent, when my powers are greater, I dispensed with Colonel Clifton's tenants when his son came of age, & I would have done so in this case, had I thought that it came within my powers. Perhaps I was more indulgent than I had a right to be in the Clifton case. As long as the men have bread & cheese, I don't think they will be entitled to grumble. Truly Yrs A. Goss.

---

690 James Fairhurst, Catholic Liberal councillor in Liverpool, 1850s–1870s; see n. 140.

401. *Mrs. Anderton, Haighton House, Preston 12 May 1866 5/5/109*

"Communion in P. [*sic*] Oratory"

My dear Mrs Anderton,

I am in receipt of your letter, asking for a continuance of Mass at Haighton House & for leave to communicate thereat not only during the winter, when the doctor has certified that it could be injurious for you to go out early, but also at other times in consequence of the difficulty you experience in going out fasting. Knowing the delicate state of your health in this matter, I grant for one year the permission asked; but such communion shall not fulfil the Easter precept, nor, according to the Instruction of our Predecessor printed & circulated, shall it be lawful to have Mass or to communicate in the Oratory on the following days:– Easter Sunday, Ascension Day, Pentecost, the Annunciation, the

Assumption, Christmas day, the Epiphany, Feast of Sts. Peter & Paul & All Saints. With every best wish to yourself & family I remain truly Yrs in Xt. Alexander Goss.

402.   *Rev. Mr. Stirzaker,*[691] *Skelmersdale   12 May 1866   5/5/111*
                          Returns: Admission charge.

Dear Rev. Sir,

I have searched in vain for any return made by you of the numbers present at Mass, cathechism, & afternoon prayers, on the 2nd Sunday of Lent, as also of the Easter communicants. It is possible that they may have arrived in my absence & may have been mislaid. I shall be glad, then, to have a duplicate return. Any Sunday will furnish returns sufficiently accurate for my purpose. I would not have you to make any change in the admission charges: it would be calculated to produce ill feeling as it has done at Poulton. Your best plan would be to get Can. Hodgson to propose it, some Sunday, to the people, you exchanging duty with him for the occasion: he is a persuasive speaker.

With every best wish I remain truly Yrs A. Goss.

---

691   William Stirzaker 1838–1912(?), first r. of St Richard's, Skelmersdale; not listed after 1899. The letter seems to be the only mention of admission charges; they were not uncommon but most churches just had voluntary entry contributions.

403.   *Sr Lucy, Convent, St. Wilfrid's, Preston   13 May 1866   5/5/112*
                          "One God shalt thou adore"

My dear Sister in J.C.

Our Lord says that the first commandment of all is, "the Lord thy God is <u>one</u> God". Now if it be, as our Lord says it is, that there is only one God, you must make your choice between the statue of the Holy Child, & Jesus Christ, whose body & blood, soul & divinity are truly present in the Blessed Eucharist. You cannot set up both for adoration, nor can you divide with a graven image the worship due to the God of heaven. By the law of the Church as laid down by the Cong: of Rites, you not only cannot set up for honour but even leave unveiled an image in the presence of the B.S. tho' it is allowed when a hundred of years [*sic*] was alleged in its favour.

With every best wish to yourself & community I remain, sincerely Yrs in Xt. Alexr. Goss.

404.   *Rev. S. Walsh, Belle Vue, Derby Road   20 May 1866   5/5/146*
                          "Exeat"

Rev. Sir,

I am in receipt of your letter of the 18th in which, as you allege by the

Vicar General's advice, you ask to be removed to another Mission, & in case I have not one at my disposal for permission to apply to some other Bp. Had you been ordained for my Diocese, I should not have considered myself called on to grant your request, but as you voluntarily gave yourself to me, I feel bound in courtesy to release you from an obligation voluntarily contracted. On your receiving from another Bp. a promise of incorporation, I will expedite to you letters of excorporation from the Diocese of Liverpool. Until then you will consider yourself as heretofore bound to the Mission of St. Alexander. Praying God to have you in his holy keeping I remain Yrs in Xt. +Alexander Goss.

405.   *Mr. J. T. Cullen, 37 Tithebarn St., Liverpool*   *30 July 1866*
5/6/2/163

"Superstitious Prayer"

Dear Sir,

The Bishop is away from home. I know, however, that nearly two years ago his Lordship sent a priest to you forbidding you to sell or reprint any more, as it was most superstitious, if not more than that. A few days ago, hearing that it was still sold by you, the Bishop directed me to call & insist upon its suppression, under pain of excommunication. I may add that whilst serving the Church at Eldon St. & seeing the same prayer in the window of your shop in Vauxhall Road, I told the shopkeeper of the Bishop's opinion of it, & she promised to inform you of what I had said.

I remain Your's [*sic*] truly, Edward Powell, Sec.

406.   *Very Rev. Canon Oakeley,*[692] *St. John's, Islington*   *24 April 1867*
5/5/147

My dear Canon,

I write to thank you for your generous & fearless defence of the great Champion, who is too humble & retiring to defend himself. It is lamentable to see the persistent efforts of little men to lift themselves into note by assailing a name that is without stain. I think a national church is a national curse; but I have never been able to be persuaded that a man to be a sound Catholic must cease to be a true Englishman. The Holy Father has about him a set of men who have much zeal, but little discretion, & the Bp. of Orleans[693] was not the first to see that Rome could not stand, as it was divided against itself; for when I was there in 1860, the prime minister & the camerilla were ever at cross purposes. The gossip of Rome is a thing to shudder at. A Bp. may never weary of doing good, but should he not come out with something strong & pungent whenever these fussy busy bodies choose to dictate, he is denounced as a Gallican & put down in their black books to be denied favour. If such men were in England, they would hardly be entrusted with the charge of a mission,

& yet they do not hesitate to criticise the acts of Bps even in the presence of their own subjects. They mistake their own rambling notions for the sentiments of the Holy Father & if we did not know the true state of things at Rome, they would make the Holy See a bye word amongst us. If they be not less free with the Holy Father's name they will create a Gallicanism in England.

We all owe you a thousand thanks for your truthful, firm, generous & respectful letter. I do not think there is a Priest in my Diocese that does not endorse it.

With every best wish I remain sincerely Yrs in Xt. Alexr. Goss

---

692   Frederick Oakeley, 1802–80, tractarian convert in 1845; canon of Westminster in 1852. His letter appeared in *The Tablet* on 20 April 1867: it was a very strong defence of Newman against rumours that his orthodoxy was suspect in Rome, and described him as so pure and saintly that he could not be spoilt by shafts of malignity. 'The monument of whose work for the Church of God is around us in that vast company of converts … one whose writings have contributed more than those of any one of the present generation to uphold the principles of sound doctrine … and ecclesiastical obedience.' He spoke of busybodies and gossip-mongering in Rome, hence Goss's reactions.

693   Felix Dupanloup, 1802–78; bishop of Orleans in 1849; well known as a liberal, his commentary on the Syllabus of Errors of 1864 was influential in defusing opposition to it; an 'inopportunist' on infallibility; in reality a very complex figure. See *Catholicisme*, and Peter Doyle, 'Pope Pius IX and Religious Freedom', *SCH* 21 (1984), 329–41, esp. 330–1.

407.   *Provincial of the Good Shepherd,*[694] *Hammersmith*
                          24 April 1867   *5/5/148*

Dear Mother Provincial,

I make it a principle never to interfere with the domestic concerns of Religious, that is with mere internal matters that concern only the regulation of their intercourse with their Superiors, for I hold that it is a dangerous thing to stand between the Governor & the governed. There are times, however, when I think this should be done. As regards your Institute I have never done it before, tho' I have had occasion to feel aggrieved, & hence I trust that my words will not be without effect now. On the occasion of my first Visitation I was struck by the religious bearing of two Sisters, one is now present Prioress, the other is Sister Mary of the Presentation. The latter was ordered to Scotland, much against her own inclination & much against the wishes of the then Prioress & her assistant, who did not hesitate to manifest this to me. Sister M. of the P. neither murmured nor complained nor even hinted her reluctance, which however showed itself by the tears which streamed down her face & which she, in vain, attempted to laugh away. This incident made me feel her departure from my diocese because I saw that she had the true spirit of Religion. I grieve to learn from the Prioress that it is now proposed to remove her – why I know not – nor can I conjecture that it can be for the good of souls, as the duty she has to fulfil at Hammersmith is exactly the same as she fulfils at Walton. The Children are happy under her cheerful care & unless it is her own wish to go & not to stay, I shall be sorry if the attempt to remove her is persisted in. I shall like due time to consider before I sign her obedience. Except made on good grounds changes betray weakness of government & I shall not be able to disabuse my mind of Suspicion that there are seeds of instability. Her recent bereavement makes her an object of universal sympathy.

With every best wish I remain truly Yrs in Xt. Alexr. Goss.

---

694 The Good Shepherd nuns were at Ford.

408. *Rev. P. Kane*[695]   *27 May 1867*   *5/5/150*
"Status animarum"

My dear Mr. Kane

In your Reply [*sic*] to the Visitation Questions & to Schedule 1 of Schools, you state your congregation to be about 300 souls; don't you know the exact number? If you do, why don't you state it? If you do not, how can you think that you are fulfilling your duty? Does not the good Shepherd know his sheep, & is he not known by them? Have you no school? What is the aisle used for that is boarded off from the Church? With every best wish truly Yrs in Xt. +Alexander Goss.

---

695 Peter Joseph Kane, 1831–1909; o. 1863; r. Anderton to 1881.

409. *Rev. S. Walsh, Belle Vue, Derby Road, Bootle*   *28 May 1867*
5/5/151

"Monition of Suspension"[696]
Monitio Suspensionis Prima

Rev. Sir,

I had hoped that, on my promise to give you an Exeat, provided you could find a Bishop to incorporate you, my Diocese would have been relieved from your presence, & St. Alexander's from a burden. Your dilatoriness has baffled my good intentions in your regard, & I am now under the painful necessity of warning you that unless you pay over to the Rev. Edward Powell within three days from the receipt hereof such sums as you have received towards the new Church or the Mission, I shall suspend you *a divinis*: & this is the first Monition. Furthermore you must notify to me the said payment or present the receipt of the Money from the Rev. Edward Powell. I am etc.

Alexander, Bishop of Liverpool

---

696 See letter 415.

410.   *'Extract from Instruction of Bishop Goss'*[697]   *May 1867   RCLv*

Housekeeping

The keep of the house shall be left as heretofore to the discretion of the Senior Priest, but he should be guided by the following general rules:

1. The style of the table to be always good in its kind, but plain and substantial. Beer to be allowed.

2. The Coadjutor to have no <u>right</u> whatever to wine or spirits either after dinner or supper or at any other time. The Senior Priest not to allow the ordinary use of either, especially of spirits, but to exercise a very cautious discretion on occasionally allowing it on certain days or in certain seasons.

3. No one to have the right of ordering meals, or inviting to the house, except the Senior Priest; and no meals to be permitted except at fixed hours.

4. All wines and spirits to be kept under lock and key, and no one to be allowed possession of the key except the Senior Priest.

5. Coadjutors to be most strictly forbidden to keep at their own disposal, either in their rooms or in the house, any wine or spirits of their own.

6. Every Coadjutor to be required to give notice at breakfast to the Senior Priest when he intends to be absent from dinner.

---

[697]   The Instruction was the result of a commission established in 1867 by the Chapter, at Goss's request, to inquire into diocesan financial matters and clerical life; its report is in RCLv 'Report of the Commission, 1867'.

411.   *Rev. T.A. Bury O.S.B.,*[698] *Hindley nr. Wigan   1 July 1867*
                                                            5/5/152

My dear Fr. Bury

I am glad to learn that, with the sanction of your Superior, you propose to erect a new church at Hindley.[699] As I expressed to you at my Visitation it is not before it is wanted, for in its present ruinous condition it is not fit to be the home of the Blessed Sacrament, & is not large enough to accommodate the people that belong to your district. Your own people will, no doubt, do their best to aid you, but you will have to appeal to the generosity of the faithful at large, & I have great pleasure in recommending that appeal to the faithful of this Diocese, & to pray for the success of your efforts as well as for the blessing of God on all those who come to your aid.

With every best wish, I remain truly Yrs in Xt. +Alexander Goss.

---

[698]   Thomas (Austin) Bury OSB, 1827–1904.

[699]   St Benedict's, Hindley, was an ancient Benedictine mission. For its dilapidated state, see the 1866 Visitation Report, RCLv 3/B, 4/117; a new church was opened in 1869.

412. *Rev. J. B. Quinn,*[700] *Wavertree Road, Nr Ash Grove, Lpool*
                              8 July 1867   5/5/153

Rev. Sir,
Your letter has relieved me of the duty of summoning you by an Edict on Scholes Church door[701] to return under pain of suspension within two days. I am not unforgiving, but I am a lover of Church discipline & aim to maintain it. I count therefore on your return to Scholes, to which you were appointed, & from which you have not obtained your release. The Clergy go into Retreat next week; accompany them. Wine & women have undone many; if you do not abstain from the first, you will soon fall prey to the second. I speak advisedly. Praying God to guide & direct you.
I remain Yrs in Xt. Alexander Bishop of Liverpool
How comes it that your letter is dated Liverpool & was posted the same day in Wigan?

---

[700] John Barry Quinn, b. 1839, o. 1864; St Patrick's Wigan 1866–8; no trace after 1868. See letters 414 and 421.
[701] Scholes Church was St Patrick's, Wigan, founded 1847.

413.   *CIRCULAR*   *9 July 1867*   5/5/155

Dear Rev. Sir,
The Bishop instructs me to request that you insert the following Monition in your Note Book, & read it at every Mass & public Service on Sunday next.
   "The Bishop instructs us to request that, in case any anti Catholic lecturers exhibit in this town, you will not congregate about the place in which they lecture, or enter the lecture room, or mass together in the neighbouring streets, or offer any opposition, or get up counter lectures, or answer in the public prints or by placards the calumnies & slanders they may utter."[702]
I remain Yrs sincerely in Xt. James Ray

---

[702] See Neal, *Sectarian Violence*, 180–2, on local problems at this time.

414.   *Mr. George Vaughan, Scholes*   *16 July 1867*   5/5/156
                    (Petition – Rev. John Quinn)
Dear Sir,
I beg to acknowledge the receipt of your Petition accompanied by the signatures of a large number of St. Patrick's Congregation, praying that the Rev. John Quinn may not be removed from St. Patrick's, but may be allowed to continue his missionary labors [*sic*] amongst you. It is

to me exceedingly gratifying to find that my Clergy enjoy the esteem and respect of their flocks, and it shall always be my aim to provide such pastors for my people as will not only discharge their duties, but discharge them in such a way as shall win the hearts & affections of their people. I have now to assure you that Mr. Quinn's leaving was entirely his own act. It seems to have arisen from some doubts in his own mind regarding his suitableness for the duties he had to discharge, and not from any dislike that he had to his work or the Congregation. I am happy to say that he and your respected pastor Mr. McCormick lived on the most agreeable terms, and were mutually satisfied and pleased with each other. Communicate my sentiments to the gentlemen who signed the address, and rest assured that if Mr Quinn leaves St. Patrick's, it will be because he thinks that he can do more good elsewhere. Wishing every blessing to all the Congregation of St. Patrick's, I remain Your Father in Xt.

+Alexander Goss.

415.   *Rev. S. Walsh, 46 Spellow Lane, Lpool   25 August 1867*
5/5/157

"Exeat"

Rev. Sir,

If you are in an anomalous position, you have no one to blame for it but yourself: it is your act, not mine, that has placed you where you are.

I inclose a Latin letter as you claim the English one insufficient: both are as ample, probably more so, than the one you bore to my Predecessor on leaving the Congregation of which you were a member.[703] Whatever may be my faults, want of forbearance to you is not amongst them.

I remain Yrs in Xt. Alexander Goss.

---

703   See letters 404, 409. The Latin letter is on p. 158 but is too faint to be legible.

416.   *[To Bp. Ullathorne]   10 September 1867*   5/5/160

My dear Lord,

Many thanks for the inclosed letters which I return. It is very useful to know the opinions of one's brother Bps. I must confess that I am not hopeful about our future relations. The treatment of Dr. N is infamous. What has he done to be cast aside in so contemptuous a manner? How insolent the expression used by Stonor[704] who is only of yesterday. I think we should sustain our position by presenting a firm remonstrance, couched not in the flattering words of the day but in the more English style of St. Thomas. We are little better than Vicars general, & we shall soon be something less. I think we should remonstrate before publishing the brief, & if we publish it, we should do so simply, leaving to Rome the responsibility of its own act. If Germans & Americans are allowed to attend mixed universities how can we condemn of mortal sin, or being in occasion of sin, those who do the same thing in this country.[705]

Ever truly Yrs in Xt. A. Goss.

---

[704] Edmund Stonor, 1831–1912, third son of Lord Camoys; he spent his priestly ministry in Rome, becoming Dean of St John Lateran, and Abp of Trebizond in 1888; see Robert J. Stonor OSB, *Stonor, A Catholic Sanctuary in the Chilterns from the Fifth Century till To-*day (Newport, 1951), 344–6.

[705] *Decreta*, 330–2: Barnabò's letter to Manning, 6 August 1867, forbidding attendance at non-Catholic universities. It ordered individual bishops to issue pastorals on the subject. See also Champ, *William Bernard Ullathorne*, 315–18. Goss did write a pastoral, concentrating on the dangers of mixed education for all ages, not just university students; AAL, Pastoral Letters, Second Sunday of Advent, 1867. See letter 418, to Manning.

417. *Rev. P. Van Hee,*[706] *52 Gt. Mersey St., Lpool* 2 October 1867
5/5/178

Rev. & dear Sir,

I am surprised to learn that a Coadjutor Priest can introduce a female into a private room, can call for drink, can lock the door, & remain there without challenge till 11.30, & then leave the house to accompany her home.

Now I beg to observe 1. that no one ought <u>to be able</u> to enter the house or to leave it after 11 o'clock without your knowledge: after that hour, the outer key should be in your custody. 2. No priest ought to be allowed to see a female in any other room than the waiting room or dining room, whatever her respectability, & never with the door locked or for a long period or at suspicious hours. 3. All wine & spirits should be kept under lock & key, the key ought to be kept by the Senior priest; the use of either should not be <u>ordinarily</u> allowed even at dinner or supper, but may occasionally be allowed at the discretion of the Senior priest. Beer should be allowed at dinner. 4. No priest can keep a private store in his room of either wine or spirits. 5. No priest but the Senior can order meals or invite others to dine: no meals to be permitted except at the fixed hours. 6. Any priest dining out must notify the same to the Senior priest at breakfast time, & say <u>where</u> he is dining, so that if he be wanted it may be known where he is to be found. 7. Smoking must not be allowed in any room of the house, unless it be the water closet. 8. The salary of Coadjutor priests must not exceed £25 per an. for the first three years after ordination, & may be increased every three years by the addition of £5 until it reaches the maximum of £40. In addition to this he is entitled to his retributions, but not to fees. You will consider these regulations obligatory both as regards yourself & others, i.e. you will see that they are followed.

Mr. Nixon will succeed Mr. Sheedy,[707] & will be with you on Friday or Saturday. A. Goss.

---

[706]   Peter Van Hee 1837–94, b. Belgium, edu. Bruges; r. at Eldon Street 1866–82.

[707]   John Nixon, 1839–1912; o. 1867; Peter Sheedy: b. 1840; edu. All Hallows, o. 1866, but no trace after 1867.

418.   *His Grace the Archbishop of Westminster*   *6 October 1867*
5/5/179

"Circular on University Education"

My dear Grace,

I cannot think it necessary to hold a meeting for securing uniformity of utterance on the subject of university education. The Holy See has secured the object in view by laying down instructions for our guidance. Unless the Pastoral had been written for us, I do not see that more could have been done.[708] I should hope that the Bishops who happened to be in Rome when this question was raised did not undertake to act as representatives of the Episcopate, for I had my own procuator there, & I do not hear that he was consulted.

With every kind wish Very sincerely Yrs in Xt. +Alexander Goss.

---

[708]   This letter is a little odd: Goss had already written to Manning (letter 5/5/160, 5 September) against the idea of a common letter on the subject, because it would 'smack of synodal action' without the advantage of 'synodal discussion'; was Manning now offering that advantage? Goss had added that the question was never raised in his diocese.

419.   *V.R. A. Weld, Prov. S.J.,*[709] *9 Hill St., Berkeley Sq, London*
21 December 1867   *5/5/187*

"Faculties & Synod"

My dear Fr. Provincial,

I beg to reciprocate your kind wishes, & write to say that you may signify to the gentlemen named that I grant the usual Missionary faculties, & on their writing for a *pagella* I will forward one, if one be wanting.

Is it not usual for official personages, on hearing rumours calculated to give pain, to write & inquire into their accuracy before commenting on them? Your Reverence knows best why you have not so acted. There is however no truth in what you have heard, not a single Fr. of your Society was read up as a defaulter. The changes or contemplated changes made in the Missionaries of the Society rendered it difficult for the officers of the Synod to compile an accurate list of those bound to attend. Hence some omissions both of secular & religious priests, &

some names read out of persons that have gone away or been removed. As soon as I noticed it, I called the attention of the Secretary & required a new list to be made out. He told me that he asked Fr. Porter[710] to furnish one. If your Reverence heeds such groundless & mischievous & false rumours I fear you will alter the good relations that have subsisted for a dozen years. Be it so. I shall regret it, but should have the satisfaction of feeling that it has not originated with me.

With every best wish, I remain Yrs in Xt. Alexander Goss

---

[709] Alfred Weld SJ, 1823–90; Provincial 1864–70; English Assistant in Rome, 1873–83; sometime editor of *The Month* and *The Messenger.*

[710] George Porter SJ, 1825–89, at St Francis Xavier's, Liverpool; he was not on good terms with Goss; see letters 422, 427.

420. *His Grace The Archbishop of Westminster* 17 February 1868

5/5/188

My dear Grace,

I did not express any opinion on the subjects raised in your letter of the 6th as I supposed my silence would be taken as an approval of the sentiments expressed by you. My letter was posted with others which I know reached London for the first delivery on Tuesday. Many of my clergy think that it would be advantageous to have the children off the streets at any cost, whether they learned any thing or nothing, for they would thereby be for a certain number of hours out of harm's way. I don't see any particular objections to a rate, unless it be part of a system formed for the elimination of denominational education.

It seems to me that by right education is a parental not a state duty, for if the state has a right to prescribe education it must have a right to prescribe the kind of education, & is only prevented doing so by the force of public opinion; but how long that opinion may be in favour of denominational education, we cannot say, & therefore it is unwise to recognize in the state a power which it may abuse. The addition of a conscience clause to a school bill, would reduce schools to the same position as the Irish national schools:[711] still, in poor localities such schools are better than none. We should, however, resist any innovation, even tho' not injurious itself, if it would have the effect of weakening or damaging the denominational system.

I have the honour to remain Your Grace's Obedient Servant in Xt. Alexander Goss.

---

[711] The Irish National School system had been set up in 1831, with government funding of multi-denominational schools for primary-age children and state control of teachers and curricula; attendance was not compulsory. By mid-century the schools in practice had become denominational and control passed to the churches, though technically the

state was still in control; the number of schools and pupils steadily increased. See D. H. Akenson, *The Irish Educational Experiment* (London, 1970). An attempt by the Corporation to run a similar system in Liverpool in the 1830s began promisingly but eventually failed through sectarian opposition; see James Murphy, *The Religious Problem in English Education: The Crucial Experiment* (Liverpool, 1959).

421.   *Rev. Thos. Tobin*   *2 March 1868*   *5/5/189*
"Conduct of Rev. Mr. Baines"[712]

My dear Mr. Tobin,

You write me that a respectable young priest has told you that "all say that you get the worst class of fellows in the Diocese, & that you are not called upon to put up with blackguardism". Now that priest, whatever his name, is a slanderer, & likely a knave or fool to boot. Mr O'Gorman[713] was surely above cavil. Mr. Quinn, when appointed to St. Michael's, had the reputation of being a brilliant and able man; he was educated, like myself, at Ushaw & Rome, & came out of both places with a flaming character. I could not foresee, certainly did not expect that he would be faithless to his gifts. Mr. Parkinson[714] had done his duty at Lancaster, from which place he came to you, & enjoyed & enjoys still the reputation of being one of the most amiable priests in the Diocese. Mr. Baines passed through his studies with honour: he gained the £50 prize for his theological ability, & he came to you fresh from the grace of ordination. If your caviller be, as you say he is, a respectable man, let him say to these gentlemen's faces what he has said behind their backs. If Mr. Baines does not do as he is bid in matters in which he is subject to you, summon him before the Vicar, & let him reprimand him: such breaches of duty it is his province to correct, not mine. From Mr. Walker's letter, it appears that Mr. Baines behaves with you at table no worse than he behaved with him when his guest. I cannot force him to speak, however I may regret his silence. Be good enough to tell him I must have his status returns on the inclosed paper, & admonish him from me that the payment of his salary will depend thereon, besides the further chance of being sent into retreat.

With every best wish I remain Yrs in Xt. Alexander Goss.

---

712   Baines: *vere* Richard Baynes 1842–99; o. 1867, left St Michael's 1868 for St Vincent's, Liverpool.
713   Michael O'Gorman, 1839 (Ireland), o. 1864; died of typhus 1866.
714   James Parkinson, 1838–83, o. 1863; at Lancaster to 1866 and St Michael's to 1867.

422.   *Rev. G. Porter S.J., St. Francis Xavier's, Lpool*   *29 April 1868*
5/5/190
"Irregular marriage"

My dear Fr. Porter,

The V.R. Can. Carr complains that a marriage has been celebrated at St. Francis Xavier's between persons belonging to his District who were related in the 3rd degree.

1o.   I wish to know whether William Aindow & Anne Swift were married in the April of last year at your church & if so, by whom?

2o.   I wish to know whether a dispensation was procured for the said parties, they being within the prohibited degrees?

3o.   If the parties concealed the relationship, & were married at your church, how came they to be married without a certificate of the publication of banns in the church to which they belonged?

If the parties were married by dispensation there is no ground of complaint on the ground of irregularity, & I do not take cognisance of want of courtesy. You have a copy of Can. Carr's Complaint. With every best wish I remain Yrs in Xt. Alexander Goss.

423.   *Rev. D.F. Barry O.S.B.,*[715] *Seel St., Lpool*   *25 June 1868*
5/5/192
"Marriage Case"

Dear Rev. Sir,

I feel it my duty to call your attention to the marriage case of Thomas McGoldrick & Margaret McQuale. On the 7th of May you made application for a Dispensation, alleging that they were related *in gradu 3o. consanguinitatis.* On the 10th I signed the Dispensation, but requested my Secretary not to forward it, till you had made inquiry from the Parish Priest of the parties whether they were free to marry. On the 18th of May you married them, after having, as you state, made the necessary inquiries.

Now 1o. In your letter to Rev. W. Quinn of May 11 you inquire whether T. McGoldrick has ever been married in his parish, but you do not ask whether there is any other canonical impediment. 2o. You make no inquiry about the woman McQuale, on whose side there might also be impediment. 3o. The Rev. Mr. Quinn says that the man is a profligate, that he is the father of two illegitimate children by different women, one of whom alleges a promise of marriage, & that the woman McQuale was own cousin[716] to Goldrick [*sic*], in gradu 2o. not 3o; that he informed you 'how the man stood there', & requested you 'not to marry them'.

I wish to know 1o.what proof you had that the parties had ceased to be parishioners of Rev. Mr. Quinn; 2o. what proof you sought or

had of the free state of the woman; 3o. whether or not he alleged that
the parties were <u>own</u> cousins; 4o. whether he mentioned the alleged
promise of marriage to one of the mothers of his illegitimate children.
    I remain very truly Yrs in Xt. Alexander Goss Bp. of Lpool.

---

715   David (Francis) Barry OSB, 1836–96.
716   'Own' cousin: i.e. first cousin. A promise of marriage, whether formal or informal,
did not compel the parties to marry, though it might be grounds for compensation.

424.   *Rev. Wm. Bradshaw,*[717] *St. Joseph's Preston*   *30 August 1868*
5/5/197

"Excorporation"

Rev. Sir,
You write as if you thought that my forbearance sprang from pusilla-
nimity. If this be your belief you will be led into mistakes, of which you
may have all your life to regret the consequences. I am slow to act, but
I am slower still to retrace my steps.
    You do not say whether you hold in writing the consent of any Bishop
to <u>in</u>corporate you in case I consent to <u>ex</u>corporate you: such consent in
writing is necessary. Until you have it, you need not write again to me,
but you shall hear from me in due time. I am Yours in Xt. +Alexander
Goss.

---

717   William Henry Bradshaw, 1834–1912; he served in the diocese until retirement in
1909; a man of many missions.

425.   *Rev Wilfred Cooper O.S.B., St. Augustines, Lpool*
30 August 1868   *5/5/198*

Dear Rev. Sir,
There is no law to prevent political meetings, as there is to prevent
dancing in school rooms, under censure, but duty requires that quasi
ecclesiastical buildings should be used for the purposes for which they
were erected, a school room for the teaching of the young & ignorant,
a young men's room for the purposes of the young men's society, from
which politics are excluded. The Church, as such, has no politics, tho'
it is conservative of what it finds, constitutionalism in England, abso-
lutism in Russia, republicanism in America, but its mission is not to
interfere except so far as its jurisdiction requires. You are the pastor of
all the Catholics of your mission, whatever may be their political principles, & whilst, as a man, you are free to vote on any side, yet, as a priest,
you should not ally yourself with parties among your people. I have had
a vote for a quarter of a century, but never exercised it but once. My

politics are the good of the Church & the welfare of my people: I belong to no party. Some years ago, the liberal papers denounced me because I published a note saying that the Conservatives had promised to appoint Chaplains to our gaols: I should have acted the same if the Whigs had made the promise, i.e. I should have promulgated it.

If Government come to know of such meetings, it may affect the educational grant to our schools. If they dare not <u>sanction</u> Mass to be said, will they sanction or allow political meetings? Besides many of your subscribers may be conservative. My greatest & most intimate personal friend, Lady Scarisbrick,[718] is for the Whigs: the best Contributor to the Charities, the general charities of the Diocese, Sir Robt. Gerard, is Conservative. My advice then is disinterested: Let neither school room, nor Church, nor young men's room be used for political purposes. I say nothing of Monday's meeting as it is convened. Truly Yrs in Xt, A. Goss.

---

[718] Lady Scarisbrick – *vere* Dame Anne Hunloke, widow of Sir Thomas Windsor Hunloke, fifth baronet, Catholic, of Wingerworth, Derbyshire (md.1807, he died 1816). Born Anne Eccleston in 1788, she was the sister of Charles who inherited the Scarisbrick estates and changed his name to Scarisbrick. When he died in 1856, the estate passed to Anne, now a widow, who also took the name Scarisbrick; she lived until 1872. Goss often stayed at the Hall in later years. Hilton, *Catholic Lancashire* (86–7) describes Scarisbrick Hall near Ormskirk as 'the apogee of Gothic Catholic houses'; it still has a suite named 'Bishop's Rooms'. See *VCH* III, 269.

426. *Rt. Rev. Dr. Turner*   *15 September 1868*   *5/5/199*
"Common Letter on Ushaw"

My dear Lord,

The letter of the 19th of August on the Colleges was addressed by Propaganda to Archbp. Manning, who was directed to ascertain the sentiments of the Bps. cointerested in the three Colleges, & to report their several opinions. It appears to me that several may apply to the three batches of Bps. or to each Bp. individually. I understood it in the first sense, because I had previously had a letter, in which the Secretary of Prop. requested that I would communicate with the bps. cointerested in Ushaw & learn their opinions whether anything could be done, & if so what, to preserve St. Cuthbert's College & at the same time carry out the instructions of the Holy See for the erection of Seminaries in the respective dioceses. Before I could carry out the suggestion, the printed letter arrived. I think we fully comply with the instructions of Propaganda by a joint letter; but at the same time each Bp. may stand on his own bottom & write his own letter. Further I think he may, if he likes, sign the common letter, if he approves of its contents, & add a private letter if he have any thing further to suggest. For my own part I should have preferred to have had the whole matter referred to the next Synod. There can be no lasting settlement of any question till justice, full & impartial, be done, we cannot for the sake of peace allow the interests of our Dioceses to be further sacrificed.

We can send the letter with whatever signatures are attached as expressing the views of those who sign it, without questioning the undoubted right that each Bishop possesses of stating his own individual views.

Ever truly Yrs Alexander Goss.

427. *Rev. George Porter S.J.   16 September 1868*   *5/5/200*
"Fraudulent Marriage"

My dear Fr. Porter,
I am in receipt of your answer to Can. Carr's complaint about the unlawful & invalid marriage of Wm. Aindow & Lucy Swift, which I find to be unsatisfactory. You allege that the addresses given are places within your district, that Aindow represented himself as a sailor, & that you cannot say whether or not you verified the residences. A reference to the *Liber status animarum* would have shown that the parties did not reside at the places named, & the profession of a sailor, to say the least, should have suggested additional caution. As the matter now stands, qualified by your letter, you appear to have neglected every precaution ordered by the Church, & the result is an invalid & incestuous marriage to the scandal of their native village. By the common law of the Church you were bound to inquire, <u>before</u> putting up the banns, *"ex his ad quos spectat, qui et quales sint qui matrimonium contrahere velint. An inter eos sit aliquod canonicum impedimentum"*.[719] The Ritual cautions you against admitting strangers, as these were to you, *"ignotos non facile ad matrimonium admittat"*.[720] You say the banns were published but the Council of Trent says that banns are ordered only to aid in the discovery of impediments *"ut si aliqua subsunt impedimenta facilius detegantur"*. The Council of Lateran expressly says *"Et ipsi presbyteri nihilominus investigent, utrum aliquod impedimentum obsistat"*. Barbosa warns priests against putting up the banns of persons such as these, whose absence from your status book must have shown them to be exteri, *"nisi eorum conditionem noverit legitimo in scripto testimonio, quod alium virum vel uxorem non habeant, & quod omni impedimento canonico matrimonii careant"*. The gravity of this case requires a more satisfactory reply than that contained in your letter of May 2nd.

With every best wish Yrs in Xt. Alexander Goss.

---

719 Trans: 'from those concerned, who and what sort of people they may be who wish to marry. Whether there may be any canonical impediment between them.'
720 Trans: *Ritual*: 'he should not easily admit to marriage unknown people'. *Trent*:

'so that any other underlying impediments may be discovered easily'. *Lateran*: 'And nevertheless let the priests themselves investigate whether any other impediment exists'. *Barbosa*: 'unless he knows their condition from a legitimate written testimony, that they do not have another wife or husband, and that they are without any canonical impediment to marriage'.

428. *Rev. Fr. Francis OSF, Franciscan Convent, West Gorton,*
Manchester   *18 September 1868*   *5/5/203*
Dear Rev. Sir,
The V.R. Dr. Fisher, who is acting for my Vicar General now dangerously ill, assures me that he issued no prohibition against your preaching, but only declined to license you, for which he cannot be called upon to give a reason, as it is not the deprivation of a right, but only the refusal of a favour. His refusal to sanction your giving a Mission may be sought in the fact that the priest had usurped the Bp's functions by making arrangements without enquiring whether it were expedient to do so, & because, as there are several bodies of religious established in the Diocese for the purpose of giving Missions, he may have judged it to be not in accordance with Ecclesiastical usage to solicit your assistance at a distance from your Monastery in aid of a Diocese which had no claim on your services.[721] With every best wish I remain Yrs in Xt. +Alexander Goss.

---

[721] Neither Goss nor O'Reilly wanted Franciscans in the diocese; see Peter Doyle, 'Bishop O'Reilly and the Franciscans', *NWCH* 27 (2000), 45–54.

429. *Rt. Rev. Dr. Ullathorne, Bp of Birmingham*   *19 September 1868*
5/5/204
"Theologian to Gen. Coun."
My dear Lord,
What answer do you propose to return to the letter of the Archbp. dated Sep. 17? 1o. Why should the person named be from our respective Dioceses? Why may not each Bp. name or suggest one from any of our Dioceses? 2o. Why has he to be capable of transmitting information in our future Provincial councils; for, as our nominee to prepare for a Gen: Coun: he will have no place in our Prov: Synod? 3o. What can Eng: Missionary experience have to do with the decrees of an oecumenical Council? Missionary experience & great theological knowledge seldom go together. 4o. Why must he be from the Secular Clergy? He is not a representative, but a worker to take his part in a great business. I suggested to the Archbp. to send round the names already proposed, with the name of the Proposer: we could then have transferred our vote

from our own nominee to some body that seemed more eligible whom we might not previously have thought of. I suggested Dr. Newman. Why should we restrict ourselves when the Holy See has not restricted us?[722]

Jos. Pyke Esq, Winckley Sq, Preston will be my address till Wednesday, after which Queen's Hotel, Harrogate. I remain truly Yrs in Xt. Alexr. Goss.

---

[722] Manning got his own nominee accepted as consultor on the dogmatic commission: William Weathers, 1814–95, President of St Edmund's 1851–68 and later auxiliary to Manning. See Cwiekowski, *The English Bishops*, 74, 78–80.

430.   *Rev. Fr E. Whyte S.J.,*[723] *St. John's, Wigan*   *14 October 1868*
5/5/208

Dear Rev. Fr.
There has arrived at this office a letter addressed to the V.R. Canon Carr, without signature, stating that Fr. Di Petro[724] will remain at home to attend to the congregation on the day of Synod. As the Bishop is under the impression that he only who summons the Synod can dispense with attendance, he would be glad to know by whose order Fr. Di Pietro remains at home. He does not care to interfere with your arrangement but he wants to know for future guidance by whom that arrangement was made.

[*signed by*] John Wallwork

---

[723] Edward Whyte SJ, 1827–1904. On the issue of non-attendance, see also 5/5/207 of 14 October 1868, Wallwork to Porter, in charge of the Jesuit mission in Liverpool: his claim for exemption from attendance at Synod had been received, but Goss refused to express any opinion on its validity; in practice, Porter need not attend as long as he sent a suitable representative in his place.

[724] John Baptist Di Pietro SJ, b. 1820, was curate at St John's; no other biographical detail is given. Fitz-L also lists a Salvator Di Pietro, but he is not in the *Directory*.

431.   *Rt. Rev. Bp. Brown, Bullingham, Hereford*   *9 December 1868*
5/5/211

"Visitation of Regulars"

My dear Lord,
As I take it, Monasteries, with less than 12 inmates, are subject to the Visitation of the Ordinary. The Missionary Regulars in England claimed exemption from such Visitation as they were living out of their monasteries for the public service: the claim I neither admitted nor denied, but abstained from making the visitation. Such claim of exemption did not prevent their visitation in whatever concerned the cure of souls, to

the same extent as secular priests. If I did abstain from the full exercise of my rights, it was for the sake of peace, as I had so many of them in my Diocese; but I have no recollection of any denial of such rights, tho' they did claim not to be dealt with as vagabonds living outside of their Monastery. Archbishop Errington both in Plymouth & London asked for a return of the Missionary income of the Regulars having cure of souls, & it was provided to him without question. If at a Mission there was property held by them in their capacity of Regulars, & not of missionaries, such property would escape visitation unless the ordinary refused to recognise a claim of exemption where there were not 12 inmates. Whether at any of their Missions there be such property remains to be decided by the Holy See. After the letter of July 9 from Card. Barnabò there can be no doubt of their obligation to have the Bishop's leave for absence beyond a few days, & of their obligation to spend on their Missions all that remains over & above their suitable maintenance, & consequently of the Bishop's duty to see by an examination of accounts whether this be done.[725] If it be necessary to have a representative in Rome on this matter, I think we should meet & depute one ad hoc; for the Archbp. has gone for his own purposes not ours, & I don't know what his sentiments are on the matter. I return your letter, as after my explanation you may modify it. I have not made any visitation of Regulars since July 9, but I shall act up to Card. Barnabò's letter when I do.

Ever truly Yrs Alexander Goss.

---

[725] Barnabò's letter is in *Decreta*, 313–15.

432. [*Dr. Newman*]   *12 May 1869, Scarisbrick Hall, Nr. Ormskirk, Lancs.*   ABO

My dear Dr. Newman,

Our Bps, when in London, decided to issue pastorals on the Feast of the Sacred Heart, in favour of denominational Education. I was not present, but shall follow their example, though I do not like the Archbishop's policy of united legislation for matters over which in the respective Dioceses there can be admitted no control but that of the Diocesan. The object of my letter is to ask if you will be good enough to write me such a Pastoral. You can, I cannot. The subject is great & wants a masterly hand. Pious Pastorals that suit well for family homilies, will not suit a great occasion or a great subject: we want a national document. I often regret that we write in so slipshod a way, when the times demand something more telling & authoritative. I seek an excuse, independently of want of ability, in my ailment which prevents me writing, so that I reserve most of my utterances for extemporary sermons, unless chance throws in my way an amanuensis. When not engaged in actual work,

I live at the quiet address which heads my letter, amusing myself with collecting materials for a Catholic history of my Diocese.

I cannot conceal from you my regret that you are not in Rome preparing for the Council. I don't suppose they wanted you there, but your friends did & do. Dr. Weather's appointment was, I think, managed by the Archbp. more adroitly than straightforwardly. It is much to be regretted that English opinion cannot be suitably represented. Mgr. Talbot has too long influenced the head of the Church, & the views of a few headstrong & venturesome young men have been taken as English public opinion. Long ago I heard it hinted that if the personal infallibility of the Pope were proclaimed, all England would come over, at least the clerical element. My sermon at Preston was not fully reported, but I said that the Newspapers uttered blasphemy when they ventured to prescribe to the Holy Ghost both what had to be done, & how it had to be done, & I stigmatized as an insult offered to the Catholic hierarchy of the world, the supposition that they would, without adequate examination, proclaim the dogma of Papal Infallibility by acclamation as boys welcomed a favourite toast by shouts of a viva. The Italian officials about the Pope treat every body as school boys & children. Our press is in the hands of incompetent bigots, & if any man dares to speak honestly upon open questions he is denounced to Rome as a Gallican. Nobody dares to tell the Pope the truth. He has now ceased to be called any thing but the Vicar of Xt: nay they seem to claim for him powers that do not belong to Christ as Redeemer, but to Xt as God. Pardon this hurried & hodge podge letter – I write to you without either restraint or reticence.[726]

With every best wish I am ever Yrs truly, Alexander Goss.

---

[726] Newman replied the following day (see Dessain, XXIV, p. 255), calling Goss's request a 'flattering proposal' and an 'extraordinary honour', but declining it on the grounds of having no experience of poor schools and being too busy anyway. Goss wrote a pastoral letter in September, 1870, on the 1870 Education Act (AAL, S1/2/C/18)

433.   [*Card. Barnabò*]   *13 August 1869*   *AAL, S1/3/A/16*
                                                                          [*draft*]

Eminent Prince[727]

I write to acknowledge the receipt of a letter dated July 30 with which Your Eminence has honoured me on the ['subject' *crossed out*] case of the Rev. James Berry,[728] & to assure you that I did reply to it as speedily as possible. I would have done so at once, but my Vicar General who has in his care the most recent correspondence on the subject, is not here, & I have to sail to day to the Isle of Man – a six hours sail over a rough & treacherous sea – in order to make the visitation of that distant outpost. My work in Lent brought on sickness which lasted over Easter, and since my recovery I have been engaged in my 5th canonical Visitation, a fatiguing labour in hot weather, so that I feel it hard, whilst cultivating the vineyard of the Lord with one hand, to be obliged to defend myself with the other against the importunities of a priest which I had hoped I had long ago set at rest. Meanwhile I thank your Eminence for the personal kindness which you have always exhibited to me, & kissing the sacred purple beg to remain the most humble & devoted servant of your Eminence,

Alexander Goss Bishop of Liverpool.

---

727 The draft is in Goss's hand.

728 James Berry had worked in a number of missions in the diocese; he was less than zealous, neglecting the church fabric and alienating the people by intemperate language. He had also worked in Shrewsbury 1853–55 and 1866; he seems to have belonged to the diocese of Menevia. Barnabò, rather strangely, took up his case and threatened Goss that it would go to a full meeting of Propaganda if Berry was not supported. Correspondence between Goss and Barnabò erupted irregularly between May 1867 and August 1869; see AAL, S1/3/A/14–16, Roman Correspondence. Goss had put a strong case that he had no obligations to Berry in either justice or equity. This is the final letter on the subject.

434. [*Very Rev. Fr. Weld, Provincial SJ*]   *23 October 1869   5/5/209*
Very Rev. and dear Fr.

Your proposition regarding the abandonment of Portico & the building of a school Chapel at Thatto Heath[729] is too grave to be settled in the limited time at my disposal before leaving for the Council. I can quite understand your desire for your Fathers to live together; but you cannot be ignorant that non-residence amongst the people of whom they have the spiritual care, would be fatal to religion. This is not a proposition that admits of doubt, for the Church has placed it beyond the sphere of private opinion by enforcing residence under severe penalties. Fifteen years ago I expressed myself strongly on this subject when a similar propositon was made to me, & again when the removal of the Pastor from Portico actually took place, though I had the Provincial's assurance that a priest should always remain there on Saturday night & should say mass on weekdays when there was anybody to hear it. This promise was not fulfilled; & you may remember Mr Stokes's[730] complaint on the subject two years ago.

I do not ask you to violate your rule either in this or any other instance; but if you find that missionary duty is incompatible with religious life, or the rules of the order, or your superior's wish, you have the remedy in your own hands; but, whatever may be the issue, I should not like to incur the responsibility of even seeming to countenance non-residence.

With every best wish, Yours sincerely in Xt. Alexander Goss.

729   Portico and Thatto Heath: both were within easy reach of the Jesuit house in St Helens. See letter 362.

730   Perhaps John Stokes, 1837–?91; joined the Redemptorists in 1866; later worked abroad.

435.   [*Dr. Newman*]   *28 March 1870, Hotel Beau Séjour,*
             Cannes, Alpes Maritimes, France   *ABO*[731]

My dear Dr. Newman,

Ever since I came here I have been intending to write to you, but for a long time I was physically unable, & now I am almost mentally so.[732] I have, however, improved in a marked manner, for I can take a walk for an hour or even more, & I can read, & think, whereas for a long time I would hardly sleep & suffered from such a strange bewilderment in my head that waking & sleeping thoughts were equally vivid. I lived habitually as one feels occasionally from taking very strong coffee when fasting. You will say enough of self: well, it is something to feel & know & be able to own that I am what I am, a broken reed.

It has been to me a great disappointment not to be able to be in Rome, as what I once was: but if I were to go now, my voice would be not only powerless but silent. I could not stand the excitement of the strife & should not have the strength to be of use. I should be one more on the right side & *voila tout.*

I may err in my estimate of a Bp's duty, but I have always held that in matters of faith he is a witness of the tradition & teaching of ['the' *crossed out*] his Church, altho' he might scholastically hold different notions. Personally Mgr Sibour[733] believed the dogma of the Immaculate Conception before it was declared a dogma of faith; but the opinion he wrote as head of the Paris Church was one of the strongest, so strong that the Roman Curia said a <u>few</u> more of such expressions of opinion would have delayed the definition for years. Now by a few more I understand not more than half a dozen. I was in Rome at that time, end of 1854.

I find it so difficult to put my notions, that I don't think I should have ventured to write to you unless is had been for my wish to signify my adhesion to your condemnation of an aggressive & insolent faction. The Dublin Review, the Tablet, & Archbp Manning have taken upon themselves not merely to advocate the Infallibility, but to denounce every body else a little less than heretics & infidels & as committing the unpardonable sin against the Holy Ghost whose decision & ruling they forestalled. I do not know that the Archbp has written any thing harsly [*sic*] beyond what provoked speedy punishment from Dupanloup:[734] but his putting himself so prominently forward, as he does, is both insolent & aggressive: neither his learning nor his standing among

Catholics justify his assumption & his testimony is opposed to the teaching of English Catholics, which is summed up in the Act of Faith in which we accept as of faith all that the Church teaches, because the Son of Truth has revealed it in his Church. The Archbp's position is a thing to be ashamed of, rather than be assumed as a justification of his prominence, for he is standing in another man's shoes, as Archbp Errington was shoved out to make way for M. Poor Mgr. Talbot has much to answer for in that wrong doing. Dr. M. tried hard to get over Darbois,[735] saying it would be such a grand thing for the Archbps of the two great Western sees to receive the hat together; but Darbois would not bend. The Univers is, if anything more insolent than the Tablet and I see that the Tablet cites the letters of L. Veuillot without however naming him, as tho' of a learned or well-informed layman of position.[736] Truth, simple English truth, seems to have departed from the whole faction. I generally believe any assertion which they are unanimous in contradicting. Nothing ever wounded the simplicity of my faith so much as the trickery with which I became acquainted on official intercourse with the Curia. The present Council, as a friend of mine observes, will change the patriarchal sceptre into a dictator's truncheon, and the Bps who went to Rome as princes of the household to confer with their august ['chief' *crossed out*] Father will return like satraps despatched to their provinces where they may find awaiting them for obedience the very decrees which they had refused to sanction in Council. It is to be hoped that when further opposition becomes fruitless, the opposing Bps will leave the Council en masse, [&] thus add one more to the existing reasons for not considering the great meeting to be an oecumenical Council.[737] The Eastern or Armenian Church at least will I fear be lost for threats are tried when conciliation was needed. The Pope has been so flattered by the great assemblages of the Bps of the Church about him, that he has been led to think that he can rule them as a pedagogue rules his pupils. The dealings of Rome at any time with the Bps has been of the ferula & bonbons stamp: they are not dealt with as grown up men, but as difficult children: & even the best of the Italian laity cannot understand how Bps should refuse submission when by such submission they may attain honours & preferment. In case of disputes about property the Pope's *altum dominium* is used to cover every flaw in justice, & henceforth his Infallibility will be held to supply any defect of argument or revelation in matters of faith. My own opinion is that the Pope believes, feels himself now to be personally inspired & hence no argument can deflect him from an opinion: he has made his own the Wesleyan principle of conscious justification, only applying it to inspiration. For years no one has dared to contradict him & Antonelli[738] manages him by seeming to oppose him & getting some other Cardinal to propose what he really wants in opposition to what he seemingly wants. The Pope is amiable & hence has a sort of hysterical affection from ladies & young priests & he has unfortunately believed that he would be able to exercise the same fascination over the Bps. He began life as a liberal but was at heart an autocrat & he soon made known to the Cardinals that the white zuchetto covered all the red ones.[739] With him the Infallibility is a personal affair & he looks upon all who do not go in for it as enemies, personal enemies.

It has pained me much to write what I have written, but I have written it in the interests of truth. Beyond preaching months ago against the folly of supposing the Infallibility was going to be passed by acclamation,[740] I have given no public utterance either in my own Diocese or in Rome. Now ought I to do anything, & if so, can you do it for me. (1). I may remain silent, as I have hitherto done. (2). I might sign & send, if written for me, a letter strong & firm, but respectful to the Pope, either absolutely against the doctrine or the opportuneness or both: absent Bps are sending to him their adhesion. (3). A letter might be addressed par Times [sic] to Mgr. Dupanloup adhering to his last letter against the opportuneness & amplifying it from an English point of view. (4). A letter might be supposed to be written by me to a friend (5) or to my Chapter, or to my people – I leave the matter to you & will endorse or sign whatever you write for me; for my honour & integrity could not be entrusted to better hands.[741]

Dr. Alexdr. Lycurgus, Archbp of Syra & Tenus[742] has consecrated a Church & ordained Priests in my Diocese: should any protest be made to his Patriarch or to himself? Could any public good, as regards Protestants, be done by showing the schismatical or usurping power of such a proceeding – Protestants are taking him by the hand.

Further it seems they are meditating a Protestant See at Lpool. Now against this I should like to be prepared[743] – Bear in mind that personally I am a broken reed; that I shall never be myself again; that if I were I possess nothing beyond fearlessness in speaking the truth.

Adieu my dear Dr. Newman – Count on my adhesion to what you have written. If they [word or words lost] the party would try to cry you down, as they are doing Montalembert[744] & there is no knowing what the Pope might be driven to do.

With every best wish affectionately Yrs in Xt. Alexr. Goss.

---

731 The letter is printed in Cwiekowski, *English Bishops*, 169–72.

732 In November 1869 he had sent Propaganda a medical certificate, signed by three doctors, to the effect that he was far too ill to attend the Council; they added that the harsh northern climate was not good for him and he should go south for the winter (APF, *Anglia*, 18, fol. 1228).

733 Marie Dominique Auguste Sibour, 1792–1857; archbishop of Paris in 1848, in succession to Mgr Affre, who had been murdered in June 1848; Sibour himself was murdered by a priest in January 1857; the *Directory* for 1858 has a long memoir of him

(160–9), but does not avert to his views on the definition of the dogma, except to say he attended the ceremony in Rome. Cwiekowski, *English Bishops*, 169, says Sibour believed the doctrine was 'indefinable'.

734 Dupanloup, Abp of Orléans; see n. 693 above.

735 Darbois of Paris: mis-spelling of Georges Darboy, Abp. of Paris (1862–71); he was prominent at Vatican I, opposing the definition of infallibility, more on political than theological grounds. He was arrested during the Commune and shot in May 1871. Manning tried his best to save him; see E. S. Purcell, *Life of Cardinal Manning, Archbishop of Westminster*, 2 vols (London, 1896), II, 467–8.

736 Louis Veuillot, 1813–83, journalist, prolific author and editor of the extremely pro-papalist and often excessively belligerent *L'Univers* from 1843. The paper was closed down from 1860 to 1867, on the orders of Napoleon III. It was extremely popular with French rural clergy (see *New Catholic Encyclopedia*, 2nd edn, 2003).

737 Cwiekowski, *English Bishops*, 123–5, details the efforts to organise an effective opposition party.

738 Giacomo Antonelli, 1806–76: Cardinal Secretary of State from 1848 and a very powerful figure in Rome; he was regarded by opponents as an unscrupulous statesman rather than a churchman; he opposed the calling of Vatican I (*ODCC*, p. 67).

739 But see letter 449, where Goss claims the Pope remained a Whig at heart!

740 See Cwiekowski, *English Bishops*, 91–2, for pre-Council excitement and concern.

741 ibid.,, 172, for the draft of Newman's reply; while he refused Goss's request, he agreed with his view of the role of bishops as *testes* as well as *judices*.

742 Alexander Lycurgus, Greek Orthodox Archbishop of Syra, Tinos and Milo; he visited Liverpool at the end of 1869 to open a new Orthodox church and was feted by some Anglicans throughout the country in the hope of Orthodox/Anglican reunion; unfortunately, he could not speak or understand English and his views were repudiated by the official Greek Orthodox authorities. See F. Skene, *The Life of Alexander Lycurgus, Archbishop of the Cyclades* (London, 1877); see also *DTC*, IX, 1359–61.

743 Goss had already spoken against the proposal in public in June 1867, claiming it would make a 'spiritual harlot' of the see to which he was already wedded. This sparked off another spat between him and Rev. Campbell (n. 193); see Burke, *Catholic Liverpool*, 178.

744 Montalembert: some lines are almost illegible here: Cwiekowski reads 'Mistakenly' (*English Bishops*, 172), but it is much more likely a proper name.

436. [*Bp Clifford*]   *8 August 1870, Scarisbrick Hall*   ADC[745]
[*My dear Lord*]

Welcome home triumphant tho' beaten. Can you give me any news of Dr. Errington? I have written to the Archbp. to ask him to call the attention of the Bps to the anomaly of issuing common addresses <u>out</u> of Synod.[746]

I see that he [*Manning*] promises a Pastoral in vindication of the Council's method of proceeding regarding the <u>new</u> dogma: if he does give his version, I hope you will give yours, & follow him step by step; for if he has a right or privilege to make revelations that palliate the tyranny that has been used & the coertion [*sic*] employed, you have an equal right to make such revelations as will justify you in the course you took. The majority of the English Bps. were opposed to the fabrication of the new article. He says it is already of faith: but I conjecture that the decree has no force till promulgated with the other acts of the Council. It is so with a Provincial Synod. Do the opposition Bps admit the decree or do they challenge the authority of the whole Council on the score of want of liberty of action? If there be really a flaw in the Council, the Pope cannot demand interior assent to the new doctrine, tho' by a tyrannical exercise of power he may enforce its publication. With it comes the <u>obligation</u> of persecution, for the Popes have laid it down as the <u>duty</u> of sovereigns to persecute, & with it also comes the doctrines propounded by the Archbp that the Pope is not & cannot be a subject but is above not only the sovereign in whose state he lives, but above all sovereigns, with power to absolve subjects from their allegiance & to transfer empires from one ruler to another, as he gave Ireland to the English & America to the Spaniards. Popes have claimed this power in documents addressed to the whole Church as much as any truths ever are addressed to it. If the doctrine has to be published all that it entails ought to be published with it. We can no longer, laity or clergy, deny divided allegiance. By declaring the Popes to be infallible, it makes this claim of universal dominion, in temporals as well as in spirituals, to be infallible & of faith, & as much to be believed as the mystery of the Trinity. If you know what action the opposition Bps. purpose to pursue I shall be glad to learn …[747]

Excuse this long letter. I write as if I had been fighting side by side with you, as I was in spirit.

A. Goss

---

[745]   J. A. Harding, *Clifford of Clifton (1823–1893)* (Bristol, 2011); see also Cwiekowski, *English Bishops*, 293.

[746]   Cwiekowski (*English Bishops*, 292–3) omits part of this letter, and takes the 'Archbp' to be Errington, but surely it refers to Manning.

[747]   The names of the bishops who accepted the decision of the Council afterwards are in J. D. Mansi *et al.* (eds), *Sacrorum Conciliorum nova et amplissima collectio*, 55 vols (Florence, Leipzig, Paris, 1759–1927); the last five volumes (1923–27) deal with Vatican I; I have found no evidence that Goss submitted his acceptance.

437.   *His Grace the Archbp of Westminster   8 August 1870,*
                                    Scarisbrick Hall   AAL, S1/3/ C/6

My dear Grace,
I am obliged by your favour of an invitation to dine on the occasion of the meeting of the Bps with respect to the recommendation for the See of Southwark.[748] I am, however, advised not to incur the fatigue of a long journey to be followed by prolonged sittings, & deem it prudent to yield to this advice repeated from several quarters. I have the less scruple in doing so, as the meeting is deprived of its synodal character by its

being notified that the Bps will meet together in mantelletta. Unless my memory is grievously at fault, we have hitherto met in mozetta, as being supposed to be present in the exercise of a sort of jurisdiction.[749]

I hope your Grace will pardon me for calling through you the attention of the Bps to what seems to be an irregularity not in accordance with precedent. Some time after the first meeting of the Bps it was notified to the Rev. James Nugent, as a journalist, by your Secretary, that the Bps would hold him responsible for what appeared in his Paper.[750] Now I ventured to say to your Grace, when it was a question of warning the Editor of the *Weekly Register*, that Editors of papers are responsible only to the Bp of the Diocese in which they are published, & that the interference of other Bps would render them actionable at Rome. After this I was surprised to see the warning to the *Register* not in the names of the Bps who had sanctioned it, but in the name of <u>the</u> Bps. In the time of the late Cardinal, whenever the Bps agreed to act with united action, the Pastoral, though common, was issued by each Bp in his own name to his own Diocese. If I mistake not, this is in accordance with Ecclesiastical usage; but I speak as one open to correction if I am in error.

I beg to remain Yrs truly, +Alexander Goss.

---

[748]   Grant died in Rome on 1 June 1870. On 5 August Manning sent the bishops a printed invitation about a meeting to discuss the appointment and to dinner later in the day, and any day they were in London.

[749]   The *mantelletta* is a short mantle reaching to the knees, open in the front and with slits for the arms to pass through; its colour is the colour of the office of the wearer. The *moz(z)etta* is a short cape edged with fur and with a small hood; coloured purple for bishops, it should only be worn in a bishop's own diocese and so is a sign of jurisdiction; in England it is also worn by canons (*ODCC*).

[750]   Amongst his many roles, Nugent was editor/owner of the *Northern Press and Catholic Weekly Times*, later the *Catholic Times*; see Bennett, *Father Nugent*, 70–1 for details. The *Weekly Register*: this was generally anti-definition; see Beck, *The English Catholics*, 504–5, for its varied history. See also letter 440 to Newman.

438.   [*Canon James Fisher*]   *18 August 1870, Moor Park, Preston*

AAL, S1/3/E/4

My Dear Can. Jas.

You know how anxious I have been for years to have all the documents in my custody examined & calendared & lest these should be intentions unfulfilled, & instructions not carried out. This becomes the more necessary from the amalgation [*sic*] of Education Funds, so that except in cases where a boy is placed on a specific Fund it is hard to say from what Fund are drawn the resources for his education, so that we know not to whom to allocate the intentions, e.g. the student educated on the

Gerard Fund – and the capital of a £1000 is supposed to form 2 Funds according to the Doway charges – is burdened with heavy obligations.

Had you had no duties to your sister I had always contemplated you living at St. Edward's which I think would have been given a strength to my administration that I in vain look for elsewhere. However Mr. Gibson will assist in the work of calendaring, and would I think be willing to assume the care of the Diocesan Fund, and thus leave Mr. Lennon more at liberty to help you with the general accounts, which I need not Mr. Gibson's assurance to convince me is a formidable burden. Yet notwothstanding my anxiety about my own affairs I am more anxious at present that you should assist your brother. He has been away for nearly a year nursing me with a brotherly affection so that his accounts must necessarily require more attention than he is able at present to give them. It grieves me to see him for notwithstanding an affected cheerfulness he is worn down by an adverse decision in the Moreton trial,[751] & has not the courage to face the world, as he would have that the [*sic*] unanimous verdict is in his favour, and that he is considered a victim to that prejudice which militates against justice to Catholics. Do not wait for an invitation, but go at once to his aid. Two work more cheerfully than one – and the labour will occupy his mind. Besides if done at once Mr. Flynn[752] could remain to attend the cemetery, whilst you & he are employed in this necessary work. Leave the entire care of the Crosby Mission to Mr. Dawber.[753] It will have to be worked by one, when you go to Burscough, and the feeling of responsibility he may have to assume will train him for his future work. You could go down on the Saturday evening to aid him with the Sunday Masses but in all other respects leave him the entire care of the Mission, so that you may help your brother in the first instance, and afterwards assist and direct Gibson in the calendaring the papers which will be the crowning work of my administration that is already more indebted to you than this generation will be able to repay. With every best wish, I remain Yours ever A. Goss.[754]

---

751   Moreton Trial: a full account is in Burke, *Catholic Liverpool*, 205–7: John Henry Fisher, President of St Edward's, was involved in drawing up the will of wealthy Samuel Holland Moreton that left everything to Goss; a trial in June 1870 decided against the validity of the will; the local Protestant press was involved and inveighed against Fisher. Goss and he were close friends and his will speaks of their 'great affection'. There are very few letters between them, presumably because they both lived at St Edward's for all of Goss's episcopate.

752   Patrick Flynn 1840–1900; o. 1869, on the staff at St Edward's to 1870, then c. St Patrick's, Liverpool.

753   James Dawber, a nephew of John Dawber (see n. 146), o. 1866, at Great Crosby to 1870; not in *Directory* after 1876, and see O'Neill, *St Anthony's*, 138, for a sad letter about him in 1877.

754   The letter is not in Goss's hand, but the final 'ever' and his signature are.

439. [*Canon James Fisher*] [*n.d. ? mid-1870*]   *AAL, S1/3/E/6*

My dear James,

I asked you a question & you answer by asking me another. Every paper
that could enable me to answer is in your possession and my memory,
once good, fails me since my sickness. As regards Powell's £50 I have
no doubt, but write & ask him, that it was my donation to his church,[755]
it being a gift to me from Lady S. to pay my expenses in visiting her,
as her gentility makes her phrase it. The difficulty or doubt may have
arisen from money not being paid over at once. I think the papers that
I gave you will show that Mr. Bilsborrow's[756] list includes this. It is
possible that the money may have reached him before my letter & hence
he may have supposed that there was another donation. I forget whether
it was the 2nd or 3rd donation of Lady S. to Barrow: it was applicable
for his maintenance, to buy wine or what he liked, or for his church.

  Wherever the money is, it is not in my hands. What I have ever
received has been paid over to Goss & Fisher, or given to your brother
to pay Goss & Swarbrick: but a donation of that kind would never go
into the latter account.

  Bear in mind that I have <u>never</u> had a balance sheet of my own account
& none of the Public Acct since Mr. Gibson left the administration. Now
this is not right. You ask me don't I trust you? Entirely, & my conduct
has shown it: but a person in my position is not doing his duty without
having yearly balance sheets, even if he had angels for his administra-
tors. You know how I have implored you for it ever since my return
from Cannes. But you have too much on your mind & hands. The last
time I saw you at St. Edward's you promised to send me Sir Robert's
list for last year but you forgot it & no wonder. My money is hoarded
up & I know not what I have, but my Will will put it out of the reach
of any spendthrift Bishop. He shall never have the chance of laughing
at my folly. I supposed Gibson's office of Secretary ceased as it had
begun, i.e. with his connection with the Administration. I have a book
at St. Edward's which I can send to Mr. Lennon next week for the entry
of my accounts. Gibson drew it up. AG

---

[755] Edward or Austin Powell – probably the former, at St Alexander's, Bootle, 1866–85;
formerly Goss's secretary.

[756] John Bilsborrow, 1836–1903; o. 1865, first rector and founder of St Mary's, Barrow
1865–72; rector of Upholland, 1885–92; Bishop of Salford, 1892 to d; see Anne C.
Parkinson, *A History of Catholicism in the Furness Peninsula 1127–1997* (Lancaster,
1998), 61–2.

440.   [*Dr. Newman*]   *16 November 1870* [*year added later*]   ABO
                              Private

My dear Dr. Newman,

I have received a letter from Mr Dolman,[757] who asks if a card bearing my name 'be written or sent out by me or with my knowledge or approbation'. He says that the card contains 'words of a very grave nature & calculated to injure deeply his character', that he intends to publish my reply in order that the attack on his character may not be sheltered by the sanction of my name, for he cannot suppose it to be issued by me.

1.   Shall I notice his letter?
2.   Shall I content myself with simply acknowleding its receipt?
3.   Shall I ask if his letter has been written with the privity & sanction of his archbp?

NB. The Archbp most likely sent him the card. It was issued for my own Diocese & I cannot therefore be called to account by him.

4.   Shall I say that whether the card be mine or not is a matter of inquiry for me not for him, & that if it be a forgery it will be for me not him to take cognizance of it. That as regards the fact ['s' *crossed out*] stated it is true viz that he flooded my Diocese with a circular to the disgust of my clergy & the weakening of Discipline, & tho' he had his Archbp's sanction after the fact, it is none the less a piece of shameless effrontery.

5.   What do you suggest: you may rely on me.

You would probably see the Archbishop's illogical letter to him published in last week's Tablet, no doubt as a counterpoise to my decree. The Archbishop contends that the humblest Catholic has the right of immediate access to the Pope. This I did not deny, but what I denied was the right of Mr. Dolman to agitate my Diocese & request my clergy to have the document signed by my clergy. The document contains many exaggerated & some false assertions e.g. that we are all citizens of Rome.

If it be not troubling you too much I should be glad of a line. I go on Friday to Ince Blundell Hall near Liverpool.

This is hardly a private matter. No doubt the Archbp is at his back & will probably bring the matter before Rome unless he may be satisfied with the amount of dirt the Tablet may throw.

Before the Council he notified to Mr. Nugent that the B̲p̲s̲ would hold him responsible for what he published in his paper. Before the last meeting of the Bps I wrote to him to call the attention of the Bps to what I considered an invasion of my Diocesan rights. He read part of my letter about the Bps' dress & acted upon it; the other part he did not read tho' addressed to him as chairman.

Pardon me for troubling you in the midst of more useful occupations, but what used to be oaken staves have changed to reeds in this good old England.

Ever afftely Yrs. in Xt. A. Goss

---

[757] Alfred Dolman, 1824–1901, listed in the *Directories* for 1865–69 as MR in Somerstown, London; previously on the staff at St Edmund's, Ware. Self-styled Chairman of the Committee for an Address from the Catholic People of Great Britain to the Holy Father, of 21 October 1870. There is a copy of his circular in AAL; it includes the phrase 'each Catholic is a citizen of Rome'. See letters 442 and 445.

441. [*Dr. O'Bryen*] *13 September 1870, Scarisbrick Hall*
AAL, S1/4/E/7

My dear Dr. O'Bryen,

You will oblige me if you can find time amongst your multifarious labours, by translating the Bollandists [*sic*] account of the Episcopate & Saints of Man,[758] as you translated the Bulls on folio, writing on one side or doubling longitudinally the folio & writing on one half of each folio, *more Romano*. Begin the account of the Episcopate with Initio [*sic*]. The Isle of Man was first occupied by the Scoti etc. – continue to No 7 – Then on a fresh page or sheet begin the Saints at Mount George – Make the marginal notes the head, so to speak, of chapters – thus
1.   The Ecclesiastical State of the Isle of Man from the time of St. Patrick to the arrival of the Northmen.
2.   In the 12th century, after the desolation of Man by the Northmen, the See of Sodor, including most of the Hebrides, is instituted & made subject to the Archbp of York, etc.—
Do the Saints in the same way. I would put the references at the end of each chapter. This would make them easier for reference; & be careful in noting them as they are important.

Provost Cookson goes to Wigan on Thursday: would it not be well for you to meet him there about your school? Do you think Pemberton the best site? Would not a central point be better which would include the various Greens, as Goosegreen etc. He is going to Wigan to see about a school between you & Wigan, where I want to begin a new mission. The Wiganers want it to be well out of the town: I want it to be not so far away, or another will have to be built. There is a large population on your side of the railway Stations – Have you thought of the possibility of supporting a new school in addition to your own? I am glad to hear that you are carrying your usual energy into the work at Orrell. Mr. Adamson was for many years asleep; Hubbersty in his last days was never at home; & Kaye fell into a slough & dragged the mission with him.[759]

However you have my best wishes & blessing & a subscription, which I will pay in November if you will then write to me & let me know your prospects. The land owners should do something, tho' not

Catholic – Young Fred. Gerard's wife's father – Porter – has or had property at [???].

Hoping that you keep your health I am with every best wish truly Yrs in Xt.

+Alexander Goss.

---

758 The Bollandists were responsible for the monumental *Acta Sanctorum*, fifty-three volumes of which appeared between 1643 and 1794; sixty-one volumes of a new series appeared, published in Paris, 1863–67. Goss was interested in the section on the Church in the Isle of Man because of his work on the history of the Island; see Introduction, p. xlvii.

759 Thomas Adamson, 1817–69, r. at Orrell 1848–69. Robert Hubbersty: see n. 498: Kelly has him at Orrell 1841–49 (*English Catholic Missions*). Peter Kaye, 1804–56, of the Salford Diocese, formerly of the Lancashire District.

442.   [*Circular sent to the clergy*][760]   *31 October 1870, Wigan*
                                      APF, Anglia, 18, fol. 1

We forbid any Notices to be published within the Church, in Town and Country, that are not ordered by us, or that do not concern the Services or Collections or arrangements to take place within the said Church, or other Church of the Diocese, or which do not regard the Children at School or Catechism, or which are not enjoined or sanctioned by the Ritual or Canons of the Church.

Given at Wigan, October 31, 1870. +Alexander, Bishop of Liverpool.

---

760 This message was sent to all the clergy, printed on a small letter card, 10 cm by 5 cm; capitalisation as in the original. One of the cards, originally addressed to Rev. F. Dunham (see n. 641) at the Catholic Institute, found its way into the Propaganda archives. See letter 448 to Newman.

443.   [*Dr. O'Bryen*]   *12 December 1870, Scarisbrick Hall*
                                         AAL, S1/4/E/7

Dear Dr. O'Bryen

You are late in the field, as the Reports have gone up to the Crisis Committee.[761] When I wrote to you, it was intended to have built a church at Robin [? *illegible*] so as to accommodate the Greens; but circumstances have compelled me to go to the site proposed to me within the first week of my Episcopate.

You had best draw up a memorial setting forth the wants in the locality on the Bridgewater Estate, giving numbers of children & distance from existing schools, then forward it to Dr. Fisher with a request that he will send it to Mr. Eyston or Sir R. Gerard – formerly they refused land for a <u>Church</u> i.e. as a gift, but Sir Robert promised the use of his influence, & I fell ill.

They tell me you have built a young Aula Regia[762] or minor theatre at Orrell with which Government would have no concern. I have heard nothing of Mr. Adamson's will & do not know who are the Executors.

I have been scotched for a fortnight at St. Edward's, but am now again on my legs though rickety.

With every best wish to yourself and hoping the cold weather is not troubling you beyond endurance, I am ever Yrs. A. Goss

---

[761] The Crisis Committee: set up to cope with the demands on Catholics resulting from the 1870 Act; see Tenbus, *English Catholics and the Education of the Poor*, 84–6, 91–3.
[762] Trans: 'A Royal Hall'.

444.   [*Dr. O'Brien*]   *Sunday [n.d., ? December 1870]*

AAL, S1/4/E/7

My dear Dr. O'Bryen,

Next Sunday I shall be at St. Mary's, & proceed thence to Ushaw, probably staying at Lpool for the meeting. Now when at Ushaw I shall have an opportunity of consulting some books in the Library which I may not easily find elsewhere, & to which reference is made in the sheets you have from the Bollandists. I shall be obliged, therefore, if you can manage the translation by Sunday next & forward it with the original to St. Mary's. I know you are busy, but it may be done in the evening or in congenial weather.

I had some thoughts of visiting & confirming at Orrell on All Saints, but do not know whether that would suit you or whether you would prefer to have it deferred till Spring. It is not material, but yours is the only place left in the neighbourhood, as Birchley belongs to another Deanery. I leave here tomorrow for Scarisbrick.

I hope you stand the weather & the work. Ever sincerely Yrs. +Alexander Goss.

445.   *Bishop Clifford*   *13 December 1870, [Scarisbrick Hall]*

Clifford Letters[763]

My dear Lord,

I have received a letter from Card. Barnabò, as I doubt not you have also, in which he says that it has been told him that you & I have denied permission to our respective Diocesans to sign an act of protest against the invasion of Rome & the consequent captivity of the Supreme pontiff, which many hundred thousands of laity & clergy of England this a wonderful impulse of piety [*sic*] have signed. ... my prohibition is exactly the same as yours – for the preface has nothing to do with the substance of my decree – to forbid unauthorised circulars in the Church. I should think it is the Archbp's doing, but Dolman threatened me with an appeal to his & my ecclesiastical superior in the Tablet newspaper – Ought we not to ask the name of his informant & to be furnished with a copy of the charge? Ordinarily we do not reply to anonymous charges, but Bps have been snuffed out & editors of journals substitued in their place ...

We shall probably have a notice in the Tablet, in due time, boasting how certain refractive Bps have been whipped into order by Propaganda. I shall be guided in my reply by what you write. Our liberties & our jurisdiction are now surely at stake. We have an eely foe against us who does not stick at a trifle, as evidenced by his account of the peaceful & dignified demeanour of the Council at all times.

---

763 I am grateful to Canon Harding for permission to reprint this shortened version of this letter from his book, *Clifford of Clifton*, 210–11.

446.   *Eminent Prince* [*Cardinal Barnabò*]   20 December 1870
APF, Anglia, 18, fol. 151

Most Eminent Lord

I have recently received a letter from Your Eminence, dated from Rome 3rd December, in which you inform me that you have been told that I refused permission to the people of my Diocese to sign a protest against the invasion of the City of Rome and the subsequent captivity of the Supreme Pontiff; and you ask me what the truth may be in this matter. I am grateful to Your Eminence for giving me the opportunity of denying altogether the truth of what you have been told about me. You are correct in thinking that I have always shown due observance and piety towards the Holy See, since everybody knows that for 15 years, in both pastoral letters and speeches, in churches and in public, I have defended the cause of the Supreme Pontiff, perhaps more forcefully than elegantly, but nevertheless with great approval from the people, even in farflung places. In my three most recent sermons at the end of October, before the doctors, at the insistence of my Chapter and Clergy imposed a temporary silence on me, I attacked before a great crowd of people the violent injustice and impiety of the Piedmontese King, and raised my voice as strongly as I could against the injuries inflicted on the Supreme Pontiff. And behold my reward! To have my name dragged down before the Holy See, and the whole kingdom know that I have been accused of being an enemy and a traitor in the house of my Father! You say that there is no need for people to have special permission to protest against the damage done to the Supreme Head of the Church. I reply that there is not a single Catholic who does not know that he is free to sign any protest, even against the bishop's wishes or opposition, nor is there amongst the Bishops any who would wish to deny his people this common privilege.

This is what I did. Certain people, with no authority, sent to the rectors of churches and those with the care of souls a letter, ordering that it be signed by everyone, even Women and Children. In order to come to the help of the Clergy and oppose the weakening of ecclesiastical discipline, and because the rashness of the people concerned should be denounced as strongly as possible, I decided to remind the Clergy of the Diocese of the Decree, published 20th December, 1866, which forbade extraordinary announcements to be made in Churches without due permission.[764] Afterwards I heard that other Bishops had resisted these dangers in their own way, obviously lest the Ordinary with the charge of souls should be like useless salt trodden on by men. If the columns of the Church are thrown down, it will not be long before the Head of the whole edifice collapses, and I do not speak rashly when I say that we must take care lest a very powerful case be weakened by thoughtless advocacy.

I beg Your Eminence to let our Common Father know that I and my whole Diocese share with him his great sufferings, and to ask that he deign to impart his Apostolic Blessing on me, my Chapter, the Clergy and the people. I am, Your Eminence, Your most humble and devoted Servant,

Alexander Goss, Bishop of Liverpool.

---

[764] See no. 442 above, and letter to Newman, 448 below, for Propaganda's reply.

447. [*Fr. Prov. Allanson*]   *28 December 1870*   *AAA, Allanson Letters, vol. 1, pp. 149–54*

Very Rev. & dear Fr. Provincial,

Your letter has quite bewildered me: it reads like a leaf from the last century.[765] You can hardly expect me on the occasion of the question of building a school at Garston to follow you over the extensive field you have travelled, or to discuss or give an opinion about matters that are not individual to my Diocese or personal to myself, but concern every Diocese & Bp. in England as well as every Religious Body. I am unprepared to enter on this question. I have had no correspondence on it for years, & it is beyond our competency to decide.[766]

You imply that there has been a lack of courtesy in not informing you of the foundations of Missions that may interfere with Missions served by you. The Synod leaves the Bp. free liberty in the matter & implies no such act of courtesy. You ask for leave to found a new House at Garston.[767] You have not placed before me any information which would make such a foundation lawful, much less desirable or advantageous to Religion. As regards Mr. Bulbeck's application for building schools, the only subject really at issue, his statistics show that such foundation is not at all necessary. My officials will furnish you with details. I remain, etc. Alexander Goss

---

765   Allanson had written a long letter on 19 December, rehearsing some of the past history of the relations between the VAs/bishops and the Benedictines; it may be found in Justin McCann OSB, *English Benedictine Missions, A Survey* (privately published, 1940), 49–51. In it he admitted Bulbeck was wrong to think he could establish a new mission run by the Benedictines; he asked for Goss's permission for a school only because the school would lead on to the establishment of a new mission.

766   There follows a short passage here in which Goss pointed out that Benedict XIV's *Apostolicum ministerium* had been abrogated by the Bull of Restoration in 1850. The Synod of Westminster, he added, seemed to indicate that episcopal permission was needed even for building a school.

767   Rev. W. A. Bulbeck OSB was at St Austin's, Grassendale, Liverpool; the new dock area of Garston adjoined this. A Secular mission opened there in 1883. See note 143.

---

448.   *V.R. Dr. Newman*   *24 January 1871, Scarisbrick Hall,*
                                            Ormskirk   *ABO*

My dear Dr. Newman,

Whether Archbp. Manning or Dolman, I know not, but somebody carried a complaint to Rome against Dr. Clifford & myself. We both received letters of inquiry from Card. Barnabò: we both replied, & have both received answers much of the same tenor – he expresses himself perfectly satisfied: *"responsum tuum omni exceptione majus"*. He adds: *"Nihil enim magis aequum ac debito ordini consentaneum duco, quam ut omnia qua in Ecclesiis publica fiunt, licet ad optimum finem, sub dependentia ac directione Episcopi compleantur"*.[768] I had told him in my letter that the case of the Pope naturally strong would be brought to nought, if they did not mind, by jejune advocacy. Pardon me for troubling you with this & accept my best thanks for having so wisely advised me not to notice the letters of inquiry addressed to me by Mr. Dolman.

Praying God long to preserve you to us. I am with every best wish sincerely Yrs in Xt.

+Alexander Goss.

---

768   Trans: 'your response is beyond all criticism'. [*He added*] 'For I think nothing is better suited to and in line with due order than that everything that is done publicly in churches, even if done for the best purpose, should be carried out dependently on the Bishop and under his direction.'

449. [*Dr. Newman*]   *21 April 1871, 8 York Place, W.*[769]   *ABO*

My dear Dr. Newman,

You have so kindly interested yourself on various occasions in the fate of an adventurous wayfarer, that I venture to send you a copy of a message I have lately received from the Pope. It refers to my action regarding the Uhlans,[770] which had received the approbation of the Prefect of Propaganda. The same post that brought me the message sent thro' Mr. Reynolds, a layman of my Diocese, brought to Dr. Fisher a letter from Mgr Stonor[771] expressing a hope that the message would not reach me. He at the same time enclosed a copy, as there were, when he wrote, two or three erroneous versions of the message in circulation in Rome. The Pope began life as a Whig & he seems determined to end in the same principles.[772] Excuse me & believe me ever faithfully & afftely Yrs in Xt.

+Alexander Goss.

We break up today.

[*In Goss's hand in margins:*]

Dite al Vostro Vescovo di dare più aria ai laici.
Dite al Vostro Vescovo che io gli mando la mia benedizione, ma bisogna dare più libertà d'azione ai buoni Cattolici della sua Diocesi.[773]

* * *

---

[769]   The residence of Archbishop Manning; presumably Goss had at last accepted an invitation to stay overnight.

[770]   Uhlans were a type of cavalrymen with a rather fierce reputation in European armies of the nineteenth century. Goss seems to have used the term of Dolman and his supporters first of all in a visitation sermon in Wigan about November 1870; as reported in *The Tablet* (1870, 650–1), the bishop had added, 'He would have them understand clearly and distinctly that there was only one Bishop of Liverpool, and as long as he held the pastoral staff he would resist and resent any aggression … on his spiritual jurisdiction. When he (was) too feeble to <u>wield</u> it … he would resign.' Dolman replied, condemning Goss's words and saying he would report them to the 'proper ecclesiastical authorities' (*The Tablet*, 27 November, p. 682); see the previous letter – the authorities sided with Goss.

[771]   See n. 704.

[772]   For Pius IX's early reputation as a liberal, see J. N. D. Kelly, *The Oxford Dictionary of Popes* (Oxford, 1996), 309.

[773]   Trans: 'Tell your Bishop to give more room to the laity', and 'Tell your Bishop that I send him my blessing, but he needs to give more liberty of action to the good Catholics of his Diocese.'

After this letter there seem to be only a few that Goss wrote himself, though there are also a small number written by the Vicar General, Canon Fisher, but signed by Goss. In one of the latter, in May 1871, Fisher wrote to Propaganda to ask for permission for the Sisters of Mercy to have the Blessed Sacrament reserved in their chapel even though Mass was said there only once a week (APF, *Anglia*, 19, fols. 66–8; Rinaldini commented on the illegibility of Fisher's writing, a sentiment this historian can only agree with). Later that month, there is a request for a marriage dispensation (a few more of these date from 1872). A more interesting letter of April 1872 dealt with the question of stole fees (see letter 387) and whether they should go into a common fund for distribution between the priests in that mission, or be used to pay off the mission debt; whether they should go to the priest performing the sacrament, or all go to the head of the mission. Propaganda involved Manning in this discussion; he sat on the fence somewhat but in the end suggested that the Westminster practice of all fees (except Mass stipends) going to a common fund for equal distribution was the best way out of what he acknowledged was a knotty problem. (APF, *Anglia*, 18, fols 417–20). In a number of these letters Fisher says how ill Goss has been, though on 19 April 1872 he says he is now better: though still weak he has recently finished the visitation of the Diocese, preaching twice on Sundays and confirming 11,000 – it is no wonder, Fisher adds, that he has been ill!

The APF volume that covers 1872 contains no reference that I have been able to find to Goss's death on 3 October 1872; on 4th November 1872 Fisher wrote on black-edged paper thanking Propaganda for his faculties as Vicar Capitular, but without mentioning Goss at all.[774]

---

[774] Goss's will of November 1869 was proved on 25 November 1872. Surprisingly, he left a house in Bevington Bush, Liverpool, to his niece; the rest of his estate was divided equally between Canons J. H. Fisher and Thomas Cookson 'absolutely for their own use' and free from any trust deed. See n. 751 and letter 439.

APPENDIX 1

The English and Welsh Hierarchy 1850–1872

(VA indicates that the bishop had been a Vicar Apostolic before 1850)

WESTMINSTER 1850 Nicholas Wiseman (VA)
1865 Henry Edward Manning

BEVERLEY 1850 John Briggs (VA)
1861 Robert Cornthwaite

BIRMINGHAM 1850 William Bernard Ullathorne OSB (VA)

CLIFTON 1850 Joseph Wm Hendren (VA)
1851 Thomas Burgess
1855 William Joseph Clifford

HEXHAM (and 1850 William Hogarth (VA)
NEWCASTLE)* 1866 James Chadwick

LIVERPOOL 1850 George Hilary Brown (VA)
1856 Alexander Goss

NEWPORT and 1850 Thomas Joseph Brown OSB (VA)
MENEVIA

NORTHAMPTON 1850 William Wareing (VA)
1858 Francis Kerril Amherst

NOTTINGHAM 1851 Joseph Wm Hendren (VA)
1853 Richard Butler Roskell

PLYMOUTH 1851 George Errington**
1855 William Vaughan

SALFORD 1851 William Turner
1872 Herbert Vaughan

SHREWSBURY 1851 James Brown

SOUTHWARK 1851 Thomas Grant
1871 James Danell

* Newcastle was added to the title in 1861.
** When he moved to be coadjutor in Westminster he became Bishop (later Archbishop)
of Trebizond, a title Goss often used when referring to or addressing him.

APPENDIX 2

Relations between Bishop Brown and Bishop Goss

Between late 1853 and January 1856 there was an extensive correspondence between Bishop Brown and his new coadjutor, Bishop Goss. Cardinal Wiseman was also involved in the quarrel between the two men and all three were involved in correspondence with Propaganda on the subject. Something has already been said about it in the Introduction, and some of Goss's letters to Brown are included in this volume. A diary of the correspondence will illustrate the intensity of the quarrel. Goss's letters are in AAL Add.Lttrs, 1–40; the Propaganda material is in APF, *Anglia*, 14, and APF, *Lettere*, 346 (1855). Other letters are referred to in the correspondence but cannot be dated; probably there are other letters from Wiseman to Goss and, perhaps Wiseman to Brown. Goss wrote lengthy letters about the quarrel to Dr Cornthwaite, rector of the English College, Rome, and Roman agent for the bishops. To judge from Propaganda's letters to Brown, its officers became exasperated with him: the letter of 15 January 1855 orders him to give Goss full faculties for the visitation, adding, 'You will carry out these orders with the obedience which you bear towards the Holy See', while a letter to Wiseman in May speaks of Brown's *durezza* or stubbornness (APF, *Lettere*, 346, fols 49b, 50, 359; my translation). Letters marked * are reproduced in this volume.

Part 1: Diary of the Correspondence

1853   25 November: Goss to Wiseman*
1854   ? October: Brown to Chapter
        18 November: Goss to Brown*
        31 December: Brown to Propaganda
1855   15 January: Propaganda to Brown
        29 January: Brown to Propaganda*
        29 January: Propaganda to Brown
        7 February: Brown to Propaganda
        3 March: Propaganda to Brown
        ? March: Wiseman to Goss
        18 March: Goss to Wiseman*
        19 March: Goss to Wiseman*
        4 April: Propaganda to Goss
        4 April: Brown to Propaganda

7 April: Brown to Propaganda
17 April: Goss to Brown*
23 April: Brown to Goss
23 April: Propaganda to Brown
25 April: Propaganda to Goss
27 April: Wiseman to Propaganda
11 May: Brown to Goss
18 May: Propaganda to Wiseman
16 June: Goss to Brown*
? June: Brown to Wiseman*
24 August: Goss to the Chapter*
30 August: Goss to Brown*
31 August: Brown to Goss
6 September: Brown to Goss
11 September: Goss to Brown*
14 October: Brown to Goss
21 October: Goss to Brown*
9 November: Goss to Brown*
10 November: Goss to Cornthwaite*
13 November: Brown to Goss
14 November: Goss to Brown*
21 November: Brown to Goss
23 November: Goss to Brown*
26 November: Goss to Cornthwaite*
3 December: Goss to Brown*
7 December: Propaganda to Wiseman
16 December: Goss to Cornthwaite*
1856   2 January: Brown to Propaganda
16 January: Goss to Cornthwaite*

Part 2: Extracts

A: Letter of Goss to Wiseman 18 March 1855

[*The second part of this long letter is printed above, as letter 5. Apart from its content, illustrating from Goss's point of view the quarrels between himself and Brown, the letter is of some interest in showing how fully at this stage he treated the cardinal as a confidant.*]

1o. [You have asked me to explain my refusal to accept faculties.] In my memorandum book under the date of Sep. 29. 1853 – four days after my consecration – I find the following among other entries. "Dr. Brown proffered to give me the powers of <u>Vicar General</u>, as Dr. Walsh[i] had given Cardinal Wiseman when his Coadjutor, & as he had given Dr. Sharples, but I declined them <u>on the score</u> that I was <u>his</u> helper and not the Vicar's, & hence could not benefit <u>him</u> by having such faculties." Dr. Brown did not press the matter, nor did he rectify the mistake into which, it seems, I fell; for I knew nothing whatever of the faculties enjoyed either by your Eminence or by Bp. Sharples, but supposed them to be, as the entry states, the faculties of V.G., & in declining to accept them, I stated such to be the grounds of my refusal.

To show that this continued to be my impression, I will cite an extract from a letter addressed from London to the Chapter of Liverpool, May 10th 1854, in explanation of my supposed refusal to assist the Bp. After showing them that I had scrupulously carried out every commission with which I had been entrusted, & that I should expose myself to censure by acting without a commission, I continued, "the mistake may have arisen from my having declined, a few days after my consecration, to accept the faculties usually granted to Vicars. I did so on the ground [sic] that my receiving them could confer no relief on the Bp. though it might relieve Dr. Crook[ii] whom I believed, however, fully able to discharge his duties. I stated also to the Bp. that I had been appointed his Coadjutor & not his Vicar's, & that as the proposed communication of faculties could neither relieve him, nor serve the Diocese, I begged to decline them. Dr. Brown being most likely of the same opinion did not press my acceptance of them. I had before me the disedifying differences that had arisen between Dr. Sharples & Dr. Brown on the exercise of such jurisdiction, & I feared a recurrence of similar dissensions. I saw too that if Dr. Crook & myself exercised the same faculties over the same district that we might be led to act at cross purposes by one granting, & the other refusing to grant, faculties to individuals applying under similar circumstances."

Of the accuracy of this view of the faculties offered to me, I never entertained a doubt until the week after my return from Rome, when I waited on the Bp. in company with Can. Walmsley,[iii] some of the circum-stances of which interview I mentioned in a letter to your Eminence. At that interview the Bp. alluded to my refusal to accept faculties. I again stated the grounds of my refusal, when he added that the faculties were the same as those enjoyed by Dr. Sharples & your Eminence. I replied, Yes; but you assured me that they were also the same as those enjoyed by Dr. Crook. He assured me that I had made a mistake for that [sic] they contained additional powers, an announcement that I then heard for the first time. If a mistake, it affords an additional proof of the neces-sity of transacting business in an official manner, Dr. Brown's refusal to do which has given some grounds for the second charge against me. Before, however, proceeding to answer that, I ought to observe that he never in any letter pressed upon me the acceptance of the faculties. It is true that one of his letters, dated Oct. 26, accumulates instances of Bishops having been assisted by their Coadjutors, but the real object of that letter was to prove that I ought to come to confer with him; for it professed to be an answer to a letter that I had addressed to him on that subject, on the 19th of the same month. My impression up to this moment has been, that he never offered me faculties but once, & then only vicarial faculties similar to those possessed by Dr. Crook, which, though offered, I did not think he was anxious for me to accept. These I declined for reasons already stated, viz. the embarrassments likely to follow from two persons (Dr. Crook & myself) exercising the same faculties, & also because I was told that Dr. Brown would seize the opportunity of throwing upon me the responsibility of every unpopular step. [*half a page of crossing out*] Whatever impression my refusal to accept the proffered faculties may produce on others, it could not produce on Dr. Brown an idea that I declined to act under him or to aid him. In a letter dated 5 days after our interview (Oct. 4) I write, "I believe that a Coadjutor is an aid to the Bp. in the executive: he does not usurp the functions of the Chapter, which is the legal & constituted, & responsible adviser of a Bp. I am anxious to put this matter clear [*sic*] to your Lordship, for I am sorry, & your friends – one & all – are sorry to see your Lordship weary your spirit with questions already discussed. <u>Whatever commands your Lordship may lay upon me that regard the executive, I will cheerfully & punctually & faithfully fulfil</u>; but I must decline the responsibility of adviser, as the Holy See has already provided a body of advisers in your chapter." I may seem, your Eminence, in this extract to be too chary about giving advice; but circumstances must be taken into consideration. The extract is from a long letter written with a view to dissuade him from suspending Can. Newsham,[iv] contrary to the advice given him by those of the chapter whom he had consulted, by your Eminence, & by other Bps. In <u>two</u> letters written Oct. 5 I give him advice on various subjects, tho' always, I must confess, with the fear of being betrayed by him. In a letter written Oct 7. I find the following. "<u>I will ever act as your Lordship directs, but it is for you to direct. With age rests counsel, with youth action.</u>" Oct 8. another letter of advice to him; Oct 15. I write, "I feel unable to give your Lordship any advice on the subject of appointments, because in government it is necessary to follow out one line of policy, as I have before urged upon you. Individual cases may occur when I might be of service in venturing on the expression of an opinion, <u>which I would then do</u>. In all cases I do not think it good to cancel well matured & considered appointments, as it is apt to present the appearance of a vacillating policy. I am satisfied that to make a firm government, they must all flow through the same channel." I wrote thus, as he had recently taken my opinion on various appointments, settled to act accordingly, & then, without ever appraising me of any change in his views, had acted quite differently. On November 10, I got the inclosed letter from him, the passages underlined are so in the original. In a letter addressed by me to him Nov. 25 I find the following passage, "Whatever jurisdiction your Lordship has delegated to me I have exercised to the best of my power & I hope I shall continue to do so, whenever your Lordship may think it necessary to entrust me therewith. If you conceive that I do not understand my duty or that I neglect it, point out to me the omission, but do not say that I have disappointed your expectations, because I take a different view of my duties & sphere of action to that taken by your Lordship." At the close of the letter I added, "For any future exercise of jurisdiction, I must claim a *delegatio scripta*." This remark I thought called for by the first sentence in his letter of Nov. 10 (copy inclosed), "As you have written to the respective parties about confirmation, <u>it may pass</u>."

---

i   Thomas Walsh, 1780–1849, VA of the Midland District 1826, the Central District 1840, and the London District 1848; see Plumb, *Arundel*.

ii   James Crook, 1794–1856, VG from 1848, administrator of the Pro-cathedral 1851–56.

iii   John Walmsley, 1812–68, Canon 1851, VG 1863.

iv   Thomas Newsham, 1810–68, canon 1851; a major troublemaker: see Introduction, p. xxxix and later letters.

B: Bishop Brown's letters

a. To Propaganda, 29 January 1855   APF, *Anglia*, 14, fols. 207–8 [*my translation from the Latin*]

[A few days after consecration I offered Bishop Goss the same faculties as the coadjutor of Westminster had under Bishop Walsh,] but he strongly refused to accept any faculties. I tried to persuade him that it was in order and customary, that he by virtue of his office shared in my counsels, and I cited the example of more than twelve coadjutors who had acted in this way. At that time I thought he was acting from too tender a conscience. All was in vain and I was very sad, for of all the priests in my Diocese Bishop Goss was a man after my own heart and I wished to give him the faculties specifically to carry out the visitation and other business. But he refused to give way, nor would he afterwards come to confer together about the good of the Diocese. He visited certain families in my neighbourhood but did not come to my house. With regard to the visitation of the Diocese, despite all this I would have been content if my Coadjutor had acted legally and in accord with the law of the Church in this matter and remained in the Diocese. But instead he left the country on the pretext of making a journey with a Catholic merchant through France, Germany and Italy, and went to Rome, where he still is. I am deeply upset about all this, because, it seems to me, if there is a law of the Church involved, he is disobeying both it and custom. But above all there is grave wrong in this way of acting and a danger to the peace and tranquillity of the Diocese, which I will tell you about more fully later.

b. To Wiseman, ? June 1855   [*Full text in Milburn, History of Ushaw College, 213–14*]

[*This gives a fuller picture of Brown's opposition to Goss. The Ushaw authorities had objected to a letter (see above, letter 11) that Brown had sent to the College, which had been drafted by Goss. Brown defended himself:*]

At length I sent it [*i.e. the offending letter*] as a sign to Dr Goss of my willingness to receive his advice, hoping by that to draw him into a more correct and canonical line of conduct ... let me give [an] instance of Dr. G's mind. Last year he wrote me a strong letter full of indignation against Mr. Sherburne and telling me I ought to suspend him [*and if he did not pay his debts*] excommunicate him ... I regret to say that I see few encouraging symptoms of harmonious action with Dr. Goss ... I really do not understand how it can be allowed that a young man a little more than half my age, having no other experience than teaching a few boys the rudiments for eleven years should set himself above me, after my laborious labours for twelve years at Ushaw and twenty years on the mission at Lancaster and fifteen years of being Bishop, in the way he has done in violation of the Canons of the Church. I see much uneasiness looming in the distance.

BIBLIOGRAPHY

Books and Pamphlets

Anstruther OP, Godfrey, *The Seminary Priests: A Dictionary of the Secular Clergy of England and Wales 1558–1850*, 4 vols (Ware and Ushaw, Great Wakering, 1968–77)

Baines, Edward, *History of the County Palatine and Duchy of Lancaster*, 4 vols (London, Paris, New York, 1836; new edn, 1868–70)

Barker, T. C. and Harris, J. R., *A Merseyside Town in the Industrial Revolution: St. Helens 1750–1900* (London, 1959)

Beck, G. A. (ed.), *The English Catholics 1850–1950* (London, 1950)

Belchem, J., *Irish, Catholic and Scouse: The History of the Liverpool Irish 1800–1939* (Liverpool, 2007)

Bellenger OSB, Dominic Aidan (ed.), *English and Welsh Priests 1558–1800: A Working List* (Bath, 1984)

Bennett, Canon, *Father Nugent of Liverpool* (Liverpool, 1949; 2nd edn 1993)

Berton, C. (ed.), *Dictionnaire des cardinaux: contenant des notions générales sur le cardinalat* (Paris, 1857; repr. Gregg, 1969)

Billington, R. N. and Brownbill, J., *St Peter's, Lancaster: A History* (London, 1910)

Birtill, Tony, *A Hidden History. Irish in Liverpool: An Ghaelige i Learpholl* (Liverpool, 2013)

Blundell OSB, F. O., *Old Catholic Lancashire*, 3 vols (London, 1925–41)

Boase, F., *Modern English Biography*, 3 vols (Truro, 1892)

Bossy, John, *The English Catholic Community, 1570–1850* (London, 1975)

Bouscaren, T. L. and Ellis, A. C., *Canon Law: A Text and Commentary* (3rd edn, Milwaukee, 1957)

Brady, W. M., *The Episcopal Succession in England, Scotland and Ireland* 3 vols (Rome, 1876; repr. London, 1971)

Bridge, John, *The Lowe House Story 1743–1993* (St Helens, 1993)

Broadley, Martin John, *Bishop Herbert Vaughan and the Jesuits: Education and Authority* (CRS 82, London, 2010)

Burke, Thomas, *Catholic History of Liverpool* (Liverpool, 1910)

Burscough, M., *The History of Lark Hill, Preston, 1797–1989* (Preston, 1993; repr. 2003)

Bush, Jonathan, *'Papists' and Prejudice: Popular Anti-Catholicism and Anglo-Irish Conflict in the North-East of England, 1845–70* (Newcastle upon Tyne, 2013)

Butler, Cuthbert, *The Life and Times of Bishop Ullathorne 1806–1889*, 2 vols (London, 1926)

Catholicisme: Hier, Aujourd'hui, Demain, 15 vols (Paris, 1954–2010)

Champ, Judith, *William Bernard Ullathorne 1806–1889: A Different Kind of Monk* (Leominster, 2006)

Condon CM, Kevin, *The Missionary College of All Hallows, 1842–1891* (Dublin, 1986)

Crispino, G., *Trattato della visità pastorale* (?Rome, 1711)

Cross, F. L. and Livingstone, E. A., *The Oxford Dictionary of the Christian Church* (2nd rev. edn, Oxford, 1983)

Cwiekowski, Frederick J., *The English Bishops and the First Vatican Council* (Bibliothèque de la Revue d'Histoire Ecclésiastique 52, Louvain, 1971)

Decreta Quatuor Conciliorum Provincialium Westmonasteriensium. 1852–1873 (2nd edn, London, n.d.)

Denvir, J., *The Irish in Britain* (London, 1892)

—— *The Life Story of an Old Rebel* (Dublin, 1910; repb. 1972)

Dessain, C. S., *et al.* (eds), *The Letters and Diaries of John Henry Newman*, 32 vols (London and Oxford, 1961–2008)

Dodd, Charles, *The Church History of England from the Commencement of the Sixteenth Century to the Revolution of 1688*, 5 vols (Brussels, 1737–42; new edn by Mark Tierney, London, 1839–43)

Doyle, P., *Mitres and Missions in Lancashire: A History of the Roman Catholic Diocese of Liverpool 1850–2000* (Liverpool, 2005)

Doyle, P. and McLoughlin, L., *The Edwardian Story* (Wirral, 2003)

Duckworth, Jeannie, *Fagin's Children: Criminal Children in Victorian England* (London and New York, 2002)

Evans, Bob, *The Training Ships of Liverpool* (Birkenhead, 2002)

Finnegan, R. and Hagerty, J., *The Bishops of Leeds 1878–1985* (Leeds, 2005)

Fitzgerald-Lombard OSB, C. (ed.), *English and Welsh Priests 1801–1914: A Working List* (Bath, 1993)

Flanagan, Thomas, *History of the Church in England: From the Earliest Period to the Re-Establishment of the Hierarchy in 1850*, 2 vols (London, 1857)

Foster, Harry, *Southport: A History* (Chichester, *c.* 2008)

Furnival, John, *Children of the Second Spring: Father James Nugent and the Work of Child Care in Liverpool* (Leominster, 2005)

Galloway, P., *The Cathedrals of Ireland* (Belfast, 1992)

Gavanti, B., *Praxis Synodi Dioecesanae Celebrandae* and *Praxis Visitationis Episcopalis* (Rome, 1628); republ. as *Praxis Synodi Dioeces-*

anae Celebrandae ex opere D. B. Gavanti redacta (London, Dublin, Derby, 1853)

Gilbert, P., *This Restless Prelate: Bishop Peter Baines 1786–1843* (Leominster, 2006)

Gooch, Leo, *The Revival of English Catholicism: The Banister–Rutter Correspondence 1777–1807* (Wigan, 1995)

Gore, J., *et al.* (eds), *Gore's Directory of Liverpool* (Liverpool, 1849–1919)

Gregson, Matthew, *Portfolio of Fragments, Relative to the History and Antiquities of the County Palatine and Duchy of Lancaster*, in 3 parts (Liverpool, 1817)

Hamer, Edna, *Elizabeth Prout 1820–1864: A Religious Life for Industrial England* (Downside, 1994; re-issued 2011)

Harding, J. A., *Clifford of Clifton (1823–1893): England's Youngest Catholic Bishop* (Bristol, 2011)

—— *The Diocese of Clifton 1850–2000* (Bristol, 1999)

Hastings, G. (ed.), *Transactions of the National Society for the Promotion of Social Science 1858* (London, 1859)

Heimann, Mary, *Catholic Devotion in Victorian England* (Oxford, 1995)

Henson, E. (ed.), *Registers of the English College at Valladolid 1589–1862* (CRS 30, London, 1930)

Hewitson, A. ('Atticus'), *Our Country Churches and Chapels: Antiquarian, Historical, Ecclesiastical and Critical Sketches* (Preston and London, 1872)

Hilton, J. A., *Catholic Lancashire: From Reformation to Renewal 1559–1991* (Chichester, 1994)

Holmes, J. Derek, *More Roman than Rome* (London, 1978)

Hume, A., *The Condition of Liverpool, Religious and Social* (Liverpool, 1858)

Kelly, Bernard W., *Historical Notes on English Catholic Missions* (London, 1907; repr. 1995)

Kelly, James and Keogh, Dáire (eds), *A History of the Catholic Diocese of Dublin* (Dublin, 2000)

Kelly's Directory of Lancashire (London, 1858–1924)

Keogh, Dáire and McDonnell, Albert (eds), *Cardinal Paul Cullen and His World* (Dublin, 2011)

Kirk, John, *Biographies of English Catholics in the Eighteenth Century* (ed. by J. H. Pollen SJ and E. Burton, London, 1909)

Lowe, W. J., *The Irish in Mid-Victorian Lancashire: The Shaping of a Working-Class Community* (New York, 1989)

MacRaild, D. M., *Culture, Conflict and Migration: The Irish in Victorian Cumbria* (Liverpool, 1998)

—— *Faith, Fraternity and Fighting: The Orange Order and Irish Migrants in Northern England, c. 1850–1920* (Liverpool, 2005)

—— *The Irish Diaspora in Britain, 1750–1939* (2nd edn, Basingstoke, 2011)

Mangion, C. M., *Contested Identities: Catholic Women Religious in Nineteenth Century England and Wales* (Manchester, 2008)

Manning, H. E., *The Good Soldier's Death* (Liverpool, 1872)

Marmion, J. P. (ed.), *Shrewsbury: Millennium Essays for a Catholic Diocese* (Downside, 2000)

Marsh, V., *St. Joseph's, Wrightington: A History* (Chorley, 1969)

McCann OSB, Justin, *English Benedictine Missions, A Survey* (privately published, 1940)

McClelland, V. A. and Hodgetts, M., *From Out the Flaminian Gate: 150 Years of Roman Catholicism in England and Wales* (London, 2000)

McIntire, C. T., *England against the Papacy 1858–1861: Tories, Liberals and the Overthrow of Papal Power during the Italian Risorgimento* (Cambridge, 1983)

Milburn, David, *A History of Ushaw College: A Study of the Origin, Foundation and Development of an English Catholic Seminary* (Durham, 1964)

Mitchinson, Allan (ed.), *Catholicism in Standish: From Persecution to Parish 1559–1884* (Wigan, 2005)

—— *The Registers of Standish Hall Chapel 1742–1884* (Wigan, 2001)

Monacelli, F., *Formularium legale practicum fori ecclesiastici* (Venice, 1732)

Morris, Michael and Gooch, Leo, *Down your Aisles: The Diocese of Hexham and Newcastle 1850–2000* (Hartlepool, 2000)

Murphy, James, *The Religious Problem in English Education: The Crucial Experiment* (Liverpool, 1959)

Neal, Frank, *Black '47: Britain and the Famine Irish* (Basingstoke, 1998)

—— *Sectarian Violence: The Liverpool Experience, 1819–1914* (Manchester, 1988)

Norman, Edward R., *Anti-Catholicism in Victorian Britain* (London, 1968)

—— *The English Catholic Church in the Nineteenth Century* (Oxford, 1984)

Oliver, V. Rev. George, *Collections, Illustrating the History of the Catholic Religion of the Counties of Cornwall, Devon, Dorset, Somerset, Wiltshire and Gloucester* (London, 1857)

O'Neill, Michael, *St Anthony's, Scotland Road, Liverpool* (Leominster, 2010)

Orrell, T. A., *A History of the House of Orrell* (privately published, Bolton, 1990)

Parkinson, Anne C., *A History of Catholicism in the Furness Peninsula 1127–1997* (1998)

Paz, D. G., *Popular Anti-Catholicism in Mid-Victorian England* (Stanford, CA, 1992)

Pelczar, G. S., *Pio IX e Il Suo Pontificato*, 3 vols (Turin 1910)

Petit, L. and Martin, J. B. (eds), *Collectio Conciliorum Recentiorum Ecclesiae Universae*, vol. XVII (Arnhem and Leipzig, 1927). This is volume 53 of the series originally edited by Mansi and generally referred to as 'Mansi'

Phillips, Peter (ed.), *John Lingard, Priest and Historian* (Leominster, 2004)

—— *Lingard Remembered* (CRS Monograph Series 6, London, 2004)

Phillips, Canon P. (ed.), *The Diaries of Bishop William Poynter, VA (1815–1824)* (CRS 79, London, 2006)

Plumb, Brian, *Arundel to Zabi: A Biographical Dictionary of the Catholic Bishops of England and Wales (Deceased) 1623–1987* (Warrington, 1987)

—— *'Found Worthy'. A Biographical Dictionary of the Secular Clergy of the Archdiocese of Liverpool (Deceased), 1850–2000* (2nd edn, Wigan, 2005)

—— *St. Mary's, Little Crosby: A History* (Little Crosby, 1997)

Purcell, E. S., *Life of Cardinal Manning, Archbishop of Westminster*, 2 vols (London, 1896)

Quinn, Dermot, *Patronage and Piety: The Politics of Roman Catholicism, 1850–1900* (Basingstoke, 1993)

Rimmer, J., *Yesterday's Naughty Children: Training Ships, Girls' Reformatory and Farm School: A History of the Liverpool Reformatory Association, Founded 1855* (Manchester, 1986)

Roche, J. S., *A History of Prior Park College and Its Founder Bishop Baines* (London, 1931)

Schiefen, Richard J., *Nicholas Wiseman and the Transformation of English Catholicism* (Shepherdstown, WV, 1984)

Schofield, N. and Skinner, G., *The English Vicars Apostolic 1688–1850* (Oxford, 2009)

Sharp, John, *Reapers of the Harvest* (London, 1989)

Sharples, Joseph, *Liverpool* (Pevsner Architectural Guides, New Haven, CT, and London, 2004)

Shimmin, H., *Life in Liverpool* (Liverpool, 1856)

Singleton, F. J., *Mowbreck Hall and The Willows: A History of the Catholic Community in the Kirkham District of Lancashire* (Kirkham, 1983)

Skene, F., *The Life of Alexander Lycurgus, Archbishop of the Cyclades* (London, 1877)

Stonor OSB, Robert J., *Liverpool's Hidden Story* (Birchley, 1957)

—— *Stonor, A Catholic Sanctuary in the Chilterns from the Fifth Century till To-day* (Newport, 1951)

Swarbrick, J., *Marriage: A Sermon Preached at St. Augustine's* (Preston, 1858)

Swarbrick, M., *The Story of Pantasaph and the Coming of the Capuchin Friars* (Pantasaph, 1993)

Swift, R. and Gilley, S. (eds), *The Irish in the Victorian City* (London, 1985)

—— *The Irish in Britain* (London, 1989)

—— *Irish Identities in Victorian Britain* (London, 2011)

Tenbus, E., *English Catholics and the Education of the Poor, 1847–1902* (London, 2010)

Trappes-Lomax, John, *The Lingard–Lomax Letters* (CRS 77, London, 2000)

Tyrer, Frank (ed.), *The Great Diurnal of Nicholas Blundell*, 3 vols (Record Society of Lancashire and Cheshire, Liverpool, 1968–72)

The Victoria History of the Counties of England: Lancashire, 8 vols (London, 1906–14; repr. 1966)

Waller, P., *Sectarianism and Democracy: A Political and Social History of Liverpool, 1868–1939* (Liverpool, 1981)

Walsh, B., *Roman Catholic Nuns in England and Wales, 1800–1937: A Social History* (Dublin, 2002)

Walsh, Michael, *The Tablet 1840–1990: A Commemorative History* (London, 1990)

Ward, Bernard, *The Sequel to Catholic Emancipation, 1830–1850*, 2 vols (London, 1915)

Ward, Wilfrid, *The Life and Times of Cardinal Wiseman*, 2 vols (London, 1897)

Warren, Leo, *Through Twenty Preston Guilds: The Catholic Congregation of St. Wilfrid's, Preston* (Preston, 1993)

Articles/Short Pamphlets

Anon., *Centenary Memoir, Convent of Notre Dame Mount Pleasant* (Liverpool, 1956)

Anon., *The Story of Ince Blundell Hall: A Short History of the House and the Weld-Blundell Family* (Ince Blundell, *c.* 2000)

Atkinson, R., *The Shefford Catholic Mission, 1728–1823* (Shefford, 1973)

Burscough, Margaret, *The History of Lark Hill, Preston, 1797–1989* (Preston, 1989, repr. 2003)

Conlan OFM, P., *St Cuthbert's, Wigton* (n.p., *c.* 1990)

Davies, J., 'Father James Nugent, Prison Chaplain', *NWCH* 22 (1995), 15–24

Doyle, P., 'Bishop Goss and the Gentry: The Control of Private Chapels', *NWCH* 12 (1985), 6–13

—— 'Bishop Goss of Liverpool (1856–72) and the Importance of Being English', *Studies in Church History* 18 (1982), 433–47

—— 'The Education and Training of Roman Catholic Priests in Nineteenth-Century England', *Journal of Ecclesiastical History*, 35:2 (April 1984), 208–19

—— 'Episcopal Authority and Clerical Democracy: Diocesan Synods in Liverpool in the 1850s', *RH* 23:3 (May, 1997), 418–33

—— 'An Episcopal Historian: Alexander Goss of Liverpool (1856–1872)', *NWCH* 15 (1988), 6–15

—— 'Jesuit Reactions to the Restoration of the Hierarchy: The Diocese of Liverpool, 1850–80', *RH* 26:1 (May 2002), 210–28

—— 'Lancashire Benedictines: The Restoration of the Hierarchy', *EBC History Composium* (1983), 4–21

—— 'Missed Opportunities: Clerical Conferences in the Nineteenth Century', *The Downside Review* (October 1982), 263–73

—— '"A Tangled Skein of Confusion": The Administration of George Hilary Brown, Bishop of Liverpool 1850–1856', *RH* 25:2 (October 2000), 294–313

Dudley SND, Margaret Mary, *Treasured Memories of St Joseph's 1845–2001* (Liverpool, 2001)

Duffy, Eamon, 'Doctor Douglass and Mister Berington: An Eighteenth-Century Retraction', *The Downside Review* 88 (July 1970), 246–69

—— 'Ecclesiastical Democracy Detected I: 1779–87', *RH* 10:4 (January, 1970), 193–210,

Dunleavy, J., '"Mr Hansom of Coventry": the Lancashire commissions of Charles Francis Hansom, architect, 1817–88', *NWCH* 37 (2010), 10–19

Feheny, J. M., 'The Poor Law Board August Order, 1859: A Case Study of Protestant-Catholic Conflict', *RH* 17:1 (May 1984), 84–91

Foster, S.,'The Life and Death of a Victorian Seminary: the English College, Bruges' *RH* 20:2 (October 1990), 272–90

Giblin, J. F., 'The Gerard Family of Bryn and Ince and the Parish of Ss Oswald and Edmund', *NWCH* 17 (1990), 1–17

—— 'The History of Birchley Hall and The Mission of St Mary's, Birchley, in Billinge, Lancashire', *NWCH* 4 (1972–3), 1–26

—— 'The Molyneux Family and the Missions at Scholes Hall and Our Lady's, Portico', *NWCH* 21 (1994), 1–13

—— The Orrell Family and the Mission of St. Mary's, Blackbrook in Parr, St. Helens', *NWCH* 7 (1980), 6–19

Goddard, Gillian, *St. John the Evangelist Catholic Church, Burscough: A Celebration of the Tercentenary of the Foundation of Burscough Hall Mission (1700–2000)* (Burscough, 2000)

Griffin, Brian, 'Anti-Catholicism in Bath from 1820 to 1870', *RH* 31:4 (October 2013), 593–611

Hewlett, M., *Our Lady of Mount Carmel, Liverpool, 1878–1978* (Liverpool, 1978)

Hilton, J. A., 'Brown, George Hilary', in *ODNB* (2004)

—— Catholic Congregationalism in Fleetwood, 1841–42', *NWCH* 26 (1999), 62–9

—— 'Dicconson, Edward', in *ODNB* (2004)

—— 'Our Lady's, Bryn, 1903–2003: Coal and Catholicism', *NWCH* 32 (2005), 69–76

—— *St Joseph's Wrightington, A History* (Wrightington, 1994)

Marmion, J. P., 'The Beginnings of the Catholic Poor Schools in England', *RH* 17:1 (May 1984), 67–83

McCarren FCJ, Mary Campion, Trotman, F., and Piggin, M., *With Devotedness and Love – 150 Years of Service to Catholic Education: The Faithful Companions of Jesus 1844–1994.* (Liverpool, 1994)

McCartan, E., *Centenary Year 1872–1972: Short History of the Parish* (Coniston, 1972)

Milburn, David, 'The Origins of the Junior House at Ushaw', *The Ushaw Magazine*, 69:206 (July 1959), 65–77

Mullett, Michael, '"Composed Entirely of the Poorest Class": The Establishment of the Parish of St Catherine, Penrith, Cumbria, 1833–50', in Davies, J. and Mitchinson, A. (eds), *Obstinate Souls: Essays presented to J. A. Hilton* (Wigan, 2011), 29–47

Noble, A. J., 'Thurnham Hall Chapel' (with illustration), *NWCH* 36 (2009), 100–4

Pennington, Anne-Marie, *Celebrating 150 Years: A History of Mount Pleasant Teacher Training College* (Liverpool Hope University, 2006)

Pope, D. J., 'Lancaster's Late Eighteenth-Century Catholic Shipowners and Merchants – The Gillows and Worswicks'. Part One, *NWCH* 31 (2004), 21–50; Part Two, *NWCH* 32 (2005), 21–35

Smith, Tom, '"Let justice be done and we will be silent": A Study of Preston's Catholic Voters and their Parliamentary Election Campaigns, 1832 to 1867', *NWCH* 28 (2001), 5–54

—— 'Religion or Party? Attitudes of Catholic Electors in Mid-Victorian Preston', *NWCH* 33 (2006), 19–35

Whitehead, M., 'The English Jesuits and Episcopal Authority: The Liverpool Test Case, 1840–1843', *RH* 18:2 (October, 1986), 197–219

Worrall SND, Jennifer (ed.), *Jubilee: Sisters of Notre Dame de Namur Celebrate 150 Years in Britain* (n.p., 1995)

INDEX OF PEOPLE AND PLACES

Numbers refer to pages not letters. Page spans may indicate repeated mentions rather than continuous discussion.

GENERAL INDEX

Numbers refer to pages, not to letters. Page spans may indicate repeated mentions, rather than continuous discussion.